Inventory and Hinge
Entangled Fields of Research in the Arts

Institute for Contemporary Art Research 2001–2022

Inventory and Hinge
Entangled Fields of Research in the Arts

Institute for Contemporary Art Research 2001–2022

Ed. Christoph Schenker

DIAPHANES

The Institute for Contemporary Art Research (IFCAR) at Zurich University of the Arts (ZHdK) stands for networked research in art, and thus for an expansion of the field of art. Through this focus, it makes a decisive contribution to the contemporary discourse on artistic research.

This publication provides an overview of the research projects performed over the last two decades at the IFCAR. The title refers to the twofold nature of the publication. On the one hand, it is an inventory that lists all the projects that were realized during this period: with concise texts that depict the subject of research and the course it took; with basic information on their organization in tabular form along with references about their main results and publications. The images—an unorthodox selection—are traces of the research activity and thus also part of the inventory. On the other hand, the publication is a hinge, because clicking on the websites or scanning the QR codes grants access to nearly all publications and websites that were created in the context of the individual projects. In this respect, the publication is also a hinge in the service of future research.

The projects, aside from a few exceptions, are located in the field of artistic research in the fine arts. This field is not a monoculture. Artistic work is an undertaking that intrinsically interconnects multiple competencies and areas of knowledge, ways of life and working. The IFCAR generally performs research in the form of projects that run for a limited period and have a specific focus, with teams whose members belong to a variety of disciplines. The way the research project is organized thus corresponds to the transgressive gesture of artistic work. Here it becomes manifest as interdisciplinary, networked knowledge production. From its very conception, the cultivation of these entanglements, which also bring with them particular freedoms, has been a mission statement of the IFCAR. It remains for a second publication to launch a deeper discussion on the specific contribution of artistic work to this manifold and antagonistic activity, a discussion which will, for its part, integrate the multifarious perspectives of art and of science and technology studies, philosophy and semiotics, all the way to the social sciences.

The IFCAR was inaugurated in 2005 as one of several research institutes at the ZHdK. The other institutes are dedicated to research in the fields of theater and film, music, and design, to theory, cultural studies, and art education. In the subsequent fifteen years, over thirty research projects were performed at the IFCAR with the support of external funding, primarily from the Swiss National Science Foundation (SNSF). Even before the institute's founding, research projects in the fine arts were being realized with funding from the Swiss government. The IFCAR and these precursor projects were the first at the ZHdK to perform research in the field of art; they were also the first projects in Switzerland in which artists worked as researchers. In 2005, research at Swiss art academies (as universities of applied sciences) was just getting started. In other German-speaking countries, the discourse on artistic research began to take root several years later, linked with the development of the doctoral degree in the arts. In Switzerland, however, artistic research developed over a ten-year period into project research—encouraged by project funding from the Innovation Promotion Agency KTI and the SNSF. This constellation helped foster high-quality research of great relevance within a short time. Because of their status as universities of applied arts, even today it is not possible for art universities in Switzerland to grant doctorates independently of international partnerships.

Throughout all these pioneering years, the IFCAR, as the smallest possible organization, has always seen its mission as the promotion of research competency in the field of fine arts at the ZHdK, and support for the conception and execution of concrete projects. Although art as research (outside of institutions) has a long tradition, this meant nothing less than the introduction of a new discipline into the context of the academic research and establishing a new genre in the context of art. These developments require time and continue to progress. As the first research projects at the IFCAR were developed from the interests of the artists and theorists at the ZHdK, the two research emphases that have become established are "art, urban studies and the public sphere" (art and public sphere) and "forms of artistic knowledge" (art and science). These are not explicitly identified in this volume, however. Each of the publications that appeared as a consequence of the projects constitute practice-led research—or rather, research as creation—but often also conduct a metadiscourse on artistic research. This metadiscourse—or somewhat more humbly: this commentary—has been elaborated separately in three volumes. These are *Kunst des Forschens—Praxis eines ästhetischen Denkens* (ed. Elke Bippus, 2009*), Künstlerische Forschung—Ein Handbuch* (ed. Jens Badura et al., 2015) and *Natures of Data—A Discussion between Biology, History and Philosophy of Science and Art* (ed. Philipp Fischer et al., 2020).

Christoph Schenker
Head of the Institute for Contemporary Art Research

Contents

Pictures have never been and are not simply "here." They emerge, arise, occur, appear, "originate," and develop. Thus, pictures have a history, and with this an early history. But how do pictures appear, "come into being"? In ontogeny, in the development of an individual, what qualities, structural formations and developmental tendencies can be observed in early graphic expressions? Are early pictures products or processes? Are early pictorial characteristics cross-contextual, contextual, or individual? What do early pictorial cognition and aesthetics consist of? What general aspects of early symbolic behavior do early pictures indicate? What picture concept arises from picture genesis?

These questions were addressed in several individual projects concerning early pictures in ontogeny with regard to several main topics: namely, morphology, the difference between the picture process and its product, cross-contextual and contextual manifestations, the emergence of depiction, and aspects that have to be considered in relation to phylogeny, general picture theory and aesthetics.

Comprehensive image and video archives were created during the research project, presenting over fifty-five thousand reproductions of early pictures from Europe and Asia (most of them produced by children aged one to six), and some two hundred videos of the early picture process. In addition, the historical archive of Rhoda Kellogg was reedited, and the archive of Gilles Porte published. All archives are accessible online, in open access form.

Three main results were obtained: First, the ongoing controversy on the matter was addressed, revisiting and renewing the structural assessment of the morphology of early pictures (the appearance of graphic forms, form configurations, form systems and denotations, as well as their developmental tendencies). The documentary and experimental evidence provided indicated that early pictures are in part structurally inter-individual and cross-contextual. Second, "abstract" graphic form structurally precedes, enables, and parallels graphic analogy formation, depiction, denotation, and other types of graphic referencing in the early development of pictures. Third, the intention and meaning of early pictures are in part inherent in the process of their emergence and cannot sufficiently be assessed on the basis of the products.

These findings allow for several conclusions with regard to pictures and picture genesis: The early development of pictures—and with it, the general concept of pictures—raises the question of a picture-inherent agency, positing the existence of a "picture act" (Bredekamp) that is related to a "logic" of the early development, a "consistent generation of sense and meaning with picture-inherent and picture-related means" (Boehm). As for aesthetics, reflection on the character of form is posited to precede the grading of form (form precedes beauty). As for meaning, form precedes function, indicating a "syntactical" pictorial cognition that is in part autonomous.

Early Pictures consisted of several subprojects:

- Morphology of early pictures in ontogeny, sub-projects 1–3: 1999–2001, 2002–2004, 2005–2007
- Cross-contextual and contextual aspects of early pictures in ontogeny, sub-projects 1–3: 2004–2008, 2009–2011, 2017–2018
- Early pictures and early picture process in ontogeny: 2007–2009
- Early pictures and early depiction (book project): 2012–2013

The following side studies were performed as part of *Early Pictures*:

- Early human figure drawing in different contexts of their production: 2013–2014
- Inherent Crossing. Observing chimpanzees acting with utensils and color: 2013–2016 (see related projects)
- Studies on the "abstract" and self-referential character of early pictures in onto- and phylogeny, and related aspects of a picture concept: 2009–2018
- Early picture development in ontogeny. A textbook: 2018–ongoing

Dieter Maurer

Project Title
Frühe graphische Äusserungen in der Ontogenese

Project Period
1 January 1999–ongoing

Keywords

- Early pictures
- Drawing
- Painting
- Aesthetics
- Picture theory

Heads of Project

- Dieter Maurer (head), semiotician
- Claudia Riboni (co-head), cultural researcher

Research Team

- Birute Guje, art educator
- Christina Hemauer, artist and art educator
- Judith Herren, psychologist
- Xenia Guhl, artist and art educator
- Nicole Schwarz, artist and art educator
- Regula Stettler, artist and art educator
- Karin Wälchli, artist
- Guido Reichli, artist
- Adrian Brazerol, technician
- Ursula Vogel, head of NGO
- Shammi Davis, NGO project manager
- I Nyoman Witama, NGO project manager
- I Made Yudiana, NGO project manager
- Li Kadek Liatini, NGO administrator

Software Development

- Christian d'Heureuse, software developer, Inventec Informatik AG
- Jürgen Ragaller, software developer, null-oder-eins GmbH
- Yves Schmid-Dornbierer, software developer, GarageCube, Ultrapepita

Outputs

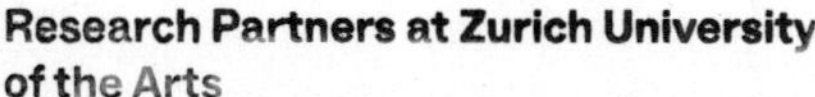

Research Partners at Zurich University of the Arts
- Institute for Cultural Studies and Art Education (until 2008)
- Institute for Critical Theory

Project Partners
- Prof. Dr. John S. Matthews, National Institute of Education (NIE), Nanyang Technological University Singapore (NTU)
- Prof. Dr. Hans-Günther Richter, University of Cologne
- PD Dr. Peter Brugger and Prof. Dr. Marianne Regard, University Hospital Zurich, Neuropsychology
- Hans Diethelm, Thomas Hermann, Jens Kistler, and Ruth Kunz, Zurich University of Teacher Education (PH Zürich)
- Dr. Heidi Simoni, Marie Meierhofer-Institute for the Child, Zürich
- Kinderhaus Entlisberg (Social Department of Zurich City)
- Ursa Vogel, NAMO Inter-Cultural Projects, Switzerland
- Joyce Scott, Linda Moselle Venter, BaliChildrensProject, Indonesia/U.S.A.

Project Funding
- Swiss National Science Foundation (SNSF)
- Commission for Technology and Innovation CTI
- Z Zurich Foundation
- Mercator Foundation
- Baugarten Foundation
- Ernst Göhner Foundation
- Lotteriefonds Zürich
- National Assurance
- Alfred Richterich Foundation
- Vontobel Foundation
- Claire Sturzenegger-Jeanfavre Foundation
- Susan Bach Foundation
- Mobiliar Switzerland Foundation

Related Project
- Inherent Crossing, Zurich University of the Arts, 2014–2017
  P. 178

Publications
- Dieter Maurer and Claudia Riboni (2019): *Wie Bilder "entstehen"*. Volumes 1–3, revised second edition. Bern: Peter Lang.
  Volume 1: "Eigenschaften und Entwicklung."
  A Open access: https://doi.org/10.3726/b15835
  Volume 2: "Bildarchiv Europa und Materialien."
  B Open access: https://doi.org/10.3726/b15846
  Volume 3: "Beschreibende Methode."
  C Open access: https://doi.org/10.3726/b15847
- Dieter Maurer, Claudia Riboni, Xenia Guhl, Nicole Schwarz, and Regula Stettler (2013): *Wie Bilder "entstehen"*. Volume 4: "Prozess und Produkt." Bern: Peter Lang.
  D Open access: https://doi.org/10.3726/978-3-0351-0628-2
- Dieter Maurer, Claudia Riboni, and Birute Gujer (2018): *Wie Bilder "entstehen"*. Volume 5: "Produkt und Kode." Bern: Peter Lang.
  E Open access: https://doi.org/10.3726/b15138

Monograph
- Dieter Maurer, and Claudia Riboni (2013): *Wie die Bilder zu den Häusern finden und das Haus ins Bild kommt. How pictures find houses and the house comes into the picture*. Zurich: Edition Patrick Frey (d/e).

Anthology
- Dieter Maurer and Claudia Riboni (eds.) (2010): *Bild und Bildgenese*. Bern: Peter Lang.

Archives
- Rhoda Kellogg (1967/2007): *Rhoda Kellogg Child Art Collection*. Digital reedition by Dieter Maurer, Claudia Riboni, Karin Wälchli, and Birute Gujer. Picture archive. First published 1 September 2007.
  www.early-pictures.ch/kellogg
- Dieter Maurer and Claudia Riboni: *Morphologie Europa*. Picture archive. First published in 2010.
  www.early-pictures.ch/eu/de
- Gilles Porte, Dieter Maurer, and Birute Gujer (2012): *Portrait—Selfportrait. Digital Edition of the Picture Archive of Gilles Porte*. Part 1: Text. Part 2: Picture Archive. Part 3: Commentary by Gilles Porte. First published in 2012.
  www.early-pictures.ch/porte1
- Dieter Maurer, Xenia Guhl, Nicole Schwarz, Regula Stettler, and Claudia Riboni: *Prozess und Produkt*. Picture and Video archive. First published in 2013.
  www.early-pictures.ch/process/de
- Dieter Maurer (ed.): *Early Human Figure Drawing in Ontogeny—Cross-contextual Aspects*. Picture archive. First published in 2014.
  www.early-pictures.ch/porte2
- Dieter Maurer, Claudia Riboni, and Birute Gujer: *Produkt und Kode*. Picture archive. First published in 2018.
  www.early-pictures.ch/as/de
- Erika Wagner and Dieter Maurer: *Archiv Wagner*. Picture and video archive, Beta Version. First published in 2018.
  www.early-pictures.ch/wagner/archive

Fig. 1 Processual characteristics of early pictures: documentation and analysis, 2009

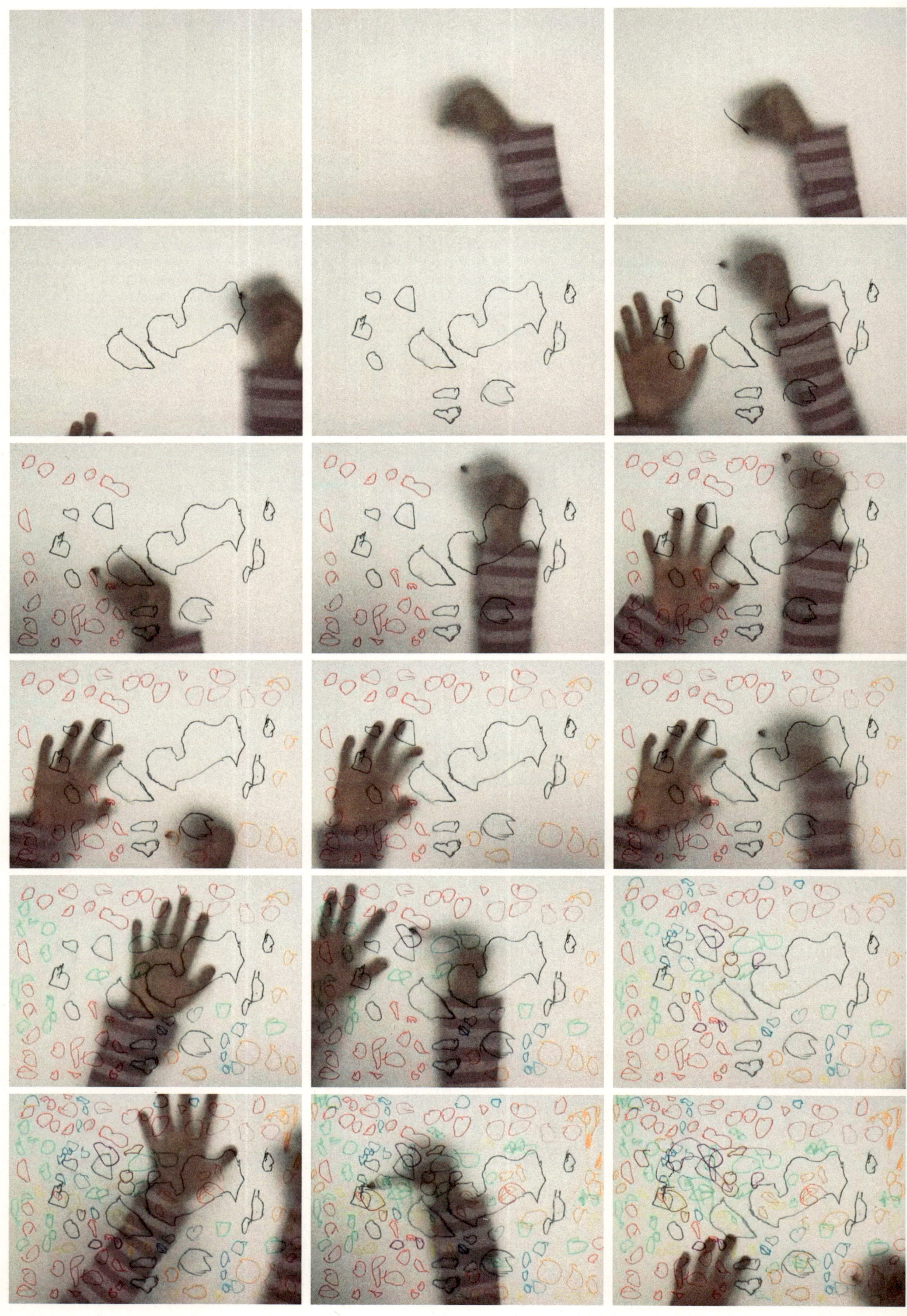

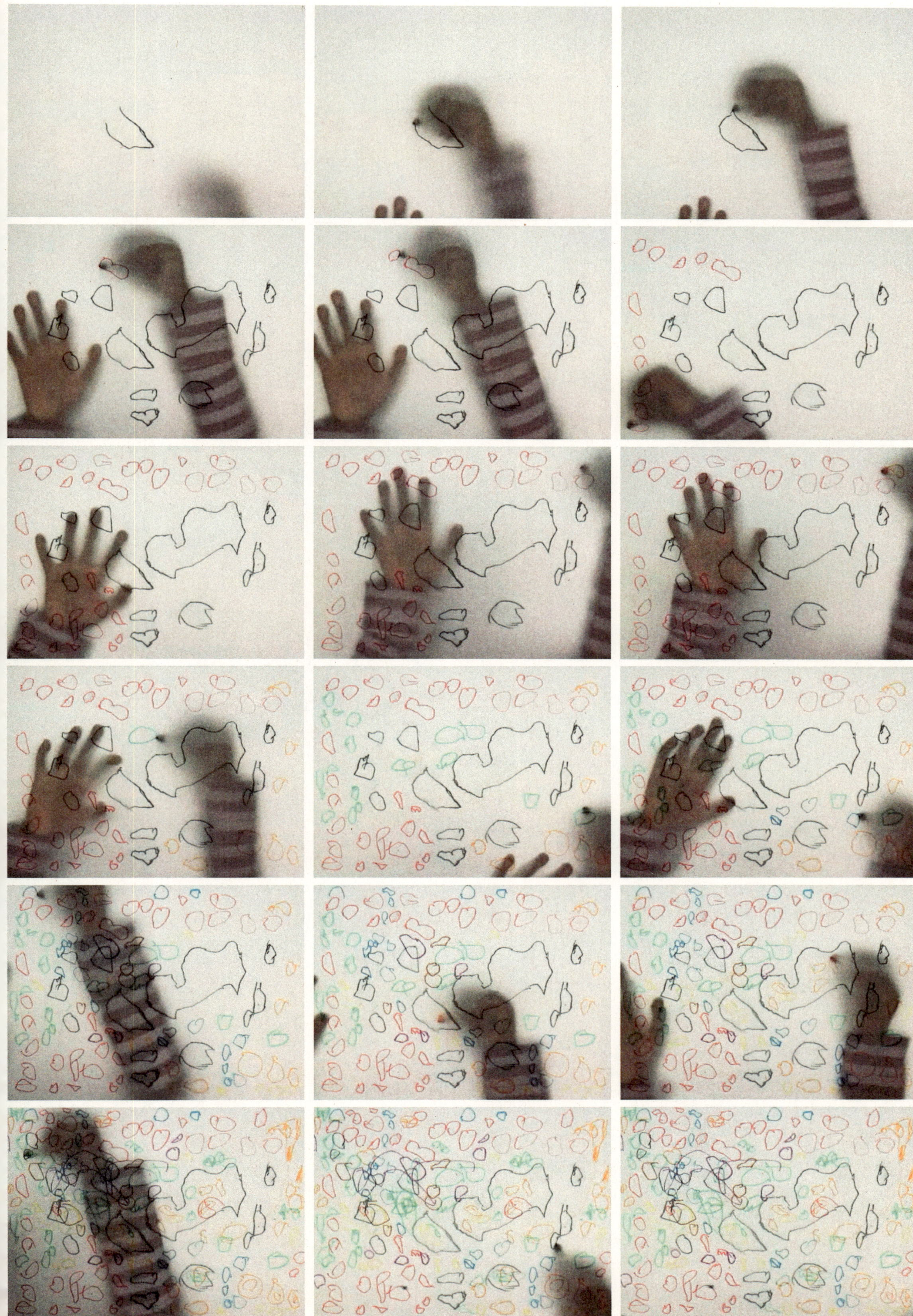

Fig. 2 Structural and aesthetic characteristics of early pictures: documentation, analysis and comparison of early drawings, 2017

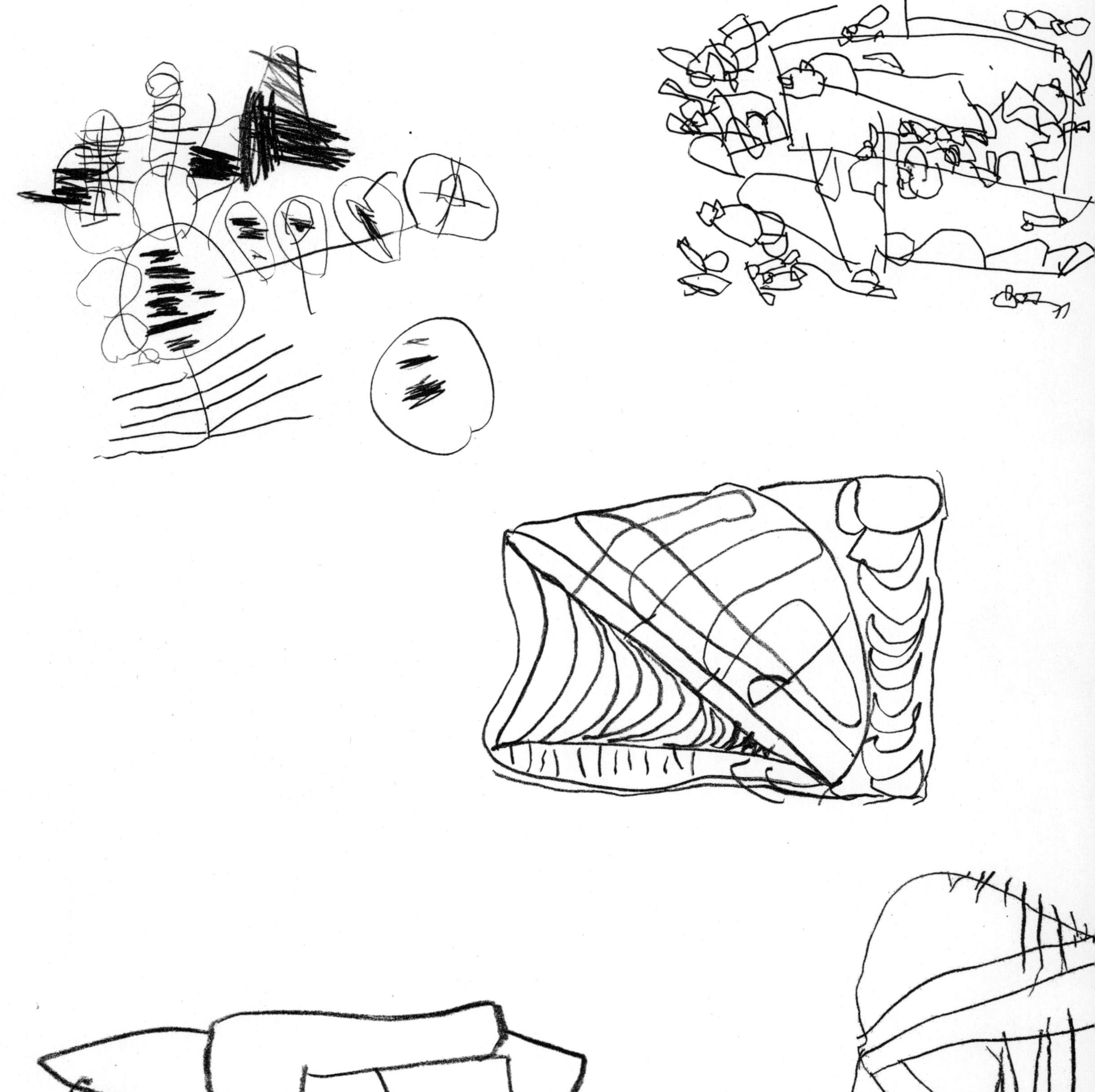

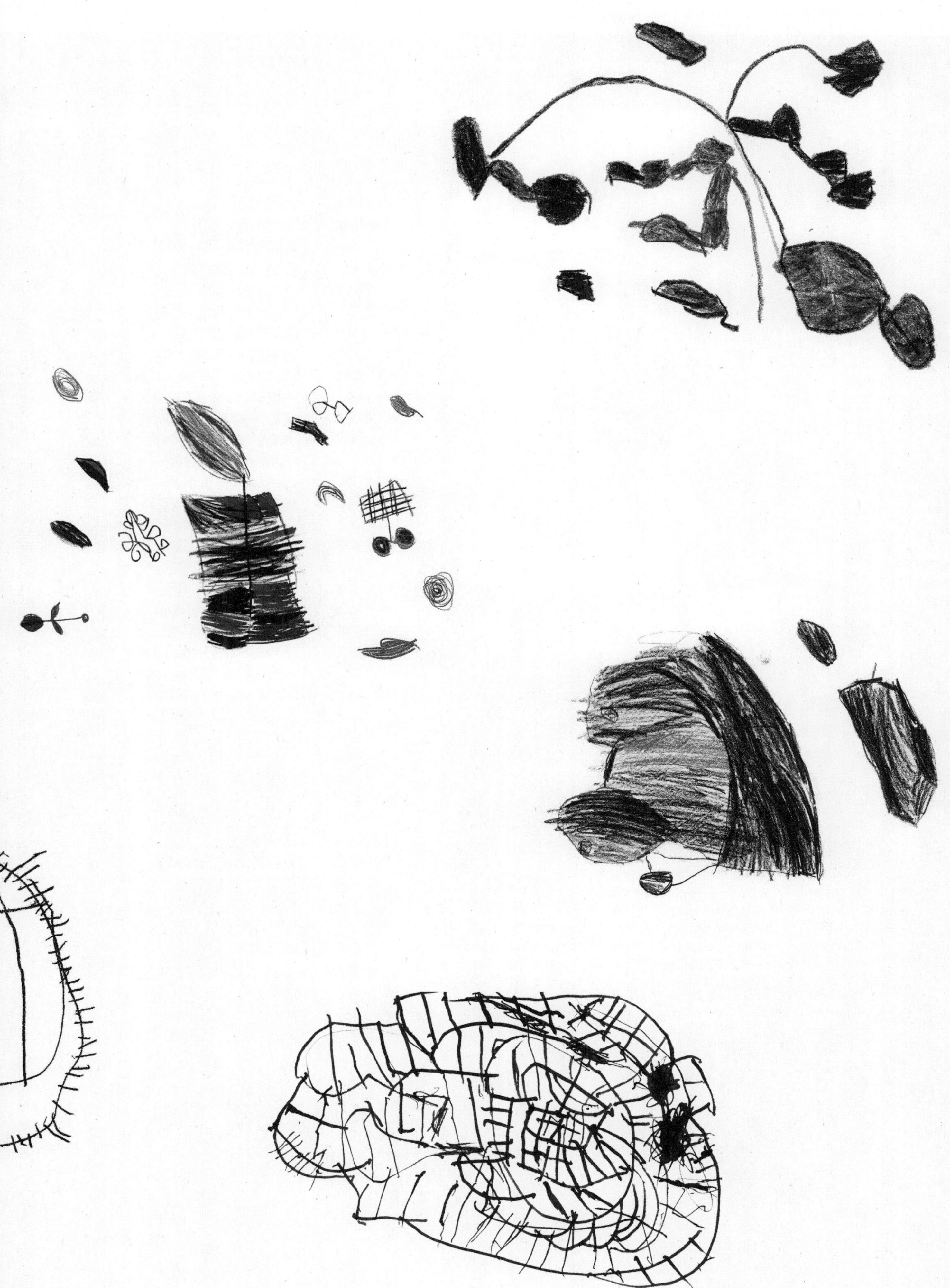

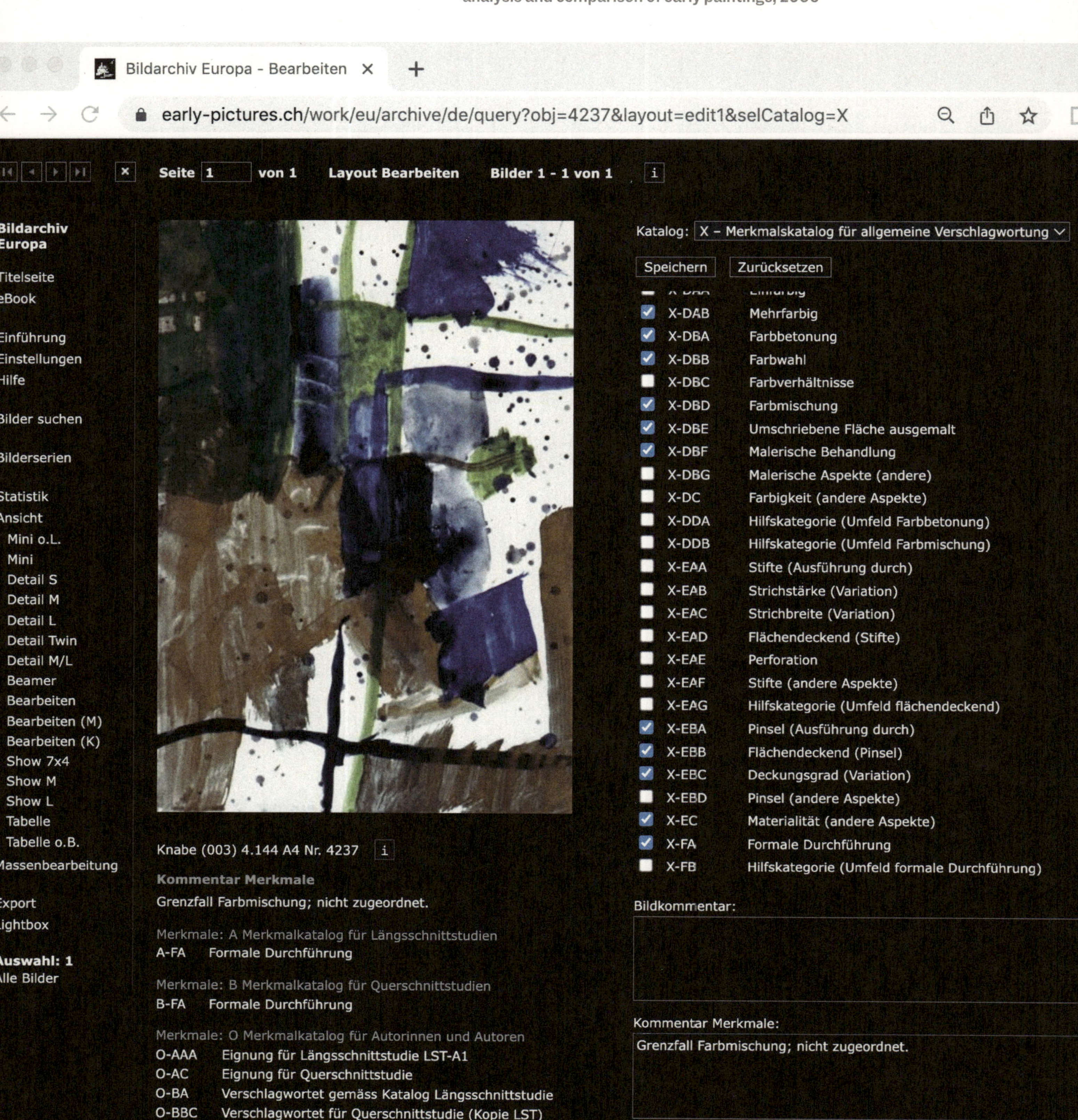
Bildarchiv Europa - Bearbeiten
early-pictures.ch/work/eu/archive/de/query?obj=4237&layout=edit1&selCatalog=X
Seite 1 von 1 Layout Bearbeiten Bilder 1 - 1 von 1
Bildarchiv Europa
Titelseite
eBook
Einführung
Einstellungen
Hilfe
Bilder suchen
Bilderserien
Statistik
Ansicht
Mini o.L.
Mini
Detail S
Detail M
Detail L
Detail Twin
Detail M/L
Beamer
Bearbeiten
Bearbeiten (M)
Bearbeiten (K)
Show 7x4
Show M
Show L
Tabelle
Tabelle o.B.
Massenbearbeitung
Export
Lightbox
Auswahl: 1
Alle Bilder
Knabe (003) 4.144 A4 Nr. 4237
Kommentar Merkmale
Grenzfall Farbmischung; nicht zugeordnet.
Merkmale: A Merkmalkatalog für Längsschnittstudien
A-FA Formale Durchführung
Merkmale: B Merkmalkatalog für Querschnittstudien
B-FA Formale Durchführung
Merkmale: O Merkmalkatalog für Autorinnen und Autoren
O-AAA Eignung für Längsschnittstudie LST-A1
O-AC Eignung für Querschnittstudie
O-BA Verschlagwortet gemäss Katalog Längsschnittstudie
O-BBC Verschlagwortet für Querschnittstudie (Kopie LST)
O-C Eignung für den Vergleich von Bildern von Geschwistern
O-DBA Nachkontrolle anhand der Originale durchgeführt
Merkmale: X Merkmalskatalog für allgemeine Verschlagwortung
Katalog: X – Merkmalskatalog für allgemeine Verschlagwortung
Speichern
Zurücksetzen
X-DAB Mehrfarbig
X-DBA Farbbetonung
X-DBB Farbwahl
X-DBC Farbverhältnisse
X-DBD Farbmischung
X-DBE Umschriebene Fläche ausgemalt
X-DBF Malerische Behandlung
X-DBG Malerische Aspekte (andere)
X-DC Farbigkeit (andere Aspekte)
X-DDA Hilfskategorie (Umfeld Farbbetonung)
X-DDB Hilfskategorie (Umfeld Farbmischung)
X-EAA Stifte (Ausführung durch)
X-EAB Strichstärke (Variation)
X-EAC Strichbreite (Variation)
X-EAD Flächendeckend (Stifte)
X-EAE Perforation
X-EAF Stifte (andere Aspekte)
X-EAG Hilfskategorie (Umfeld flächendeckend)
X-EBA Pinsel (Ausführung durch)
X-EBB Flächendeckend (Pinsel)
X-EBC Deckungsgrad (Variation)
X-EBD Pinsel (andere Aspekte)
X-EC Materialität (andere Aspekte)
X-FA Formale Durchführung
X-FB Hilfskategorie (Umfeld formale Durchführung)
Bildkommentar:
Kommentar Merkmale:
Grenzfall Farbmischung; nicht zugeordnet.
Kommentar Archivierung:
Vorlage für exemplarische Illustration früher malerischer Äusserungen

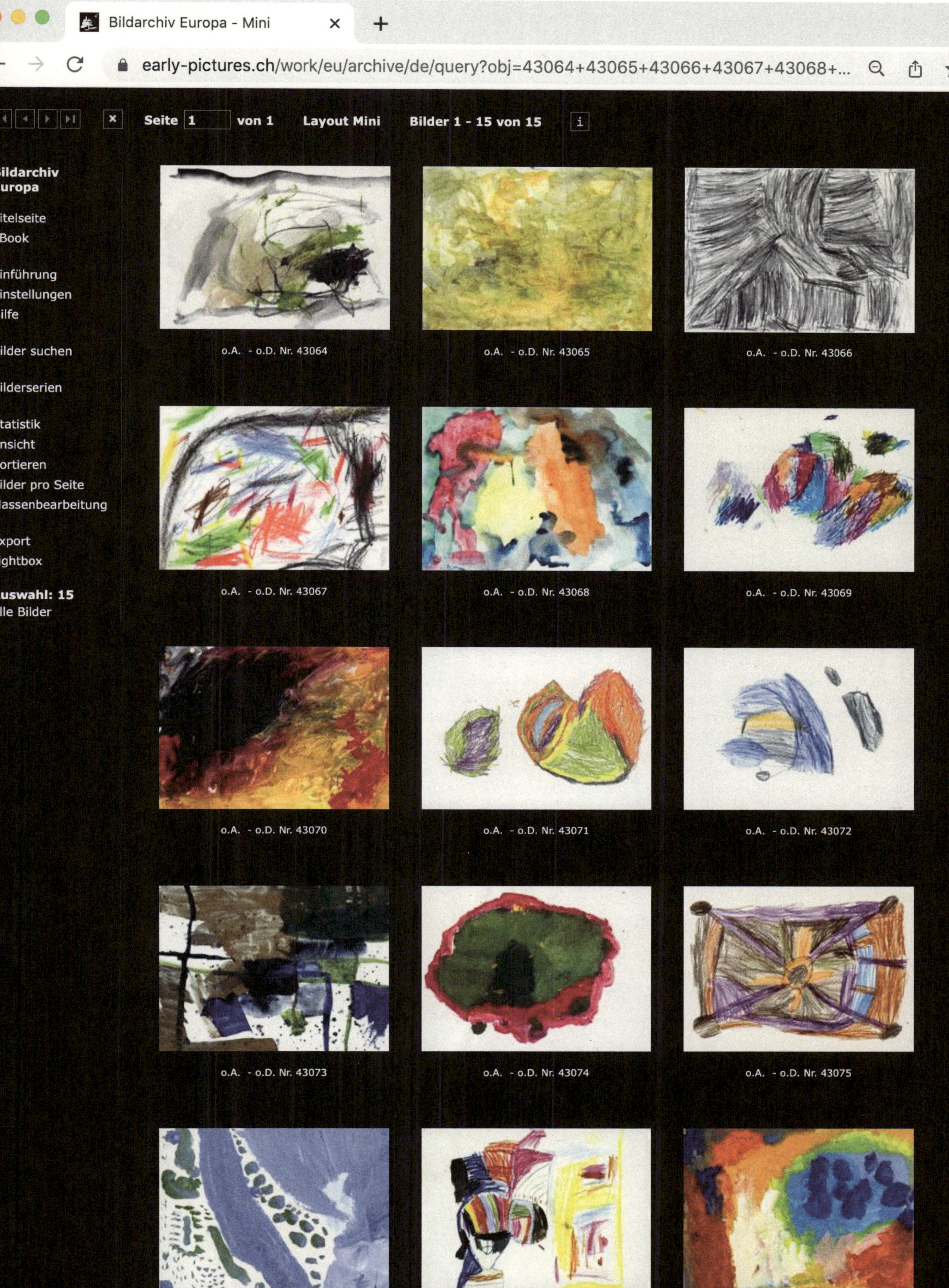
Bildarchiv Europa - Mini
early-pictures.ch/work/eu/archive/de/query?obj=43064+43065+43066+43067+43068+...
Seite 1 von 1
Layout Mini
Bilder 1 - 15 von 15
Bildarchiv Europa
Titelseite
eBook
Einführung
Einstellungen
Hilfe
Bilder suchen
Bilderserien
Statistik
Ansicht
Sortieren
Bilder pro Seite
Massenbearbeitung
Export
Lightbox
Auswahl: 15
Alle Bilder
o.A. - o.D. Nr. 43064
o.A. - o.D. Nr. 43065
o.A. - o.D. Nr. 43066
o.A. - o.D. Nr. 43067
o.A. - o.D. Nr. 43068
o.A. - o.D. Nr. 43069
o.A. - o.D. Nr. 43070
o.A. - o.D. Nr. 43071
o.A. - o.D. Nr. 43072
o.A. - o.D. Nr. 43073
o.A. - o.D. Nr. 43074
o.A. - o.D. Nr. 43075
o.A. - o.D. Nr. 43076
o.A. - o.D. Nr. 43077
o.A. - o.D. Nr. 43078

The *Public Plaiv. Contemporary Art in the Landscape and Settlement Area La Plaiv, Oberengadin* project explored the functions of artworks in public spaces which generate a relevance and effectiveness that can be identified in the concrete environment of a lifeworld. The participating artists conceived their art projects as "sensoria" with which hidden lines of conflict in the region were detected, expressed, and made experienceable and debatable for both individuals and the public.

The initial constellation of the project was bipolar. *Public Plaiv* was the first research project in the field of art at the Zurich University of the Arts (ZHdK), and the first ever at a Swiss art academy in which artists participated as researchers. It was sponsored by the Swiss Federal Innovation Promotion Agency, which required significant involvement from business shareholders. Correspondingly, it is understood to be "application-oriented research and development." The partners were the Gemeindeverbund La Plaiv in Oberengadin (along with Zuoz, the most populous municipality in the region) and the Walter A. Bechtler Foundation. The municipal association hoped that contemporary public art for the La Plaiv region would help it develop a cultural identity to differentiate it attractively from the fashionable tourist destination St. Moritz.

Another key element in the initial constellation of the project was the wave of development that public art had experienced internationally in the 1990s. The level of development of public art at that time can be described with concepts like new genre public art, socially engaged art, site specificity, and interventionism, as well as participation and activism. With special attention to the function of the artwork, the project picked up on a neglected aspect in the production and reception of contemporary art, and did so independently of the art form, genre or trend. The focus was on the performative character of the artwork.

The artistic exploration of lines of conflict in the region, on the one hand, and the exploration of the functions of artworks, on the other, built on the groundwork of the four-member interdisciplinary project team and on cooperation with local experts. The research and studies dealt with such topics as the regional Rhaeto-Romanic language, the historical and contemporary building culture, the economy (tourism) and politics, as well as the transformation of the cultural landscape. The areas of conflict between local identity and touristic added value received particular attention, as did the tension between regional ties and mobility.

At the invitation of the project team, thirteen international artists analyzed the cultural, in part latent antagonisms on site, and worked out designs for art projects. Four designs were ultimately realized. In a fictitious museum, Ken Lum thematized the emigration of natives from the mountain valley that has already been underway for centuries. Bethan Huws's film showed the region's specific architectural forms as a trace of the bodily interaction between work, living, and the rough environmental conditions in the Alps. In a nocturnal action with professional skiers, Peter Regli presented the mythical dimension of the landscape experience. Sophie Thorsen, finally, used hidden speakers under a bench overlooking the mountainside over the valley to broadcast facts and statistics on the large seasonal population variations and the immense infrastructure of Oberengadin, which subsequently cloud the viewer's pleasure in viewing one of the most beautiful mountain valleys in the world. These artistic installations were preceded by two temporary, mobile artworks by Martin Kippenberger and Roman Signer, which introduced the dialog between art and the public. In this project, artworks should be conceived as instruments with which insight can be gained and knowledge generated through sensory experiences.

Christoph Schenker

Project Title
Public Plaiv. Gegenwartskunst im Landschafts- und Siedlungsraum La Plaiv, Oberengadin

Project Period
1 July 2001–31 December 2002

Keywords
- Public art
- Functions of art
- Artwork as an instrument
- Transdisciplinarity
- Oberengadin

Head of Project
- Christoph Schenker, art theorist

Research Team
- Lilian Pfaff, art and architecture historian
- Susann Wintsch, art historian
- Tim Zulauf, artist and author

Participating Artists
- Marie José Burki
- Hans Danuser
- Michel François
- Christine and Irene Hohenbüchler
- Felix S. Huber and Florian Wüst
- Bethan Huws
- Constance DeJong
- Korpys/Löffler
- Ken Lum
- Aernout Mik
- Jos Näpflin
- Peter Regli
- Sofie Thorsen

Outputs

A

Research Partner
- Institute of Art History at the University of Zurich, Chair at the Department for Modern and Contemporary Art, Prof. Dr. Stanislaus von Moos

Project Partners
- Walter A. Bechtler Stiftung
- Wirtschaftsorganisation Plaiv (WOP)
- Hauser & Wirth Collection, St. Gallen
- Hotel Castell, Zuoz

Project Funding and Support
- CTI The Innovation Promotion Agency (now Innosuisse — Swiss Innovation Agency)
- Georges und Jenny Bloch Stiftung
- Migros Culture Percentage
- Erziehungs-, Kultur- und Umweltschutzdepartement Graubünden
- Biblioteca Engiadinaisa
- Hulda und Gustav Zumsteg-Stiftung

Related Projects
- Art Public Zurich, Zurich University of the Arts, 2004–2012
  P. 36
- Draft, Zurich University of the Arts, 2014–2017
  P. 166

Website
- www.artpublicplaiv.org

Publication
- Christoph Schenker (ed.) (2002): *Public Plaiv. Art Contemporauna Illa Plaiv. Gegenwartskunst im Landschafts- und Siedlungsraum La Plaiv, Oberengadin*. Volume 1 of the Institute for Contemporary Art Research series, Zurich University of the Arts. Zurich: Museum für Gestaltung Zürich.
  A Open access: https://doi.org/10.5281/zenodo.3897216

Interview and Article
- Jacqueline Burckhardt (2005): "Kunst im öffentlichen Raum: Theorie und Praxis. Gespräch mit Birgit Sonna und Christoph Schenker." In: Bice Curiger (ed.): *Before the Sun Rises. Walter A. Bechtler Stiftung*. Zurich: JRP Ringier, 65–88.
- Christoph Schenker (2013): "Fontana di Piaggio von Roman Signer." In: Brita Polzer (ed.): *Kunst und Dorf. Künstlerische Aktivitäten in der Provinz*. Zurich: Scheidegger & Spiess, 262–263.

Works
- Bethan Huws: *Architecture*. 2005. Film, 16 mm, color, no audio, 7 min., transferred to DVD, Madulain train station waiting room.
- Ken Lum: *Il Museum Buolf Mus-chin*. 2003. Wooden shed with figure, cabinet, ladder, plaque, and dirt mound, La Punt-Chamues-ch.
- Peter Regli: *Reality Hacking #199*. 7 March 2002. Performance on Pizzet mountain with eighteen skiers from the region equipped with signal lamps, Zuoz.
- Sofie Thorsen: *Village fig. 4/Einige öffentlich zugängliche Informationen und 20 Ereignisse, die sich um das Jahr 2002 in der Plaiv zugetragen haben könnten*. 2002. Audio, 27 min., electronic sound system, Madulain.

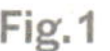

Fig. 1 Ken Lum: *Il Museum Buolf Mus-chin*. La Punt-Chamues-ch, 2003

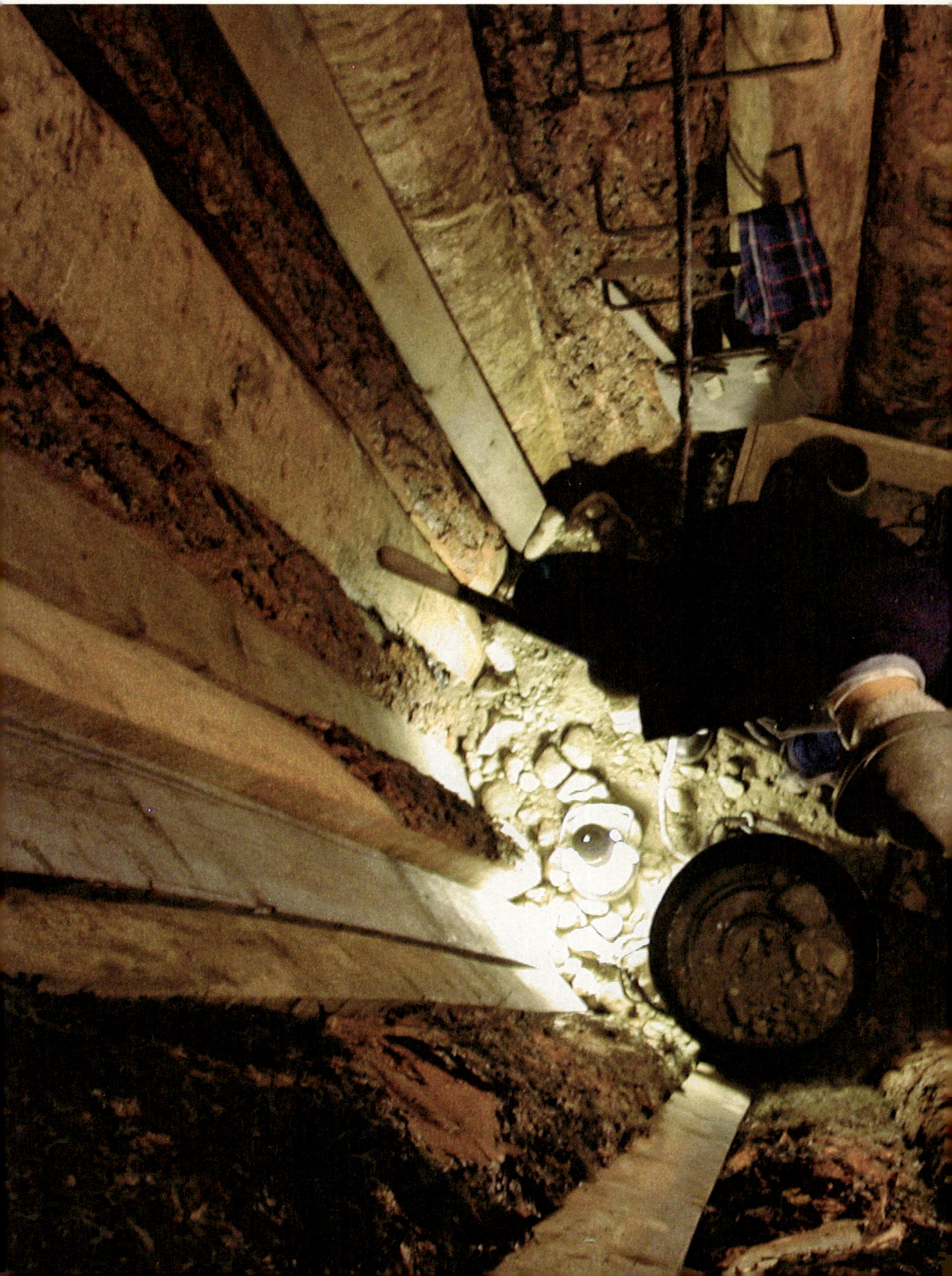

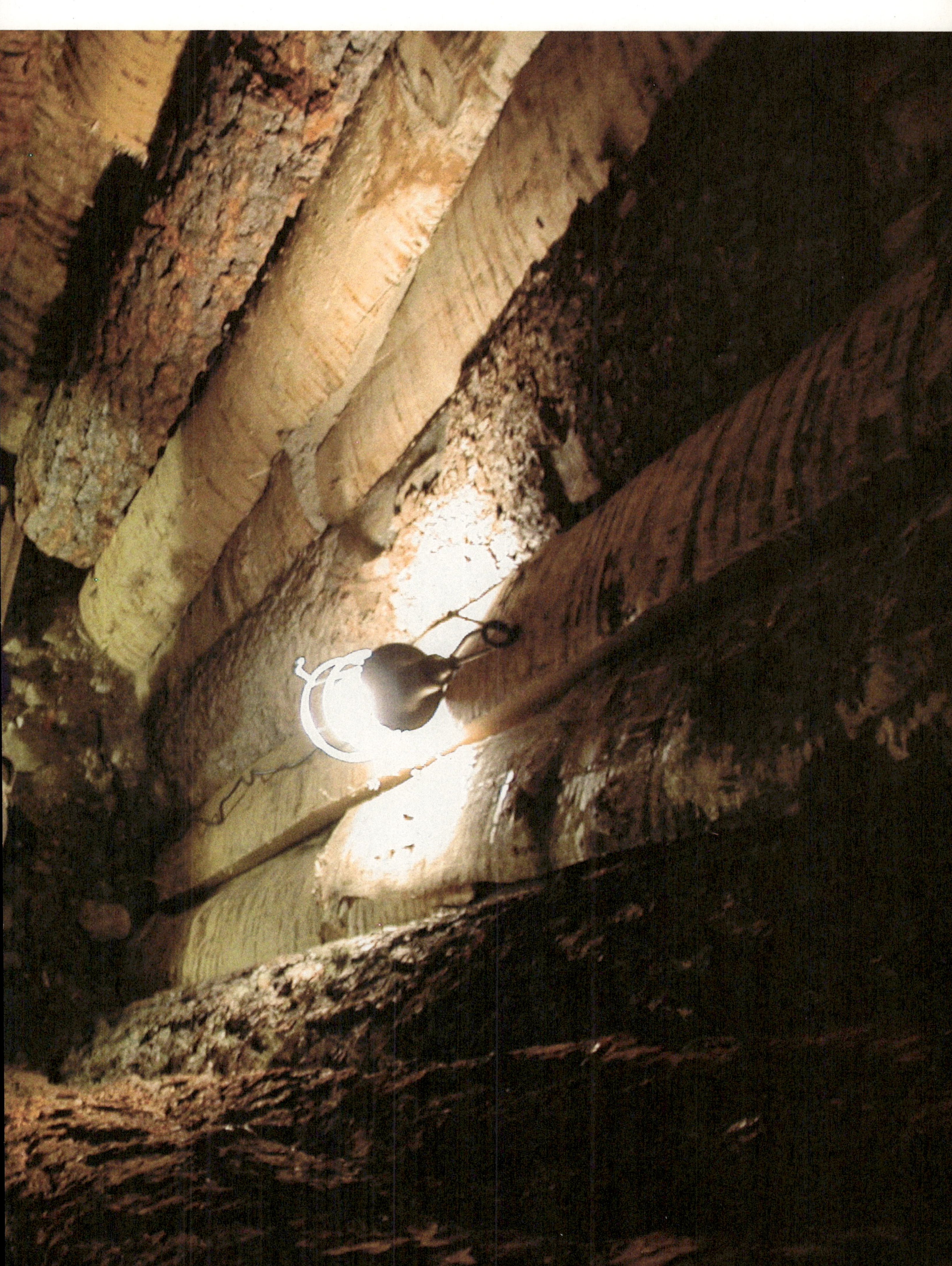

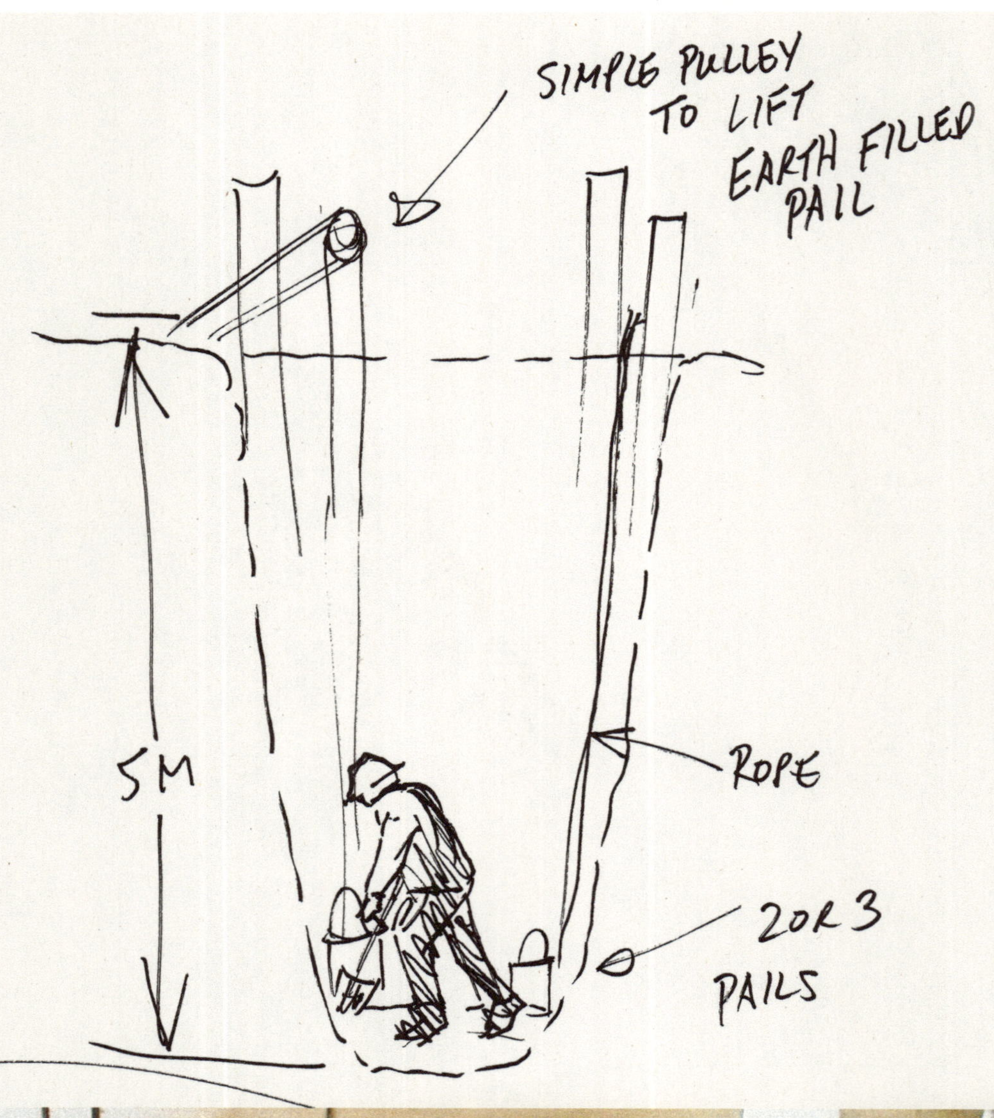
SIMPLE PULLEY
TO LIFT
EARTH FILLED
PAIL
5M
ROPE
2 OR 3
PAILS

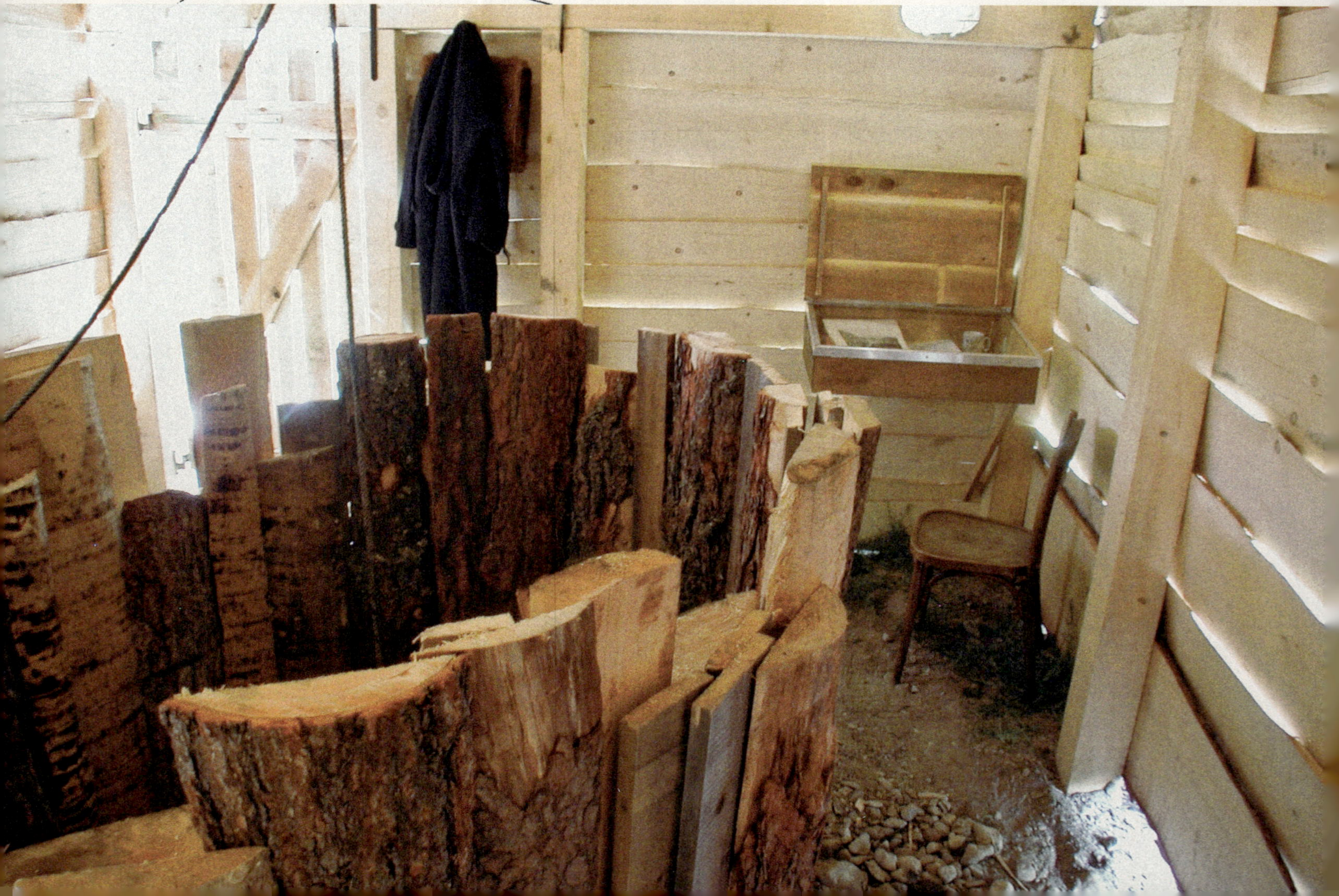

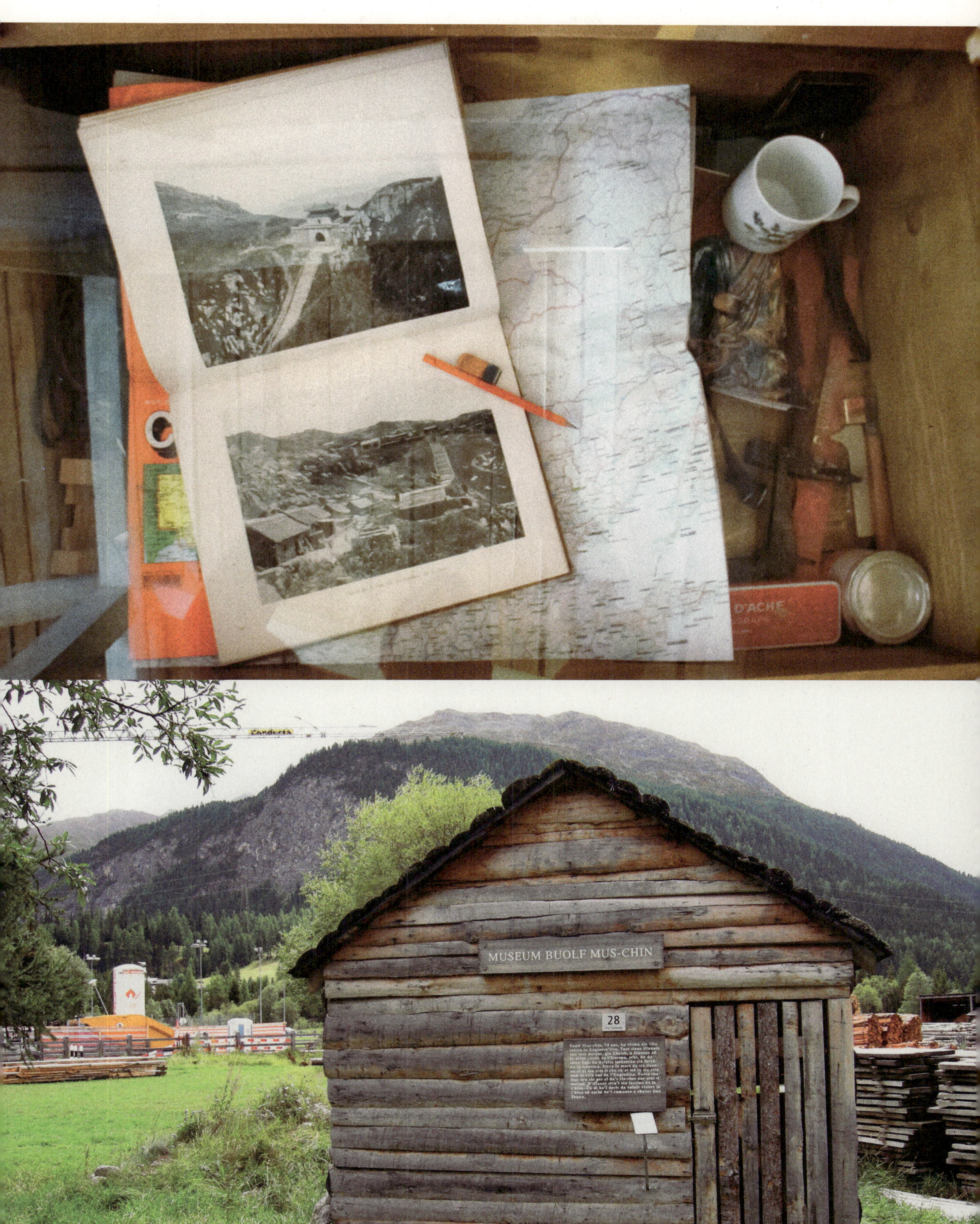
D'ACHE
MUSEUM BUOLF MUS-CHIN
28

Fig. 6–7 Bethan Huws: *Architecture*. Film still, 2005, and drawing from the proposal, 2002

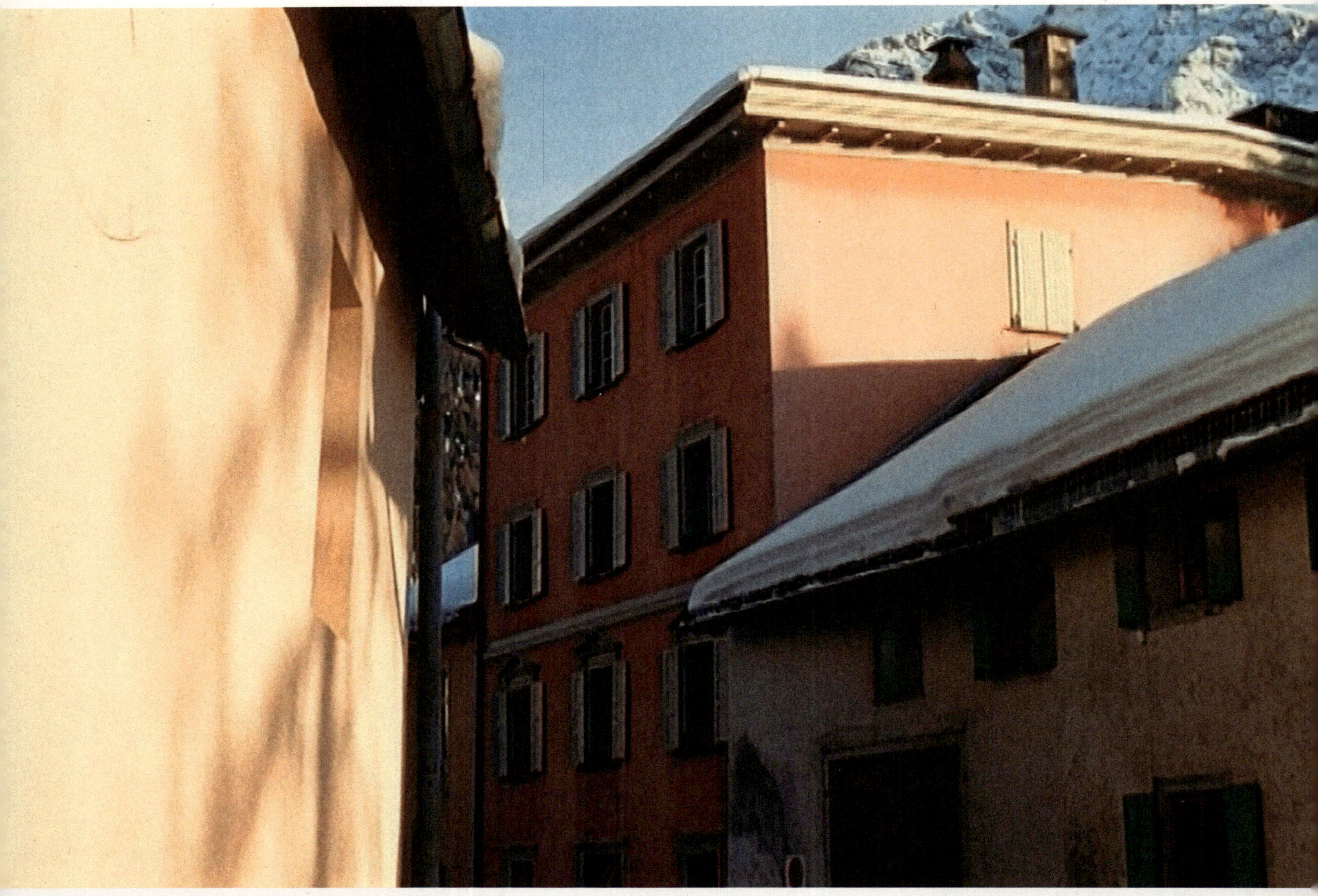

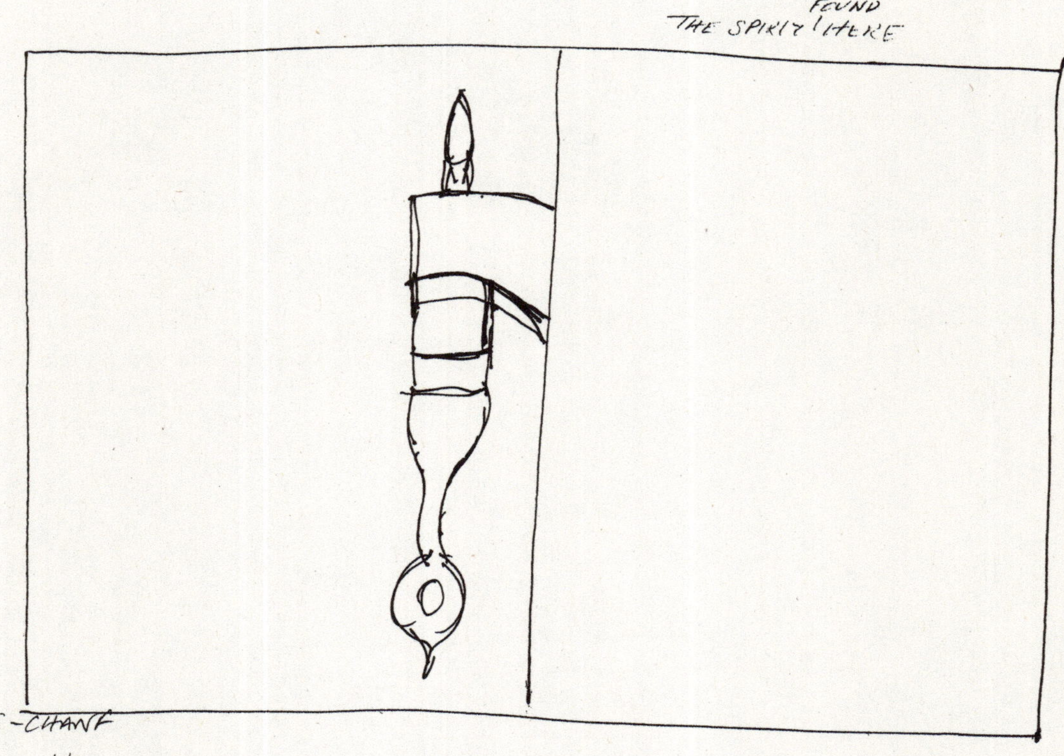

Fig. 8 Peter Regli: *Reality Hacking #199*. Intervention, Zuoz, 2002
Fig. 9 Sofie Thorsen: *Village fig. 4* (see p. 21: Works). Sound installation, Madulain, 2002

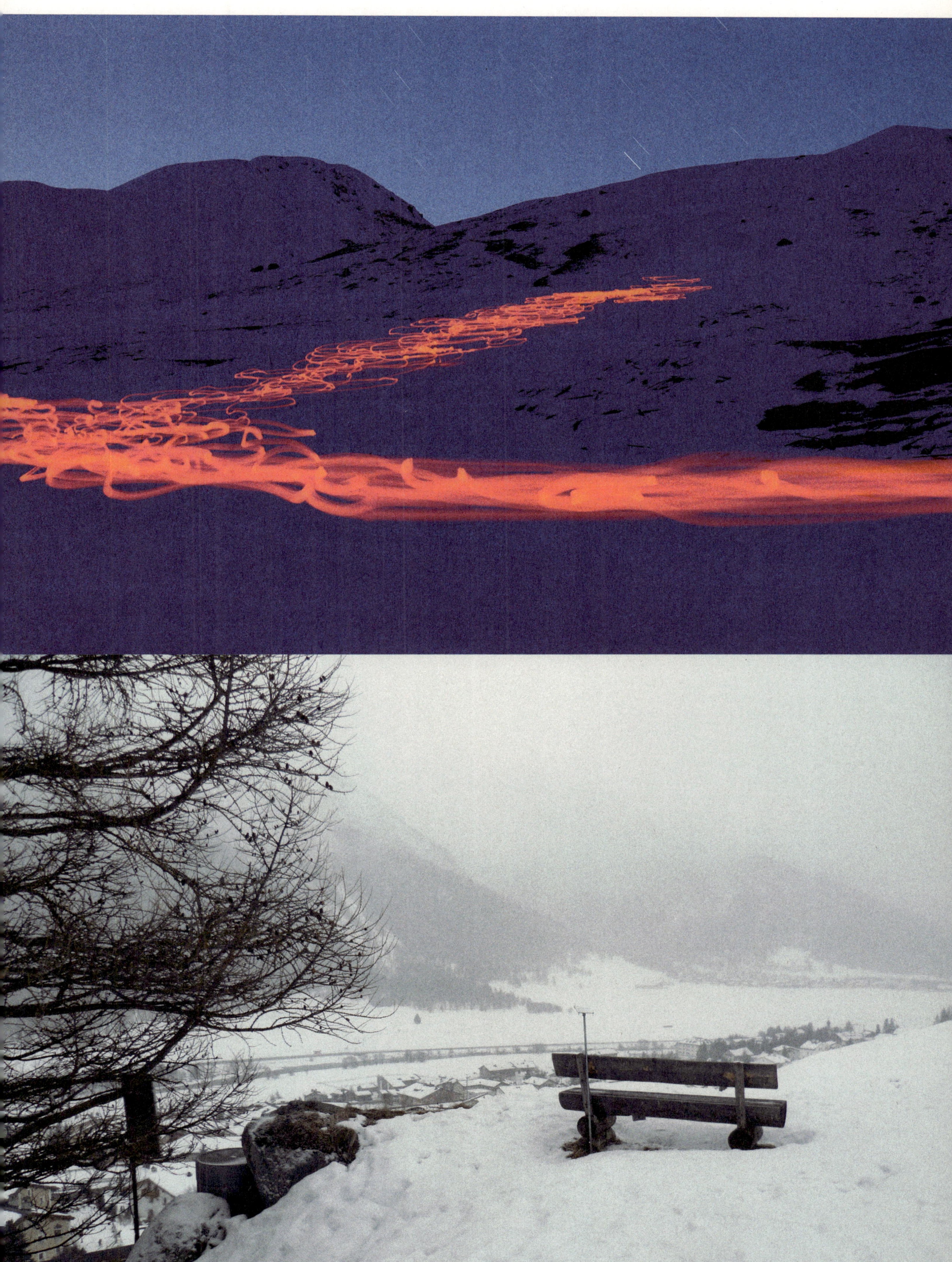

The two-part *Now* research project dealt with questions and problems concerning audio artworks, primarily in the context of the visual arts. In the 1990s, digitalization advanced the use of audio in exhibition spaces. Yet there was a lack of knowledge about how to handle sampling, loops, and timelines. Similarly, there were few references in art theory for the novel auditory experiences offered by many of these works. *Now I* focused on perception in time and sought to make knowledge from scientific fields fertile for art practice. In *Now II* this knowledge was applied to develop narrative forms for radio which forgo ritualized starting points and endings.

To accomplish the treatment mentioned above, it seemed necessary to reach a deeper understanding of how hearing functions in time. Music and composition practice were expanded by adding insights from neuroinformatics, philology, music psychology, linguistics, and semiotics, and translated into or tried out with artistic forms of representation. The knowledge was processed in the form of interviews, which then also constituted the raw material for the audio experiments. The interviews focused on nonlinear processes of consciousness and memory.

The research interviews and audio experiments were published in the form of texts and educational exercises. A key contribution to the artistic discourse was supplied by the observations and experimental explorations of the phenomena of prosodic interaction and periodic noise. In these phenomena, sound—guided appropriately—acts as a knowledge carrier (as opposed to an illustration or atmospheric background music). The work with these phenomena yielded works and cycles of works which were further developed and performed in various contexts in the subsequent fifteen years.

The *Now I* research project succeeded in making knowledge from other disciplines fruitful for event structures in audio sculptures. It also contributed to the discussion about how artistic research can enter into a constructive exchange with scientific research.

In retrospect, what makes the *Now* research project relevant was its insistence on reading the aesthetic. It showed the potential of hearing as a form of knowledge and formulated the central importance of synchronization for interpersonal, societal processes. These include swings in the pitch of conversations, group processes, and rhythms of interactions with machines. The observation and description of prosodic interaction opened up an artistically fertile field. Now that speech melodies are being scanned by algorithms to assess psychological states, this artistic field has become increasingly relevant for society.

Jörg Köppl

Project Title
Now I. Nichtlineare Bewusstseins- und Gedächtnisprozesse als Ausgangslage für neue Ereignisstrukturen in der Audioskulptur

Project Period
1 March 2003–31 December 2005

Keywords
- Hearing
- Time perception
- Audio art
- Sound art
- Artistic research

Head of Project
- Jörg Köppl, artist

Project Team
- Belinda Betsch, neuroinformatics scientist
- Volker Böhm, musician, audio designer and programmer
- Susann Wintsch, art historian and literary scholar
- Tabea Lurk, archivist

Interview Partners
- Aleida Assmann, Anglicist and German philologist
- Urs Boeschenstein, linguist
- Wolfgang Heiniger, composer
- André Vladimir Heiz, semiotician
- Monika Kasper, literary scholar
- Peter König, neuroinformatics scientist
- Annette Schmucki, composer
- Bernhard Sollberger, music psychologist

Research Partners
- Electronic Studio Basel, Musik-Akademie Stadt Basel
- Institute of Neuroinformatics, University of Zurich/ETH

Project Partners
- Radio LoRa
- Radioschule klipp+klang
- Shedhalle Zürich
- Aktive Archive

Project Funding
- Swiss National Science Foundation SNSF, DORE

Related Project
- Now II, Zurich University of the Arts, 2005–2006
  P. 60

Article
- Jörg Köppl (2005): "Arbeiten in und an der Zeit," essay with audio samples. In: Udo Israel, Andreas Reimann, and Bildungszentrum BürgerMedien e.V. (eds.): *A&F Handreichungen. Materialien zur radiojournalistischen Aus- und Fortbildung in nichtkommerziellen Radios*. With music CD. Kopaed: Munich, 463–502.

Lectures and Live Performance
- *Forum 1 Zeitmodelle*. 21 August 2003. Shedhalle, Rote Fabrik, Zurich. Lectures by Belinda Betsch, Reto Friedmann, and Bernhard Sollberger.
- *Forum 2 Erzählungen*. 21 November 2003. Shedhalle, Rote Fabrik, Zurich. Live performance by Volker Böhm and Jörg Köppl.

Exhibitions
- *hier ist niemand*. 5 November–9 December 2005. Kunsthof Zürich. Sound installation by Jörg Köppl and Mirjam Bürgin.
- *Ich höre Deine Stimme in meinem Kopf*. 23 September–20 November 2011. Kunstmuseum Thun. Solo exhibition by Jörg Köppl.

Radio Broadcast
- Jörg Köppl and Volker Böhm: *Fragen über Fragen. Eine computergenerierte Komposition*. Non-stop from 31 July–6 August 2003 and at night from 24 November–8 December 2003. Radio LoRa 97.5 MHz.

Fig. 1 Jörg Köppl and Mirjam Bürgin: *hier ist niemand*. Kunsthof Zürich, 2005

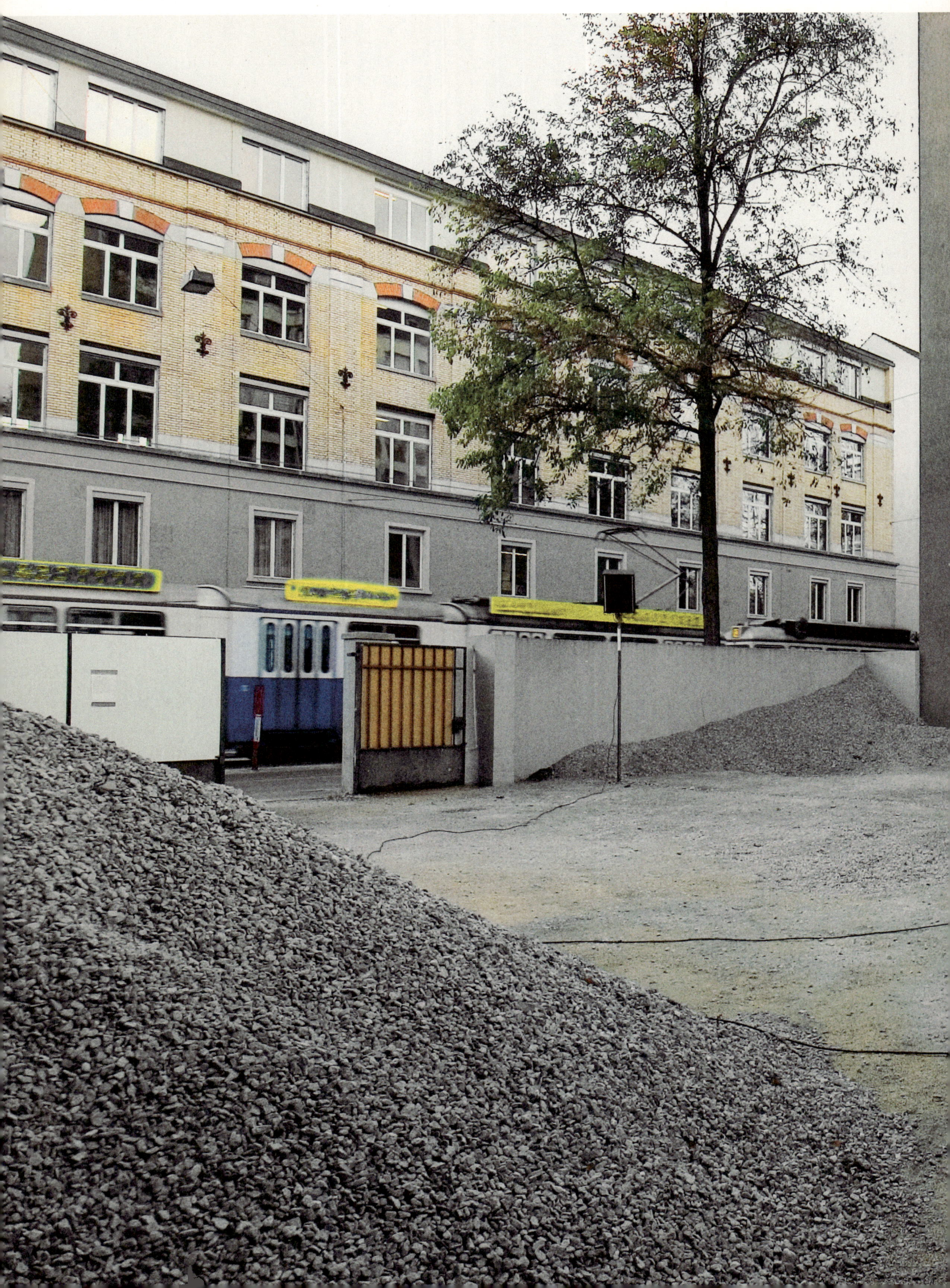

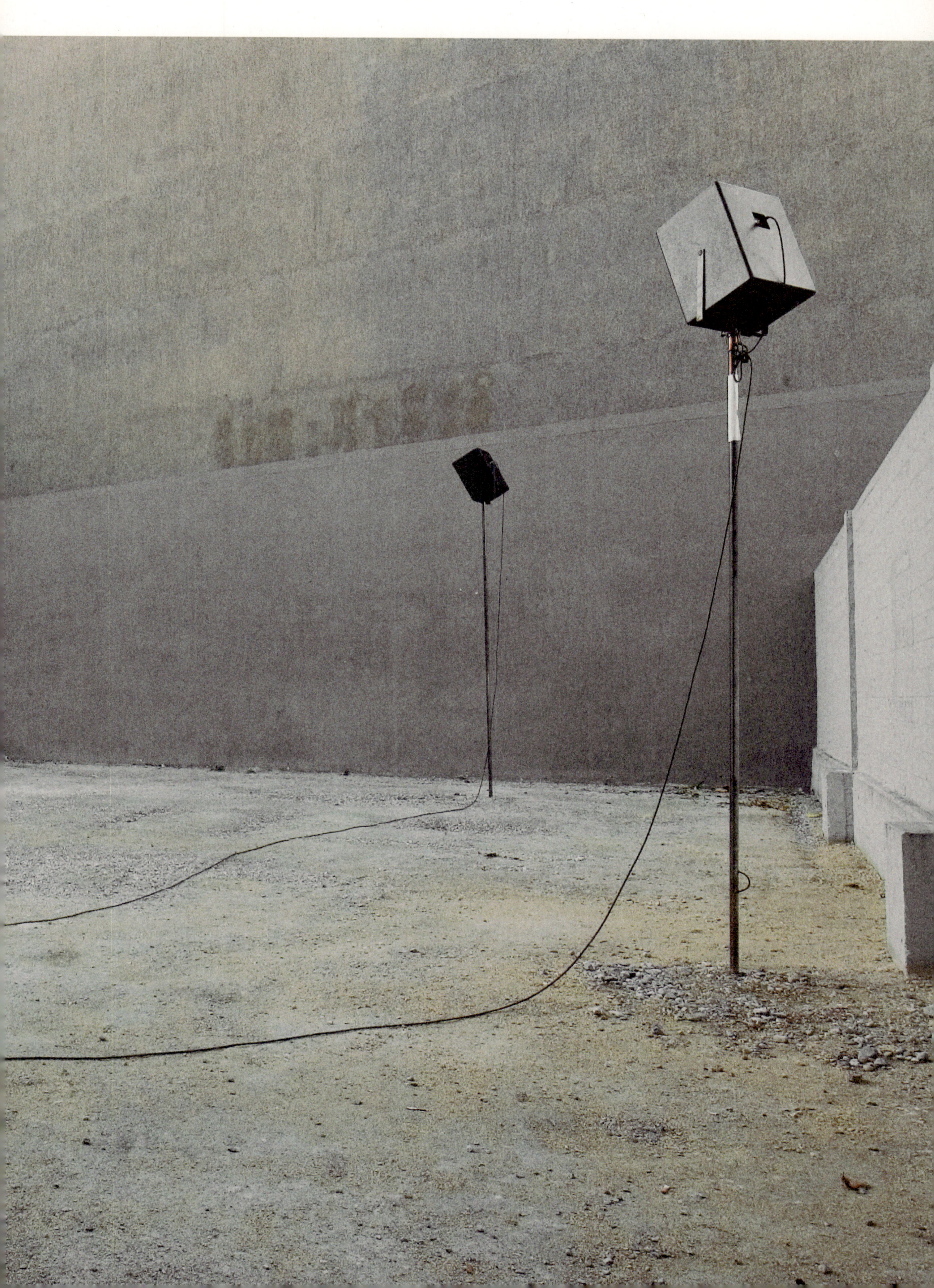

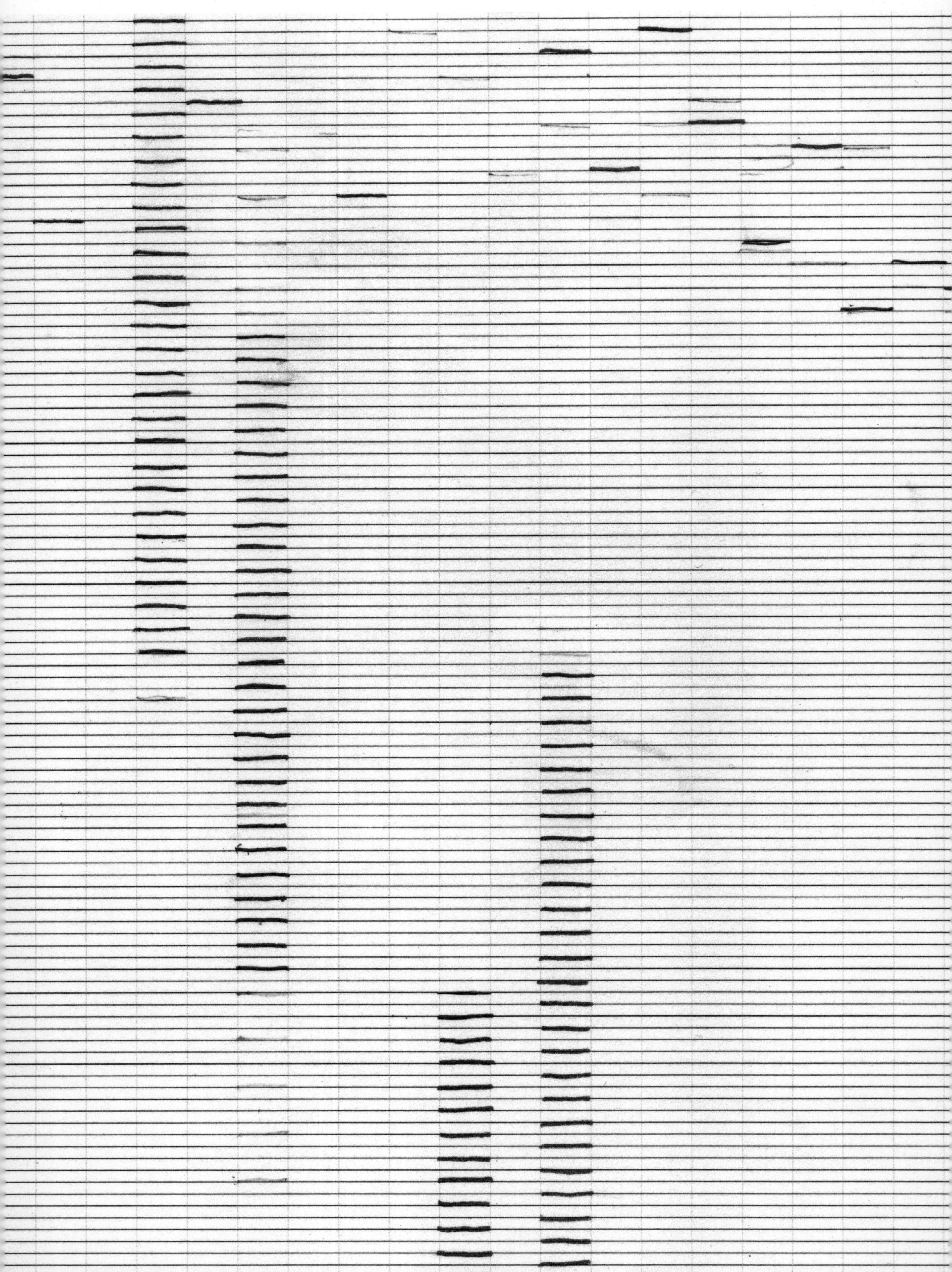

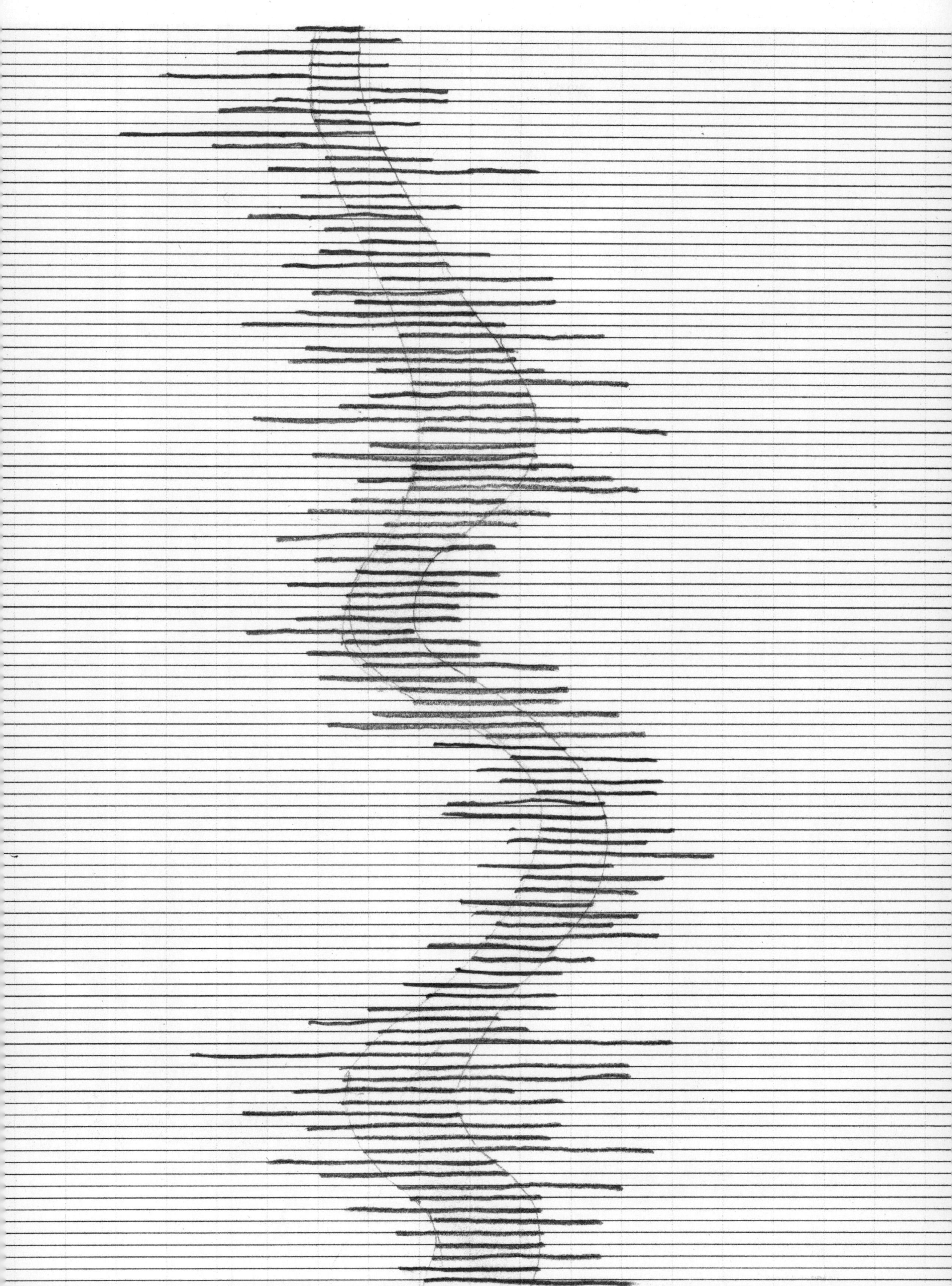

Fig. 4 Jörg Köppl in collaboration with Franziska Bruecker: *inhale – inhalt*
Fig. 5 Jörg Köppl with Markus Hochuli and Léo Collin: *palaver*
Both Kunstraum Walcheturm, Zurich, 2021

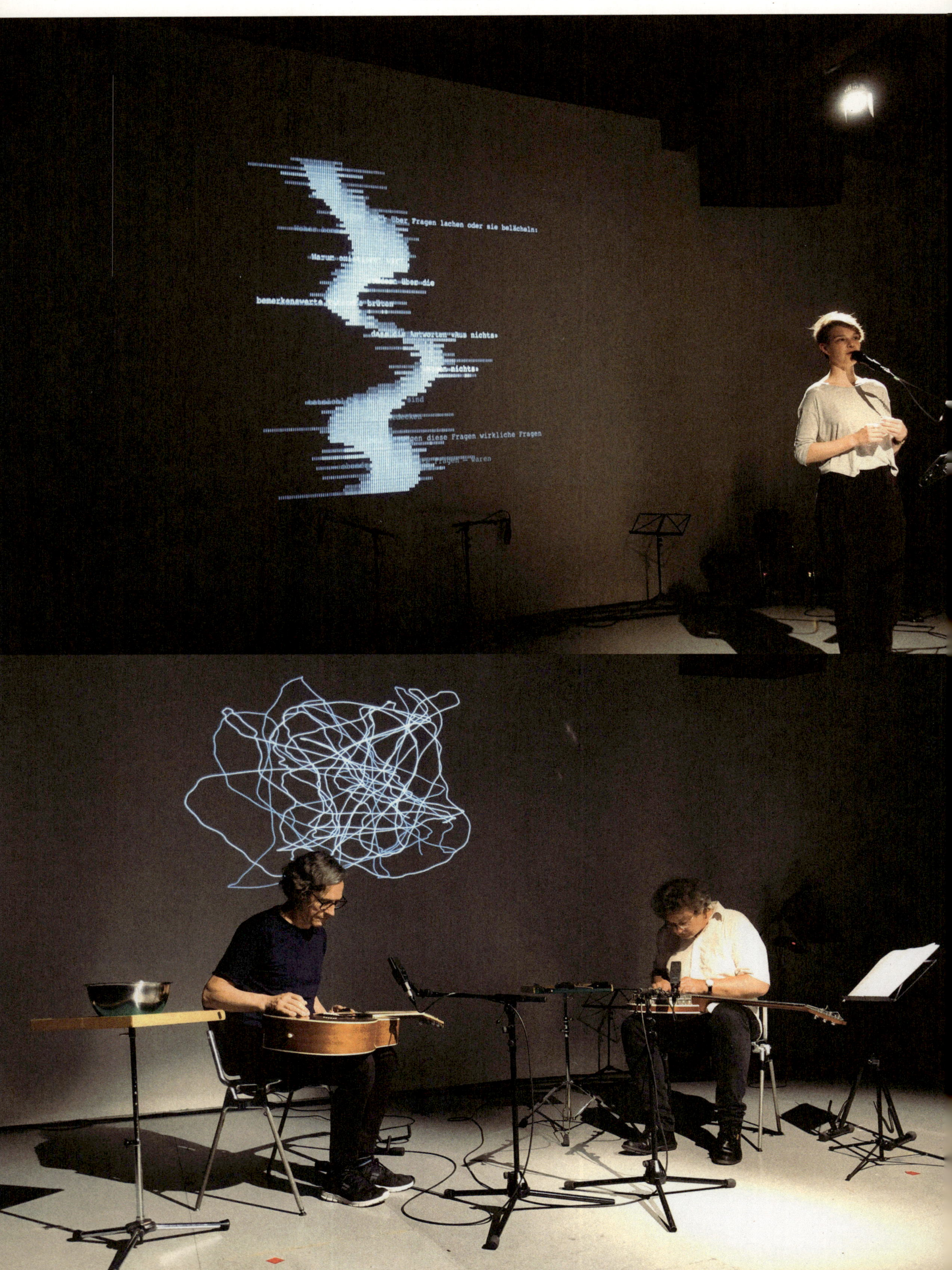

Fig. 6 Jörg Köppl/scenic design by Mirjam Bürgin: *mono*. Kunstraum Walcheturm, Zurich, 2018

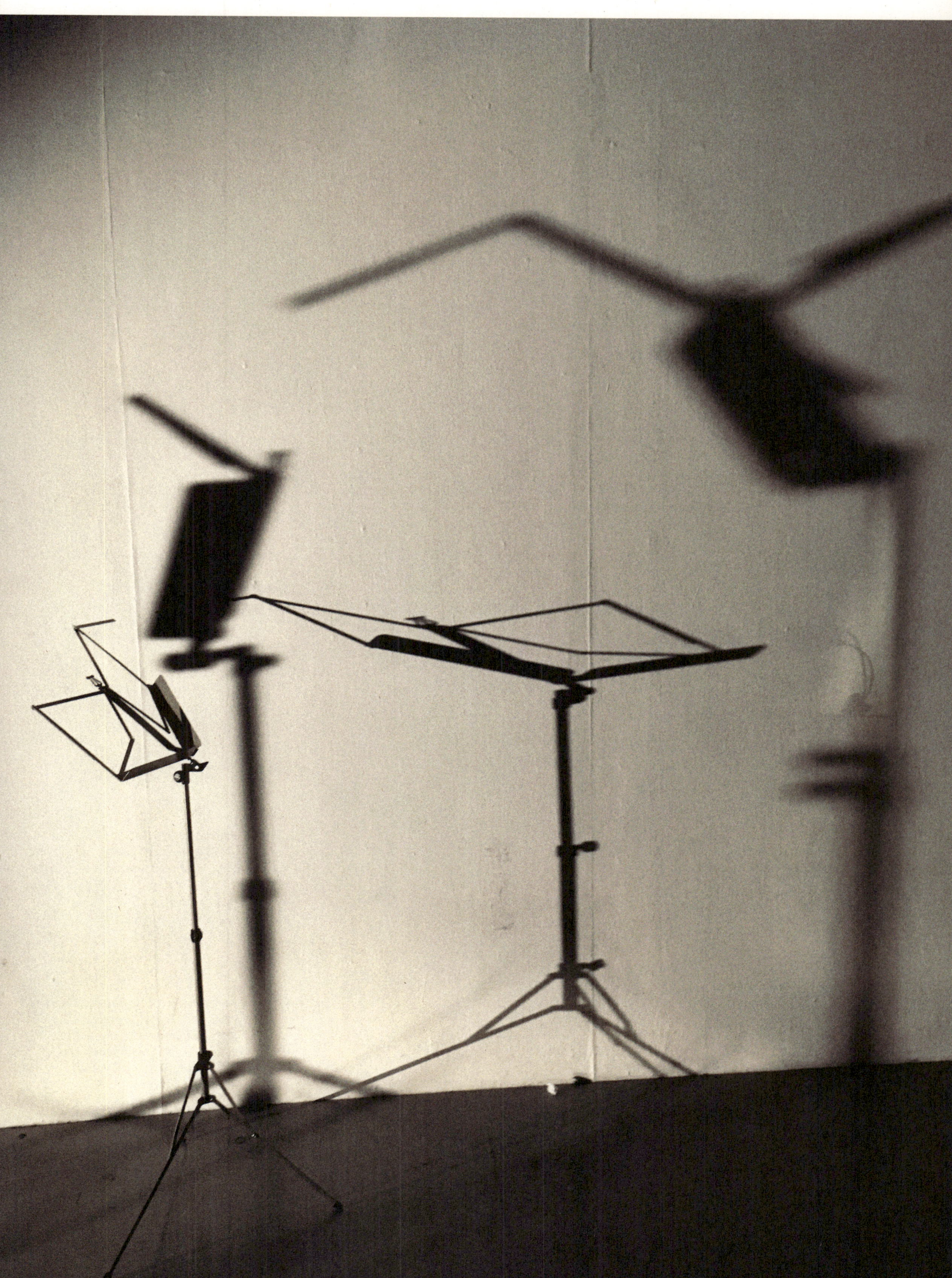

In the early 2000s, the city of Zurich had a great deal to do, in comparison with other global cities, to cultivate public art and to encourage its discourse. Art in public space played no significant role in city marketing. And while the Zurich art market had soared to international renown in the 1990s, the city made hardly any contribution to the internationally established discourse about and through contemporary public art.

This was the constellation from which the research project was launched in 2004. One of its emphases was on development work in the city administration, another on research for and in artistic projects. Together with the city administration, it created structures and instruments that provided for active promotion of the future development of public art. In late 2006 the project team submitted its mission statement for art in public space in the city of Zurich. Shortly after the mission statement was approved, the city council initiated the permanent "Task Force Art in Public Space."

A second emphasis of the research project was the design of several artistic pilot projects, some of which were partially realized. They were based on a concept of public art geared less toward public space and more toward the context of the public sphere. The art projects were the result of a transdisciplinary process developed within the research project, which was later dubbed the "Zurich Model" by Hedwig Fijen, director of *Manifesta*, the European Biennale of Contemporary Art. Simply put, the process consisted of two separate phases. The first was to perform both extensive research and focused studies in order to determine societal, political, economic, ecological, and cultural factors that were of particular and critical relevance for the city of Zurich as a whole or for a segment of the public. The second step was to invite artists who had expertise in the identified fields to develop projects specific to the identified situations. The artists then did their own research and consulted with experts from other disciplines to work cooperatively on each topic and object. The fact that the projects referred to the factors identified lent a new quality to public debates.

Viewed from the perspective of the sociology of science, the process that took place in the research organization was largely congruent with the "Mode 2 Knowledge Production" that emerged in the mid-1990s, as described by Helga Nowotny, Peter Scott, Michael Gibbons and others. The individual pilot projects followed this logic as well. For example, in their transdisciplinarity as a form of knowledge production that incorporates heterogeneous, and even non-scientific and non-artistic knowledge; and in the site-specific and problem-oriented production of knowledge, that is, in the production of knowledge for a concrete application context. It is not as if "Mode 2" were not already being practiced in the field of contemporary art. But the project succeeded in making this process explicit, performing it systematically, structuring it transparently, and advancing its development. The reference to "Mode 2 Knowledge Production" made it possible to integrate the artists into the project as researchers.

Unfortunately, it was not possible to execute all of the artistic projects for which comprehensive proposals were submitted. The projects by Monica Bonvicini and Matthew Buckingham fell by the wayside, and the one by knowbotic research was realized only in part. Such processes can take a long time in the context of public art. Because some of the projects were realized only after the actual period of financing by the KTI, the project is listed in two parts here.

Christoph Schenker

Project Title
Kunst Öffentlichkeit Zürich

Project Period
Phase 1
- 2004–2007 (City of Zurich)

Phase 2
- 2008–2012 (Hardau residential complex; project director: Christoph Lang)

Keywords
- Public art
- Public sphere
- Artistic research
- Mode 2 knowledge production
- The Zurich model

Head of Project
- Christoph Schenker, art theorist

Project Team
- Bettina Burkhardt, architect
- Bernadette Fülscher, architect
- Michael Hiltbrunner, cultural anthropologist
- Christoph Lang, artist and scenographer
- Ulrich Vonrufs, historian
- Tim Zulauf, artist and author

Participating Artists
Phase 1
- Monica Bonvicini, Matthew Buckingham, Harun Farocki, knowbotic research, Lawrence Weiner; San Keller, Claudia & Julia Müller; Ana Axpe, Christoph Hänsli, David Renggli, Shirana Shahbazi, Till Velten

Phase 2
- Zilla Leutenegger, Sislej Xhafa

Outputs

A

D

B

C

Research Partner
- Philip Ursprung, SNSF Professor for the History of Contemporary Art, ETH Zurich

Project Partner
- City of Zurich

Project Funding and Support
- KTI/CTI The Innovation Promotion Agency (now Innosuisse—Swiss Innovation Agency)
- Hans Hüssy
- G + B Schwyzer Stiftung
- Swiss Re
- Mai 36 Galerie
- Stiftung der Schweizerischen Landesausstellung 1939 Zürich
- Migros-Kulturprozent
- Homburger Rechtsanwälte
- Baugenossenschaft Zurlinden
- Zumtobel Lighting GmbH

Related Projects
- Public Plaiv, Zurich University of the Arts, 2001–2002
  P. 20
- Draft, Zurich University of the Arts, 2014–2017
  P. 166

Project Websites
- https://www.stadtkunst.ch
- https://blog.zhdk.ch/y-hardau/

Publications
- Christoph Schenker and Michael Hiltbrunner (eds.) (2007): *Kunst und Öffentlichkeit: Kritische Praxis der Kunst im Stadtraum Zürich*. Volume 2 of the Institute for Contemporary Art Research series. Zurich: JRP Ringier.
  A Open access: https://doi.org/10.5281/zenodo.3979250
- Christoph Schenker (2021): *Art as Compact Knowledge—Art Public Zurich: A Research Project*. Volume 2A of the Institute for Contemporary Art Research series. Zurich: IFCAR.
  B Open access: https://doi.org/10.5281/zenodo.5636780
- Stadt Zürich and Institute for Contemporary Art Research (eds.) (2012): *Kunst und Bau – Die Hardau*. Zurich: Amt für Hochbauten, Stadt Zürich.
  C Open access: https://doi.org/10.5281/zenodo.5116228
- Selma Dubach and Christoph Schenker (eds.) (2011): *Public Issues. OnCurating*, Issue 11.
  D Open access: https://doi.org/10.5281/zenodo.5256145

Conference
- *Kunst Öffentlichkeit Zürich*. 17–18 November 2005. Kunsthalle Zürich. With Jean-Christophe Ammann, Marius Babias, Ursula Biemann, Beatrice von Bismarck, Boris Buden, Gabriela Christen, Peter Ess, Martin Heller, Jean-Pierre Hoby, Daniel Robert Hunziker, Anne Keller, Oliver Marchart, Bessie Nager, Christoph Schenker, Hito Steyerl, Philip Ursprung, Martin Waser, and Ingrid Wildi.

Panels and Lecture
- *Kunst Öffentlichkeit Zürich*. 4 November 2005. Zurich University of the Arts. With Stefan Römer, Michael Hiltbrunner, Hanspeter Huber, Susanne von Ledebur, Shirana Shahbazi, Dorothea Strauss, and Till Velten.
- Harun Farocki: Presentation of the video *Übertragung* and panel discussion with Georges Didi-Hubermann and Ludger Schwarte. 9 September 2008. Schaulager Basel.
- Tim Zulauf: "Der berührende Bildschirm," lecture about the video *Übertragung* (2007) by Harun Farocki. In: *Praktiken ästhetischen Denkens*, 4–5 April 2019, FHNW Academy of Art and Design, Basel.

Works
- San Keller: *Freinacht in der Hardau* and *Best of Hardau*. 5 March and 4 June 2005. Two participatory art performances. Hardau residential complex, Zurich.
- Ana Axpe, Christoph Hänsli, David Renggli, Shirana Shahbazi, Till Velten: Multipart poster project. March–December 2005. Hardau residential complex, Zurich.
- knowbotic research: *BlackBenz Race*. 2005/06. Art performances, interventions (realized in part). Zurich—Pristina—Zurich.
- Claudia and Julia Müller: *Glocke*Hardau*-BimBam*2006*. 2006. Bronze bell. 120 × 100 × 100 cm. Hardau II, Zurich.
- Harun Farocki: *Übertragung*. 2007. Video (color, sound). 43 min. Limmatplatz, Zurich.
- Lawrence Weiner: *Ball Bearings or Round Stones*. 2007. Work in three parts in English, German, and Italian. Sheet metal. Each 310 × 220 cm. Bellevueplatz, Helvetiaplatz, and Limmatplatz, Zurich.
- Zilla Leutenegger: *Das Haus im Haus*. 2009. Work in five parts. Wall drawings and fittings. Oberstufenschulhaus Albisriederplatz, Zurich.
- Sislej Xhafa: *Y*. 2011. Sculpture. Various materials. 15 m high. Hardaupark, Zurich.

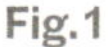

Fig.1 Shirana Shahbazi: Poster. Hardau, Zurich, 2005

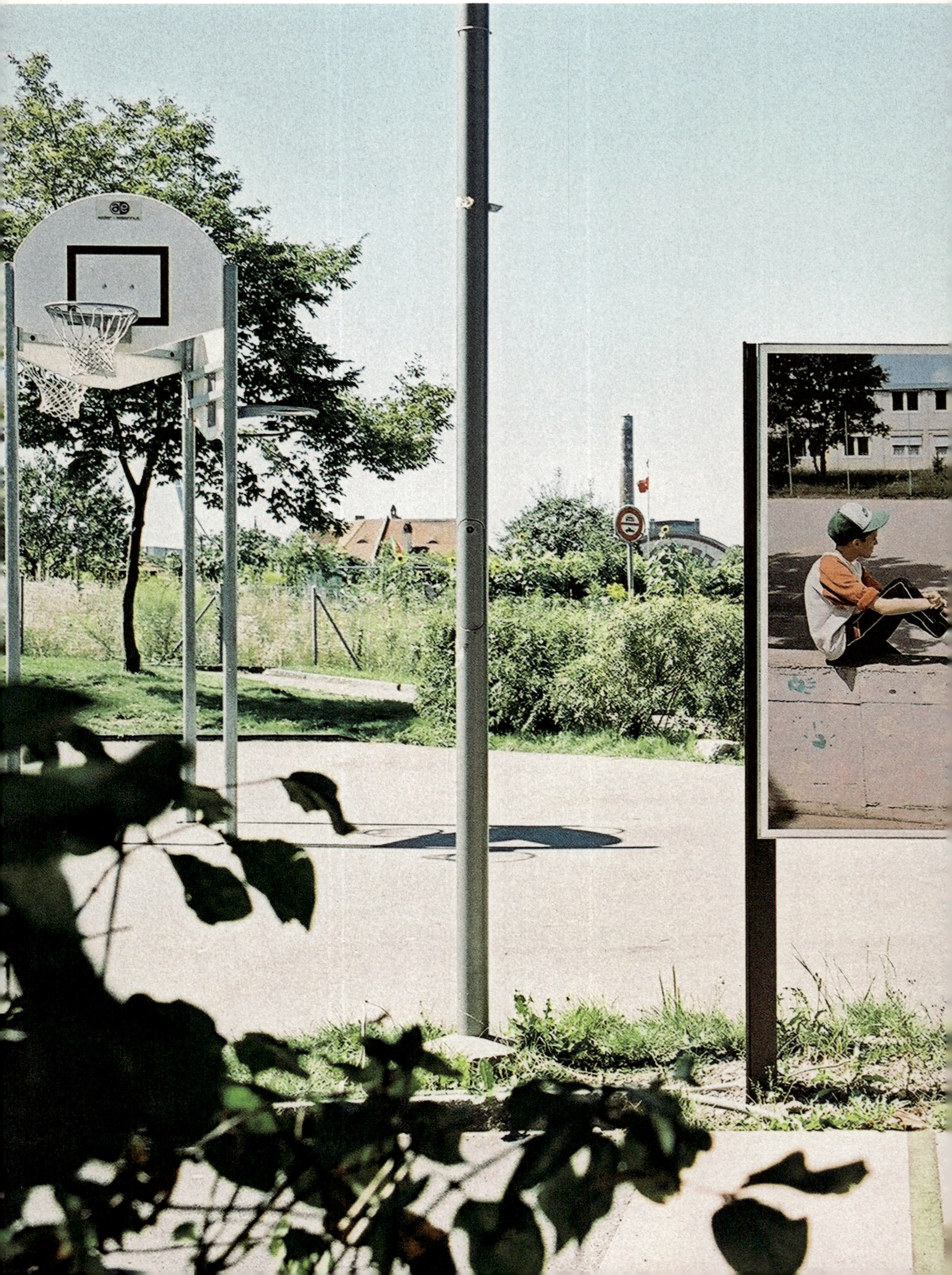

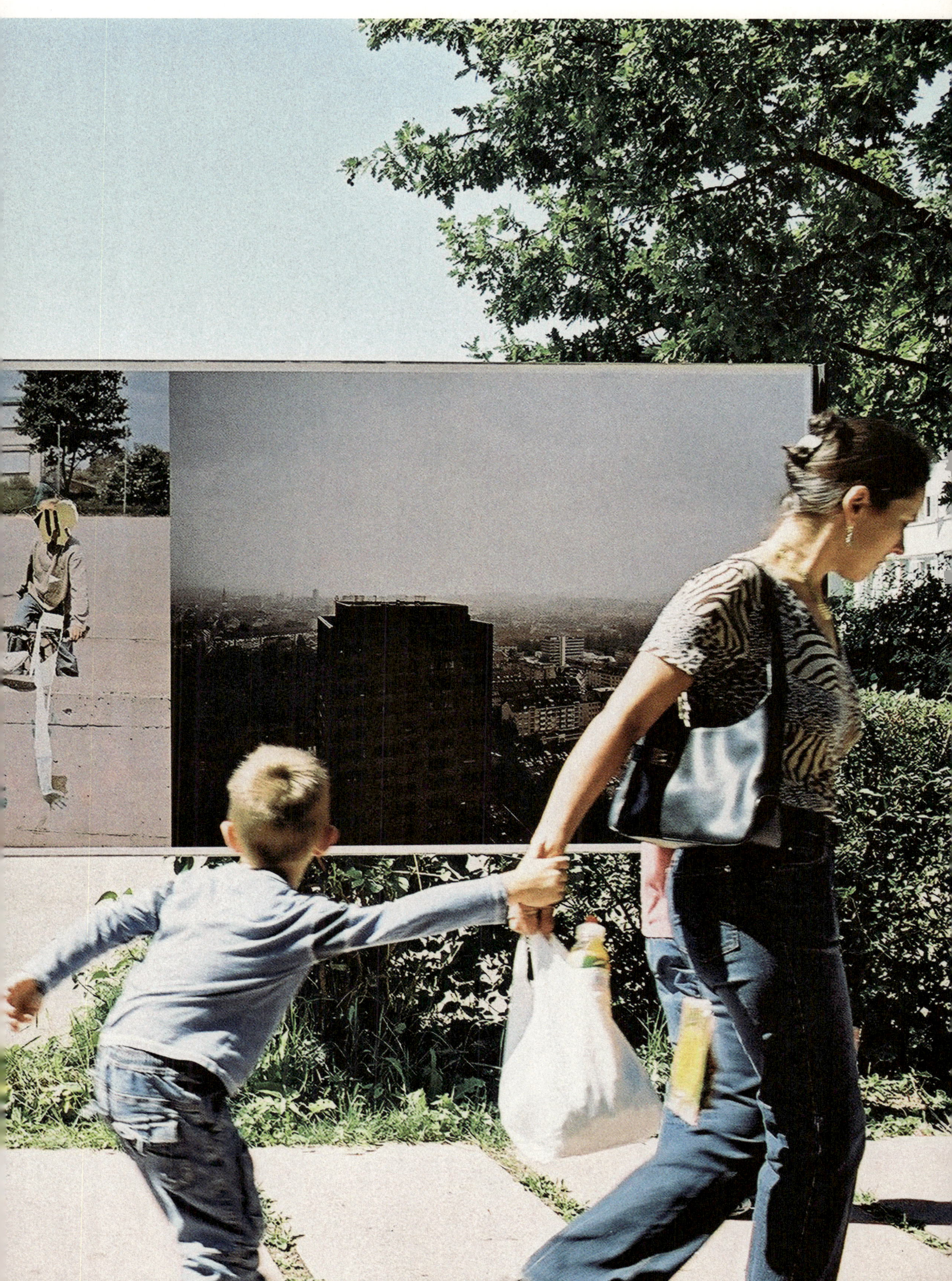

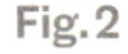

Fig. 2 Sislej Xhafa: *Y*. Hardaupark, Zurich, 2011

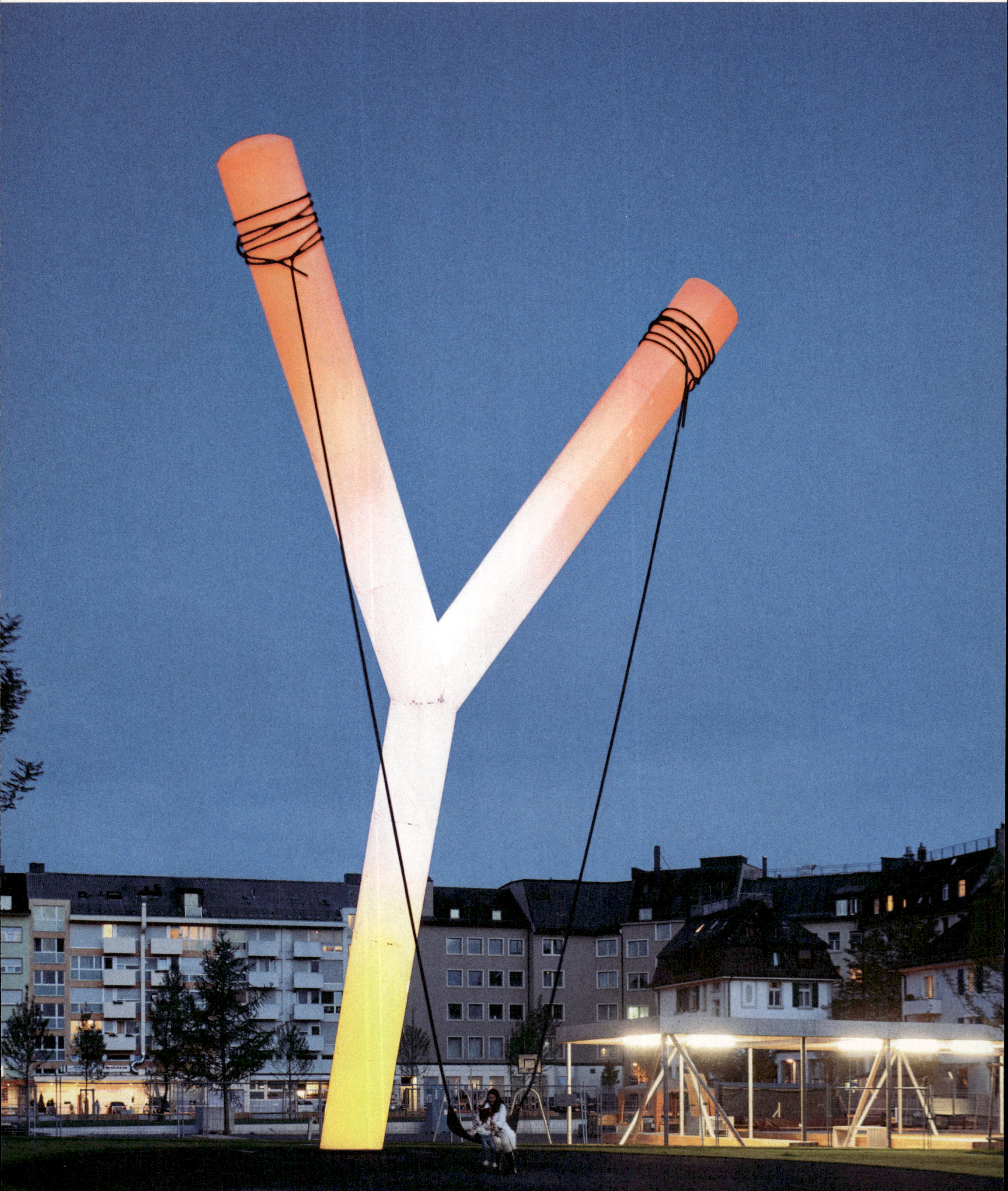

Fig. 3–4 San Keller: *Best of Hardau* and *Freinacht in der Hardau*. Zurich, 2005

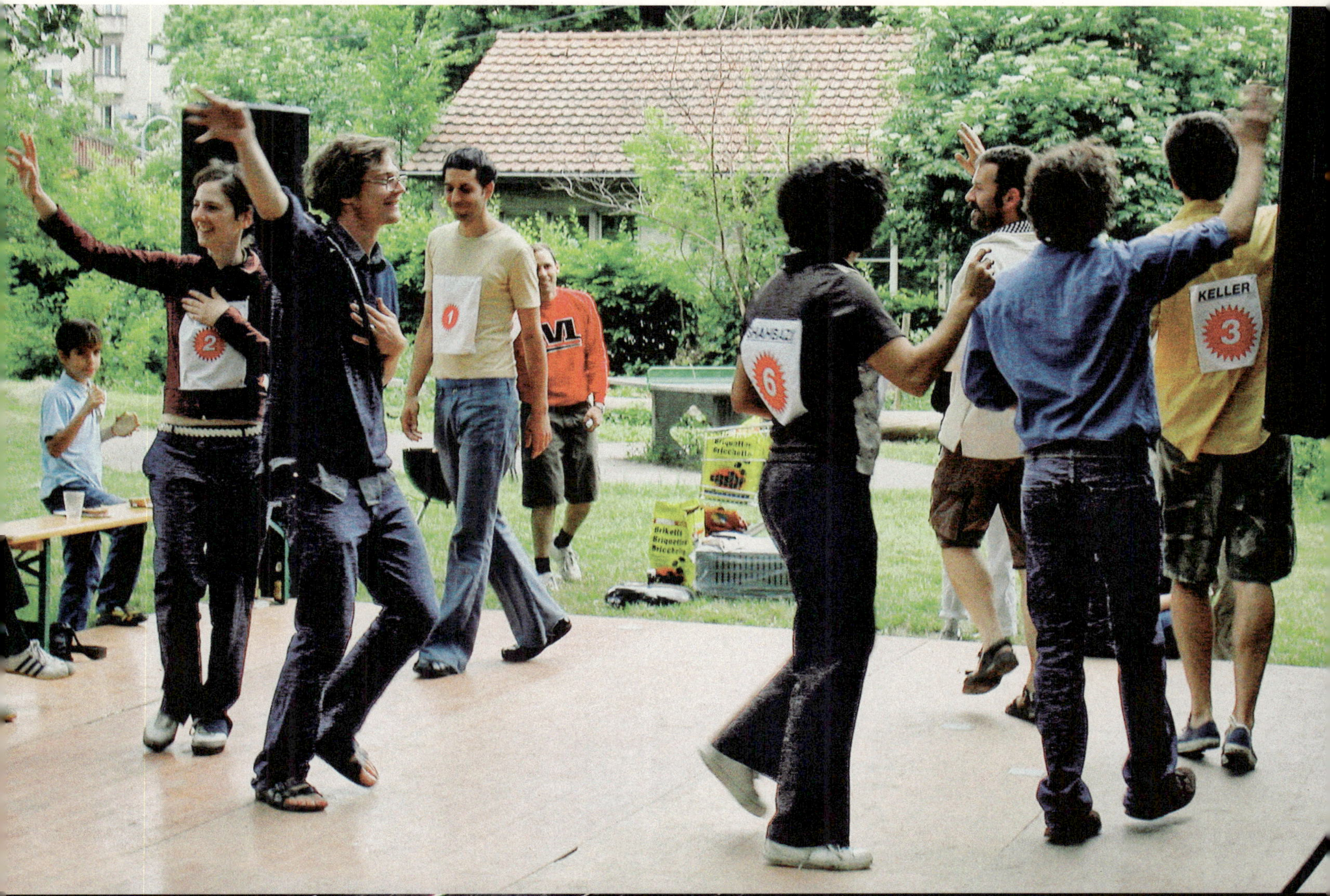

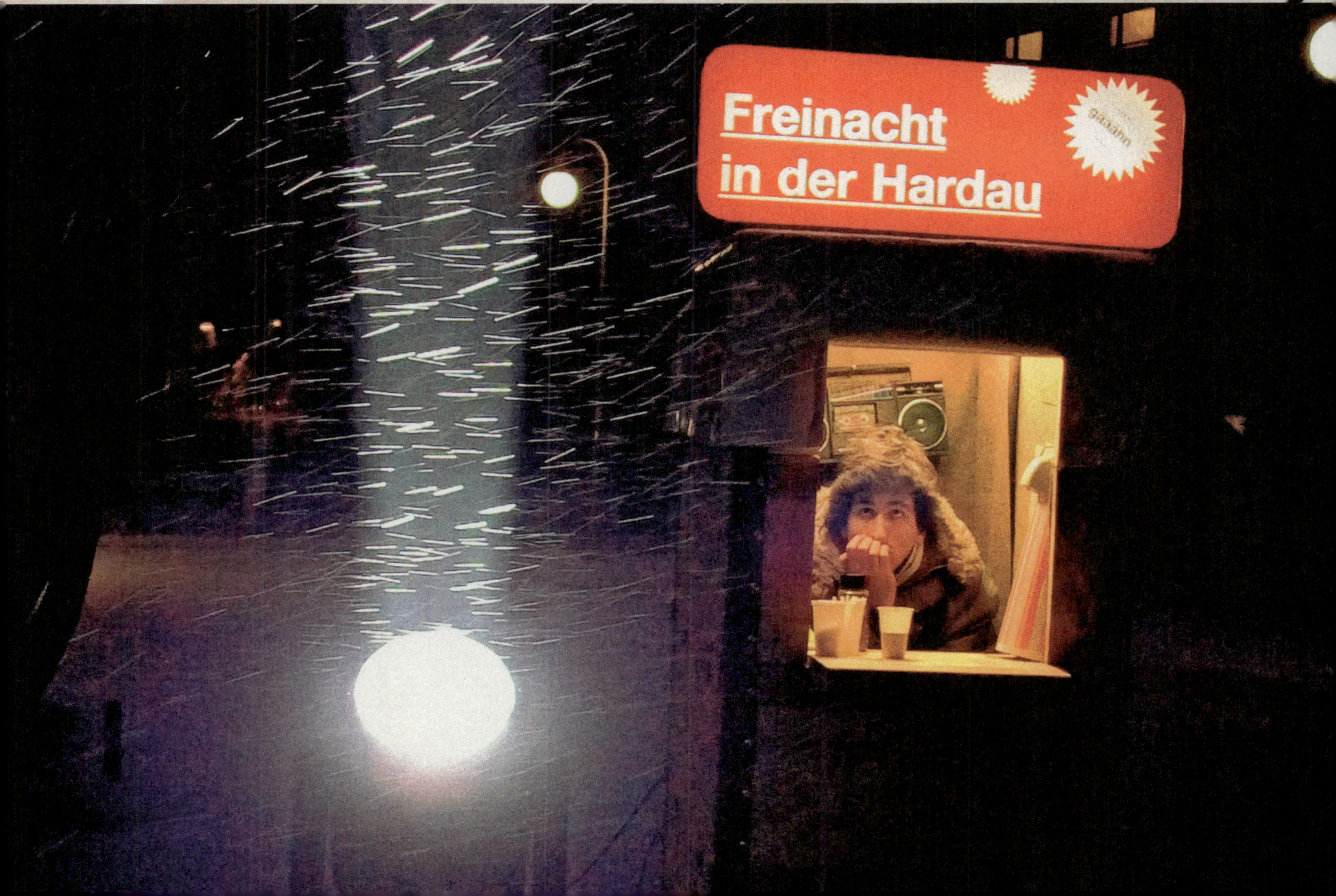

Fig. 5 Lawrence Weiner: *Ball Bearings or Round Stones*. Helvetiaplatz, Zurich, 2007

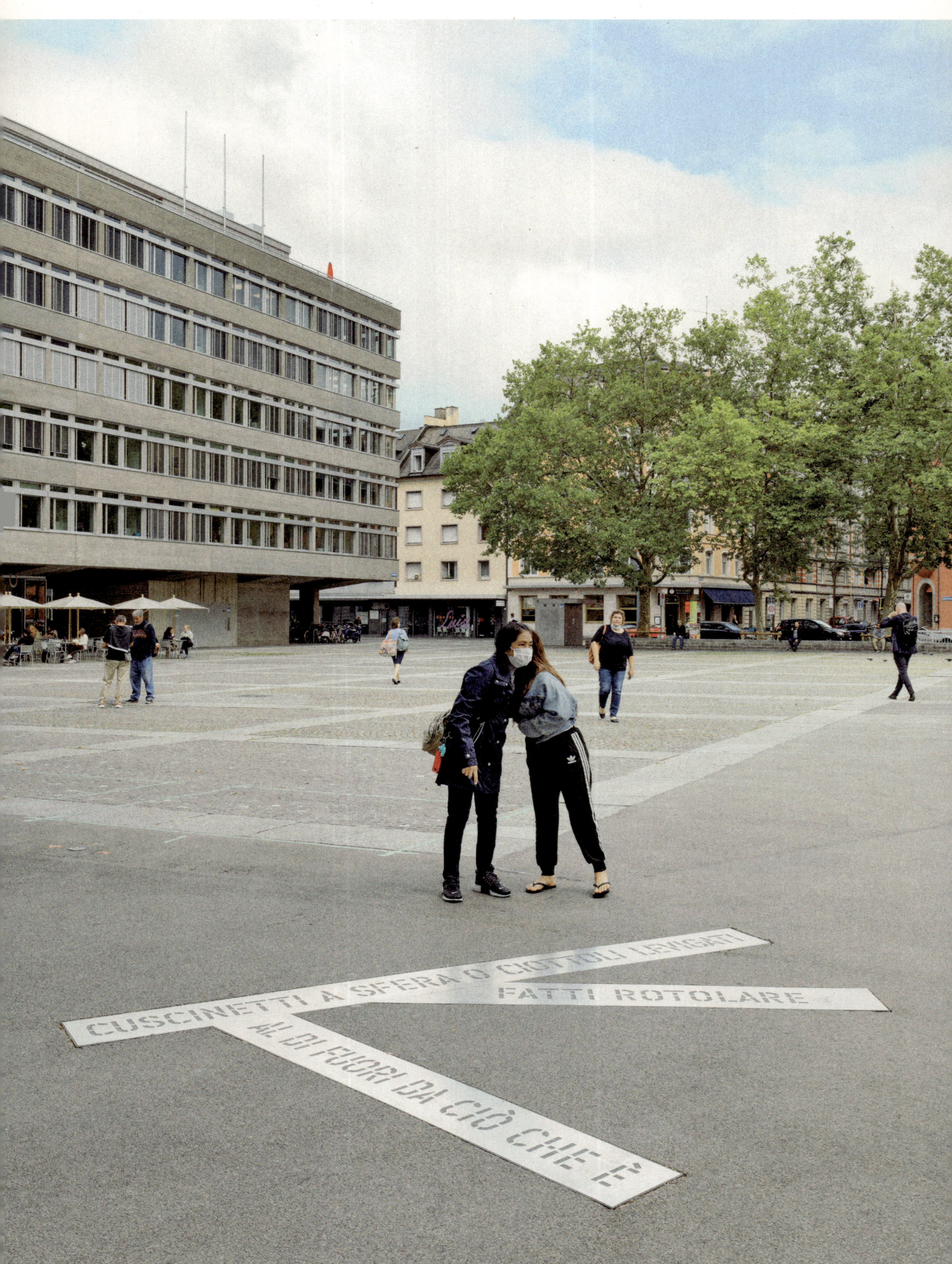

Fig. 6 Harun Farocki: *Übertragung*. Limmatplatz, Zurich, 2007

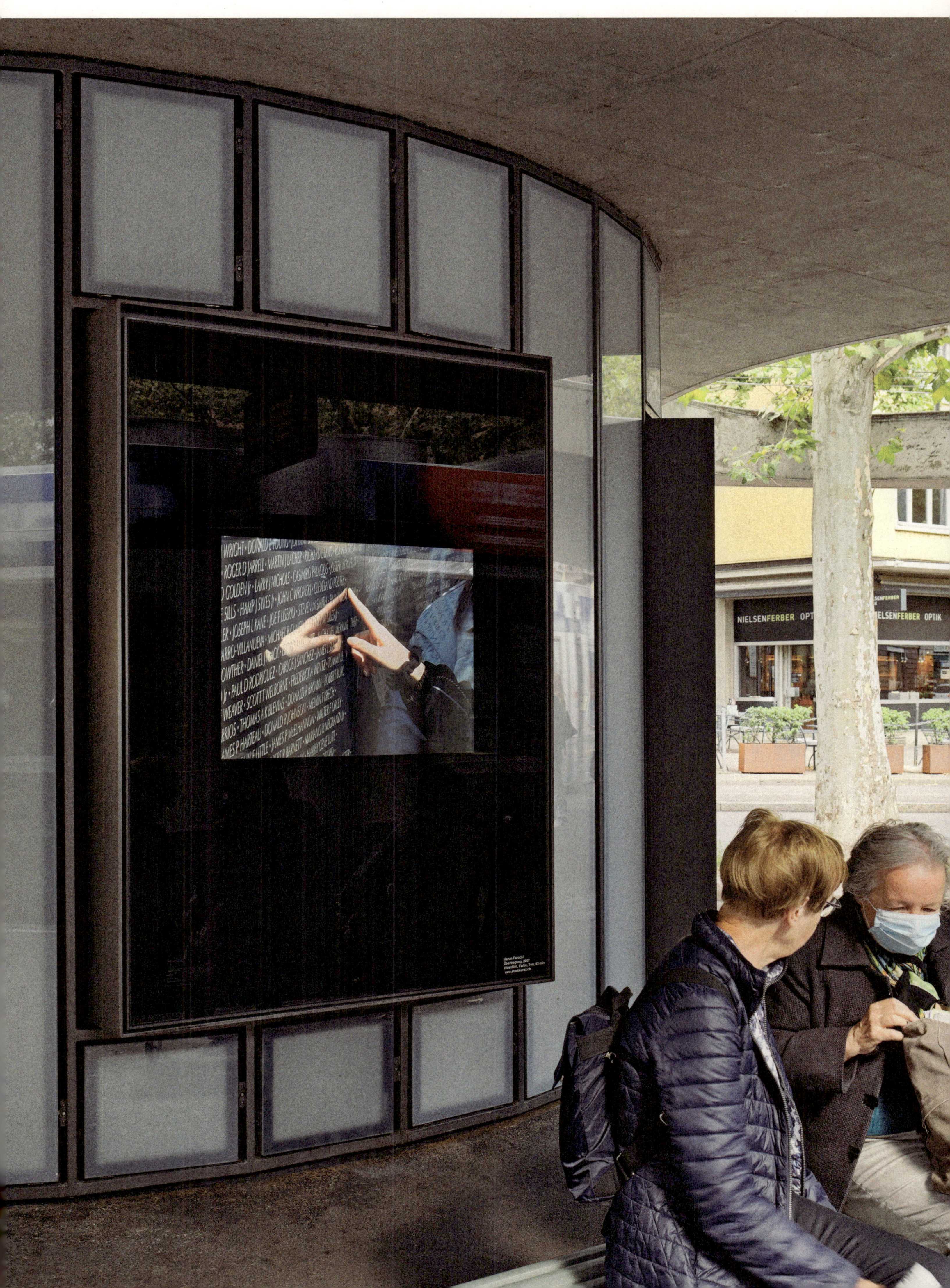

The research project *The Art of Research* investigated methods of art that are similar to practices in cultural studies. How is knowledge produced in these fields and at their boundaries? In close cooperation with artists, we examined techniques of knowledge creation, knowledge structuring, and knowledge transfer. We worked out criteria for an artistic-scientific practice that renounced the limitations of the classical division between theory and practice. Our intention was to identify performative formats as well as aesthetic and formal criteria that are sporadically used in cultural studies, and to reinforce these formats for processes of knowledge creation in art and science. The study focused on artistic research and on visual representation as a scientific activity. At its center were concrete production processes, issues of materials, aspects of experience, issues of creativity and of artistic expression, gender-specific issues, spaces of knowledge production, and, finally, strategies of representation.

The project had three emphases. In a historical and philosophy of science section, functions and the importance of images and representation in the sciences were discussed. In a second emphasis, forms of research and research in contemporary art were investigated in order to identify specific characteristics of artistic knowledge production. In a third section, the team developed criteria relevant to research and representation that would define an artistic-scientific practice of socio-political relevance. On the basis of close cooperation between scientists and artists, and the experimental testing of approaches in teaching projects, we were able to activate knowledge cultures in which knowledge became more strongly oriented to actions and processes for the duration of the project. Through this it was possible to partially break down hierarchical differentiations, like that between theory and practice. The project devised a "poetology of knowledge." A poetology of this kind conceives and describes the emergence of new knowledge objects and areas of knowledge; it makes visible the means of representation upon which the knowledge systems are based, that is, the rules and methods of a representational context. A knowledge that also visualizes a process of becoming holds promise for an open knowledge structure, which invites active participation in knowledge-creating processes. Yet it is unsettling as well, since knowledge, as something certain in itself, and something that affirms itself, is put into question, to the extent that space is created for self-transgression, contingency, and ignorance. The research performed in the project was visualized in exhibitions, publications, lecture performances, teaching projects, and symposia. The four exhibitions, entitled *Kunst des Forschens—dazwischen* (Art of Research—in between) offered artists who do research the opportunity to present their projects, to contextualize them in events accompanying the exhibitions, and to offer them up for discussion. In the three teaching projects called *Kunst des Forschens—dazwischen-projekt* (Art of Research—project in between), which were held jointly by Zurich University of the Arts (ZHdK) and the University of the Arts Bremen (HfK), methods of artistic research were tested. The publications that arose from these were combined in a ring binder (A5 format). These binders were economical and had such a flexible design that they could be adjusted to the demands of each given project. The lecture performances followed phases of collective research.

The project started in Bremen 2005 and then followed its project head to Zurich, where it was continued at the ZHdK. The connection to the HfK Bremen remained in the form of cooperation in the framework of the *Kunst des Forschens—dazwischen-projekt* (#1–3) teaching projects.

Elke Bippus

Project Title
Kunst des Forschens. Techniken der Wissensbildung und -strukturierung in einer künstlerisch-wissenschaftlichen Praxis

Project Period
1 January 2005–31 December 2007

Keywords
- Artistic research
- Poetology of knowledge
- Aesthetic practices
- Theory and practice
- Visibility

Head of Project
- Elke Bippus, art theorist and art historian

Project Team
- Frank Hesse, artist
- Bärbel Zindler, artist

Research Partners
- Katharina Hinsberg, artist
- Beate Terfloth, artist

Project Partners
- University of the Arts, Bremen
- Insel Hombroich, Neuss-Holzheim
- Stadt der Wissenschaft, Bremen
- White Space, Zurich

Outputs

Project Funding
- Fritz Thyssen Stiftung für Wissenschaftsförderung (Interdisciplinary field "Image and Imagery")

Related Project
- Forschung in den Künsten und die Transformation der Theorie, Zurich University of the Arts, 2009–2010

Website
- http://kunstdesforschens.zhdk.ch

Publications
- Frank Hesse (2006): *„N" Strahlen*. Kulturbehörde der Freien und Hansestadt Hamburg (ed.), Hamburg.
- Elke Bippus and Frank Hesse (eds.) (2007/08): *Kunst des Forschens/dazwischen*, dazwischen #1–4 und dazwischen-projekt 1–3, Zurich.
  - A Open access: https://doi.org/10.5281/zenodo.5701961
- Elke Bippus (ed.) (2009): *Kunst des Forschens. Praxis eines ästhetischen Denkens*. Volume 4 of the Institute for Contemporary Art Research series, Zurich University of the Arts, 1. edition. Zurich & Berlin: diaphanes.
  - B Open access: https://doi.org/10.5281/zenodo.4882690

Conference
- *Kunst des Forschens*. 6–8 December 2007. Zurich University of the Arts. With Sigrid Adorf, Beatrice von Bismarck, Elke Bippus, Kathrin Busch, Oswald Egger, Gabriele Gramelsberger, Frank Hesse, Katharina Hinsberg, Jörg Huber, Christoph Keller, Daniel Kurjakovic, Christopher Lindinger, Dieter Mersch, Eva Meyer, Peter Piller, Dagmar Reichert, Hannes Rickli, Eran Schaerf, Christoph Schenker, Marcus Steinweg, Ute Vorkoeper, Daniel Zehntner, and Gesa Ziemer.

Teaching Projects
- dazwischen-projekt 1: "Strichweise Verzeichnen. Untersuchung eines Protokolls. Protokoll einer Untersuchung." 12–16 November 2007. Zurich University of the Arts.
- dazwischen-projekt 2: "Parameter | Transformation_Reflexion." 8–11 January 2008. University of the Arts Bremen.
- dazwischen-projekt 3: "Arbeiten im Feld." 3–7 November 2008. Field Institute Hombroich.

Lectures and Film Screening
- Daniel Eschkötter: "dazwischen #1." 23 August 2007. Lecture in the framework of *dazwischen #1–4*. White Space, Zurich.
- Oliver Kotcha: "dazwischen #3." 19 December 2007. Lecture in the framework of *dazwischen #1–4*. White Space, Zurich.
- Fred Truniger: "dazwischen #4." 5 March 2008. Film screening in the framework of *dazwischen #1–4*. Zurich University of the Arts.

Exhibitions:
- *dazwischen #1–4*. 2007. Exhibition project in cooperation with White Space. Zurich. With Eske Schlüters and Katrin Mayer: *dazwischen #1. ZwischenFiguren or* dependency is a marvelous thing. 22–26 August 2007.
- Karolin Meunier and Mirjam Thomann: *dazwischen #2. no projects were undertaken*. 27 October–4 November 2007.
- Oliver Kochta, Frank Lüsing, and Alexander Rüscher: *dazwischen #3. Science Club's Knuttihaus*. 12–19 December 2007.
- Volko Kamensky and Julian Rohrhuber: *dazwischen #4. Walla, walla, walla*. 5–12 March 2008.

Fig. 1 Katrin Mayer: *Zwischenfiguren*. White Space, Zurich, 2007

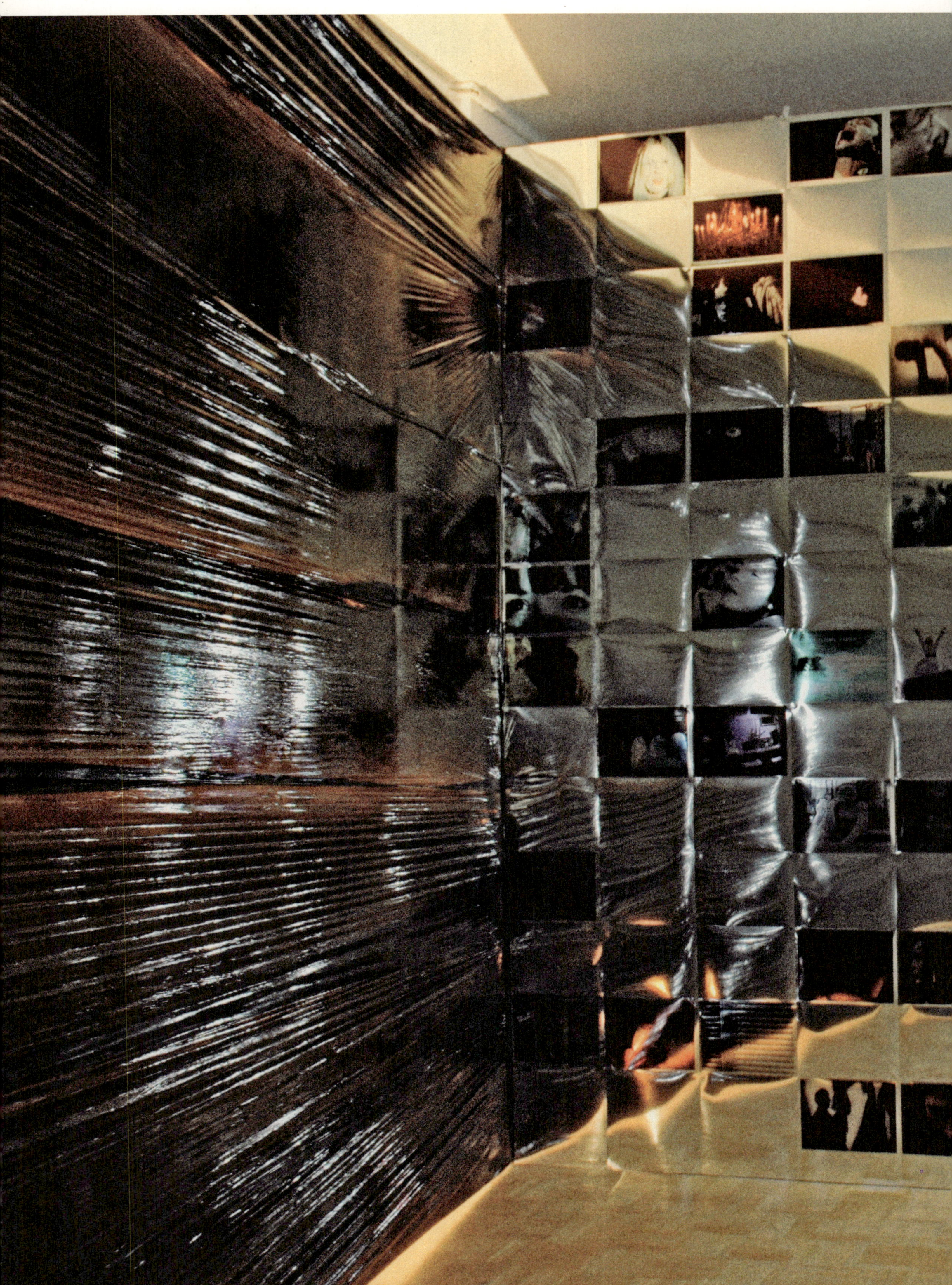

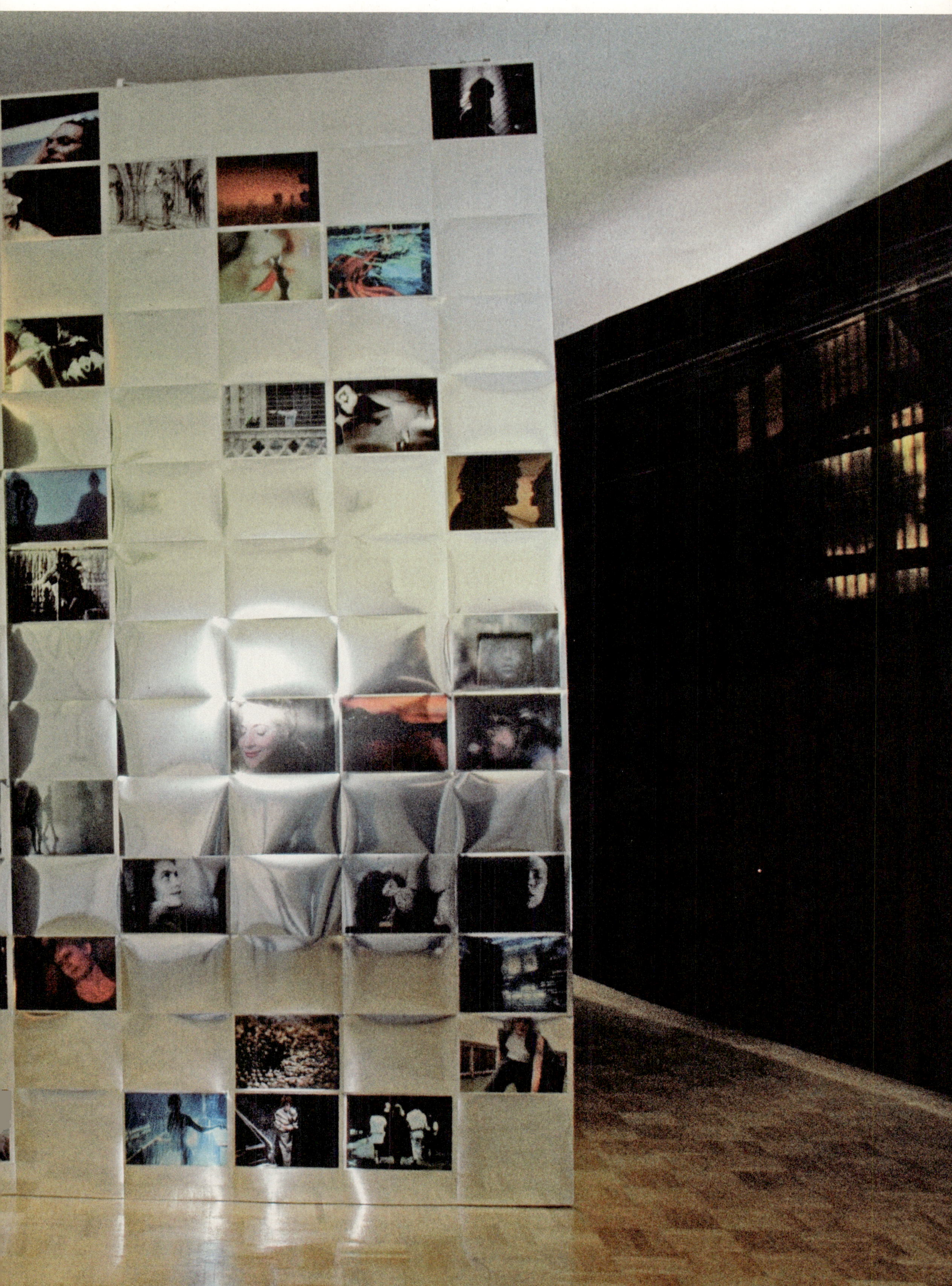

Fig. 2 Oliver Kochta, Frank Lüsing, and Alexander Rischer: *Science Club's Knuttihaus*
Fig. 3–5 Karolin Meunier and Mirjam Thomann: *no projects were undertaken*
Both White Space, Zurich, 2007

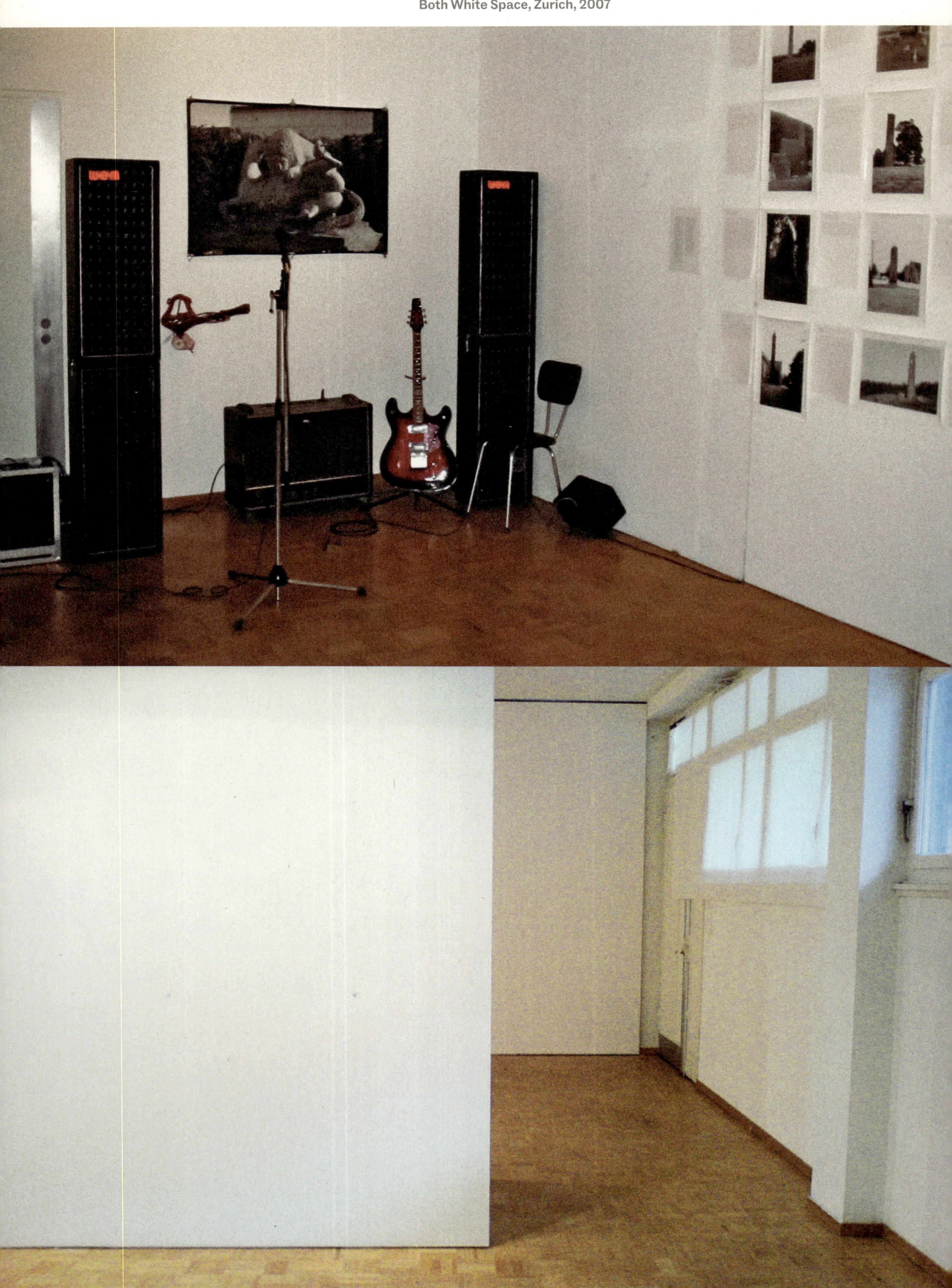

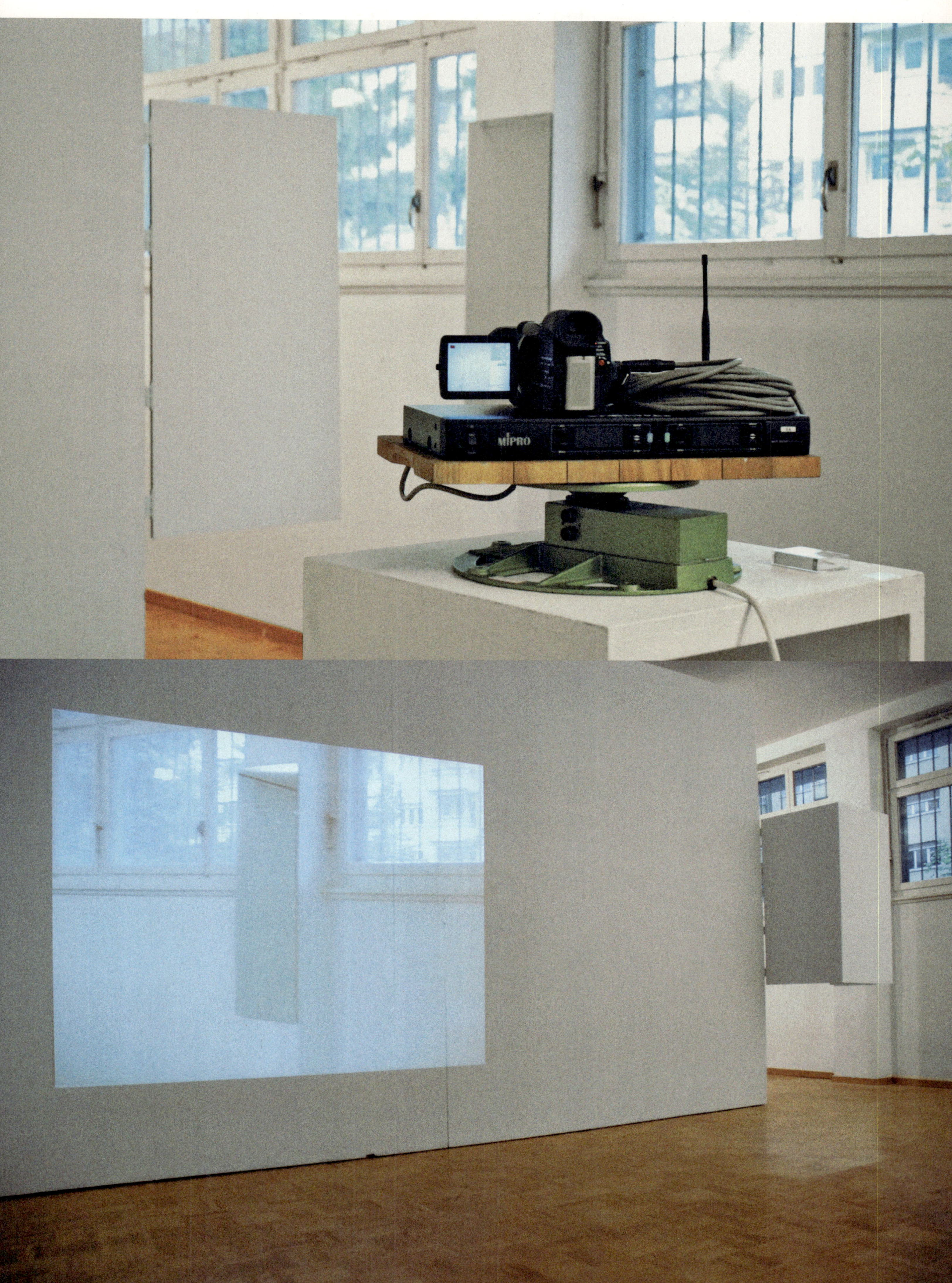
MIPRO

The photographic long-term observation focused on the example of the city of Schlieren on Zurich's western border, to show how urban transformations took place in an agglomeration municipality over the past fifteen years. Schlieren was one of the first agglomeration municipalities in Switzerland that attempted to control its development using an urban development concept ("Stadtentwicklungskonzept," STEK). This STEK 1, developed by the Metron company, served as the starting point for the photographic long-term observation. In the first project phase a photographic observation concept was developed. Every two years, the changes in spatial interaction among buildings, streets, and green spaces was documented at sixty-three defined locations throughout the urban area. Recording parameters were standardized for all these overview photos so that the processes of change in the different types of space could be compared. The photo locations chosen were not only in the developing areas, which experienced spectacular change over the course of the study, but also in stable residential districts and landscapes. Parallel to the overview photos, every five years a themed series of close-up photographs was taken. These focused on individual objects that were characteristic for the use and atmosphere in the various types of spaces. They depicted the appropriation, design, and aesthetics of the living spaces. Overviews and close-ups composed two separate, complementary forms of spatial representation.

The photographic long-term observation of concrete sites makes topical issues of spatial development and urbanization comprehensible, like densification of urban structures, the new usage of industrial areas, the upgrading of public spaces, and the development of the center. This method can be used as a new instrument for the monitoring of spatial changes. Photography thus constitutes an addition to existing methods of spatial observation, as it allows spatial change to be perceived and experienced by the senses, just as they are seen by the eyes of residents and users.

From an artistic perspective, the long-term observation of Schlieren is situated in the context of topographic photography projects in Europe: contemporary photography at the interface between documentary photography and art, which conceives of itself as a discipline designed especially for the acquisition of knowledge on space and landscape. Photography is one of the most important media for the documentation of spatial change: our knowledge of space is also a knowledge of photographic images. Not only do they document space; they also shape the conceptions we have about our living space. The question of which photographic strategies can be employed, aesthetically or technically, to make spatial transformation perceptible, and of how temporality can be experienced in space, served as the starting point of all projects by Meret Wandeler and Ulrich Görlich at the IFCAR. The result of the long-term observation is an image archive with around 1500 photographs. The conceptual artistic work with this image archive and the analysis of issues of photographic seriality, combined with the development of the observation concept, were at the core of the artistic research. They developed special methods to exploit the artistic potential of rephotography (repetition of photographs at regular time intervals under identical recording conditions). This generates a specific view of the space that undermines the conventional perception patterns of urban and architecture photography.

This photographic long-term observation produced a documentation of the transformation of everyday life spaces that is unique for Switzerland and contributes to a contemporary image of an urbanized Switzerland.

Meret Wandeler

Project Title
Fotografische Langzeitbeobachtung Schlieren. Räumliche Entwicklungsprozesse in Agglomerationsgebieten

Project Period
2005–2006
- Development of the photographic observation concept and photographic inventory

2007–2020
- Continual documentation

Keywords
- Urban transformation
- Spatial development
- Agglomeration
- Documentary photography
- Seriality

Heads of Project
- Ulrich Görlich, artist
- Meret Wandeler, artist

Project Personnel
- Christian Schwager, photographer
- Elmar Mauch, photographer

Project Partners
- Metron Raumentwicklung AG
- City of Schlieren, Abteilung Bau und Planung
- Staatsarchiv des Kantons Zürich

Project Funding
- Swiss National Science Foundation SNSF
- Metron Raumentwicklung AG
- City of Schlieren
- Sophie und Karl Binding Stiftung
- Volkart Stiftung

Outputs

A

Sponsors

- Zürcher Kantonalbank
- Halter AG
- Gewerbe- und Handelszentrum Schlieren AG
- Hauseigentümerverband Schlieren
- Reformierte Kirchgemeinde Schlieren
- Vereinigung für Heimatkunde Schlieren
- Wirtschaftskammer Schlieren

Related Projects

- Archive of Places, Zurich University of the Arts, 2008–2010
  P. 90
- Visual and Auditive Dispositives of Perception, Zurich University of the Arts, 2012–2013
  P. 134

Website

- http://www.beobachtung-schlieren.ch

Publications

- Ulrich Görlich and Meret Wandeler (2006): *Fotografische Langzeitbeobachtung Schlieren 2005–2020. Bericht zur ersten Projektphase 2005/06*. Non-numbered volume of the Institute for Contemporary Art Research series.
  A Open access: https://doi.org/10.5281/zenodo.4297670
- Meret Wandeler, Ulrich Görlich, and Caspar Schärer (2022) (eds.): *Fotografische Langzeitbeobachtung Schlieren 2005–2020*. Zurich: Scheidegger & Spiess. In press.

Articles

- Ulrich Görlich and Meret Wandeler (2011): “Fotografische Langzeitbeobachtung Schlieren 2005–2020.” In: Nanni Baltzer and Kersten Wolfgang (eds.): *Weltenbilder*. Berlin: Akademie-Verlag, 203–216.
- Meret Wandeler and Hubert Locher (2015): “Fotografische Forschung. Ein Interview.” In: *Rundbrief Fotografie: Analoge und digitale Bildmedien in Archiven und Sammlungen*. 22, 1 [N.F. 85], 37–47.
- Ulrich Görlich and Meret Wandeler (2019): “Observación fotográfica a largo plazo de Schlieren/Long-term photographic observation of Schlieren.” In: Gierstberg, F. (ed.): *Paisajes enmarcados. Misiones fotográficas europeas, 1984–2019—Framed landscapes. European photography commissions, 1984–2019*. Madrid: Museo ICO, 338–388.

Presentations

- Ulrich Görlich and Meret Wandeler: “Fotografische Langzeitbeobachtung Schlieren.” In: *Photographic observation as a tool for landscape policies*. European seminar, Ministry of Ecology, Energy, Sustainable Development and Territory Management, Paris, November 2008.
- Ulrich Görlich and Meret Wandeler: “Fotografische Langzeitbeobachtung Schlieren.” In: *Recollecting Landscapes*. Colloquium at deSingel Internationale Kunstcampus Antwerpen, organized by the Flanders Architecture Institute and Ghent University in cooperation with KU Leuven, October 2018.

Exhibitions

- Ulrich Görlich and Meret Wandeler: *Fotografische Langzeitbeobachtung Schlieren*. Installation with 4 monitors. In the exhibition *Concrete – Fotografie und Architektur*. 2 March–20 May 2013, Fotomuseum Winterthur.
- Ulrich Görlich and Meret Wandeler: *Long-term photographic observation of Schlieren*. In the exhibition *Paisajes enmarcados. Misiones fotográficas europeas 1984–2019. Framed landscapes. European photography commissions 1984–2019*, 7 June–8 September 2019, Museo ICO Madrid.

Works

- Meret Wandeler and Ulrich Görlich designed each contribution to the exhibition as an installation in the form of digital slideshows on monitors and/or inkjet prints specific to the given space and oriented to the theme of the exhibitions. These constituted stand-alone works, realized from the image archive of the long-term observation of Schlieren. The images of sequences in publications are comparable.

Fig. 1 Rietbach development area, detailed view, 2005

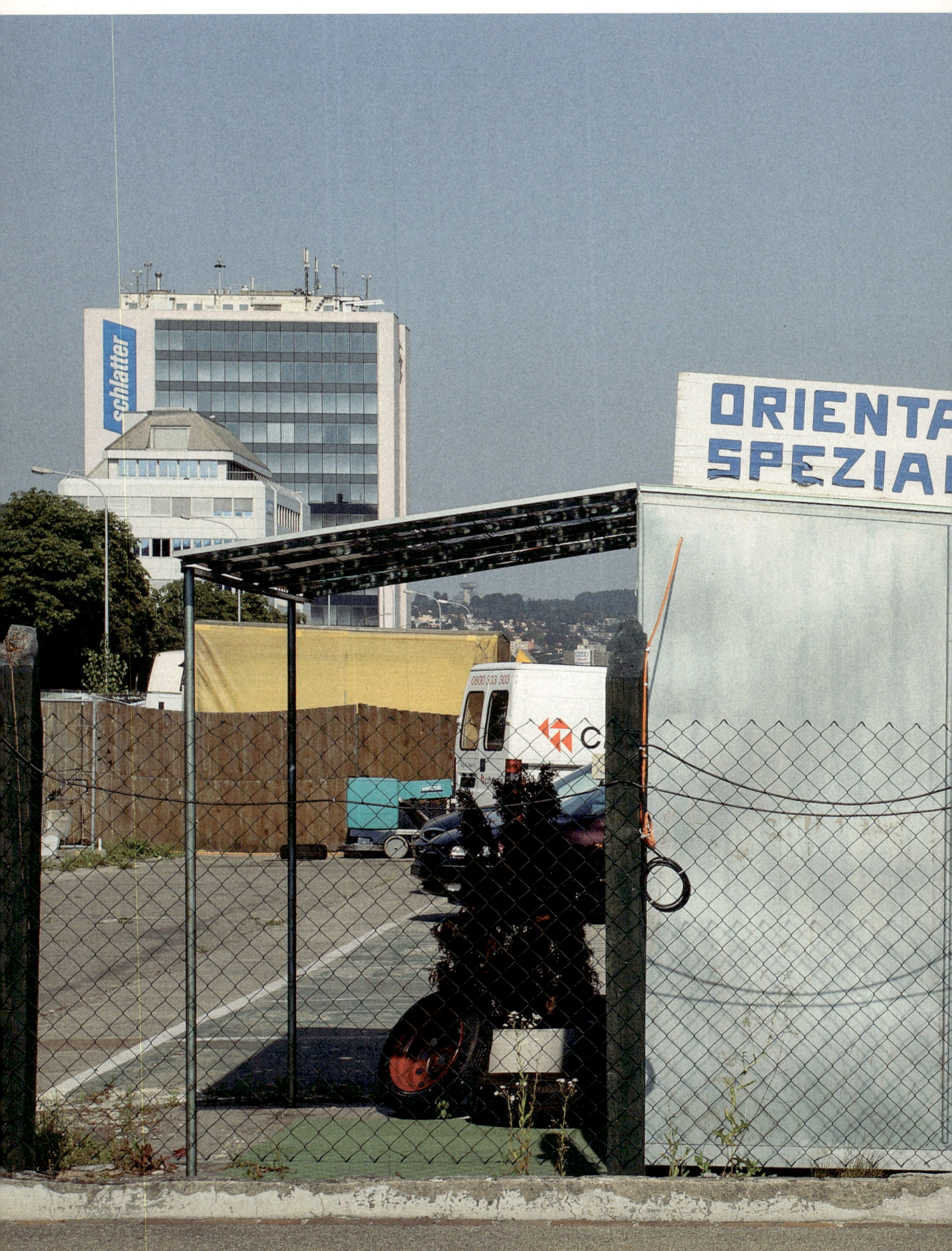

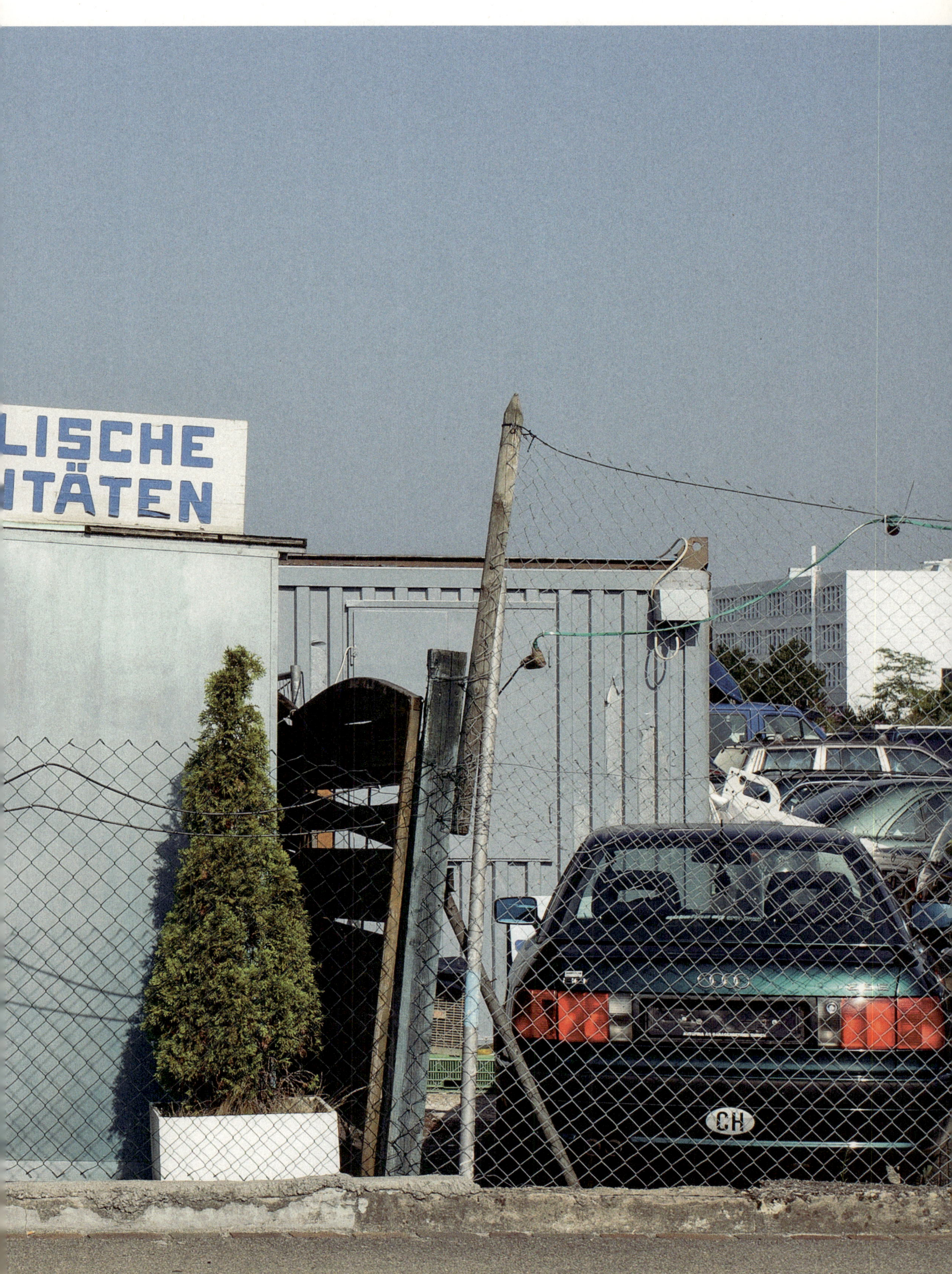
LISCHE
ITÄTEN
CH

Fig. 2 Schlieren West development area, intersection of Nassackerstrasse and Badenerstrasse. Complete series of overviews from 2005–2019. Photograph, 2005

Fig. 3 Photograph, 2007

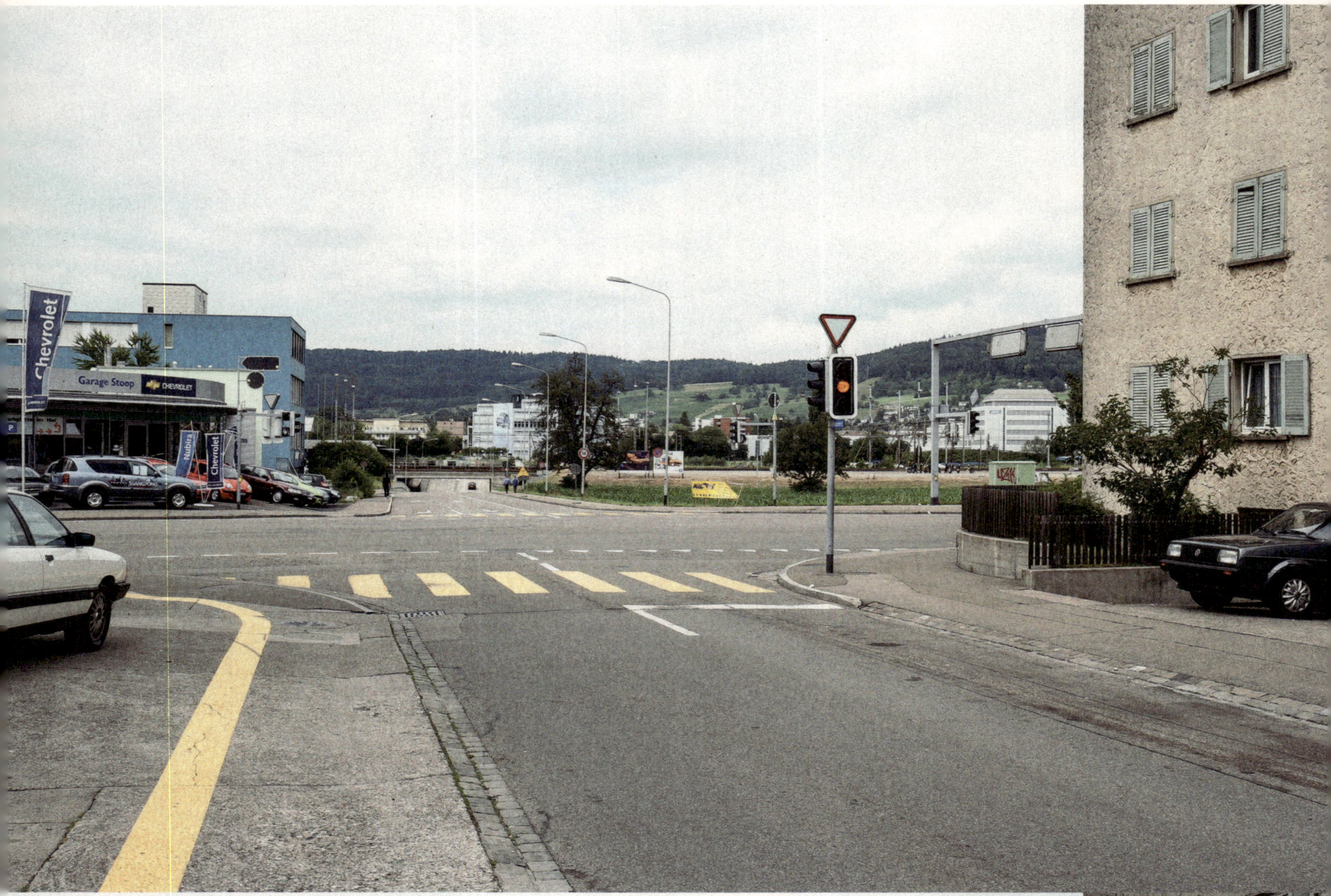

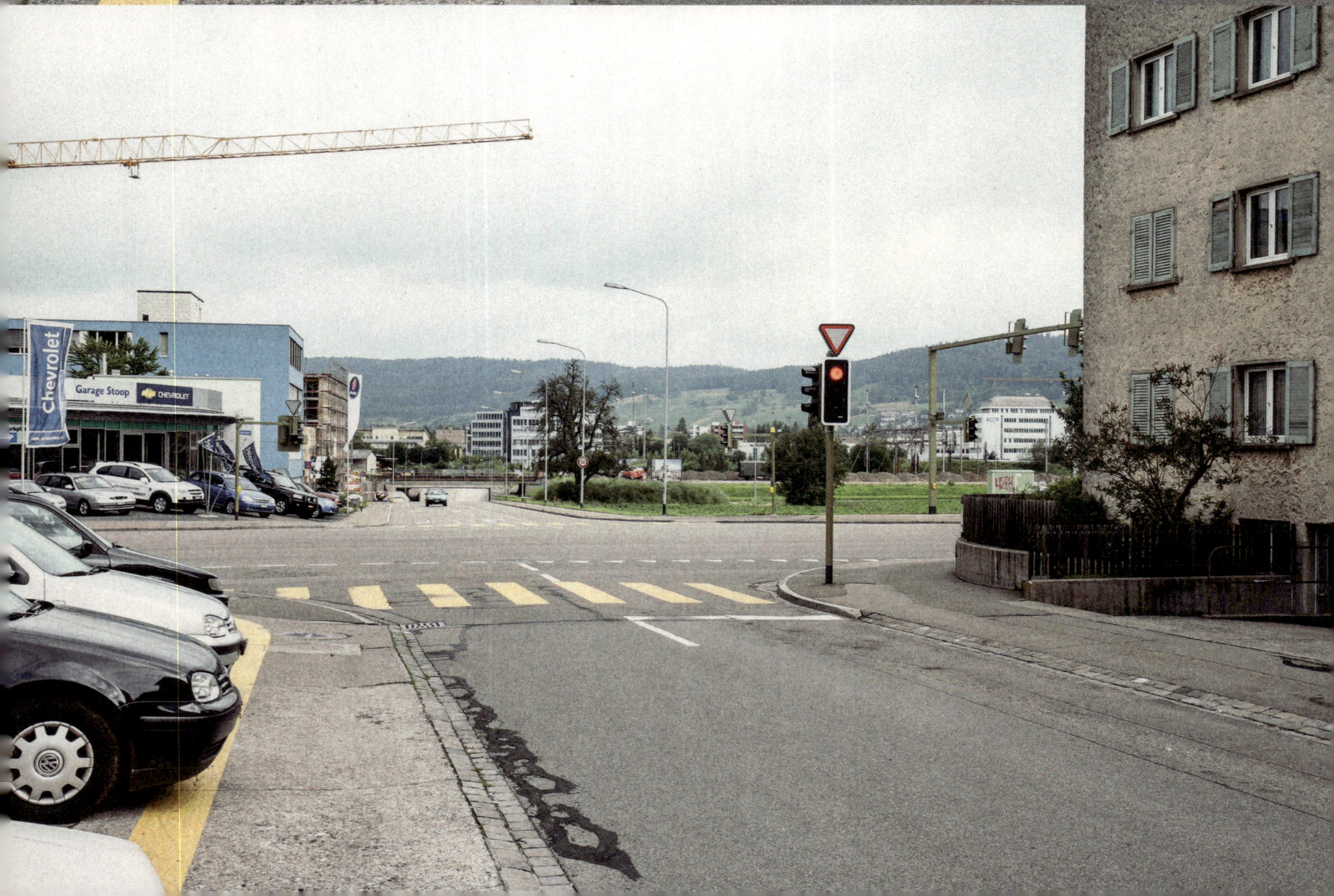

Fig. 4 Photograph, 2009
Fig. 5 Photograph, 2011

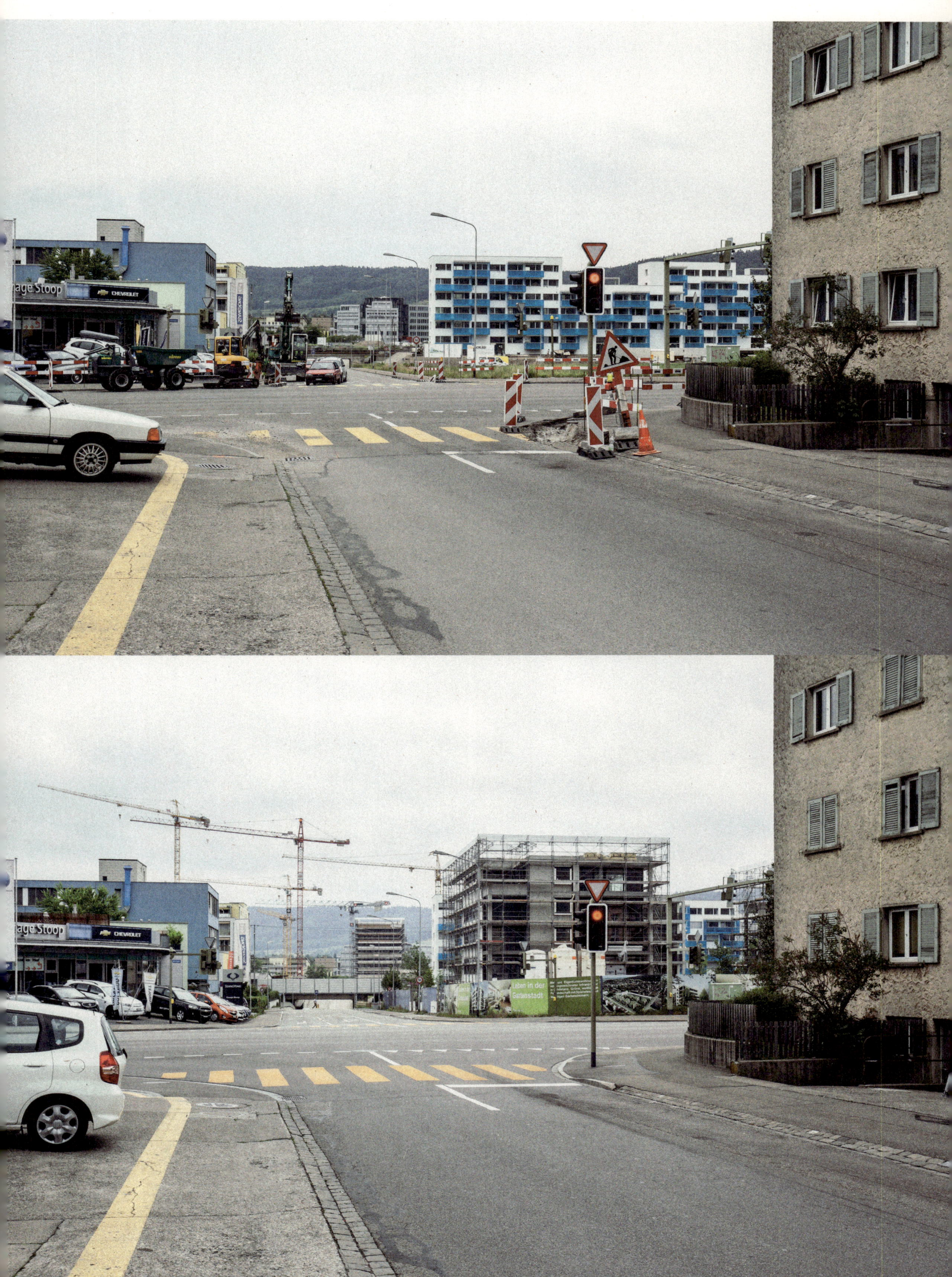

Fig. 6 Schlieren West development area, intersection of Nassackerstrasse and Badenerstrasse. Photograph, 2013

Fig. 7 Photograph, 2015

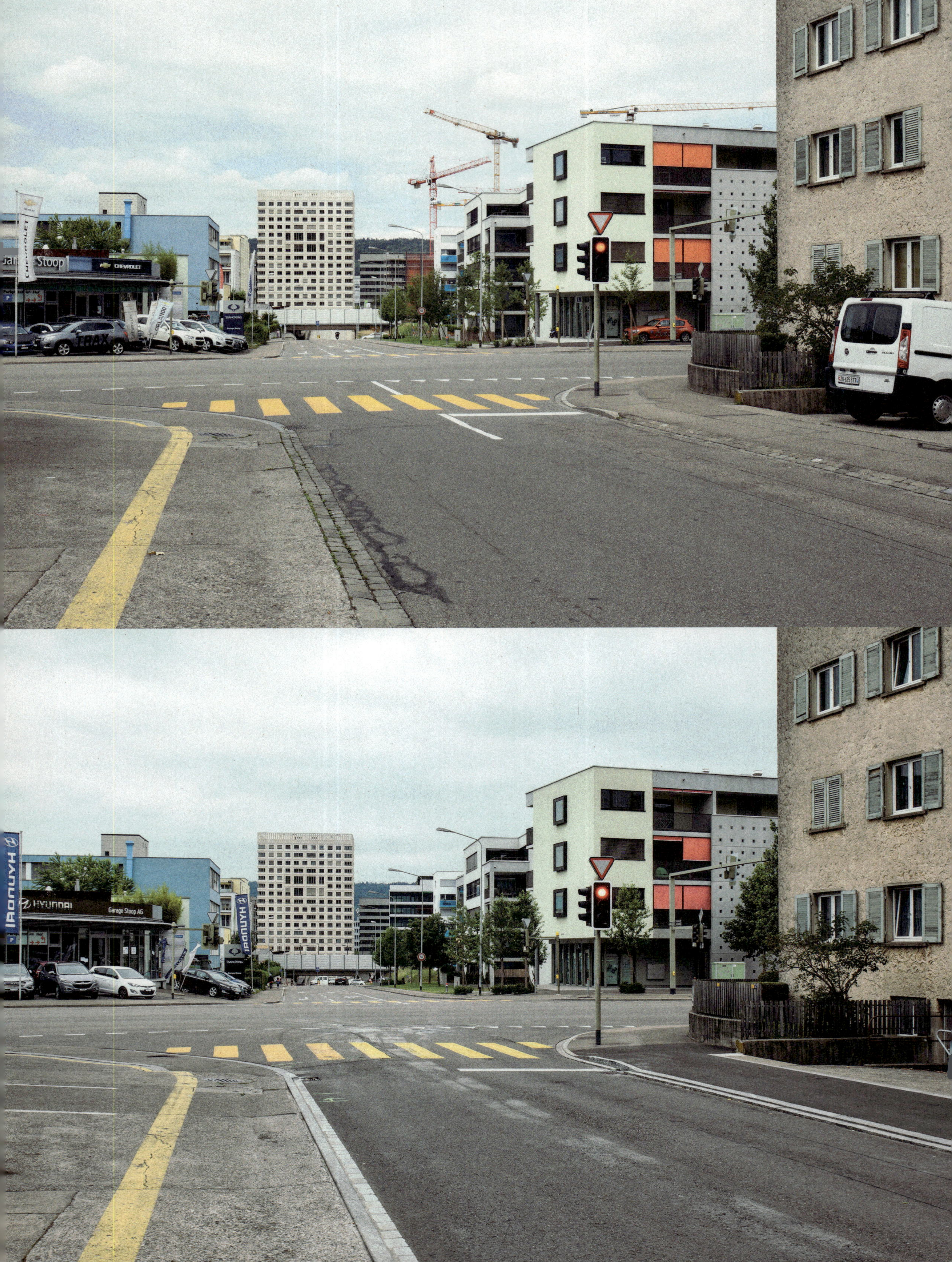

Fig. 8 Photograph, 2017
Fig. 9 Photograph, 2019

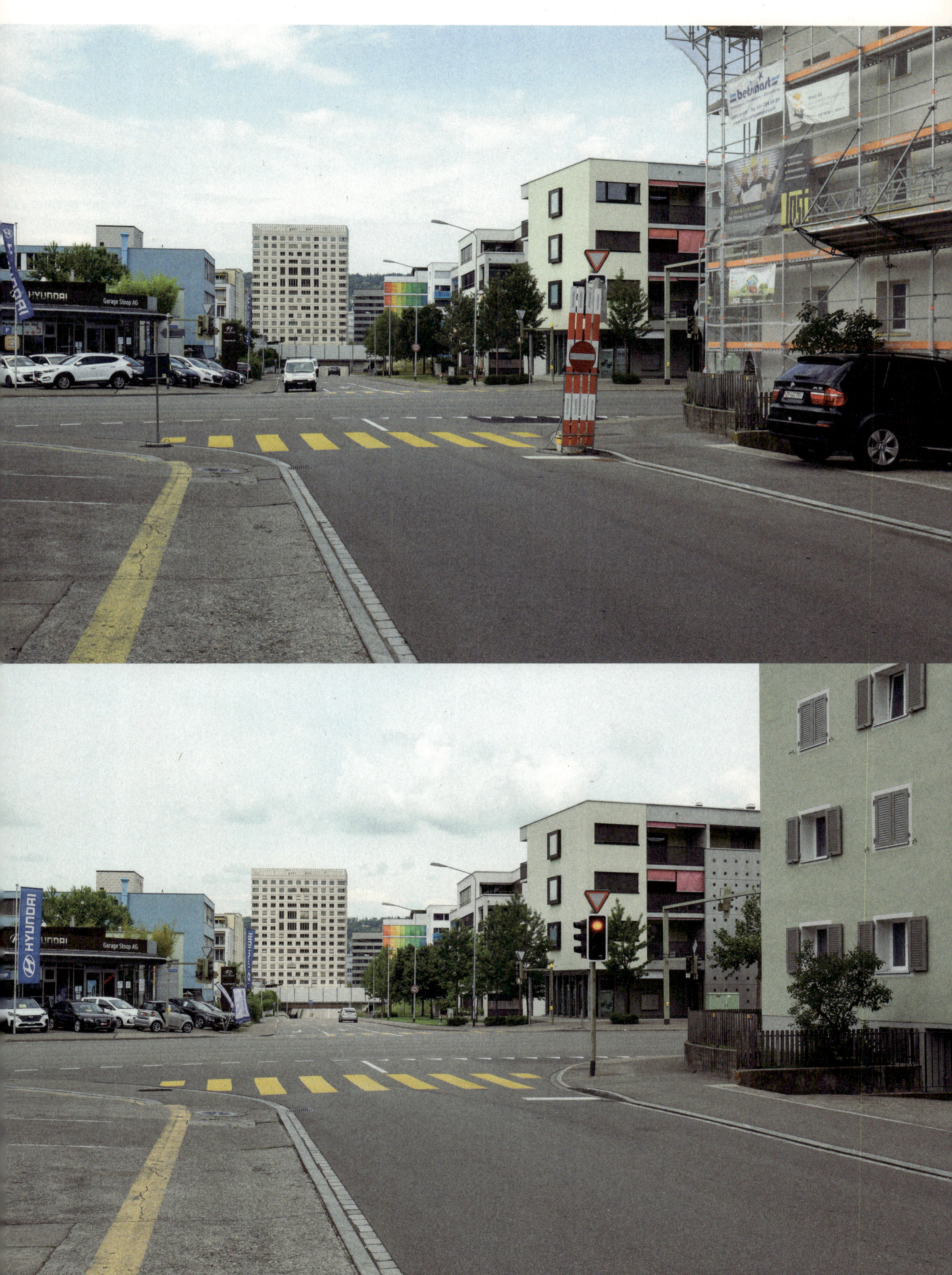

Fig. 10–13 Rietbach development area, detailed views, 2005

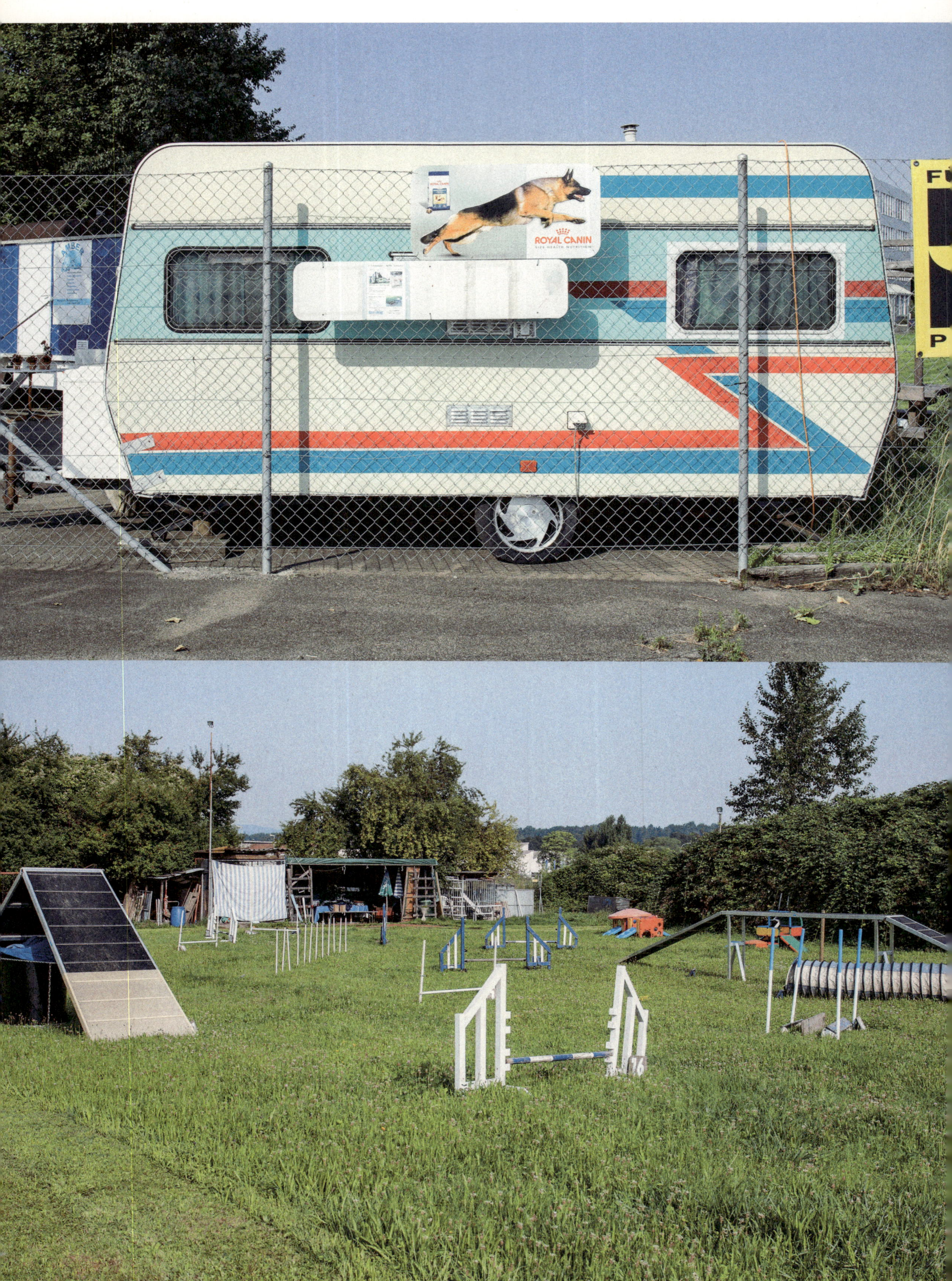

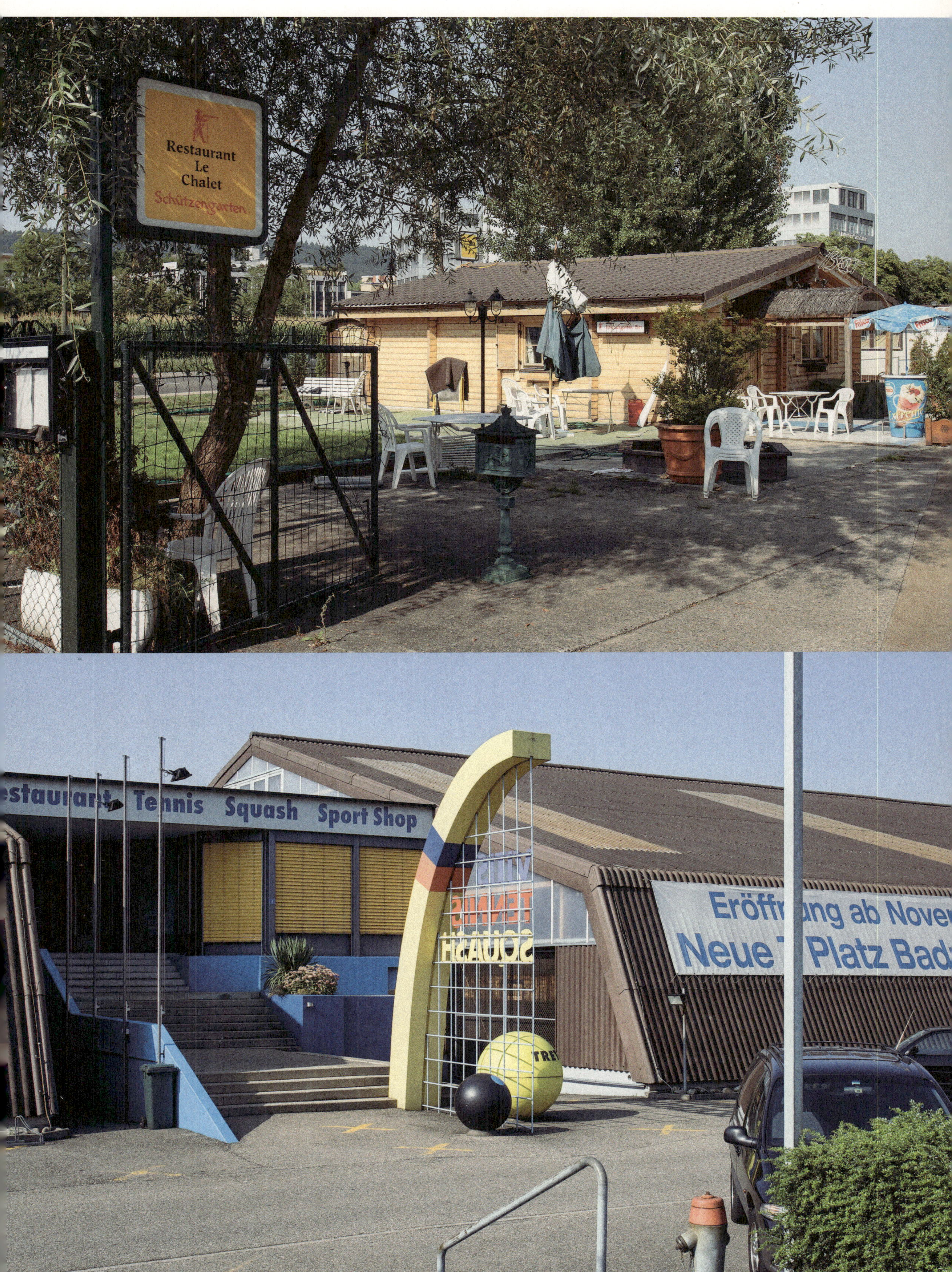
Restaurant
Le
Chalet
Schützengarten
Restaurant Tennis Squash Sport Shop
Eröff ung ab Nove
Neue Platz Bad

The two-part *Now* research project dealt with questions and problems concerning audio artworks. The first part of the research project compiled and processed knowledge from related disciplines for art practice to make them fertile for art research. In *Now II* this knowledge then flowed into a collaborative practice in order to develop narrative forms for extremely long periods on the radio.

The interdisciplinary texts, exercises, and audio artworks worked out in the first part provided information about how our hearing works in time. The background of the investigation was the increasing prevalence of artistic audio works in exhibitions during the 1990s. Among the questions asked was how audio works can be conceived for exhibition spaces where they are usually performed without any ritualized starting and end point. In the night hours and in the summer shutdown of Radio LoRa we found a suitable field to apply the experiences and findings from *Now I* and develop forms of nonlinear narrations.

LoRa, a local radio station in Zürich, which had already appeared as a project partner in *Now I*, serves numerous migrant and cultural communities as both an important voice and a social center. At the same time, it offers space for experimental forms of radio and radio art. How, the research question asked, can the findings from *Now I* be applied to realize attractive programming for the night hours and the summer break, which normally feature playlists? Through close cooperation between artists and Jörg Köppl it was possible to implement, examine, and enhance experiences and insights about auditive time perception.

As a result, the project cooperated with Radio LoRa to develop the pilot projects *Der elektromagnetische Sommer* (The Electromagnetic Summer) and *Nachtschichten* (Night Shifts) for the night hours during regular broadcasting operation. *Der elektromagnetische Sommer* was played for two weeks during Radio LoRa's summer transmission break, featuring live artistic and experimental broadcasting. A competition was advertised for the first *Elektromagnetische Sommer*. For the *Nachtschichten*, eleven artists were invited to conceptualize audio artworks. The operative components of the curatorial concept for *Nachtschichten* were the nocturnal timeslot as well as the topical and aesthetic practices of the artists. Representatives of audio art, electronic music, and audio design were brought together along with improvising musicians. This added a local connection to Zurich's art community.

The collaborative realization of the individual contributions allowed the differentiation of algorithmic composition techniques, without which the long program lengths cannot be mastered. The works produced are distinguished by their strong emphasis on the imaginary—be it through an extremely epic structure, through fragmentation, or through the use of noises. They thus could be comprehended as an alternative to conventional radio practice (music and information). The project also managed to generate interest in audio works and their contents, techniques, and methods among a broader audience. This was achieved thanks to the broadcasting of the contributions on Radio LoRa and their discussion in radio features, as well as their advertising and discussion in other media. *Der elektromagnetische Sommer* continued as a radio art event on Radio LoRa until 2011.

Jörg Köppl

Project Title
Now II. Ereignisstrukturen für offene Dauern am Radio

Project Period
1 June 2005–31 January 2006

Keywords
- Radio art
- Algorithmic composition
- Long durations
- Artistic research

Head of Project
- Jörg Köppl, artist

Project Team
- Volker Böhm, musician and audio designer
- Christoph Schenker, art theorist

Research Partners
- Electronic Studio Basel, Musik-Akademie Stadt Basel
- Projekt AktiveArchive, Hochschule der Künste Bern
- Schweizerisches Institut für Kunstwissenschaft, Zürich

Project Partner
- Radio LoRa

Project Funding

- Swiss National Science Foundation SNSF, DORE

Related Projects

- Now I, Zurich University of the Arts, 2003–2005
  P. 28
- Radio Lewa, Artellewa, Cairo, 2013

Outputs

A

D

B

C

Websites

- www.lora.ch/projekte/nachtschichten
- www.lora.ch/40-projekte/108-elektromagnetischer-sommer

Publication

- Jörg Köppl (ed.) (2008)*: Nachtschichten – Radioarbeiten von Stini Arn, Jackie Bruce, Mirjam Bürgin, Benjamin Federer, Karen Geyer, Anja Kaufmann, Jörg Köppl, José J. Navarro, Philipp Schaufelberger, Lorenz Schuster, Ana Strika*. Volume 3 of the Institute for Contemporary Art Research series. Zurich: Edition Fink. With 3 audio CDs (Nachschichten 2006).
  - A Open access: https://doi.org/10.5281/zenodo.6501542
  - B Open access Audio CD 1: https://doi.org/10.48504/1885-5r97-001
  - C Open access Audio CD 2: https://doi.org/10.48504/1885-5r97-002
  - D Open access Audio CD 3: https://doi.org/10.48504/1885-5r97-003

Radio Broadcasts

- *Der elektromagnetische Sommer 2005*. 18 July–10 August 2005, Radio LoRa 97,5 MHz. Audio works: *Kanal 7* by Mario Purkathofer, Roli Roos, Valentina Vuksic, Anja Kaufmann, Florian Merkur, Marc Widmer, Patrick Kaufmann, Jonas Ohrstrom, Regula Erni, Monya Pletsch, Julia Tabakhova, Cristin Wildbolz, Q&A, and pilot.fm et al., *Langstrasse Live* by Rolf Simmen, *Air Vent* by Kate Donovan.
- *Nachtschichten 2006*. 1 January–16 July 2006, Radio LoRa 97,5 MHz, Radio FRO Linz, Radio FLORA Hannover, and Radio FREE FM Ulm. Audio works: *RadioSolarKompass* by Anja Kaufmann, *KLANG:ZEIT:KLANG* by Benjamin Federer, *microscopic trips* by Stini Arn, *Nachtgestrika* by Ana Strika, *DRS 4* by Philipp Schaufelberger, *Graufilter* by Karen Geyer, *El Piano de Trapo* by Jose J. Navarra, *LoRa 2.0 – jetzt neu!* by Lorenz Schuster; *dichten* by Jörg Käppi, *Verzehnfachung* by Jackie Bruce, and *Mille et une nuits* (now: *Machin/machine*) by Mirjam Bürgin.
- *Der elektromagnetische Sommer 2006*. 17 July–6 August 2006. Radio LoRa 97,5 MHz. Audio works: öppis – *some etwas schwyzerdütsch* by Katja Jug and Ulrike Hug, *Mitkochen – eine Kochsendung in akustischer Gemeinschaft* by Cornelia Heusser, *Effedege* by Fabio Gaggetta and *Kanal 7—Travelling New Territories* by and with Wildprovider and Atelier Anorg, with Chaostreff Zürich, Trash.net, SheGeeks, Digitale Allmend and the platforms Sonicsquirrel.net, Sofatrips.com, PizQuit.net and Mediapedia.ch. Curated and moderated by Mario Purkathofer.
- *Der elektromagnetische Sommer 2007*. 16 July–8 August 2007. Radio LoRa 97,5 MHz, Radio Orange, Halle, and live at Kunsthof Zürich. Audio works: *Radioerevan_Yurt* by Marold Langer-Philippsen, *Johnny Head_In_Air Show* by Sarah Washington, *Installations-Feedback* by Knut Aufermann and *Kanal 7*, a radio exhibition with over 50 contributions by Andrea Thal, Anna Kanai, San Keller, Al Andalus, Unabhängige Kunsträume Schweiz, Stefan Seydel, and Bit Tuner, among others.

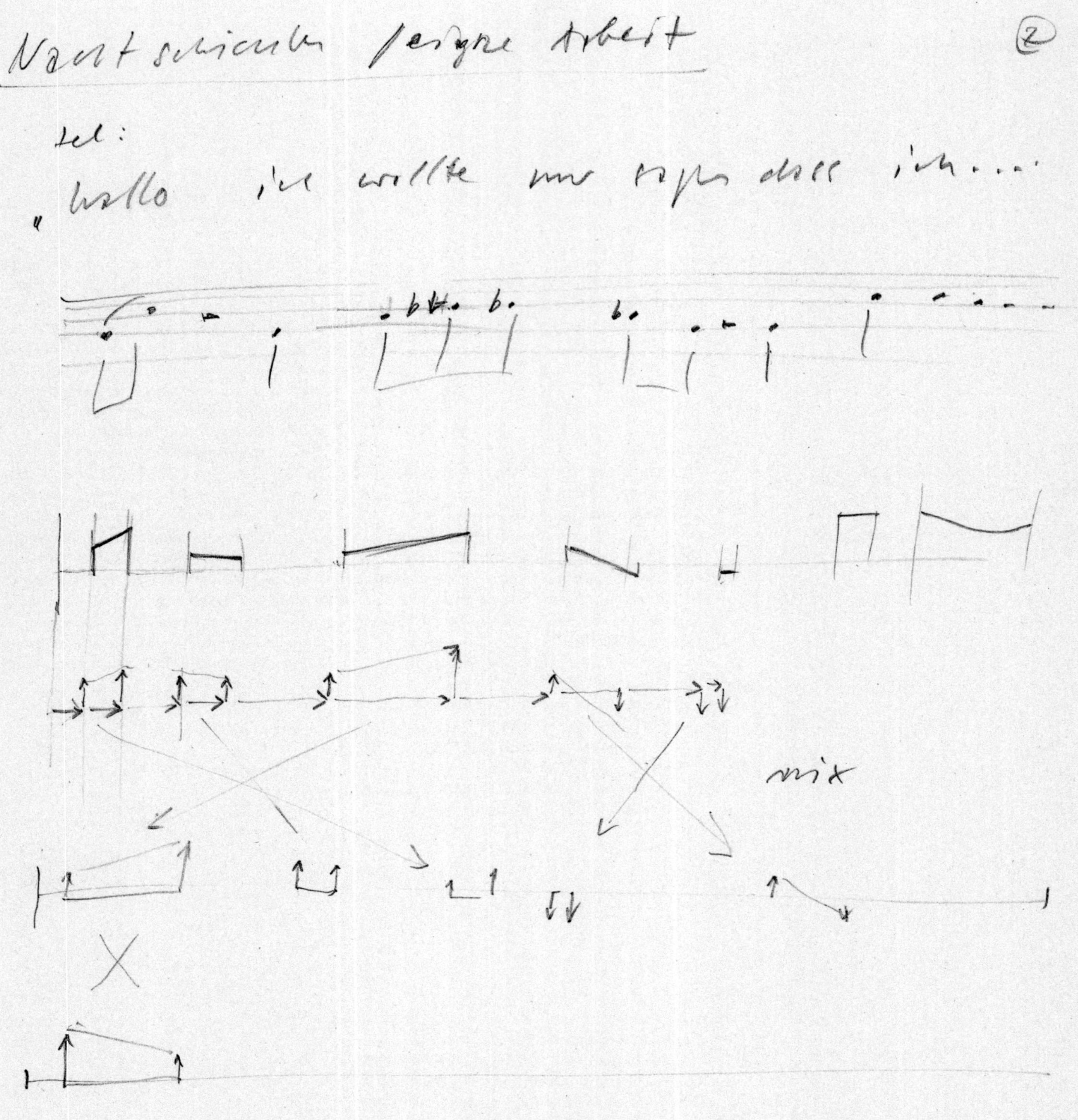
Nachtschichten / eigene Arbeit
②
tel:
„hallo ich wollte nur sagen dass ich...
mix
ECHO / KLAGEMAUER / ORAKEL
„da ist niemand" ... „das Echo wird
nur deine Einsamkeit verstärken" ... „deine
Klage verhallt ungehört" ...
„niemand versteht dich"

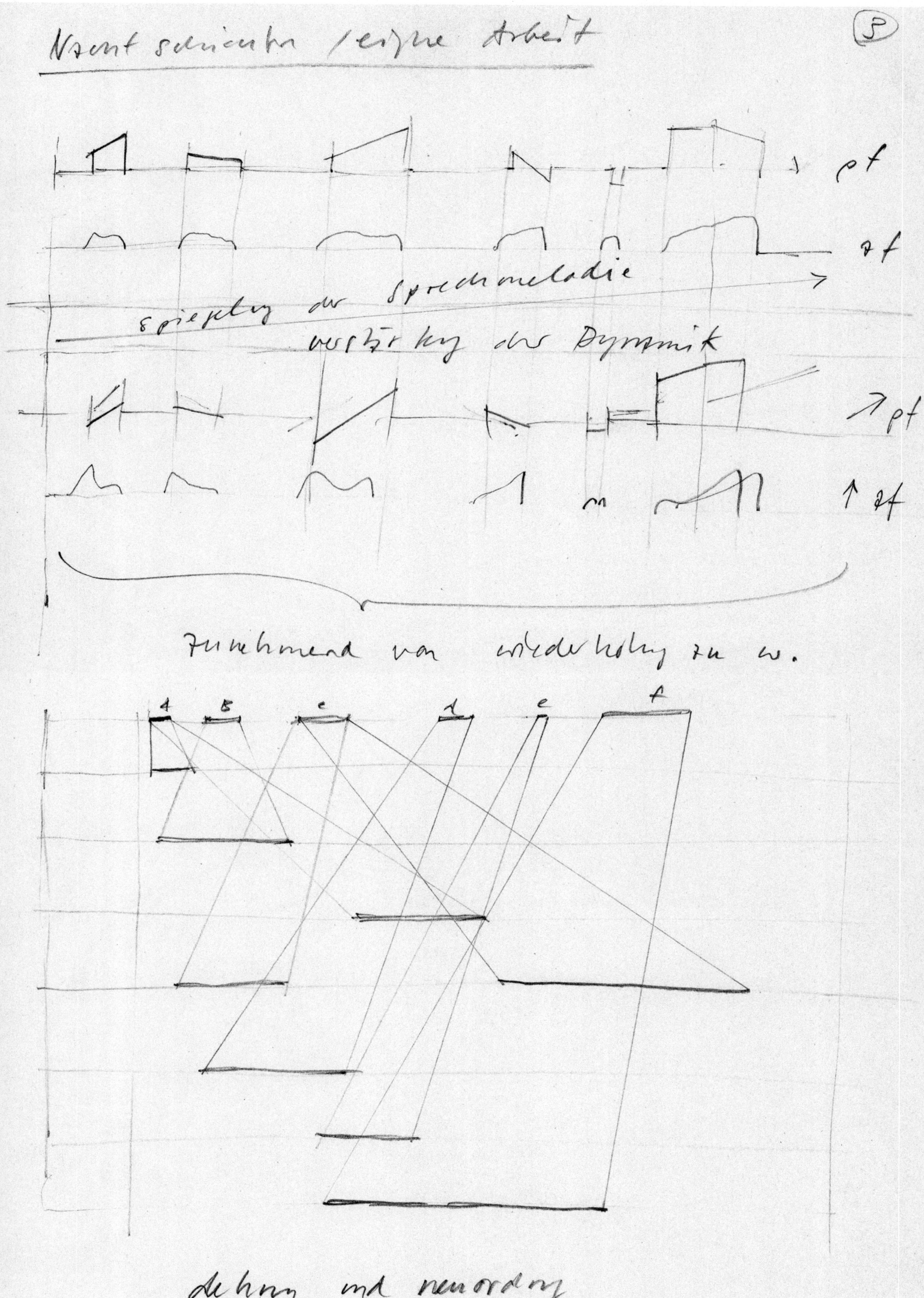
3
pf
Spiegelung der Sprechmelodie
Verstärkung der Dynamik
pf
Zunehmend von Wiederholung zu W.
a b c d e f
Dehnung und Neuordnung

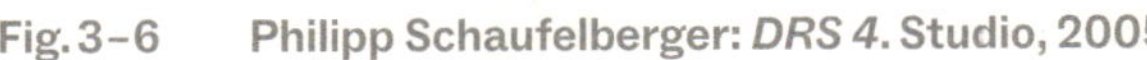

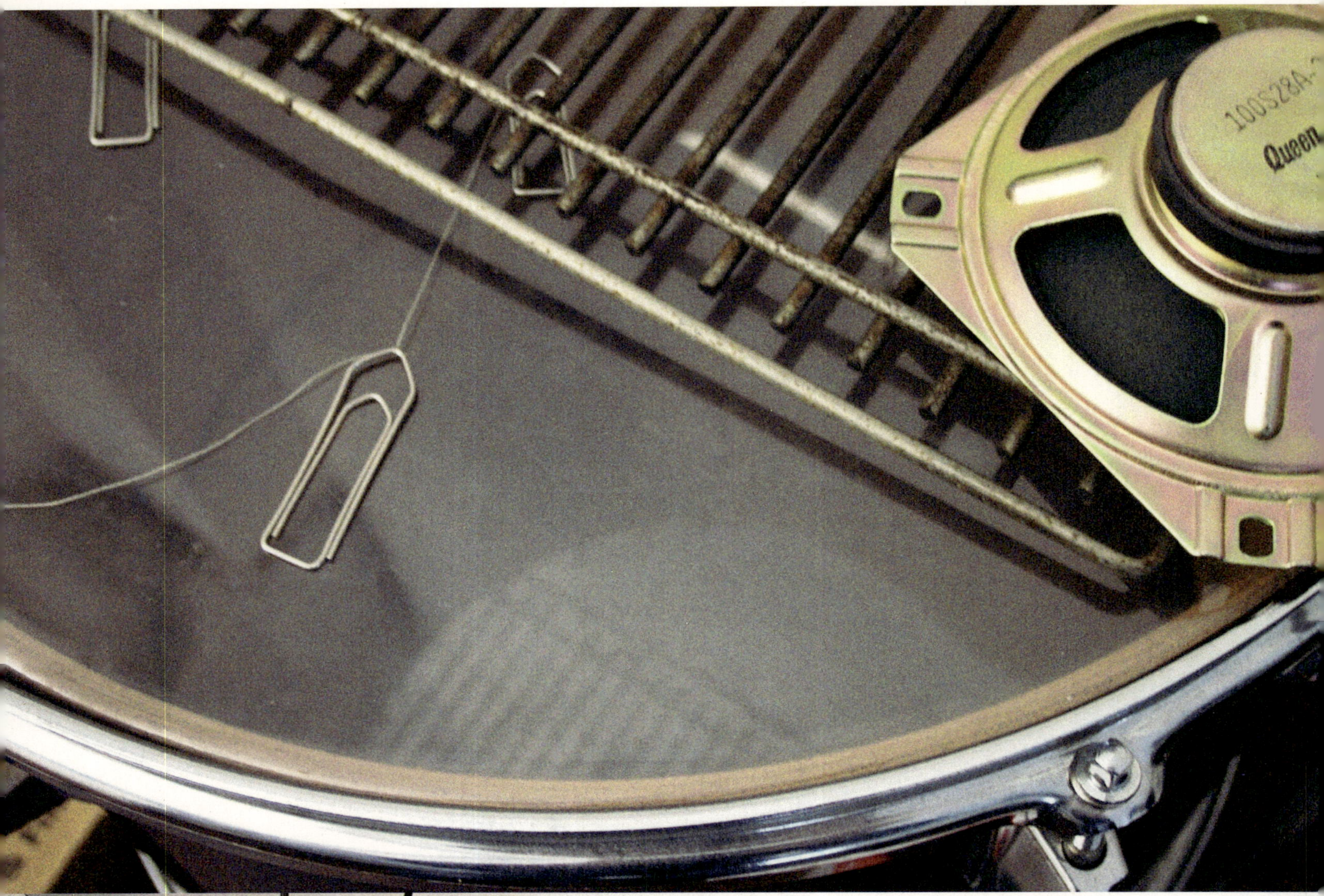

Fig. 3–6 Philipp Schaufelberger: *DRS 4*. Studio, 2005

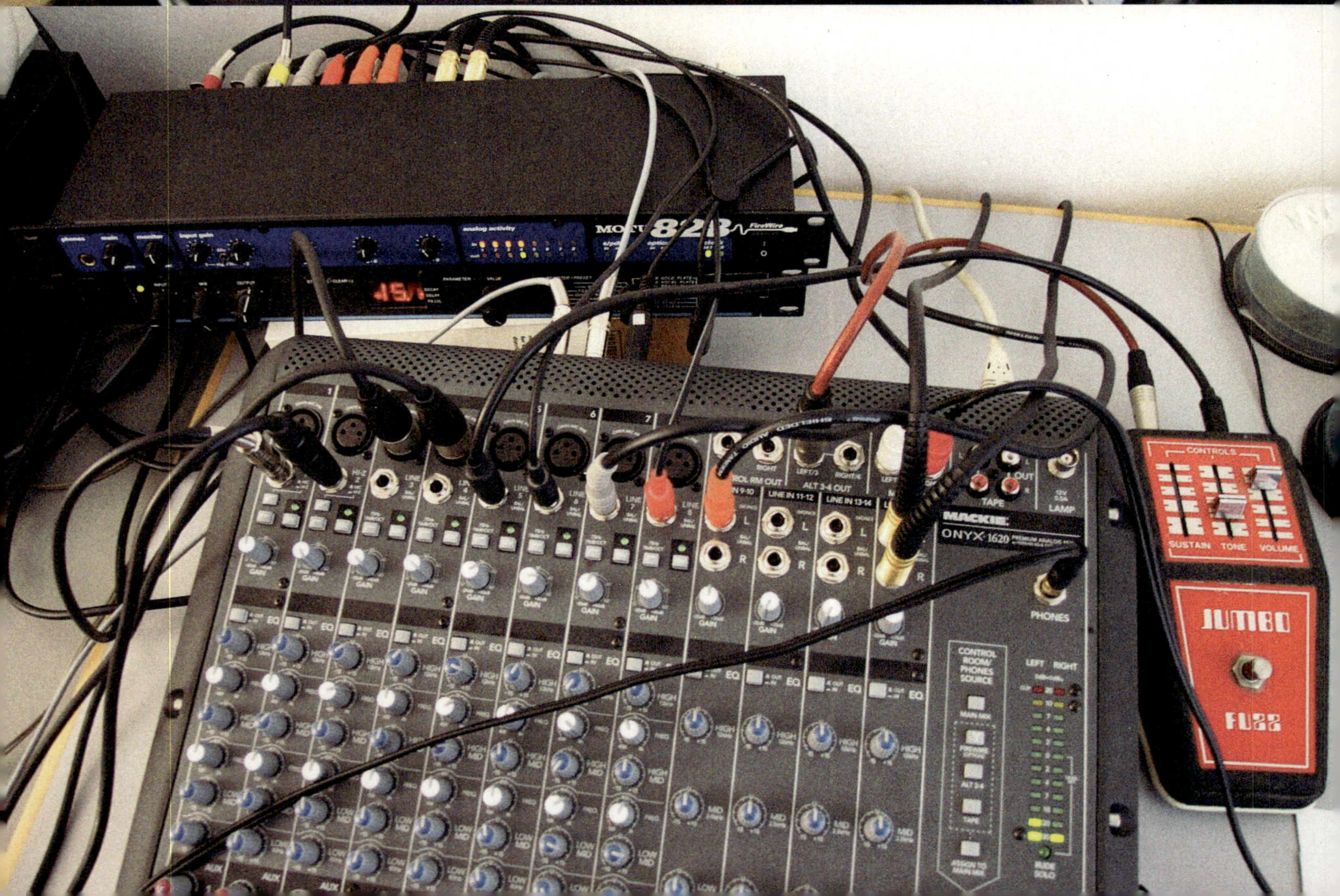

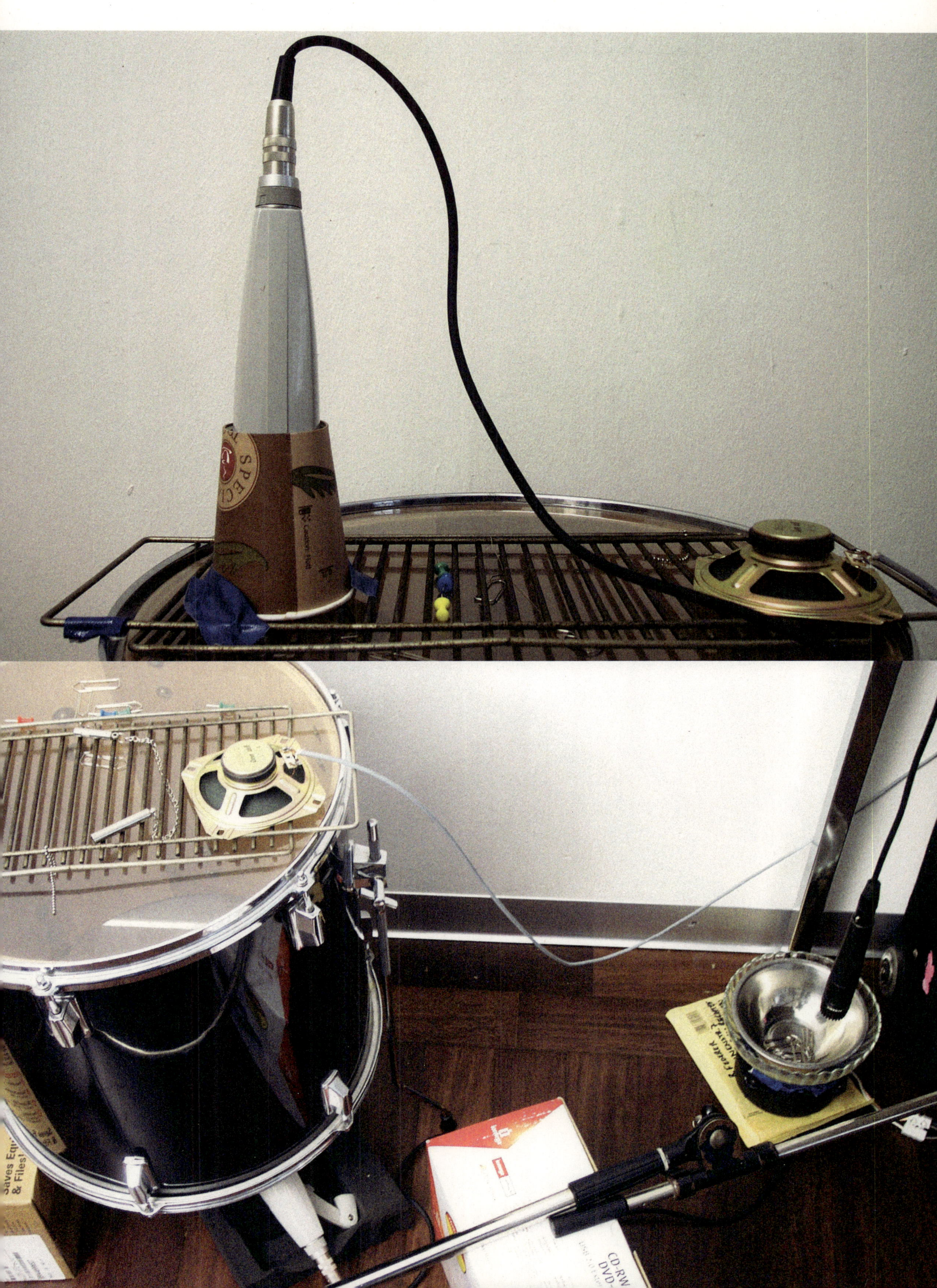
SPEC
Saves Equ
& Files!
CD-RW
DVD

Fig. 7 Karen Geyer: *Grauton*. Kunsthalle Zürich, 2005

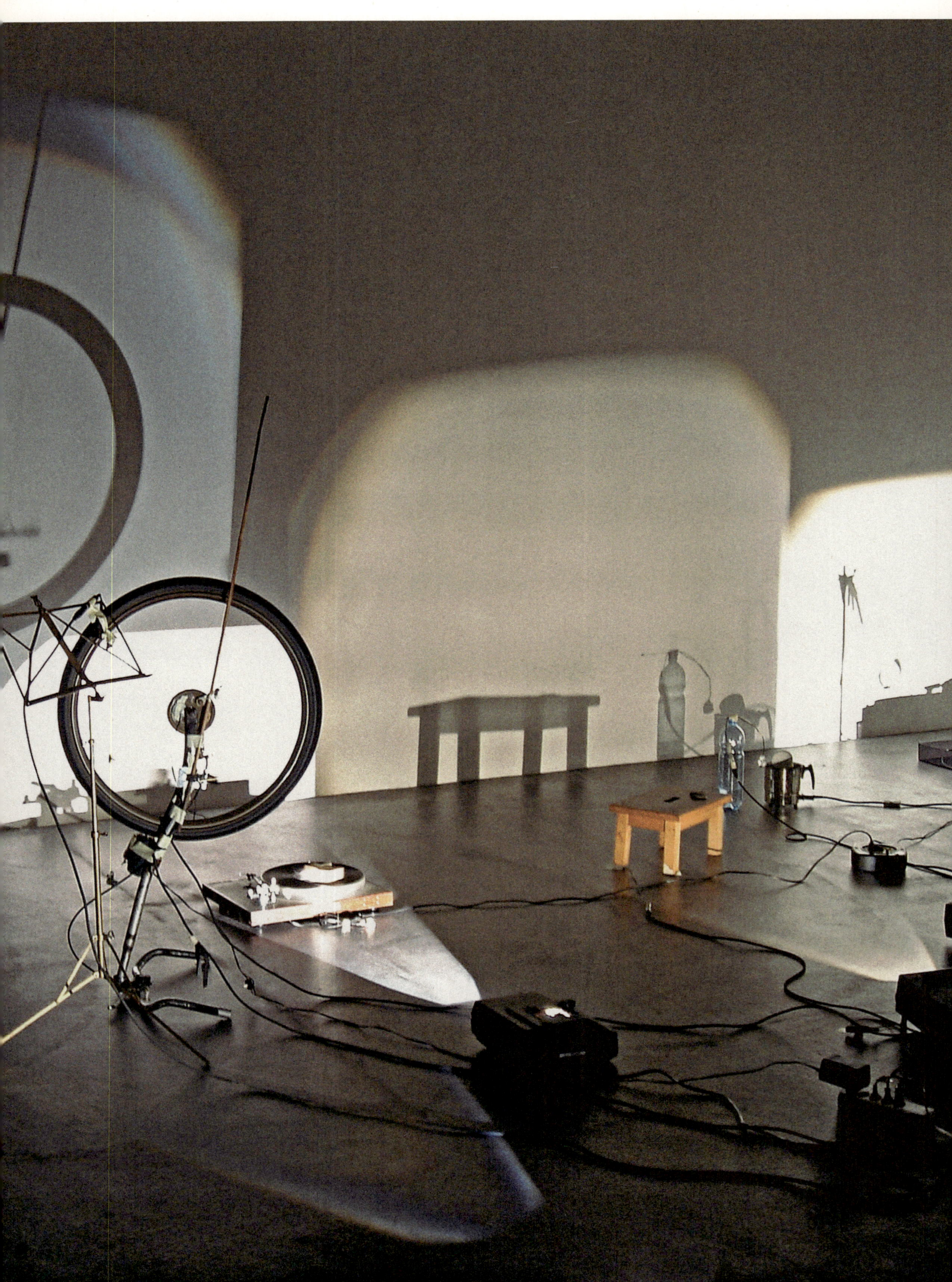

Fig. 8 Lorenz Schuster: *LoRa 2.0 — jetzt neu!* Algorithmic composition, screenshot, 2005

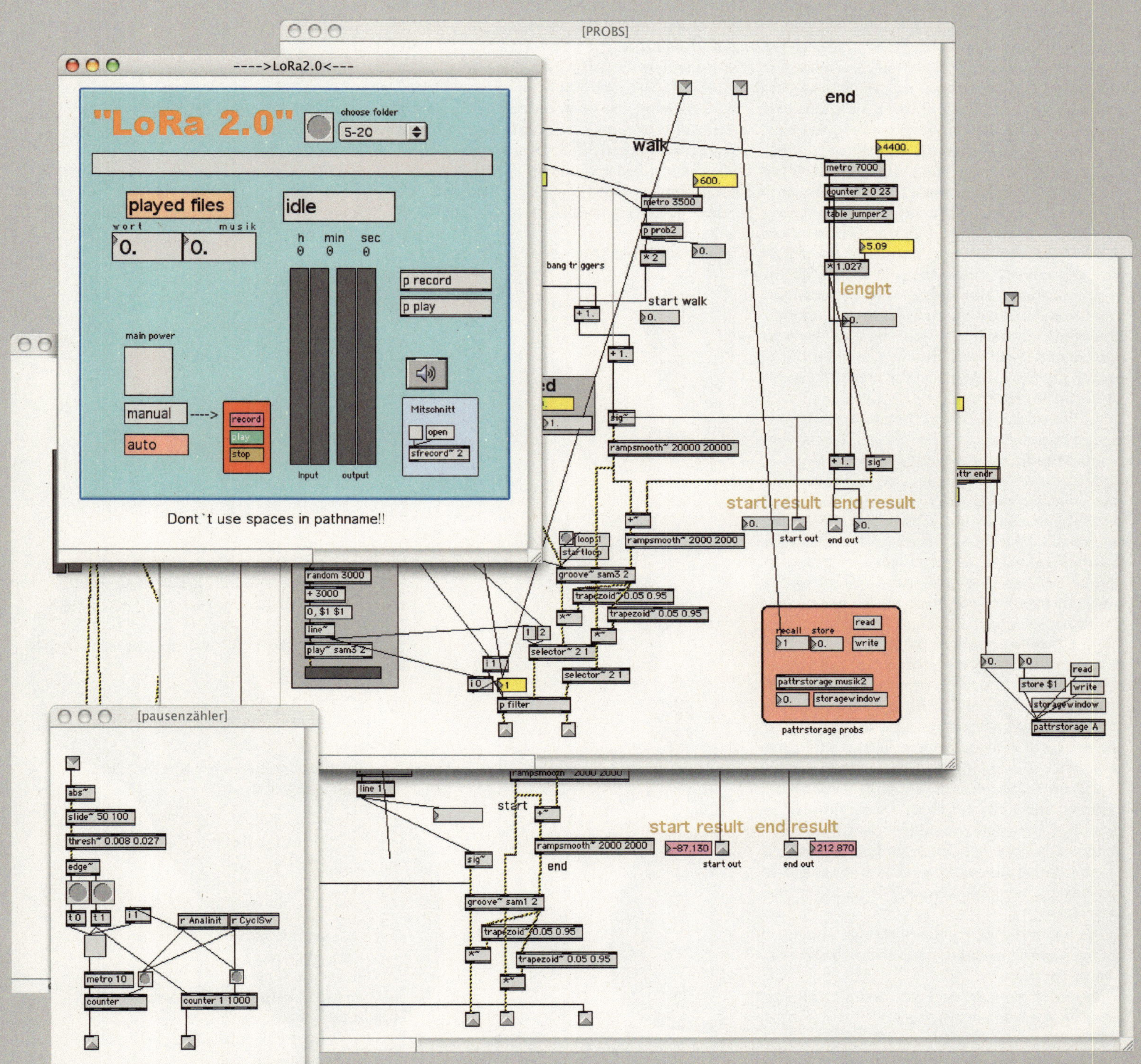

The background of this artistic research project was the fact that, in view of increasing globalization and the process of digitalization brought with it, many societal phenomena can no longer be defined as local; instead, they must be understood as dynamic fields of many locations and forces that influence each other despite being separated by geographical distances. This change in negotiation spaces has increasingly entered the focus of researching artists. How are artistic practices changing that take place simultaneously with active performances in public spaces at different locations? What topics are genuinely connected with these translocal localizations? How can translations between local and networked, local and mass media, analog and digital find their audiences? How do artists establish relationships to art and research publics in which artistic practice can be seen and interpreted?

From these questions the concept of "translocality" was developed and refined. The starting point of the *Translocal Practices* research practice was the art in public space project *BlackBenz Race,* realized by knowbotic research from 2005 to 2007 and sponsored by the IFCAR. *BlackBenz Race* dealt actively with the Kosovan diaspora in Zurich, reflecting on its public representation and perception. This culminated in a performative, translocal intervention in the form of a semifictive car race from Zurich to Pristina.

These experiences triggered the wish to discuss translocality more intensively with other artists, theorists, and curators, and to examine how this concept is negotiated artistically and scientifically. A project group was established consisting of knowbotic research (at that time this artist group included Christian Huebler, Alexander Tuchacek, and Yvonne Wilhelm), Felix Stalder, and Fabian Vögeli. During multiple meetings, the group compiled, compared, and analyzed various artistic practices. Afterward these were discussed with experts at a two-day conference. The project group then defined three topic areas:

1 The understanding and knowledge about the theoretical-analytical conception of translocal spaces.
2 The positioning of one's own artistic projects within the translocal spaces.
3 Formats that are developed in order to make the content and materials generated in these artistic projects accessible to a broader public.

For the conference, artists were asked to team up with one of the critics/curators they invited. These teams prepared points of discussion and related them during the workshops to the three topic areas listed above.

Following the conference, the concept of translocality became consolidated in the further artistic research activities of knowbotic research, Felix Stalder, and Fabian Vögeli. knowbotic research, since renamed knowbotiq, has conducted further research activities on translocality.

Yvonne Wilhelm and Christian Huebler

Project Title
Translokale Praktiken. Künstlerische Praktiken in vernetzten Räumen

Project Period
1 October 2006–30 September 2007

Keywords
- Translocality
- Public
- Translocal space
- Globalization
- Artistic research

Heads of Project
- knowbotic research, artist group (Christian Huebler, Alexander Tuchacek, and Yvonne Wilhelm)
- Felix Stalder, cultural and media researcher

Project Team
- Fabian Vögeli, student at VMK, Zurich University of the Arts

Research Partners
- Azra Aksamija
- Ute Meta Bauer
- Jochen Becker/metroZones
- Ursula Biemann
- Andreas Broeckmann
- Carles Guerra
- Stefan Kaegi/Rimini Protokoll
- Karl-Heinz Klopf
- John Palmesino
- Pelin Tan
- Srdjan Jovanovic Weiss

Conference Funding
- Swiss National Science Foundation SNSF, DORE

Related Projects
- Swiss Psychotropic Gold, Zurich University of the Arts, 2015–2020
  P. 184
- The Aesthetics of the Translocal, Zurich University of the Arts, 2019–2020
  P. 246

Website
- www.translocal-practices.net (no longer available)

Articles
- Felix Stalder (2006): "Tracing Translocality: The BlackBenz Race." In: Networked Cultures. www.networkedcultures.org/index.php?tdid=14
- knowbotiq and Felix Stalder (2012): "Translocal Practices—In the Possibilities between Spaces and Conflicts." In: *Practices of Experimentation, Research and Teaching in the Arts Today*. Edited by the Department of Art & Media, Zurich University of the Arts, 70–87.

Conference
Translocal Practices, Artistic Practices in Networked Spaces, 4–5 June 2007. Kunsthalle Zürich and Zurich University of the Arts. With contributions by:
- Azra Aksamija and Ute Meta Bauer: "Antagonistic Fields in the Translocal Space." Keynote Lecture.
- Ursula Biemann and Carles Guerra: "The Maghreb Connection."
- John Palmesino and Srdjan Jovanovic Weiss: "Undecidability: Observations on Architecture and Extraterritoriality."
- Pelin Tan and Karl-Heinz Klopf: "Conflictuous Localities."
- Stefan Kaegi/Rimini Protokoll and Jochen Becker/metroZones: "Scenarios of New Old Europe."
- Andreas Broeckmann, workshop moderation and closing analysis.

Lectures
- knowbotic research: "Translocal Practices." In: *Immediate Art—Lecture Series*. 4 August 2008. Centre for Contemporary Art Laznia in Gdansk (PL).
- knowbotic research: "Kunst und translokale Praktiken." In: *BASICS. MEDIEN|KUNST|GESELLSCHAFT*. 6 November 2008. Galerie 5020, Salzburg.

Exhibition
- *be prepared! tiger!* 30 January–24 February 2008. Kulturprojekte Berlin in cooperation with the Haus der Kulturen der Welt. Solo exhibition as part of *transmediale.08 CONSPIRE*. knowbotic research with Peter Sandbichler.

Works
- knowbotic research: *BlackBenz Race*. 2003–2005. Two to five black Mercedes limousines, performative intervention between Pristina, Zurich, Rotterdam, and London. With Bim Bimma (.NR.) rapper Pristina, Gabriel Sandro (live video), and Felix Stalder.
- knowbotic research with Peter Sandbichler: *be prepared! Tiger!* 2006. Stealth boat, radar station. Performative intervention in the urban space of Duisburg, Duisburger Akzente: *PubliCity—Constructing the Truth*.
- knowbotic research: *newborn_undeliverable?* 5–7 June 2008. Performative intervention on the occasion of the 2008 World Cup in Zurich, 2 m-high wooden letters, 25 t truck, with rapper EKI NOX. In cooperation with Fabian Vögeli and Felix Stalder, Kunsthof Zürich.

Fig. 1–2 knowbotic research: *be prepared! tiger!* Wilhelm Lehmbruck Museum, Duisburg, 2006

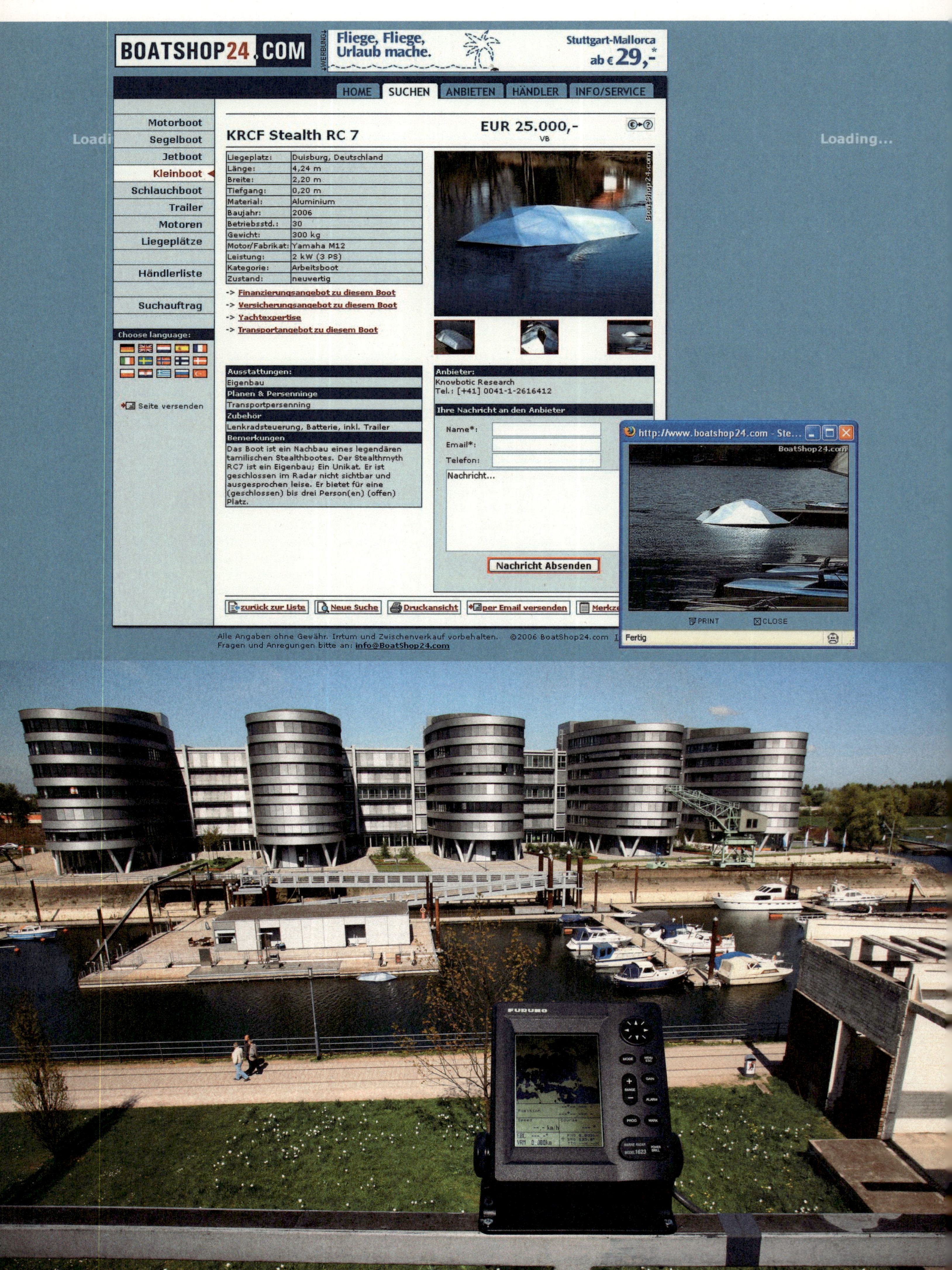

Fig. 3 knowbotic research: *be prepared! tiger!* Skuc Gallery, Ljubljana, 2006
Fig. 4 Field research. Pristina and online media, 2008

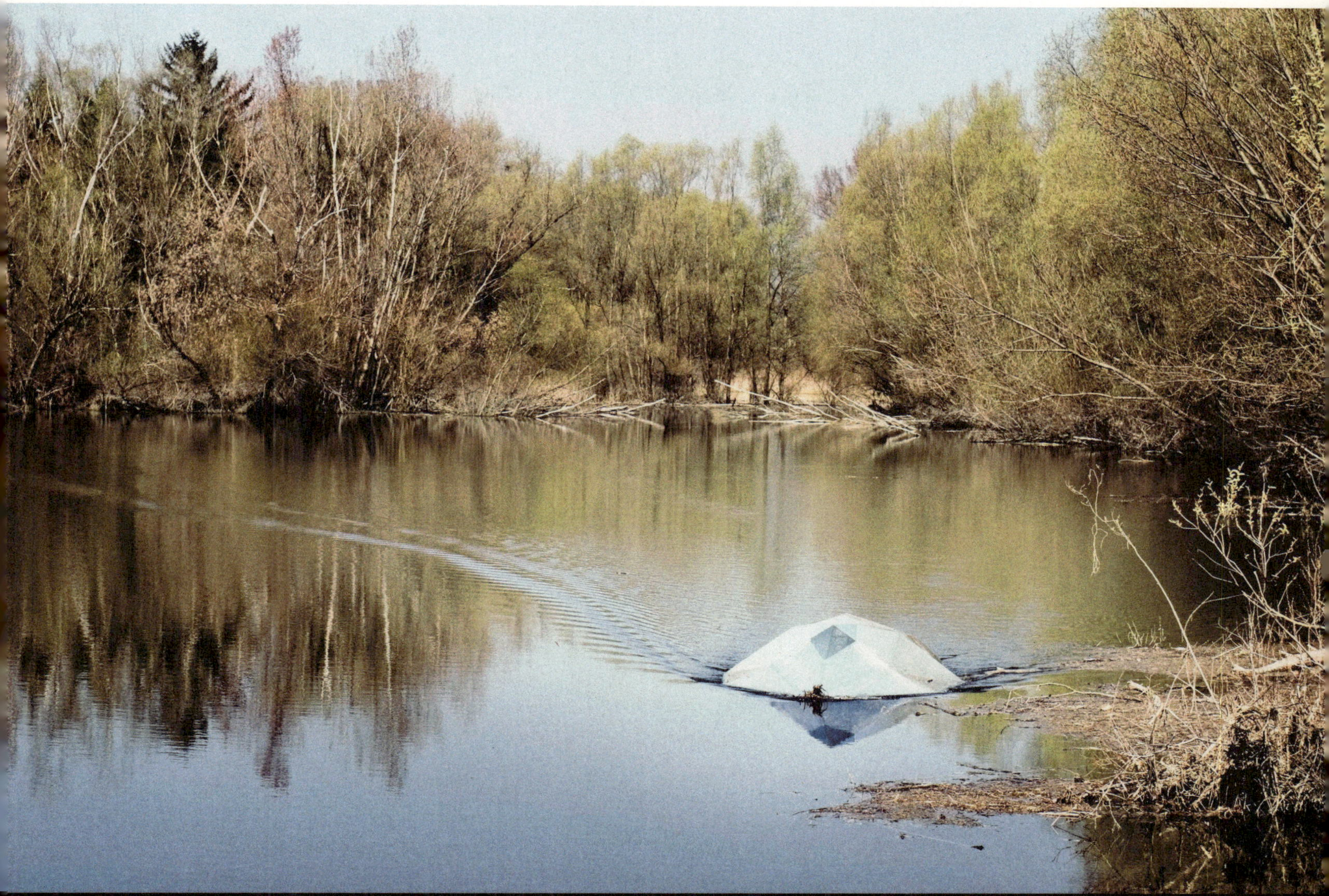

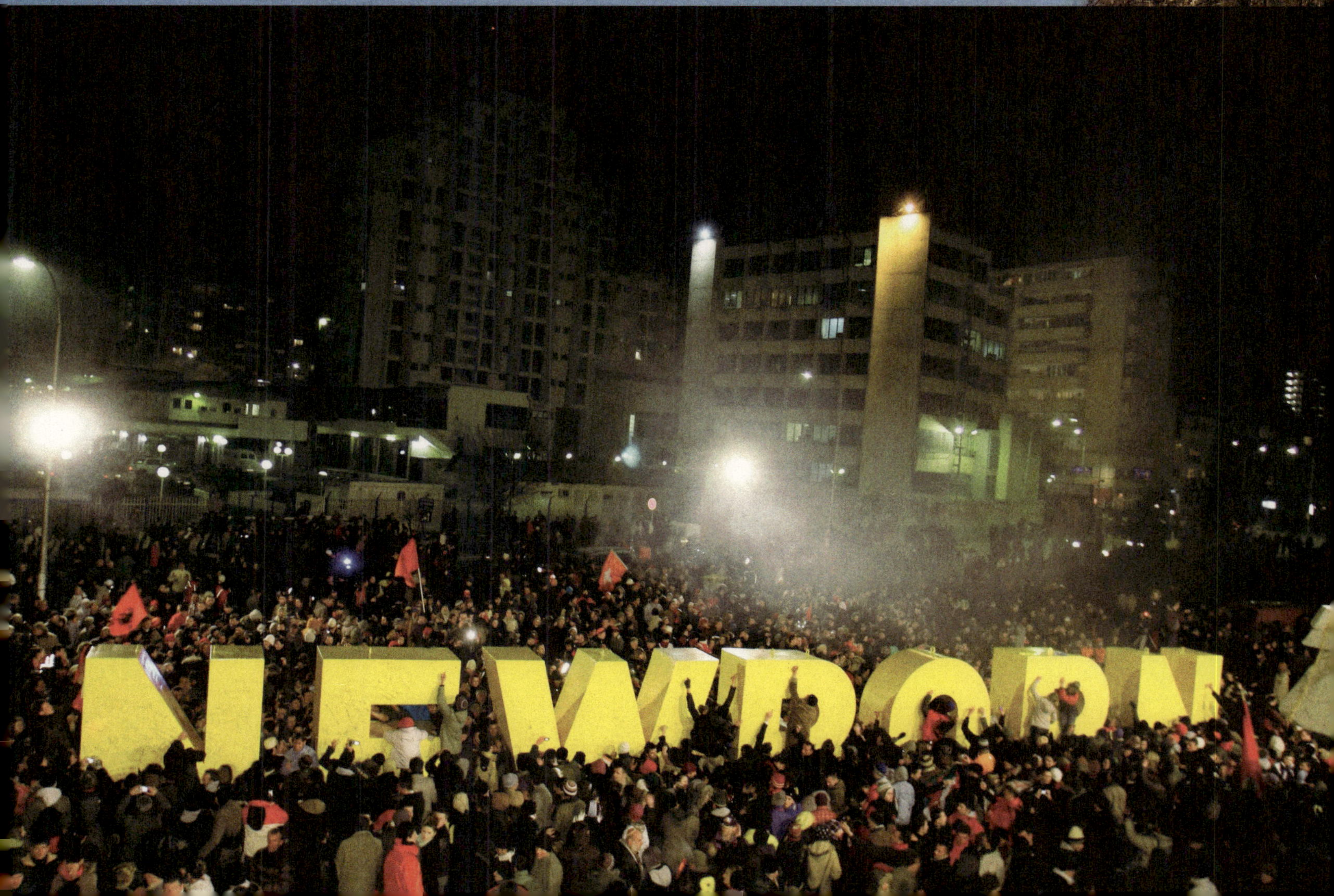

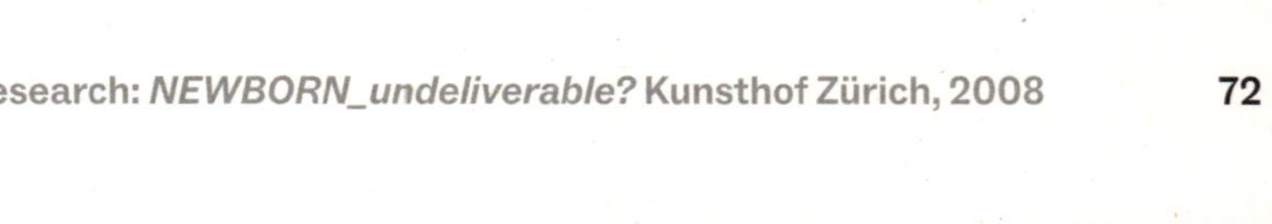

Fig. 5 knowbotic research: *NEWBORN_undeliverable?* Kunsthof Zürich, 2008

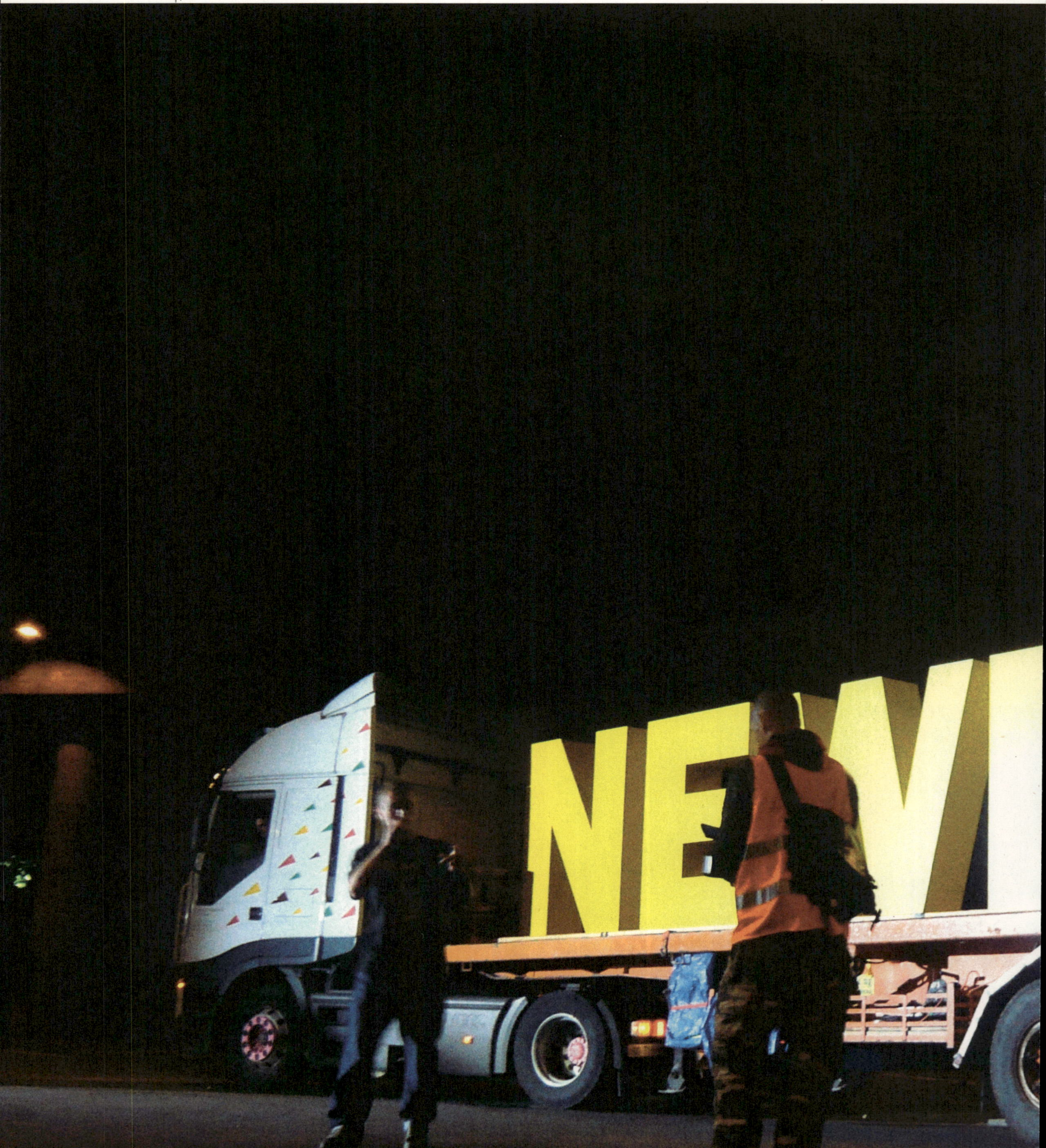

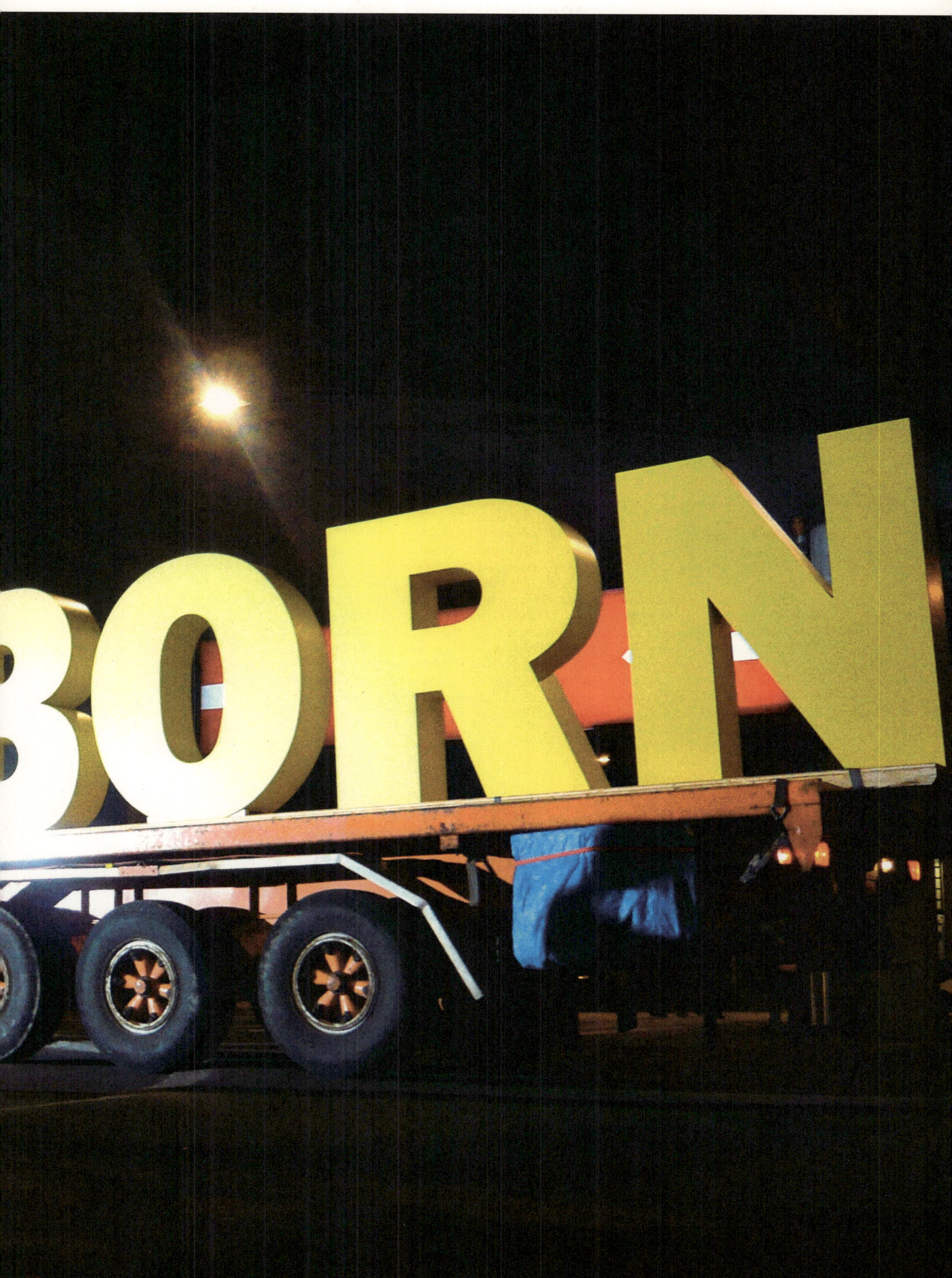

This project launched by Hannes Rickli investigated audiovisual material from the context of behavioral biology. It did so by means of a corpus of functional films that emerged from measurement cameras and microphones of experimental systems during research work. These unedited videos (videograms) were recorded starting in the 1990s, first on magnetic tape and later on hard disks, and unsystematically collected by Rickli during laboratory visits. They are the remnants of earlier phases of experimentation, in which research media, spatial settings, and experimental animals (fish, mites, mosquitos, and flies) were explored by synchronizing and matching recordings. Because the biologists removed this material from the scientific process after it was evaluated, it did not circulate in biological publications. The genre of instrumental or operative film did not attract the attention of film sciences until around 2005.

Five studies conducted in parallel in the disciplines of art, history of science, sociology of science, media science, and art history/art research, in collaboration with three partner laboratories, investigated this instrumental image refuse. The artistic study reconstructed the original recording situations of the videos on a 1:1 scale and rendered them as ready-mades in the form of audiovisual installations in the art space. The history of science study used the example of audio and video recordings to investigate acoustic communication in fish to investigate how the design of an experimental system can be understood as an act of practical philosophizing. The sociology of science study conducted interviews with three laboratory partners on the North Sea island of Heligoland; in Austin, Texas; and in Zurich. They discussed how the scientists posed questions about the fish and the insects, and how they dealt with disturbances in the collected data. In collaboration with the artist Hannes Rickli, the study was transformed into a video installation. The media science study analyzed the videograms as physical traces of experimentation and described the spillover of signs they contain which makes it possible to interpret the human-animal-apparatus relationship. From this confrontation emerged the first international and interdisciplinary conference on functional film, which took place in Zurich in 2009 at the conclusion of the research project. On the basis of other contemporary examples, the art research study allocated the work of reading traces and archiving from the artistic *Spillover* project to a practice that increasingly uses resources of what is vague and unofficial to bring a "different" knowledge to representation and to societal negotiation.

The understanding of the video material collected out of artistic interest and the understanding of its production in the scientific context was worked out in workshops at the partner laboratories, featuring close exchange among the disciplines involved in the project. The workshops also facilitated theory development by asking when (≠ what) an image is (in contrast to a diagram, for instance). Over the project period the studies developed in loose pairings or independently of each other. The methods and forms of presenting the studies were oriented to their given specialized practice and manifested themselves in art installations, texts, and conferences.

The *Spillover* project was succeeded in 2012 by a research cooperation that played a key role in the subsequent *Computer Signals I* and *II* projects as well as the SNFS Agora project *Data Flows* (project period 2021–2024). Members: Professor Philipp Fischer (Alfred Wegener Institute), Professor Gabriele Gramelsberger (RWTH Aachen University), Professor Christoph Hoffmann (University of Lucerne), Professor Hans Hofmann (University of Texas at Austin), Professor Emeritus Hans-Jörg Rheinberger (Max Planck Institute for the History of Science, Berlin.

Hannes Rickli

Project Title
Überschuss. Videogramme des Experimentierens

Project Period
1 October 2007–31 March 2009

Keywords
- Experimental systems
- Materiality of experimentation
- Materiality of media
- Traces
- Art & science

Head of Project
- Hannes Rickli, artist

Research Team
- Michele Dell'Ambrogio, programmer
- Thomas Galler, artist
- Roman Keller, artist
- Christoph Hoffmann, science researcher
- Michael Guggenheim, sociologist
- Nicola Müllerschön, art researcher

Additional Staff
- Peter Geimer, art historian
- Christoph Schenker, art theorist

Research Partners
- Biological Institute Heligoland, Alfred Wegener Institute, Helmholtz Centre for Polar and Marine Research
- Institute of Neuroinformatics UZH/ETH
- Max Planck Institute for the History of Science
- University of Texas, Section of Integrative Biology

Outputs

A

Project Partners
- Helmhaus Zürich
- videocompany.ch

Project Funding
- Swiss National Science Foundation SNSF

Related Projects
- Computer Signals I, Zurich University of the Arts, 2012–2015
  P. 118
- Computer Signals II, Zurich University of the Arts, 2017–2021
  P. 214
- Listening to Data Flows, Zurich University of the Arts, 2021–2024

Publication
- Hannes Rickli (ed.) (2011): *Videogramme/Videograms. Die Bildwelten biologischer Experimentalsysteme als Kunst- und Theorieobjekt/The pictorial worlds of biological experimentation as an object of art and theory.* Volume 6 of the Institute for Contemporary Art Research series. With English-language text supplement. Zurich: Scheidegger & Spiess.
  A Open access: https://doi.org/10.5281/zenodo.6330789

Articles
- Hannes Rickli (2009): "Livestream Knurrhahn." In: Elke Bippus (ed.): *Kunst des Forschens. Praxis eines ästhetischen Denkens*. Zürich/Berlin: Diaphanes, 49–63.
- Hannes Rickli (2012): "Precarious Evidence. Notes on Art and Biology in the Age of Digital Experimentation." In: Florian Dombois, Ute Meta Bauer, and Michael Schwab (eds.): *Intellectual Birdhouse. Artistic Practice as Research*. London: Koenig Books, 101–115.
- Hannes Rickli and Christoph Schenker (2012): "Experimentieren." In: Departement Kunst & Medien, Zürcher Hochschule der Künste (ed.): *Praktiken des Experimentierens. Forschung und Lehre in den Künsten/Practices of Experimentation. Research and Teaching in the Arts Today*. Yearbook 4. Zurich: Scheidegger & Spiess, 150–163.

Conference
- *Latente Bilder. Erzählweisen des Gebrauchsfilms*. 10–12 September 2009. Collegium Helveticum, Filmpodium Zürich, and Helmhaus Zürich. Concept and organization: Peter Geimer, Vinzenz Hediger, and Hannes Rickli. With Scott Curtis, Philipp Fischer, Steven N. Fry, Oliver Gaycken, Vinzenz Hediger, Christoph Hoffmann, Hans Hofmann, Florian Hoof, Nicola Müllerschön, Cord Richelmann, Hannes Rickli, Georg Rüppell, Dan Streible, Margarete Vöhringer, Susanne Witzgall, Florian Wüst, and Yvonne Zimmermann. Moderation: Peter Geimer, Michael Guggenheim, Vinzenz Hediger, and Hans-Jörg Rheinberger.

Lecture
- Hannes Rickli: "Der unsichtbare Faden. Motive biologischer Gebrauchsfilme." In: *Motifs of the Moving Image*. 28–30 March 2012. Internationales Kolleg für Kulturtechnikforschung und Medienphilosophie IKKM, Weimar.

Film Screening
- *Schwarzbäuchige Fruchtfliege #1, First Tests 2006/2011.* Part of *Das Kino der Tiere. Eine kurze Geschichte des Tierfilms*. 5–10 May 2011. 57. Internationale Kurzfilmtage Oberhausen.

Exhibition
- *Videogramme*. 6 September 2009–25 October 2009. Helmhaus Zürich. 10 Installations by Hannes Rickli.

Work
- Video and audiovisual installations in the *Videogramme* exhibition, 2009, Helmhaus Zürich. See Rickli (2011), 94–107.

Fig. 1–2 Field research. Agroscope Bee Research Centre, Liebefeld Köniz, 1991

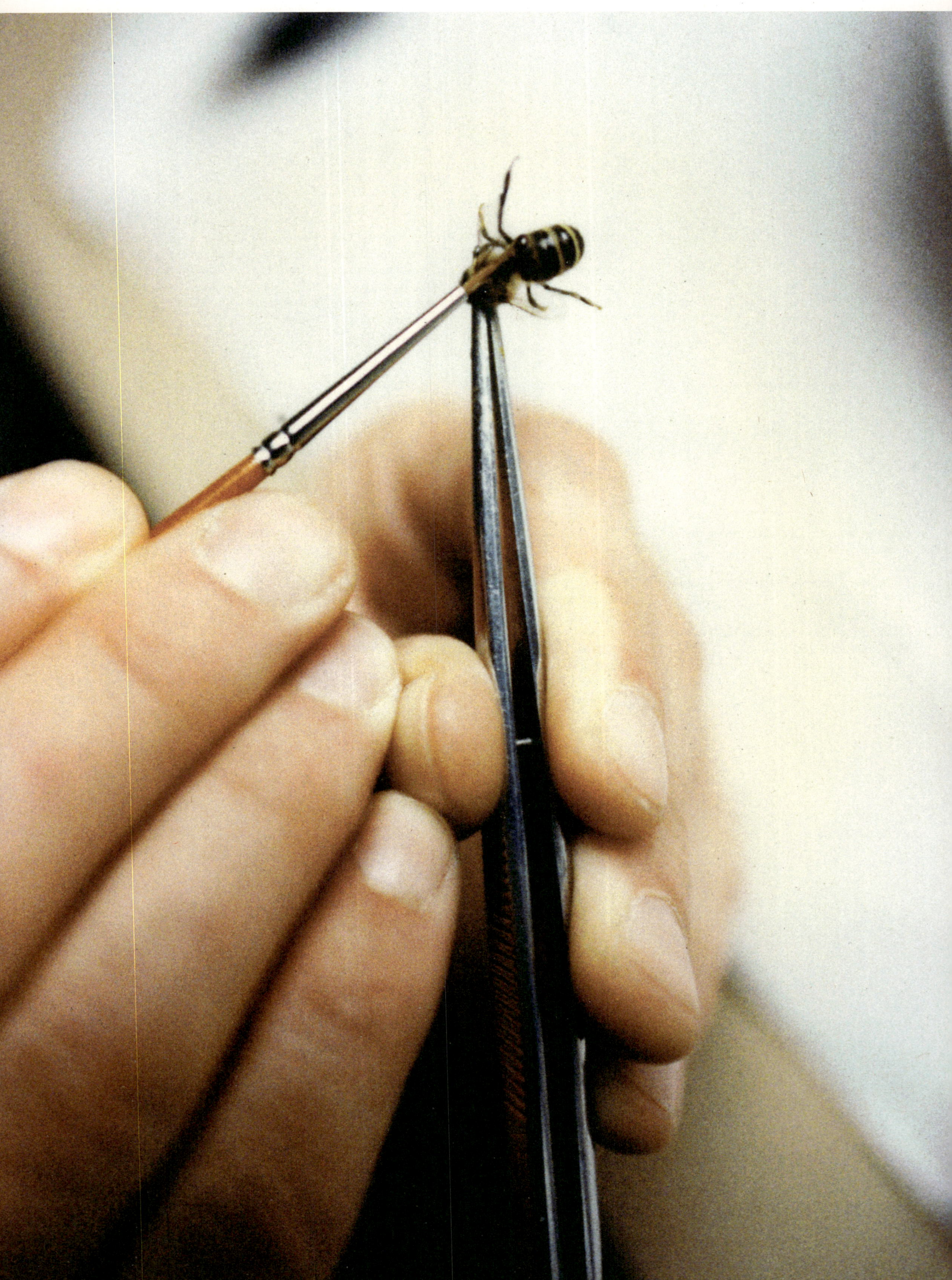

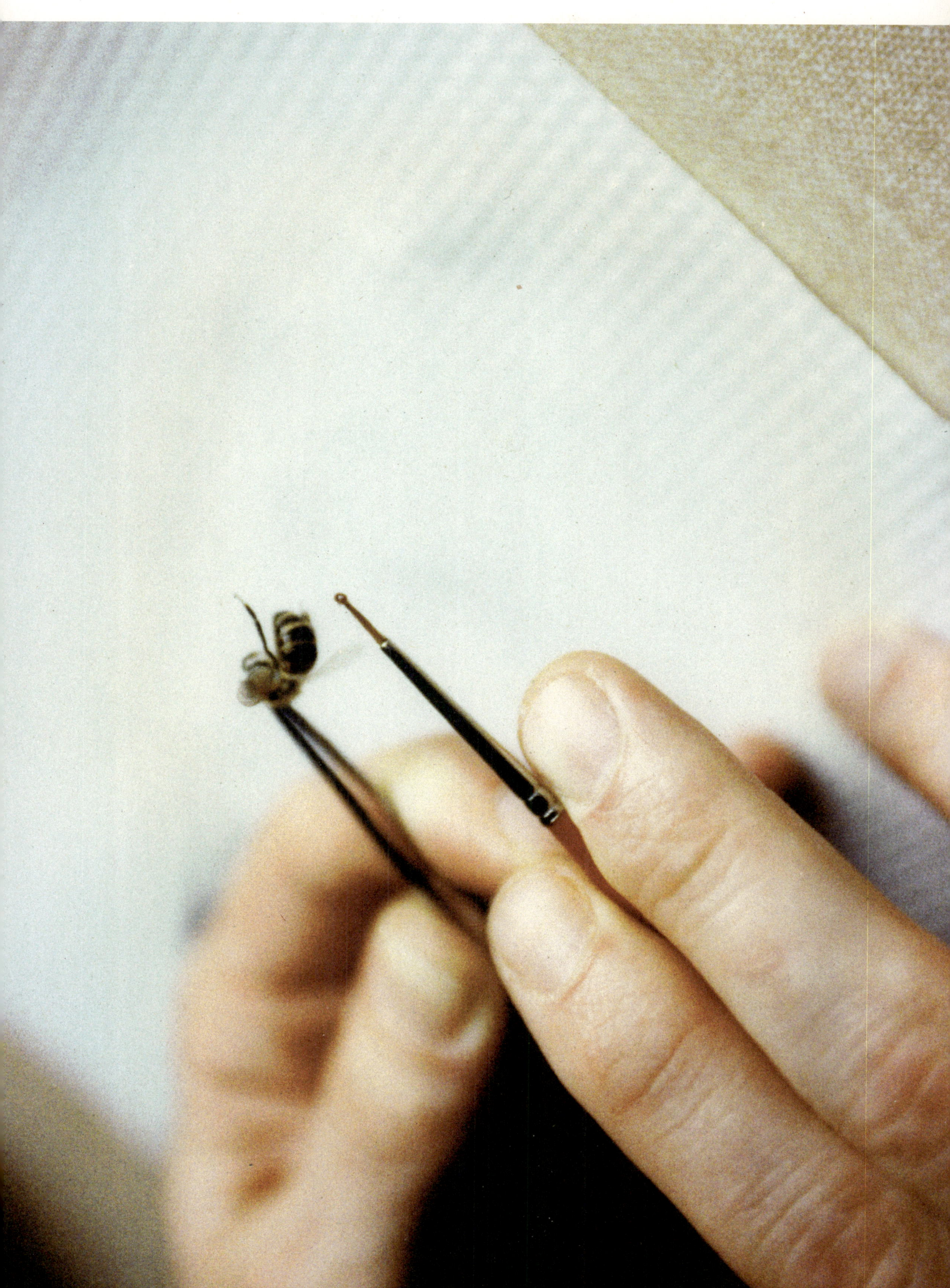

Fig. 3 Hofmann Lab. University of Texas, Austin, 2008
Fig. 4 Arrival at Heligoland workshop, 2008

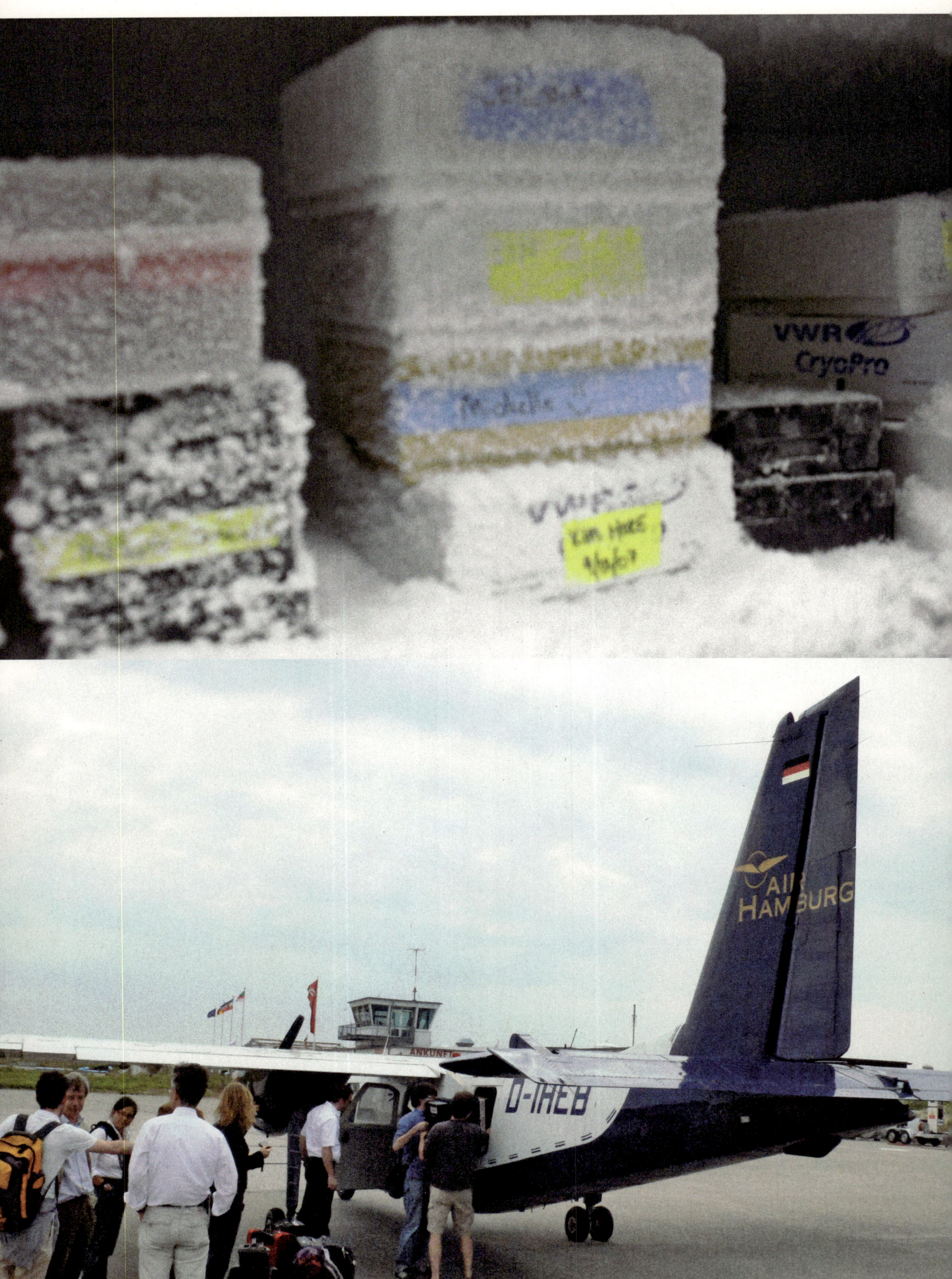

Fig. 5 Publication proofs of *Videograms*, 2011

Fig. 6 RemOs1. Limnological Institute, University of Konstanz, 2005

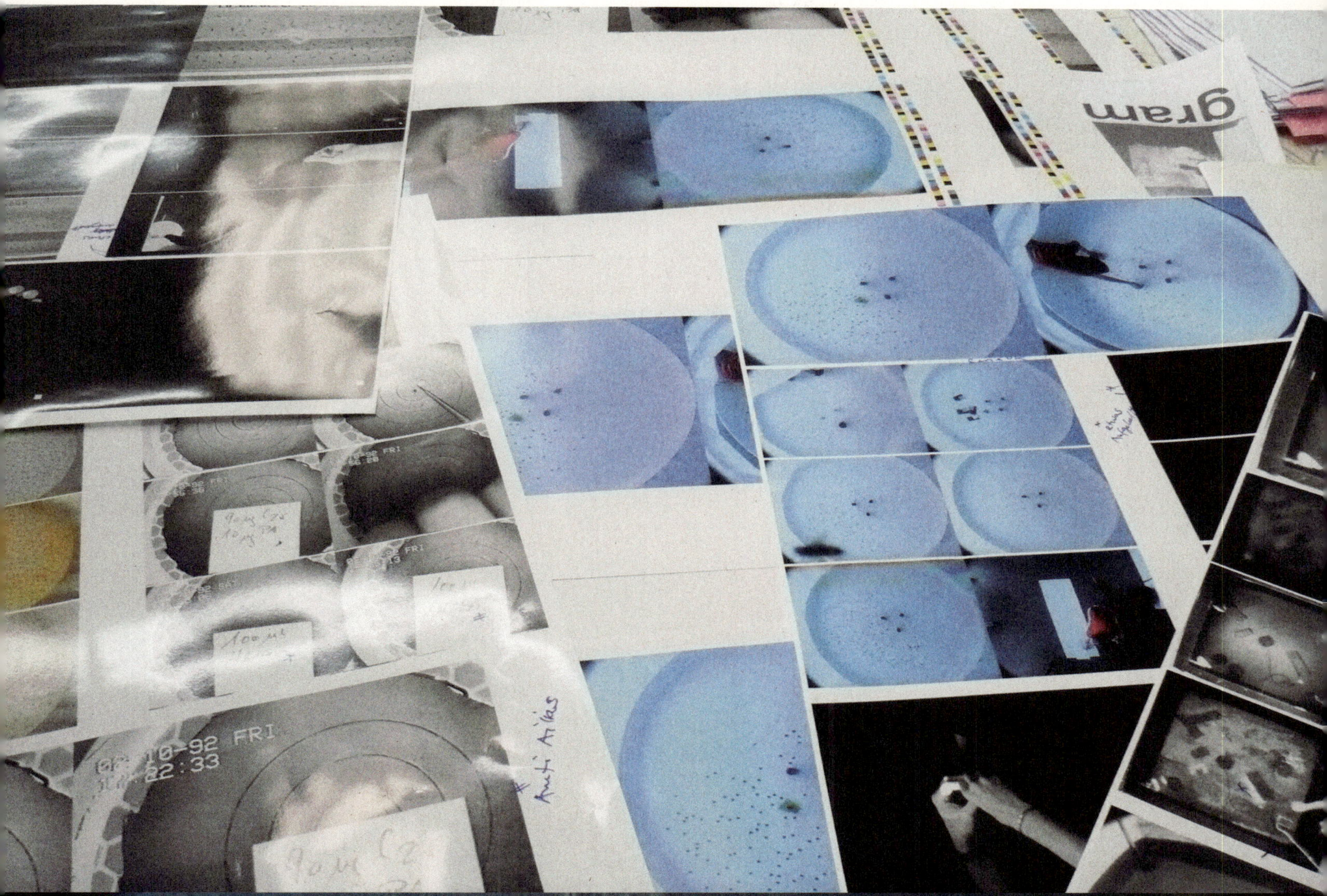

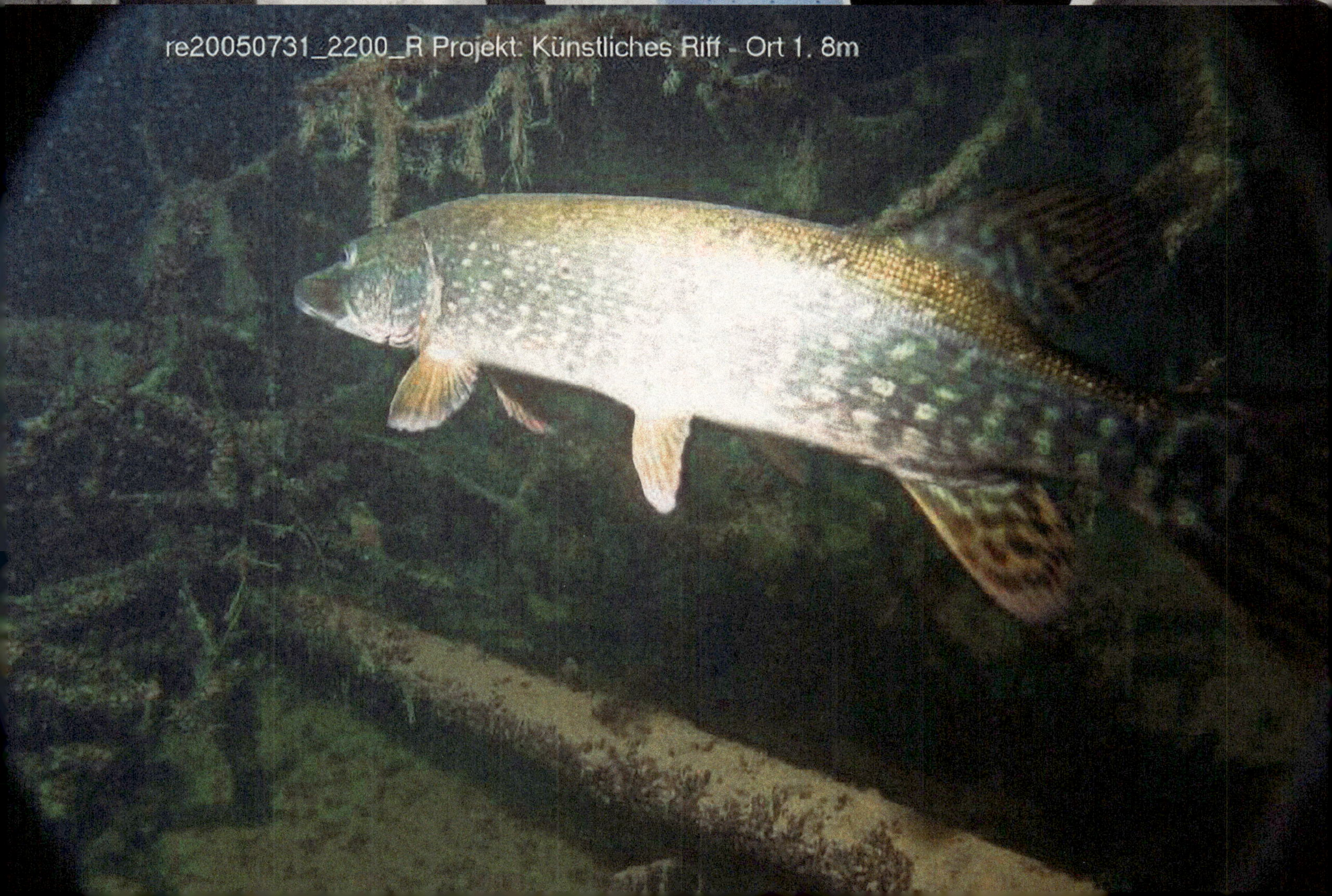

re20050731_2200_R Projekt: Künstliches Riff - Ort 1. 8m

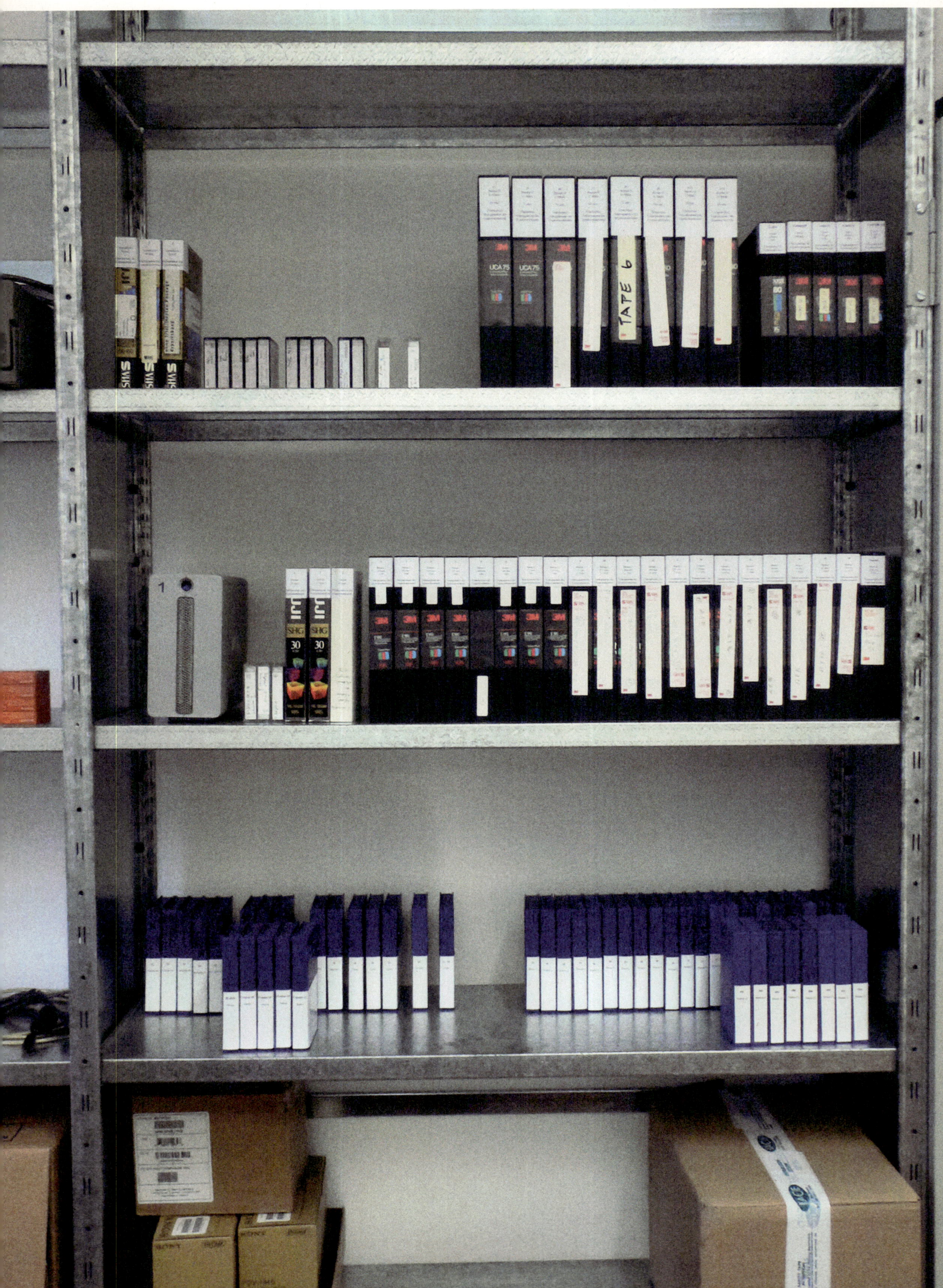

Fig. 7 Videograms archive. Analog and digital image carriers, 2007

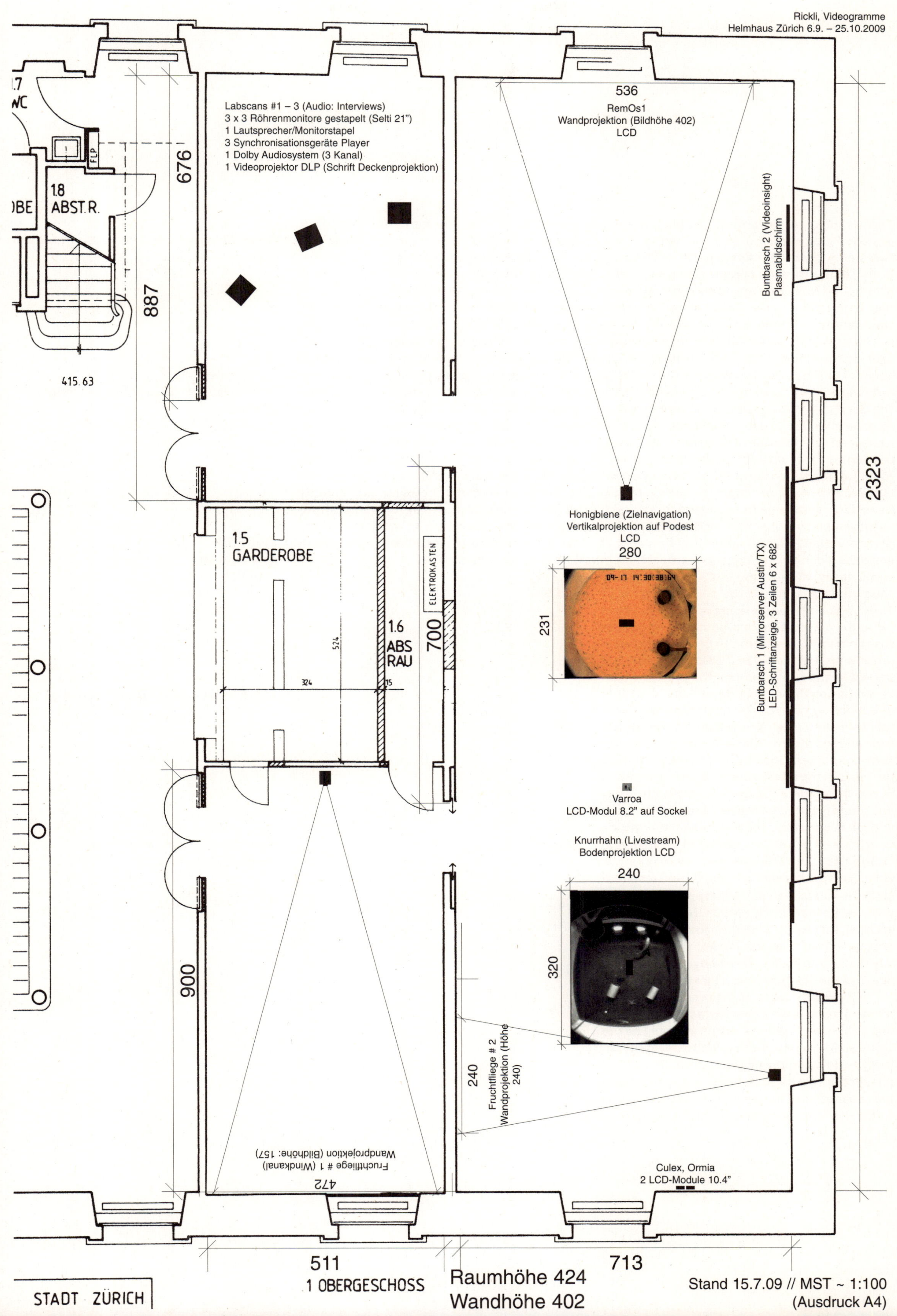
Rickli, Videogramme
Helmhaus Zürich 6.9. – 25.10.2009
Labscans #1 – 3 (Audio: Interviews)
3 x 3 Röhrenmonitore gestapelt (Selti 21")
1 Lautsprecher/Monitorstapel
3 Synchronisationsgeräte Player
1 Dolby Audiosystem (3 Kanal)
1 Videoprojektor DLP (Schrift Deckenprojektion)
536
RemOs1
Wandprojektion (Bildhöhe 402)
LCD
Buntbarsch 2 (Videoinsight)
Plasmabildschirm
676
887
1.8
ABST.R.
415.63
2323
Honigbiene (Zielnavigation)
Vertikalprojektion auf Podest
LCD
280
231
1.5
GARDEROBE
ELEKTROKASTEN
1.6
ABS
RAU
700
524
324
15
Buntbarsch 1 (Mirrorserver Austin/TX)
LED-Schriftanzeige, 3 Zeilen 6 x 682
Varroa
LCD-Modul 8.2" auf Sockel
Knurrhahn (Livestream)
Bodenprojektion LCD
240
320
900
240
Fruchtfliege # 2
Wandprojektion (Höhe 240)
Fruchtfliege # 1 (Windkanal)
Wandprojektion (Bildhöhe: 157)
472
Culex, Ormia
2 LCD-Module 10.4"
511
713
1 OBERGESCHOSS
STADT ZÜRICH
Raumhöhe 424
Wandhöhe 402
Stand 15.7.09 // MST ~ 1:100
(Ausdruck A4)

The first phase of the project, the photographic project *Parallel*, addressed the visible structures of migrant lifeworlds in the metropolis Berlin. It investigated opportunities and limits, attempting to represent and demonstrate complex correlations in the discourse of the migration debate by means of photography. Linda Herzog posed the question as to whether a parallel society of Turkish origin exists in Berlin. The concept of the parallel society is used to designate the political tensions that are dealt with in the German-language discourse on migration. *Parallel* intended to use photography to create a space where the issue of different cultural values and norms could be broached. One challenge to make this space lay in the fact that certain cultural and moral concepts of German majority society can diverge from those in Turkey, such as the understanding of democracy and solidarity, individualism, and education in terms of linguistic diversity and language competence. In some cases, integration into German society thus implies rejecting the societal norms of Turkish society, a phenomenon that harbors potential for sociopolitical conflict. The deeper research in Turkey from the preceding photographic project *Mihriban. Türkei 2004 bis 2007* served as the foundation for the project's concentration on the various lifeworlds of migrants of Turkish origin in Berlin. *Mihriban* used documentary photography to describe different cultural and societal realities in Turkey. Herzog presumed that these societal structures would also be visible in the altered cultural setting of urban Berlin. In *Parallel* she experimented with different photographic patterns of representation and clichés that evoked the idea of integration or expressed non-belonging to the German majority society. In Berlin she visited various interest groups, cultural associations, and individuals in the Turkish-language diaspora, conversing with and taking photographs of the protagonists and their lifeworlds. With the consent of the photographed persons, the images were continually discussed and analyzed by migration experts, photographers, and other participants.

Over the course of the project, however, this approach proved unsatisfactory. The photographic examination focused strongly on the cultural differences between the German majority society and the migrants from Turkey and their progeny in Berlin. It became apparent that the conception of the project exhibited an intercultural orientation based on the discrepancy between "self" and "foreign." Consequently, Herzog redirected the perspective of the project in order to propose photographic alternatives to counter the understanding of "us" and "not-us," and to visually renegotiate the idea of integration in the transcultural context. Over the second phase of the project, transculturality as cultural understanding, a concept introduced by Wolfgang Welsch, developed into a vision in which people can possess multiple cultural belongings and move within and between different cultural formations. The concept of culture was defined by interrelationships and commonalities, which allowed new photographic perspectives. The final product of the project, entitled *Samimi. Fotografien zu Identität und Zugehörigkeit* (Samimi. Photographs of Identity and Belonging), consists of forty-six photographs and one textual work that discusses the visibility of migration phenomena in the photographic representations.

Linda Herzog

Project Title

Parallel. Fotografisches Projekt zur türkischen Migration in Berlin

Project Period

First project phase at Zurich University of the Arts

- 1 May 2008–31 December 2009

Second project phase

- 2010–2017

Keywords

- Migration
- Photography
- Parallel society
- Transculturality

Head of Project

- Linda Herzog, photographer

Project Funding (First Project Phase)

- George Foundation Winterthur
- Aargauer Kuratorium

Website

- www.grad.ch/samimi_text.html

Monographs

- Linda Herzog and Tan Cemal Genç (2017): *Dört Göz. Four Eyes. Journeys with Photographs and Drawings*. Dresden: Hesperus print* Verlag and Istanbul: Karşı Sanat.
- Linda Herzog (2017): *Samimi. Ein Fotoessay zu Identität und Zugehörigkeit*. Master's thesis at FHNW Academy of Art and Design, unpublished.

Article

- Linda Herzog (2016): "Samimi – Warum ist das Leben nicht schön." In: Kunstverein Kärnten (ed.): *Sichtfeld – das Eigene und das Fremde*. Catalog on the occasion of the exhibition at Künstlerhaus Klagenfurt, 9 June–13 August 2016. Klagenfurt: Kunstverein Kärnten, 32–37.

Exhibition

- *Warum ist das Leben nicht schön*. 12 February–3 April 2011. Kunstmuseum Thun. Labor exhibition series. Solo exhibition by Linda Herzog.

Work

- Linda Herzog: *Samimi. Ein Fotoessay zu Identität und Zugehörigkeit*. 2008–2017. Forty-six photographs.

Fig. 1 Photograph. Berlin, 2009

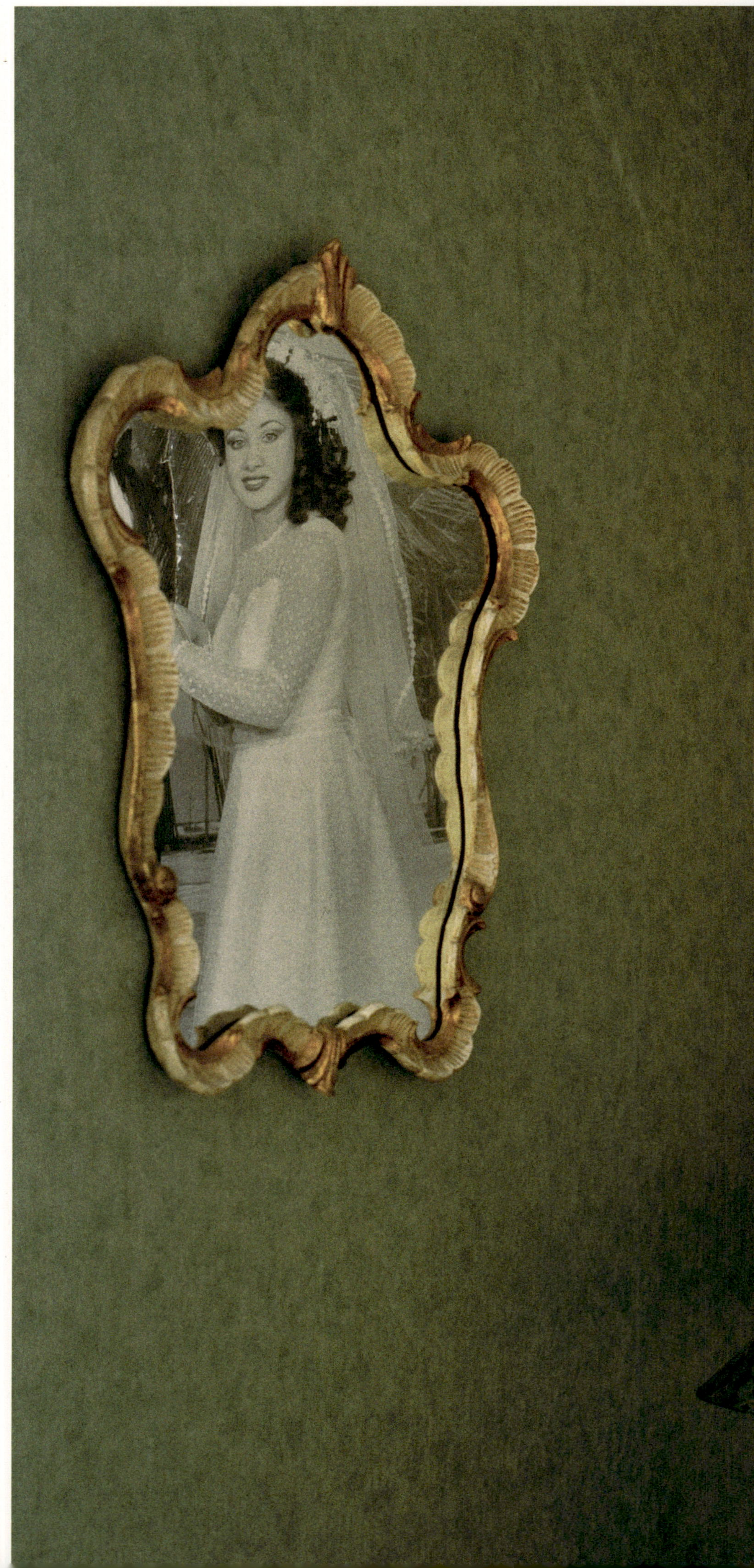

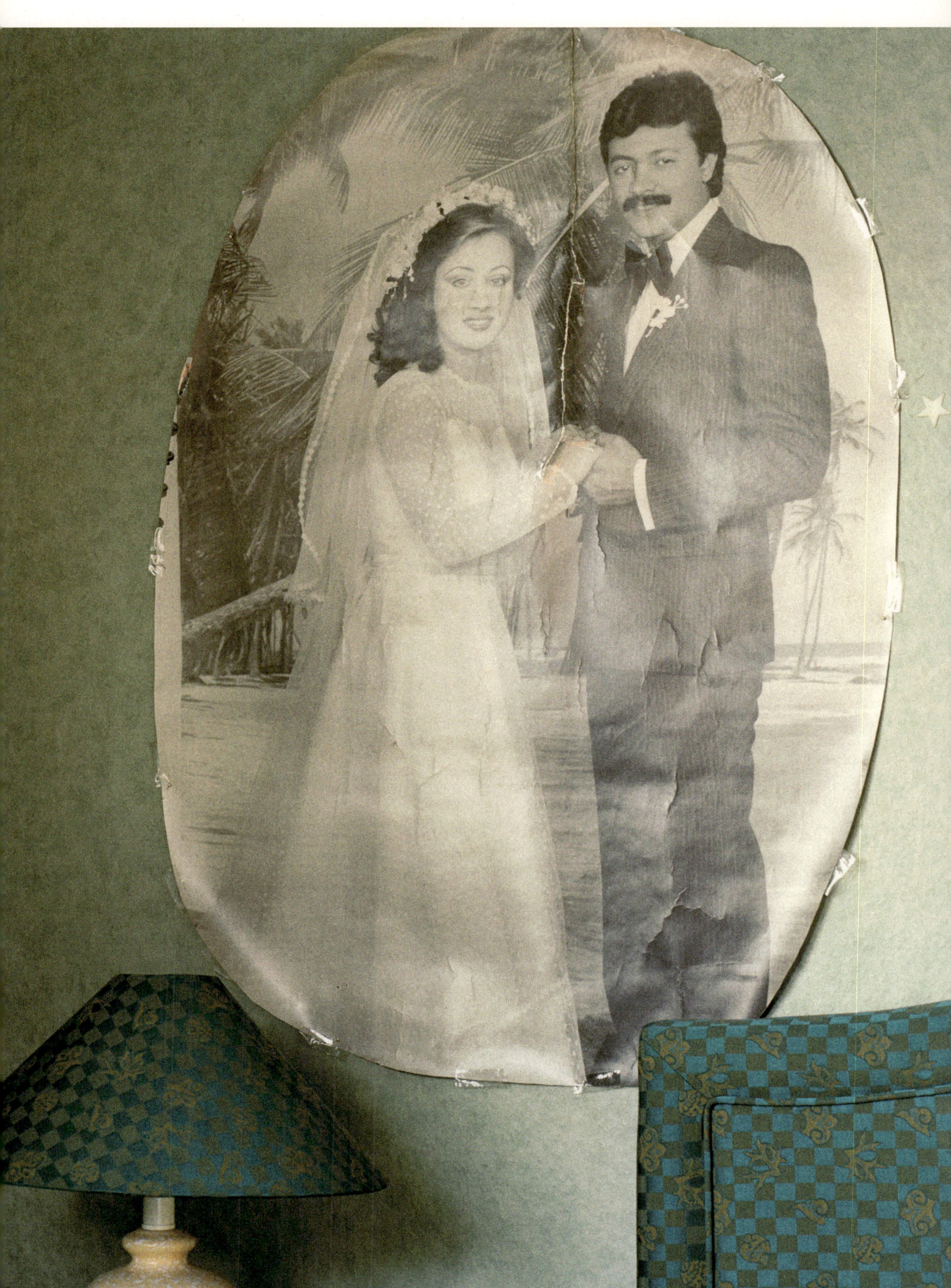

Fig. 2 Photograph. Berlin, 2015
Fig. 3 Photograph. Berlin, 2009

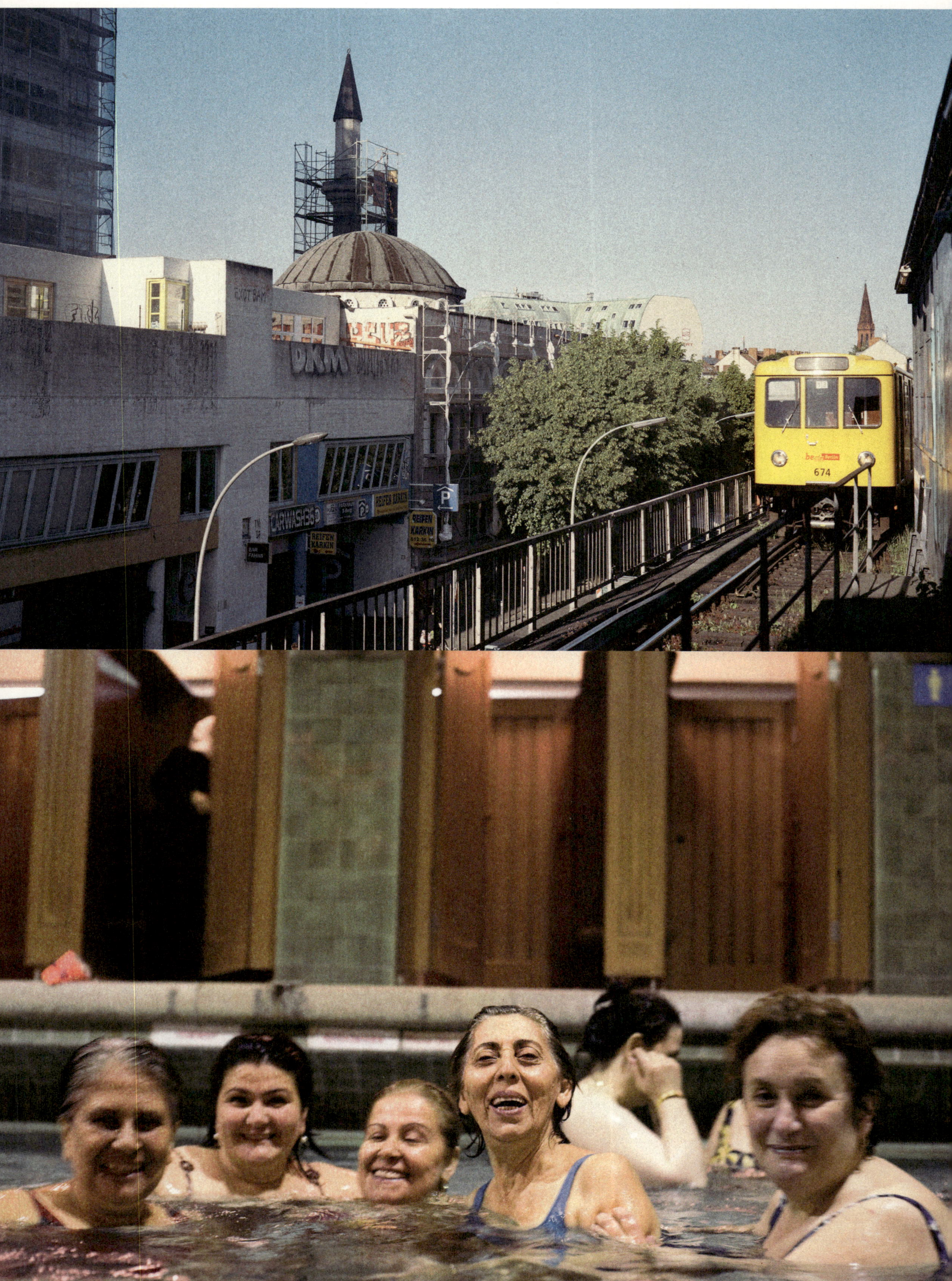

Fig. 4 Photograph. Berlin, 2009
Fig. 5 Photograph. Berlin, 2010

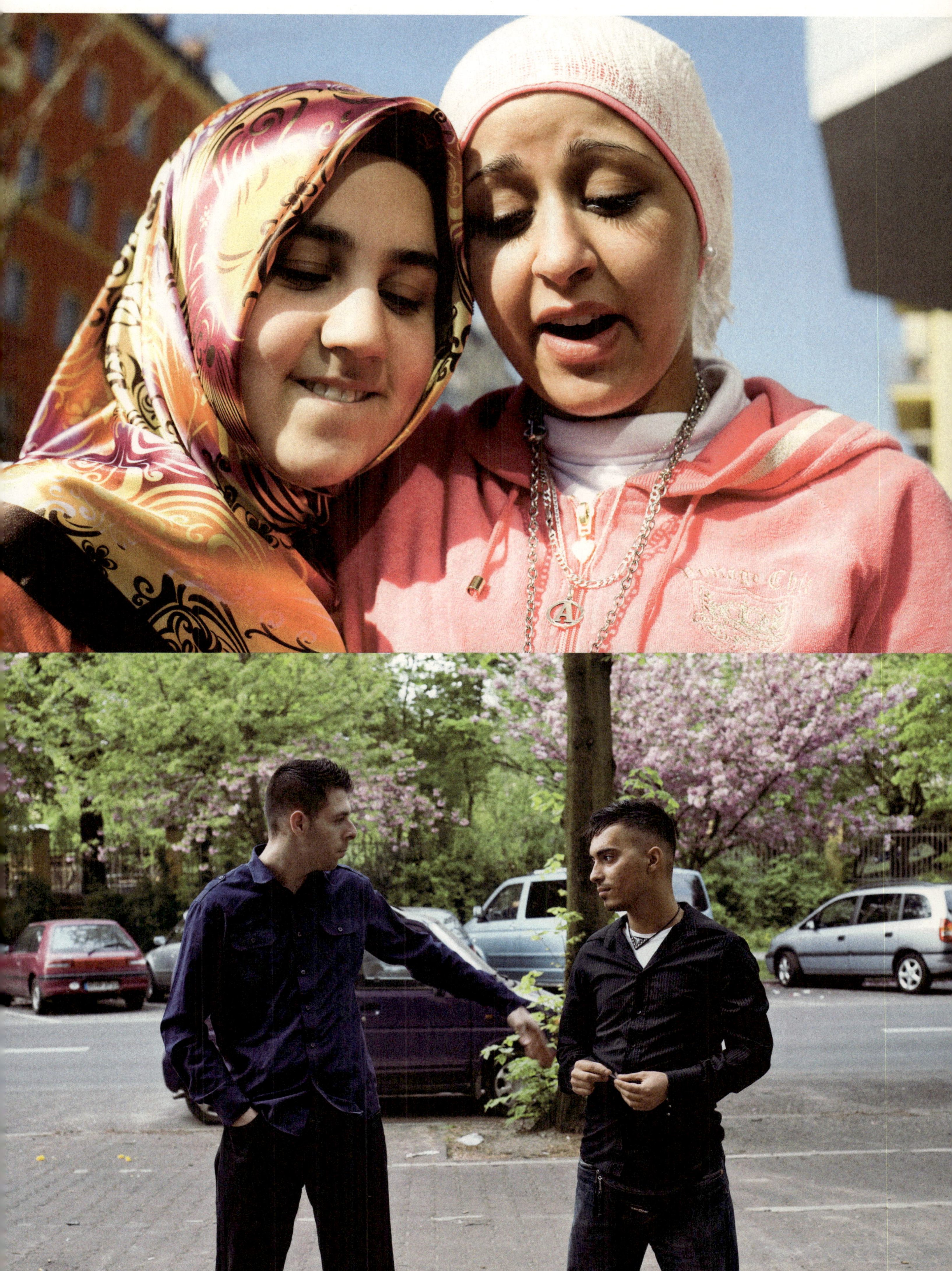

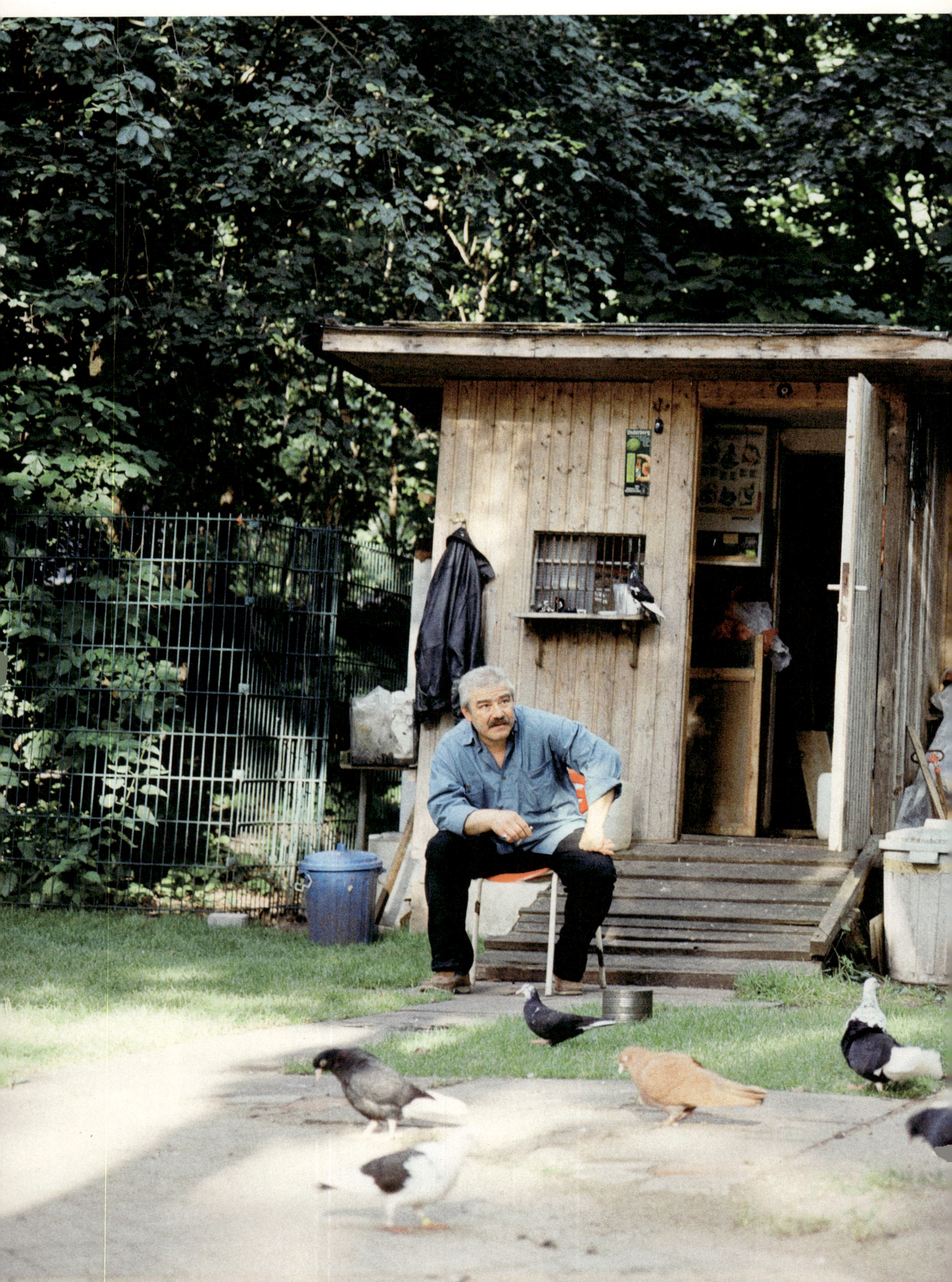

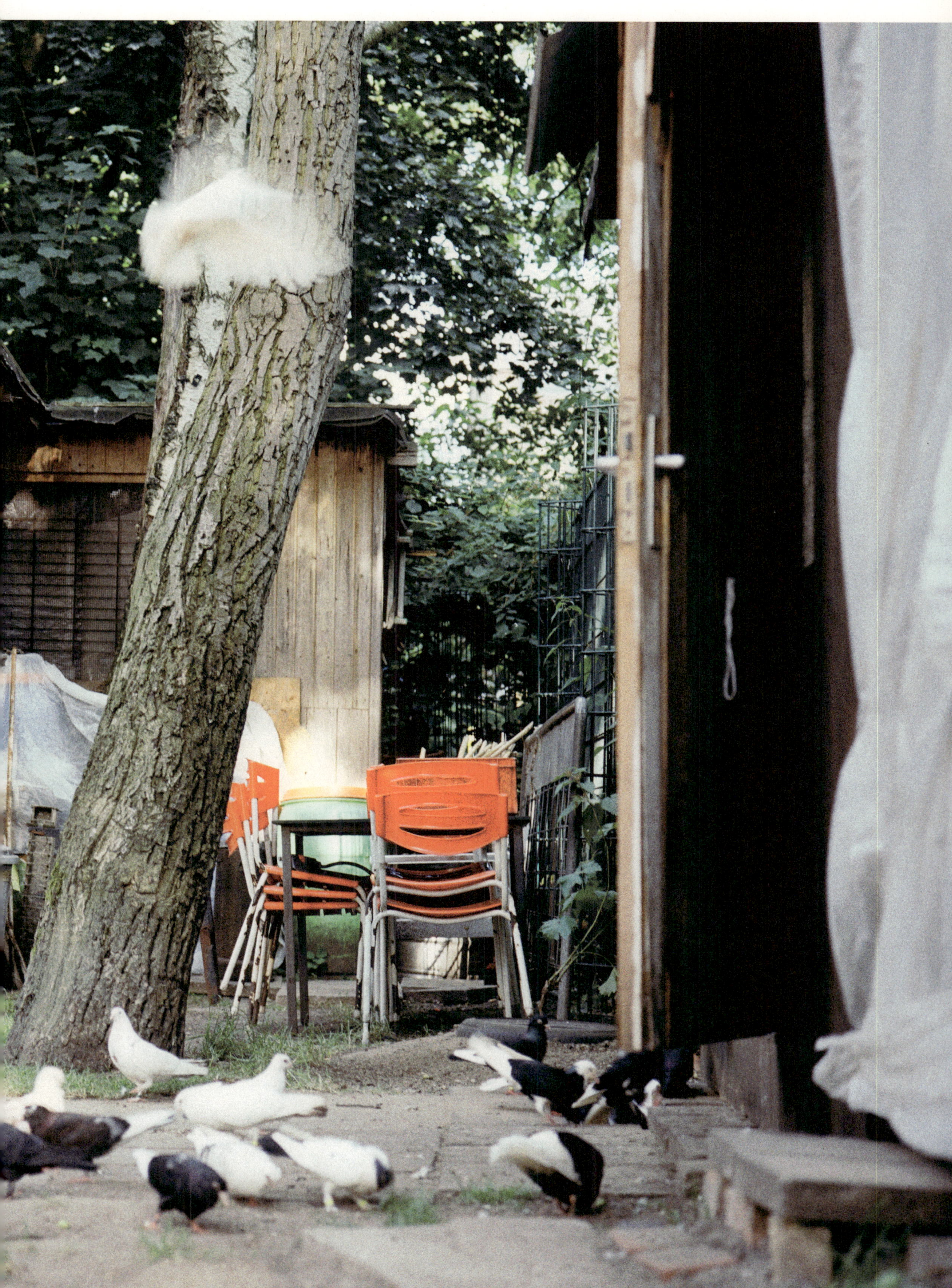

As a consequence of the changes that have taken place in construction, architecture, the economy, and society in Switzerland since the 1950s, new urban landscapes have emerged. Institutions that deal with the pictorial documentation of the landscape and settlement areas are faced with the question as to how they can illustrate these transformations in their collections. The *Views of Places* collection of the Swiss National Library's Prints and Drawings Department is tasked with collecting photographs that are important because they are typical for the country and promote identification with the Swiss nation. The existing holdings are primarily picture postcard photographs from the period before 1945. This photographic genre is not ideally suited for capturing the spatial developments important in the postwar era, such as the formation of agglomerations. The *Archive of Places* project developed proposals for how the *Views of Places* in the National Library can react to the urbanization of Switzerland and the changed production conditions in the photography of towns and landscape. The project investigated the spatial development of two cultural areas representative of Switzerland on the basis of existing documentary photographs. Comprehensive pictorial research was performed on site in Schlieren, an agglomeration community in the Midlands, and in the tourist area Oberengadin near St. Moritz, by reviewing holdings that were largely unknown and not accessible for research: archives of construction companies, of architecture and planning firms, of locally based companies, of postcard publishers, of local authorities, of the regional and supra-regional press, and local private archives and collections. These industrial photographs, which were produced and used as "operational images" in planning and construction processes, for advertising, or in the political discourse, constitute an extremely rich source for the documentation of spatial changes in the fields of architecture and agriculture, as well as in traffic and tourism.

Proceeding from the findings from this research and based on a relational understanding of space (Martina Löw, Henri Lefebvre), the project formulated collection strategies for a photographic archive on spatial development based on the areas Schlieren and Oberengadin. It formulated recommendations for image sources and photographic production contexts to be viewed, made suggestions for the objects to be documented, and for aesthetic criteria for selecting which photographs to collect. Since the collection strategies and selection criteria developed in the framework of the project can be applied to other regions of Switzerland as well, they contributed to the further development of the collection concepts of the Prints and Drawings Department of the Swiss National Library.

The result of this research project, besides the recommendations for collection strategies, are two exemplary photographic collections on Schlieren and Oberengadin for the period from 1945 to 2008, with around three thousand images each. From this photographic material, the project developed thematic series that present different views of the changes in towns and landscapes in Schlieren and in Oberengadin. Combining material from different production contexts creates a relation between various forms of photographic perception to the representation of space. They served as the foundation for the picture section of the monograph *Auf Gemeindegebiet – On Common Ground.*

In the *Fotografische Langzeitbeobachtung Schlieren 2005–2020* project, Meret Wandeler and Ulrich Görlich documented the continuous transformation of an agglomeration municipality with their own photographs. *Archive of Places* extended this timeline into the past and added to the photographic view photographs from production contexts on site.

Meret Wandeler

Project Title
Archiv des Ortes. Sammelstrategien für ein fotografisches Archiv zur Raumentwicklung

Project Period
1 October 2008–31 May 2010

Keywords
- Urbanization
- Midlands
- Alps
- Switzerland
- Documentary photography

Heads of Project
- Ulrich Görlich, artist
- Meret Wandeler, artist

Research Associate
- Lydia Lymbourides, artist and photographer

Practice Partners
- Prints and Drawings Department of the Swiss National Library
- Stadt Schlieren
- Engadin St. Moritz Tourismus AG

Project Funding
- Swiss National Science Foundation SNSF, DORE

Sponsors
- Hotel Laudinella, St. Moritz
- Gemeinde Samedan

Related Project
- Long-term Photographic Observation of Schlieren 2005–2020, Zurich University of the Arts, 2005–2020
  P. 50

Website
- www.archiv-des-ortes.ch

Publication
- Ulrich Görlich and Meret Wandeler (eds.) (2012): *Auf Gemeindegebiet. Schlieren – Oberengadin. Fotografien zum räumlichen Wandel im Mittelland und in den Alpen seit 1945; On Common Ground. Schlieren—Upper Engadine. Photographs of Spatial Development in Suburban Regions and in the Alps Since 1945*. Volume 7 of the Institute for Contemporary Art Research series. Zurich: Scheidegger & Spiess. With contributions by René Hornung, Werner Huber, Christian Schmid, and Meret Wandeler.

Articles
- Ulrich Görlich and Meret Wandeler (2009): "Archiv des Ortes. Zur fotografischen Visualisierung von Raumentwicklung." In: Corina Caduff, Fiona Siegenthaler, and Tan Wälchli (eds.): *Kunst und künstlerische Forschung*. Zürcher Jahrbuch der Künste 2009. Volume 6. Zurich: Scheidegger & Spiess 2009, 224–240.
- Susanne Bieri, Nicole Graf, Thomas Meyer, and Meret Wandeler (2011): "Fotoarchive zur Dokumentation von Ort, Raum und Landschaft." In: *disP—The Planning Review*, vol. 184, 1/2011. 68–76.
- Susanne Bieri, Christophe Brandt, and Meret Wandeler (2011): "Archiv des Ortes." In: *Rundbrief Fotografie*, vol. 70, 2011. 14–24.

Conference
- *Archiv des Ortes – Sammelstrategien für ein fotografisches Archiv zur Raumentwicklung* conference, held by the Prints and Drawings Department of the Swiss National Library and the Institute for Contemporary Art Research of Zurich University of the Arts, 14 October 2010. With contributions by Susanne Bieri, Ulrich Görlich, Christian Schmid, Meret Wandeler, and Thomas Weski. Participants in podium discussion: Angelus Eisinger, Jann Jenatsch, Nora Mathis, Peter Pfrunder, and Martino Stierli.

Exhibitions
- *Archiv des Ortes, Installation auf Monitoren*. 10 December 2011–22 January 2012. Kunstmuseum Thun. *Labor* exhibitions series. Solo exhibition by Ulrich Görlich and Meret Wandeler.
- Ulrich Görlich and Meret Wandeler (2013): "Archiv des Ortes, Digitale Slide Show." In: *Terra Nostra*, 3–7 April 2013, Photoforum Pasquart, Biel.

Fig. 1 Picture research at Kulturarchiv Oberengadin. Samedan, 2010
Fig. 2 Picture research at Vereinigung für Heimatkunde. Schlieren, 2010

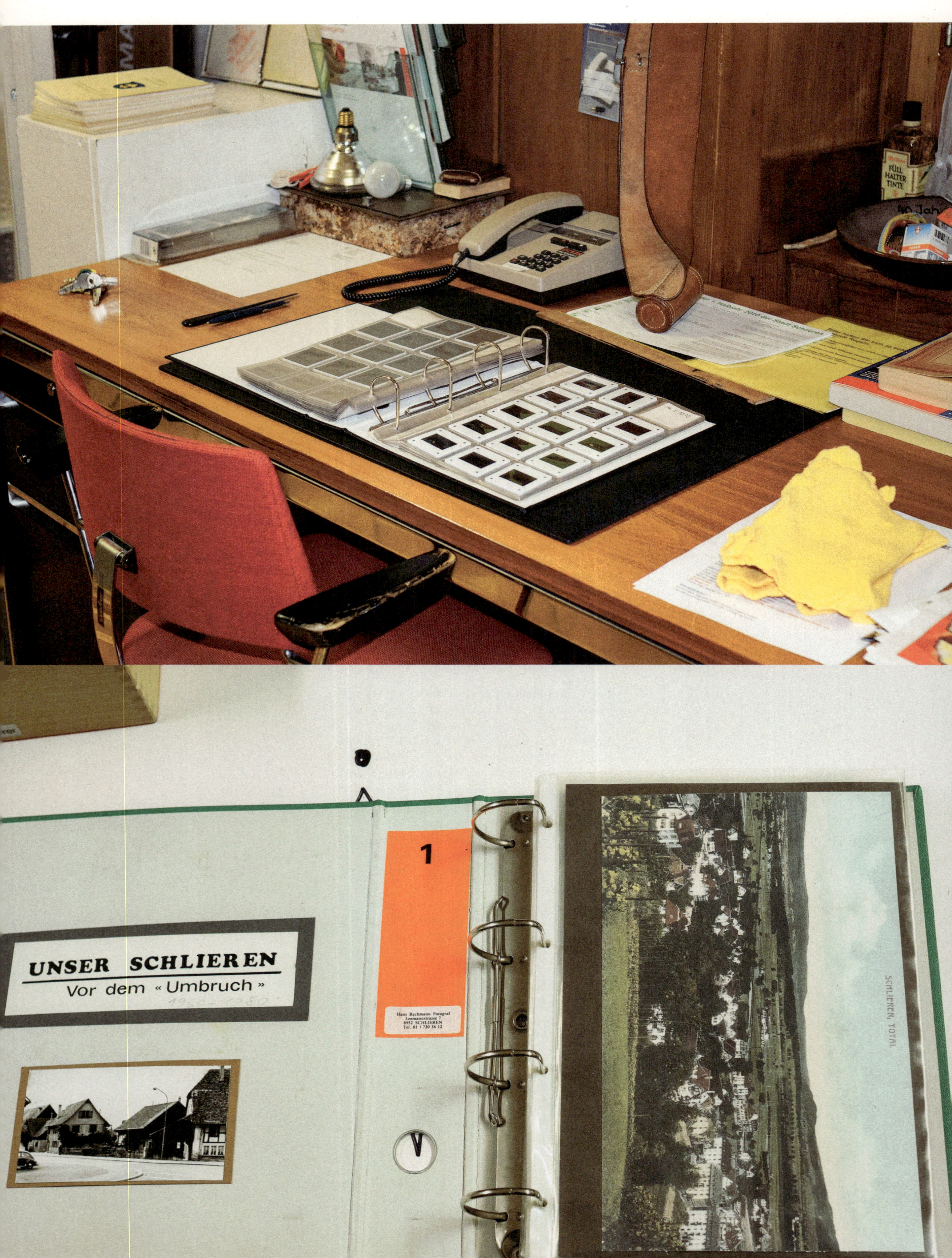

Fig. 3 Picture research at Vereinigung für Heimatkunde. Schlieren, 2010

Fig. 4 Picture research at Kulturarchiv Oberengadin. Samedan, 2010

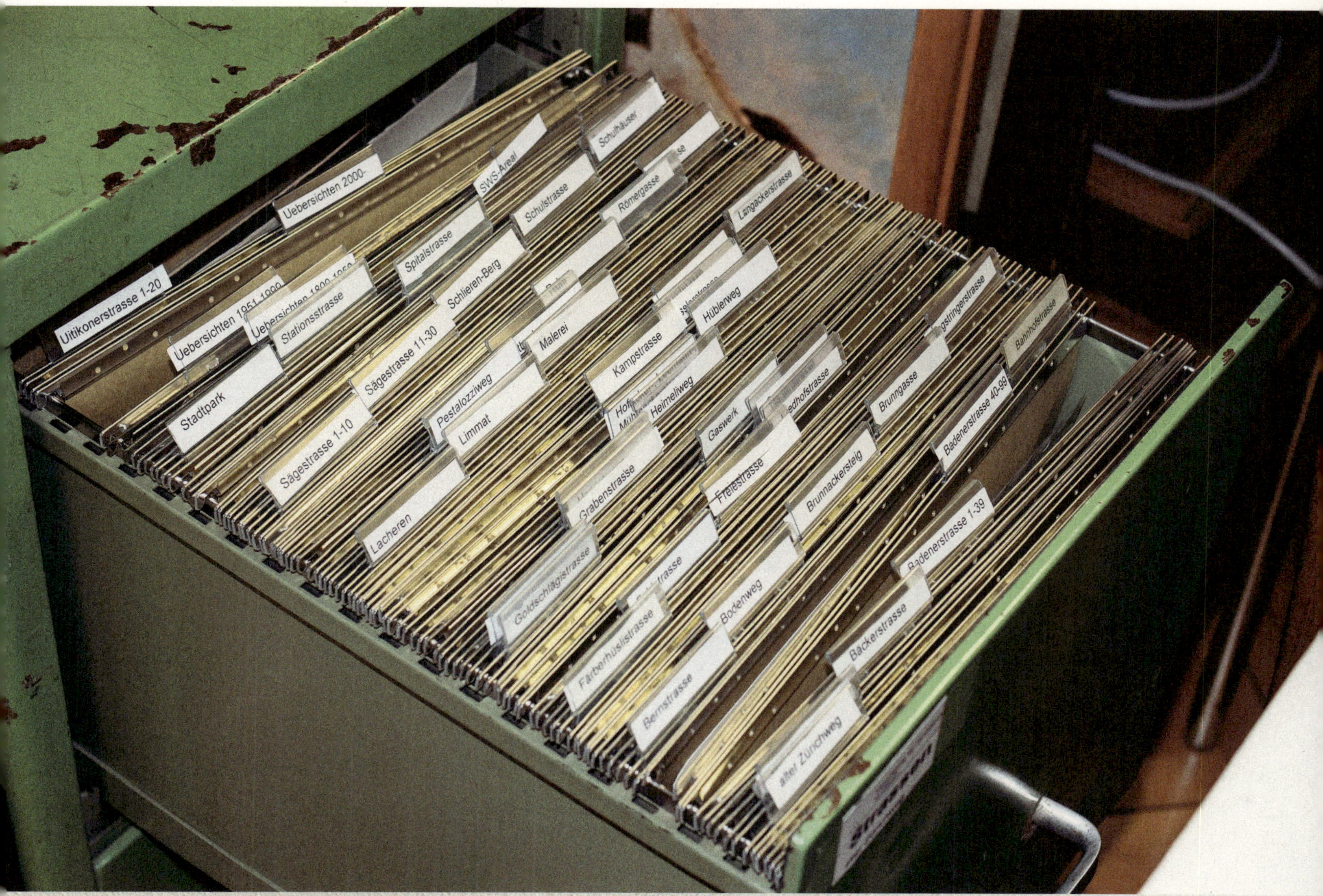

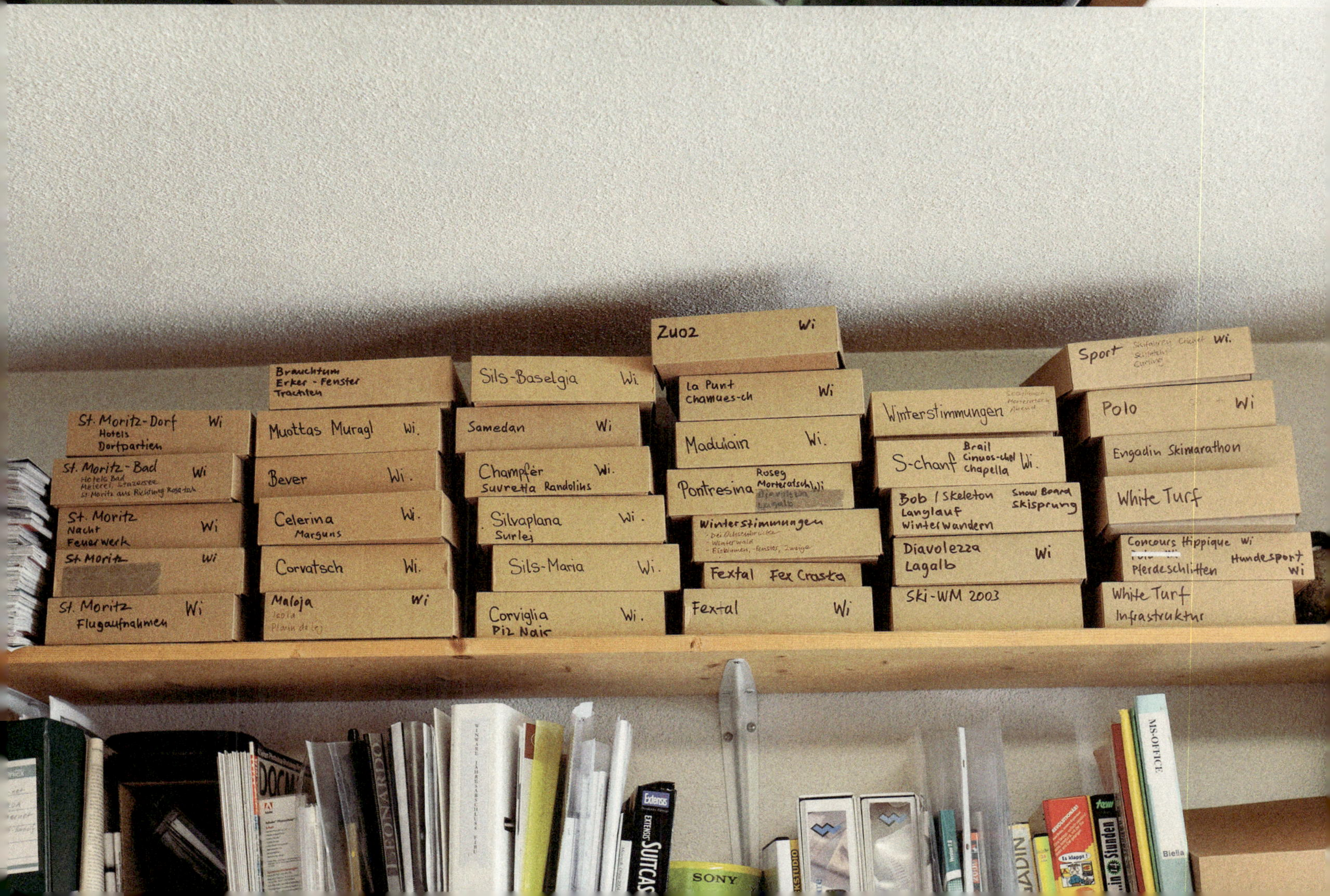

Fig. 5 Oberengadin, Silvaplana-Surlej, Surlej cable car village station — Corvatsch, undated

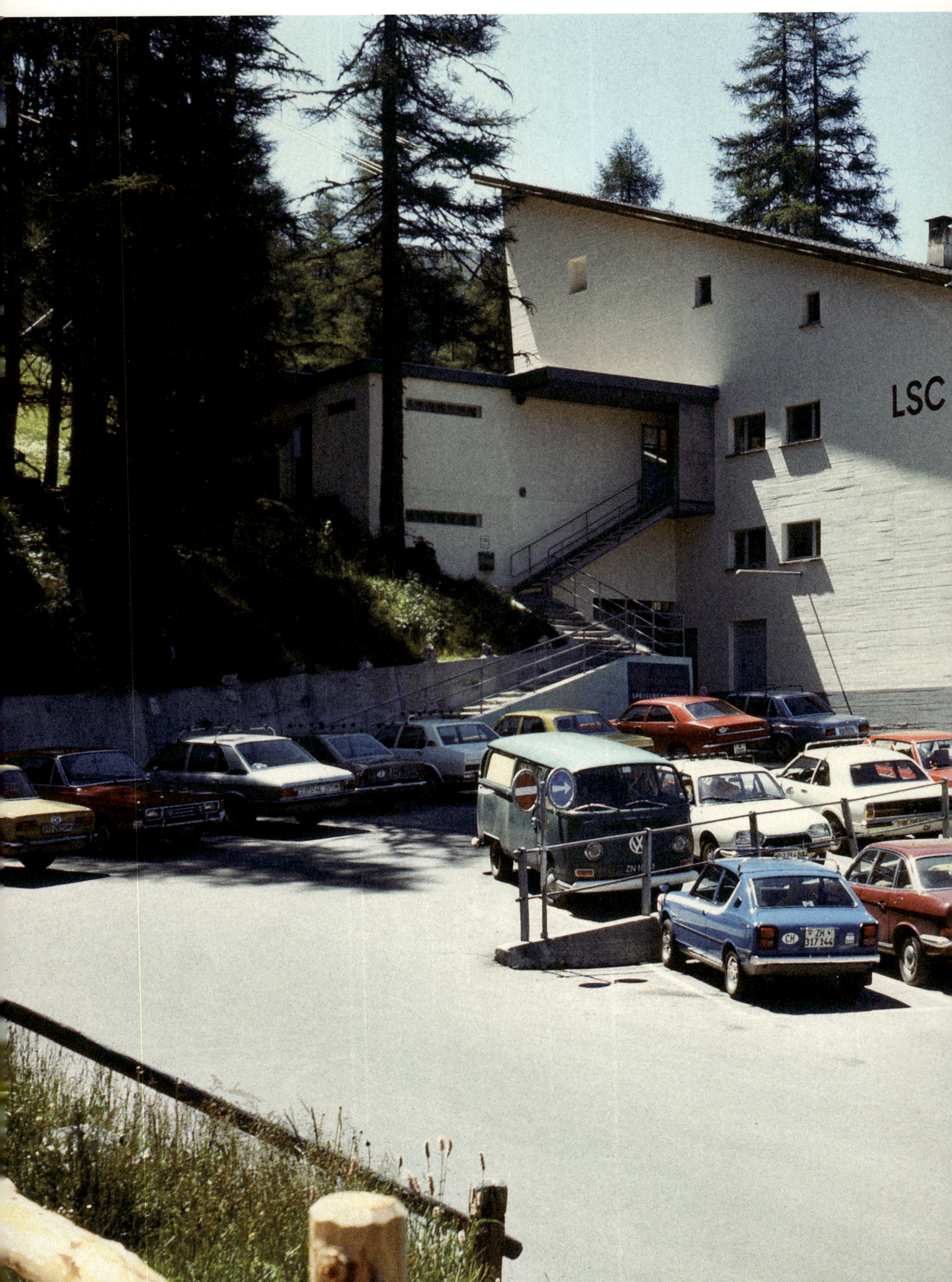

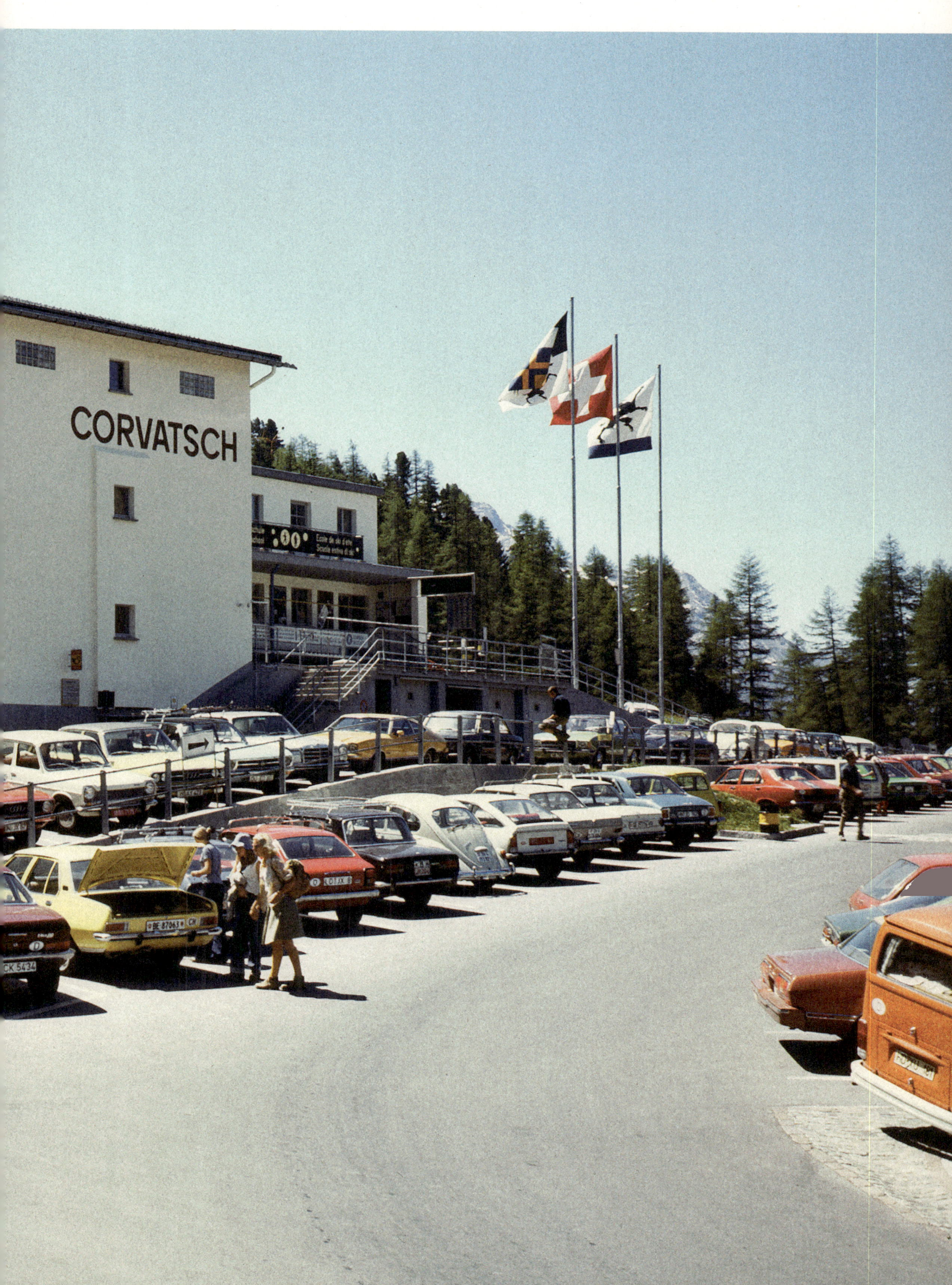
CORVATSCH

Fig. 6 Oberengadin, St. Moritz, Via Maistra, undated
Fig. 7 Schlieren, junction of Zürcherstrasse and Engstringerstrasse, Gasthaus Lilie, undated

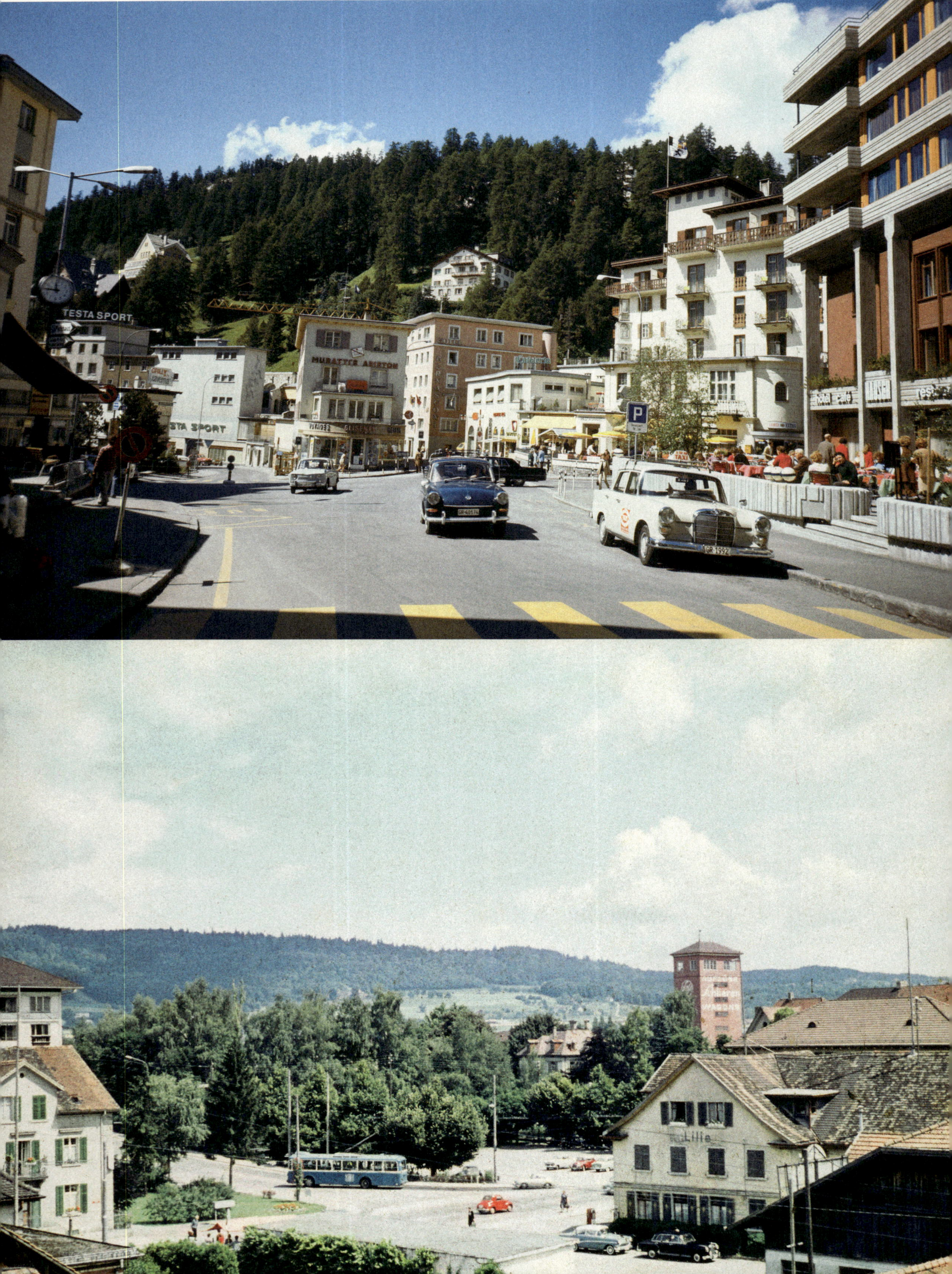

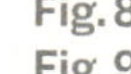

Fig. 8 Schlieren, Mercedes-Benz Automobil AG, Zürcherstrasse, 1969

Fig. 9 Oberengadin, Silvaplana, undated

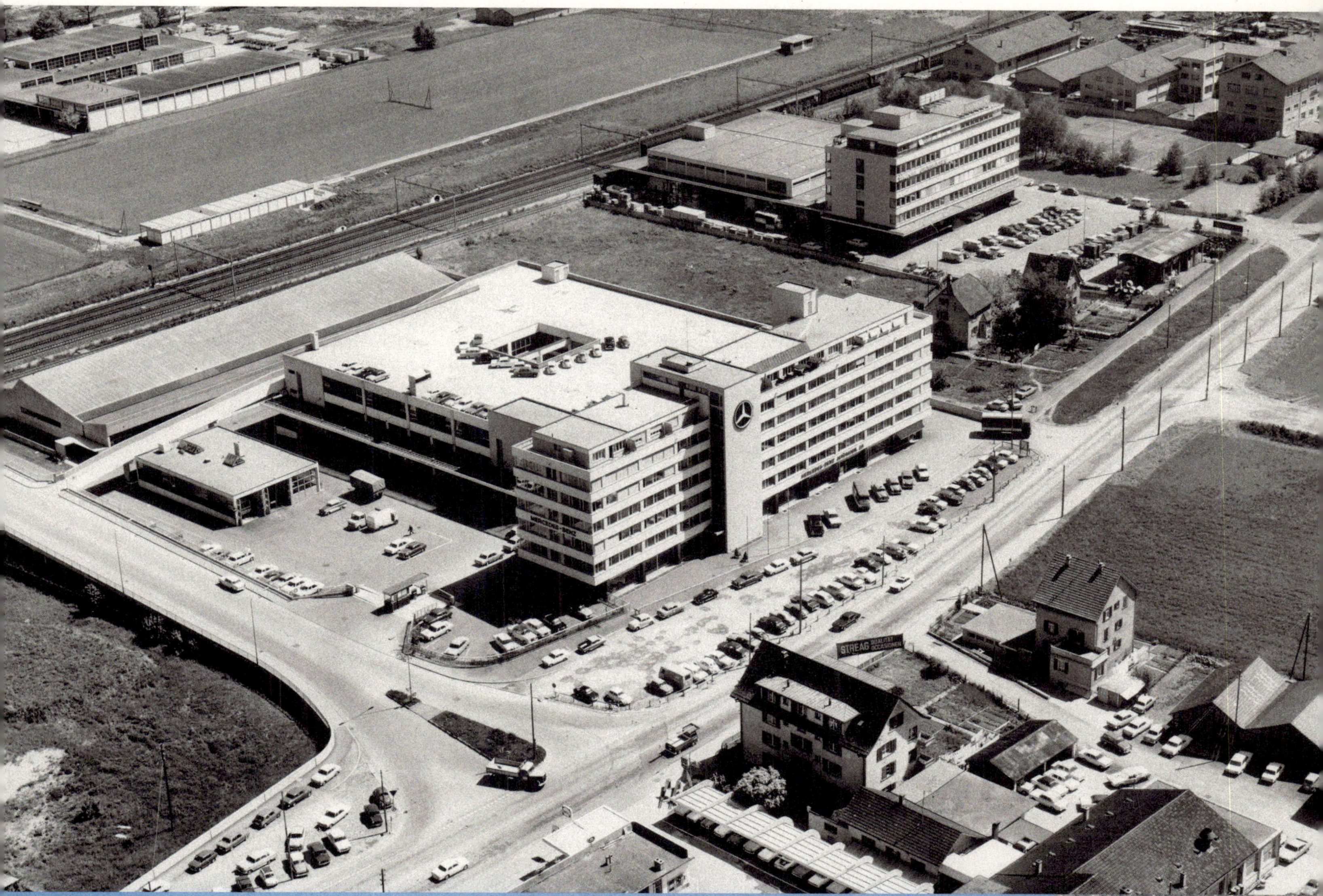

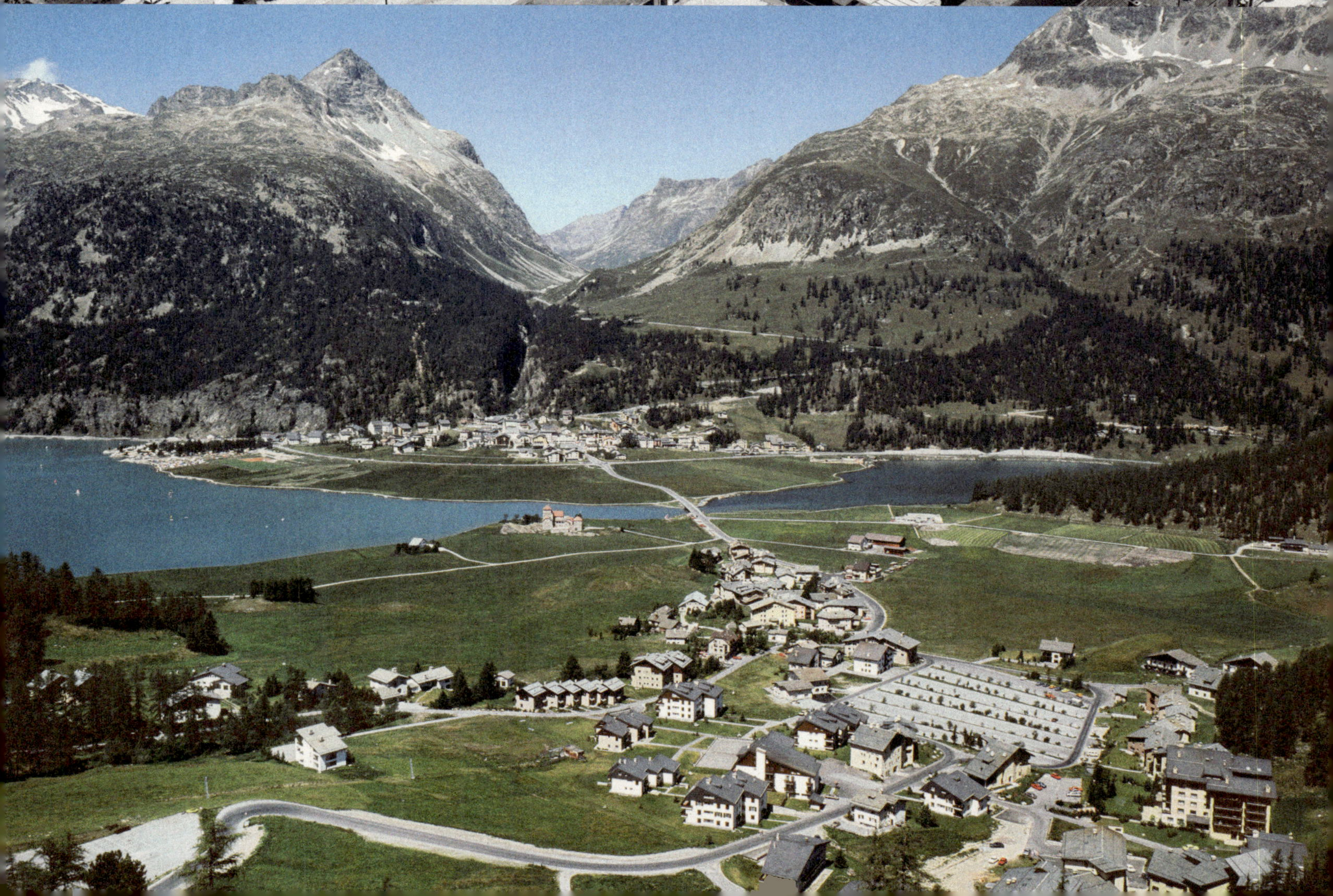

The surge in popularity of contemporary art in the second half of the twentieth century is closely linked with structural changes in the field of art. An important characteristic of this development is a phenomenon that has received so little academic attention that it has not even been assigned its own name: smaller, frequently self-organized organizations, within which the respective art is not only presented but also produced, made visible and significant, and conveyed. Even though such spaces have been around for decades, there are hardly any historically and empirically derived theorizations of this small art institutions. Instead, they generally continue to be assessed along the same criteria that are used for large institutions, and this has grave effects on cultural policy.

This research project was the first to examine the beginning of the "small-scale visual arts organizations," and the phase during which they became increasingly established, with a focus on London. Questions guiding the work included: What cultural and social policy diagnoses were the basis for founding these organizations? What new structures were put in place to meet the needs of the artistic tendency they promoted? How did the protagonists take action within these new structures, and what attitudes and values did they enforce? The analysis revealed that the structures for artistic production and art institutions are far more interwoven than has been portrayed in the conventional narratives, and that the thesis presented in Boris Groys's 2001 text *Ästhetik der Finanzierung* (The Aesthetics of Financing) describes the situation much more precisely and realistically. Thus, the study advocates that art scholarship conceive the emergence of artistic, curatorial and art criticism production as the result of interaction and negotiation. The traditional parameters of narrative, such as authorship, style, or work, should be decentralized and the factors of structure and production brought into balance with the creative process.

The phrase "small-scale visual arts organisations" used by the Arts Council England designates art spaces that are rather small and manageable in terms of both their premises and their personnel and organizational infrastructure. They rarely have paid, full-time positions at their disposal, are often concentrated on certain content (as regards artistic, cultural, or societal aspects), often work on a project-oriented basis (exhibitions are frequently only one part of a project), and are generally based on self-organization. Financing usually comes from several sources of different kinds; their self-conception often includes a dissociation from the programs and presentations of traditional art institutions. The scene in London presented itself as the object of investigation not only because of the unique density and diversity of institutions. The historical constellation within which the "arts centres," as they were initially called by the Arts Council, emerged also generated a cultural policy constellation that was exemplary in Europe. Exemplary for the fact that these art spaces soon became a central pillar of culture promotion in the developing social welfare state, but even more so during the political transformation initiated by Margaret Thatcher, which subjected these institutions to the same entrepreneurial dictates as all other policy areas.

The starting point for the project were inquiries in the field, which were overwhelming in multiple senses: Not only did the institutional landscape in London turn out to be quite extensive and diverse (more than hundred organizations of these types were found), but as a scholar faced with gigantic, largely unprocessed archives, I found it a challenge to choose a restricted but meaningful selection of institutions as examples for the development and specificity of "small-scale visual arts organisations." A further aspect of the project was its aspiration to create a new connection between empirical observation and theoretical superstructure; the project is thus located in the field of use-inspired basic research.

Rachel Mader

Project Title
Die Organisation der Innovation: Künstlerische Praxis und Kulturpolitik seit 1980

Project Period
1 November 2009–31 August 2014

Keywords
- Institutional studies
- Cultural policy
- Structures of contemporary art

Head of Project
- Rachel Mader, art researcher

Project Team
- Franz Krähenbühl, art researcher and curator

Project Funding
- Swiss National Science Foundation SNSF, Ambizione

Related Projects
- Off OffOff Of? Schweizer Kulturpolitik und Selbstorganisation in der Kunst seit 1980, Hochschule Luzern, 2014–2019

Publication

- Rachel Mader and Signe Meisner Christensen (eds.) (2020): *New Infrastructures, Performative Infrastructures in the Art Field*. Special issue of *Passepartout (Skrifter for Kunsthistorie)*, Aarhus: Narayana Press.
- Rachel Mader (2017): "Art for Society, Whitechapel Art Gallery, London, 1978." In: Elisabeth Fritz and Verena Krieger (eds.): *When Exhibition becomes Politics*, Cologne, Vienna: Böhlau, 95–110.

Articles

- Rachel Mader (2011): "Der Künstler als Unternehmer und die Folgen." In: Sabine Fastert, Alexis Joachimedes, and Verena Krieger (eds.): *Die Wiederkehr des Künstlers. Themen und Positionen der aktuellen Künstler/innenforschung*. Cologne, Vienna: Böhlau, 206–215.
- Rachel Mader (2011): "The Institute would be experimental in that… – Institutionelle Bedingungen experimenteller Kunstpraxis in historischer Perspektive." In: *Akten zum Kongress "Experimentelle Ästhetik" der Deutschen Gesellschaft für Ästhetik*. 4–7 October 2011, Kunstakademie Düsseldorf.
- Rachel Mader (2013/14): "How to move in/an institution." In: *(New) Institution(alism). On Curating*, no. 21, 33–43.
- Rachel Mader (2014): "Narrating Structures—On how to write analytically on walking experiences, digital self-representation and fragmentary archives in contemporary arts." In: Catalin Gheorge (ed.): *Critical Theories and Creative Practices of Research,* special issue of the *Vector—critical research in context* series, 103–110.
- Rachel Mader (2014): "Begegnen, interagieren, verhandeln – zur Neukonzeption von Öffentlichkeit in der partizipatorischen Kunstpraxis." In: *Perspektiven der Kunstsoziologie II. Kunst und Öffentlichkeit, Kunst und Gesellschaft* series, Springer VS, 95–111.
- Rachel Mader (2016): "Art follows institution – Kunst verhandeln." In: Lucie Kolb, Christoph Lang, Wolfgang Ullrich, and Judith Welter (eds.): *Art Handling. Partituren der Logistik*, Zurich: JRP Ringier, 41–49.
- Rachel Mader (2017): "Who sets the agenda? Changing Attitudes Towards the Relevance of Small-Scale Visual Arts Organisations in the UK." In: Charlotte Bonham-Carter, and Nicola Mann (eds.): *Rhetoric, Social Value and the Arts. But How Does It Work*, Basingstoke (Hampshire): Palgrave Macmillan (Pivot), 17–33.
- Gabriel Flückiger, Rachel Mader, and Peter Spillmann (2017): "Permanent Negotiation. Artistic Self-Organisation between Self-Determination, Cultural Policy, and Urban Development." In: Hilke Marit Berger and Gesa Ziemer (eds.): *Perspectives in Metropolitan Research. New Stakeholders of Urban Change: Q Question of Culture and Attitude?,* Berlin: Jovis, 148–158.

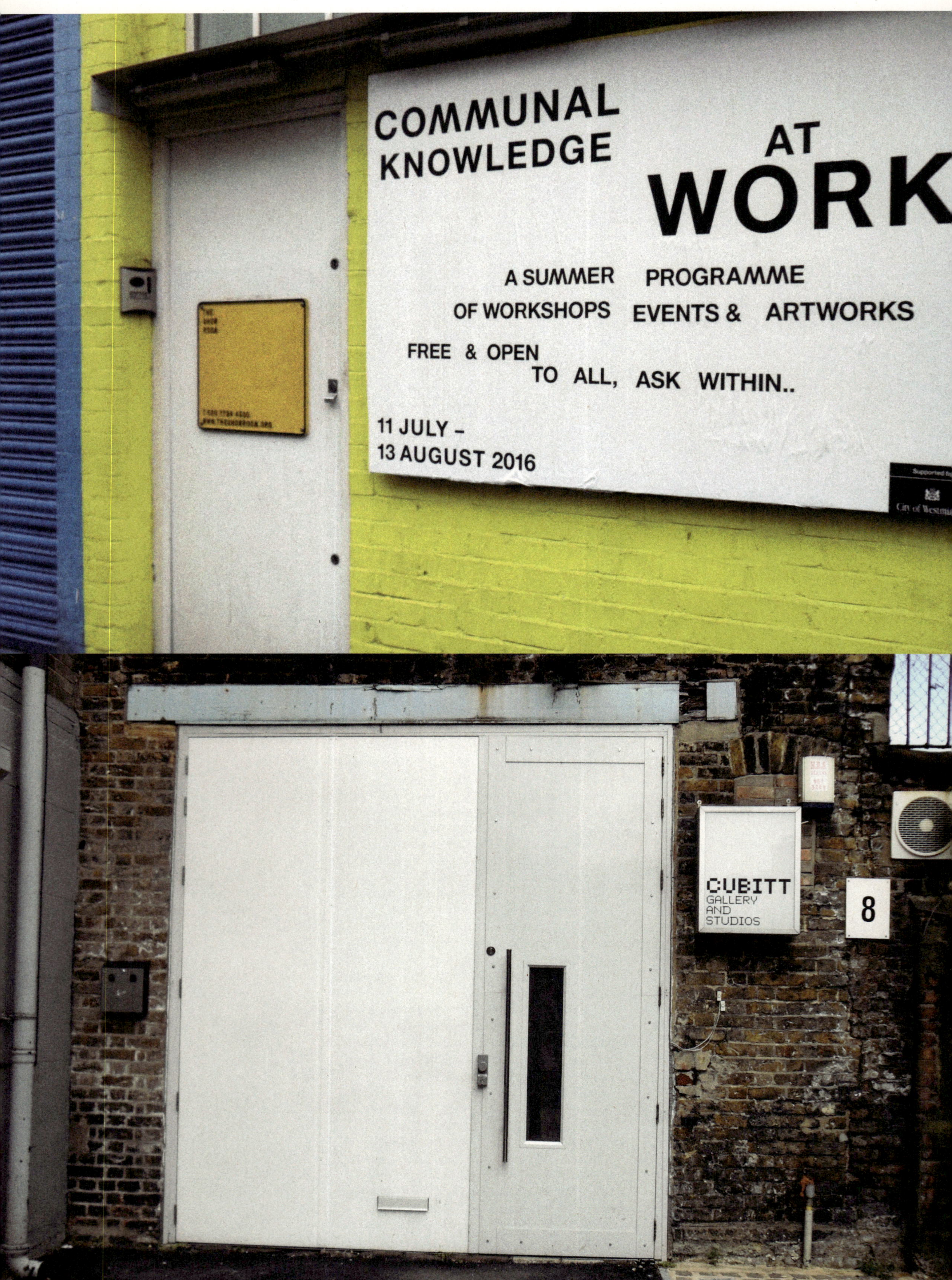
COMMUNAL
KNOWLEDGE
AT
WORK
A SUMMER PROGRAMME
OF WORKSHOPS EVENTS & ARTWORKS
FREE & OPEN
TO ALL, ASK WITHIN..
11 JULY –
13 AUGUST 2016
CUBITT
GALLERY
AND
STUDIOS
8

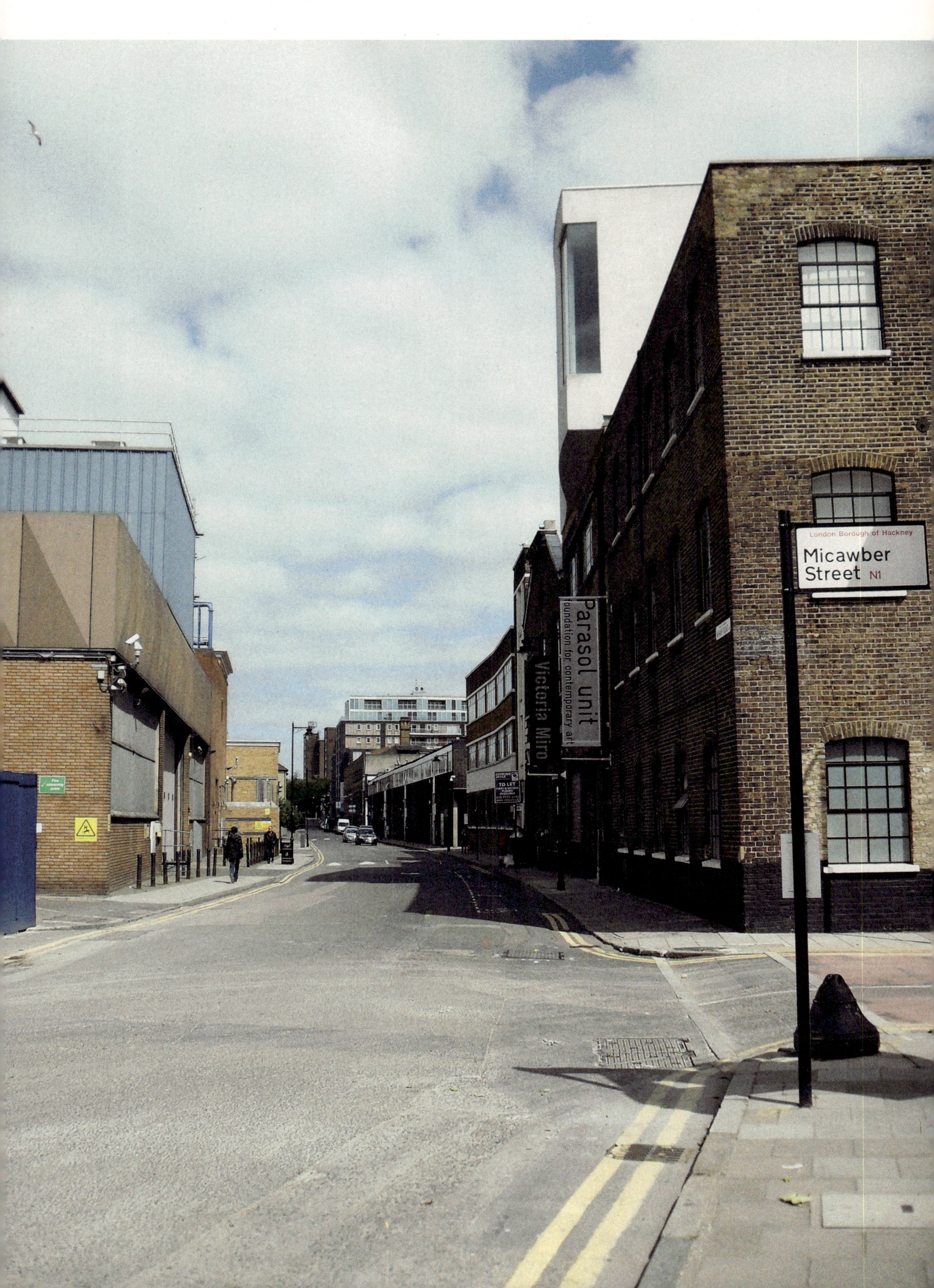

London Borough of Hackney
Micawber Street N1
Parasol unit
foundation for contemporary art
Victoria Miro
TO LET

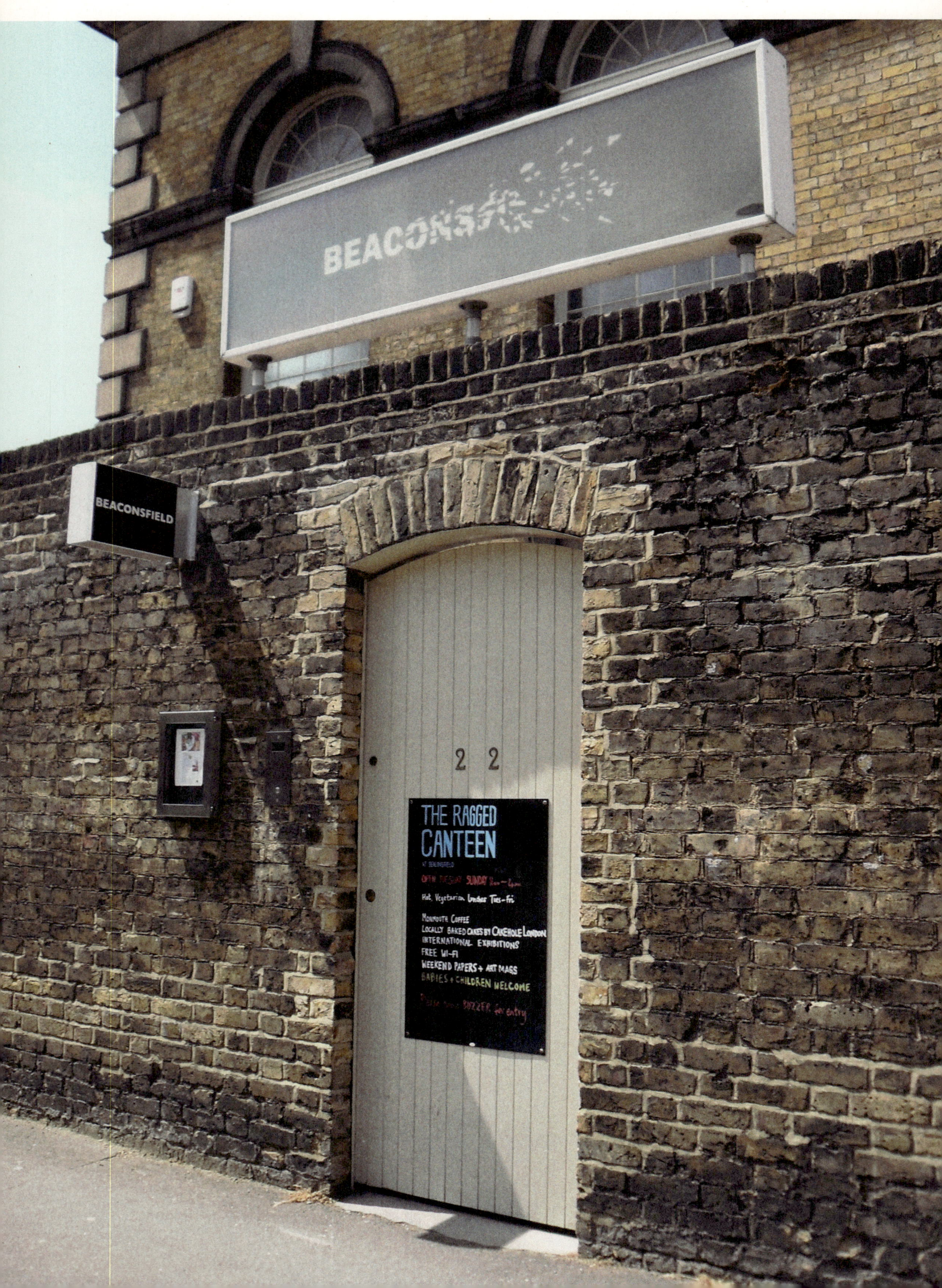
BEACONSFIELD
2 2
THE RAGGED
CANTEEN
Hot, Vegetarian Lunches Tues–Fri
MONMOUTH COFFEE
LOCALLY BAKED CAKES BY CAKEHOLE LONDON
INTERNATIONAL EXHIBITIONS
FREE WI-FI
WEEKEND PAPERS + ART MAGS
BABIES + CHILDREN WELCOME

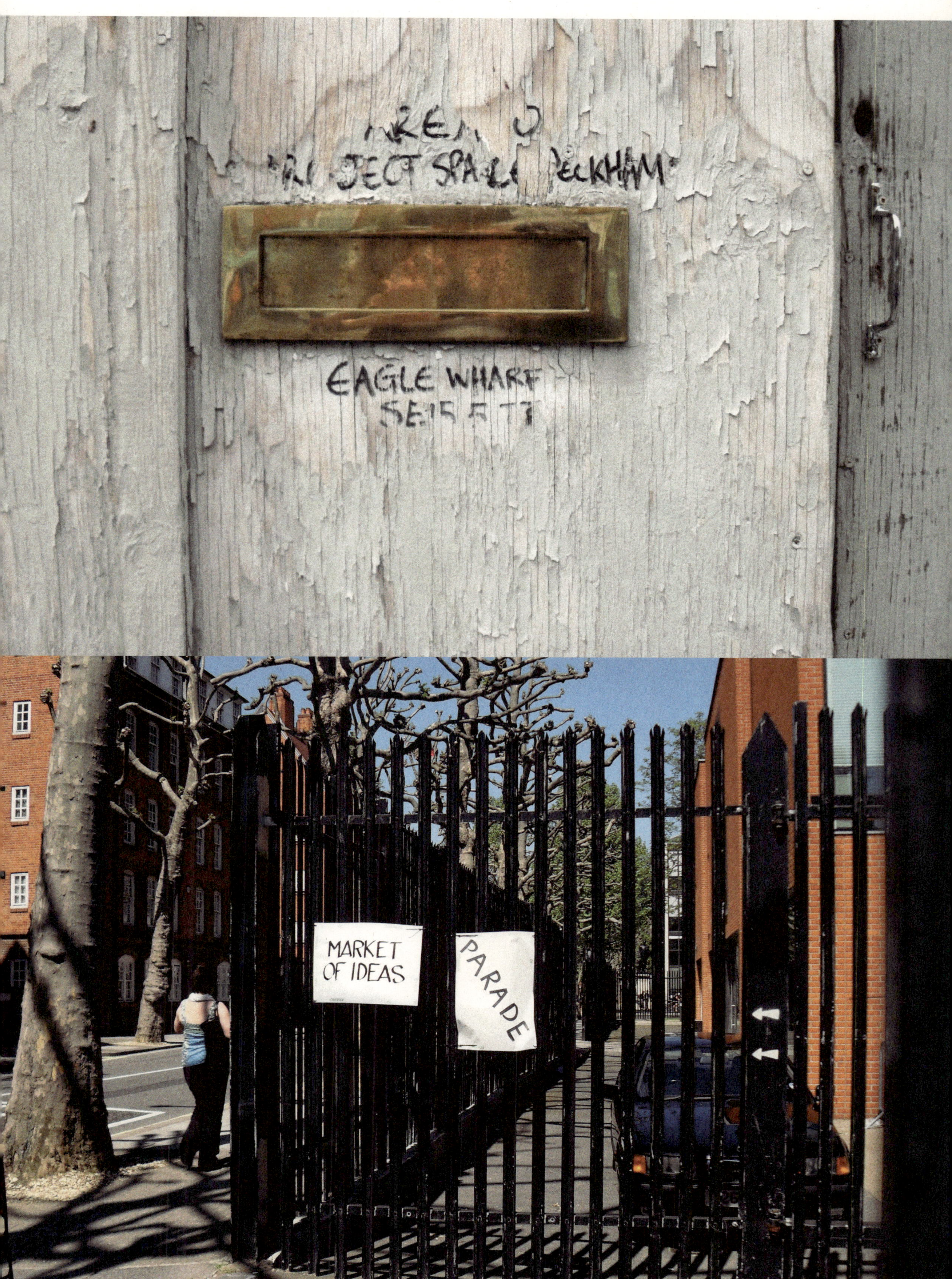
EAGLE WHARF
MARKET
OF IDEAS
PARADE

In a conversation with Nils Röller for the art journal *Kunstforum International* (2003:164) in 2003, historian of science Hansjörg Rheinberger compared scientific work with artistic work. The research project pursued this comparison asynchronously with a methodological shift in emphasis. Röller's monograph *Magnetismus — Eine Geschichte der Orientierung* (Munich: Fink, 2010) served as the premise. This discursive history demonstrated how scientific research on the "invisible" force of magnetism led to the development of instruments to assist in its perception, which, in turn, correlated with theses and visualizations (like those of the magnetic field). The project team worked with the Zentralbibliothek Zürich to specify a body of illustrations from the history of research on magnetism in the seventeenth and eighteenth centuries. The illustrations from that period document that diagrams, like those in the work of René Descartes, strengthen the paradigm of vortex theory, but also popularize it, as in the anonymously published tract *Magnetologia Curiosa*. The illustrations were digitized and posted chronologically in the WordPress blog *Journal für Kunst, Sex und Mathematik* from 1 August 2010 through 30 November 2011. The project was designed to have three artists approach the historical documents using their various practices for image production (hand drawings, video, and digital images), and publish their experiences in the form of posts to the blog. In so doing, the project brought historical scientific image productions into a relation with artistic processes today. The project design was framed by that WordPress blog, in which the participants had been exchanging texts and images since 2006 (with Judith Albert joining in 2008). Even before the conclusion of their work, the researchers were able to show a "track" made up of all 517 posts of the artistic works and annotated historical images, and to open them up for discussion in an exhibition at Kunstmuseum Thun.

While the representation of instruments in the history of natural science publications developed and refined iconographic constants, their artistic appropriation tended toward individual differentiations that resisted homogenization. In this process, intuition meant controlled perception, guided by the interest in adapting what was perceived using the artists' own creative means of expression, and thus aspiring to individual differentiation. The contributions by Judith Albert, for example, were guided by the aspect of integration, while those by Barbara Ellmerer explored pictorial possibilities, and Yves Netzhammer's concentrated on irreconcilabilities. Because the individual renderings were guided by the given means of representation, the instruments used in the artistic process played a decisive role in the product. They did not strictly determine the visualizations but became objects of investigation themselves through their interplay with the historical diagrams and the context of the blog. In relation to the posts, the artistic work produced a "surplus" of sketches. At the end of the project, it turned out that the 287 posts published by the artists were based on twice (Judith Albert and Barbara Ellmerer) or three times (Yves Netzhammer) as many sketches. This yielded the follow-up project *Ikonografie der Trostschrift* sponsored by the SNFS. This project combines the process of selecting and following up on pictorial ideas or discarding them with the method of the "image protocol."

Nils Röller

Project Title
Indirekte Erfahrungen

Project Period
1 August 2010–30 November 2011

Keywords
- Magnetism
- Display formats of physics
- *Magnetologia Curiosa*
- Iconography
- Diagrams

Head of Project
- Nils Röller, philosopher

Project Team
- Judith Albert, artist
- Barbara Ellmerer, artist
- Yves Netzhammer, artist

Research Partners
- Institut für Algebra/Algebraische Strukturtheorie, Fakultät Mathematik und Naturwissenschaften, TU Dresden
- Siegfried Zielinski, Institute of Time-Based Media, University of the Arts Berlin
- Christoph Schenker, Institute for Contemporary Art Research, Zurich University of the Arts

Project Partners
- Zentralbibliothek Zürich
- Kunsthaus Thun

Project Funding
- Swiss National Science Foundation SNSF, DORE

Related Projects
- Iconography of the Consolation, Zurich University of the Arts, 2018–2019
P. 226

Website
- www.journalfuerkunstsexundmathematik.ch

Monograph
- Nils Röller, Barbara Ellmerer, and Yves Netzhammer (2014): *Über Kräfte*. Berlin: Merve.

Articles
- Nils Röller (2010): "Der Kompass als Mittel raumzeitlicher Orientierung." In: Marcus Maeder (ed.): *Milieux sonores*. Bielefeld: transcript, 137–156.
- Nils Röller (2010): "Thinking with Instruments. The Example of Kant's Compass." In: Steven R. Palmquist (ed.): *Cultivating Personhood: Kant and Asian Philosophy*. Berlin: Walter de Gruyter, 300–307.

Lecture Series
- Lecture series in the framework of the exhibition *Magnetische Erfahrungen – Kunst begegnet Naturwissenschaft*. 13 January–16 June 2010. Zentralbibliothek Zürich. With contributions by Susanna Bliggenstorfer, Nils Röller, Peter Bexte, Siegfried Zielinski, and Olaf Räderer.

Conference
- *Zwischenstadien*. 9 December 2014, Zurich University of the Arts. With Armen Avanessian, Barbara Pfeiffer, Nils Röller, Konrad Tobler, and posts by Judith Albert, Oliver van den Berg, Darya von Berner, Johannes Binotto, !Mediengruppe Bitnik, Reto Boller, Olaf Breuning, Sarah Burger, Sampurna Chattarji, Jann Clavadetscher-R. Rashidi, Pascal Danz, Barbara Ellmerer, Klodin Erb, Felix Philipp Ingold, Daniela Keiser, Christoph Keller, Ferro Knopp, Thomas Krempke, Lang/Baumann, Katja Loher, Jso Maeder, Vera Marke, Yves Netzhammer, Florian Neuner, Caro Niederer, Elodie Pong, Zuzana Ponicanova, Thomas Ravens, Peter Rawert, Samoa Rémy, Roland Roos, Mario Sala, Marina Sawall and Stefan Wilke, Bernd Schurer, Markus Schwander, Loredana Sperini, Julia Steiner, Marcus Steinweg, Leif Trenkler, Christian Vetter, Jan St. Werner, Ingrid Wiener, Lydia Wilhelm, Rolf Winnewisser, Maria Magdalena Z'Graggen, Siegfried Zielinski, and Tim Zulauf.

Presentations
- Nils Röller: "Tote Rennen. Kunst und Wissenschaft." In: *Oswald Wiener. Innenschau*. 25 September 2009, Kunsthaus Mürz, Mürzzuschlag.
- Nils Röller: "Empfindungskörper." In: *International Flusser Lectures Day*. 30 June 2010, University of the Arts, Berlin.
- Nils Röller: "Indirect Experiences." In: *Modes of Collaboration between the Arts and Sciences*. 29 April 2011, Zurich University of the Arts.

Exhibitions
- *Magnetische Erfahrungen – Kunst begegnet Naturwissenschaft*. 13 January–16 June 2010. Zentralbibliothek Zürich. With exhibits from the collection of the Zentralbibliothek Zürich and by Judith Albert, Ian Anüll, Barbara Ellmerer, and Yves Netzhammer.
- *labor 2: Indirekte Erfahrungen. Ein Projekt aus dem Journal für Kunst, Sex und Mathematik*. 21 April–22 May 2011. Kunstmuseum Thun.

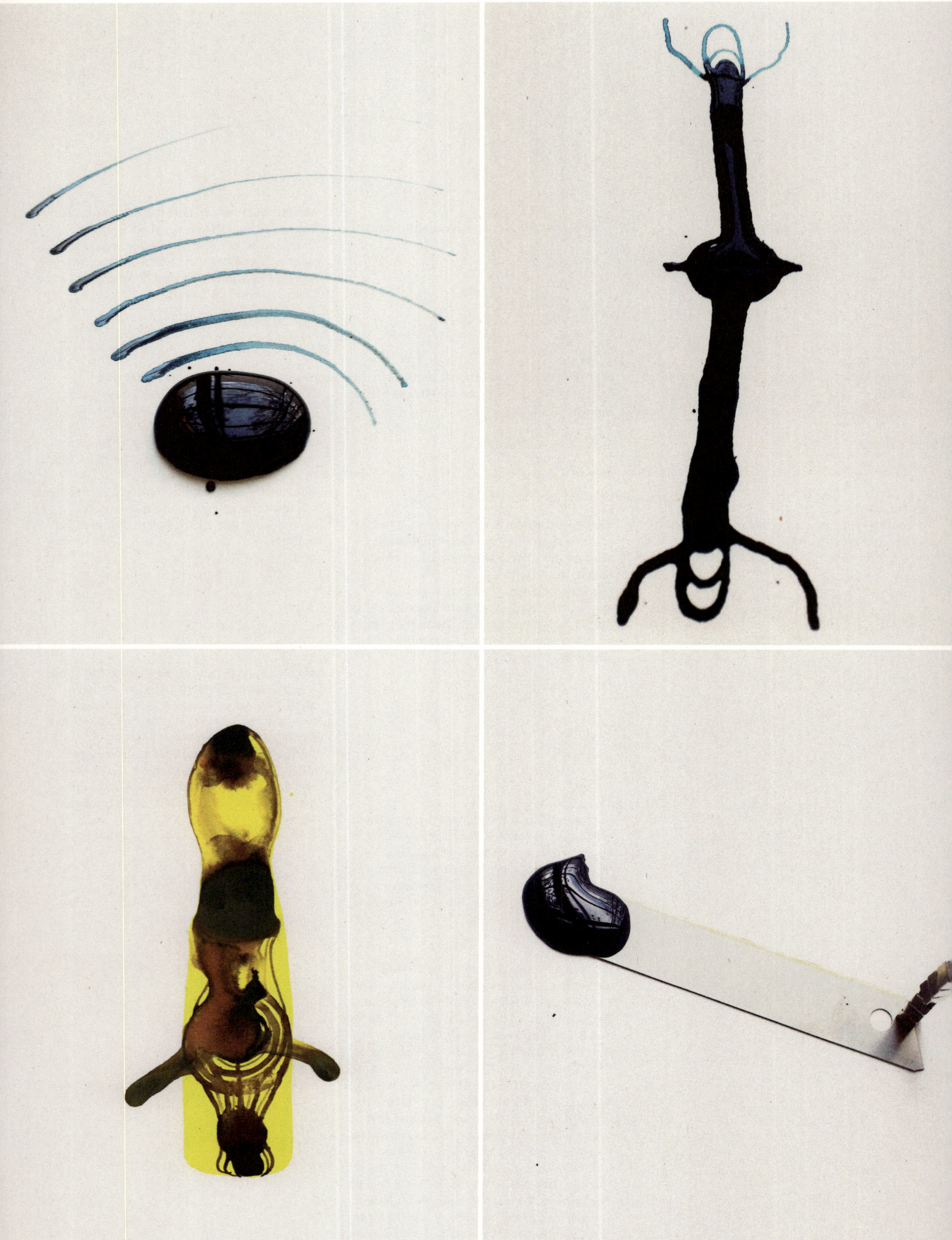

Fig. 5 Judith Albert: Blog entry, November 2011

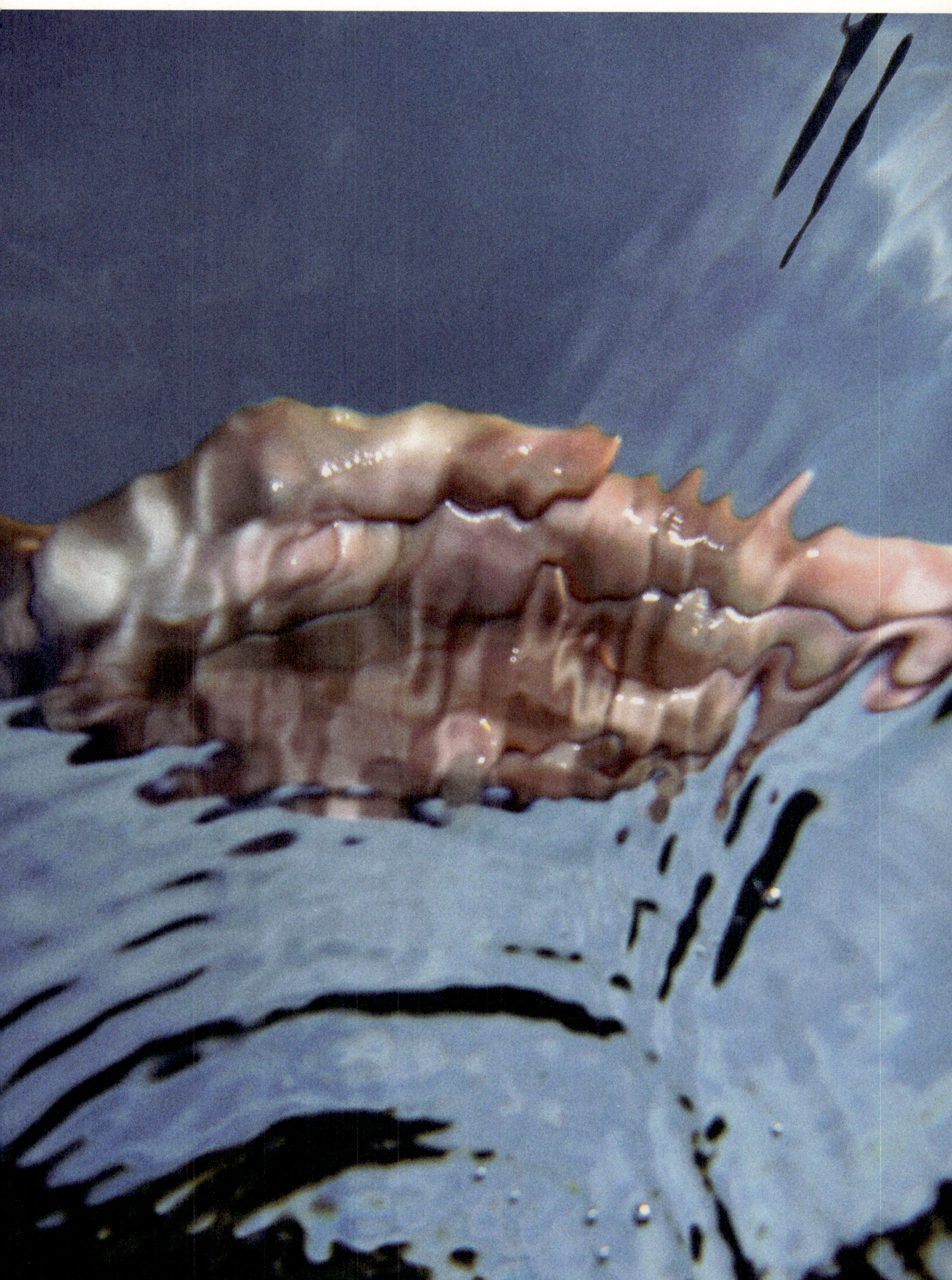

Fig. 6 Media library with image files by Judith Albert, Barbara Ellmerer, Yves Netzhammer and historical illustrations. journalfuerkunstsexundmathematik.ch, November 2011

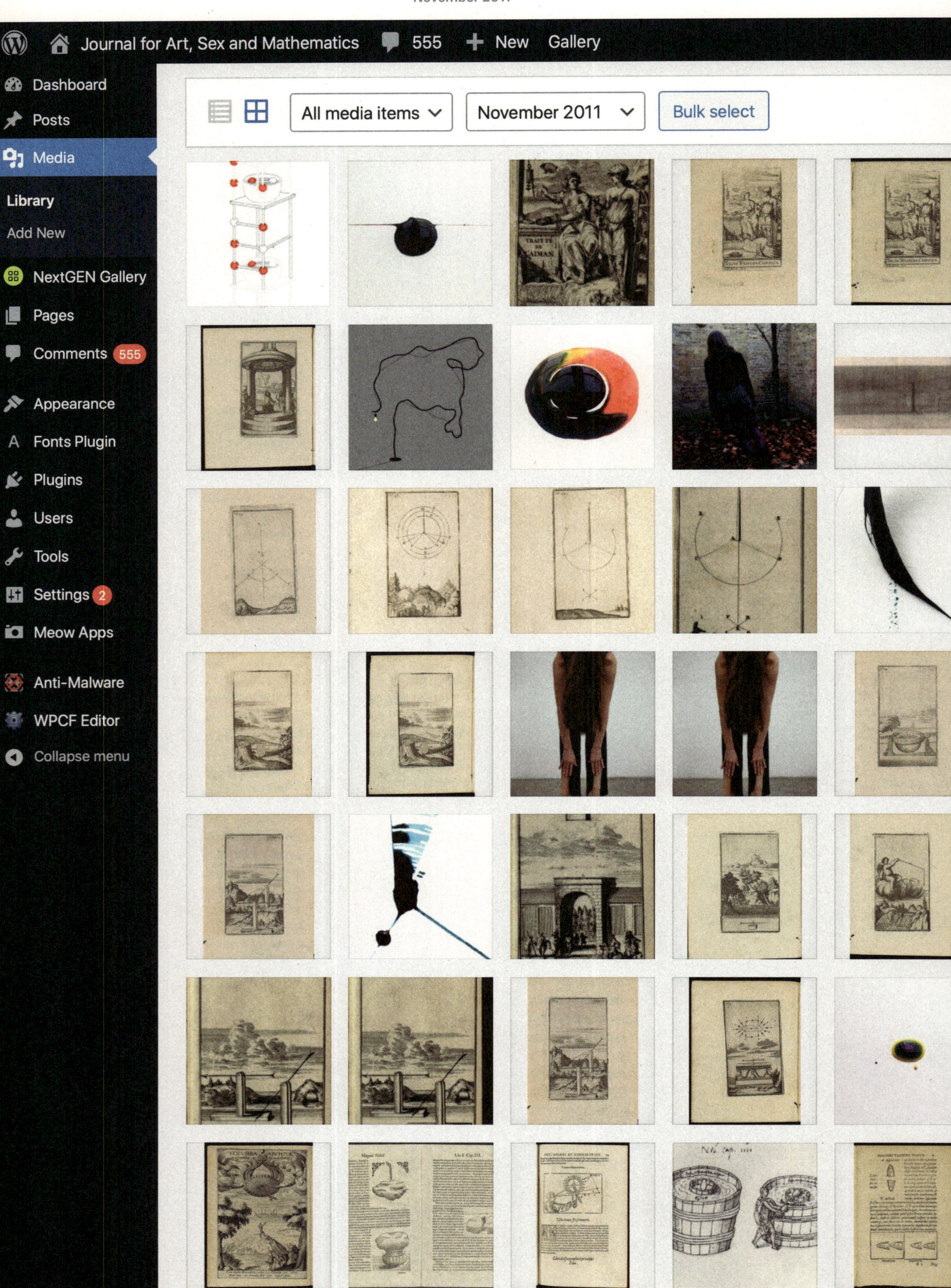

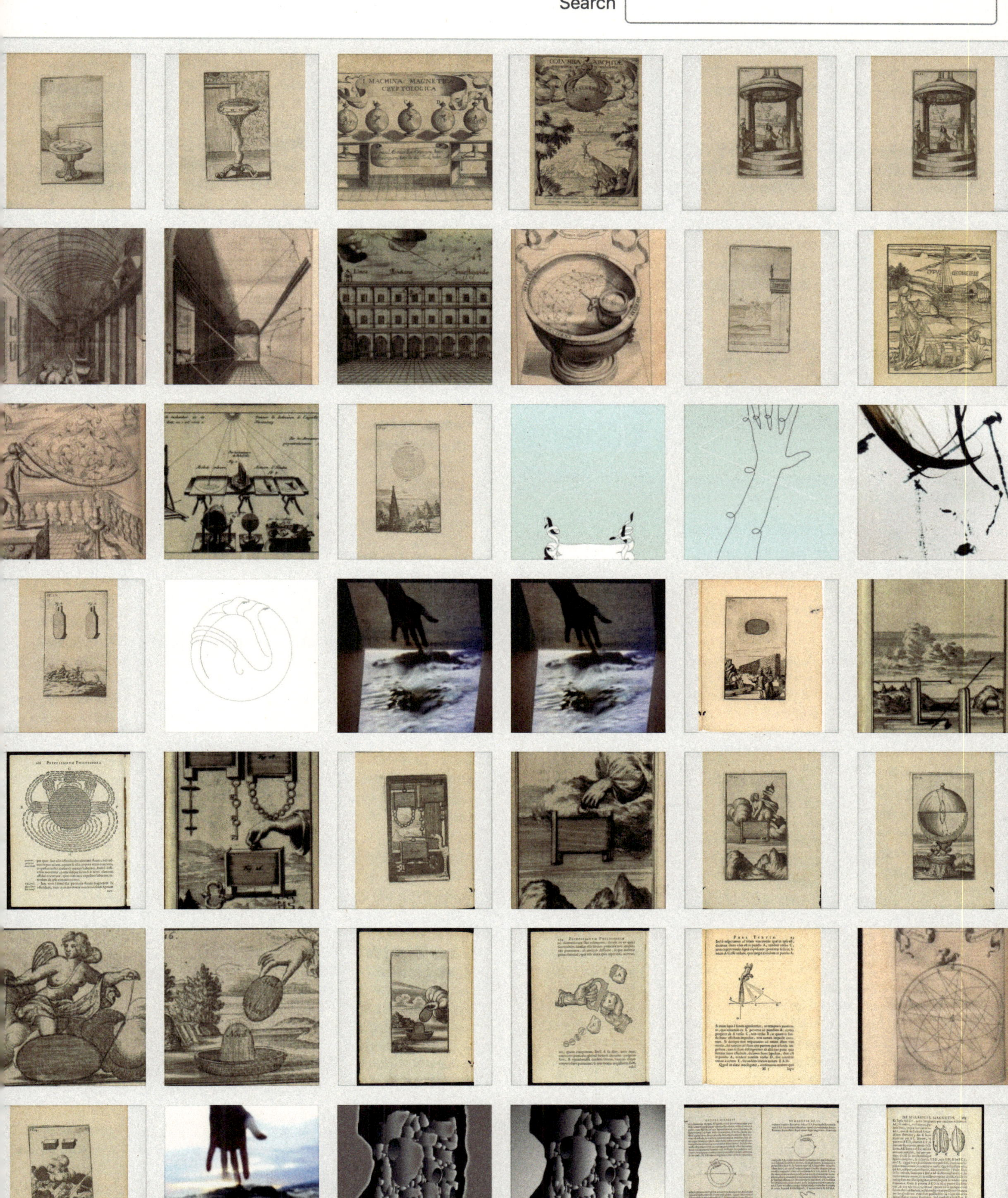
Howdy, IFCAR
Search
MACHINA MAGNETICA CRYPTOLOGICA

The extensive, little investigated estate of Serge Stauffer (1929–1989), Swiss art theorist, cofounder of the F+F School of Experimental Design and expert on (or perhaps better, artist colleague of) Marcel Duchamp, served as the foundation for the 2013 exhibition *Serge Stauffer. Kunst als Forschung* at Helmhaus Zürich curated by Michael Hiltbrunner, and the accompanying volume of the same name with writings by Serge Stauffer. The exhibition brought works by Marcel Duchamp, Doris Stauffer, André Thomkins, Klaudia Schifferle, Oliviero Toscani, and other persons from Serge Stauffer's sphere together with his own works. The diverse exhibits visualized the playfulness and the experimental and societal awakening in Stauffer's work that had influenced an entire generation in Zurich.

The review and cataloging of the estate, which yielded an organized archive that was presented to the Swiss National Library's Prints and Drawings Department in Bern in 2013, also served as the starting point for the SNSF research project, which had the goal of working through this bundle and indexing Stauffer's work.

Questions about how to classify Serge Stauffer's place in art history as a pioneer of artistic research accompanied the study, which also focused on his artistic oeuvre. The investigation dispelled any doubts about considering Stauffer to be a researching artist in the contemporary understanding of the term. Yet his position in art history is better compared with that of the Art & Language collective than with Joseph Beuys. This first reappraisal of the important historical sources on artistic experimentation and experimental art education in Switzerland from 1950 to 1970 showed that Stauffer wanted to develop a permanent laboratory for researching art in an academic environment. There were no precedents for this pathbreaking idea.

The emphases of Stauffer's work are found in drawings, collages, and photographs, most of which were found stashed away in unsorted portfolios. According to contemporary witnesses, Stauffer gave away many works like these. His disposing this way over such artifacts, which conventionally would be interpreted as his actual artistic output, suggests that what Stauffer considered important was not necessarily artistic works in their own right; he also believed that studies, teaching, and performances were an immanent part of his work and artistic activity. As such, he once again characterized and affirmed the self-conception of the researching artist. The *Öffentliche Bibliothek Serge Stauffer* project, the studies on Marcel Duchamp and André Thomkins, the work materials like school papers, notes, and invitations which Stauffer called "material," and the documents on F+F are neatly filed and were therefore also indexed here as part of his "oeuvre."

It became apparent that a reappraisal of the history of F+F as a class (1965–1970) and as a school (from 1971) with these materials would be very productive. The central role of the school both in Stauffer's work and in his research has since been confirmed and led to the follow-up project *F+F 1971*.

Michael Hiltbrunner

Project Title
Serge Stauffer. Kunst als Forschung

Project Period
1 October 2011–28 February 2014

Keywords
- Radical education
- Marcel Duchamp
- F+F Schule
- Male emancipation
- Photography

Head of Project
- Michael Hiltbrunner, cultural anthropologist

Research Team
- Gina De Micheli, art historian
- Philipp Messner, archivist and cultural researcher
- Romy Rüegger, artist

Project Partners
- F+F Schule für Kunst und Design, Zurich
- Helmhaus Zürich
- The Swiss National Library's Prints and Drawings Department

Project Funding
- Swiss National Science Foundation SNSF

Outputs

A

Related Projects

- Archives on Research-based Art, Zurich University of the Arts, 2013–2020
  P. 152
- F+F 1971, Zurich University of the Arts, 2020–2022
  P. 252

Publication

- Helmhaus Zürich (ed.) (2013): *Serge Stauffer. Kunst als Forschung. Essays, Gespräche, Übersetzungen, Studien*. Exhibition catalog. Volume 8 of the Institute for Contemporary Art Research series. Zurich: Scheidegger & Spiess.
  - A Open access: https://doi.org/10.5281/zenodo.6472260

Articles

- Gina De Micheli, Michael Hiltbrunner, and Andrea Portmann (2014): "Experimentelle Kunst im Archiv. Das Archiv von Serge und Doris Stauffer wurde erschlossen." In: Zurich University of the Arts (ed.): *Zett*, no. 1, 41–43.
- Michael Hiltbrunner (2015): "Serge Stauffer. Biographical and Emancipatory Matters." In: Simone Koller and Mara Züst (eds.): *Doris Stauffer. A Monograph*. Zurich: Scheidegger & Spiess, 43–46.
- Michael Hiltbrunner (2018): "Fragen, Methoden, Prozesse, Archive. Forschende Kunst bei Serge Stauffer und an der frühen F+F Schule." In: Ute Holfelder, Klaus Schönberger, Thomas Hengartner, and Christoph Schenker (eds.): *Kunst und Ethnografie – zwischen Kooperation und Ko-Produktion?* Zurich: Chronos, 113–126.
- Michael Hiltbrunner (2020): "Serge Stauffer and the Film de recherche. Traces of a friendship." In: François Bovier, Adeena Mey, Fred Truniger, Anton Rey, and Thomas Schärer (eds.): *Minor Cinema. Experimental Film in Switzerland*. Genève: JRP Editions, 300–317.
- Michael Hiltbrunner (2022): "Serge Stauffer – Dada und Anti-Dada in Zürich um 1960." In: Agathe Mareuge and Sandro Zanetti (eds.): *Le Retour de DADA. Die Wiederkehr von DADA. The Return of DADA*. Volume 2. Dijon: Les Presses du Réel, 103–118.

Lectures

- Michael Hiltbrunner: "Experts on Serge Stauffer and F+F School researchers, experimentelles Gespräch." In: *SARN. Unconference*. 15–16 January 2014. HEAD Geneva University of Art and Design, Geneva.
- Michael Hiltbrunner: "Serge Stauffer–Art as Research. A Utopic Theory from 1976/77." In: *Inventing Futures. Artistic Research with/in Educational Institutions*. 13–14 June 2013. ArtEZ, Arnhem.

Workshop

- *Fragen, Methoden, Prozesse, Archive. Forschende Kunst bei Serge Stauffer und an der F+F*. 25 May 2013. By Michael Hiltbrunner, Department of Social Anthropology and Cultural Studies, University of Zurich.

Exhibition

- *serge stauffer – kunst als forschung*. 15 February–14 April 2013. Helmhaus Zürich. With works by Ruedi Bechtler, Peter Blegvad, Peter Blumer, Chintan Bolliger, Anton Bruhin, Ellen Classen, Liliane Csuka, Rudolf de Crignis, Marcel Duchamp, Bendicht Fivian, Max Frei (ALMA), Karl Gerstner, ppa. Good/Könz/Weidmann, Emanuel Halpern, Felix Kälin, Christina Kubisch, Lawrence Lee, Rut Maggi, Hansjörg Mattmüller, Fredi M. Murer, Jürg Nutz, Nam June Paik, Chrig Perren, Walter Pfeiffer, Urs Plangg, Georg Radanowicz, Markus Raetz, Dieter Roth, Klaudia Schifferle, Peter Schweri, Roman Signer, Michael Simpson, Doris Stauffer, Salome Stauffer, Serge Stauffer, Veit Stauffer, M. Vänçi Stirnemann, Peter Storrer, Reinhard Storz, Ida Szigethy, André Thomkins, Clara Tice, Oliviero Toscani, Peter Trachsel, Wessely/Wildi, and others. Curated by Michael Hiltbrunner.

Archive Indexing

- *Archive Serge Stauffer*. The Swiss National Library's Prints and Drawings Department, Bern. Collection received in 2013.

Fig. 1 *Kunstlabor für Fortgeschrittene*, summer course with Serge Stauffer. F+F Schule, Zurich, 1979

Fig. 2 Serge Stauffer: *Jardin public*. Four dice, game object, model, ca. 1960

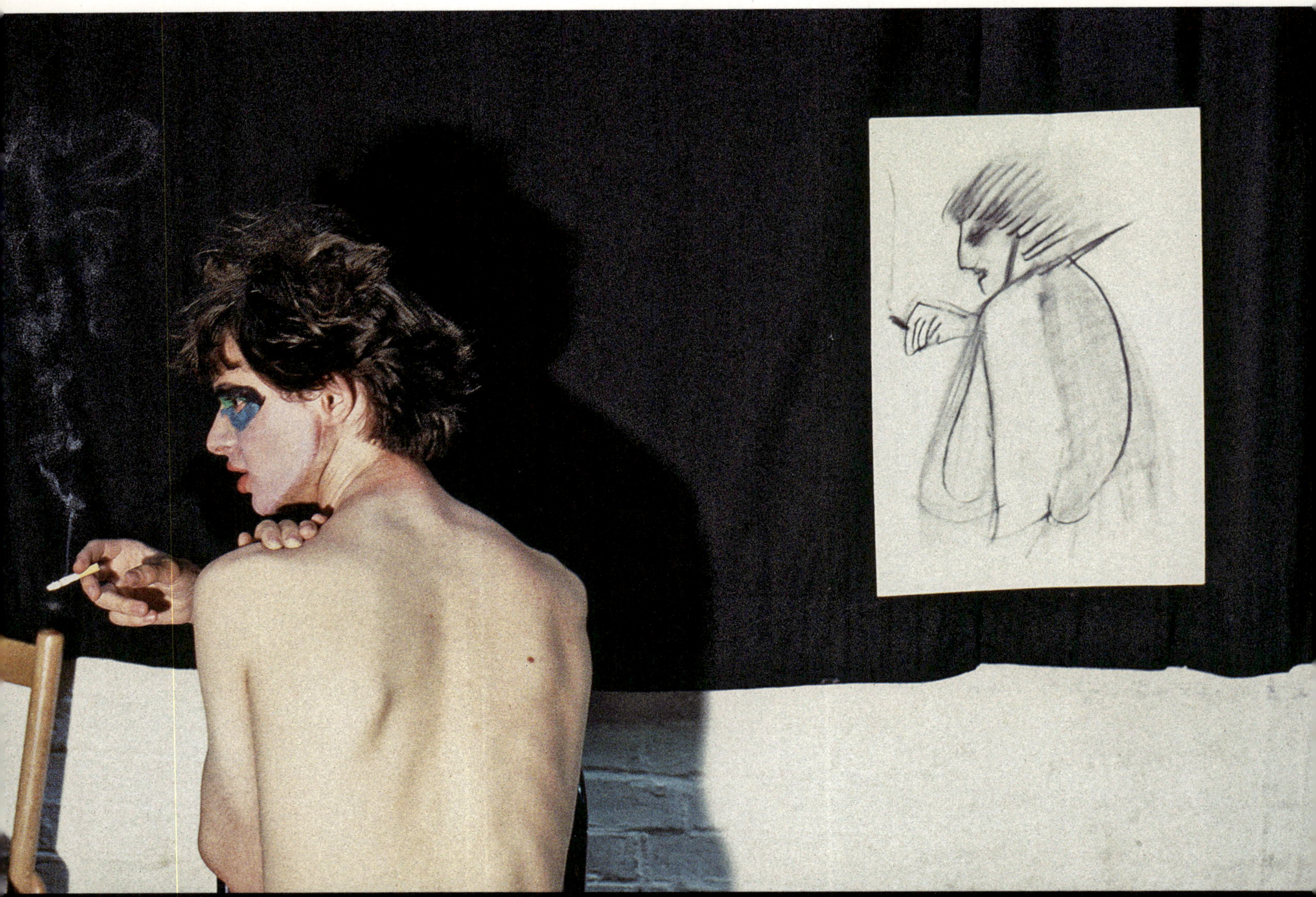

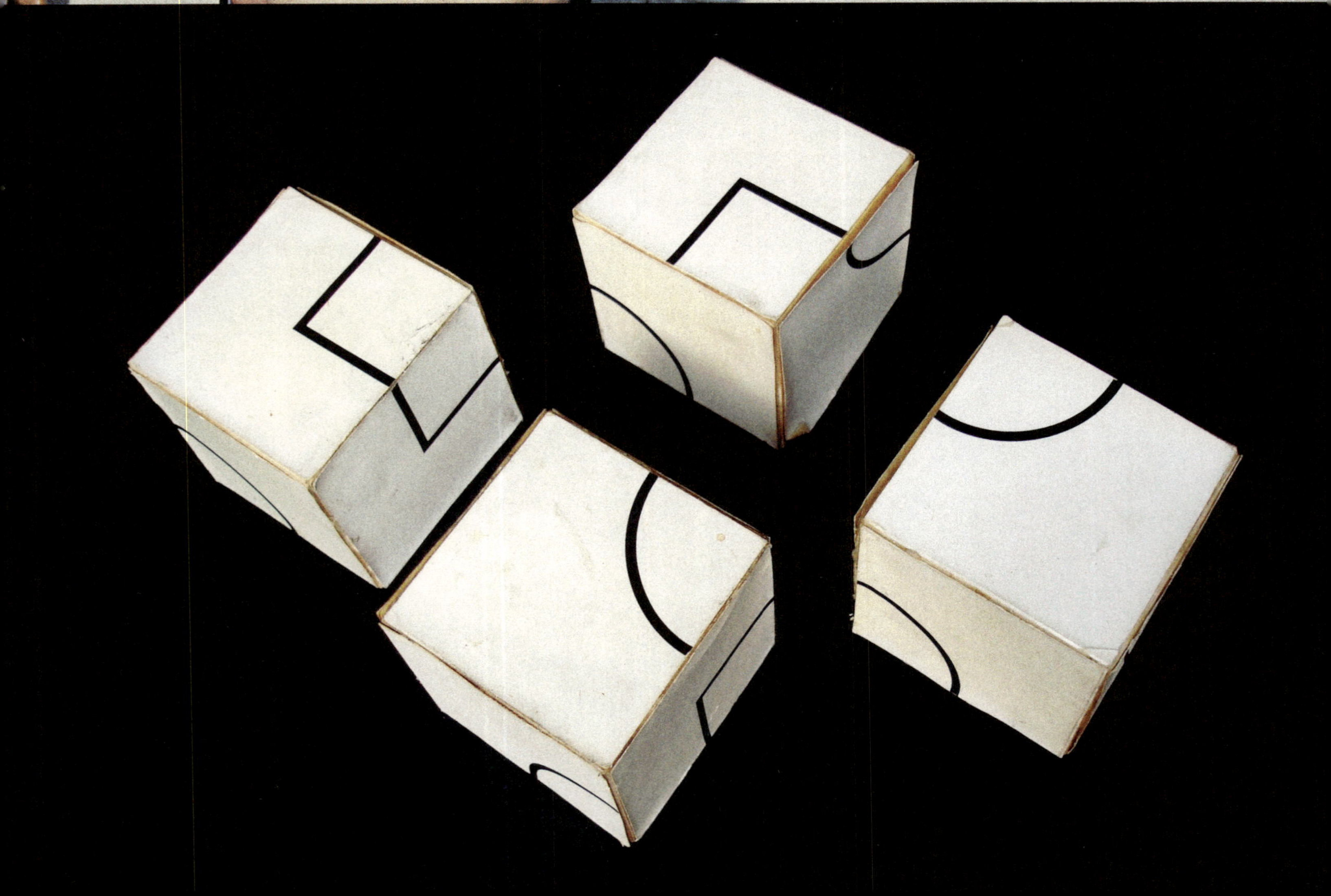

Fig. 3 Serge Stauffer: *The nine sense show*. Kleintheater Luzern, 1968
Fig. 4 F+F class: Teamwork, music-making in the art school auditorium. Zurich, 1969

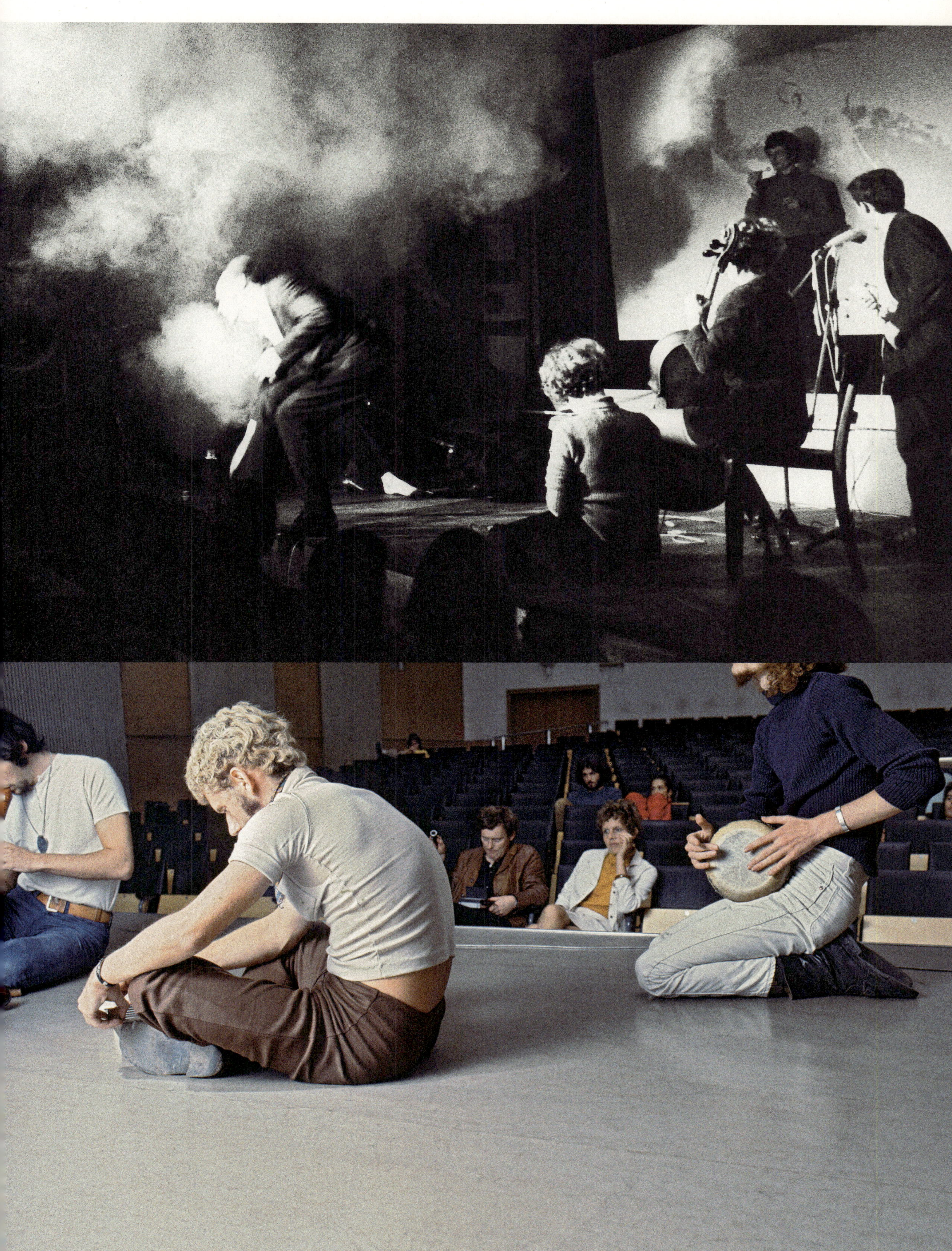

Fig. 5 *serge stauffer – kunst als forschung*. Exhibition. Helmhaus Zürich, 2013

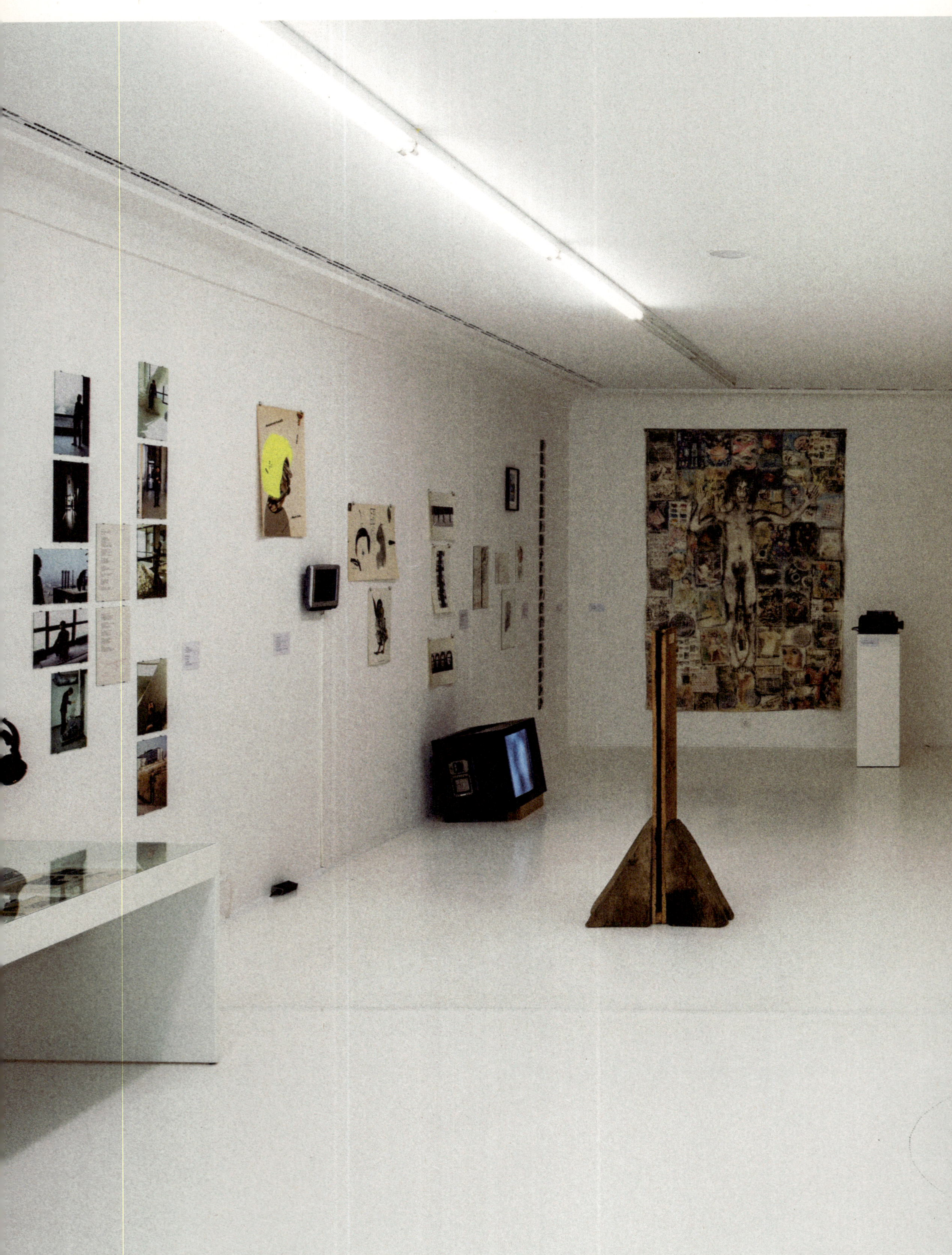

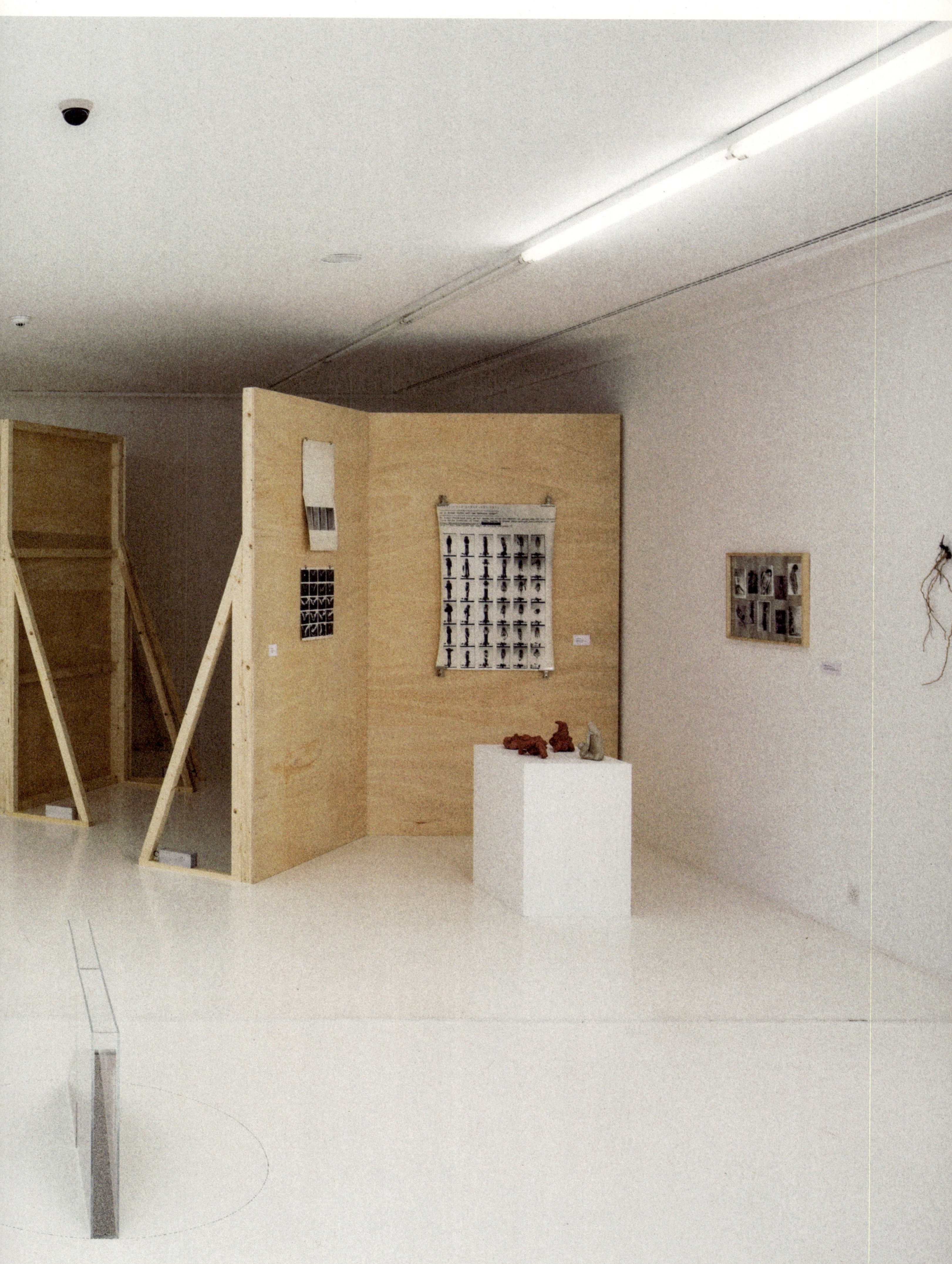

Fig. 6–11 Serge Stauffer: *Studie zu geometrisch-optischen Täuschungen.* Panels 15 × 15 cm, ca. 1962–1964

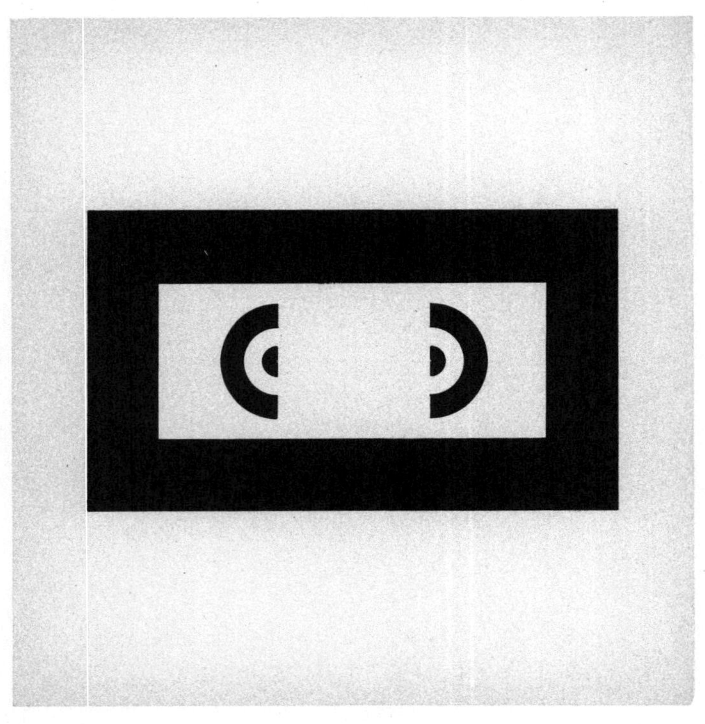

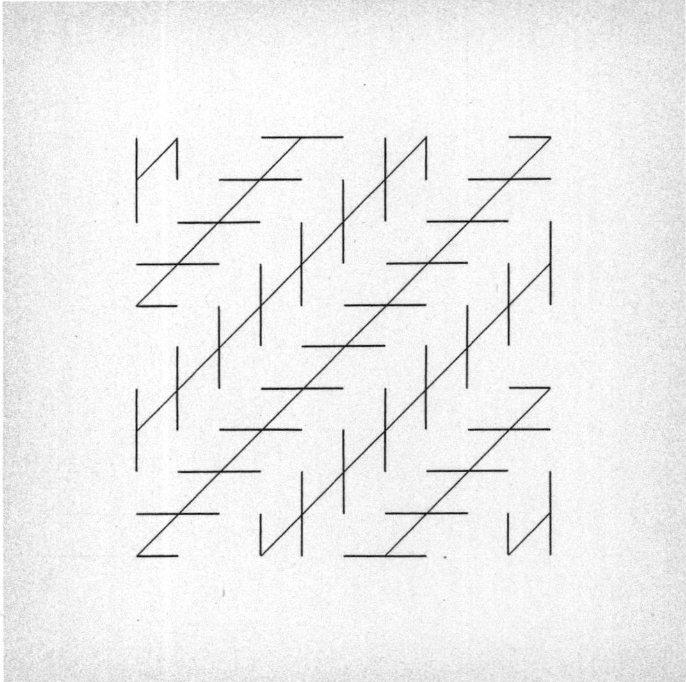

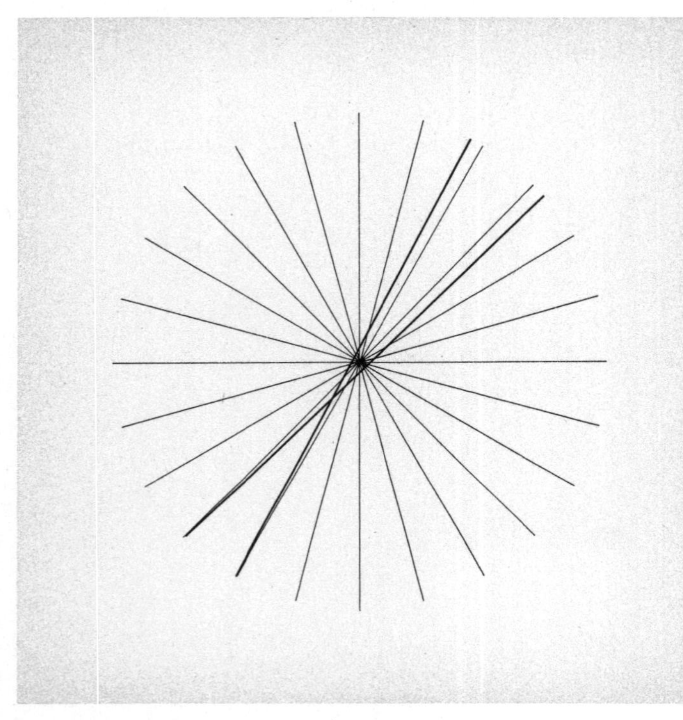

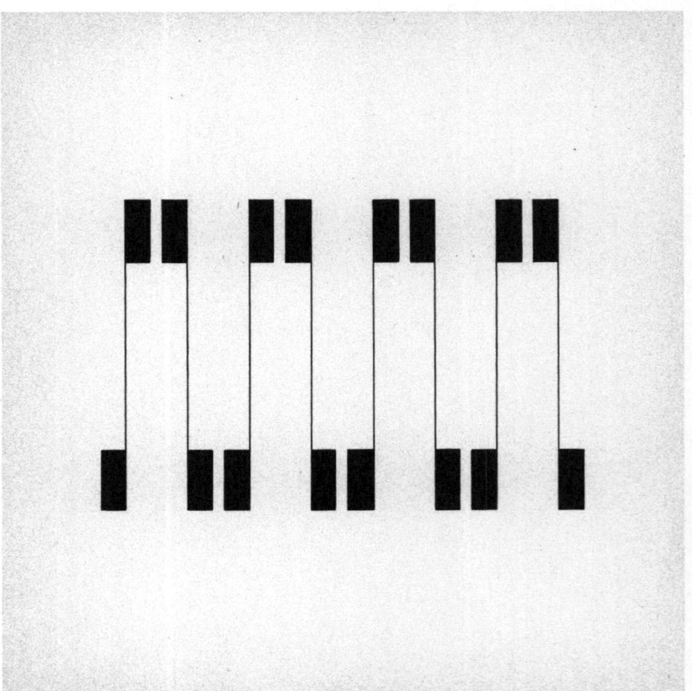

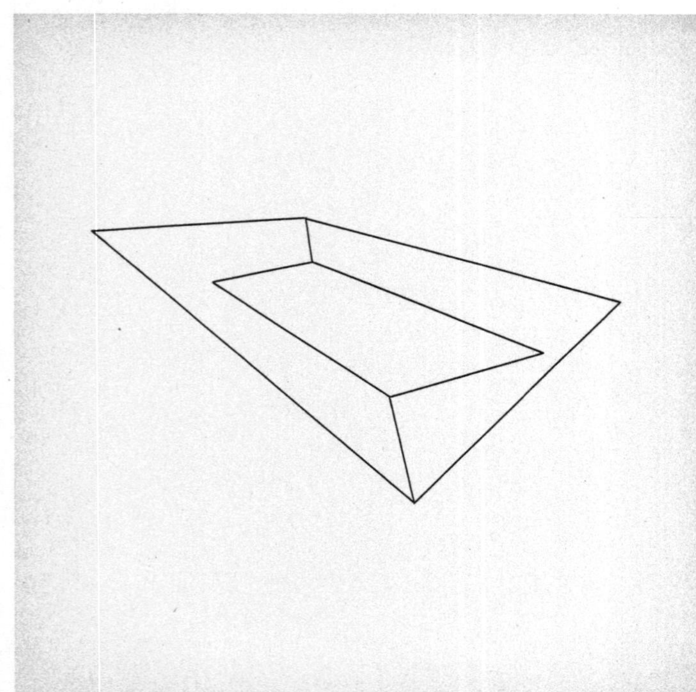

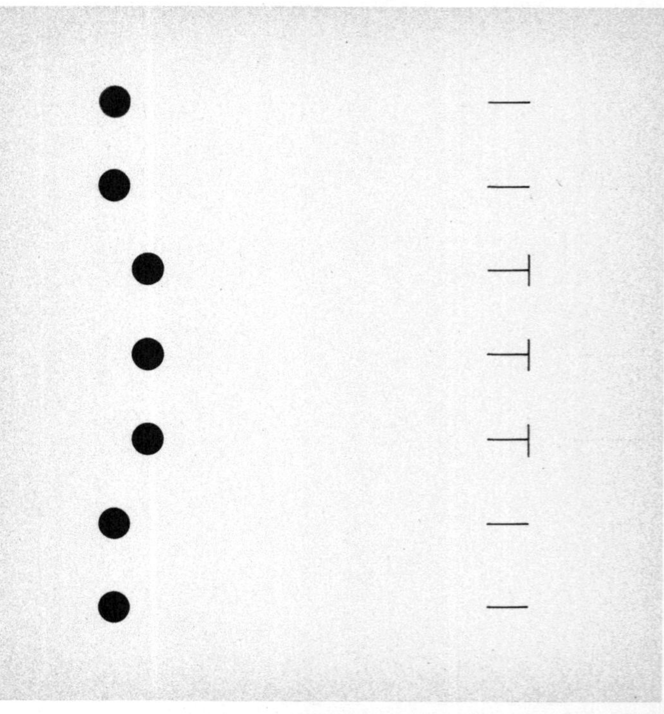

Fig. 12 Men's course with Serge Stauffer. F+F Schule, Zurich, 1978

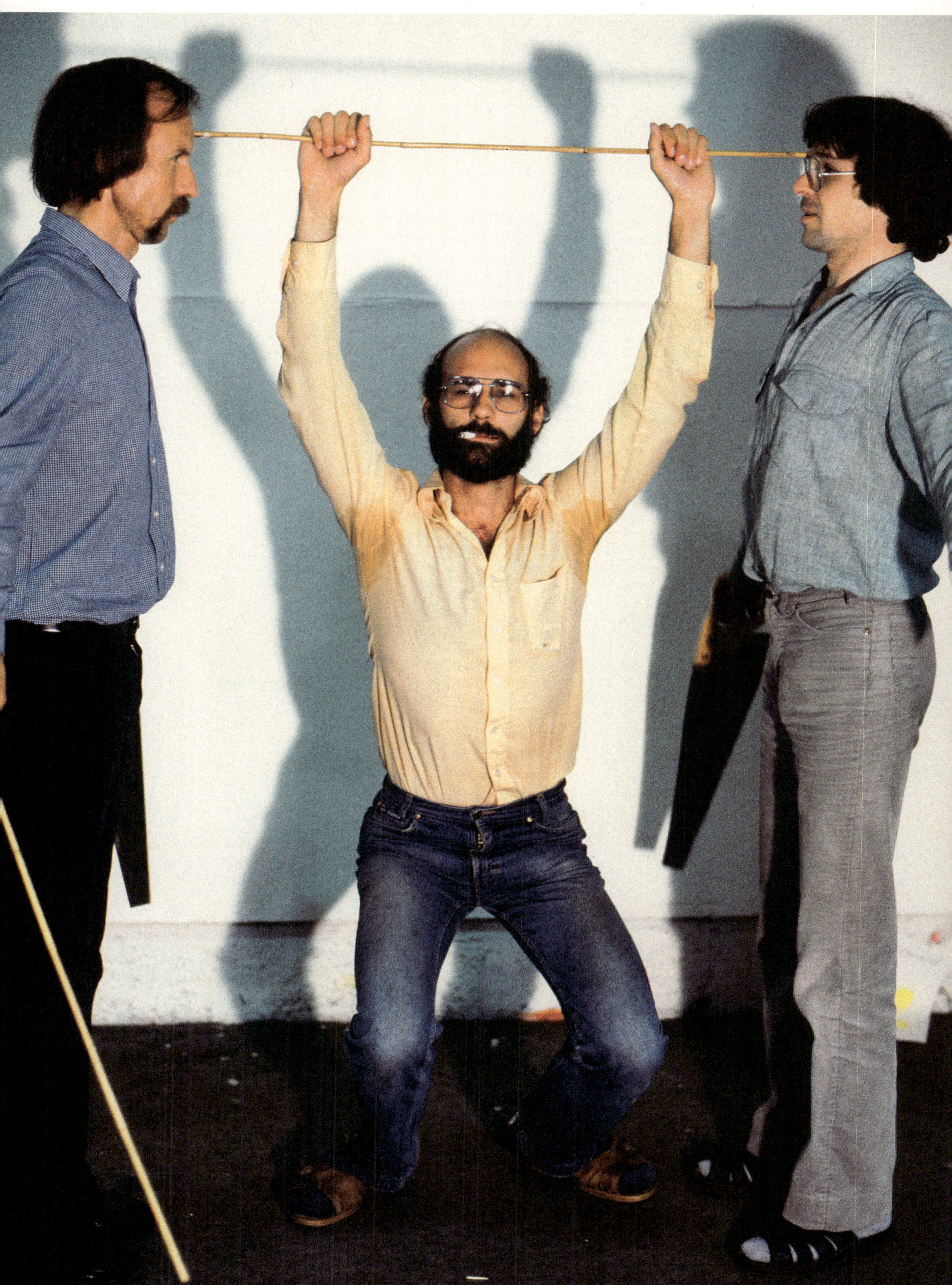

The ongoing process of digitalization penetrates all areas of life and has far-reaching consequences for the practices of biology and art. In the natural sciences a shift from theory-driven to data-driven research is under way, which constitutes not only another technological revolution but also an epistemological one. *Computer Signals. Art and Biology in the Age of Digital Experimentation I* traced this development, performing five parallel studies which looked at the research practice of two working groups that study the behavioral biology of fish. Both laboratories were research partners in this project. Their cooperation had already begun with the previous *Spillover* project (2007–2009) and continued in the subsequent *Computer Signals II* project (2017–2021). On the basis of these laboratory examples on Heligoland and in Austin, Texas, the *Computer Signals I* project asked about the concrete implications which the methods of increasingly automatized data acquisition, selection, evaluation, and processing have on research operations, their organization and activities.

Until recently, the empirical experiment and the instrumentally generated, material traces it generated—which also include images—played a key role in the analysis of knowledge processes. Under the new conditions, where images are still produced in optical sensors but often further processed as data rather than images, today this role is being taken over by "data work." What can be understood under the term "data work"? How can we describe the status of a computer that no longer merely transports media between the various analog and digital work steps performed by human and non-human actors, but configures these media interactively? What does the incipient fading of images in the natural sciences mean for the arts and for research in art?

The studies pursued such questions in the disciplines of visual arts, science studies and philosophy, media and art research: The artistic practice developed an experimental system of its own in order to observe and document data processes that take place within "black boxes" and to make them sensually perceptible. They implanted small pickups (induction coils and piezoelectric microphones) in the measurement apparatus, the computers, and the infrastructures of the biologists, which convert the physical emissions like power consumption or mechanical vibrations into audio signals. From the perspective of the devices, these "parasites" listened to the electronic work of the research apparatus. On the basis of these laboratory examples, science research concretized the shift from work with images to work with data. Philosophy of science investigated the metrification of biology and the influences of software that encourage a shift from the *wet* to the *dry* lab. Researchers reflecting on media observed the transition from analog to digital practices, in which media, as an apparatus of knowledge production, no longer convey messages but generate their own worlds by automatizing the observer. The art research study analyzed relationships like (co-)authorship and works under the conditions of cooperating with media from the life sciences.

After the first third of the research work, artists verified the envisaged negotiability of their intermediate results in an exhibition accompanied by a conference. There a wider audience of specialists and the general public discussed the results of the artistic research. The events served, first, to further develop the artistic experimental facilities installed in Heligoland and in Austin. Second, they refined the aesthetic and theoretical approaches to other, generally invisible but influential digital processes in everyday life, such as room monitoring and the control of spaces of production and consumption.

Hannes Rickli

Project Title
Computersignale. Kunst und Biologie im Zeitalter ihres digitalen Experimentierens

Project Period
1 May 2012–30 October 2015

Keywords
- Data work
- Digitization
- Art and science
- Experimental system
- Hybrid lab

Head of Project
- Hannes Rickli, artist

Research Team
- Roman Keller, artist
- Franz Krähenbühl, art researcher
- Valentina Vuksic, artist
- Birk Weiberg, art researcher

Research Partners
- Philipp Fischer, Biological Institute Heligoland, Alfred Wegener Institute, Helmholtz Centre for Polar and Marine Research
- Gabriele Gramelsberger, Institute of Philosophy, Freie Universität Berlin, Philosophy of Science Program
- Christoph Hoffmann, University of Lucerne, Seminar for Cultural and Science Studies
- Hans A. Hofmann, University of Texas at Austin, Department of Integrative Biology, College of Natural Sciences

Outputs

Project Partners

- Smartronic GmbH
- Schering Stiftung
- Berlin-Brandenburg Academy of Sciences and Humanities

Project Funding

- Swiss National Science Foundation SNSF
- Ernst und Olga Gubler-Hablützel Stiftung
- Schering Stiftung
- STEO Stiftung
- Volkart-Stiftung

Related Projects

- Spillover, Zurich University of the Arts, 2007–2009
  P. 74
- Computer Signals II, Zurich University of the Arts, 2017–2021
  P. 214
- Listening to Data Flows, Zurich University of the Arts, 2021–2024

Publication

- Hannes Rickli and Valentina Vuksic (2016): *RemOs1: Beginn einer Datenarbeit in der Arktischen See/RemOs1. Beginning Data Work in the Arctic Sea*. Volume 16 of the Institute for Contemporary Art Research series. Zurich: Zurich University of the Arts.
  - A Open access: https://doi.org/10.5281/zenodo.5077957 (DE)
  - B Open access: https://doi.org/10.5281/zenodo.5077999 (EN)

Articles

- Hannes Rickli (2013): “Electrical Images. Snapshots of an Exploration.” In: Michael Schwab (ed.): *Experimental Systems. Future Knowledge in Artistic Research*. Leuven: University Press, 26–40.
- Hannes Rickli (2016): “Der unsichtbare Faden. Materialität und Infrastrukturen digitaler Tierbeobachtung.” In: Lorenz Engell, and Bernhard Siegert (eds.): *Zeitschrift für Medien- und Kulturforschung ZMK*, no. 2/7. Hamburg: Felix Meiner, 137–154.

Conference

- *Fragile Daten*. 1–2 March 2013. Berlin-Brandenburg Academy of Sciences and Humanities (BBAW), Berlin. Organized by Hannes Rickli, Gabriele Gramelsberger, and Christoph Hoffmann. With contributions by Peter Bexte, Philipp Fischer, Kathrin Friedrich, Gabriele Gramelsberger, Christoph Hoffmann, Hans Hofmann, Franz Krähenbühl, Staffan Müller-Wille, Rubert Munzel, Hans-Jörg Rheinberger, and Hannes Rickli.

Workshop

- *Computersignale. Kunst und Biologie im Zeitalter ihres digitalen Experimentierens*. 26–27 November 2014. Leuphana University Lüneburg. In cooperation with Media Cultures of Computer Simulation “mecs,” funded by the German Research Foundation, organized by Gabriele Gramelsberger and Hannes Rickli. With contributions by Philipp Fischer, Gabriele Gramelsberger, Christoph Hoffmann, Jan Müggenburg, Hannes Rickli, and Sebastian Vehlken.

Exhibition

- *Fischen lauschen/Listening to Fishes. Beginn einer Datenübertragung aus der Arktischen See/Beginning of Data Transmission from the Arctic Sea*. Solo exhibition by Hannes Rickli. 24 January–23 March 2013. Schering Stiftung, Berlin.

Works

- Hannes Rickli: *RemOs1*. 2013. Sample. Ten-channel audio-video installation. Two video projectors, seven speakers, LED display, steel construction. 380 × 570 × 484 cm.
- Hannes Rickli: *RemOs1*. 2013. Archive. Eight-channel audio-video installation. Six 10.4" monitors, one 17" monitor, headphones.
- Hannes Rickli: *RemOs1*. 2013. Live. Seven-channel video installation. 15" monitors, internet transmission.
- Valentina Vuksic: *RemOs1. Beginn einer Datenarbeit in der Arktischen See*. 2015. Sound composition, 10 min. Commissioned by ORF musikprotokoll as part of the *steirischer herbst* program.

Fig. 1 Field research. Texas, 2014

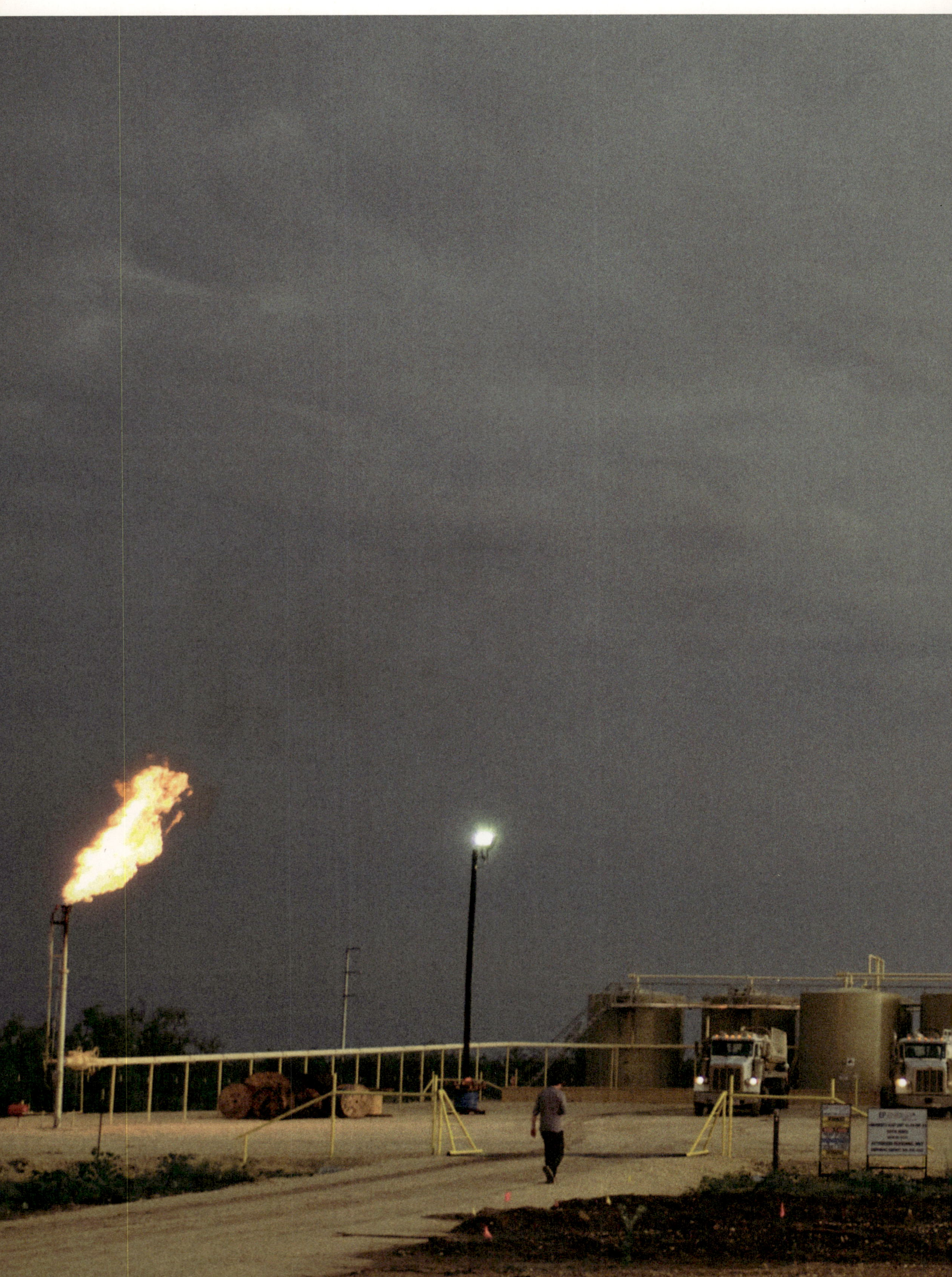

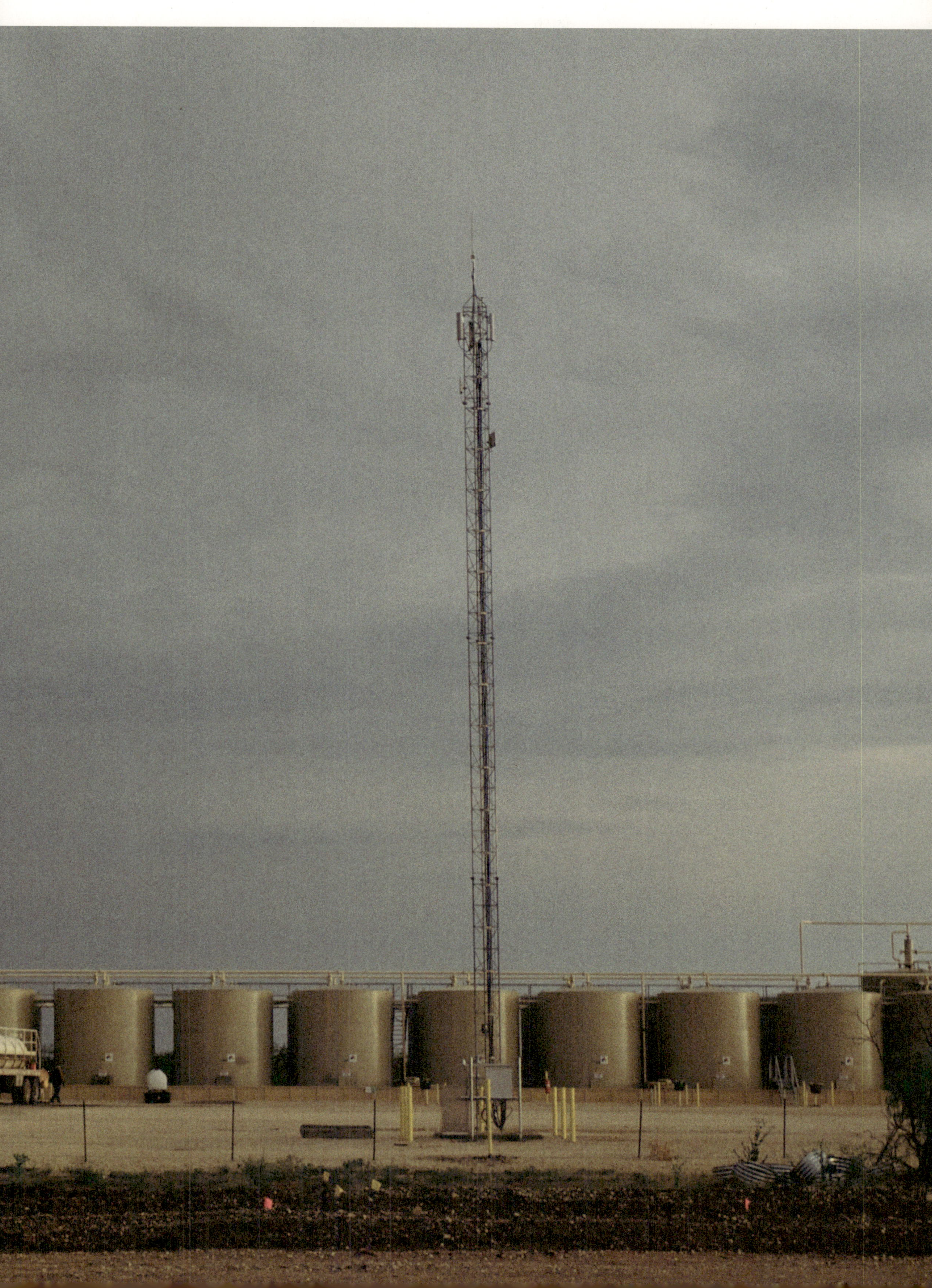

Fig. 2 Field research. Texas, 2014

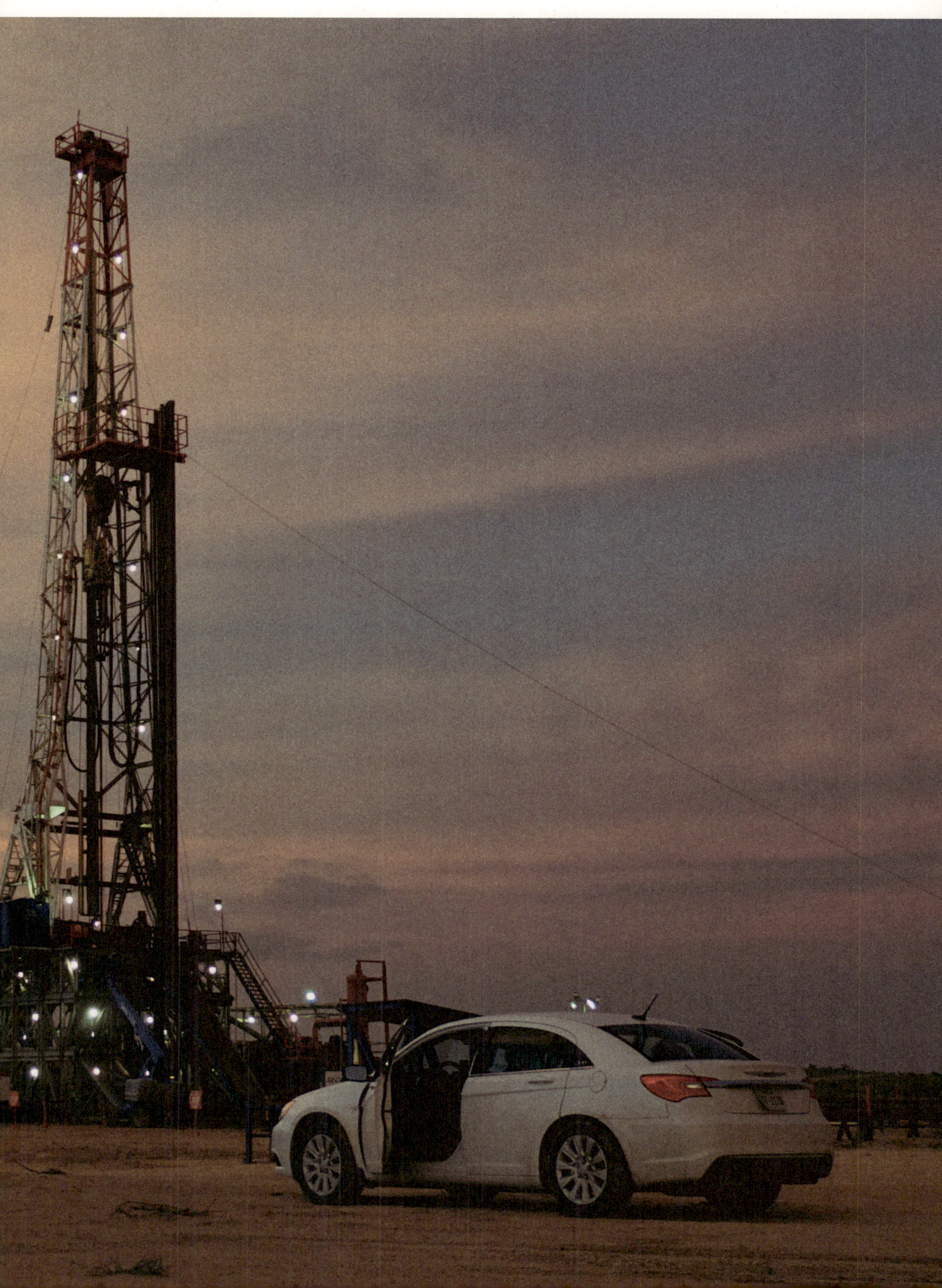

Fig. 3 RemOs1 in the test basin. AWI Centre for Scientific Diving, Heligoland, 2012
Fig. 4 Preparing the implementation of electromagnetic pickups. Texas Advanced Computing Center, University of Texas, Austin, 2014

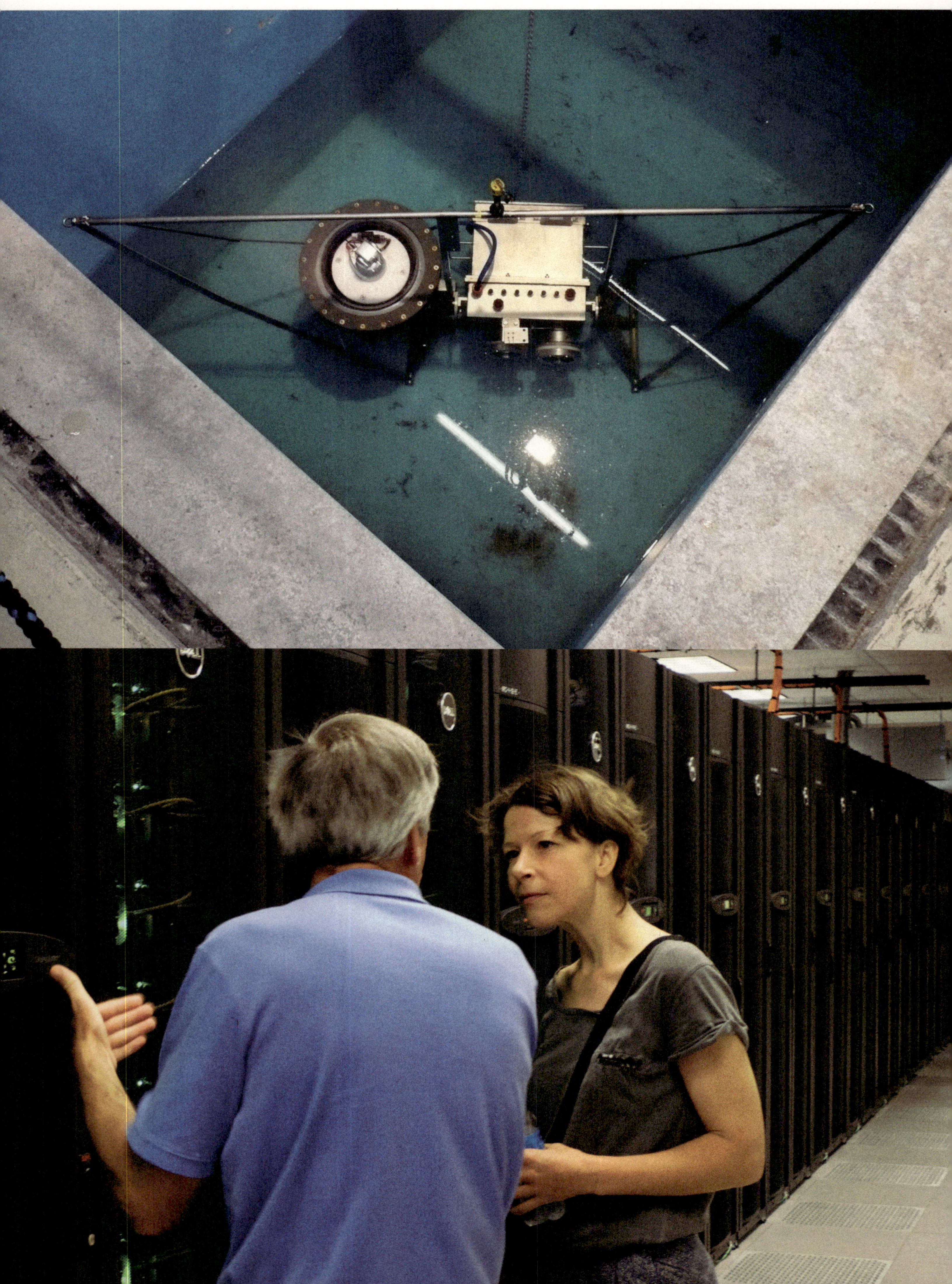

Fig. 5 Testing the lens of the stereometric camera. Ny-Ålesund, Spitsbergen, 2012

Fig. 6 Implementation of the electromagnetic pickups. AWI Centre for Scientific Diving, Biological Institute Heligoland, 2012

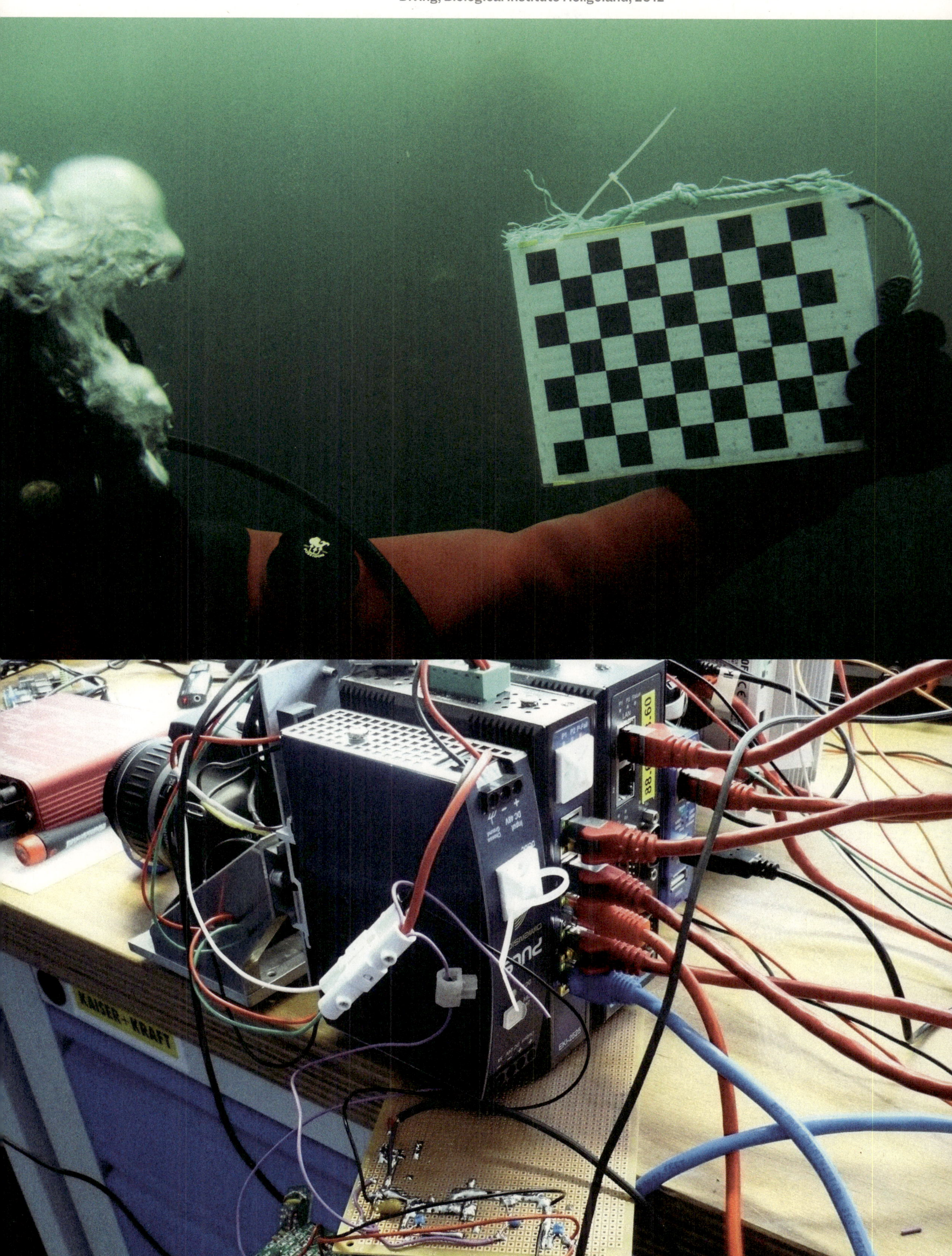

At the invitation of *Urbane Künste Ruhr*, between January and October 2013, the Institute for Contemporary Art Research (IFCAR) set up a research laboratory to investigate questions and problems specific to the Ruhr region, especially to Mülheim. Artists and lecturers at the University of the Arts Zurich as well as additional consulted specialists and artists developed four independent but topically closely interlaced projects, each with its own focus on the urban transformation process taking place in the Ruhr region.

The *battle the landscape* project by the artist duo knowbotiq (Yvonne Wilhelm, Christian Huebler) was concerned with various traditional and new landscape concepts through which it became possible to reinterpret the Ruhr region as a cultural landscape or political landscape.

In their project *Ruhrlabor on_off*, !Mediengruppe Bitnik and Kreativitätskombinat Klein Riviera collaborated to develop a new perspective on the relationship between creativity and precarity. It considered various forms of organized begging and linked them with the current discourse on creativity, which yielded such interventions as begging for creativity in Mülheim's pedestrian zone.

The Phonorama *City Telling Ruhr* by art historian Ingo Starz and musician Tobias Gerber consisted of stories told by residents of Mülheim about this city. Contents and narrative styles in an audio collage created a forum which made the city's societal debates audible.

Finally, in *Sonozones Mülheim*, musician and composer Jan Schacher collaborated with the sound artists Cathy van Eck (University of the Arts Bern), Kirsten Reese (UdK Berlin) and Trond Lossius (Bergen Academy of Art and Design, Norway) to pursue the societal aspects of hearing. On the level of sound, the city of Mülheim also accessed a complex problem area that was able to be investigated with the tools of sound art.

The projects shared the approach of an artistic research directed toward urban development, sociological, or ethnographic issues. In addition to these questions about the urban development of Mülheim within the structural change underway in the Ruhr region, they also focused on questions of methodology: How do the arts perform research? Which media require which methods? What kind of knowledge can the arts generate—to contrast with or supplement traditional forms of knowledge?

All interventions, actions and sound installations in public space should be understood as both artistic activities and parts of a research process. The Dezentrale project space in the center of Mülheim served as a laboratory for all project participants and also as a place for exchange with specialists from the region and the residents of Mülheim.

The project closed with a conference in the Dezentrale project space as well as with a publication and website.

Jürgen Krusche

Project Title
Labor Mülheim. Künstlerisches Forschen in Feldern urbaner Prekarität und Kreativität

Project Period
1 July 2012–31 October 2013

Keywords
- Public space
- Urban transformation
- Creativity
- Precarity
- Kinds of knowledge

Head of Project
- Jürgen Krusche, artist and urbanologist

Research Team
- knowbotiq (Yvonne Wilhelm, Christian Huebler), artist duo
- !Mediengruppe Bitnik (Carmen Weisskopf, Doma Smoljo), artists
- Kreativitätskombinat Klein Riviera (Ute Holfelder, Klaus Schönberger), cultural researchers
- Ingo Starz, art historian
- Tobias Gerber, musician
- Jan Schacher, musician and composer
- Cathy van Eck, sound artist
- Kirsten Reese, sound artist
- Trond Lossius, sound artist

Research Partner
- Katja Assmann, curator

Outputs

A

Project Partners
- Urbane Künste Ruhr, Kultur Ruhr GmbH, Gelsenkirchen
- Ringlokschuppen Mülheim

Project Funding
- Urbane Künste Ruhr
- Bundesamt für Berufsbildung und Technologie BBT

Related Projects
- Bureau Savamala Belgrade, Zurich University of the Arts, 2013–2014
  P. 140
- Politics of Space, Zurich University of the Arts, Connecting Spaces Zurich–Hong Kong, 2014–2018
  P. 158
- The Fragmented City, Zurich University of the Arts, 2017–2021
  P. 206

Website
- https://blog.zhdk.ch/labormuelheim/labormuelheim

Publication
- Jürgen Krusche (ed.) (2015): *Labor Mülheim. Künstlerisches Forschen in Feldern urbaner Prekarität und Kreativität*. Volume 14 of the Institute for Contemporary Art Research series. Berlin: Jovis.
  A Open access: https://doi.org/10.5281/zenodo.5744460

Article
- Jan Schacher, Cathy van Eck, Kirsten Reese, and Trond Lossius (2013): "Sonozones. Sound art investigations in public places." In: *Researchcatalogue, Journal for Artistic Research*.

Conference
- *Prekäre Landschaften. Eine künstlerisch forschende Auseinandersetzung mit (Ge)Schichten wiederkehrender Umbrüche*. 25–26 October 2013. Ringlokschuppen Mülheim. With contributions from the project team and from Katja Assmann, Klaus Ronneberger, Idrissa Aponda, Random Boi and Gurl Wave aka Rock, Stefan Goch, Mats Staub, Jochen Becker, Astrid Kusser, Salomé Vögelin, and Holger Bergmann. Moderation: Jürgen Krusche and Christoph Schenker.

Works
- Cathy van Eck: *Extended Ears*. 2013. Sound walks with listening horns and an iPhone app.
- Tobias Gerber: *City Telling Ruhr*. 2013. Audio collage, stereo, 24:34 min.
- knowbotiq: *battle the landscape!* 25 October 2013. Online cartography and live performance with vaudeville costumes, camouflage suits. Urban intervention at the entrance of a former coal mine. 2 h. In collaboration with Idrissa Aponda, Random Boi (dance), Gurl Wave aka Rock, Joana Aderi (sound), Heinz Auberg (voice). Mülheim an der Ruhr.
- Kreativitätskombinat Klein Riviera: *Bitte um Kreativität*. 23–26 June 2013. Ethnographic intervention, Mülheim an der Ruhr.
- Trond Lossius and Jan Schacher: *Sonozones. Losing Myself in the World*. 22–26 July 2013. Sound collage of a series of audio-visual field recordings presented as slow cinema. Mülheim an der Ruhr.
- Kirsten Reese: *Sonozones. Augmenting Urban Sounds*. 22–26 July 2013. Small scale installations/interventions in public space. Mülheim an der Ruhr.

Fig. 1 Cathy van Eck: *Extended Ears 1: Mechanisch*. Mülheim, 2014

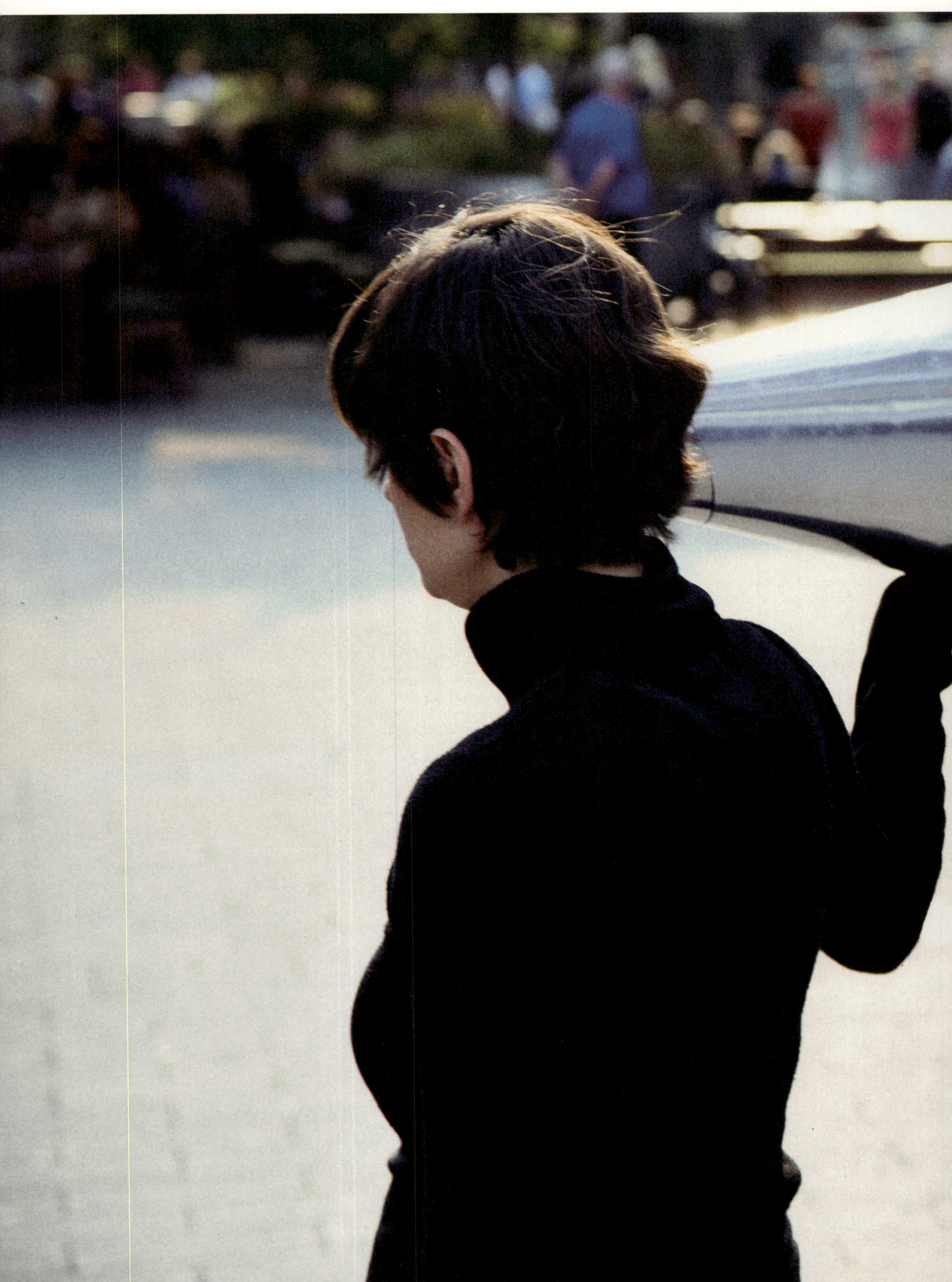

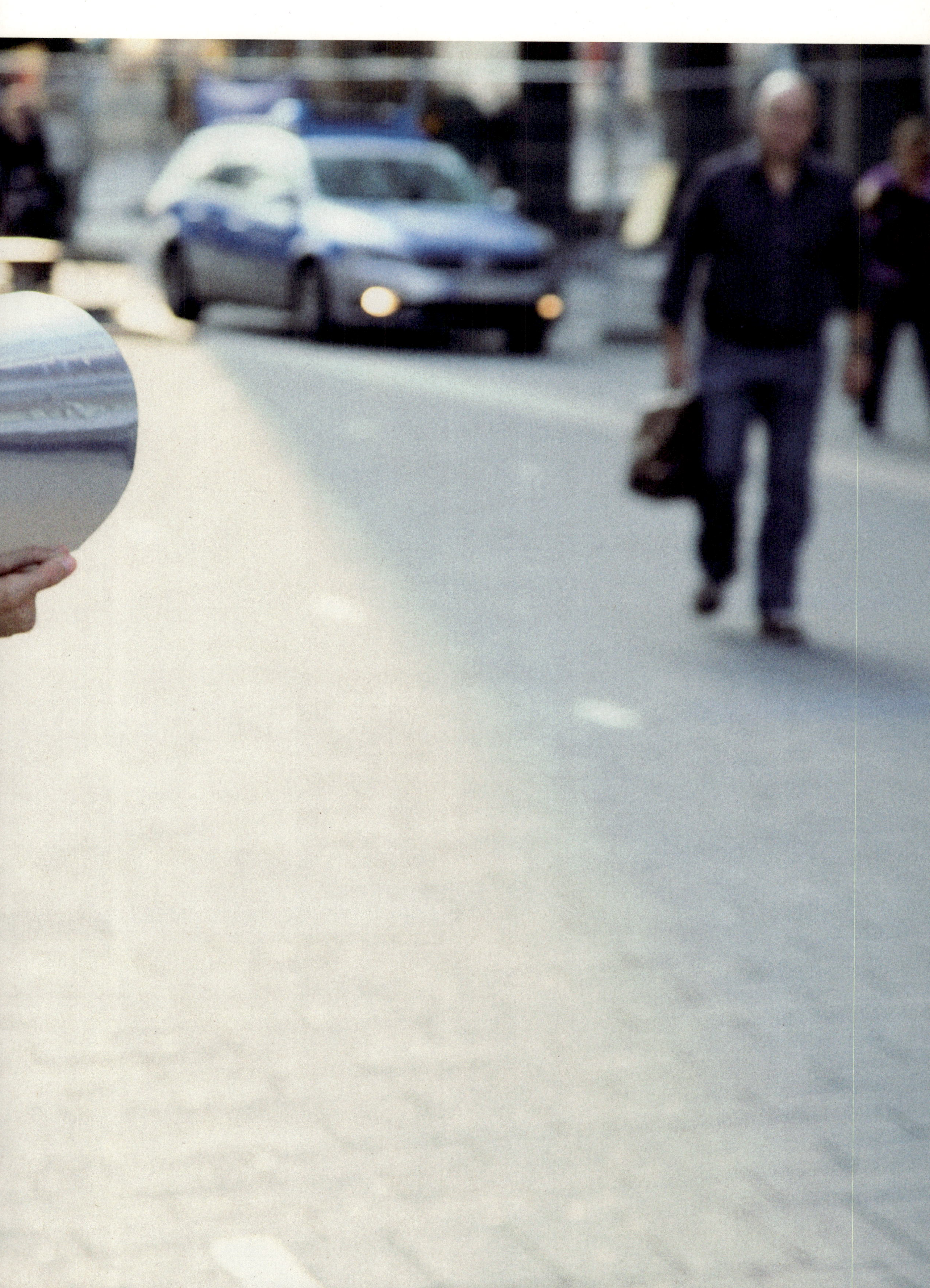

Fig. 2–4 Kirsten Reese: *Augmenting Urban Sounds*. Interventions, Mülheim, 2014

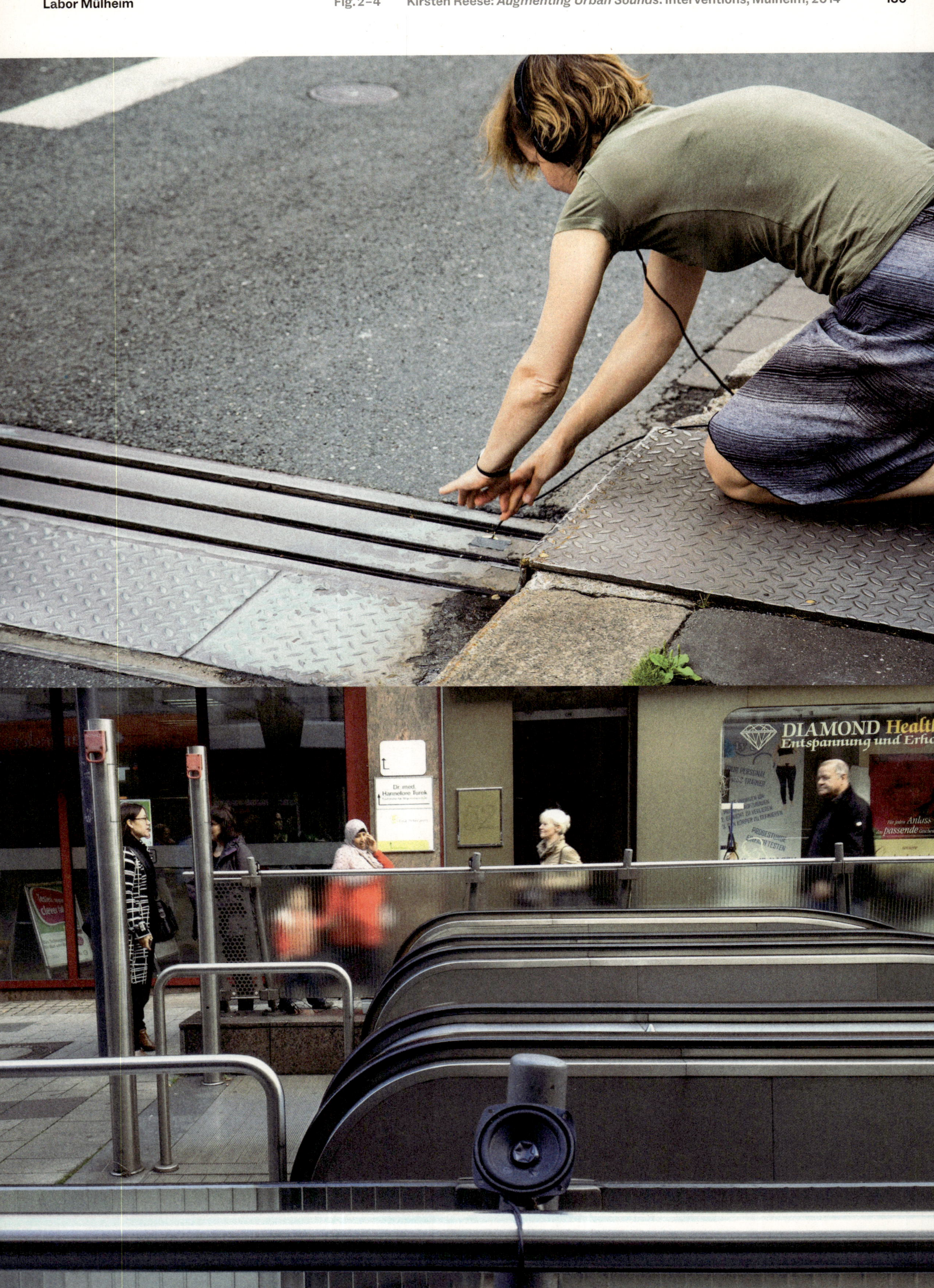

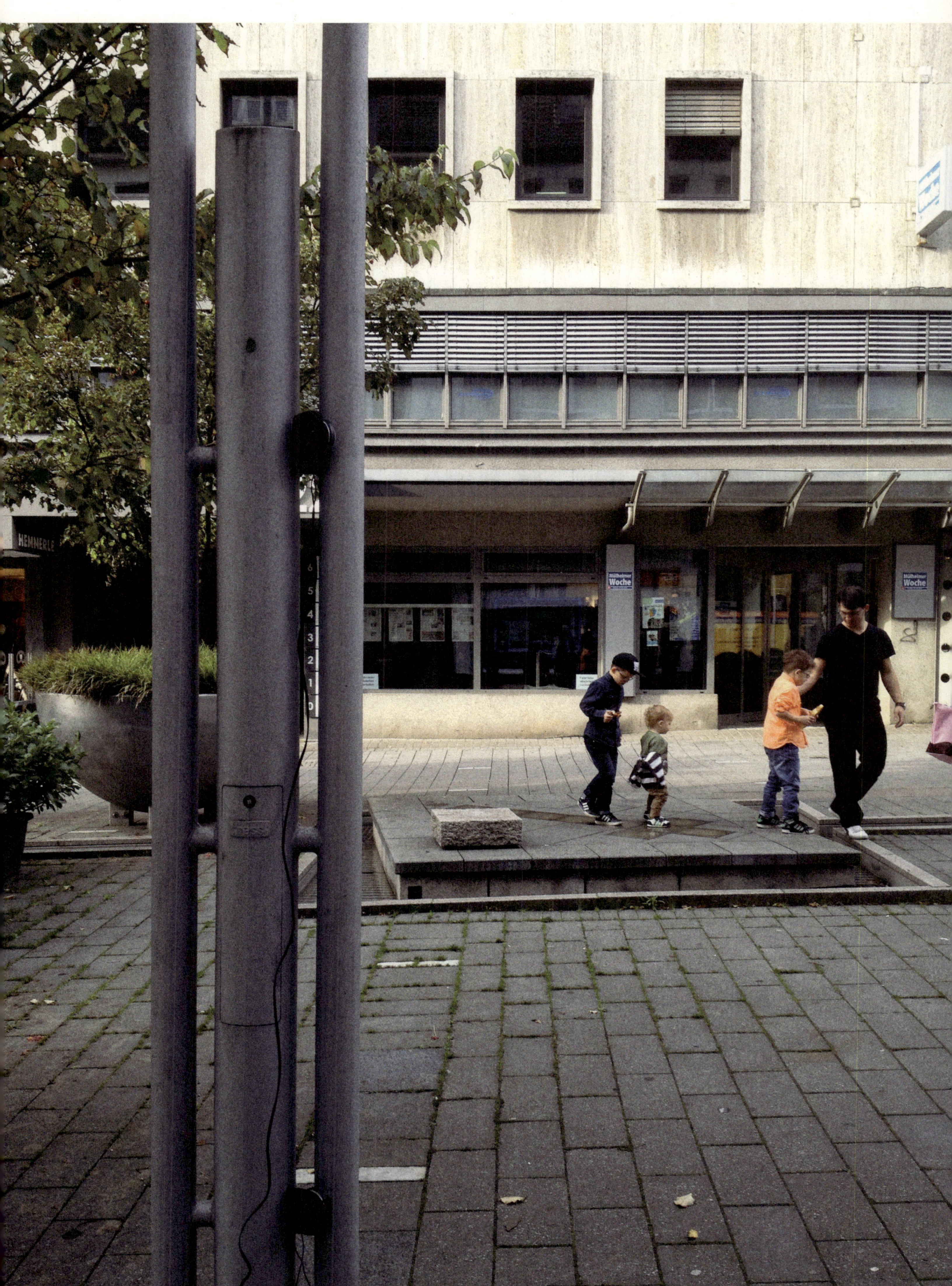
HEMMERLE
Mülheimer Woche
Mülheimer Woche

Fig. 5–7 Jürgen Krusche: Photographs from the photo essay *Leere Mitte Mülheim*, 2014

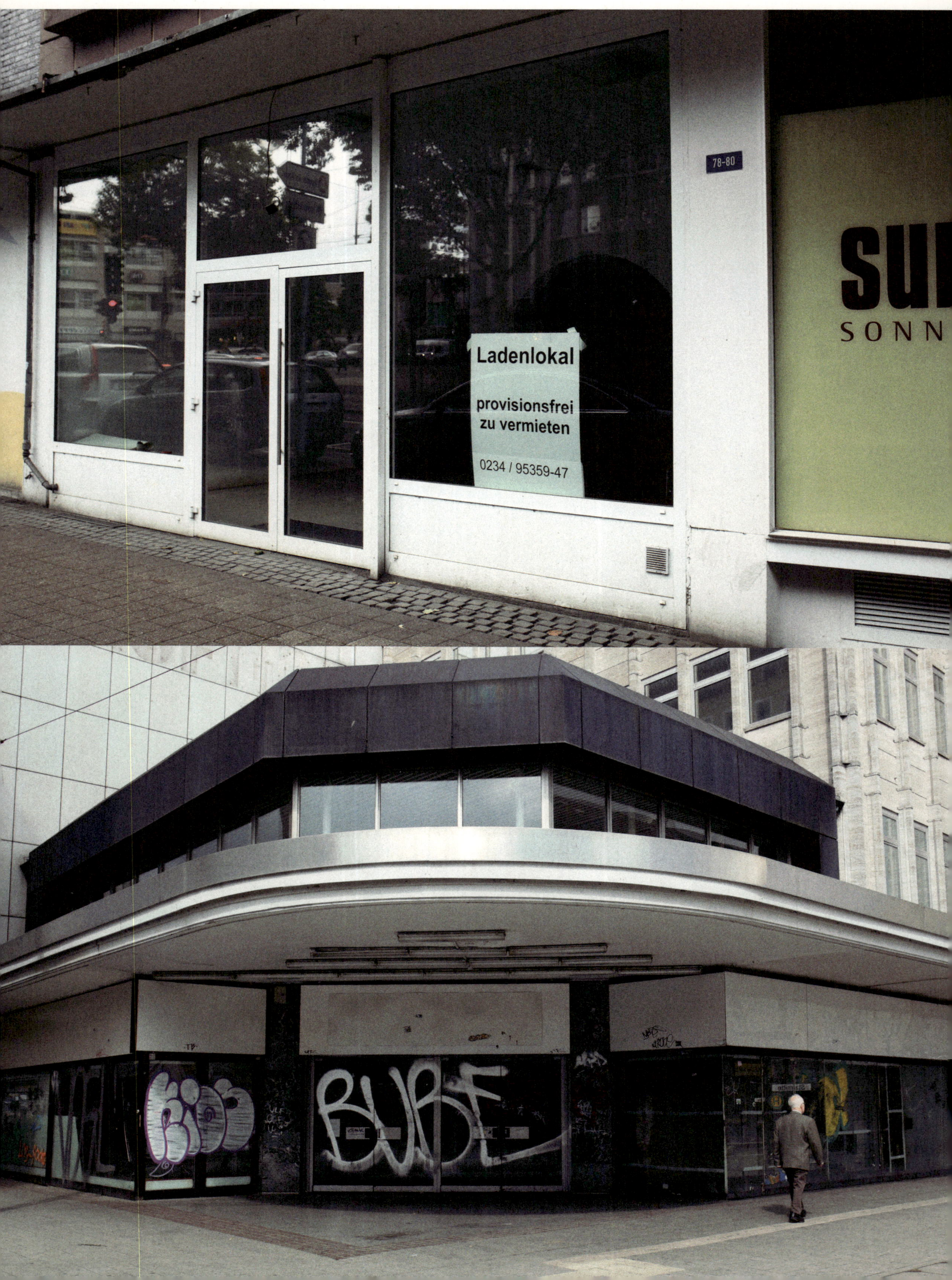

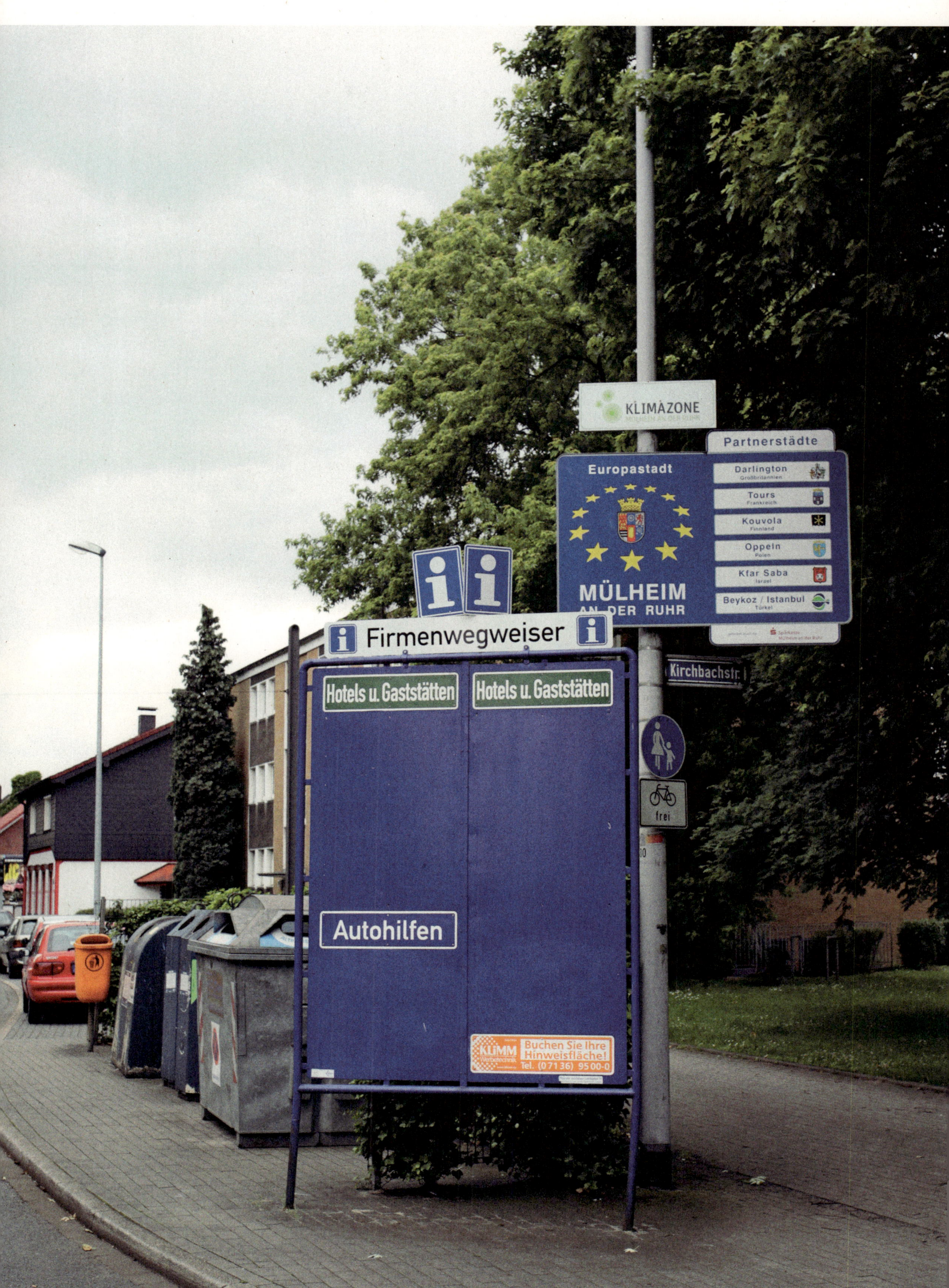
KLIMAZONE
Partnerstädte
Europastadt
Darlington
Tours
Kouvola
Oppeln
Kfar Saba
Beykoz / Istanbul
MÜLHEIM
AN DER RUHR
Firmenwegweiser
Kirchbachstr.
Hotels u. Gaststätten
Hotels u. Gaststätten
frei
Autohilfen
Buchen Sie Ihre Hinweisfläche!
Tel. (07136) 9500-0

Spatial observation works primarily with maps, plans, and statistical data. With these methods changes in the sensual and emotional, i.e., aesthetic space can be cataloged only to a limited degree. However, the dimension of space that is experienced and perceived by the senses is of essential importance for the quality of living spaces. At the halfway point of *Long-term Photographic Observation of Schlieren 2005–2020*, the project cooperated with the Auditory Architecture Research Unit (AARU) at Berlin University of the Arts (UdK Berlin) to investigate how photographs and sound recordings can be deployed to catalog the aesthetic dimension of urban transformation. The sound recordings came from the archive of the *Auditive Langzeitbeobachtung Schlieren* (Auditory Long-term Observation of Schlieren) project at the UdK Berlin/AARU, which took place in parallel to the photographic long-term observation by the Institute for Contemporary Art Research (IFCAR) at Zurich University of the Arts (ZHdK). In construction and planning, the acoustic environment was examined primarily with regard to noise pollution, i.e., according to quantitative aspects. The AARU's project in Schlieren, by contrast, was concerned with the sound of life spaces according to qualitative aspects. Every two years, sound recordings were repeated using dummy head microphones placed at twenty-four locations throughout the urban space, in order to record sound qualities of different living spaces such that they could be differentiated clearly. The shared point of reference of the photographic and auditory long-term observation was the urban development concept for Schlieren submitted by Metron AG in 2005.

The project proposed that a perception directed to the aesthetic quality of urban space by means of photographs and sound recordings demands an active, focused attitude by the recipient. By means of dispositives of perception, i.e., installations of photographs and sound recordings for interior and exterior spaces, manifold forms of hearing and seeing urban space were made possible. The dispositives consisted of various combinations of presentation formats (large- and small-scale inkjet prints, monitors, iPads, closed headphones, free-standing speakers, MP3 players) linked with a precise linguistic framing and timing instructions for viewing. The development of these dispositives, along with the testing and realization of various configurations in space, constituted the central research element in the project.

The representatives of the municipality of Schlieren and of Metron AG who participated as practice partners used these dispositives of perception in performatively designed workshops with the objective of assessing the transformation in experienced space for an upcoming evaluation of Schlieren's urban development. The project partners valued the approach focused on aesthetic perception as an extremely productive expansion of their functional, goal-oriented strategy in everyday planning. In particular, the project allowed urban planning issues and objectives to be questioned and reflected upon as they relate to the development of specific locations in the urban space. This qualitative approach, especially to the auditory aspects, was uncharted territory for all participants. Working with the dispositives allowed the workshop participants to perform a precise analysis of the qualities and deficits of specific situations in Schlieren. However, using this analysis to derive any generally valid criteria for assessing the overall transformation proved problematic. One of the reasons for this was that a linguistic formulation of qualities in a sensually perceptible space is possible only to a limited extent. The other main problem was the lack of binding criteria for the quality of spaces in urban development more generally—criteria which have been and still are the object of research and debate. The question as to how the experiences of spatial transformation generated from intensive perception can flow into planning practice therefore remained open as a concept for further research.

Meret Wandeler

Project Title
Visuelle und auditive Wahrnehmungsdispositive. Zur Erweiterung der Evaluationsmethodik von Stadtentwicklung in der Agglomeration am Beispiel von Schlieren

Project Period
1 October 2012–30 November 2013

Keywords
- Agglomeration
- Urban transformation
- Perception
- Photography
- Sound research

Head of Project
- Ulrich Görlich, artist

Project Team at Zurich University of the Arts
- Meret Wandeler, artist
- Rohit Jain, social anthropologist
- Jon Etter, photographer

Project Team at Berlin University of the Arts
- Alex Arteaga, sound researcher
- Thomas Kusitzky, sound researcher

Research Partner
- Berlin University of the Arts, Auditory Architecture Research Unit

Project Partners
- Metron Raumentwicklung AG
- Stadt Schlieren, Abteilung Bau und Planung

Website
- www.wahrnehmung-agglomeration.ch

Project Funding
- Swiss National Science Foundation SNSF/ Deutsche Forschungsgemeinschaft DFG/ D-A-CH

Related Projects
- Long-term Photographic Observation of Schlieren 2005–2020, Zurich University of the Arts, 2005–2020
  P. 50

Articles
- Sabine von Fischer (2013): “Zeitreisen als Planungsinstrumente.” In: *Tec 21*, no. 44, 12–13.
- Rohit Jain (2013): “Agglomerationsdiskurse in der Schweiz.”
  www.wahrnehmung-agglomeration.ch
- Rohit Jain (2013): “An-/Ästhetik der Agglomeration. Eine Ethnographie der Planungspraxis in Schlieren bei Zürich.”
  www.wahrnehmung-agglomeration.ch
- Sabine von Fischer (2014): “Mit den Sinnen und in vier Dimensionen.” Review of the conference *Ästhetik der Agglomeration. Dispositive zur Wahrnehmung von Transformationsprozessen.*
  https://arthist.net
- Meret Wandeler and Hubert Locher (2015): “Fotografische Forschung. Ein Interview.” In: *Rundbrief Fotografie: Analoge und digitale Bildmedien in Archiven und Sammlungen*, vol. 22, 1 [N.F. 85], 37–47.

Conference
- *Ästhetik der Agglomeration. Dispositive zur Wahrnehmung von Transformationsprozessen.* 3 October 2013, Schlieren, Festsaal Salmen. With contributions by Alex Arteaga, Gianfranco Basso, Elke Bippus, Angelus Eisinger, Ulrich Görlich, Susanne Hauser, Rohit Jain, Toni Brühlmann-Jecklin, Thomas Kusitzky, Barbara Meyer, Roberto Nigro, Andreas Sonderegger, Philip Ursprung, Meret Wandeler, Joris van Wezemael, Timo von Wirth, and Peter Wolf.

Presentations
- Ulrich Görlich and Meret Wandeler: *Visuelle und auditive Wahrnehmungsdispositive.* November 2013, Berlin University of the Arts.
- Ulrich Görlich and Meret Wandeler: *Visuelle und auditive Wahrnehmungsdispositive.* November 2013, Metron AG, Brugg.

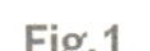

Fig. 1 Dispositive for project workshop. Schlieren, 2013

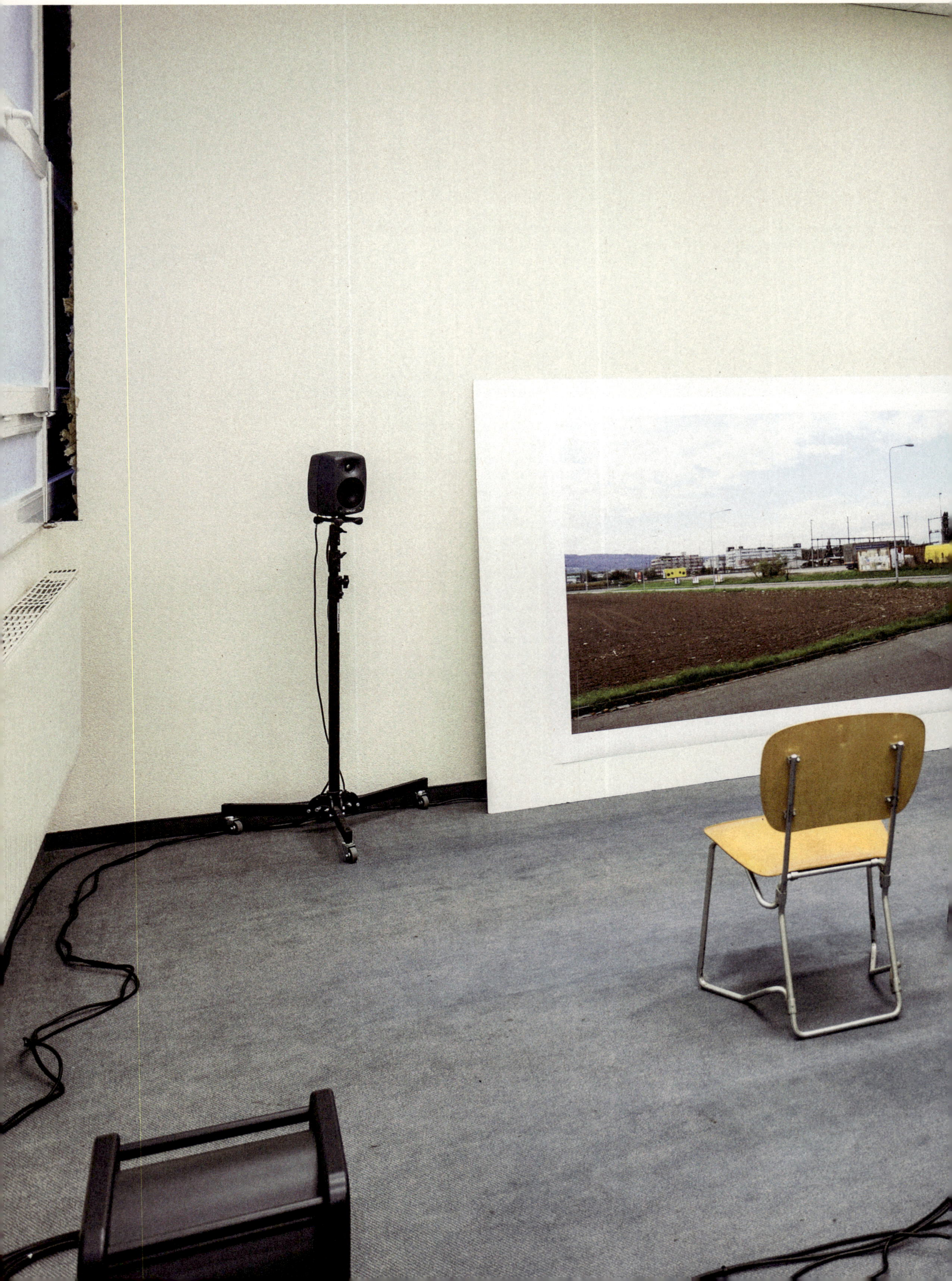

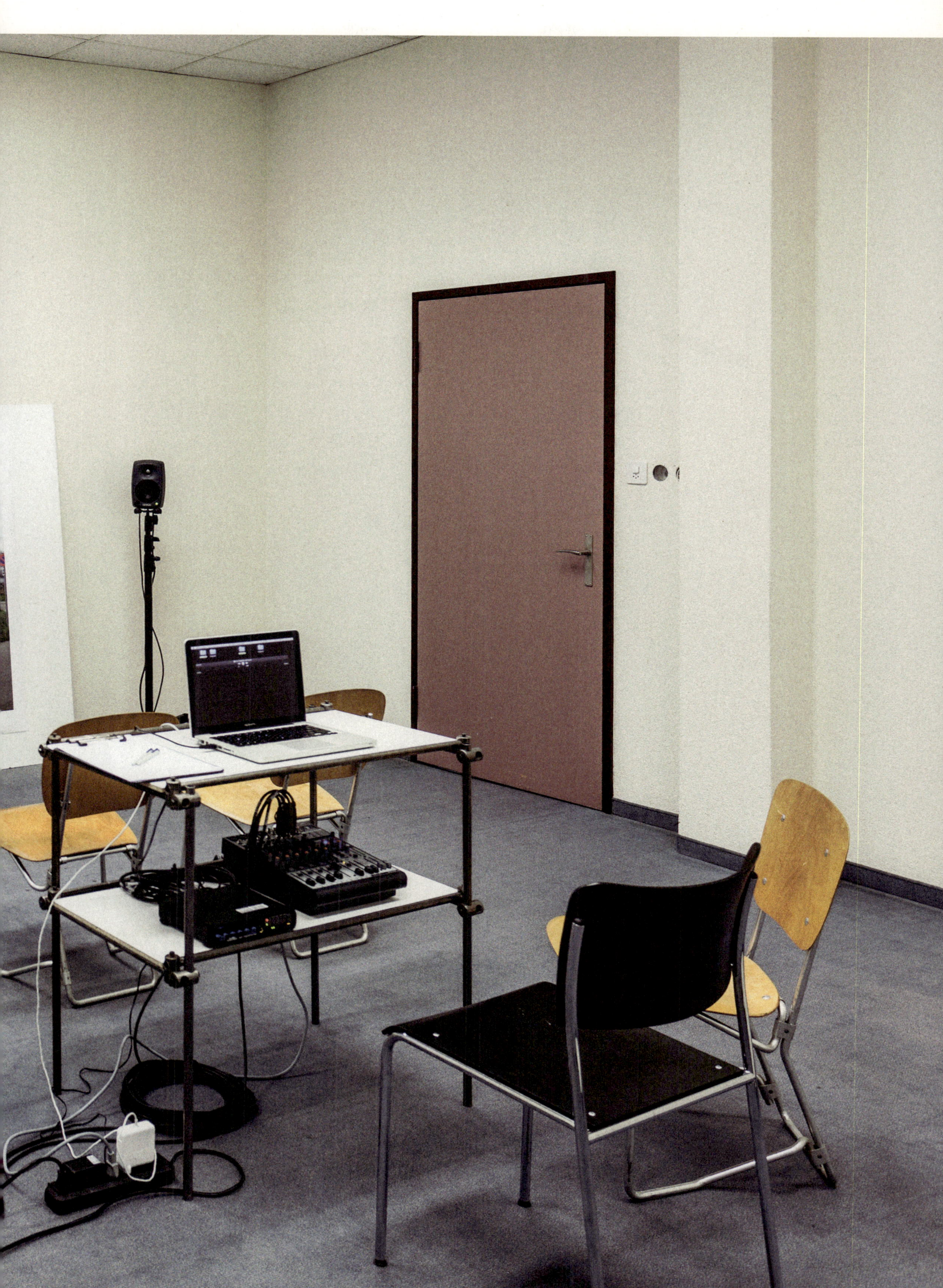

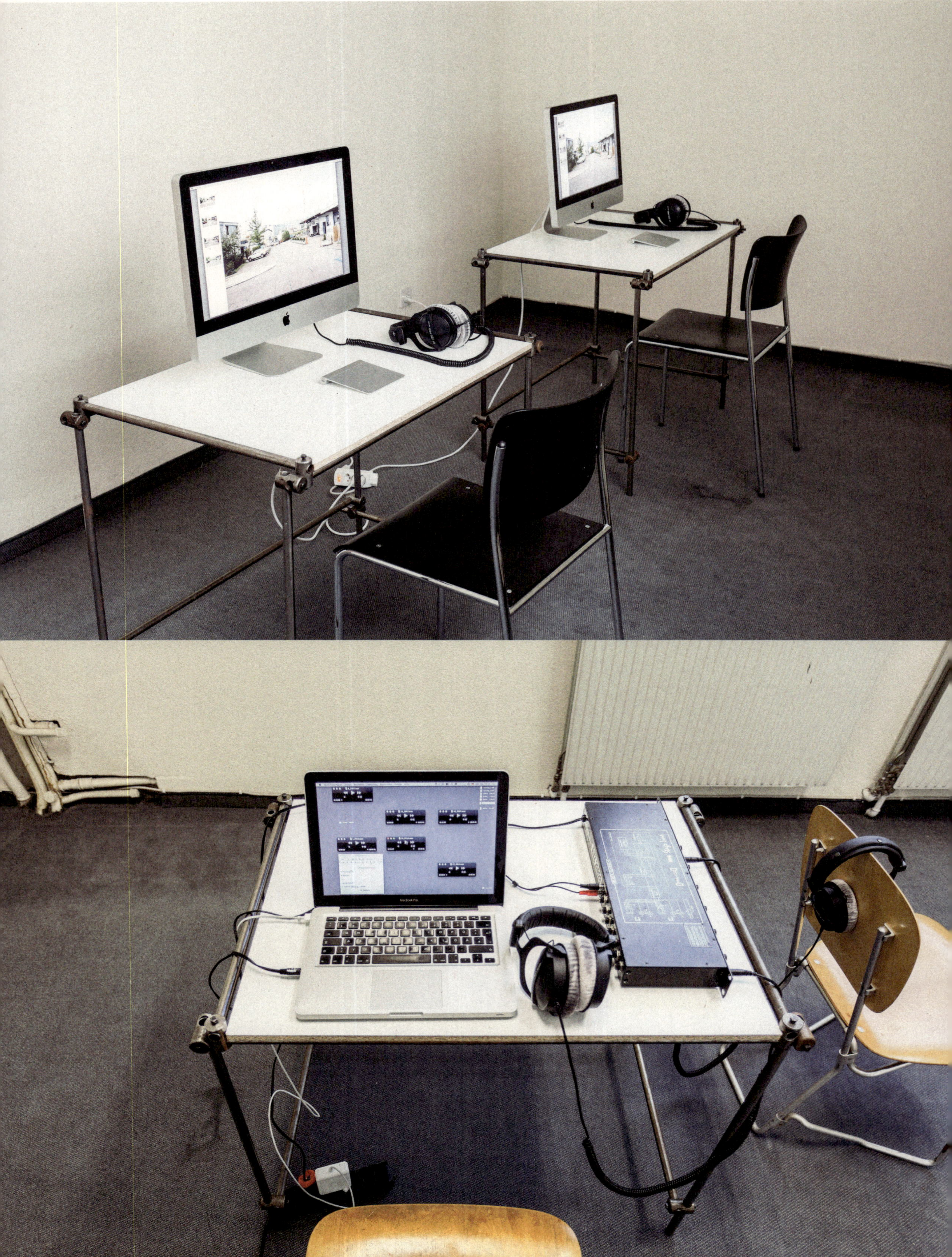

Fig. 4 Binaural sound recording with dummy head. Schlieren, 2017

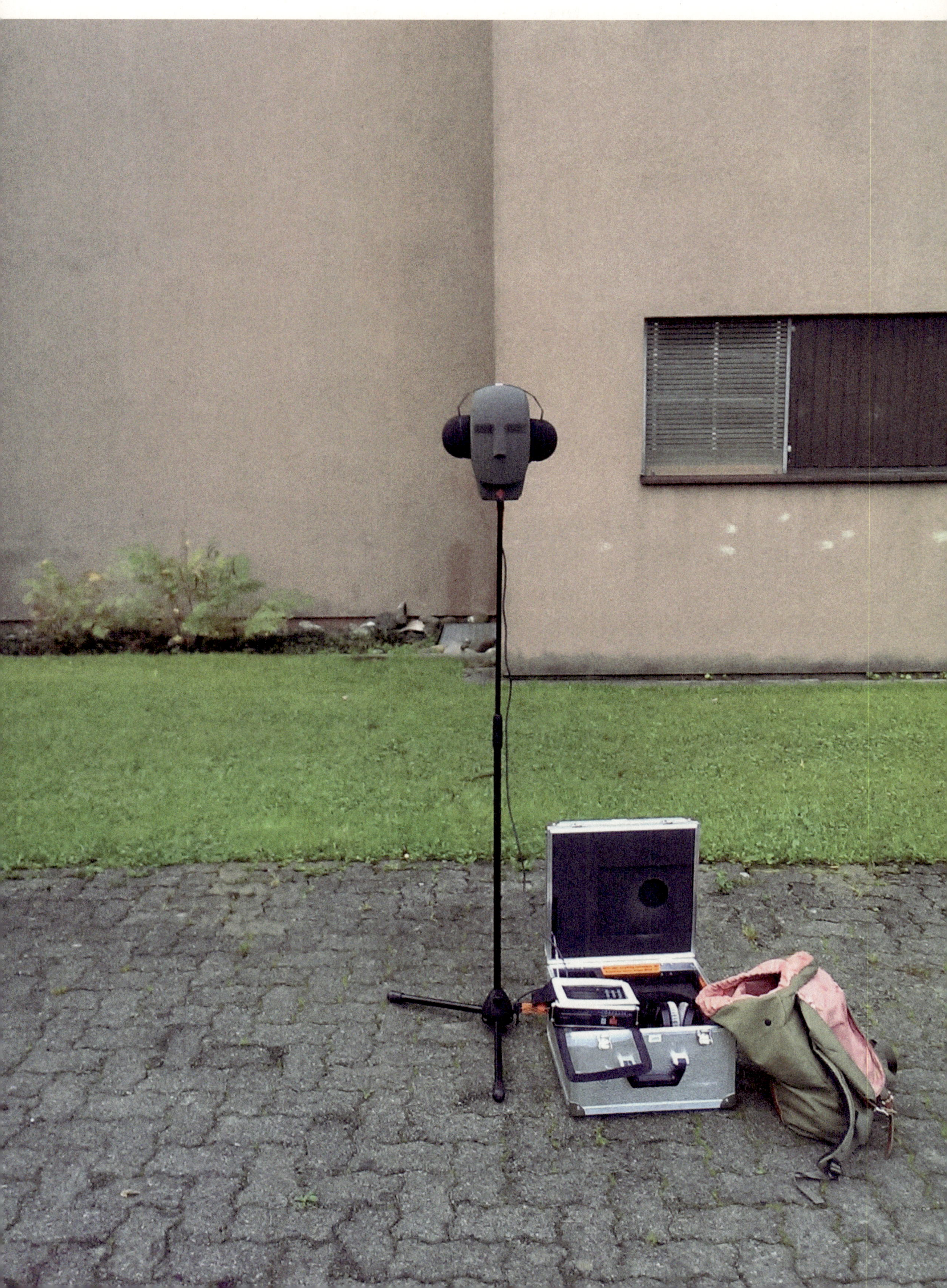

What impacts do artistic projects have on urban development? This was the initial question posed by *Bureau Savamala Belgrade*. In search of answers to this question, art scholars and social scientists from Belgrade and Zurich investigated the effects of the *Urban Incubator: Belgrade* excellence project launched by the Goethe Institute in Belgrade and conducted in cooperation with the ETH Zurich in the Savamala district of Belgrade. The project used artistic interventions in an attempt to sustainably shape the development of the heavily neglected district of Savamala in Belgrade.

Artists and creative types are frequently the unwitting midwives of urban renewal. Low rents, an inspiring atmosphere, and societal niches for alternative ways of life describe location qualities that attract the creative. While they may have little financial capital at their disposal, they invest a great deal of creative capital in their urban environment: in studios and galleries, clubs and bars, start-up companies and retail. The result is that formerly neglected urban districts are unexpectedly upgraded, often far beyond their own borders. For this reason, artists and creative people are often actively integrated in the revaluation of old buildings and desolate city neighborhoods—as was the case in Savamala. However, the consequences of such an approach are highly controversial. Critics argue that this kind of urban renewal appropriates the creative milieu for commercial and political purposes, contributing to gentrification and ultimately harming the neighborhoods and itself.

The *Bureau Savamala Belgrade* project accompanied and observed the artistic and creative contributions of the *Urban Incubator: Belgrade* project and those of other projects and events that took place in Savamala at the same time, in order to determine the extent to which they were able to contribute to socially sustainable neighborhood development. The project's focus was on the role of the arts within societal, especially urban, transformation processes. The project team was able to show how the neighborhood changed and how these changes were perceived by the residents and the broader public. They looked above all at the question of the extent to which a targeted revaluation by means of socio-artistic activities is possible without the usually inevitable gentrification that accompanies it.

Unfortunately, not all the activities undertaken by artists and architects were well received; they were often rejected entirely. In contrast, already familiar players like the new Mikser House design center and the *3rd Belgrade* art project continued to enjoy popular support. New experiments often had a hard time winning over the locals. In the end the project team had to conclude that socio-artistic activities led to hardly any relevant changes in the neighborhood that were positive for the residents.

The tools applied included discourse and media analyses; interviews with residents, municipal authorities, and other stakeholders; and photographic observations. A set of indicators was developed that was supposed to make it possible to measure and verify the strategies applied to upgrade the district.

The resulting data and documentations were compiled, archived, and exhibited in a publicly accessible office. This office understood itself to be what relational ethnography calls a "contact zone" between artists, residents, researchers, and the public. Appropriate premises were provided to the project team in Savamala by the Goethe Institute. Photos of residents of Savamala, created in the framework of the (sub) project called *Like/Dislike Savamala*, were exhibited inside and in front of the premises and annotated by the local population.

Jürgen Krusche

Project Title
Bureau Savamala Belgrade

Project Period
1 January 2013–31 December 2014

Keywords
- Gentrification
- Upgrading
- Urban studies
- Socio-artistic intervention
- Neighborhood development

Heads of Project
- Jürgen Krusche, artist and urbanologist
- Philipp Klaus, economic and social geographer

Research Team
- Dobrica Veselinović, political scientist and activist

Project Partners
- Goethe Institute Belgrade
- Ministry of Space, Belgrade

Project Funding
- Goethe Institute Belgrade

Outputs

A

Related Projects

- Labor Mülheim, Zurich University of the Arts, 2011–2013
  P. 126
- Politics of Space, Zurich University of the Arts, 2014–2018
  P. 158
- The Fragmented City, Zurich University of the Arts, 2017–2021
  P. 206

Publication

- Jürgen Krusche and Philipp Klaus (eds.) (2015): *Bureau Savamala Belgrade. Urban Research and Practice in a Fast-changing Neighborhood*. Volume 15 of the Institute for Contemporary Art Research series. Berlin: Jovis.
  A Open access: https://doi.org/10.5281/zenodo.5707105

Article

- Jürgen Krusche (2013): "Like/Dislike Savamala. Photo statements of the people of Savamala." In: *Kamenzind*, vol. 2, 48–68.

Fig. 1 Urban Incubator: Belgrade. Savamala, Belgrade, 2013

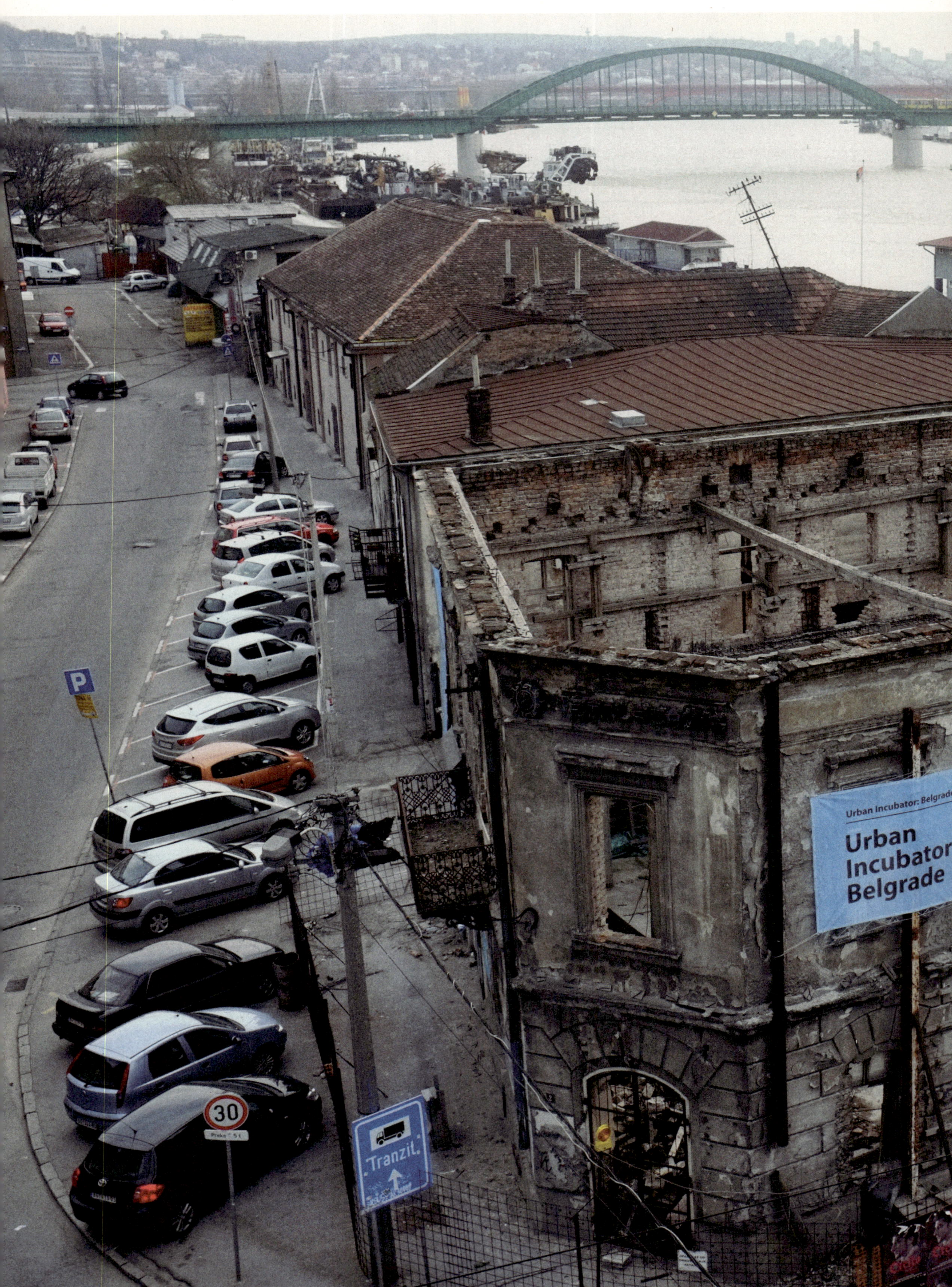

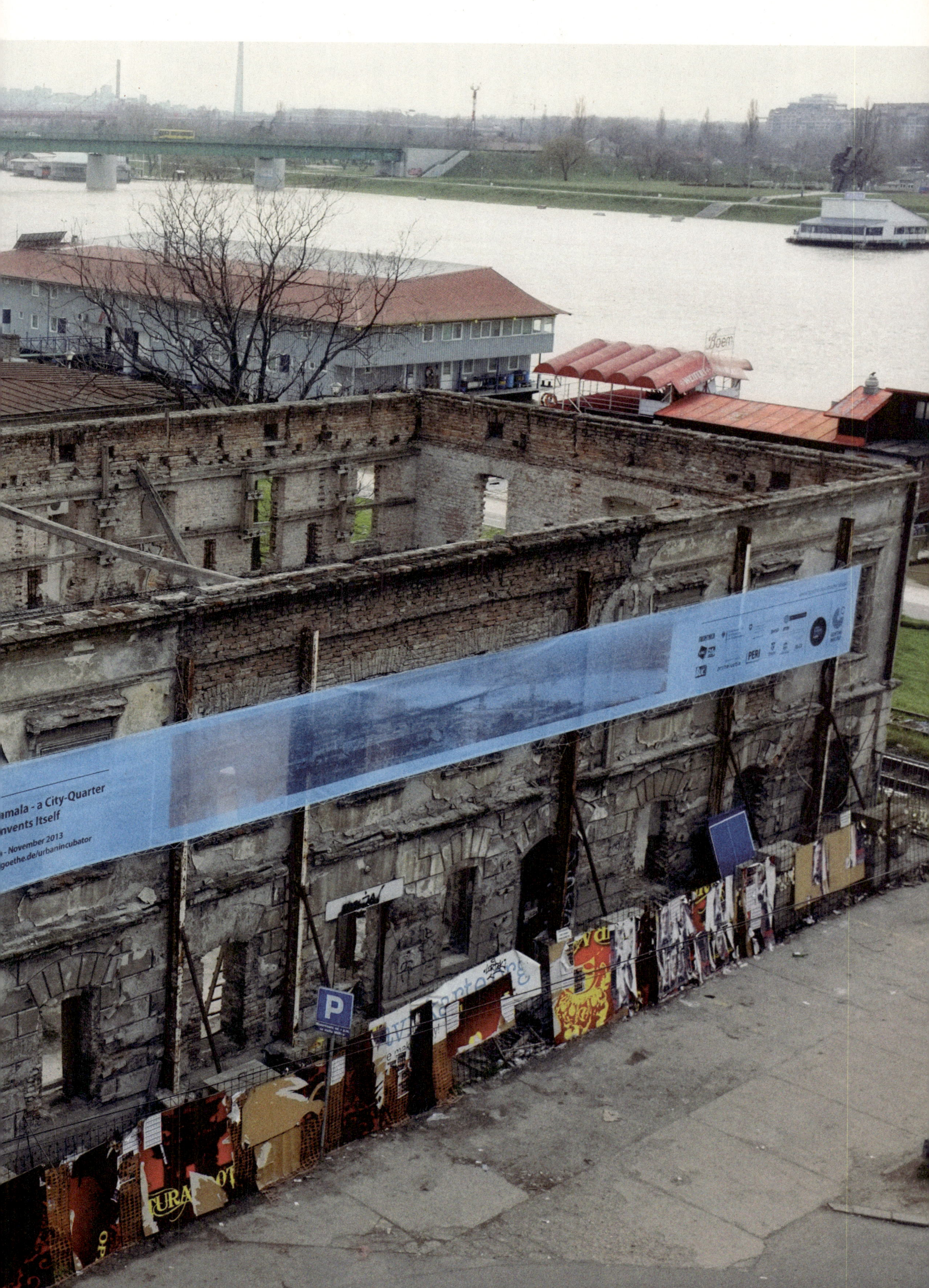
amala - a City-Quarter
nvents Itself
- November 2013
goethe.de/urbanincubator
P

Fig. 2–5 Urban transformations. Savamala, Belgrade, 2013

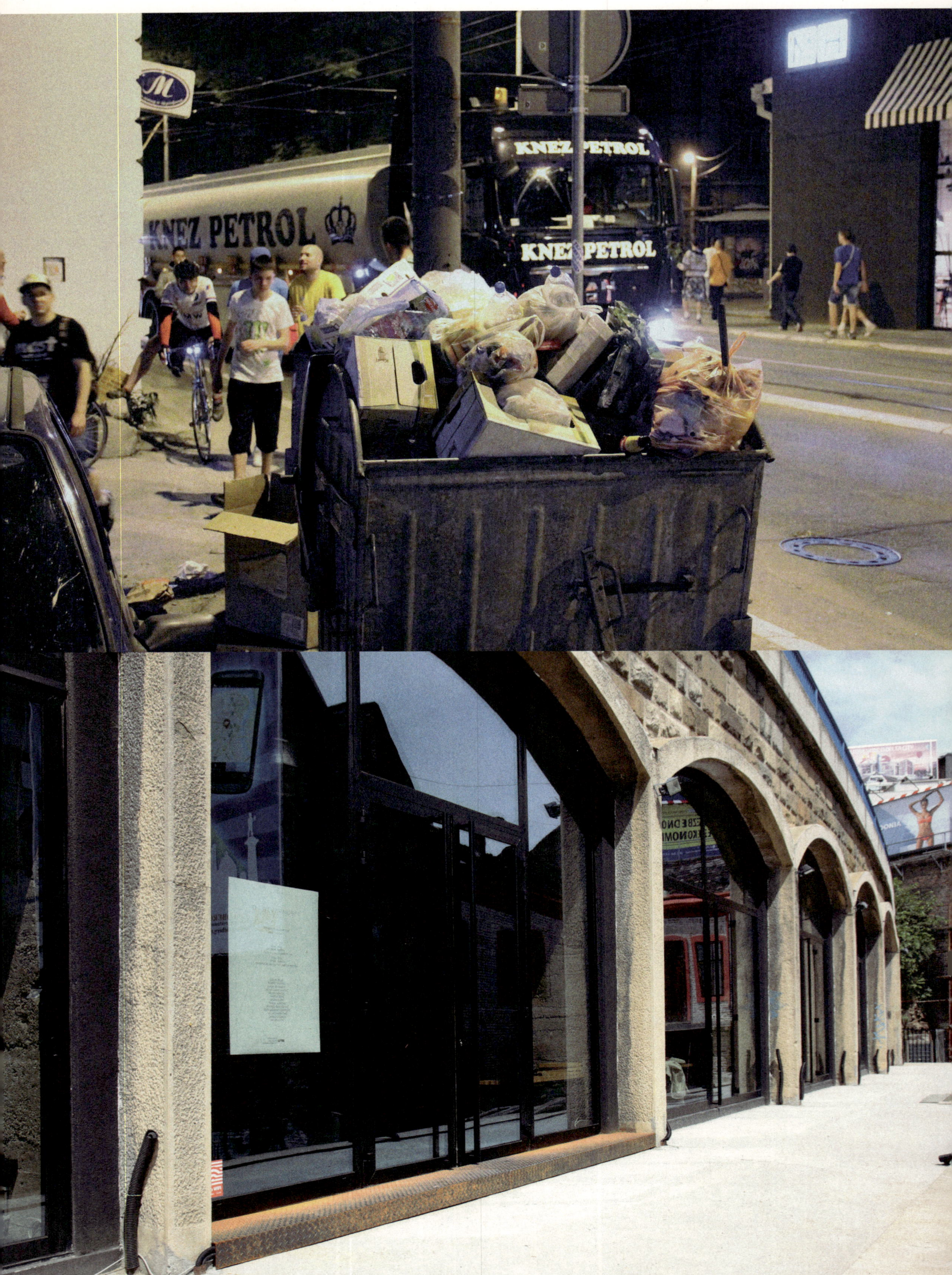

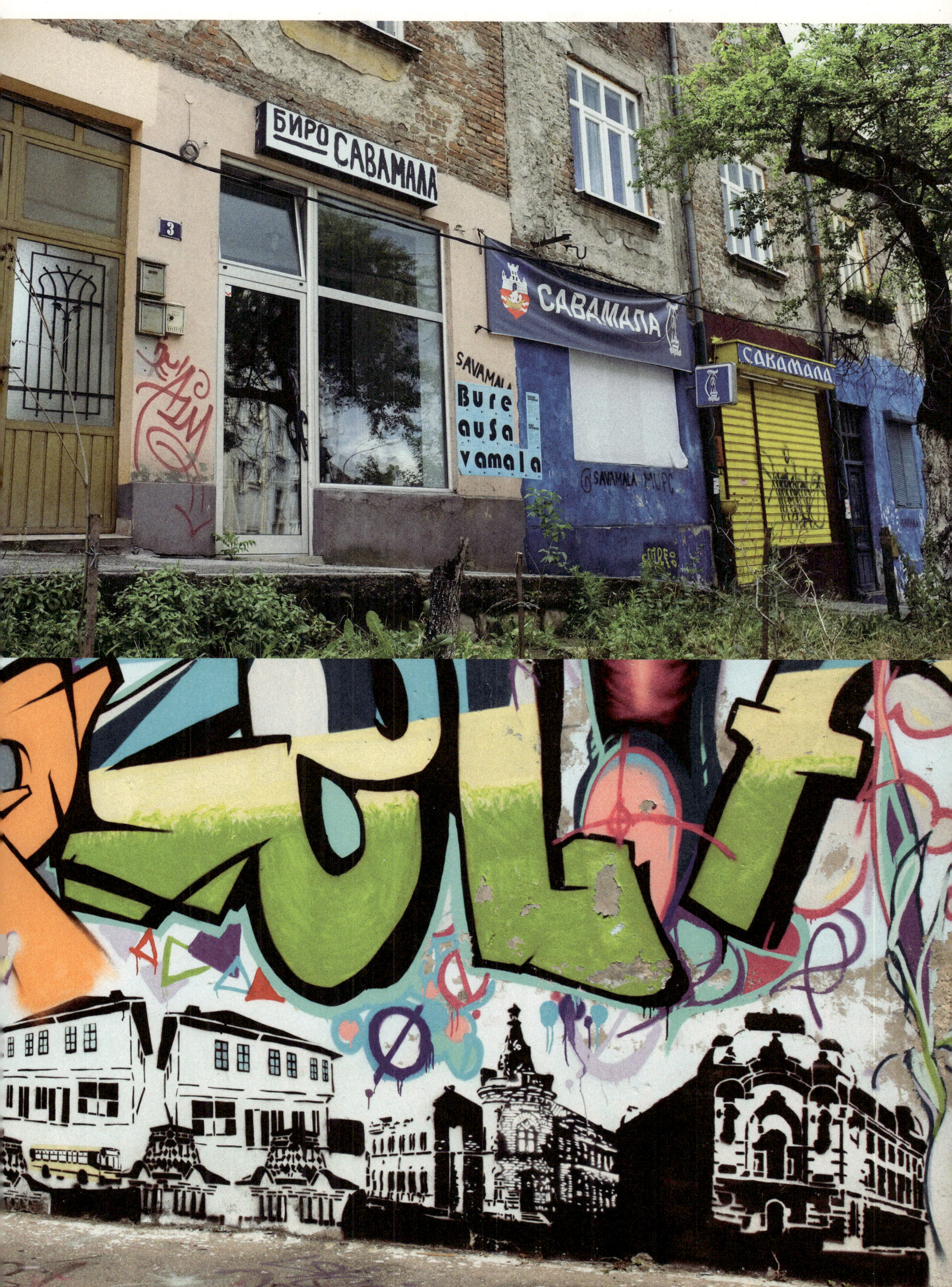
БИРО САВАМАЛА
САВАМАЛА
САВАМАЛА
SAVAMALA
Bure
auSa
vamala

Immediations: Art, Media and Event is a partnership grant that was sponsored from 2013 until 2020 by the Social Science and Humanities Research Council of Canada (SSHRC), comprising eleven universities in Canada, Denmark, Australia, Germany, Switzerland, and the Netherlands, along with nineteen partners including artist-run centers, galleries, and museums. The goal of the project was to investigate immanent relations between physical and media experience in various material, digital, and urban contexts. The project's central question was: How can experience be conceived in the sense of an indirectly lived encounter as a basis for and technique of aesthetic research? The concept of "immediation" was used to interrogate the relations between perception, embodiment, mediation, and conceptualization with regard to their shared processes of emergence that are simultaneously direct and mediated. The cooperation with scientific, artistic, and public institutions allowed experience, previously regarded as a rather abstract philosophical concept, to be investigated in terms of its sensory "mediability."

One goal was to integrate general audiences outside of academia; another was to develop procedures, methods, and techniques of "research-creation" to encourage new forms of knowledge and practices beyond the classic discursive modes of representation. On the theoretical level, approaches from affect studies and political aesthetics were interlaced with artistic practices and their institutional framings. The formats realized in the project, such as workshops, symposia, publications, collaborative digital working structures, and online platforms, opened up an ecological take on media and art, and foregrounded a concept of experience that picks up on the contemporary debates in artistic research. The project was divided into hubs along the three original geographic zones —North America, Europe and Australia—and structured in three thematic work phases which addressed different issues:

1. *Recomposing Experience* (Australia, 2013–2014): How do new creative practices between art, philosophy and society change the understanding of experience and perception, and with what political and social consequences?
2. *Anarchive* (Europe, 2015–2016): What forms of archiving and documenting are needed in order to do justice to the innovative power of research-creation activities?
3. *Event Ecologies* (Canada, 2017–2019): What possibilities are opened up by an expanded concept of the ecology of research-creation and the understanding of transdisciplinary knowledge practices?

Although different activities were performed in various work phases, at least one interhub meeting took place during each phase. These meetings were dedicated especially to testing experimental methods of research-creation and integrating them in research, teaching, and art production. External guests were usually invited for workshops, inputs, and lectures. In the context of the EU hub, monthly reading groups took place between 2013 and 2016, and working meetings with lectures and elements of artistic practice were held in various locations in Europe.

Through its connections between methods of artistic research with media and affect theory approaches, the project contributed to transdisciplinary scholarship on "research-creation" in the European context. Institutional networks were reinforced, especially between Zurich, Amsterdam, Copenhagen, Aarhus and Lüneburg. The middle phase of the project, which took place primarily at the Institute for Contemporary Art Research (IFCAR) in Zurich, placed its thematic emphasis on the *Anarchive* and was closely linked with the project plans of Elke Bippus and Michel Hiltbrunner. The research performed in this project hub played a decisive role for the project as a whole.

Christoph Brunner

Project Title
Immediations: Art, Media, Event. EU Hub, Zurich Node

Project Period
1 March 2013–29 February 2020

Keywords
- Research creation
- Affect
- Aesthetics
- Media cultures
- Speculative pragmatism

Head of Project
- Christoph Brunner, philosopher and cultural researcher

Research Team
- Nicole De Brabandere, artist and cultural researcher
- Amélie Brisson-Darveau, artist
- Verena Ziegler, designer
- Sebastian Dieterich, philosopher and historian

Research Partners
- Aarhus University
- Bauhaus-Universität Weimar
- IT University of Copenhagen
- McGill University
- RMIT University
- Université de Montréal
- Université du Québec à Montréal
- University of Amsterdam
- DAS Arts Amsterdam
- UNSW Sydney
- Deakin University Melbourne

Outputs

Project Partners (European Hub)
- Designskolen Kolding
- European Institute for Progressive Cultural Policies, Vienna
- Gerrit Rietveld Academie
- Godsbanen, Aarhus
- Het Veem Theater, Amsterdam
- Raumstation, Zurich
- Corner College, Zurich

Project Funding
- Concordia University
- Social Science and Humanities Research Council of Canada (SSHRC)

Related Projects
- Mediale Teilhabe (FOR 2252), DFG Forschungsgruppe, Universität Konstanz

Website
- http://senselab.ca/wp2/immediations

Publications
- Stavning Thomsen, Bodil Marie, Anna Munster, and Erin Manning (eds.) (2019): *Immediation Vol. I* and *Vol. II*. London: Open Humanities Press.
  Open access:
  A Vol. I http://library.oapen.org/handle/20.500.12657/23509
  B Vol. II http://library.oapen.org/handle/20.500.12657/23508
- Amélie Brisson-Darveau and Christoph Brunner (eds.) (2021): *Texturing Space: Towards an Exponential Cartography*. Hamburg: adocs Verlag. With contributions by Amélie Brisson-Darveau, Christoph Brunner, Nicole De Brabandere, Sher Doruff, Rosamund Ender, Marius Förster, Karmen Franinovic, Diego Gil, Roman Kirschner, Nuria Krämer, Yanki Lee, Erin Manning, Mariana Marcassa, Brian Massumi, Patrick Müller, Toni Pape, Peter Tränkle, and Jana Vanecek.

Article
- Christoph Brunner and Michael Hiltbrunner (2017): "Anarchive künstlerischer Forschung. Vom Umgang mit Archiven experimenteller und forschender Kunst." In: *Archivalische Zeitschrift* 95, 175–190.

Workshops
- *Water Ecologies*. 17–19 April 2014. EU hub event, DAS Arts Amsterdam.
- *Immediations—Urban Fabric, Infrastructure, Ecology*. 26–30 April 2014. Zurich University of the Arts and Corner College Zurich.
- *Techniques of Landing*. 30 April–3 May 2015. EU hub event, Aarhus/Mols, Mols Laboratoriet, Goesbanen (Denmark).
- *The Affecto-Meter*. 24–27 August 2017. Interhub meeting, Universität Weimar, IKKM.
- *Breath, Care and Surround—A Workshop on the Singular-Plural*. 17–18 November 2018. Raumstation, Zurich. With Helvetia Leal and Max Heinrich.
- *Instituent Noise and the Sensibility Soup for Collective Care*. 5–7 July 2019. Raumstation, Zurich. With Helvetia Leal and Max Heinrich.

Conferences
- *The Diagrammatic Practice of the Micropolitical—the Spatiotemporal Expression of Play between Power, Knowledge and the Aesthetics of Existence*. 14–16 November 2013. Zurich University of the Arts and Dimitrina Sevova. With Paolo Caffoni, Giusy Checola, Binna Choi, discoteca flaming star (Cristina Gómez Barrio and Wolfgang Mayer), David Dibosa, Anja Kanngieser, Maurizio Lazzarato, Isabell Lorey, m-a-u-s-e-r (Mona Mahall & Aslı Serbest), Carmen Mörsch, Daniel Morgenthaler, Roberto Nigro, Susanna Perin (S.M.U.R.), Gerald Raunig, Adrian Rifkin, Kerstin Schroedinger, Marco Scotini, Diego Segatto, Joshua Simon, Kuba Szreder, Axel Wieder, Espace Temporaire (Magdalena Ybarguen), Jens Badura, Christoph Brunner, Karmen Franinović, Roberto Nigro, Romy Rüegger, Dimitrina Sevova, Chiara Fumai, T. Melih Görgün, Michael Hiltbrunner, Franziska Koch, David Maroto, Marcelo Expósito, Silvia Maglioni and Graeme Thomson, RELAX (chiarenza & hauser & co), Wiktoria Furrer, and Sebastian Dieterich, in cooperation with Elke Bippus.
- *Matter, Memory, and the More-than-Human: New Materialist Perspectives in the Age of the Anthropocene*. 27–28 November 2014. Zurich University of the Arts. With contributions by Heather Davis, Ridvan Askin, Stamatia Portanova, and Joel McKim.

Fig. 1 *Urban Fabric*. Workshop, Corner College, Zurich, 2014
Fig. 2 *A Collaboration of Intercessors*. Adapt-r Creative Practice Conference, KU Leuven Sint-Lucas, Brussels, 2014

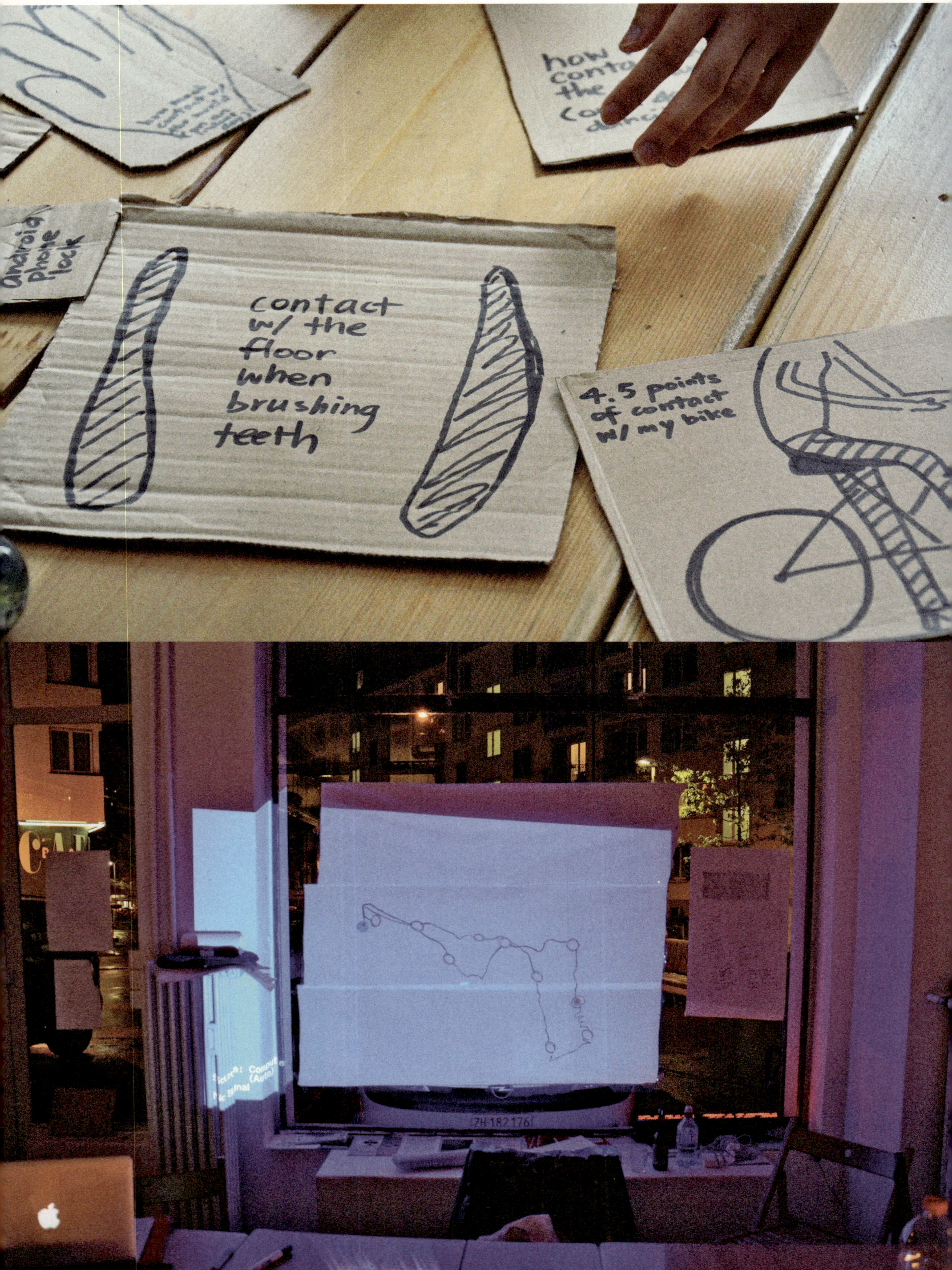

Fig. 3 *Urban Fabric*. Workshop, Corner College, Zurich, 2014
Fig. 4 *Knotting Time beyond Measure*. SARN Unconference, HEAD Geneva, 2014

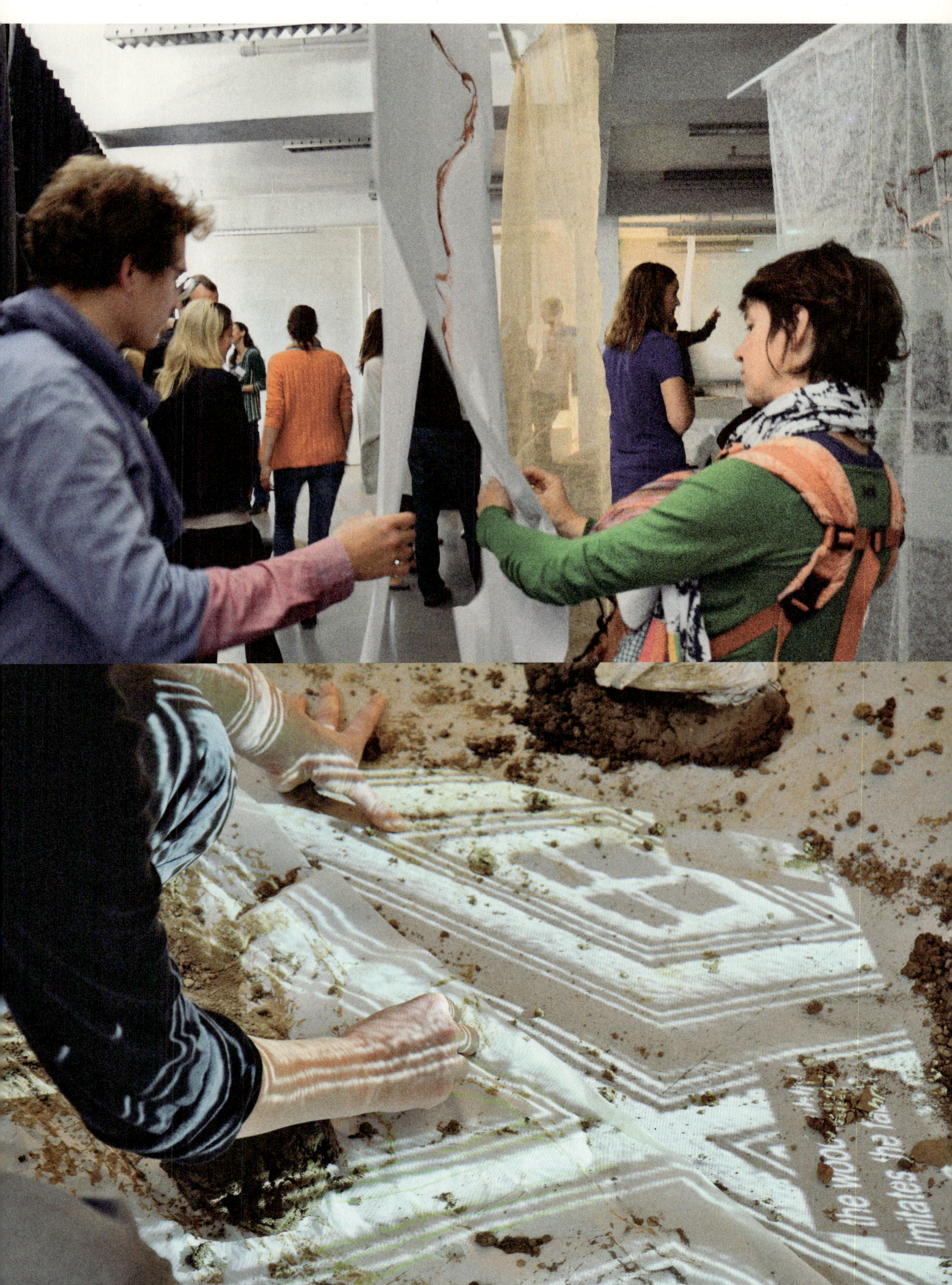

Fig. 5 *Urban Fabric*. Workshop, Corner College, Zurich, 2014
Fig. 6 *Water Ecologies*. Workshop, Amsterdam University of the Arts, 2015

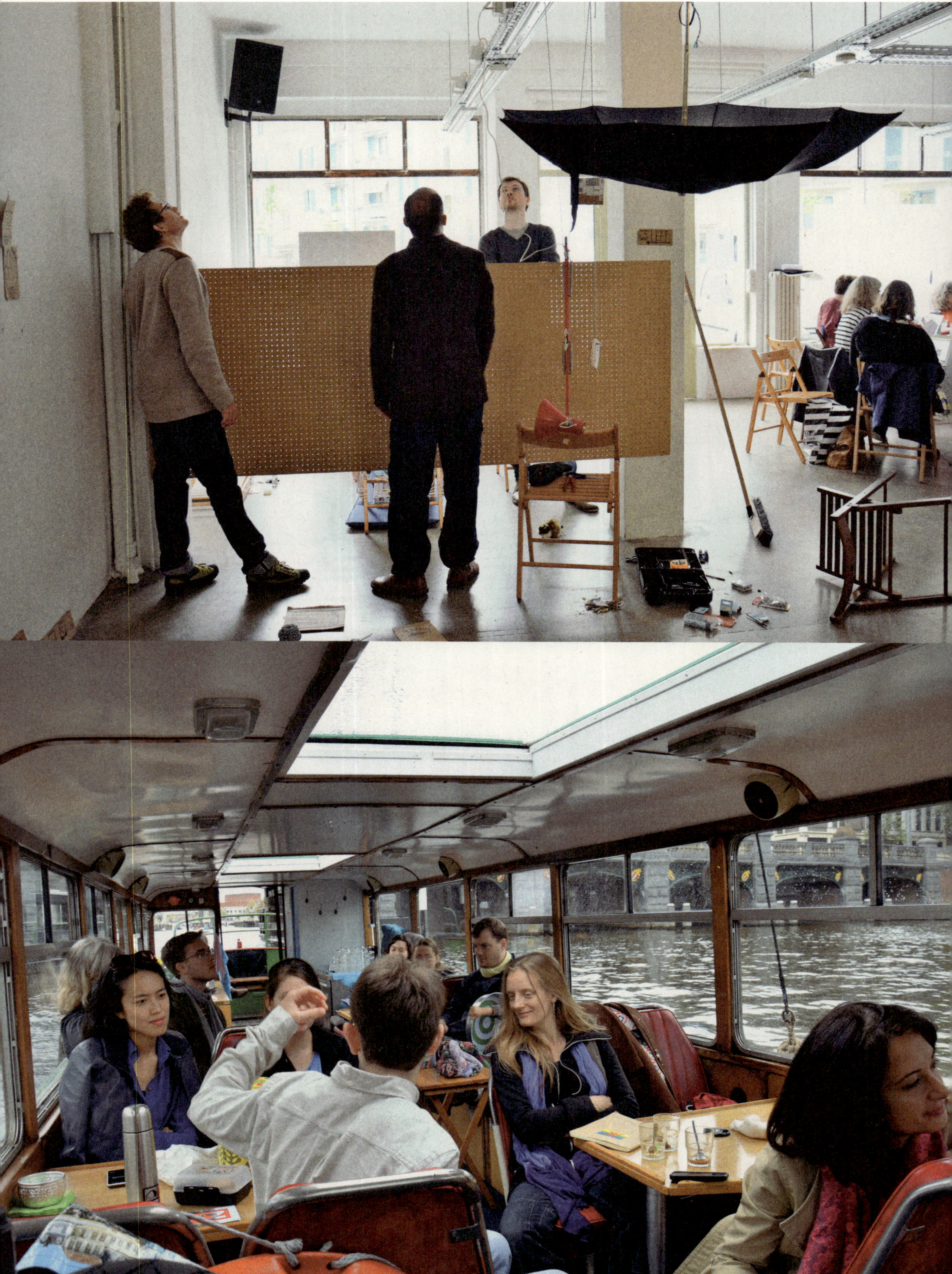

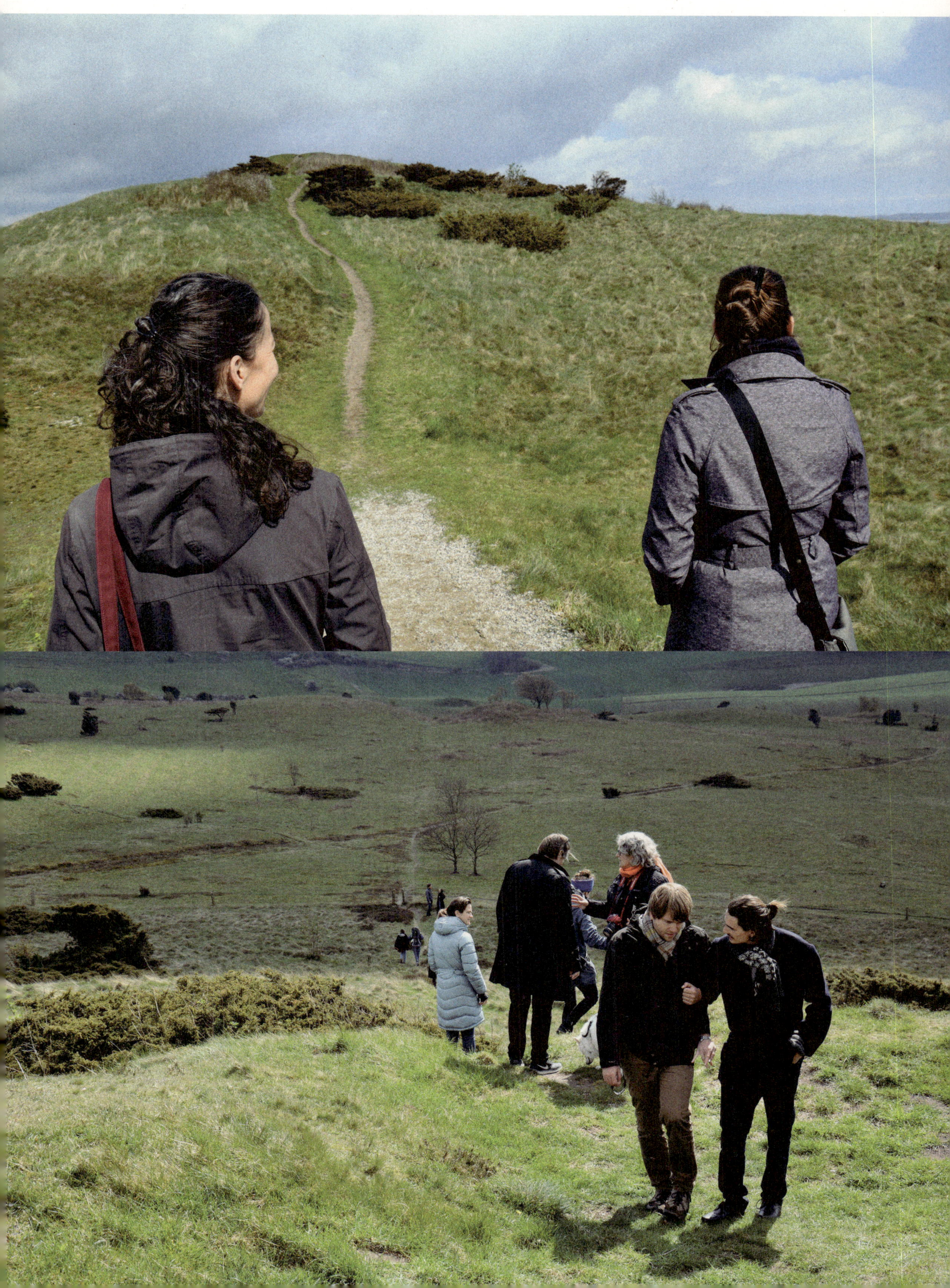

The research project *Archives on Research-based Art* delved into the archives of artists whose artistic practice indicated that they were less interested in making works than in dedicating themselves to exploring longer-term research projects. Archives of this kind are of major importance for the history and presence of research-based art. Because they are accessible only to their makers, they are often actually "anarchives" that provide insight into the character, meaning, and means of documentation of artistic work, as well as into artistic mediation and teaching. The project succeeded in preserving previously overlooked archives of artists who adhered to this artistic role, increasing their visibility.

Archives on Research-based Art proceeded from the indexing of the archive of Serge Stauffer (1929–1989), which was undertaken in the framework of the SNSF project *Serge Stauffer: Art as Research* in 2013–2014. In several subprojects, Michael Hiltbrunner and his team investigated forms and methods of self-documentation by artists. The focus was on the archive collections of Liliane Csuka, Robert A. Fischer, Hansjörg Mattmüller, Doris Stauffer, and Peter Trachsel, as well as the Marcel Duchamp archive collected by Serge Stauffer.

For the study, the team was able to secure multiple collections on the F+F School of Experimental Design in Zurich, which were of particular interest for the research project: The archive of artist, feminist, and co-founder of the F+F School Doris Stauffer (1934–2017) was reviewed in collaboration with its author. In accordance with her request, the archive was indexed posthumously as part of the Serge and Doris Stauffer Archive in the Swiss National Library's Prints and Drawings Department (NB) in Bern. The interim storage of her archive was made possible by the Zurich University of the Arts (ZHdK) Archive. Michael Hiltbrunner also contributed to the monograph (2015) on Doris Stauffer by Simone Koller and Mara Züst.

The archive of artist Peter Trachsel (1949–2013) was indexed in the Staatsarchiv Graubünden; subsequently the Bündner Kunstmuseum in Chur showed an exhibition based on this archive in 2018. Michael Hiltbrunner edited the monograph *Wir muten Ihnen alles zu – Peter Trachsel und die Hasena* (2018). After studying and teaching at the F+F School, Peter Trachsel established the Hasena as a platform for experimental art in Küblis (GR), where his projects contributed both to research-based art and to expanding rural art in a unique way.

The inventory of artist and F+F co-founder Hansjörg Mattmüller (1923–2006) was conveyed to the ZHdK Archive, where it was indexed with the existing collections. For artist Liliane Csuka (*1935), who had studied and taught at F+F, a work documentation was compiled. For this, the first step was to go through the archival material with the artist and then sort, label, and take a rough inventory of its contents. Her archive was passed on to the Stadtarchiv Zürich.

The work on the archive of journalist, media theorist, and artist Robert A. Fischer (1942–2001) required a well-founded situation analysis and a review of the archive before missing descriptions could be added and a rough inventory performed. Subsequently, the archive was transferred to the Zentralbibliothek Zürich, thus making Fischer's studies on media art, media ethnography, and documents on Zurich's fringe art scene around Plattenstrasse available to the public.

The exhibition on Marcel Duchamp (1887–1968) in the Staatsgalerie Stuttgart, founded on the archive of Serge Stauffer, was realized in consultation with Michael Hiltbrunner, who also contributed essays to the catalog. In addition, Hiltbrunner supervised the new edition of Marcel Duchamp's writings translated by Serge Stauffer. Furthermore, Hiltbrunner accompanied the auctioning of three works by Duchamp from Stauffer's estate at the Auktionshaus Grisebach in Berlin in 2021.

Michael Hiltbrunner

Project Title
Archive forschender Kunst (Liliane Csuka, Marcel Duchamp, Robert A. Fischer, Hansjörg Mattmüller, Doris Stauffer, Peter Trachsel)

Project Period
1 June 2013–31 October 2020

Keywords
- Artist archive
- Artistic research
- Cultural memory
- Artist
- F+F School

Head of Project
- Michael Hiltbrunner, art researcher and cultural anthropologist

Research Team
- Marc Matter, author and sound artist
- Pablo Müller, art historian and art critic

Project Partners
- Liliane Csuka, artist and art sponsor
- Jessie Fischer, filmmaker (estate of Robert A. Fischer)
- Doris Stauffer, artist and educator
- Aargauer Kunsthaus
- Bündner Kunstmuseum
- Stadt Zürich, Fachstelle Kunstsammlung
- Stadtarchiv Zürich
- The Swiss National Library's Prints and Drawings Department
- Staatsarchiv Graubünden
- Scheidegger & Spiess publishers
- Zurich University of the Arts, ZHdK Archive

Project Funding
- Edition Patrick Frey (Archiv Robert A. Fischer)
- Stiftung für fliessenden Kunstverkehr (Archiv Peter Trachsel)
- Georg und Bertha Schwyzer-Winiker-Stiftung (Archiv Doris Stauffer)
- UBS Kulturstiftung (Archiv Doris Stauffer)
- Private parties

Related Projects
- Serge Stauffer, Zurich University of the Arts, 2011–2014
  P. 110
- F+F 1971, Zurich University of the Arts, 2020–2022
  P. 252

Publications
- Michael Hiltbrunner and Stiftung für fliessenden Kunstverkehr (eds.) (2018): *Wir muten Ihnen alles zu. Peter Trachsel und die Hasena*. Zurich: Scheidegger & Spiess.
- Serge Stauffer (ed.) (2018): *Marcel Duchamp: Die Schriften*. Revised and extended new edition. Afterword and editing by Michael Hiltbrunner. Konstanz: Regenbogen.

Essays
- Michael Hiltbrunner (2015): "The Cthulhu News." In: Helmhaus Zürich (ed.): *Das Dreieck der Liebe*. Exhibition catalog. Zurich: Scheidegger & Spiess, 22–25.
- Michael Hiltbrunner (2015): "Serge Stauffer. Biografisches und Emanzipatorisches." In: Simone Koller and Mara Züst (eds.): *Doris Stauffer. Eine Monografie*. Zurich: Scheidegger & Spiess, 43–46.
- Christoph Brunner and Michael Hiltbrunner (2017): "Anarchive künstlerischer Forschung. Vom Umgang mit Archiven experimenteller und forschender Kunst." In: Generaldirektion der Staatlichen Archive Bayerns (ed.): *Archivalische Zeitschrift*. Volume 95. Munich: Böhlau, 175–190.
- Michael Hiltbrunner (2018): "Serge Stauffer and the Exhibition Documentation about Marcel Duchamp." In: Staatsgalerie Stuttgart and Susanne M. I. Kaufmann (eds.): *Marcel Duchamp. 100 Questions. 100 Answers*. Munich: Prestel, 252–259.

Conferences and Workshop
- *Art in the Periphery/Strategien im ländlichen Raum*. 22 June 2018. Conference on the occasion of the *Peter Trachsel – Museum in Bewegung* exhibition at the Bündner Kunstmuseum Chur, Passagenhaus Dalvazza, Küblis. Moderation: Michael Hiltbrunner.
- *Künstler fragen Künstler – Marcel Duchamp, chocolatier?* 23 February 2019. Workshop on the occasion of the exhibition *Marcel Duchamp. 100 Fragen. 100 Antworten*. Staatsgalerie and Künstlerhaus Stuttgart. With Abel Auer, Marc Matter, Birgit Megerle, and Elena Poulou. Moderated by Michael Hiltbrunner, Susanne Kaufmann, and Fatima Hellberg.
- *Publishing and archival strategies in artistic practices (The example of Peter Trachsel archive)*. 30 November 2019. Conference on the occasion of *Volumes—Art publishing days*. Kunsthalle Zürich. With Anne-Laure Franchette, Alois Baumberger, Bia Bittencourt, Sally De Kunst, Claudia de la Torre, Anita Di Bianco, and Birgit Kempker. Moderated by Michael Hiltbrunner and Gina De Micheli.

Exhibition
- *Peter Trachsel – Tun was möglich ist*. 31 August–22 September 2019. Fundaziun Nairs, Scuol. Curated by Michael Hiltbrunner and Christof Rösch.

Archives
- *Archiv Peter Trachsel*. Staatsarchiv Graubünden, 2016
- *Archiv Hansjörg Mattmüller*. ZHdK Archive, 2017
- *Archiv Liliane Csuka*. Stadtarchiv Zürich, 2019
- *Archiv Doris Stauffer*. The Swiss National Library's Prints and Drawings Department, 2019

Fig. 1 Liliane Csuka in the studio, 2018
Fig. 2 Rudolf de Crignis and Peter Trachsel: *visualisierter – zeit – gedanke*, 1973

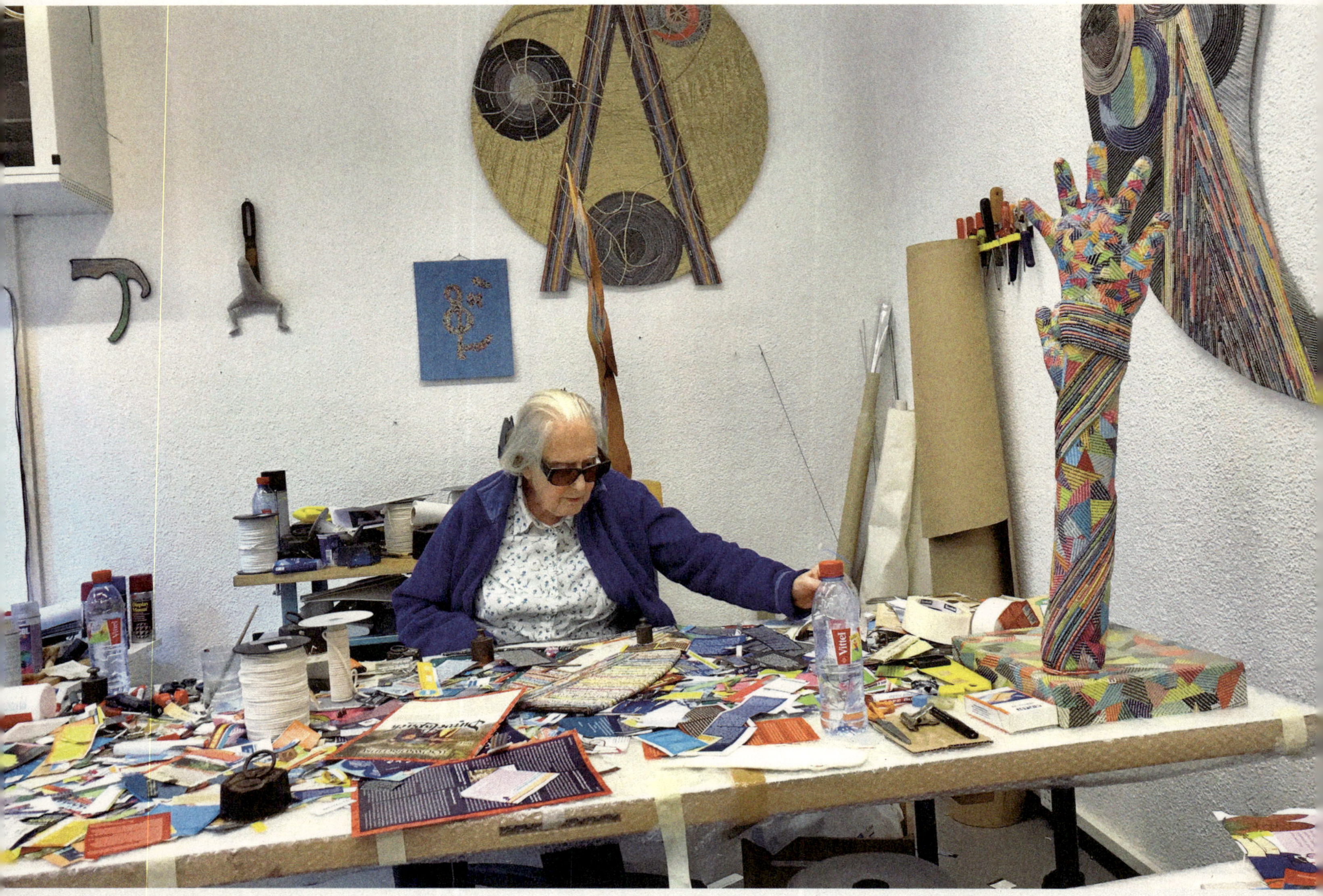

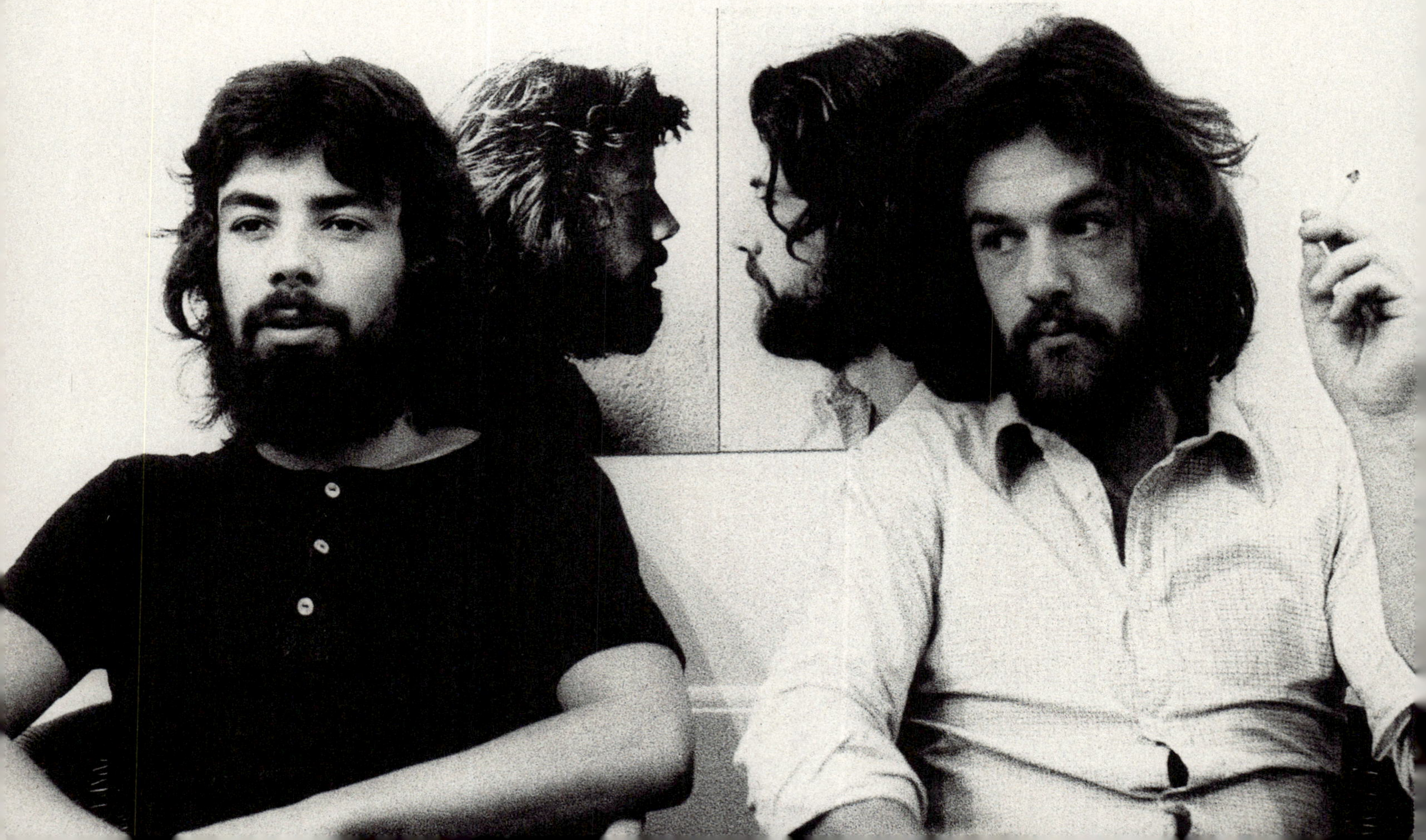

Fig. 3–4 "Witch course" with Doris Stauffer. F+F Schule, Zurich, 1977

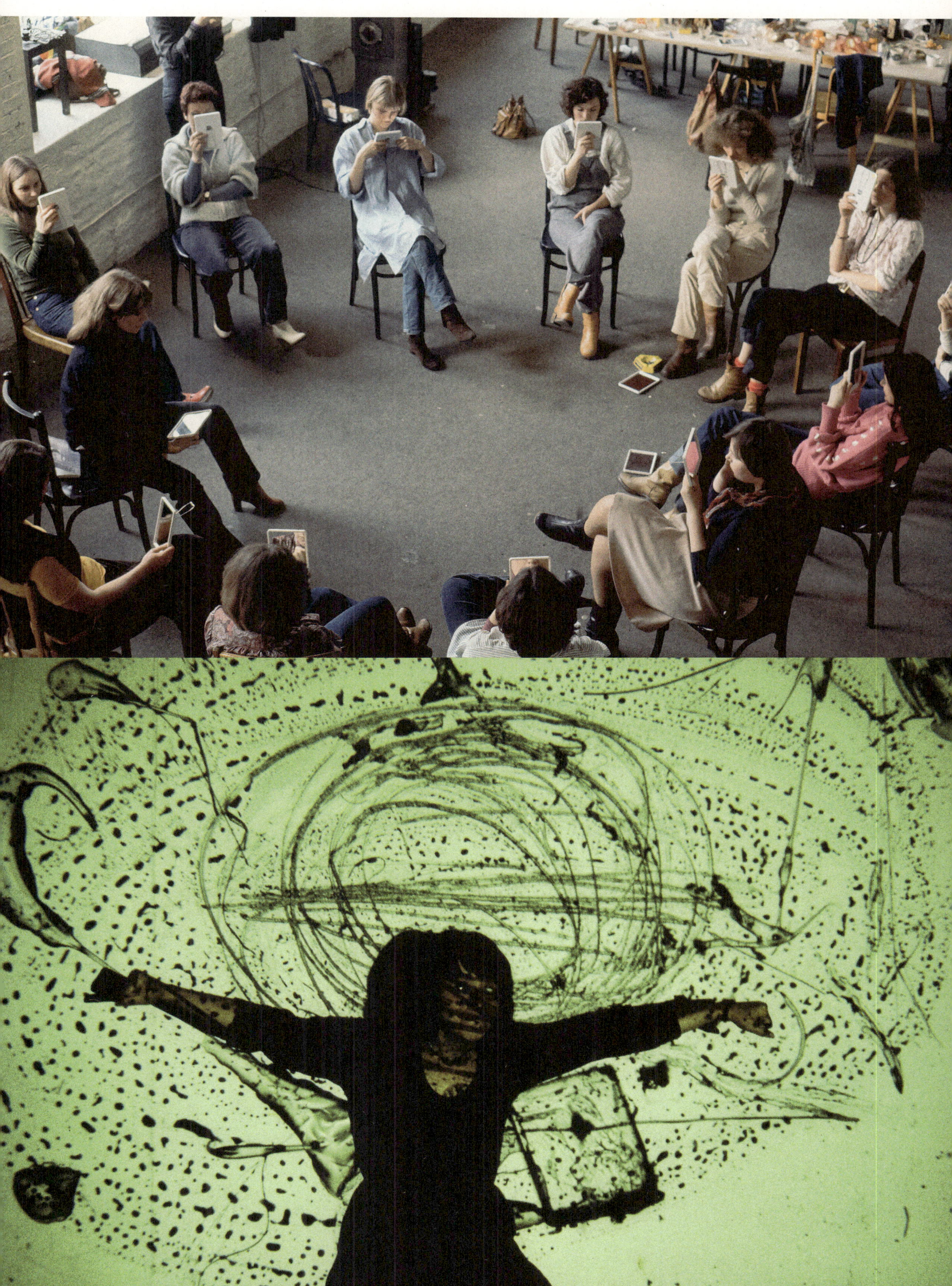

Fig. 5 Doris Stauffer Archive. Prints and Drawings Department, NL, Bern, 2019
Fig. 6 Teamwork with Doris Stauffer. Women's liberation movement protest against a beauty pageant. F+F Class, Kunstgewerbeschule, Zürich, 1969

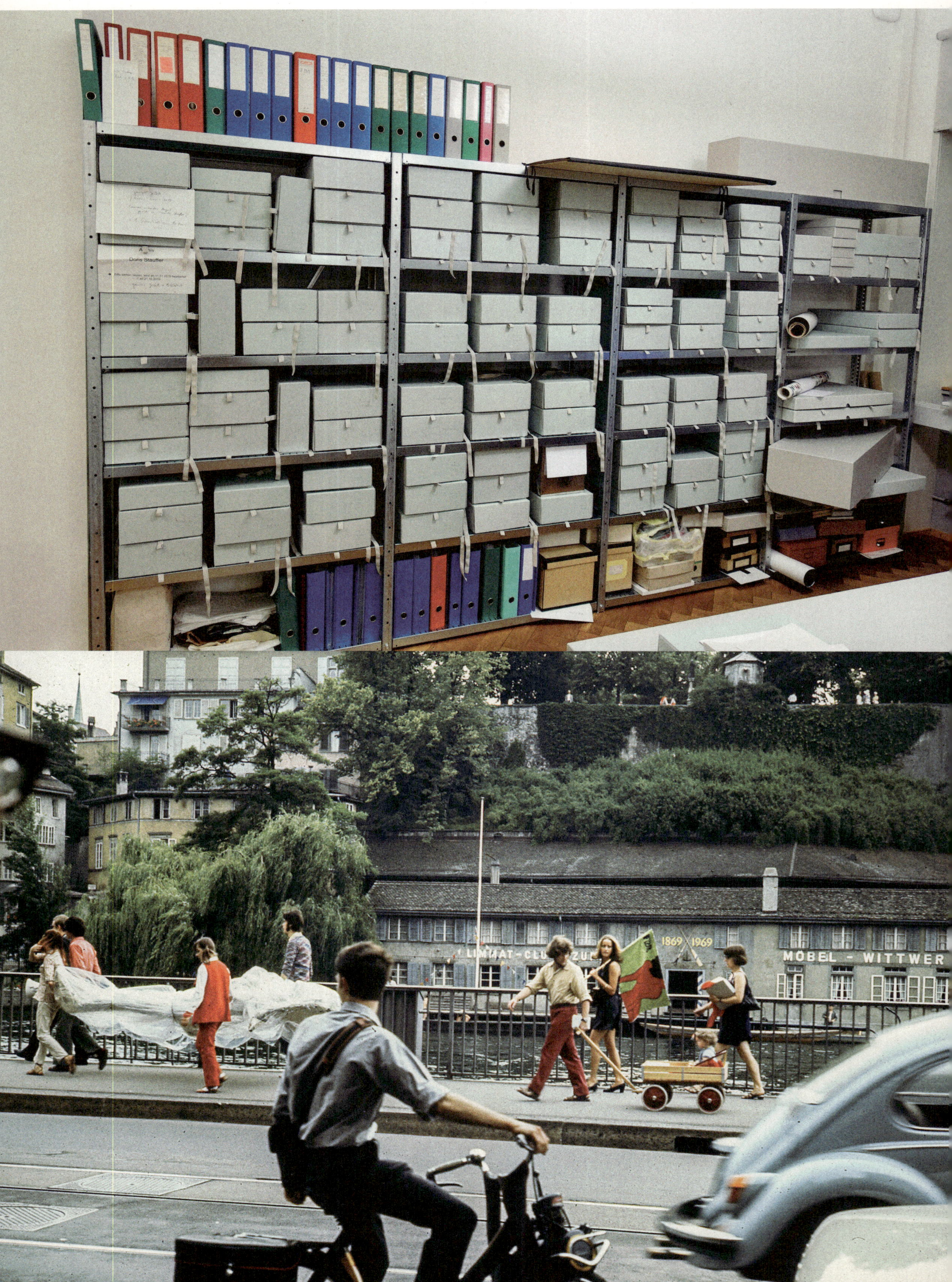

Fig. 7 Peter Trachsel Archive in the Passagenhaus. Dalvazza, Küblis, 2018

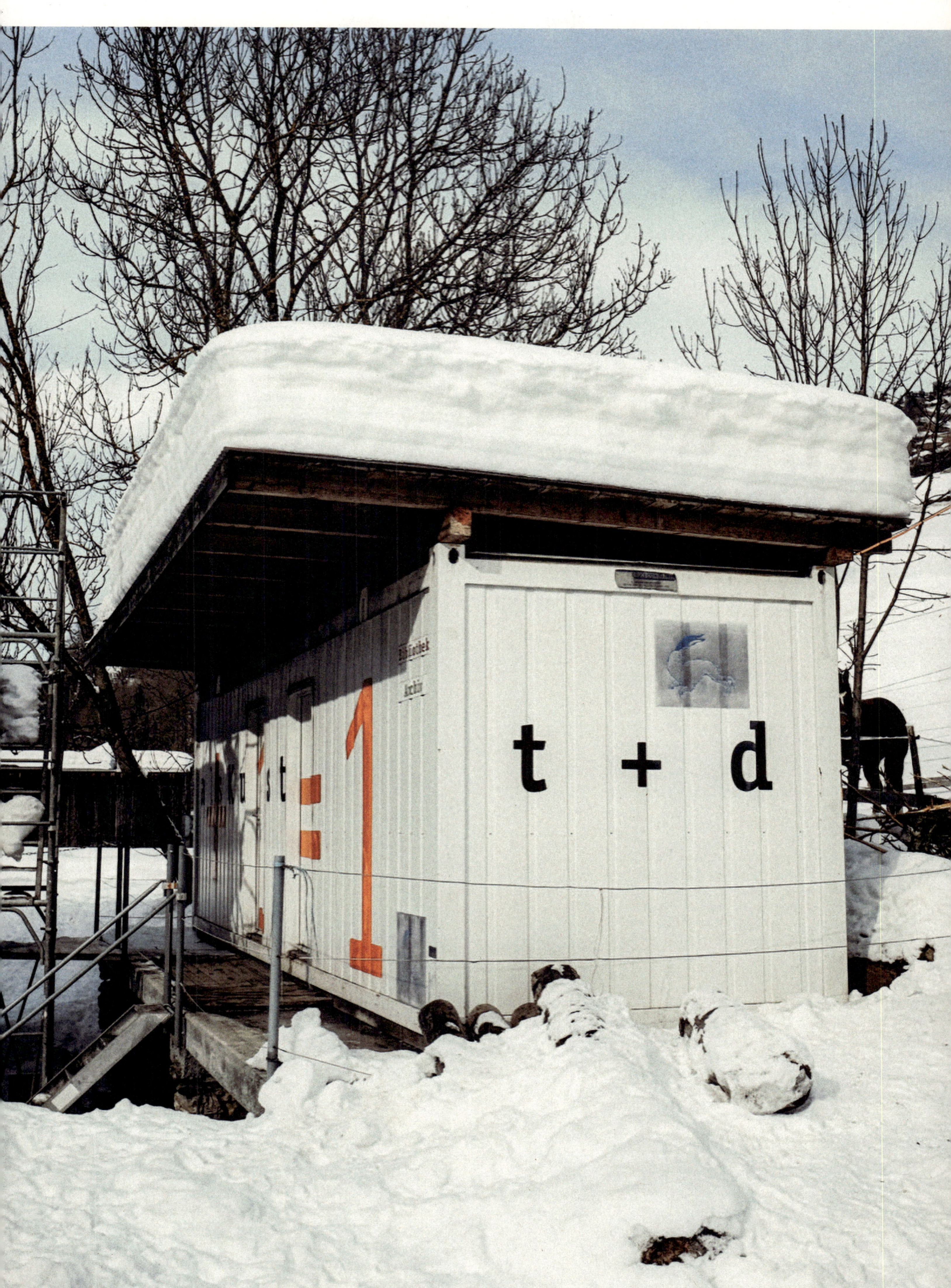

In extremely globalized cities like Hong Kong, and to a slightly lesser degree Zurich and other urban clusters, heavy development and fast transformation processes are underway, reinforced by neoliberal policies and the associated economic, social, urban, and cultural policy strategies. How to capture, describe, and interpret such fast-paced developments was the leading focus of this research. Researchers, students, and artists from the School of Design at the Hong Kong Polytechnic University and from Zurich University of the Arts collaborated on the project with community organizers like SoCO (Society for Community Organization) between 2013 and 2016. In many field trips at different times of day and during various seasons, a great amount of material was collected. The main research materials were photo and video documentaries, participatory photo observations, interviews, artistic interventions, and expert talks.

For the study a small area with open streets was chosen around the southbound side of Sham Shui Po MTR station up to the West Kowloon Corridor of Sham Shui Po, one of the poorest and most traditional districts of Hong Kong, to investigate how its public spaces were experiencing urban transformation and gentrification. The project was able to show—and present as a result in the book—interesting ways and methods in which different groups of people from different classes, different social and ethnic groups, and different nations deal with public spaces; how they use and transform, appropriate and occupy them, formally or informally, legally or illegally.

Official vendors at the daily market in Sham Shui Po often tolerate those who hawk their wares in the night market, even reaching tacit agreements that allow the night vendors to sell from unofficial stands erected on the dismantled, locked, official market stalls. A further example for creative, informal solutions is the widely accepted temporary occupation of the street space allotted for traffic by the night market vendors. Despite, or perhaps especially because of the economic pressure on public space, every last square meter of the area is used as market space by mutual agreement of all residents.

These informal solutions, which are always the result of a negotiation process, are based not on the enforcement of strict rules, but are understood by us as "politics of space." It is a continuously developed consensus among those who sell at the night market in Sham Shui Po, some of whom come from mainland China, various countries in the Arab world or Pakistan. Consensus building manifests itself as a colorful, slightly chaotic, and yet peaceful bustling of different population groups with a wide variety of social and ethnic backgrounds who converge every evening on the streets of the night market.

Jürgen Krusche

Project Title
Politics of Space. Public Spaces in Sham Shui Po, Hong Kong

Project Period
1 January 2014–31 December 2018

Keywords
- Public space
- Street space
- Artistic research
- Gentrification
- Urban transformation

Head of Project
- Jürgen Krusche, artist and urbanologist

Project Team
- Yunlong Song, filmmaker
- Baggenstos/Rudolf, students and artist duo
- Marc Latzel, photographer

Research Partner
- Siu King Chung, Head of School of Design, Hong Kong Polytechnic University

Project Partners
- Patrick Müller, musicologist and cultural researcher
- Nuria Krämer, curator and culture manager
- Connecting Spaces Hong Kong–Zurich

Outputs

A

Project Funding
- Hong Kong Arts Development Council (publication)

Website
- https://blog.zhdk.ch/politicsofspace

Related Projects
- Community Museum Project by Siu King Chung, Hong Kong, since 2002

Publication
- Jürgen Krusche and Siu King-Chung (eds.) (2017): *Deep Water. Public Spaces in Sham Shui Po, Hong Kong*. Volume 17 of the Institute for Contemporary Art Research series. Hong Kong: MCCM Creation.
  - A Open access: https://doi.org/10.5281/zenodo.6498198

Lecture
- Jürgen Krusche: "Die Strassen von Sham Shui Po als Ort 'tiefer' oder 'radikaler' Demokratie." In: *Demokratie und Frieden auf der Strasse*. Conference 29–30 June 2018. Karl-Franzens University of Graz.

Workshop and Seminar
- *Art as Diverter*. March 2015. School of Design, Poly-U, Hong Kong. With artist duo Baggenstoos/Rudolf.
- *Politics of Space—Sham Shui Po*. Spring Semester 2016. School of Design, Poly-U Hong Kong. With Siu King Chung.

Conversation
- *Zurich meets Hong Kong—A Book and a Talk*. 27 October 2017. Wontonmen, Kowloon, Hong Kong. With Siu King Chung, Yunlong Song, and Jürgen Krusche.

Exhibition
- *Public Spaces in Sham Shui Po, Hong Kong*. 16–22 November 2016. Zurich University of the Arts. With works by Siu King Chung, Yunlong Song, and Jürgen Krusche.

Fig. 1 Night market. Sham Shui Po, Hong Kong, 2016

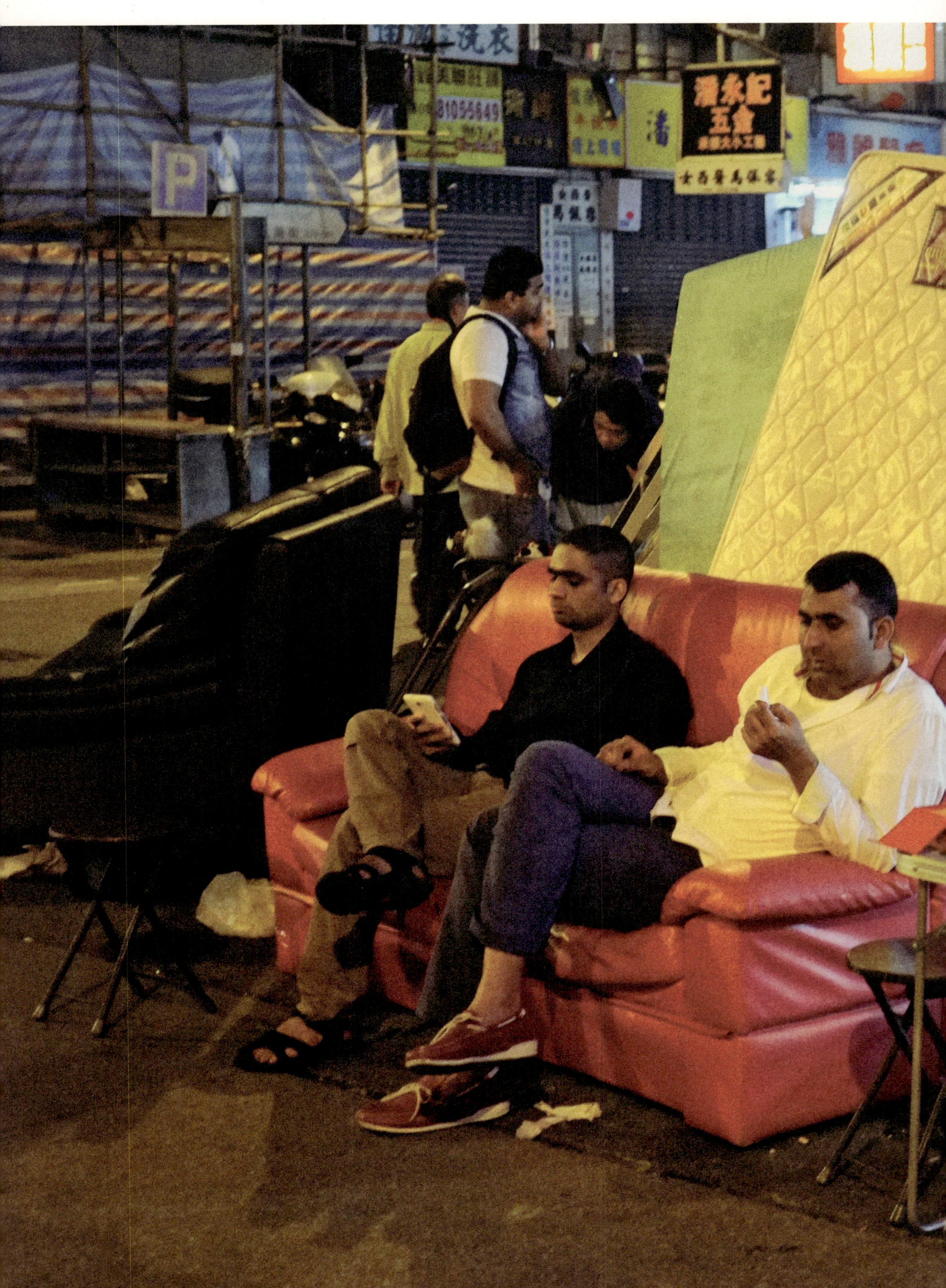

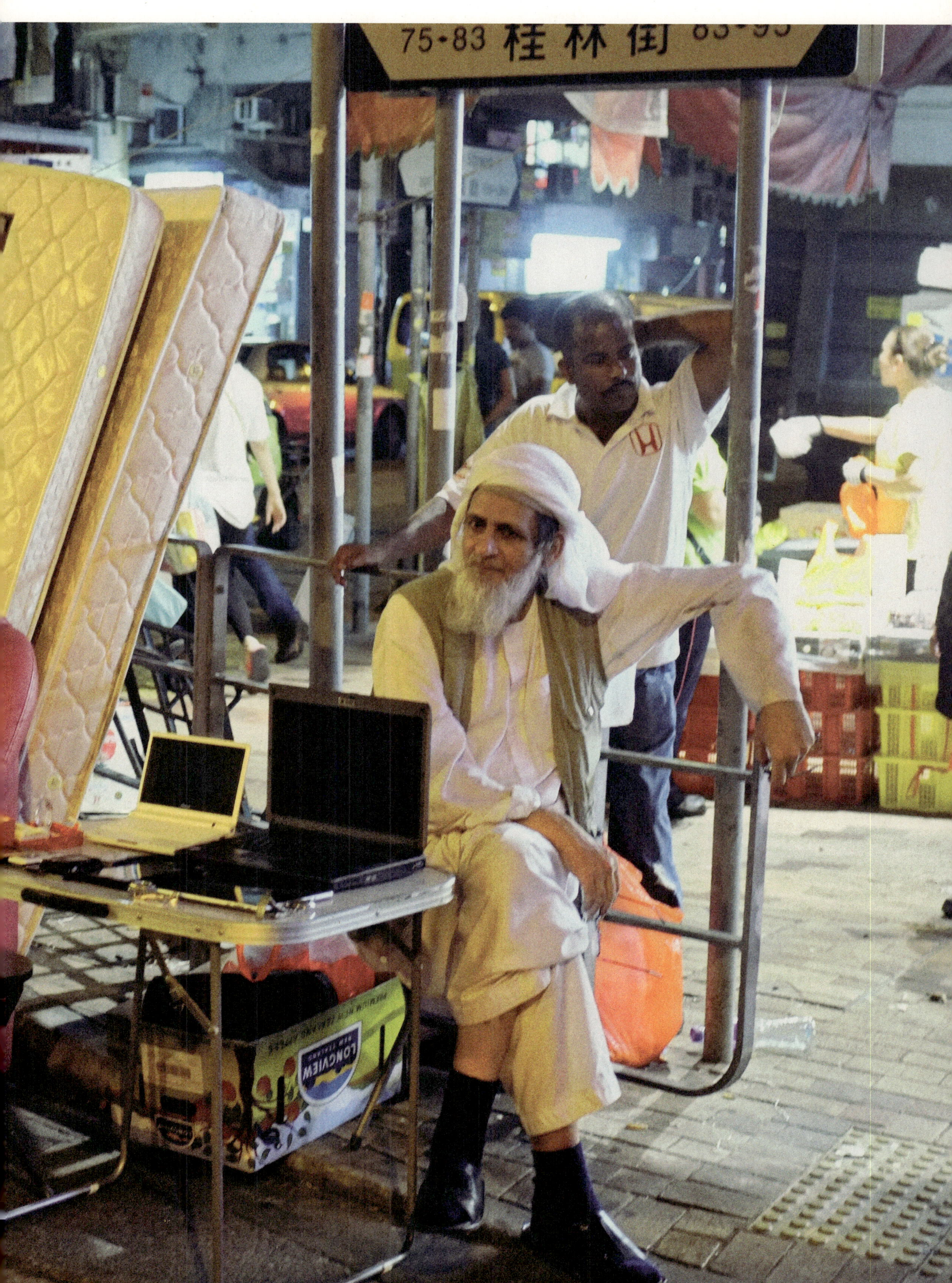
75-83 桂林街
LONGVIEW

Fig. 2 Street space. Sham Shui Po, Hong Kong, 2016
Fig. 3 Night market. Sham Shui Po, Hong Kong, 2016

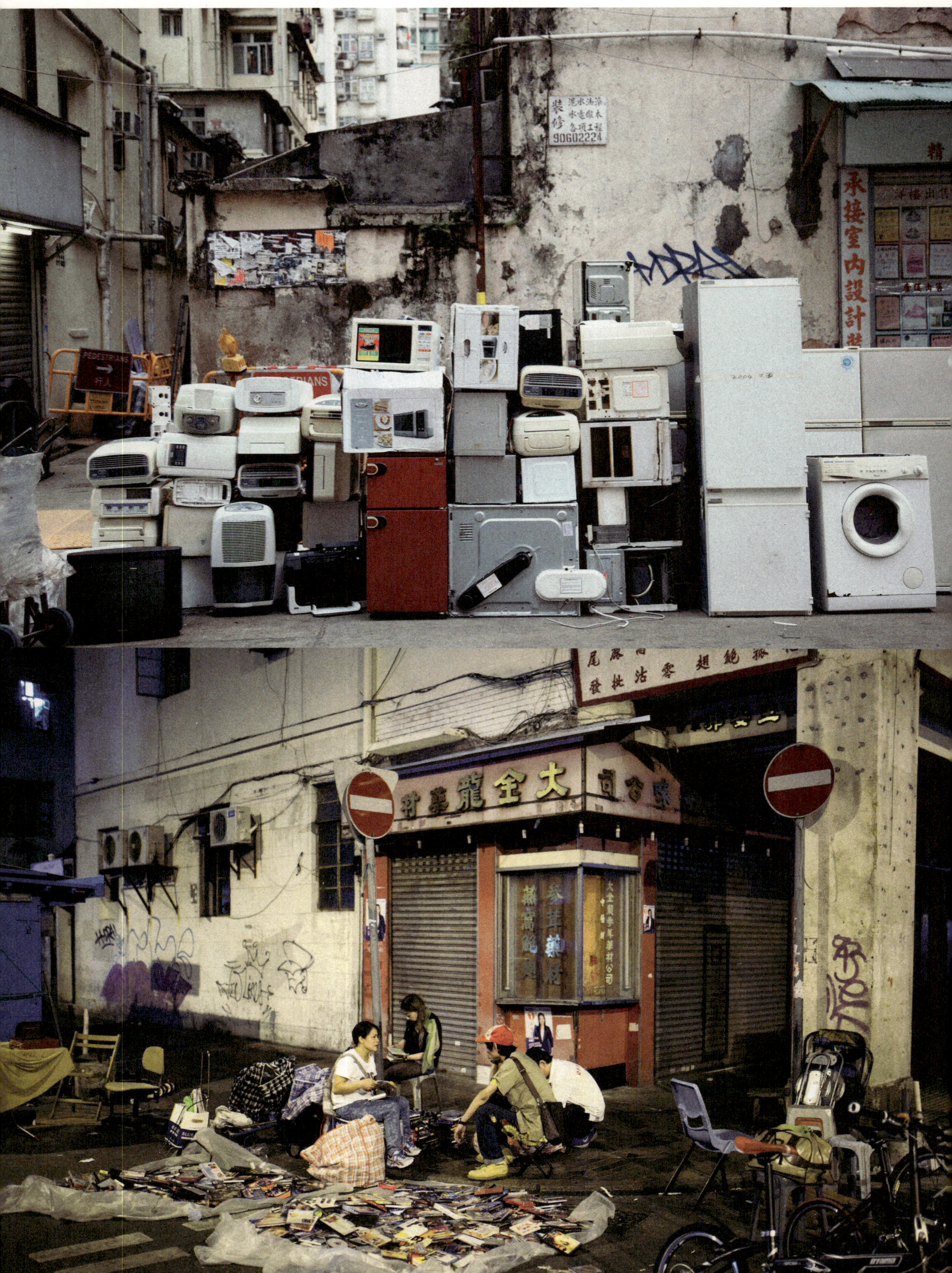

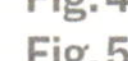

Fig. 4 Big Eye Sister. Sham Shui Po, Hong Kong, 2016
Fig. 5 Street space. Sham Shui Po, Hong Kong, 2016

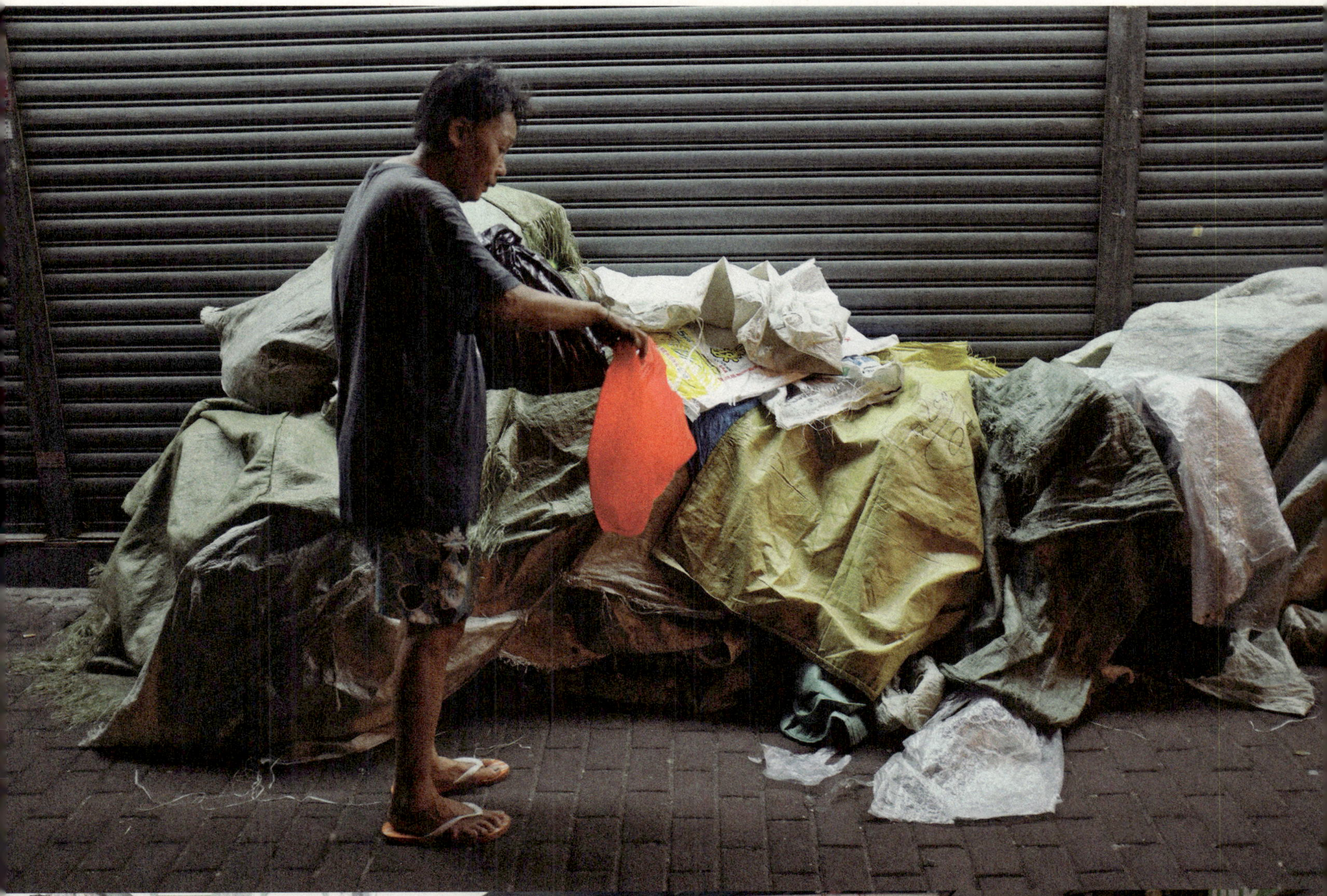

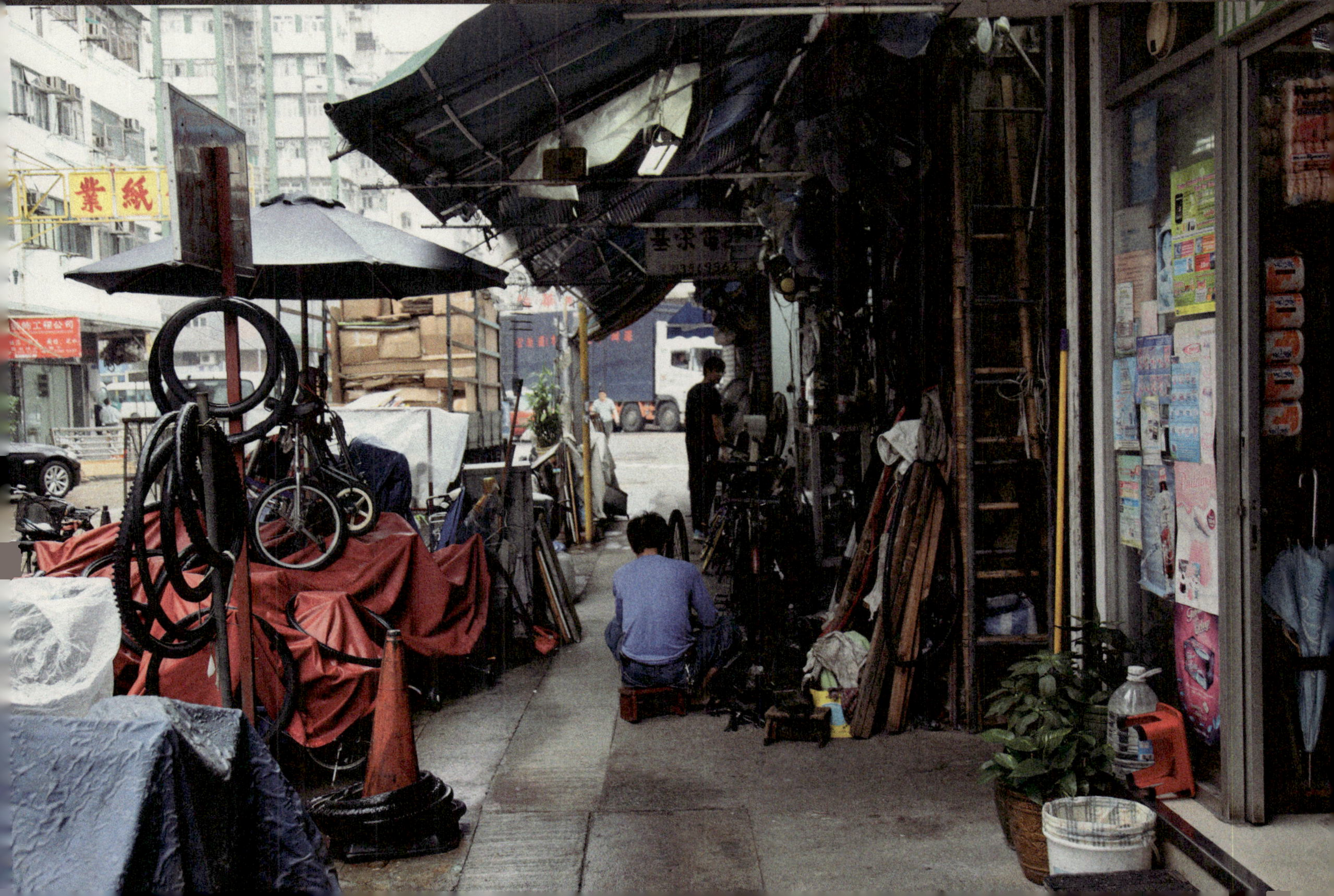

Fig. 6 Rooftops. Sham Shui Po, Hong Kong, 2016

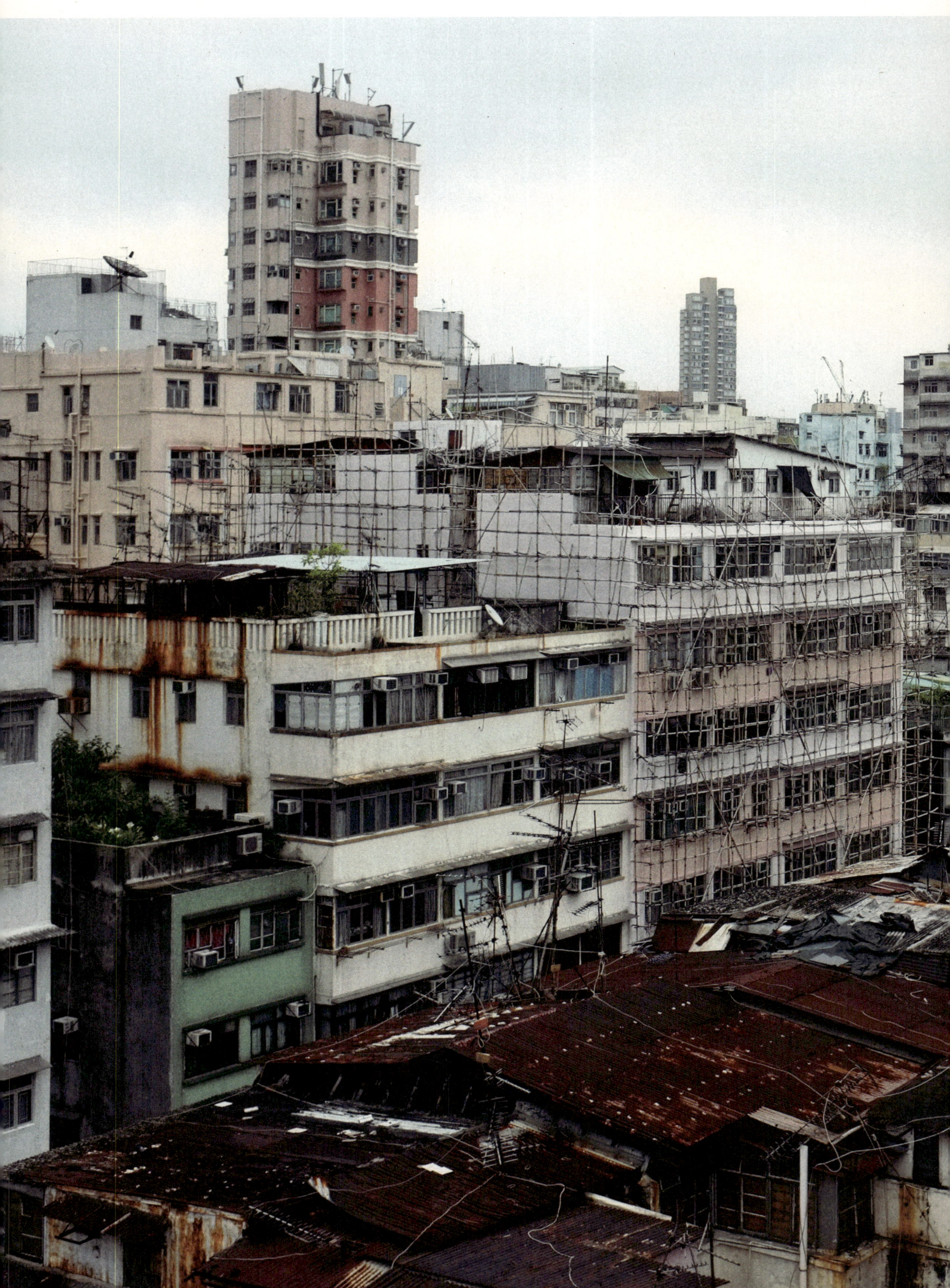

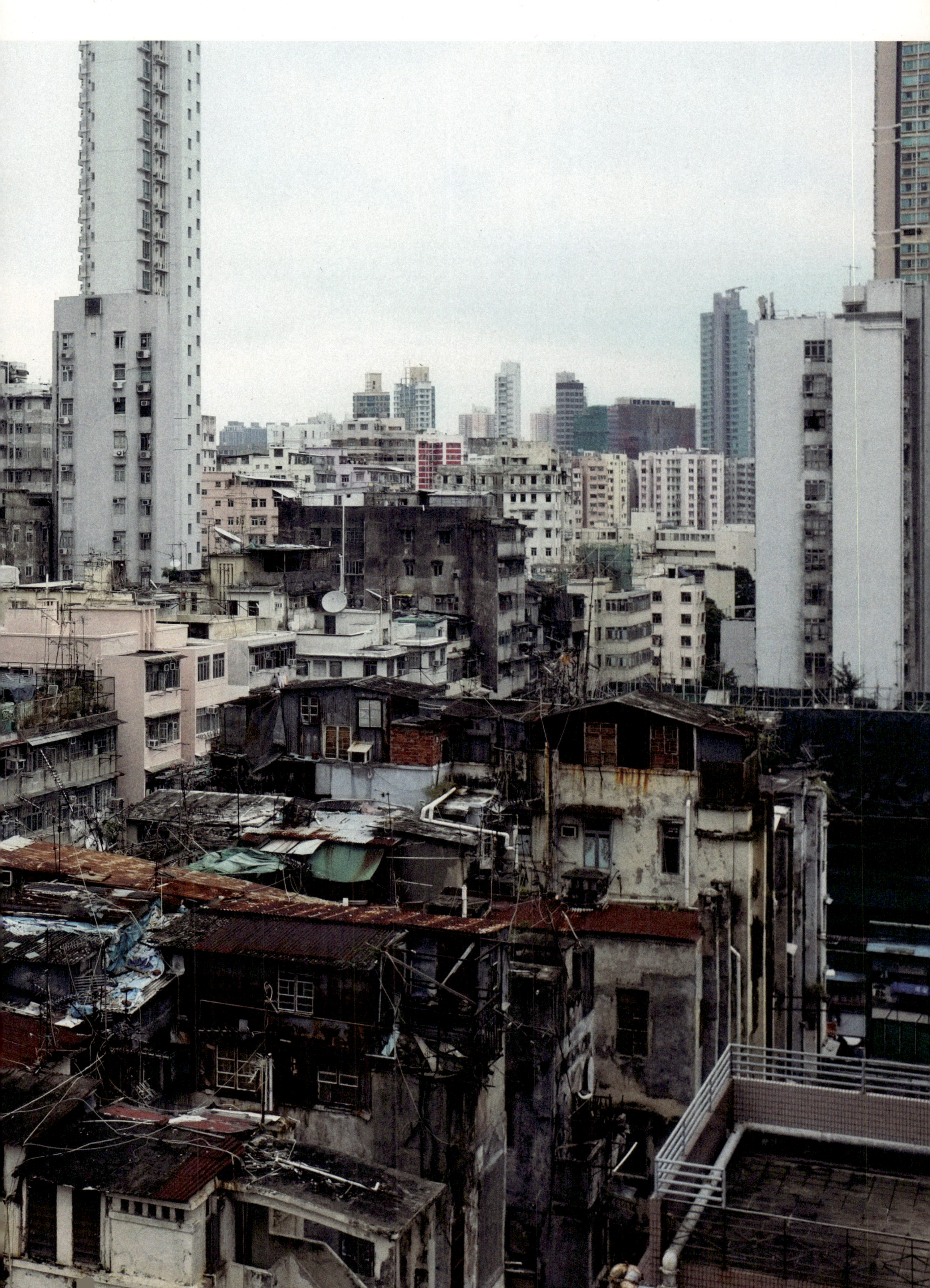

The *Draft* project built on the two projects *Public Plaiv* and *Art Public Zurich*. In *Public Plaiv* the artists examined the functions of public art, especially the function of mapping out local zones of conflict. In *Art Public Zurich* the initial constellation was changed by the shift in frame of reference from public space to the public sphere. The "experimental system" also concerned locally specific problems which the artists addressed with reference to interdisciplinary specialized knowledge. In the expanded context of globally networked contemporary art, however, it seemed advisable to conceptualize "public art" more broadly. Accordingly, the *Draft* project defined public art as contemporary art which especially addresses public issues, and thus produces, contributes to, or provokes public debate.

Draft consisted of nine interdisciplinary collaboratives in nine cities around the world: Beijing, Cairo, Cape Town, Hamburg, Hong Kong, Mexico City, Mumbai, St. Petersburg and Zurich. Each of the collaboratives was ideally composed of at least one artist, one curator, and one scholar. In early summer 2015, at the start of the joint undertaking, the collaboratives met for a public conference in Mumbai, at which all participants presented their previous work as well as their disciplinary and societal contexts. Over the course of the subsequent year, each collaborative realized one project, which was then presented at the second conference in Zurich in summer 2016. At both conferences, the different approaches and the impact of the projects on their given cultural, social, and urban contexts were explained in detail and discussed.

The approach of an individual project specific to a city can be depicted using the example of Mexico City: Supported by preliminary works, the interdisciplinary collaborative addressed the issue of the omnipresent violence in public life, organized crime, and the erosion of state structures in Mexico. It organized a public workshop at the Museo Universitario Arte Contemporáneo (MUAC) over two evenings, in which twenty-two persons from various walks of life and scientific disciplines analyzed and interpreted the images of violence circulating in public media. This was the first time in Mexico that neoliberal violence and narcoterrorism were debated in the context of a museum as an issue of cultural public life. Following the workshop, the artist collective Teatro Ojo used found footage to produce *At Night, Lightning*, forty-one very short, scary video clips which were broadcast unannounced, quasi disruptively, into the programming of the university TV station at Universidad Nacional Autónoma de México (UNAM).

The nine collaboratives investigated, each in its own way, which public issues they perceived to be especially urgent in their local contexts, and in which form they should be debated in which public. The topics ranged from real estate speculation and the refugee crisis, to censorship and the manipulation of public information, all the way to trials as a means of the repressive state apparatus.

The *Draft* project succeeded in investigating and establishing a contemporary public art whose focus is directed toward public debates (in specific contexts). At the same time, the individual, local projects could be understood as a lens through which certain societal problems—or other aspects of these problems—are perceived in the first place. In so doing, the term of artwork was discarded, or redefined as a field that proves itself to be art precisely through its ability to transgress the boundaries of art, integrate various disciplines, and participate in various discourses.

Christoph Schenker

Project Title
Draft. International Network for Research and Practice in Public Art

Project Period
1 June 2014–31 July 2017

Keywords
- Contemporary public art
- Public issues
- Public debates
- Interdisciplinary collaboratives
- Cross-cultural exchange

Heads of Project
- Gitanjali Dang, curator and author
- Christoph Schenker, art theorist

Project Associates (Conferences)
- Phalguni Desai, project coordinator and communications
- Linda Jensen, curator

Participating Collaboratives
Beijing
- Ju Anqi and Xu Peili

Cairo
- Jens Maier-Rothe, Jasmina Metwaly, Alia Mossallam, Sarah Rifky, and Philip Rizk

Cape Town
- Riason Naidoo, Jay Pather, and Richard Pithouse

Hamburg
- Sophie Goltz, Abimbola Odugbesan, Alice Peragine, and Christoph Schäfer

Hong Kong
- Giorgio Biancorosso, Cosmin Costinas, Qinyi Lim, and Samson Young

Mexico City
- Helena Chávez Mac Gregor, Cuauhtémoc Medina, and Teatro Ojo (Héctor Bourges

Valles, Laura Furlan Magaril, Karla Rodríguez Lira, Patricio Villarreal Ávila)

Mumbai
- Gitanjali Dang, Rupali Gupte, Prasad Shetty, and CAMP (Shaina Anand, Ashok Sukumaran, Zinnia Ambapardiwala)

St. Petersburg
- Chto Delat (Tsaplya Olga Egorova, Nikolay Oleynikov, Dmitry Vilensky)

Zurich
- knowbotiq (Christian Huebler, Yvonne Wilhelm), Nina Bandi, and Rohit Jain

Research Partner
- Khanabadosh, Mumbai

Project Partners
- Swiss Arts Council Pro Helvetia
- Connecting Spaces Hong Kong–Zurich
- Studio-X Mumbai

Project Funding
- artEDU Stiftung
- Stanley Thomas Johnson Stiftung
- Ifa Institut für Auslandsbeziehungen

Related Projects
- Public Plaiv, Zurich University of the Arts, 2001–2002
  P. 20
- Art Public Zurich, Zurich University of the Arts, 2004–2012
  P. 36
- Swiss Psychotropic Gold, Zurich University of the Arts, 2015–2020
  P. 184
- InOctober, Zurich University of the Arts, 2016–2021
  P. 190

Website
- https://www.draftprojects.info
  With downloads of publications and information on local conferences, workshops, exhibitions, and performances.

Publications

Beijing
- Gitanjali Dang, Barbara Preisig, and Christoph Schenker (eds.) (2019): *Ju Anqi*. DVD. Mumbai/Zurich: Draft.

Cairo
- Alia Mossallam (ed.) (2016): *"Ehky ya tarikh," Speak history: We came to Alexandria in search of....* Cairo: Self-published.
- Alia Mossallam (ed.) (2016, reprint 2018): *Speak History*. Workshop publication. Cairo: self-published.
- Jasmina Metwaly and Philip Rizk (2021): *On Trials. A manual for the theatre of law*. Berlin: Archive Books.

Cape Town
- Riason Naidoo (ed.) (2022): *Any Given Sunday*. Newspaper supplement. *Mail & Guardian*. 21 January 2022. Johannesburg: Mail & Guardian.

Hamburg
- CTC Curating the City (2020): *Beyond Welcome: Another Planning is Possible*. Postcard. Mumbai/Zurich: Draft.
- Alice Peragine (2020): *Soft Core—Protection Procedure*. Set of six postcards. Mumbai/Zurich: Draft.

Hong Kong
- Giorgio Biancorosso, Qinyi Lim, and Samson Young (2021): *Draft: Orchestration*. Zurich: Zurich University of the Arts and Mumbai: Khanabadosh.

Mexico City
- Helena Chávez Mac Gregor and Cuauhtémoc Medina (eds.) (2018): *Teatro Ojo: En la noche, relámpagos—At Night, Lightning*. Mexico: Museo Universitario Arte Contemporáneo.

Mumbai
- Gitanjali Dang (ed.), forthcoming.

St. Petersburg
- Dmitry Vilensky (ed.) (2016): *Houses of culture—Yesterday, today and tomorrow*. Newspaper *Chto Delat*, no. 38. August 2016. Reprint as no. 40. May 2018.

Zurich
- Nina Bandi, Christian Huebler, and Yvonne Wilhelm (eds.) (2020): *Swiss Psychotropic Gold*. Volume 23 of the Institute for Contemporary Art Research series. Basel: Merian Verlag.

Conferences
- *Draft Mumbai*. 4–6 June 2015. Studio-X Mumbai. With contributions by all project participants (see participating collaboratives), plus Li Zhenhua, Iris Long, Reza Negarestani, and P. Sainath. Moderators: Ranjit Hoskote and Lawrence Liang.
- *Draft Zurich*. 28–30 July 2016. Zurich University of the Arts. With contributions by all project participants (see participating collaboratives), plus Gabrielle Goliath and Buhlebezwe Siwani. Commentators: Anila Daulatzai, Uzma Z. Rizvi, Nils Röller, and Zheng Bo. Moderator: Gareth Evans.

Works and Projects

Beijing
- Ju Anqi: *Drill Man*. 2016. Video, 35:23 min.

Cairo
- Jasmina Metwaly and Philip Rizk: *Exercises On Trials*. 2016. Lecture performance.

Cairo/Alexandria
- Alia Mossallam: *Elsewehere—Struggles Across the Sea*. 17 April–31 May 2016. Research workshops.

Cape Town
- *Any Given Sunday*. 15 May–5 July 2016. Nine public performances.

Hamburg
- Alice Peragine: *Soft Core—Protection Procedure*. 5 May 2016. Site-specific performance.
- CTC Curating the City: *Beyond Welcome: Another Planning is Possible*. 28 May 2016. Choreographed parade.

Hong Kong
- Samson Young: *Orchestrations*. 2016. Video, 24:00 min.

Mexico City
- Teatro Ojo: *At Night, Lightning*. 2016. Forty-one videos of 31 seconds each.

Mumbai
- *R and R*. Since 2016. Centre for artistic and intellectual activity.

St. Petersburg
- Chto Delat: *Rosa's House of Culture*. 2015.

Zurich
- Knowbotiq: *Swiss Psychotropic Gold: Delinking Commodity Trading*. 28–30 July 2016. Performative assemblage.

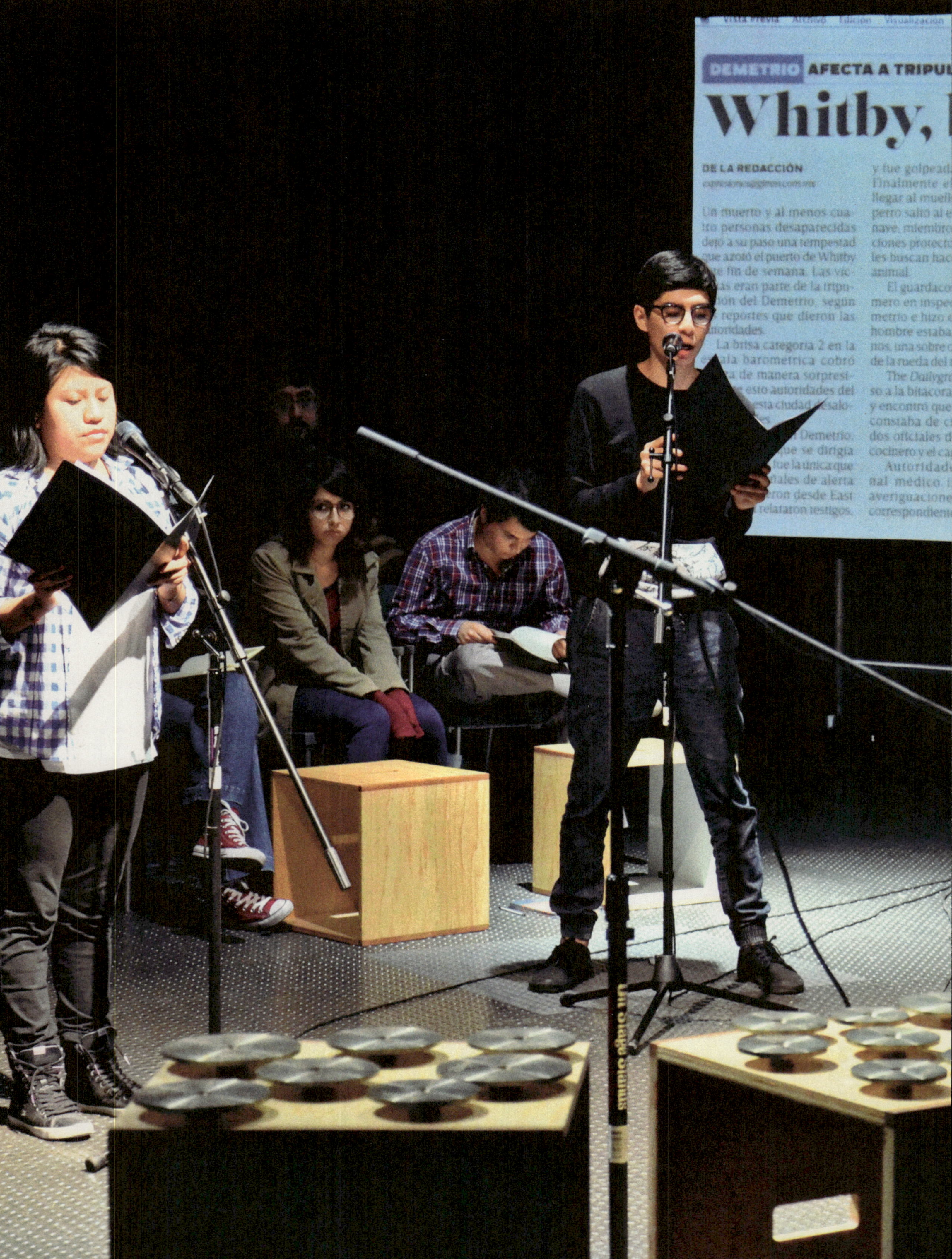

Fig. 1 Carlos Amorales and Buró Fantasma: Performance. University Museum of Contemporary Art, Mexico City, 2016

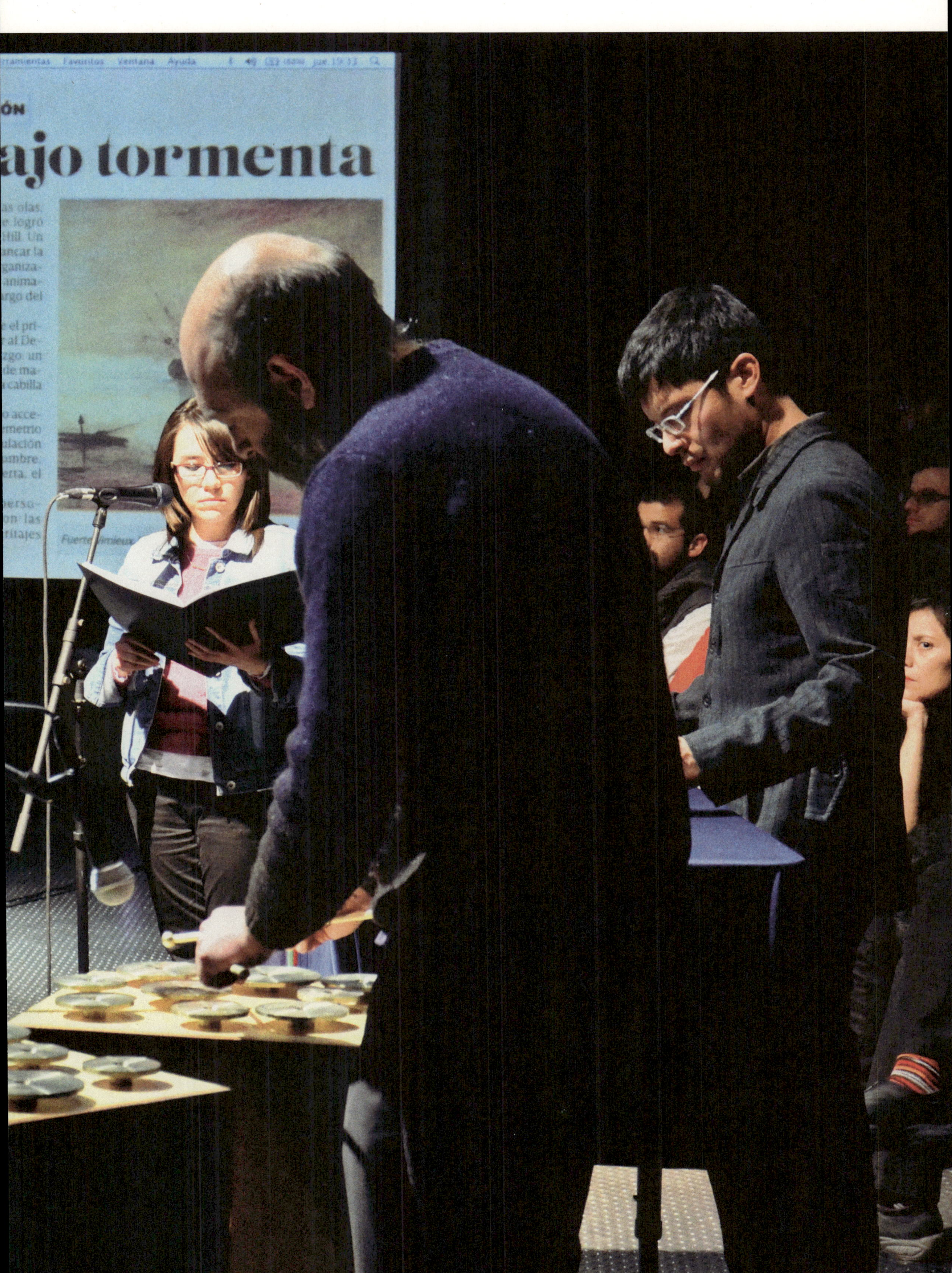
Favoritos Ventana Ayuda
ajo tormenta

Fig. 2 Teatro Ojo: *At Night, Lightning*. Video still, 2016
Fig. 3 Vecinos del Ritmo and Ilena Diéguez: Performance. University Museum of Contemporary Art, Mexico City, 2016

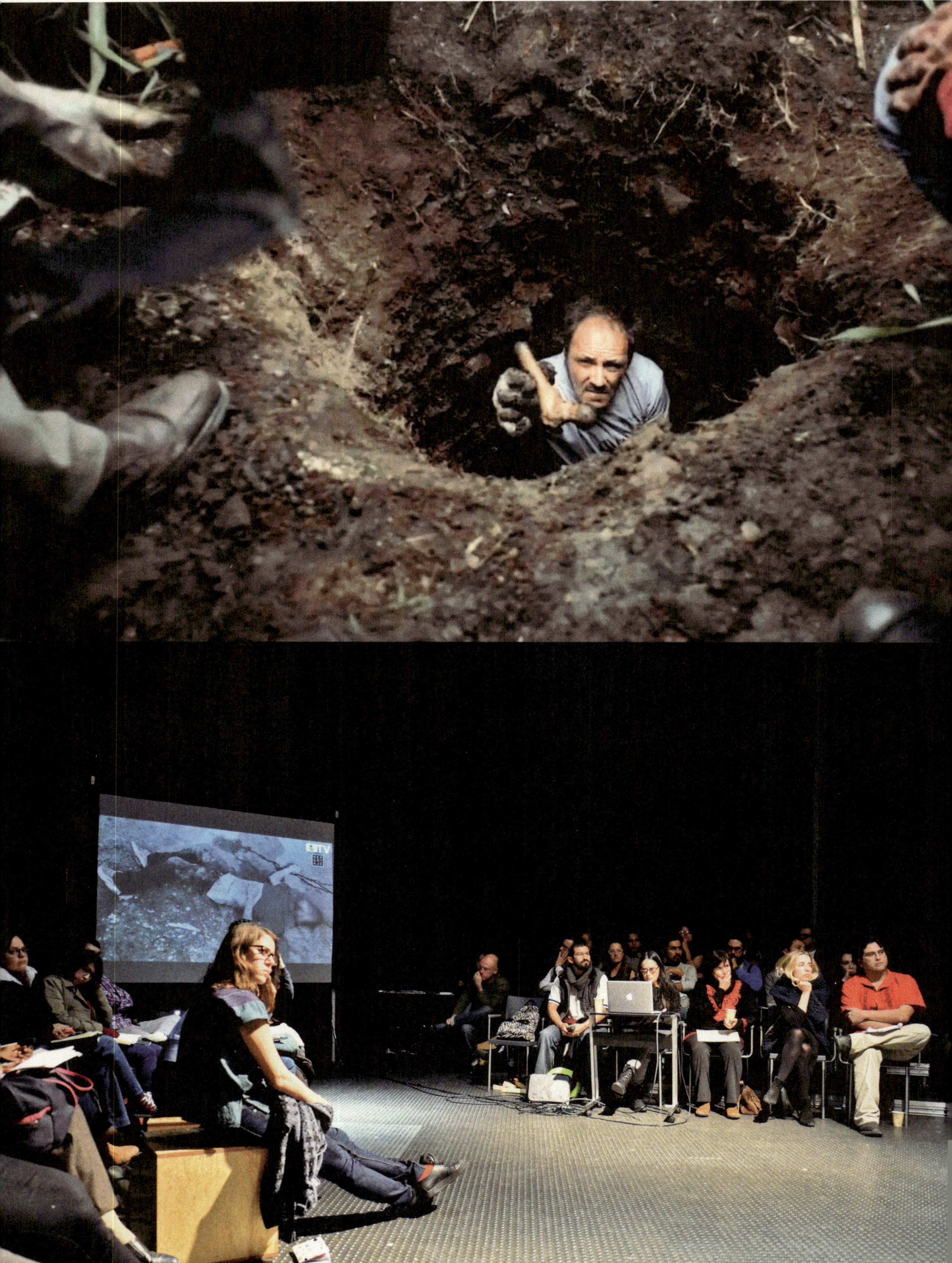

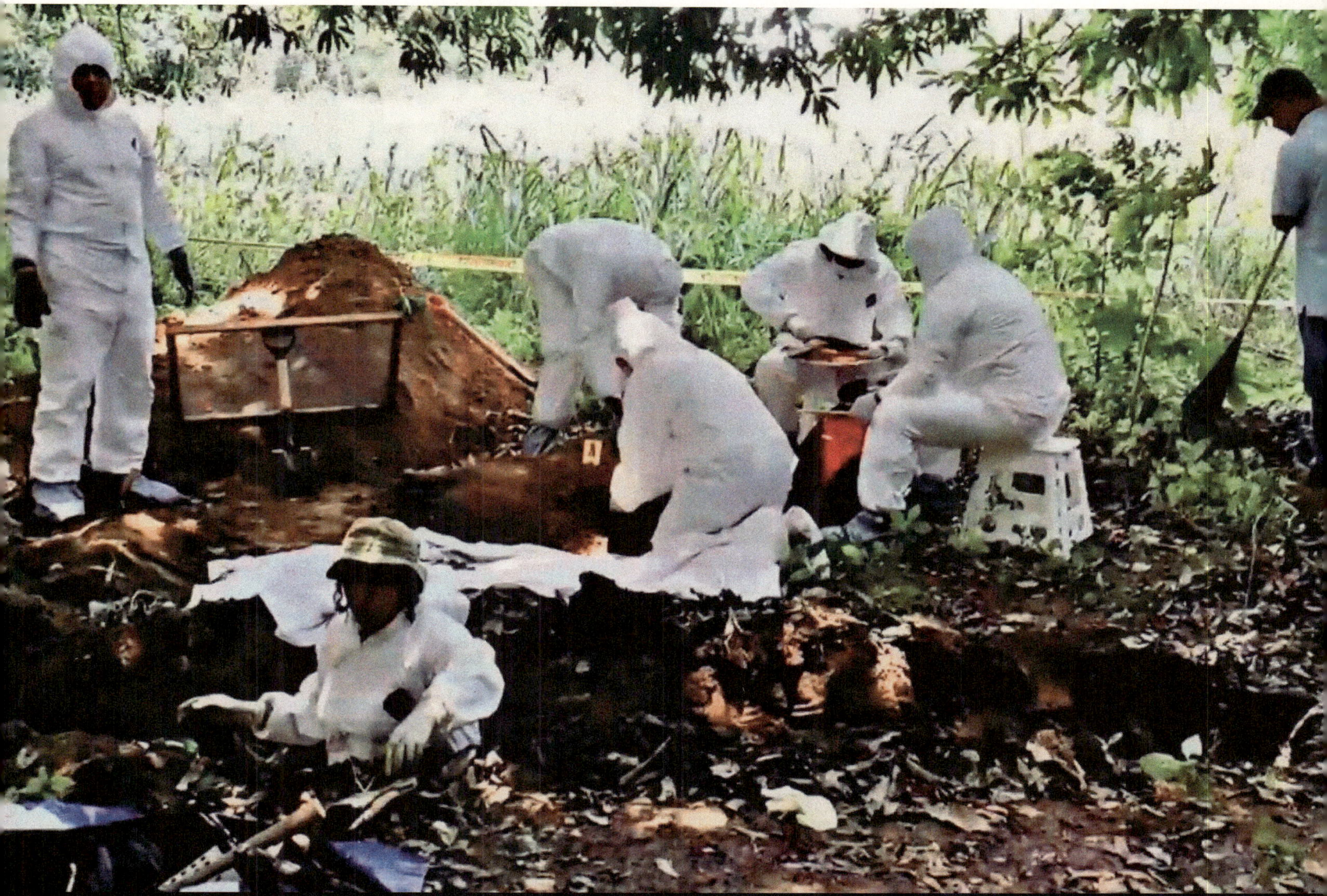

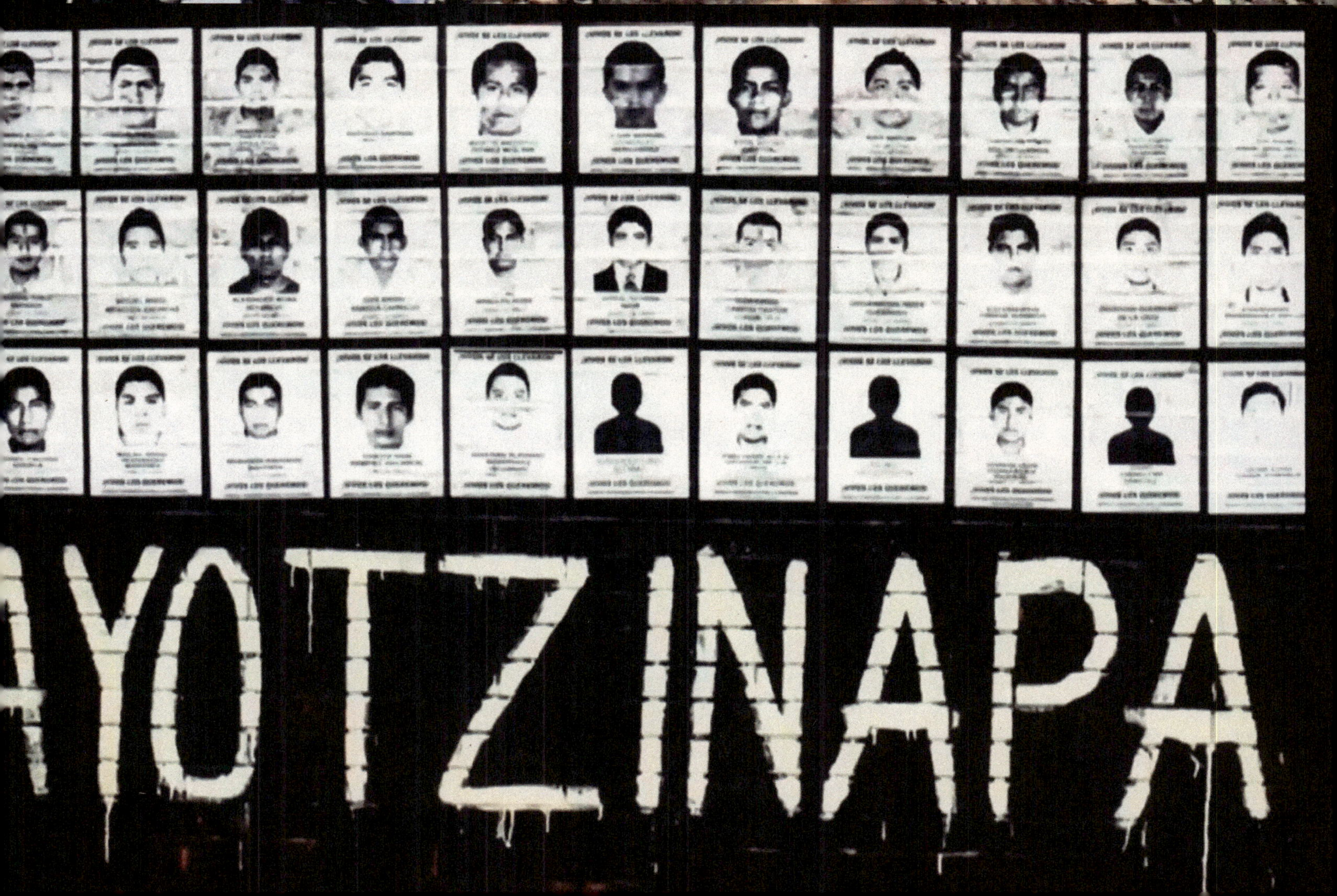

Fig. 4–5 Teatro Ojo: *At Night, Lightning*. Video stills, 2016

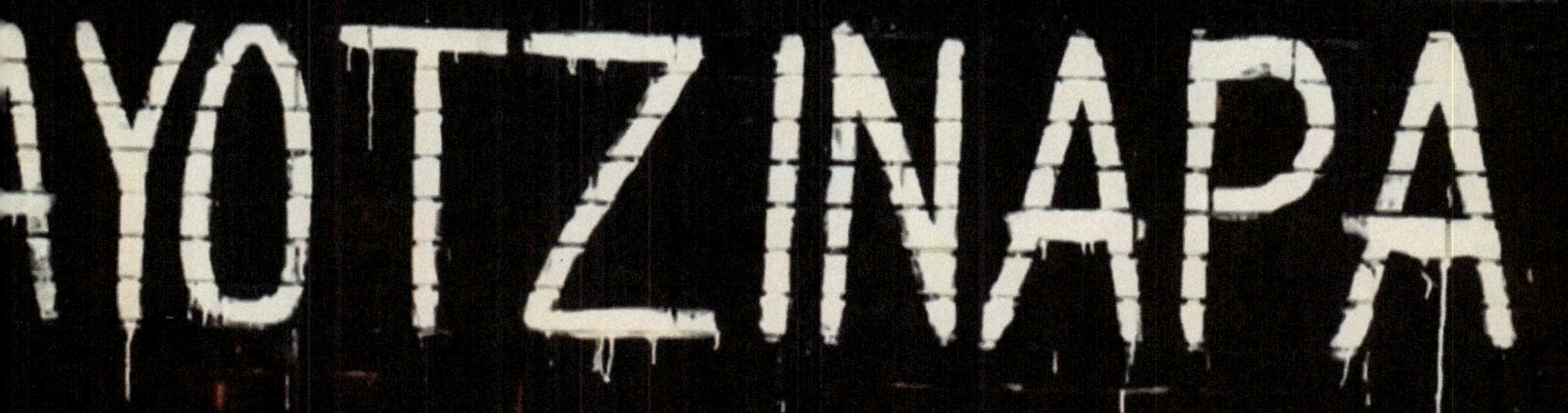

The Chinese Contemporary Art Award (CCAA), established in 1998 by the Swiss entrepreneur and former ambassador to China Uli Sigg, along with its archive in Beijing, were the starting point and reference of the investigation. The exemplary case study describes current tendencies and mechanisms of Chinese contemporary art and of the globalized art world. The objects of the analysis were the structures of relationships between persons, institutions, specialist discourses and the art market, as well as the manifold (reciprocal) influences of the CCAA. What role did the CCAA play for the circulation of artists living in China in the increasingly globalized field of art? How did the launch and promotion of the awards affect the presentation and reception of Chinese contemporary art in Europe? The art-historical and ethnographic case study allowed the questions to be differentiated and answered to some extent:

- It became clear how the growing prominence and the rising reputation of the award and the Uli Sigg Collection stimulated each other reciprocally.
- The composition of the jury of the CCAA with curators and directors of internationally renowned art institutions indicates that the members were selected strategically, with a particular focus on their social and professional networks. As a result, numerous winners of the CCAA were invited by these key figures to the Biennale in Venice or the documenta in Kassel. This contributed to the international prominence of the Chinese artists no less than did the proactive loaning policy of the Sigg Collection: Since 1986 a multitude of thematic "China exhibitions" in Europe and America have been provided with works from the collection.
- The study verifies that Sigg's targeted support for Chinese contemporary artists encouraged and enhanced the interest of European collectors and the art market in this field.
- It also became apparent that the artists benefiting from the CCAA contributed to the canon formation within the Chinese art scene, which was significantly encouraged by the permanent presentation of the Sigg Collection in the future Museum M+.
- Not only did the award serve to support artists, but it was equally important as a networking instrument for Sigg as a collector. It granted access to new segments of artists and knowledge about an art scene that was difficult for him to access. The important influence of the award is reflected in the Sigg Collection, which contains work by most of the laureates from the years 1998 to 2013. The distinction of the artists through the CCAA legitimates and ennobles the collection, and vice versa.

The study served as a knowledge base for the *CAS Contemporary Chinese Art I. Executive Education on Global Culture* pilot program, which was held in 2015 at the Zurich University of the Arts' Continuing Education Centre, and in 2016 at the Connecting Space in Hong Kong. As the basis for the instruction units, a reader was compiled, consisting of essays, interviews and several network diagrams, with a comprehensive index of persons and institutions. The networks show the social relationships Uli Sigg cultivated over years with representatives of the Chinese and European art scene, such as Ai Weiwei, Lars Nittve, Harald Szeemann, Carolyn Christov-Bakargiev and Ruth Noack, through which he was able to market Chinese contemporary art in the West. Most of the knowledge collected in the reader is based on research in the CCAA archive in Beijing, on literature reviews, and on many interviews with artists, curators, gallerists, and other actors in Beijing, Hong Kong, and Switzerland: Uli Sigg, Anna Li Liu, the director of CCAA; Pi Li, former director of the CCAA and designated director of the CCAA collection at M+.

Franz Krähenbühl and Barbara Preisig

Project Title
Contemporary Chinese Art Award

Project Period
1 August 2014–31 March 2015

Keywords
- Translocality
- Social networks
- Postcolonial studies
- Chinese contemporary art
- Global art world

Heads of Project and Team
- Franz Krähenbühl, art researcher and curator
- Barbara Preisig, art historian and art critic
- Michael Schindhelm, author and filmmaker

Project Partners
- Connecting Spaces Hong Kong–Zurich
- Continuing Education Centre, Zurich University of the Arts

A

Publication and Article

- Franz Krähenbühl, Barbara Preisig, and Michael Schindhelm (eds.) (2015): *CAS Contemporary Chinese Art I. Executive Education on Global Culture*. Zurich University of the Arts.
    - A Open access: https://doi.org/10.5281/zenodo.6341558
- Franz Krähenbühl and Barbara Preisig (2016): "Macht und Expansion im Netzwerk. Zürich, ZHdK, Pfingstweidstrasse 96–Peking, 43 Rixin Road, West Tiangezhuang." In: Franziska Koch, Daniel Kurjakovic, and Lea Pfäffli (eds.): *The Air Will Not Deny You. Zürich im Zeichen einer anderen Globalität*. Zurich/Berlin: Diaphanes, 79–91.

CAS Continuing Education

- *Chinesische Gegenwartskunst. Executive Education on Global Culture*. CAS Modul 28–30 March 2015, Continuing Education Centre, Zurich University of the Arts.

Online Course

- *CCAA Chinese Contemporary Art Award. A Case Study on Global Culture*. Online course, since 2016, Continuing Education Centre, Zurich University of the Arts.

Fig. 1 Sigg Collection art-storage facilities, 2014

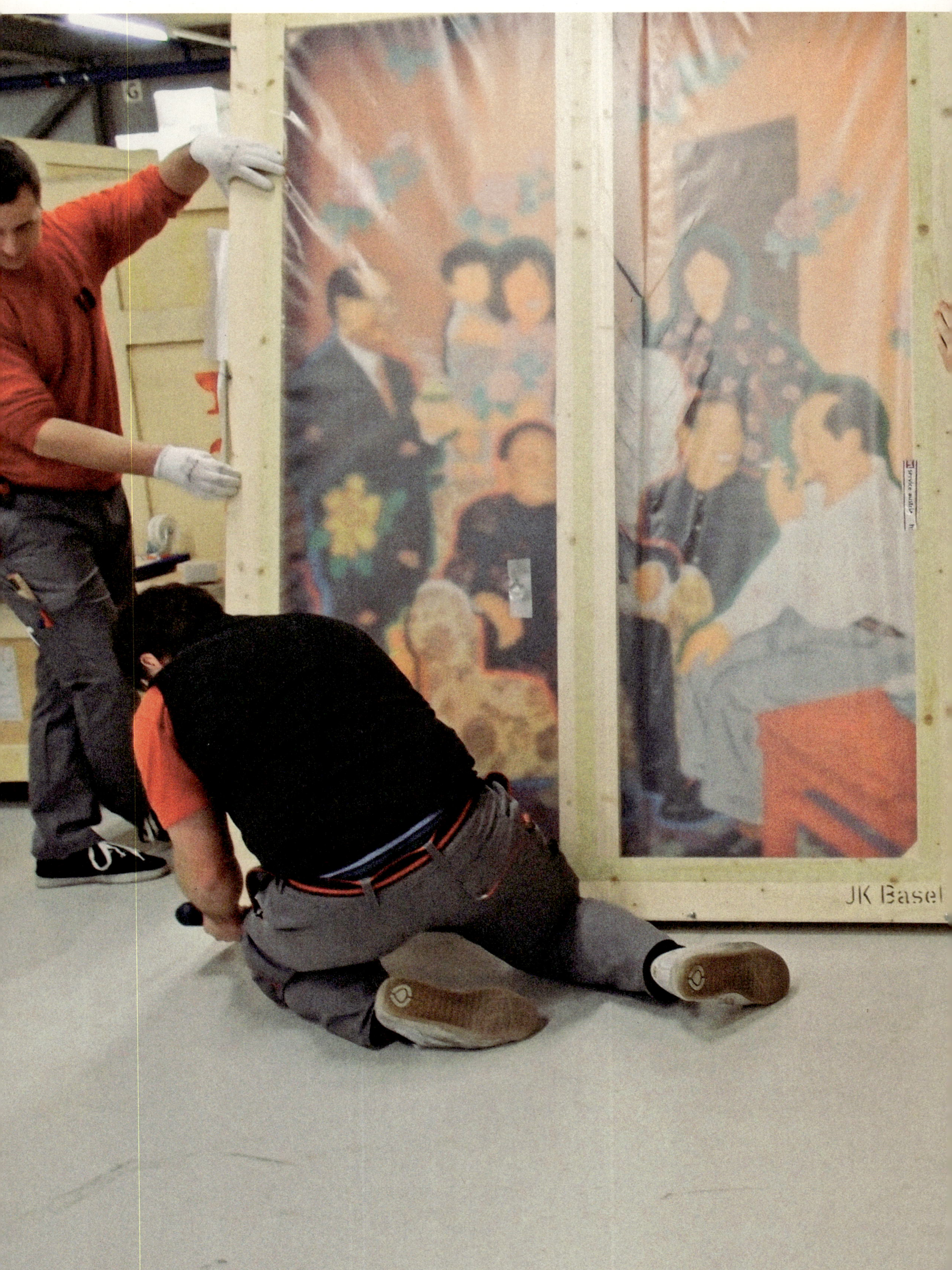

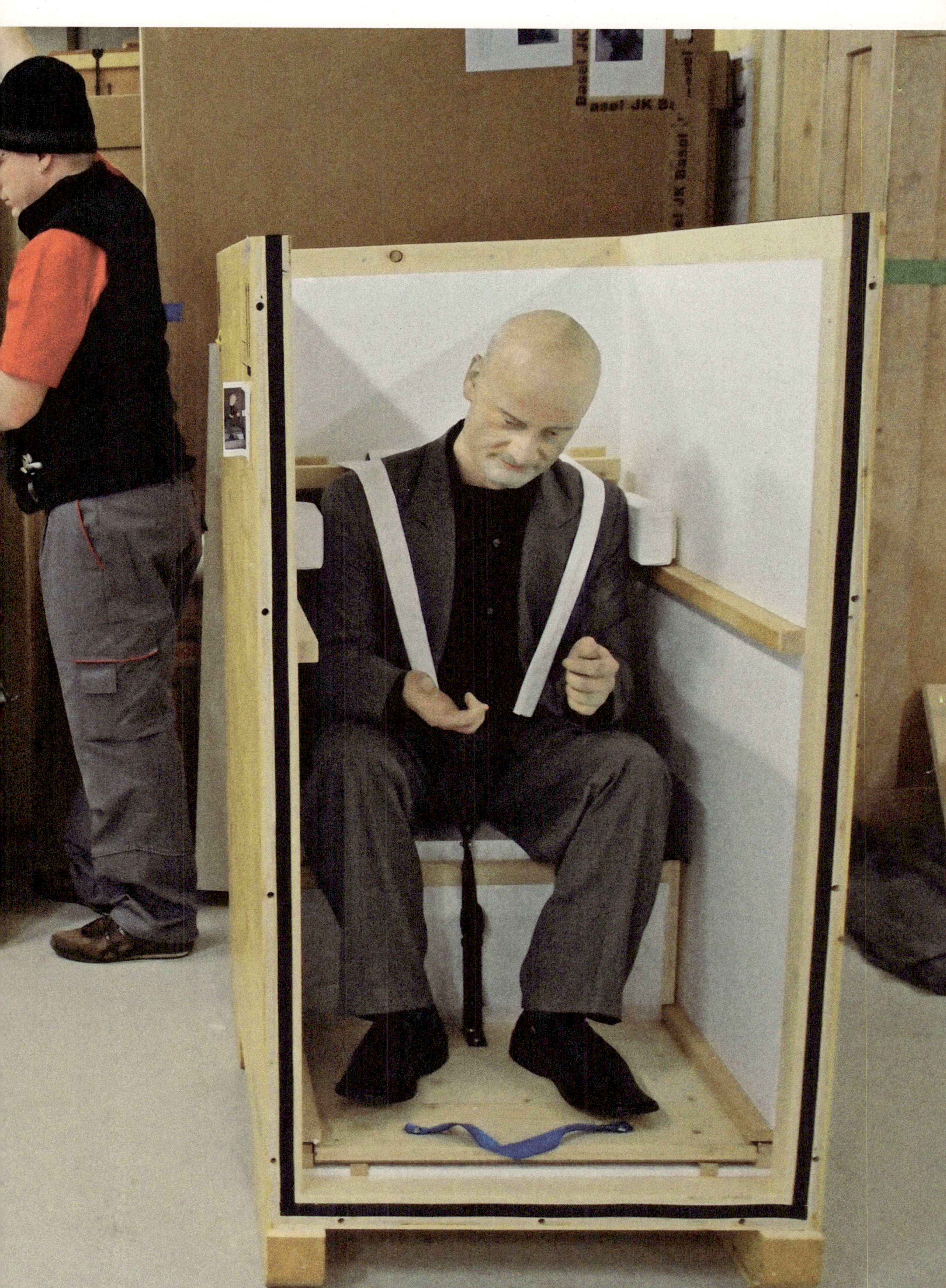

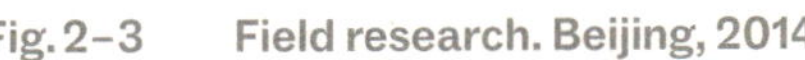

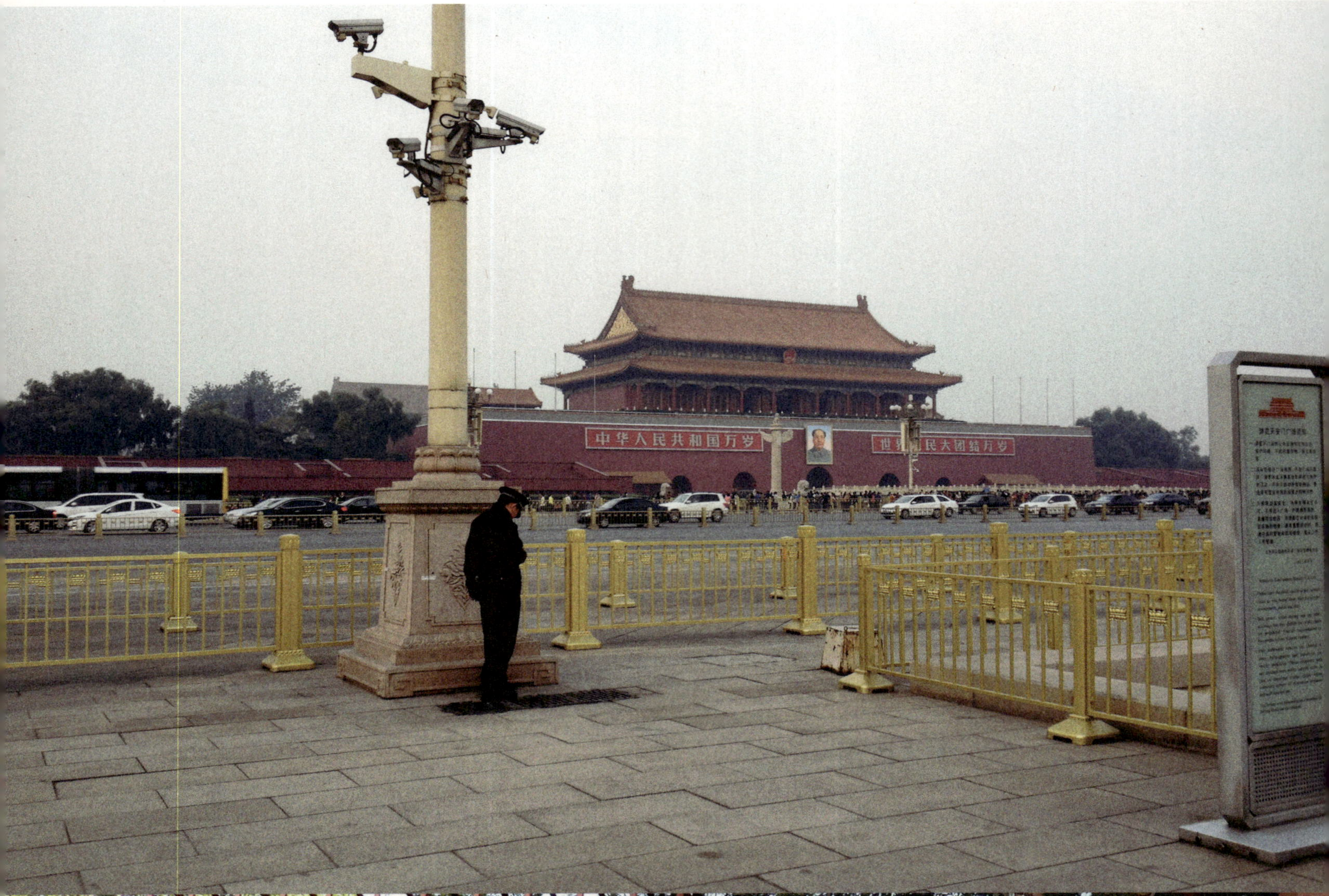

Fig. 2–3 Field research. Beijing, 2014

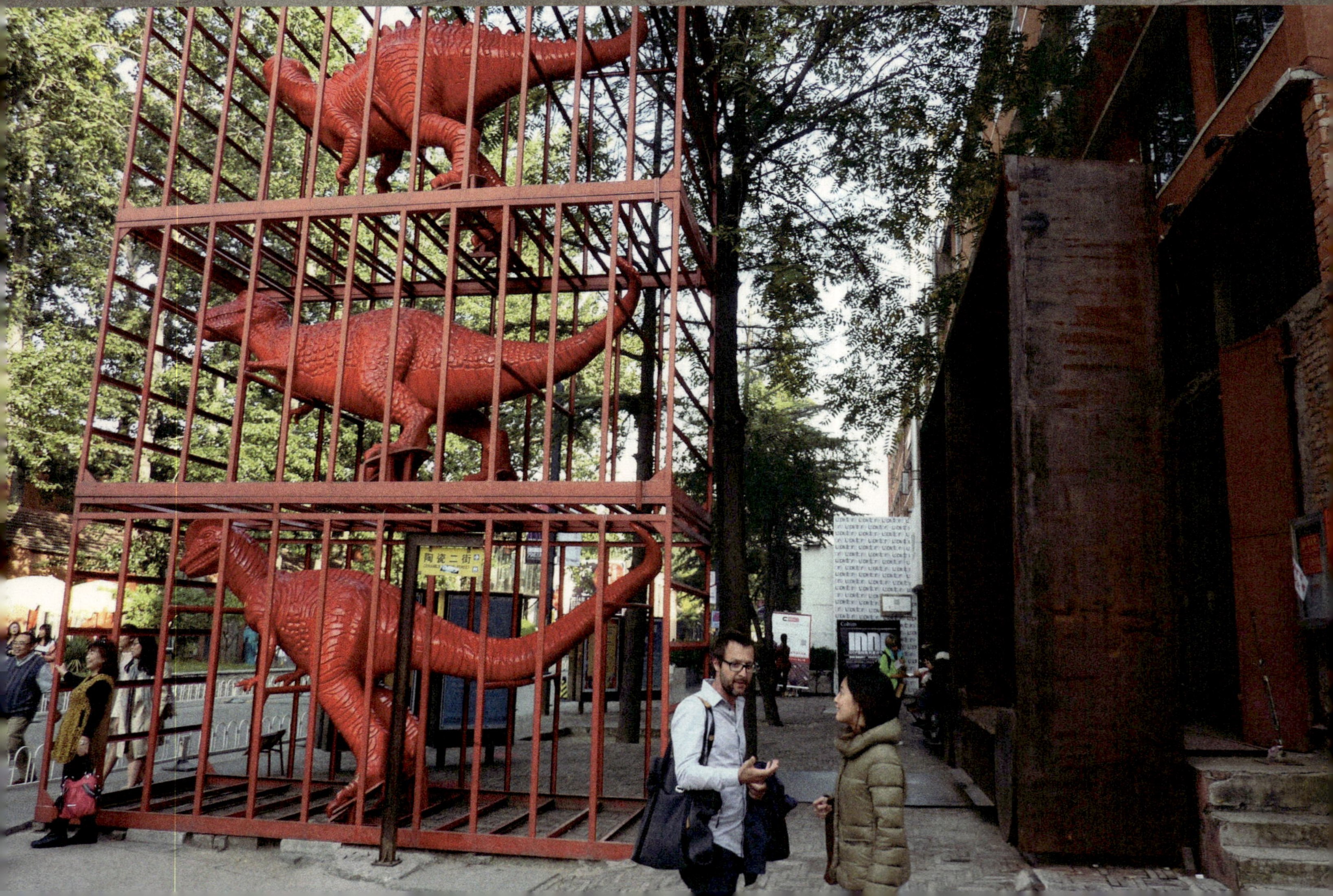

Fig. 4 Huang Yong Ping: *Circus*, 2012. Red Brick Art Museum, Beijing, 2014

Fig. 5 Exhibition *15 Years Chinese Contemporary Art Award (CCAA)*. Power Station of Art, Shanghai, 2014

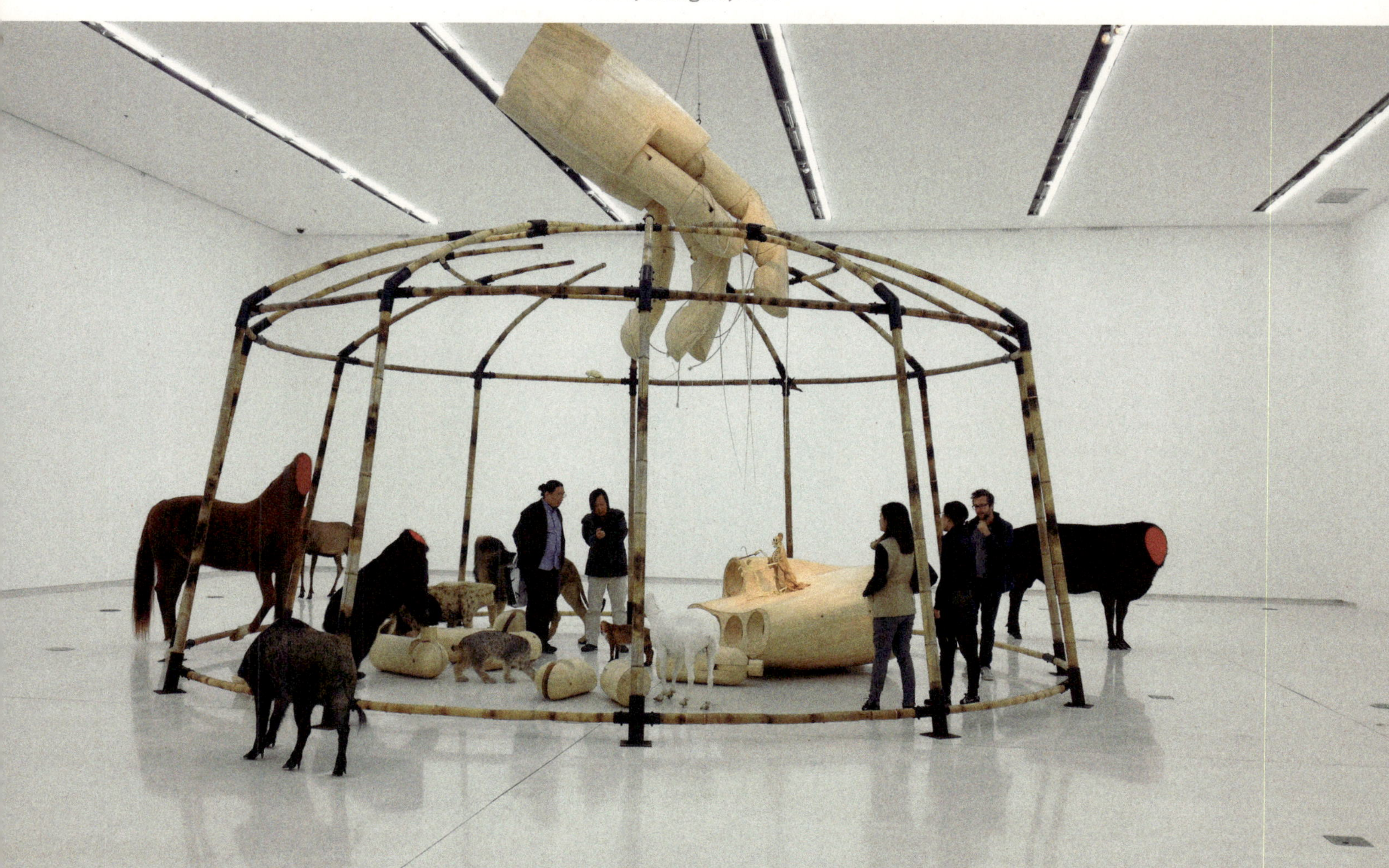

Do chimpanzees develop the self-motivation to use a paintbrush if they repeatedly are offered the opportunity to paint? Do they distinguish that handling a brush and paint is mutually related to the application of color and its visual effect? Is it ultimately possible to establish evidence of a pre-graphic or pictorial intention?

A transdisciplinary research team, composed of members of the Zurich University of the Arts, the University of Zurich, and the Walter Zoo Gossau, explored these questions. Over the course of twenty months, the *Inherent Crossing* project offered a group of sixteen chimpanzees the opportunity to participate voluntarily in sessions during which they were able to occupy themselves with painting utensils. Of the sixteen chimpanzees in the group, five were regularly responsive to the offer. One of the female chimpanzees, Blacky, repeatedly indicated a pre-graphic intention in the way she handled the painting utensils. On multiple occasions, Blacky painted solid patches of color, juxtaposed paint applications, and displayed a differentiated treatment of the liquid paint as an imaging material.

For the question of pictorial intention, the actual process in dealing with the utensils is decisive: How are the brush and the gaze directed? Are their movements varied or repeated? What is more, however, the sessions in Walter Zoo made clear that the social and spatial conditions, as well as how fit each animal is on a given day, are essential for the animal to pay any attention at all to the brush, paint, and carrier surface. The setting of the sessions, the social constellations within the chimpanzee group, and the individual relationships between the given scientists and apes proved to be central elements in this process. Accordingly, the research team recorded not only the actual act of applying paint, but also the social factors prevalent during each session. Such an expanded focus is decisive for evaluating the study, as merely interpretating the traces of paint would be inadequate.

The study demonstrates, on the one hand, that the question of early graphic behavior among chimpanzees can be discussed only when the individual prerequisites of each chimpanzee are accounted for. It makes clear that a pre-graphic or pictorial intention may potentially be inherent in individual chimpanzees, but that pictorial interest is distinctly individual. On the other hand, it shows that the social parameters that enable a space of contemplation to emerge are of decisive relevance for the participation and development of pictorial processes.

Benjamin Egger

Project Title
Inherent Crossing. Zur Evidenz früher bildhafter Intentionen

Project Period
1 November 2014–31 January 2017

Key Words
- Chimpanzee ontogenesis
- Research across species
- Early graphic manifestation

Heads of Project
- Benjamin Egger, artist
- Dieter Maurer, semiotician

Project Team
- Carel van Schaik, anthropologist
- Angela Widmer, animal caretaker
- Sabine Wiedemann, animal caretaker

Research Partner
- University of Zurich, Anthropological Institute and Museum

Project Partner
- Walter Zoo AG Gossau

Research Funding
- Ernst Göhner Stiftung

Website
- https://inherent-crossing.net

Archive
- Benjamin Egger and Dieter Maurer: *Archive: Inherent Crossing. On the Evidence of a Pre-Graphic Intention*. First published 2020. https://inherent-crossing.net/archive.

Related Projects
- Early Pictures, Zurich University of the Arts, 1999–ongoing

P. 12

Publication
- Anthropological Institute and Museum of the University of Zurich (ed.) (2016): *Kunst – Ein evolutionärer Denkansatz*. Exhibition Catalogue, University of Zurich. With contributions by Benjamin Egger, Dieter Maurer, and Carel van Schaik.

Presentation
- Benjamin Egger and Dieter Maurer: "Inherent Crossing." Research Day. 12 December 2015. Zurich University of the Arts.

Conference
- *Kunst – Ein evolutionärer Denkansatz*. In the framework of the eponymous exhibition, 28 April 2016. Anthropological Museum, University of Zurich. With contributions by Benjamin Egger, Dieter Maurer, and Carel van Schaik.

Exhibitions
- *Kunst – Ein evolutionärer Denkansatz*. 29 April 2016–30 April 2017. Anthropological Museum, University of Zurich. With contributions by Benjamin Egger, Dieter Maurer, and Carel van Schaik.
- *Inherent Crossing: Interviews*. 3–4 November 2016, Showroom Z+ N° 6, within the exhibition series Kollaborationen, Zurich University of the Arts.

Work
- Benjamin Egger: *Inherent Crossing*. 2017. Video, single channel, HD, color, 19:30 min.

Fig. 1 Angela Widmer, Madschabu, and Blacky. Walter Zoo Gossau, 2014

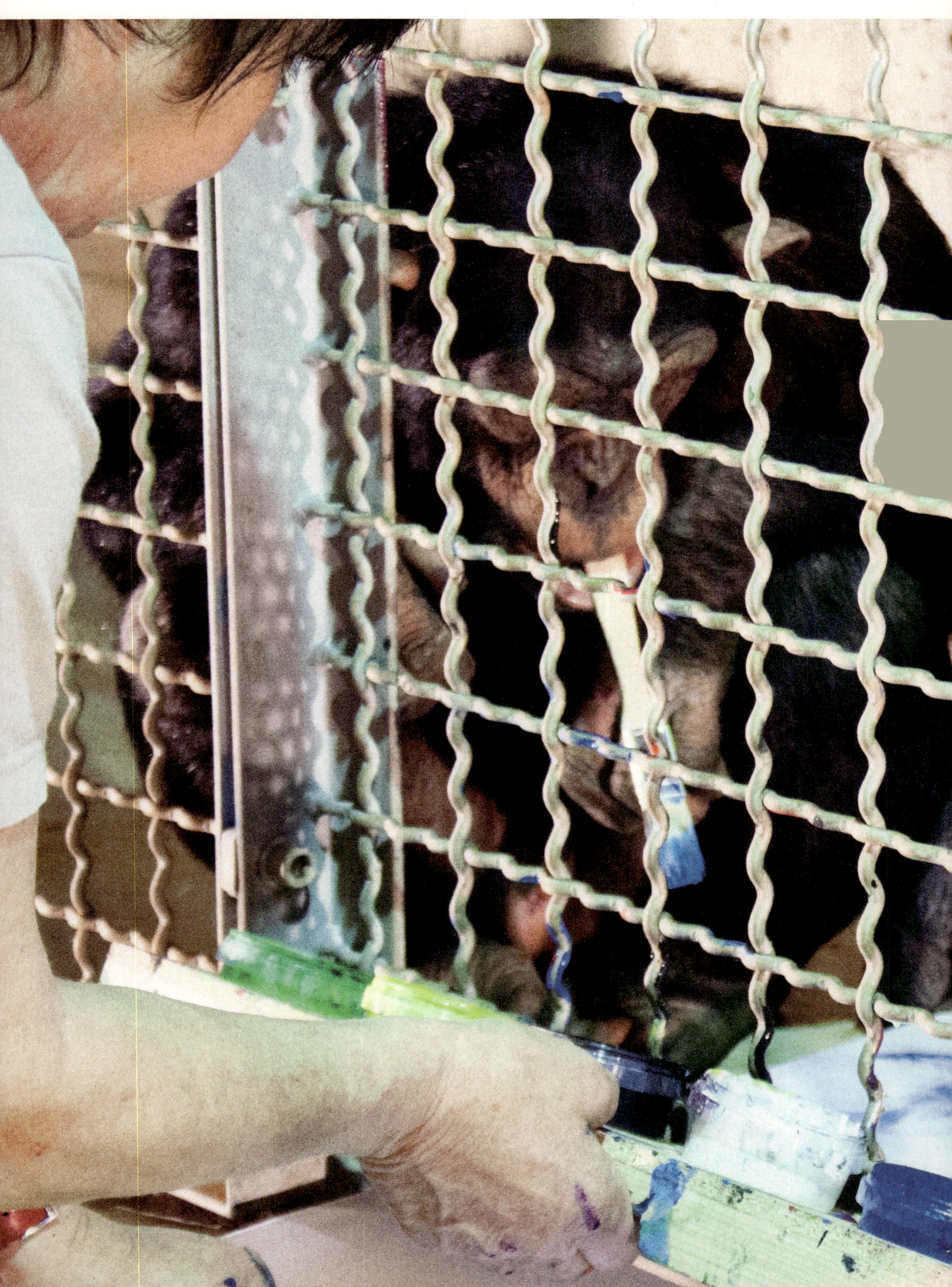

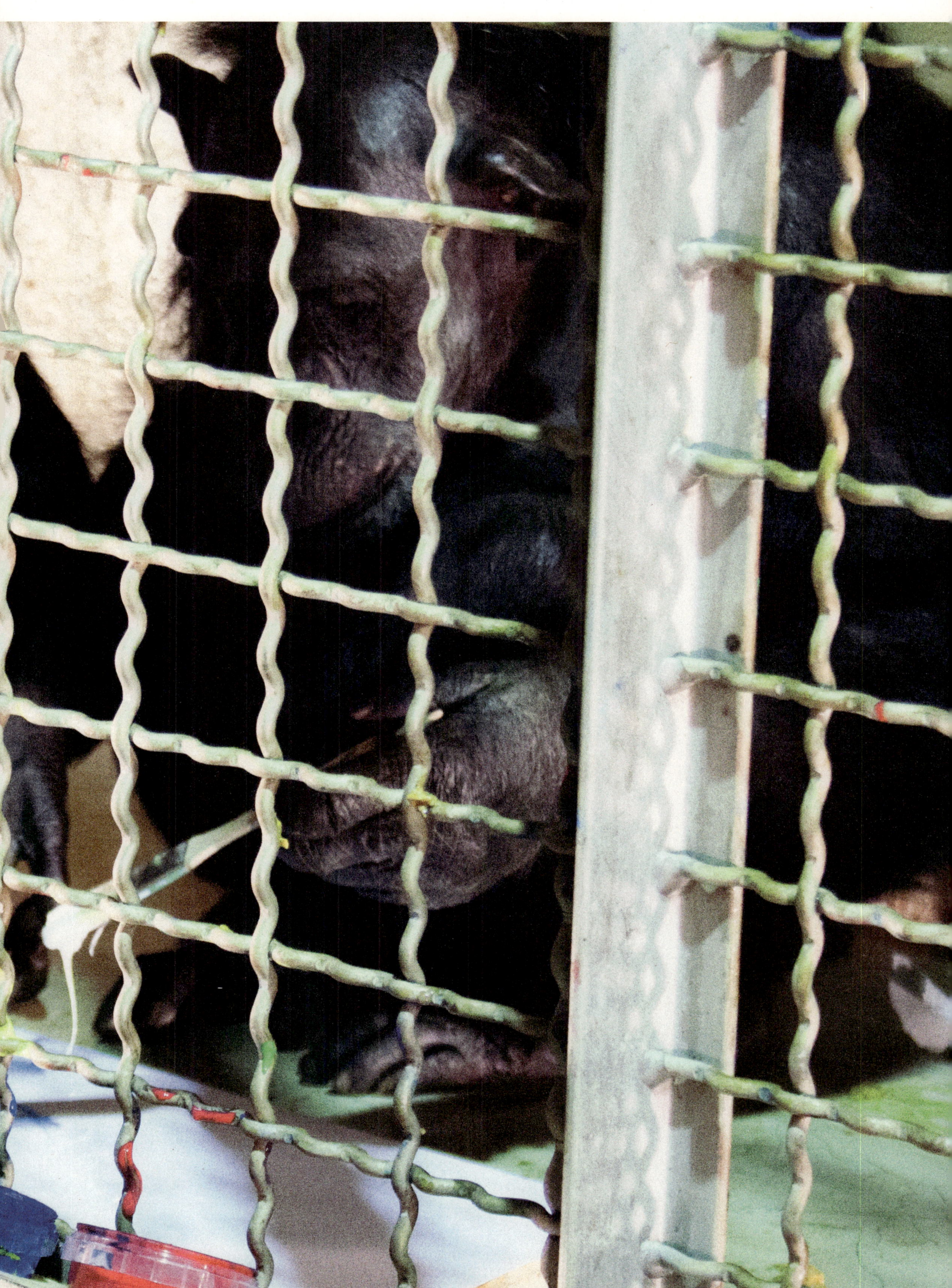

Fig. 2 Manifestation by Blacky. Walter Zoo Gossau, 2014
Fig. 3 Sketch of the setting, 2013

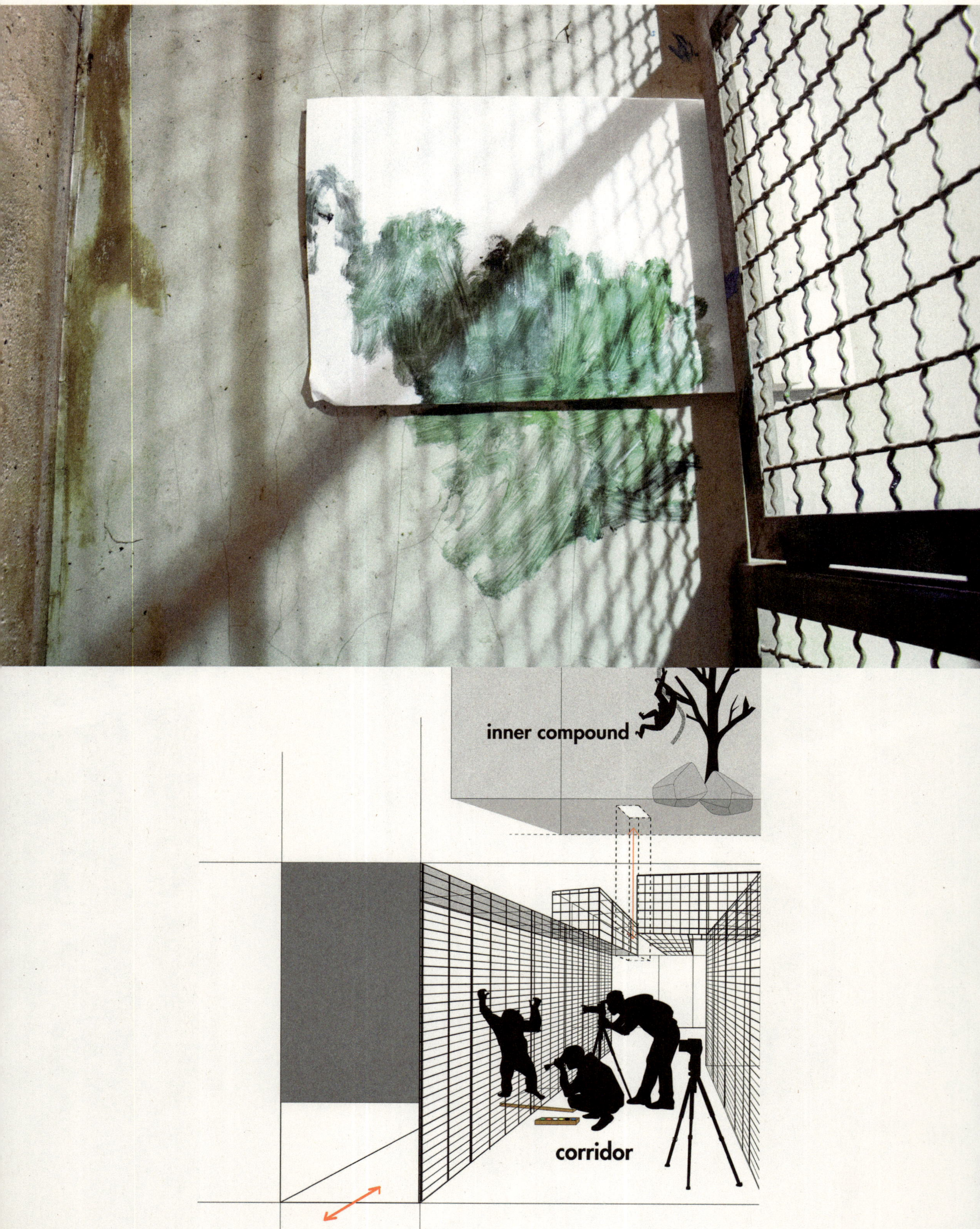

Fig. 4 Malik and Elisha. Video still, Walter Zoo Gossau, 2015
Fig. 5 Painting utensils. Walter Zoo Gossau, 2014

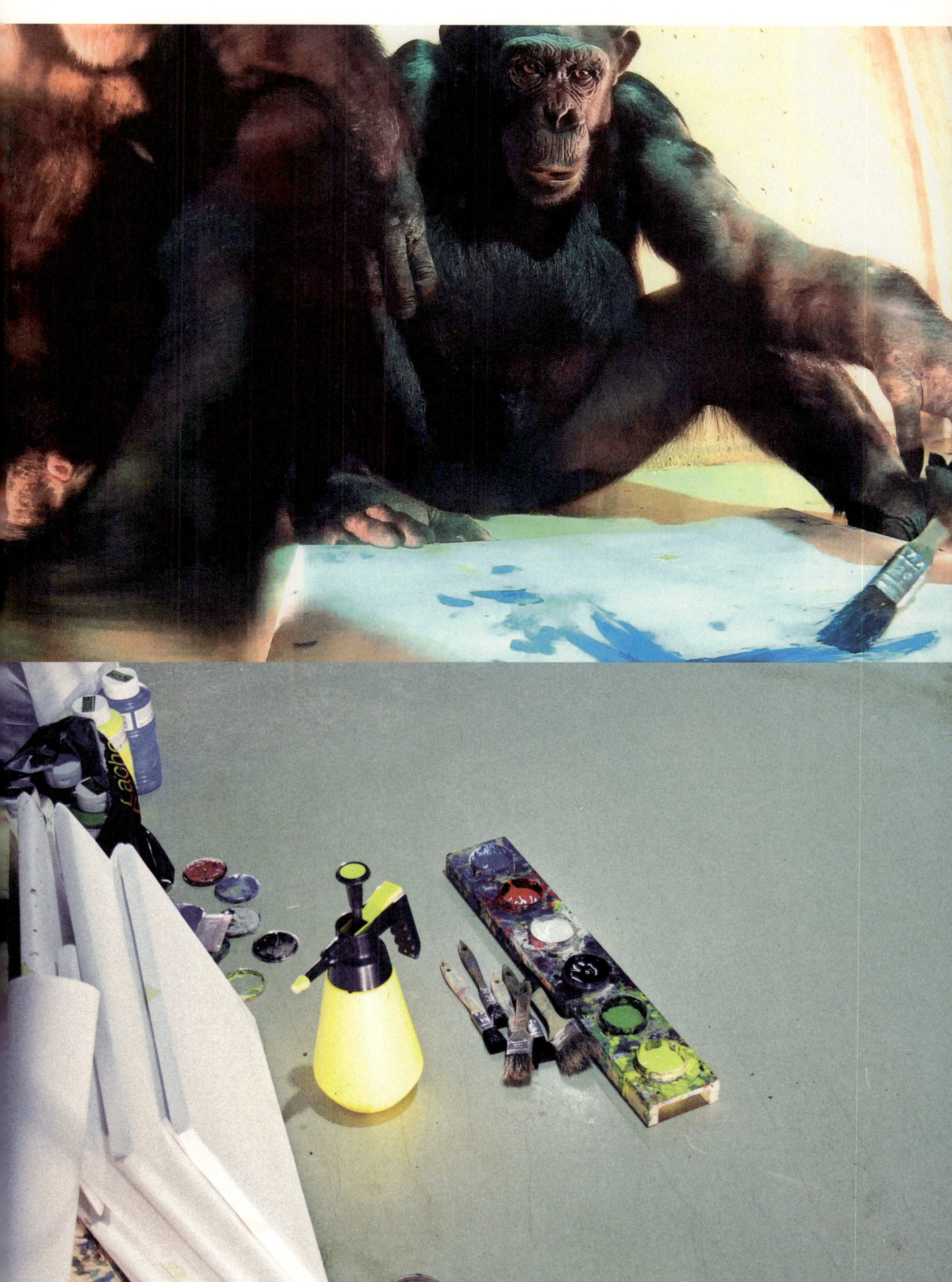

Swiss Psychotropic Gold investigated Swiss commodity trading with a focus on the extraction, refining, and symbolic acquisition of gold. Commodity trading made an essential contribution to early industrialization in Switzerland, and also to the formation of a global, technocratic financial center. Today up to 70% of the gold mined globally, including conflict gold, is refined in Switzerland. The research consisted of artistically researching encounters and confrontations with actors, materialities and affects surrounding commodity trading, and of physical sensitizations to these subjects.

We collaborated with the sound artist A Frei to trace the invisibility of the transfer of gold and its metabolism, and made audio-based field recordings at three Swiss gold refineries. We conducted conversations with historians (Jacob Tanner, Lea Haller), finance experts, and theoreticians (Stefan Leins, Jordy Rosenberg, and Achim Szepanski), gold experts, and NGOs (Public Eye). From this we gathered that considerable critical reappraisal of commodities trading in Switzerland has already taken place, both in academia and by NGOs, but hardly any projects have more closely investigated the affective economies of gold. Our aim was to trace the collective imaginations, amnesias, and excitations which official Switzerland generates in dealing with gold, and to reflect upon these critically and somatically. For this, typical narrations of neutrality, security, moral superiority, and democratic attitudes were analyzed with/in their references to the associations with the precious metal gold, and its colonial and postcolonial entanglements pointed out. In the long, intensive research phase we collected primarily materials and documents in analog and digital archives, remaining critically vigilant for that which could not be found there.

Even today we repeatedly establish how up to date the topic is: On the one hand, in the field of politics through current initiatives (cf. corporate responsibility initiatives in Switzerland, and the supply chain law in Germany); on the other, in the field of art through invitations to conferences and exhibitions. Global commodity trading with gold and its physical and mental contaminations continue to create ecological, social, and affect-economic issues that must urgently be addressed. Yet, the relations between libidinous desire, violence-oriented extractivism, and climate-critical interventions cannot be sufficiently conveyed and dealt with through historical and economic analyses and a knowledge culture based on statistics and diagrams. As a team we conceptualized critical fabulations about gold's cosmopolitan network of relationships and Switzerland's role in this mesh. We developed speculative scenarios in which we integrated gold as a material, casting the infrastructures of gold trading and the landscapes violated through gold extraction as actors whose voices must be heard. In artistically sensory treatments, performative encounters (acupuncture with gold, meditation on gold, inhalation of psychoactive stimulants), our fabulations were translated into hybrid objects of knowledge and the senses. These translations and embodiments culminated in the multimedia publication *Swiss Psychotropic Gold*.

The experiences from the project and the broader questions it raised were also included in the SNSF-sponsored pilot project *The Aesthetics of the Translocal. Methods of Artistic Research for the Negotiation of Latent Knowledges* with Ines Kleesattel and Uriel Orlow.

Christian Huebler and Yvonne Wilhelm

Project Title
Swiss Psychotropic Gold

Project Period
1 July 2015–31 December 2020

Keywords
- Commodity trading
- Epistemic disobedience
- Material semiotics
- Affective economies
- Molecularization

Head of Project
- knowbotiq (Yvonne Wilhelm and Christian Huebler), artists

Research Team
- Rohit Jain, social anthropologist
- Nina Bandi, political theorist
- A Frei, artist

Project Funding
- Pro Helvetia
- Kunstförderung Österreich, Bundeskanzleramt

Related Projects
- Draft (umbrella project), Zurich University of the Arts, 2014–2017
  P. 166
- The Aesthetics of the Translocal, Zurich University of the Arts, 2019–2020
  P. 246

Outputs

A

Website

- http://swisspsygold.knowbotiq.net

Publication

- Yvonne Wilhelm, Christian Huebler, and Nina Bandi (eds.) (2020): *Swiss Psychotropic Gold*. Volume 23 of the Institute for Contemporary Art Research series. Basel: Christoph Merian.
  - A Open access: https://doi.org/10.5281/zenodo.5896739

Article

- knowbotiq and Nina Bandi (2020): "Swiss Psychotropic Gold." In: Mihye An and Ludger Hovestadt (eds.) (2020): *Architecture and Naturing Affairs*. Basel: Birkhäuser, 70–79.

Lecture

- *Public Talks: Swiss Psychotropic Gold as part of Draft*. 16 March 2017. Valand Academy, University of Gothenburg, Public Guest Program. With Rohit Jain, Gitanjali Dang, and knowbotiq. Curated by Giorgiana Zachia.

Performative Installations and Exhibitions

- *Swiss Psychotropic Gold: Delinking Commodity. Trading Rohstoffwechsel*. 28–30 July 2016. Empty Office Building in Zurich West. Performative installation during *Draft Zurich Conference*, in collaboration with Fred Hystère, Tanja Quirici, Teresa Vittucci, and Alper Yacioglu. With the support of Nina Bandi and Rohit Jain.
- *Psychotropic Gold-Decanonizing University*. 29–30 June 2017. University of Basel. Performative Installation during the 7th European Conference on African Studies.
- *The Swiss Psychotropic Gold Refining*. 10 September–8 October 2017. Corner College. Solo exhibition.
- *Gold—Mining the Unconsciousness*. 11 February–10 April 2022. Helmhaus Zürich. Solo exhibition.

Works

- knowbotiq and Nina Bandi: *On the Division of Labour, Work, Knowledge, the Sensible*. 23–24 September 2016. Performance lecture at Vienna Academy of Fine Arts/Kunstraum Niederösterreich, Vienna.
- knowbotiq and Gabriel Flückiger: *Swiss Psychotropic Gold—abstract sex and molecular joy*. 12 December 2019. Performance at Biennale Némo, hosted by Centre Culturel Suisse Paris.
- knowbotiq and Elizabeth Gallón Droste, Claudia Howald, Fundación Mareia, Ana Garzón Sabogal, and Pablo Torres: *Mercurybodies—Many are holding*. 2022. Animated satellite maps and listening space, flatscreen, 4-channel audio installation, audio players, headset, booklet.

Fig. 1 knowbotiq: *Swiss Psychotropic Gold*. Hartware MedienKunstVerein, Dortmund, 2021

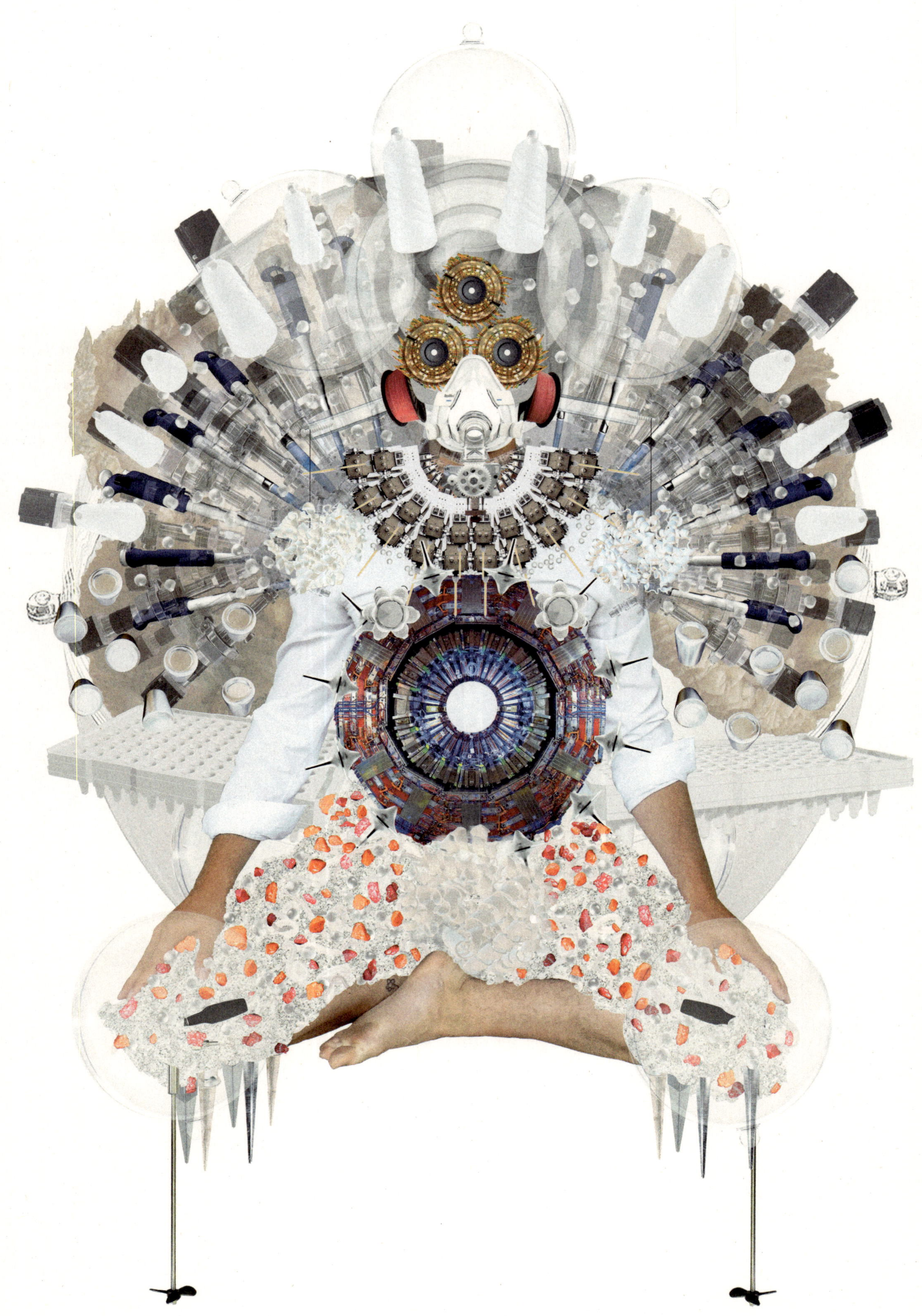

Fig. 2 knowbotiq: *The Psychotropic Refinery*. Helmhaus Zürich, 2022

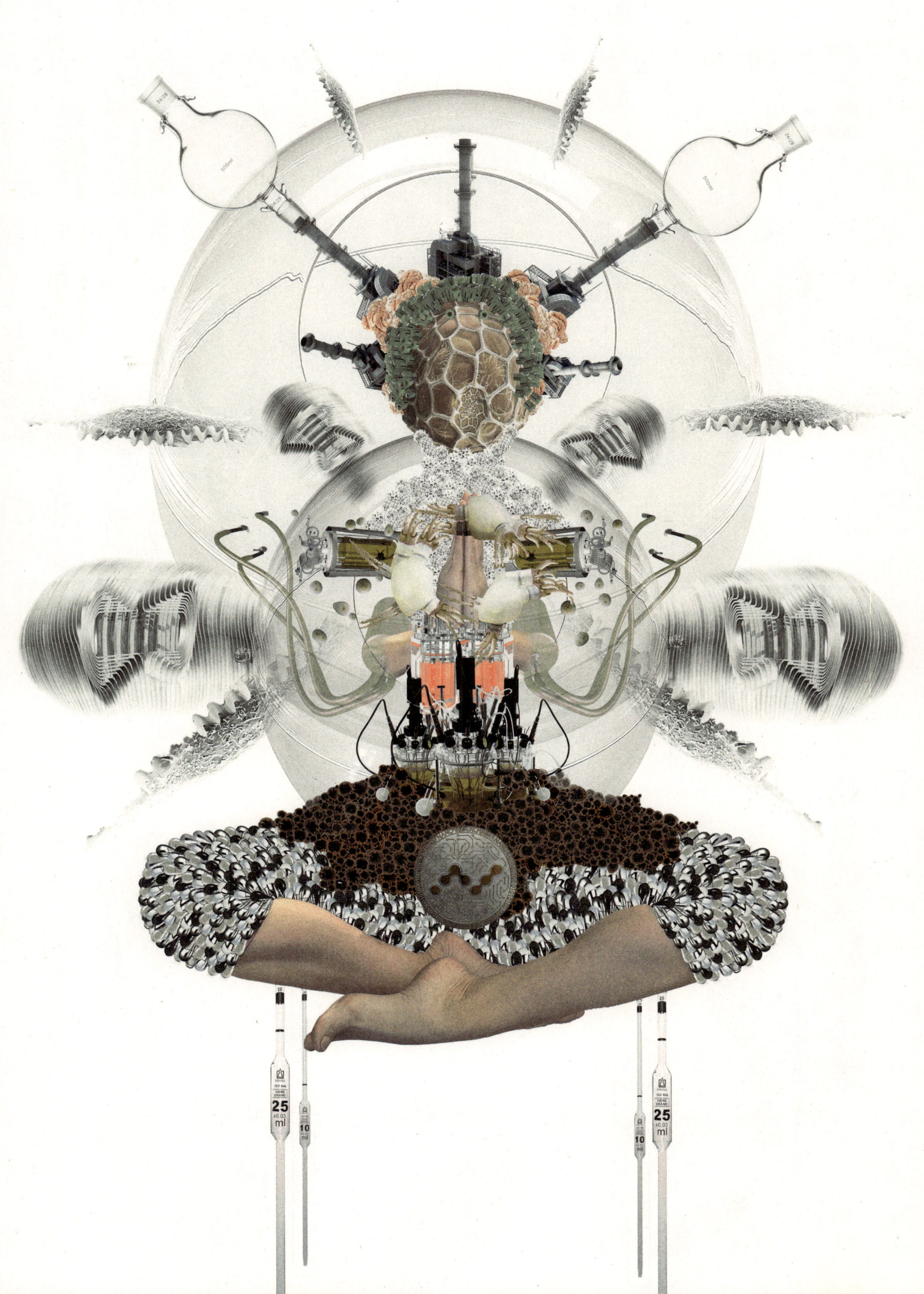

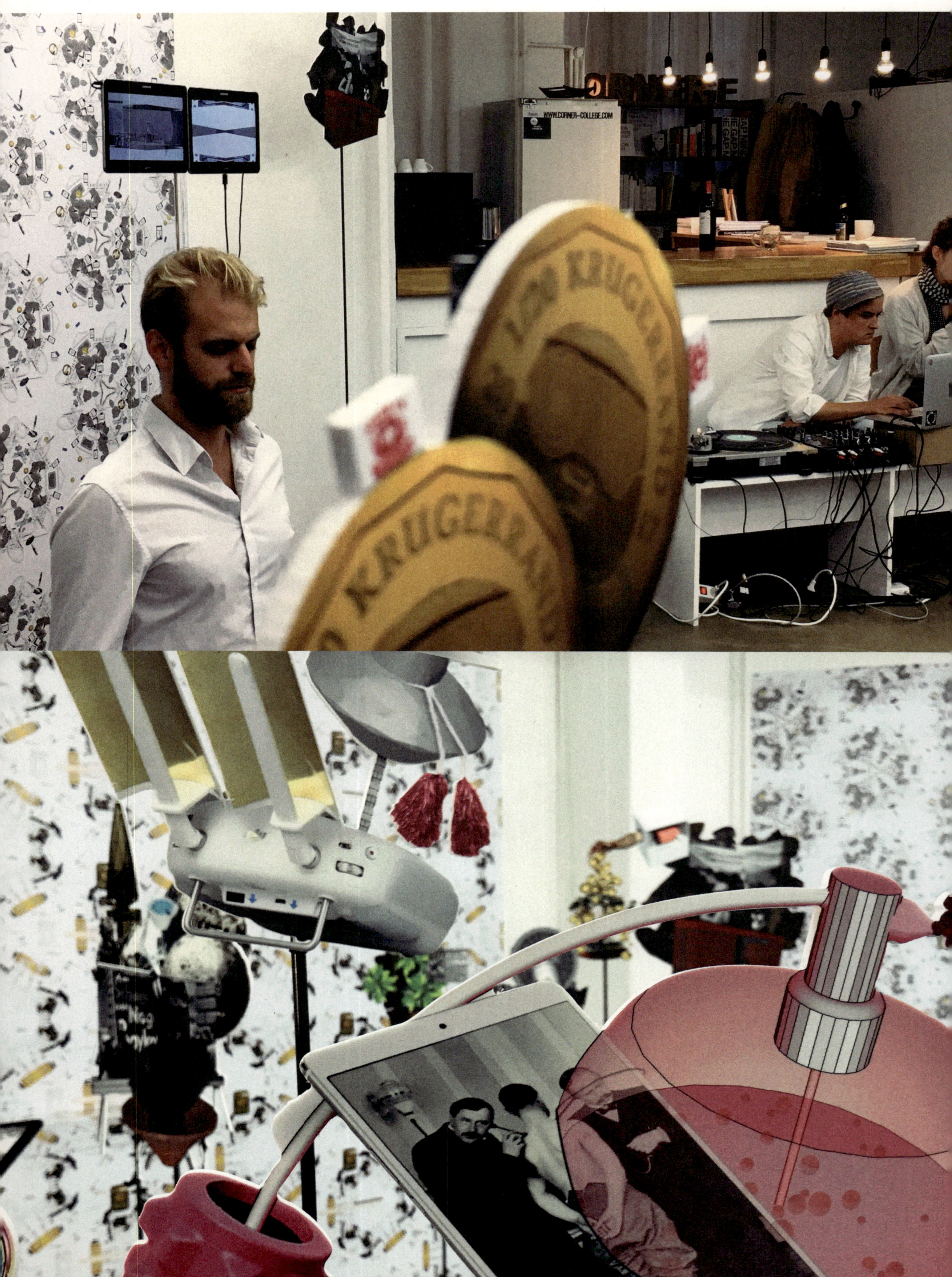
WWW.CORNER-COLLEGE.COM
KRUGERRAND
KRUGERRAND

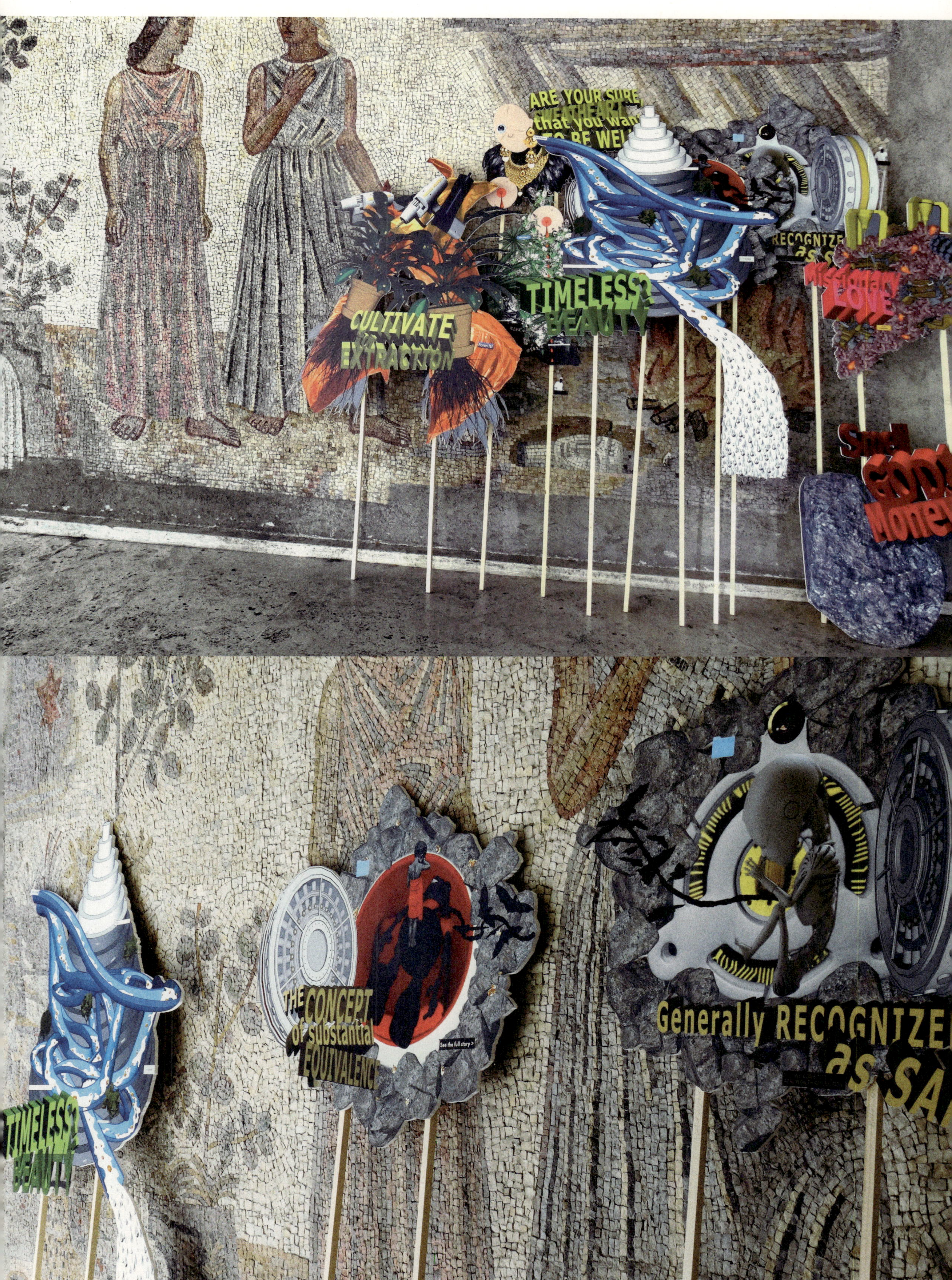

Fig. 5–6 knowbotiq: *Psychotropic Gold. Decanonizing the University*. 7th European Conference on African Studies, University of Basel, 2017

Contemporary public art engages with current societal themes by initiating or contributing to public debates. As such, art takes the position of a critical instance and contributes to fostering a democratic consciousness. Proceeding from the fact that many topics addressed by art are globally significant, but processed locally, the translocal discussion about approaches, methods, and practices is of immanent importance. A discussion of this kind promises to nurture knowledge about the public sphere, a consciousness about global challenges and their local expressions, and to glean an understanding of problems as well as insights into other life realities with their corresponding problem-solving strategies. Building on the experiences from the *Draft* project, the Institute for Contemporary Art Research (IFCAR) initiated the InOctober network of art academies and institutions in selected cities of the global South and North with a view to promoting long-term dialog, research, and teaching on the international level among equal partners in the field of contemporary public art.

The central format of InOctober was the annual October School, an open, flexible event oriented to instruction and research. The given host institution chose the thematic orientation and organized and held the event, inviting its partner institutions and other guest universities to send students and lecturers to participate in the exchange program. In workshops, thematic city tours, visits to local activist groups and community programs, and seminars and lectures held on site, around thirty-five students investigated, discussed, and negotiated a locally significant societal challenge with a global impact, such as the emotionalization of politics and the public sphere (Delhi 2017), or horizontal practices in the postcolonial discourse (Mexico City 2019). Internationally mixed groups developed models of artistic approaches to initiating and stimulating public discourse. Expert reports from various fields of knowledge like sociology, political science, and philology allowed for observation from multiple perspectives; renowned visual and theater artists, activists, and documentary filmmakers accentuated the urgency and relevance of the addressed topic areas. The intensive, direct exchange among students, lecturers, and local experts over two weeks at each October School yielded a deeper understanding of the situation on site, as well as in-depth exchange among the participants about perspectives, values, and artistic problem-solving strategies.

After the initial summer school in Zurich in 2016, entitled *Negotiating Space—Art and Dissent*, which was conceptualized and run in cooperation with Manifesta 11, the subsequent October Schools took place in Delhi and in Mexico City. Due to the Corona pandemic, during the 2020 and 2021 October Schools the meetings and exchange among the students in different cities had to take place online. The decidedly critical and political orientation of the October School resulted in the withdrawal of the important partner institution the Chinese University of Hong Kong from the program due to political pressure, while other universities' participation was restricted by their university administrations.

The program fostered exchange among students, lecturers, and researchers, and long-term cooperation with partner institutions. It supported university-level discourse on research and instruction on both the local and the international levels, and facilitated the transfer of ideas and knowledge to the generation of young artists. With this it contributed to the sensibilization and networking of its researchers, students, and lecturers in the field of contemporary public art. Moreover, it conveyed that the artistic treatment of relevant societal topics is an important field in the art.

Franz Krähenbühl

Project Title
InOctober. International Network for Contemporary Public Art

Project Period
1 January 2016–31 December 2021

Keywords
- Contemporary public art
- Interculturalism
- Globalization
- Activism
- Engaged public art

Heads of Project
- Franz Krähenbühl, art researcher and curator
- Christoph Schenker, art theorist

Staff from Zurich University of the Arts
- Nils Röller, philosopher
- Nadia Graf, artist
- Yvonne Wilhelm, artist
- Donatella Bernardi, artist

Staff from the Partner Universities
- Tushar Joag (IND), artist
- Sharmila Samant (IND), artist
- Vedant Nanackchand (SA), art theorist
- José Miguel Casanova (MX), artist
- Siu Kee Ho (HK), artist
- José Luis Macas (ECU), artist
- Javier Martinez (MX), communication representative
- Yuri Alberto Aguilar (MX), artist and art theorist
- Makiko Hara (JP), curator

A

Partner Universities
- Shiv Nadar University (SNU), Department of Art, Design, and Performing Arts, Delhi, India
- The Chinese University of Hong Kong (CUHK), Department of Fine Arts, Hong Kong, China
- University of Johannesburg (UJ), Faculty of Art, Design and Architecture, Johannesburg, South Africa
- Universidad Nacional Autónoma de Mexico (UNAM), Faculty of Arts and Design, Ciudad de Mexico, Mexico
- Pontificia Universidad Católica del Ecuador, Facultad arquitectura, diseño y artes, Quito, Ecuador
- Akita University of Art (AUA), Graduate School of Transdisciplinary Arts, Akita City, Japan
- Baptist University Hong Kong (BUHK), Academy of Visual Arts, Hong Kong, China
- MASS Alexandria, studio space and study program, Alexandria, Egypt
- China Academy of Art, SIMA School of Intermedia Art, CAA, Hangzhou, China
- University of the Witwatersrand Johannesburg, Division of Visual Arts, Johannesburg, South Africa
- School of Engaged Art, Chto Delat, St. Petersburg, Russia
- Accademia di Belle Arti di Palermo, Dipartimento Arti visive, Palermo, Italy

October Schools
- Summer School Zürich 2016
  Art and Dissent—Negotiating Space
  24 July–6 August 2016
  Zurich University of the Arts
- October School Delhi 2017
  Encountering Emotions (in the Public Sphere)
  4–14 October 2017
  Shiv Nadar University Delhi
- October School Delhi 2018
  Justice, Citizenship and the Self
  8–20 October 2018
  Shiv Nadar University Delhi
- October School Mexico City 2019
  Decolonization: Horizontal Practices
  26 October–10 November 2019
  Universidad Nacional Autónoma de Mexico
- October School online 2020
  Wronging Rights: Challenging Human Rights Through Culture
  28 September–3 October 2020
  Zurich University of the Arts and online with partner schools
- October School 2021
  Where do we stand? Cosmopolitical Turbulences in Artistic Contextualization
  1–6 November 2021
  Zurich University of the Arts and online with partner schools

Project Partner 2016
- Manifesta 11 Zurich, the European Biennial of Contemporary Art

Related Project
- Draft, Zurich University of the Arts, 2014–2017
  P. 166

Project Website
- https://inoctober.org

Publication
- Nadia Graf, Franz Krähenbühl, and Christoph Schenker (eds.) (2019): *Fanzine October School Delhi 2018*. Zurich: Zurich University of the Arts.
  A Open access: https://doi.org/10.5281/zenodo.5818050

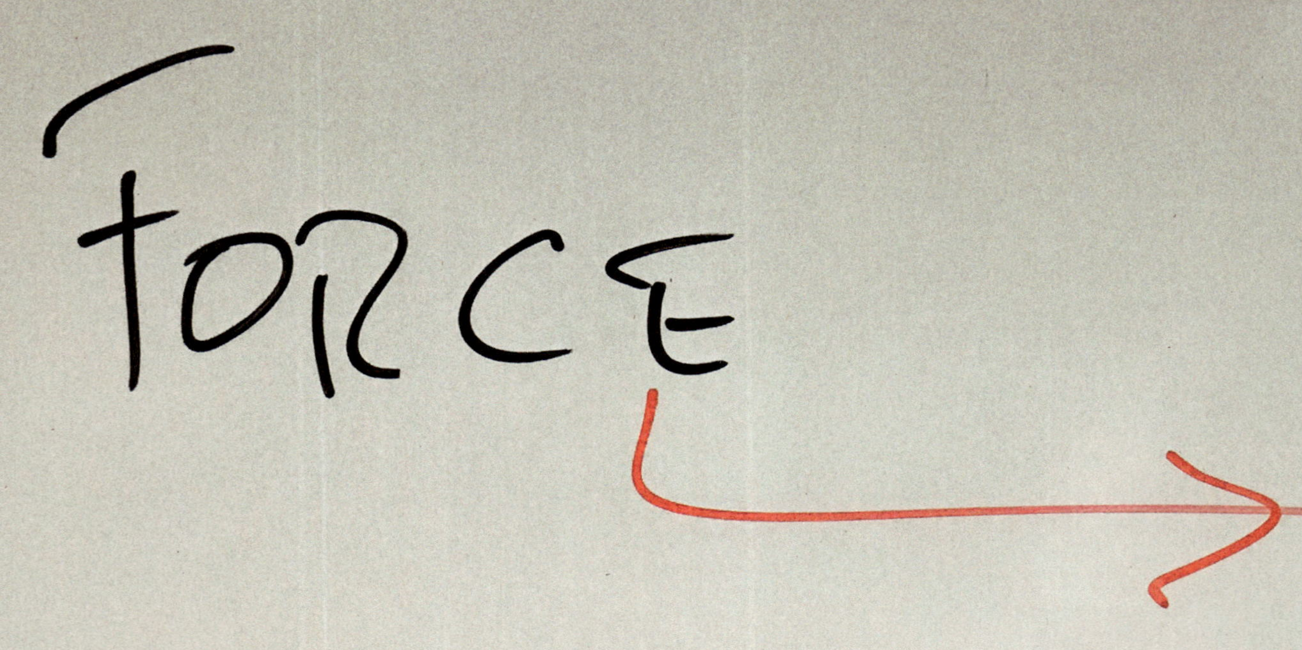
FORCE

Violation

Fig. 2–3 Field research. October School Delhi, 2018

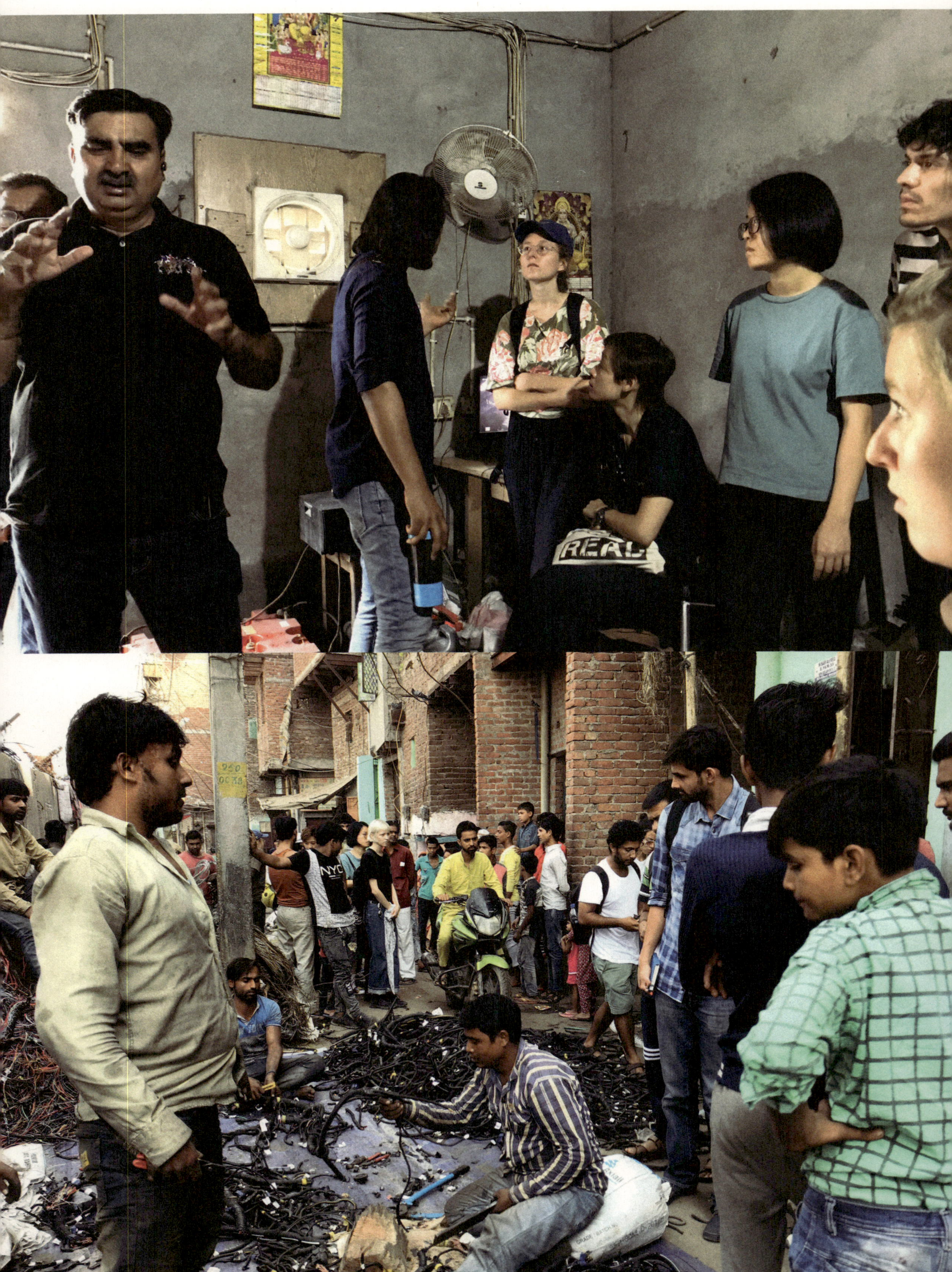

Fig. 4 Talk by Medha Patkar. October School Delhi, 2018
Fig. 5 Walk with Sohail Hashmi. October School Delhi, 2018

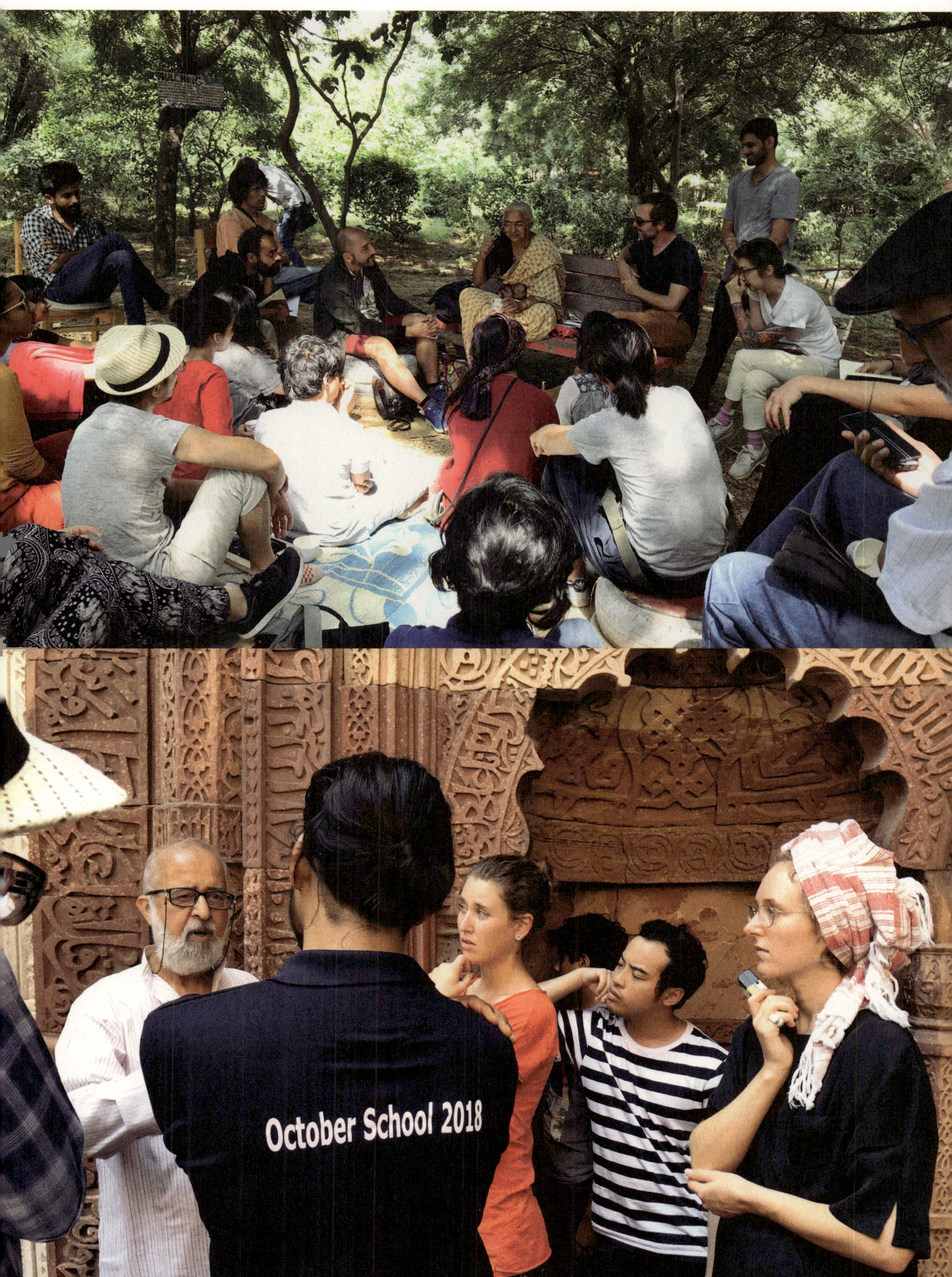

What is Critique? was an international symposium, held at Zurich University of the Arts (ZHdK) and organized in cooperation with Neuer Berliner Kunstverein e.V. and Inaesthetics. The idea that gave rise to this series of events is the present-day doxa that thinking constitutes itself as critical thought only, or, in other words, that thought must be critical or not be thought at all. This criticality or criticalness as a contemporary technology of legitimation and power calls for a critique in its own right.

Touching on the legacy of the Enlightenment, which always needs to be updated and critically analyzed, the question of what critique is was discussed in relation to its central role for civil society. Assuming a critical attitude towards all assertions and realities can enable us to reflect on such positions, instead of simply believing the discourses to be true. At the same time, we must acknowledge that a critical attitude includes affirmative traits, and thus implies and presupposes affirmations that limit its critical reach. The symposium was the third and last part of a series of events dedicated to the question "What is Critique?" This series of events began with Jean-Luc Nancy's *Unser Zeitalter ist nicht mehr das eigentliche Zeitalter der Kritik* (Our age is no longer the actual age of critique), a keynote lecture delivered at the HAU Hebbel am Ufer in Berlin on 28 January 2016. The series continued with two symposia entitled *Was ist Kritik?* (in Berlin)—*What is Critique?* (in Zurich). The first symposium was held on 6–7 February 2016 at the Neuer Berliner Kunstverein, the second on 1–2 April 2016 at ZHdK. While the Berlin Symposium invited speakers such as Elena Esposito, Eva Illouz, Sabeth Buchmann, Ann Cotton, and Maxim Biller, who shed light on philosophical aspects on the notion of critique, the Zurich symposium focused on artistic practices. How are the conditions of artistic articulation of critique—that is, one's own social contextuality and relativity—reflected in the means of art? Which methods of re-framing realities and conditions of one's own work are available for artistic practices?

The symposium comprised three main sessions during which three artists working in different social, institutional, and media fields discussed these and other questions together with a dialog partner (Artur Żmijewski and Gerald Raunig, Ursula Biemann and Emily Eliza Scott, Zheng Mahler and Roger Buergel). The dialog partners, together with the audience, explored the possibilities of critical practice, the forms of locating one's art, and the relation between critique and affirmation. In addition to the conversation on stage, the artists presented some of their key works. These artworks or art projects built the very center of the discussion.

Barbara Preisig

Project Title
What is Critique? International Symposium

Project Period
28 January 2016–2 April 2016

Keywords
- Philosophy
- Art criticism
- Artistic research
- Criticality
- Affirmation

Heads of Project
- Barbara Preisig, art historian and art critic
- Christoph Schenker, art theorist

Contributors to Zurich Symposium
- Ursula Biemann, artists
- Roger Buergel, curator and critic
- Gerald Raunig, philosopher
- Emily Eliza Scott, art and architecture historian
- Marcus Steinweg, philosopher
- Zheng Mahler (Royce Ng and Daisy Bisenieks), artist duo
- Artur Żmijewski, artist

Cooperations/Research Partners
- Marius Babias, Neuer Berliner Kunstverein
- Marcus Steinweg, Inaesthetics

Project Funding and Support

- **Allianz Kulturstiftung for Europe**

Editorship

- **Marius Babias, Barbara Preisig, and Christoph Schenker (eds.) (2017): *What is Critique? International Symposium*. ZHdK Konzert 46–49, DVD series. Box with 4 DVDs. Zurich: IFCAR in cooperation with Neuer Berliner Kunstverein e.V.**

Fig. 1 Ursula Biemann: Lecture. Zurich University of the Arts, 2016

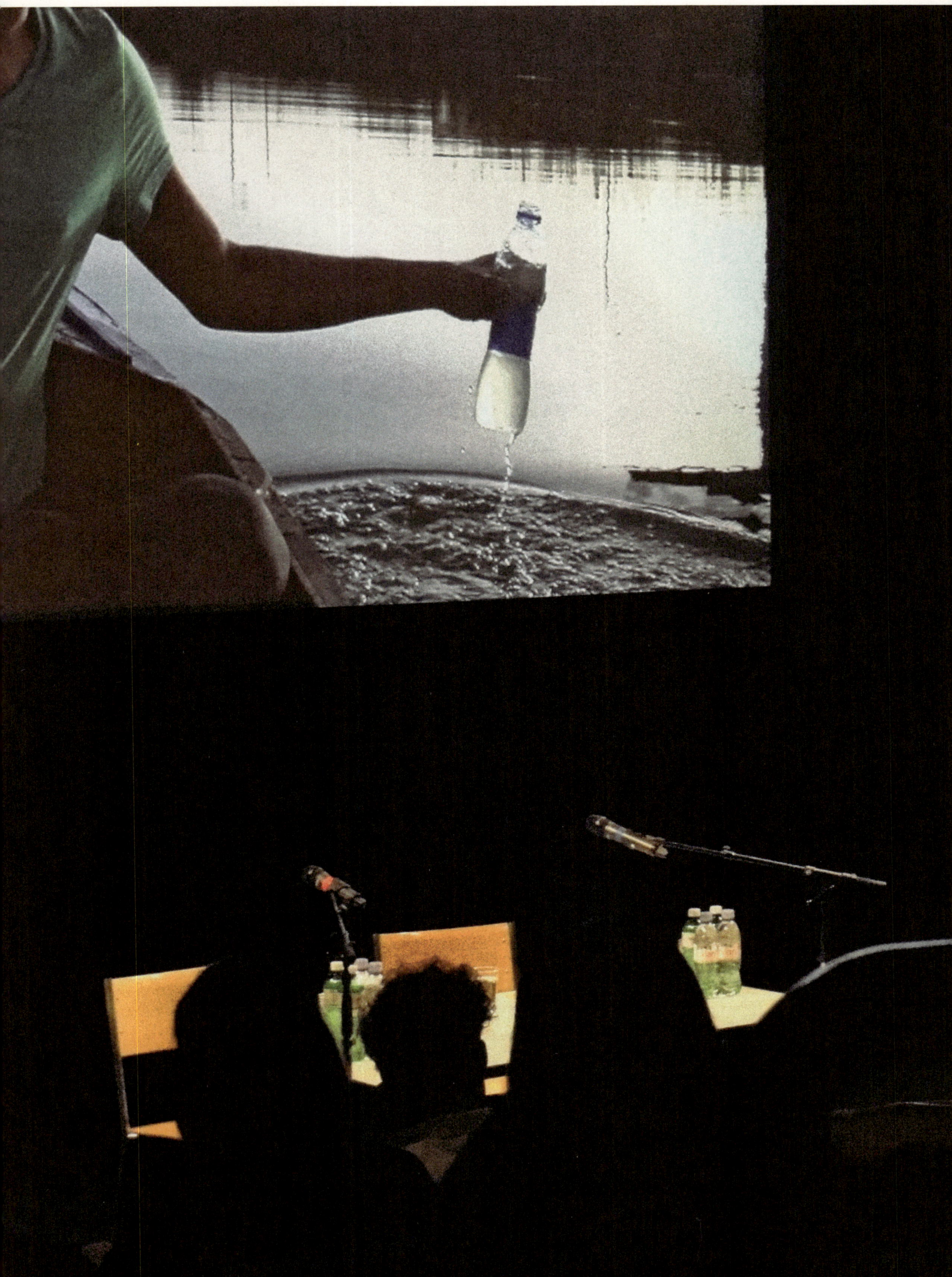

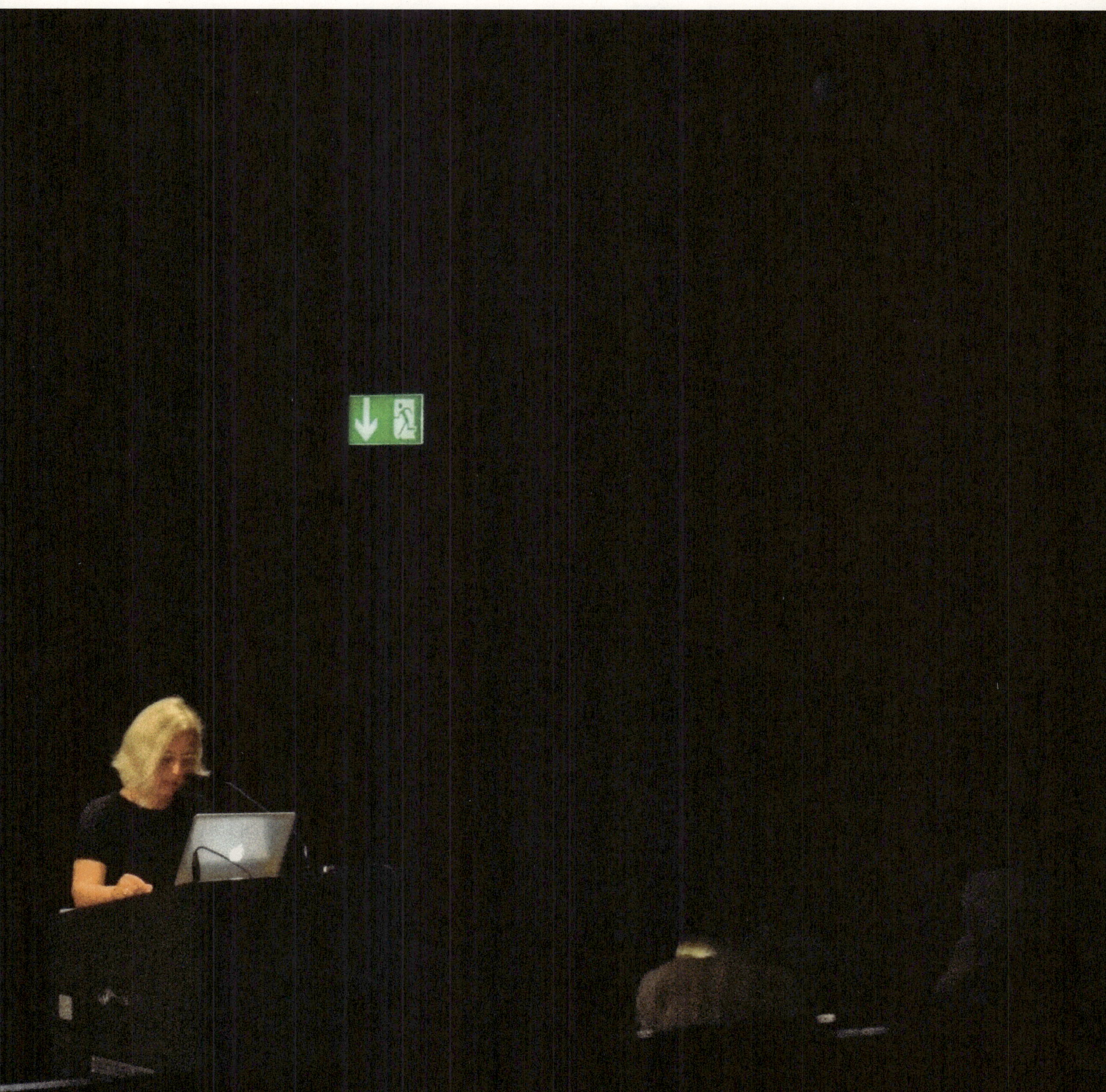

At the center of the project were fifteen (post-) digital artistic projects with a twofold character. They operate as discursive symbols, on the one hand, and as functional infrastructure, on the other. They theorize and adopt freely accessible online and offline resources like digital archives, technical infrastructures, local spaces and educative formats. In so doing they raise fundamental art theory and social science questions, which we researched under the aspect of commons. For us it was important to research not *about* these projects but *with* the artists and activists who run them, and to determine and negotiate key questions on the basis of the projects. The research project itself assumed a twofold character. On the one hand, we conveyed the research results discursively; on the other, we compiled freely accessible resources with which others can continue our work on their own.

Commons—self-organized relations for the free use of shared resources—constitute a comprehensive alternative to an order structured on private property. Its structuring element is not individual ownership but common concern. Who belongs to the community and on what goals this concern is oriented—growth, preservation, transformation—essentially determines the character of commons. From the perspective of art theory, commons pose questions such as the role of authors, the boundaries of the work, and the relationship between productive and reproductive work. From this perspective, commons projects can be understood as a form of institutional critic, whereby their critique is primarily articulated by an instituting practice and only indirectly targets existing institutions.

The central methodological element of the project was research meetings, physical meetings with the artists and theorists which lasted several days, in order to define the questions that emerged from the projects and reflect on them together. We did not proceed from the assumption that we researchers knew more than the participating artists. The goal was to create a shared space for horizontal exchange and learning.

Video interviews with all participating artists were conducted and recorded in high quality. These interviews pursued two objectives: First, to give the artists the opportunity to render in compact form the often quite fragmented, long-term and process-oriented projects, and to reflect upon them along an interview guide we compiled. Second, we generated material with which we and other persons can continue to work. For this purpose the interviews were placed on the project website and freely licensed. In a manner not atypical for (digital) commons, these interviews are simultaneously final product and raw material.

In addition to a multitude of smaller publications, lectures, and exhibition contributions, the research project generated three major outputs. First, the website, on which we documented the process from beginning to end, and which serves as the central archive for the shared materials. Second, an exhibition at panke.gallery in Berlin (Sept./Oct. 2019), in which we cooperated with the artists to develop "scores." These "scores" translated the process-oriented projects into the exhibition space, without losing the twofold character of the projects as discursive symbols and actionable materials. A comprehensive catalog was created for the exhibition as well. Finally, theorists were invited to work on a collective book. Each participant was to reflect on the projects and their potentials from their own perspective. The interviews served as a shared foundation and were provided to the authors. Thus, a collection of texts emerged that were independent but repeatedly entered into dialog with each other through their many references to the projects, and conveyed a dynamic relationship between polyphony and focus.

Felix Stalder

Project Title
Creating Commons

Project Period
1 January 2017–30 June 2020

Keywords
- Interdisciplinarity
- Expanded concept of art
- Commons
- Digital infrastructures
- Institutional critique

Head of Project
- Felix Stalder, culture and media theorist

Research Team
- Shusha Niederberger, artist and educator
- Cornelia Sollfrank, artist

Project Partners
- House of Electronic Arts, Basel
- panke.gallery, Berlin
- springerin, Vienna

Project Funding
- Swiss National Science Foundation SNSF

Outputs

Website

- https://creatingcommons.zhdk.ch

Publications

- Cornelia Sollfrank, Felix Stalder, and Shusha Niederberger (eds.) (2021): *Aesthetics of the Commons*. Volume 24 of the Institute for Contemporary Art Research series. Zurich and Berlin: Diaphanes.
  - A Open access: https://doi.org/10.5281/zenodo.4944036
- Cornelia Sollfrank, Felix Stalder, and Shusha Niederberger (eds.) (2020): *Open Scores. How to Program the Commons*. Exhibition Catalogue. Berlin/Zurich: panke.gallery & Creating Commons.
  - B Open access: https://doi.org/10.5281/zenodo.6470245

Guest Editorship and Articles

- Cornelia Sollfrank, Felix Stalder, and Shusha Niederberger (eds.) (2019): *Digital Unconscious*. Volume 4 of *Springerin*.
  - Cornelia Sollfrank: "What can we learn from the (digital) Commons? Ästhetische Praxen des Lernens und Verlernens." 4–6.
    - C Open access: https://doi.org/10.5281/zenodo.3724624
  - Shusha Niederberger, Cornelia Sollfrank, and Felix Stalder: "Open Scores. How to Program the Commons." 7.
    - D Open access: https://doi.org/10.5281/zenodo.3873267
  - Shusha Niederberger: "Feminist Server – Sichtbarkeit und Funktionalität. Digitale Infrastruktur als gemeinschaftliches Projekt." 8–9.
    - E Open access: https://doi.org/10.5281/zenodo.3895646
  - Kevin Rittberger: "Furtherfield – mit Nachahmung fangen CommonistInnen wenig an." 10–11
    - F Open access: https://doi.org/10.5281/zenodo.3724586
  - Felix Stalder: "Von der Teilnahme zur Aneignung. Ein Horizont künstlerischer Praxis?" 12–14.
    - G Open access: https://doi.org/10.5281/zenodo.3724582

Exhibition

- *Open Scores. How to program the Commons*. 21 September 2019–12 December 2019. panke.gallery, Berlin. With works by Dušan Barok (monoskop.org), Marcell Mars and Tomislav Medak (memoryoftheworld.org), Sebastian Lütgert and Jan Gerber (0xdb.org), Kenneth Goldsmith (ubu.com), AAAAARG, Zeljko Blace (#QUEERingNETWORKing), Ruth Catlow & Marc Garrett (furtherfield.org), Laurence Rassel (erg.be), Marek Tuszynski (Tactical Tech), Constant (Michael Murtaugh, Femke Snelting and Peter Westenberg), Stefanie Wuschitz (Mz* Baltazar's Lab), Panayotis Antoniadis (nethood.org), Alessandro Ludovico (neural.it), Eva Weinmayr (andpublishing.org), Spideralex, Sakrowski (curatingyoutube.net), Creating Commons, Johannes Kreidler, and Alison Knowles. Talks and screenings with Sebastina Lütgert, Cornelia Lund, and Isabel de Sena.

Archive

- Cornelia Sollfrank, Felix Stalder, and Shusha Niederberger: Video archive at https://creatingcommons.zhdk.ch with interviews and lectures (2013–2018) by and with Daphne Dragona, Olga Goriunova, Michael Murtaugh, Patricia Reis and Stephanie Wuschitz, Laurence Rassel, Femke Snelting and spideralex, Eva Weinmayr, Ruth Catlow and Marc Garrett, Sean Dockray, Kenneth Goldsmith, Mauricio O'Brian, Panayotis Antoniadis, Peter Westenberg, Z. Blace, Alessandro Ludovico, Marek Tuszynski, Marcell Mars and Tomislav Medak, Sebastian Lüttgert and Jan Geber, and Dušan Barok.

Fig. 1 Interview with Sean Dockray. House of Electronic Arts, Basel, 2018

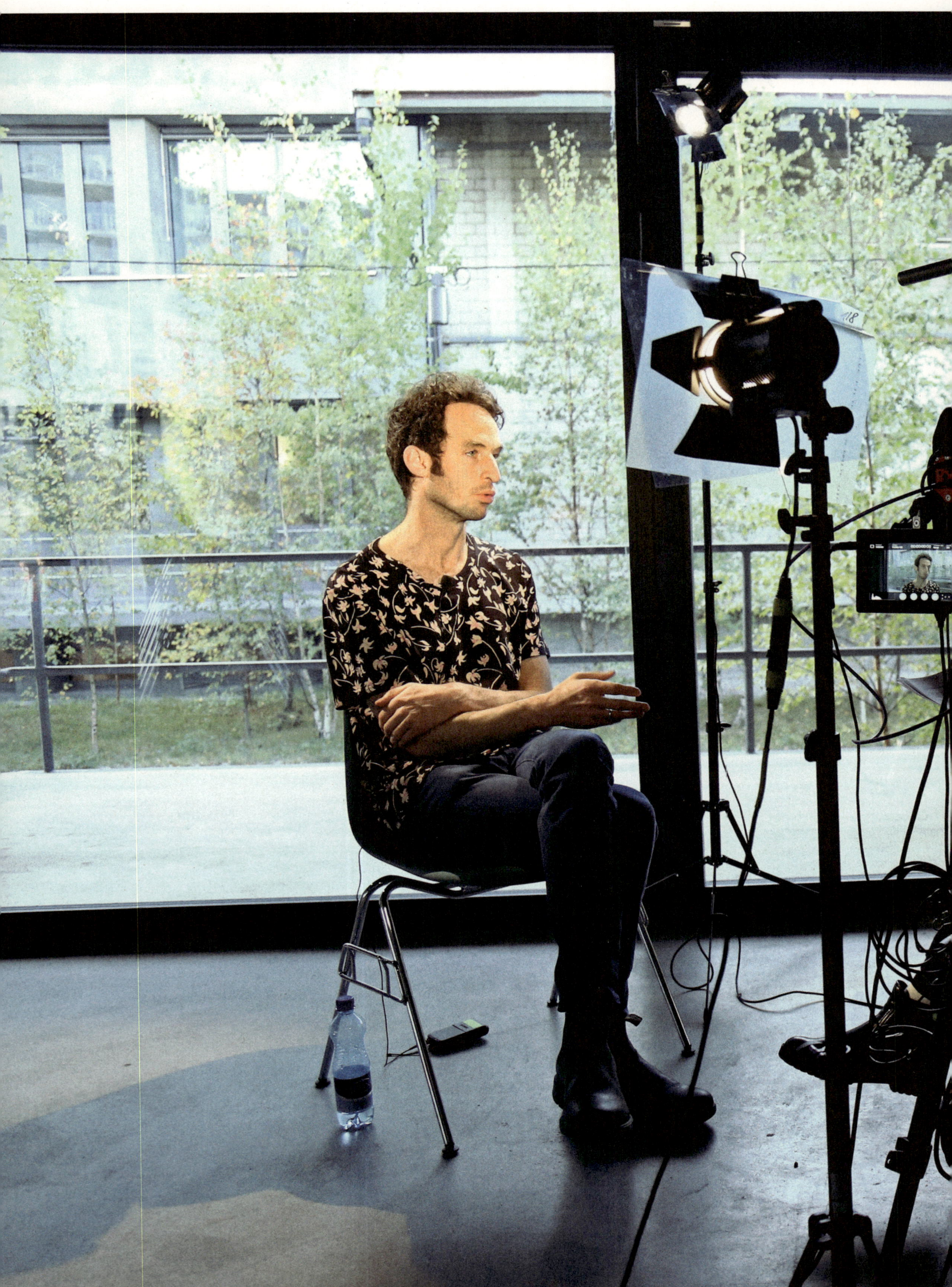

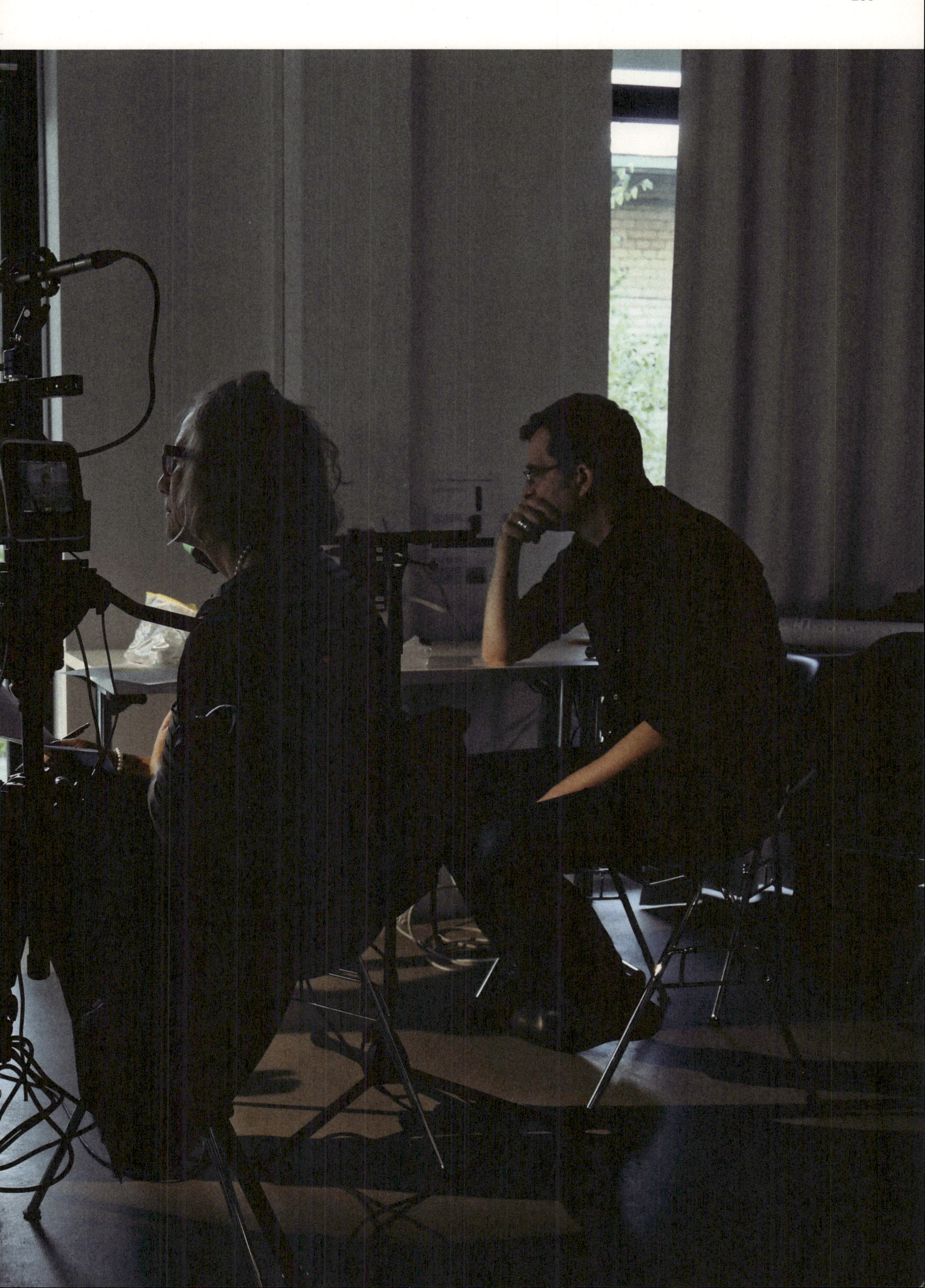

Fig. 2 Cornelia Sollfrank: *Giving What You Don't Have*. Yebisu International Festival for Art & Alternative Visions, Tokyo, 2017

Fig. 3 Eva Weinmayr: *Against Immunisation*. panke.gallery, Berlin, 2019

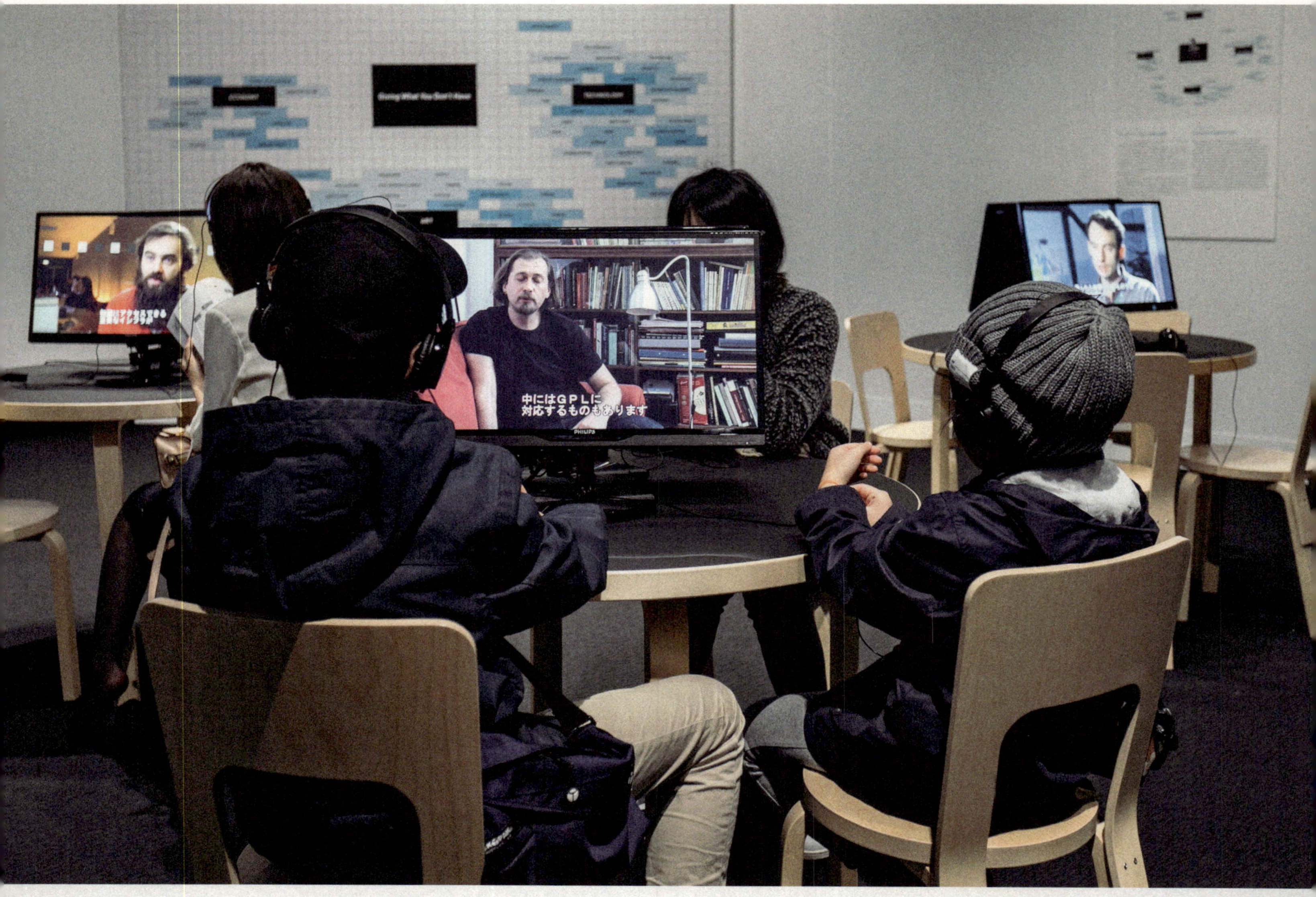

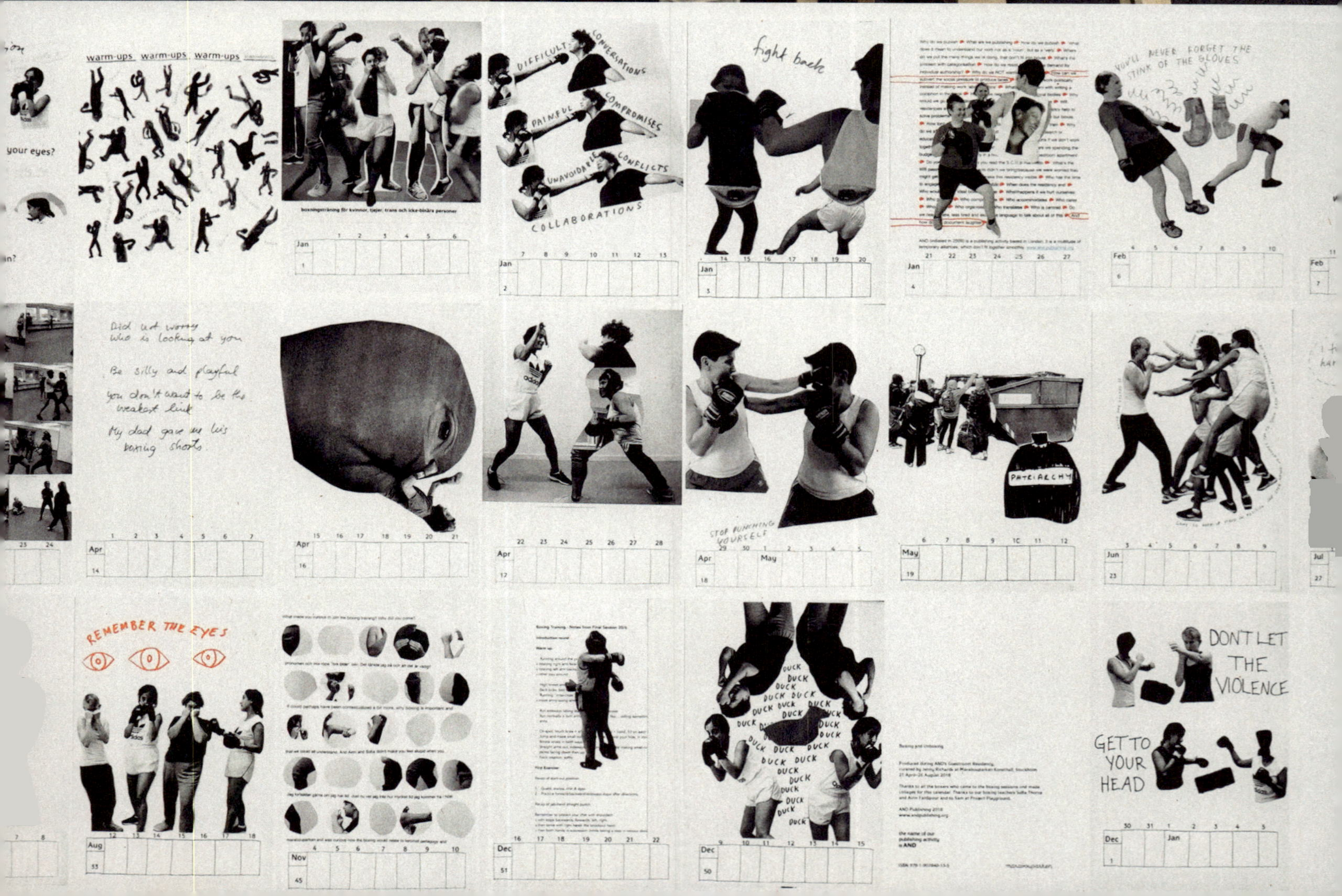

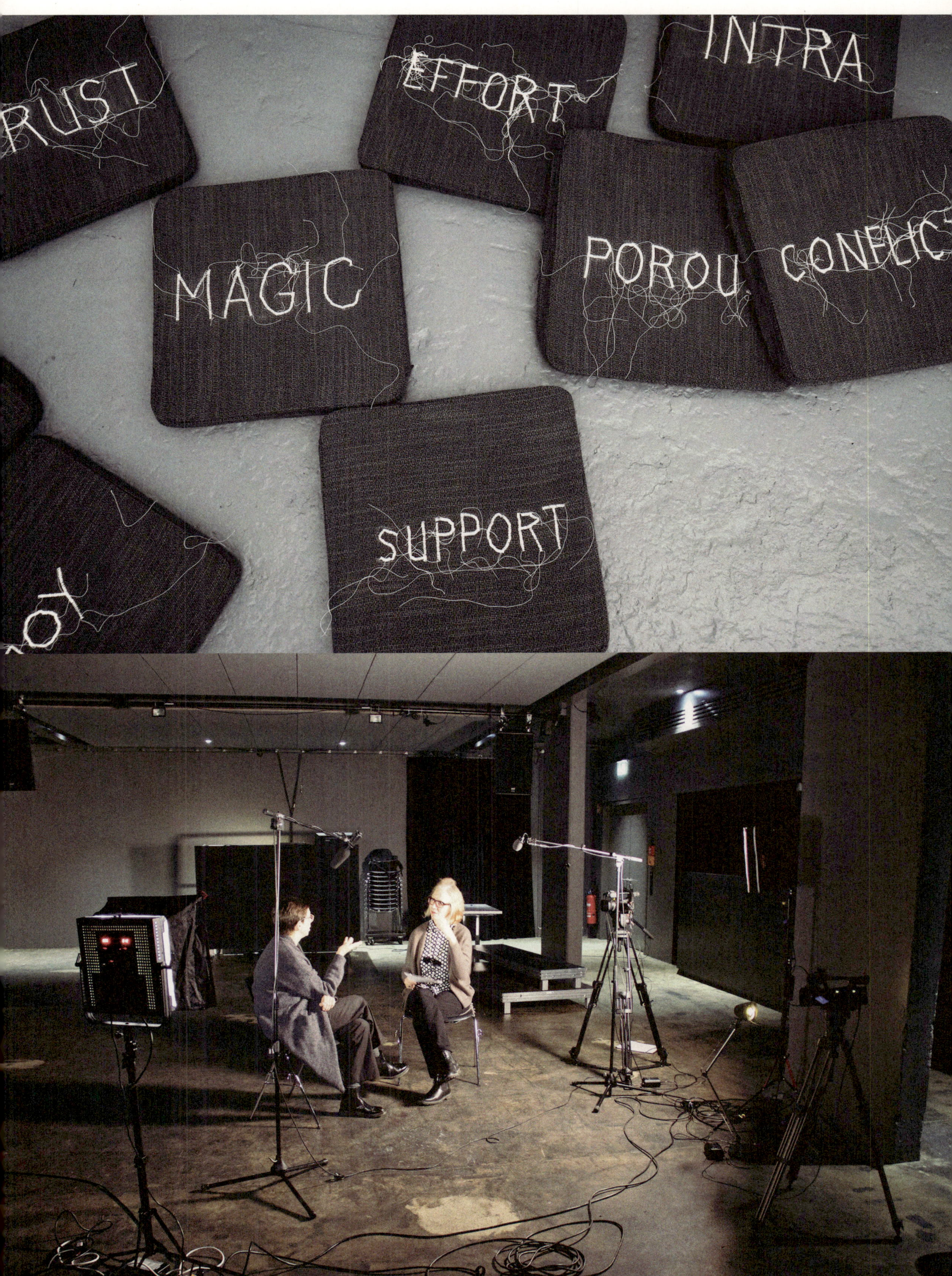

Fig. 4 Constant: *Collaboration Guidelines*. panke.gallery, Berlin, 2019

Fig. 5 Interview with Laurence Rassel. House of Electronic Arts, Basel, 2018

In the 2015 French documentary film *Mainmise sur les villes?* (Who owns our cities?) city planner Jan Gehl demands access to public spaces as a human right. In the neoliberal or entrepreneurial city, however, this access is threatened by privatization and commodification, as well as through increasing regulation and practices of exclusions and signposting. The homeless, alcoholics, rampaging youths, and otherwise undesirable persons are increasingly being driven out of many public spaces. While many city planners and sociologists call for more heterogeneity and diversity to keep cities vibrant, city administrations often work in the opposite direction. The increased cooperation of cities with private investors and globally operating companies, especially, is leading to the loss of what makes a city vibrant: free and open encounters between people from different classes and cultures. At the core of every "open city" are public spaces that can potentially by accessed by everyone.

As such, exclusion and displacement are interwoven with entrepreneurial urban policy, and are frequently deployed deliberately as strategies to redesign cities according to globally oriented ideals and economic interests. Strategies of exclusion change not only the public spaces but also social togetherness. Ever more city dwellers are affected by these complexes processes all over the world, yet their voices are rarely heard. Seldom is it shown how these top-down processes on the use of public spaces affect the residents of cities. *The Fragmented City* intended to change this, and focused on the perspective of the excluded. It showed the deliberately deployed urban strategies and measures as well as their associated impacts. It also documented the unconscious and subjective perception of the affected populations that were targeted for exclusion.

The investigation was based on three case studies in Berlin, Graz, and Zurich. They focused on three questions: In what spaces are what exclusion processes taking place? Who is affected by them in what way? How do they become visible, that is, what are their consequences on the public spaces?

Four methodological approaches were applied: In video walks, public spaces were visited by the excluded, who followed the project's key questions to comment on the spaces. Concomitantly, comprehensive photographic research was performed at selected locations. In cooperation with an actor, concrete situations experienced by the excluded in urban spaces were re-enacted and photographed. A further approach focused on participative and performative aspects of loitering.

The four different approaches were reflected in the four different methods of media representation in the final publication. These included a text illustrated with images and videos, four video portraits accompanied by longer interview passages, a long photo essay, and a brief written depiction of the field work based on field notes.

Because its methodological approach and its media presentation place the project in a transdisciplinary field between scientific and artistic practices, it makes an important contribution to artistic urbanology.

Jürgen Krusche

Project Title
Die fragmentierte Stadt. Prozesse und Strategien der Exklusion und ihre Wirkungen auf die öffentlichen Räume

Project Period
1 March 2017–30 April 2021

Keywords
- Public space
- Exclusion
- Artistic research
- Urban studies
- Gentrification

Head of Project
- Jürgen Krusche, artist and urbanologist

Research Team
- Aya Domenig, filmmaker and ethnologist
- Thomas Schärer, cultural researcher and historian
- Julia Weber, sociologist and artist (PhD)
- Miriam Gautschi, cultural researcher

Research Partners
- Sigmar Gude, Topos Stadtforschung, Berlin
- Johanna Rolshoven, Institute for Cultural Anthropology and European Ethnology, University of Graz

PhD Cooperation
- PhD program of Zurich University of the Arts, in cooperation with the University of Art and Design Linz

Outputs

A

Project Funding
Swiss National Science Foundation SNSF

Related Projects
- Labor Mülheim, Zurich University of the Arts, 2012–2013
  P. 126
- Bureau Savamala Belgrade, Zurich University of the Arts, 2013–2014
  P. 140
- Politics of Space, Zurich University of the Arts, 2014–2018
  P. 158

Publications
- Jürgen Krusche, Aya Domenig, Thomas Schärer, and Julia Weber (2021): *Die fragmentierte Stadt*. Volume 25 of the Institute for Contemporary Art Research series. Berlin: Jovis.
  A Open access: https://doi.org/10.5281/zenodo.5717776
- Julia Weber (2022): *Herumlungern?! Begegnungsräume an urbanen Orten*. University of Art and Design Linz. Unpublished doctoral dissertation.

Article
- Julia Weber (2018): "'Loitering' in Urban Public Space—Wandering with a Street Poet in Berlin." In: *WiderScreen: Kaupunkikuvitelmat ja urbaani arki—City imaginings and urban everyday life*. Volume 1–2, 1–9.

Presentation
- Thomas Schärer (2018): "Die fragmentierte Stadt: Ausschluss- und Aneignungserfahrungen." 29–30 June 2018. In: *Frieden und Demokratie auf der Strasse* Conference. University of Graz.

Exhibitions
- *Currybernd ist wieder da!* 23 October 2019. Outdoor exhibition and screening. Getränke Hoffmann, Berlin. With contributions by Aya Domenig and Jürgen Krusche.
- *Die fragmentierte Stadt*. 28 October 2021. Book presentation and interventionist exhibition in cooperation with the actor Urs Stämpfli and Jovis Verlag, Berlin Jannowitzbrücke. With contributions by Urs Stämpfli and Jürgen Krusche.

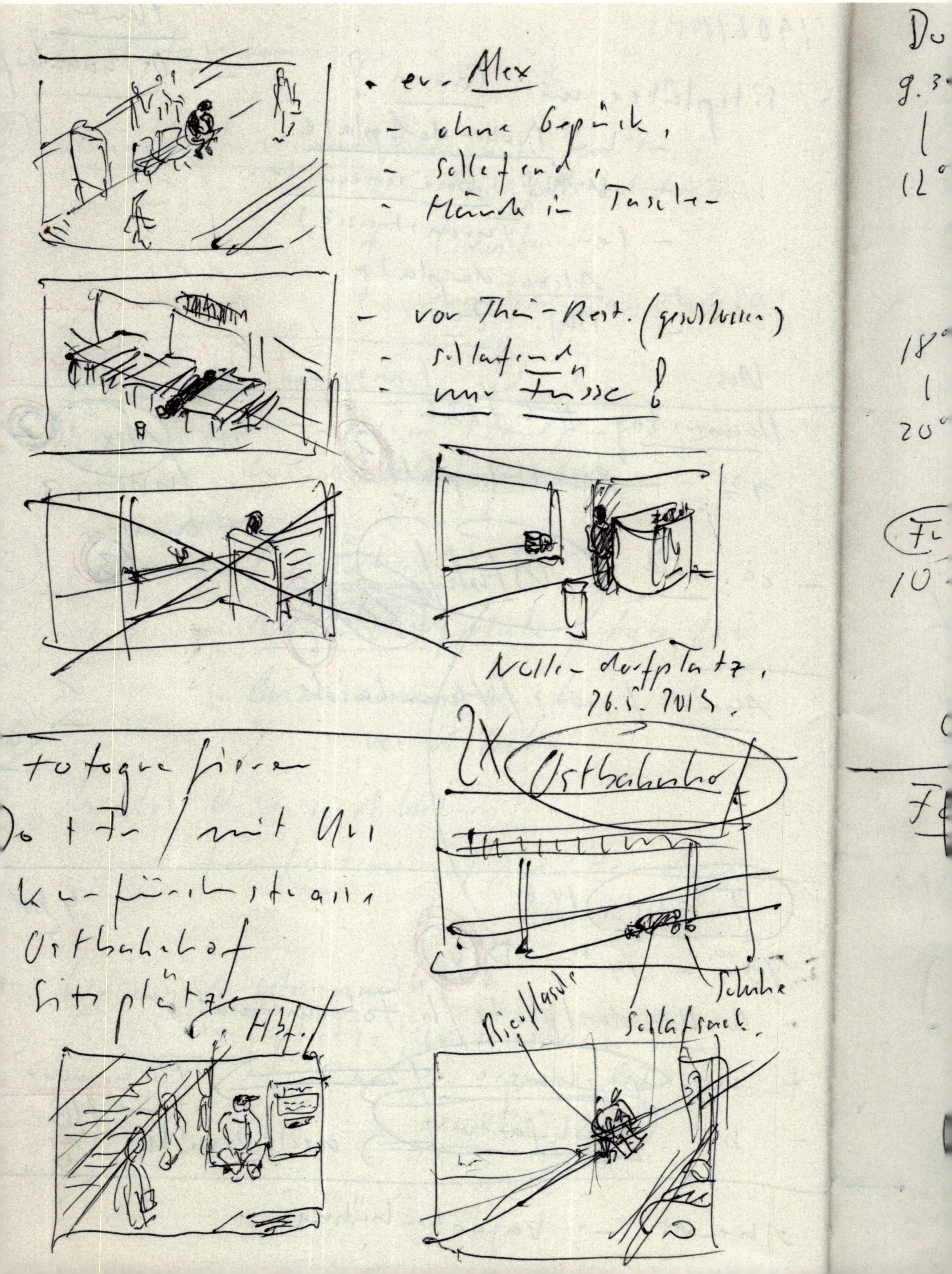

- er – Alex
- ohne Gepäck,
- schlafend,
- Hände in Taschen

- vor Thai-Rest. (geschlossen)
- schlafend
- nur Füsse!

Nollendorfplatz, 26.5.2015.

2x Ostbahnhof

fotografieren
Do + Fr / mit Uli
Kurfürstenstrasse
Ostbahnhof
Sitzplätze
Hbf.

Bierflasche
Schlafsack
Schuhe

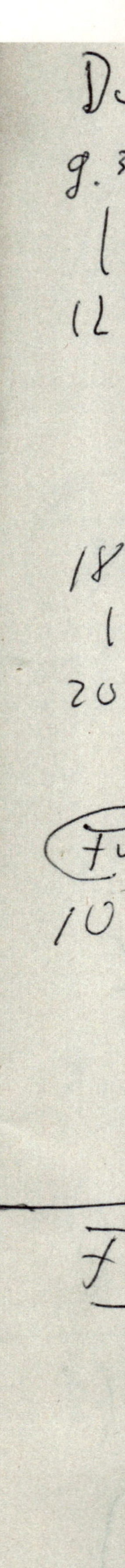

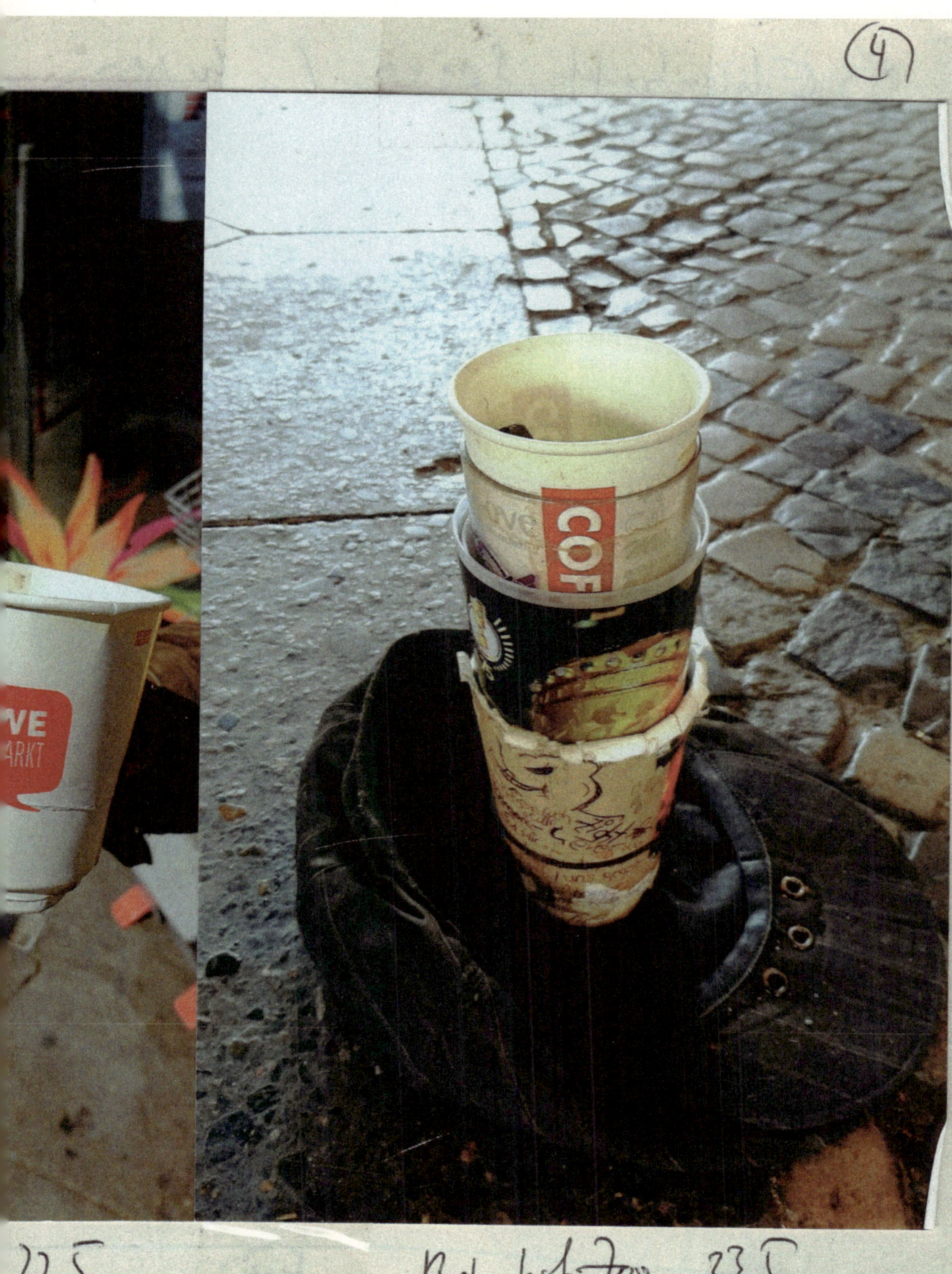

22.5.

Bahnhof Zoo, 23.5.

– Simulacrum ??

Fig. 3 Jürgen Krusche: *Currybernd ist wieder da* (detail). Berlin, 2019

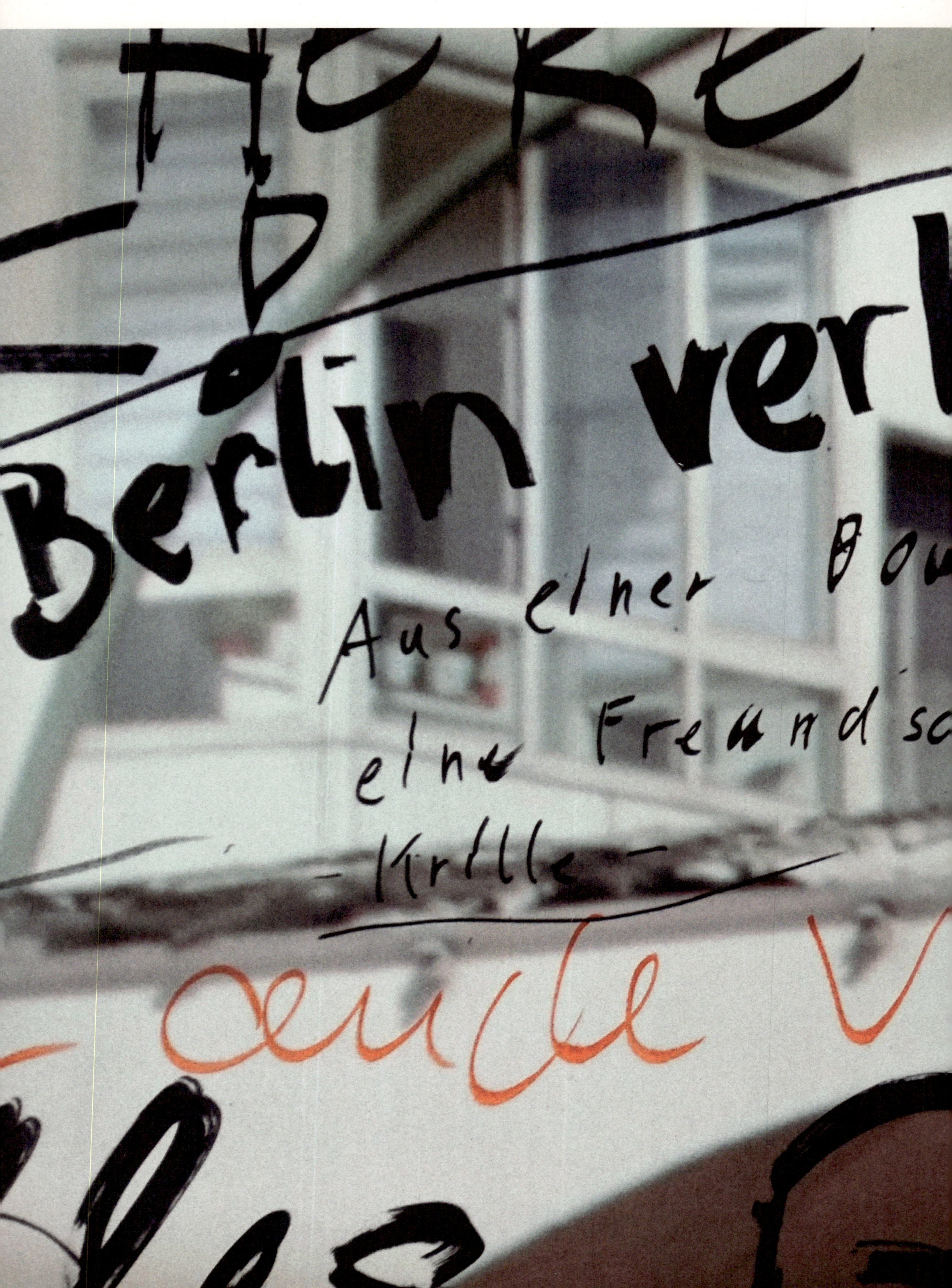

alles

or eine

wurde

Danke Bernd

Fig. 4 Julia Weber: *Wir bleiben hier. Solange die Sonne scheint*. Video still, Berlin, 2019

Fig. 5 Jürgen Krusche: Working material on *Currybernd*. Berlin, 2017

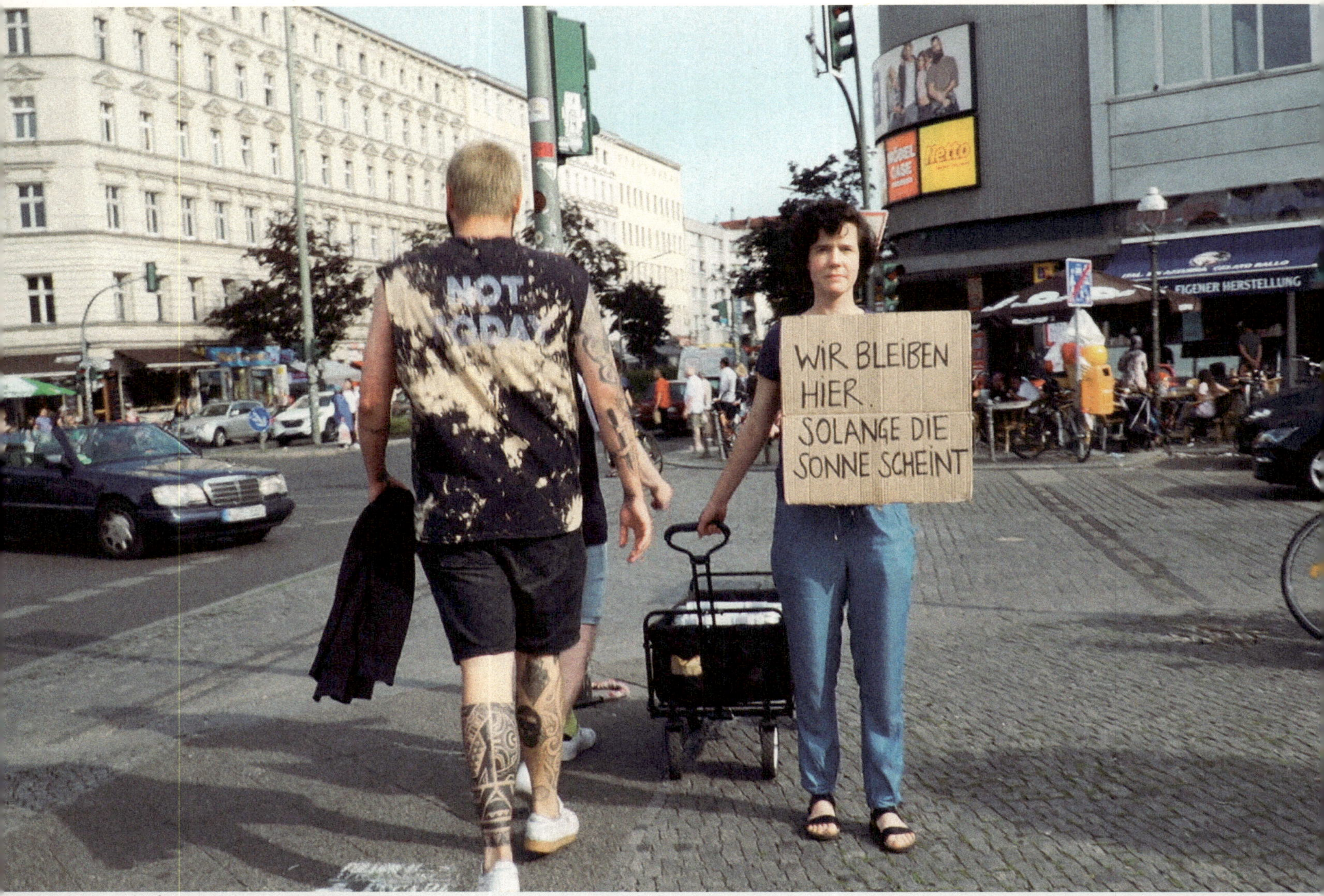

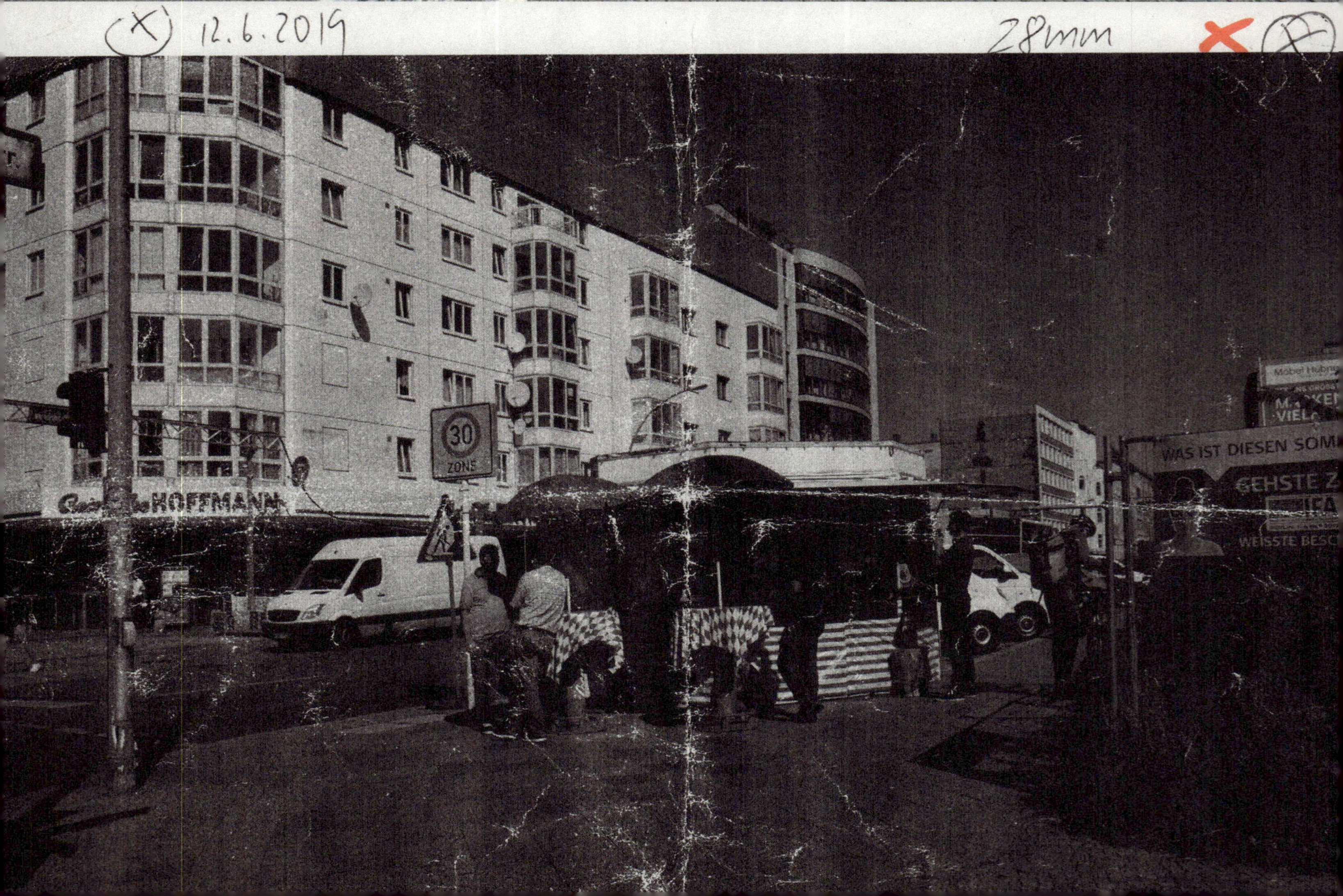

WIR BLEIBEN HIER. SOLANGE DIE SONNE SCHEINT

(X) 12.6.2019 28mm

Fig. 6 Thomas Schärer: Field research. Video still, Zurich, 2017
Fig. 7 Jürgen Krusche: Place to sleep. Tiergarten, Berlin, 2018

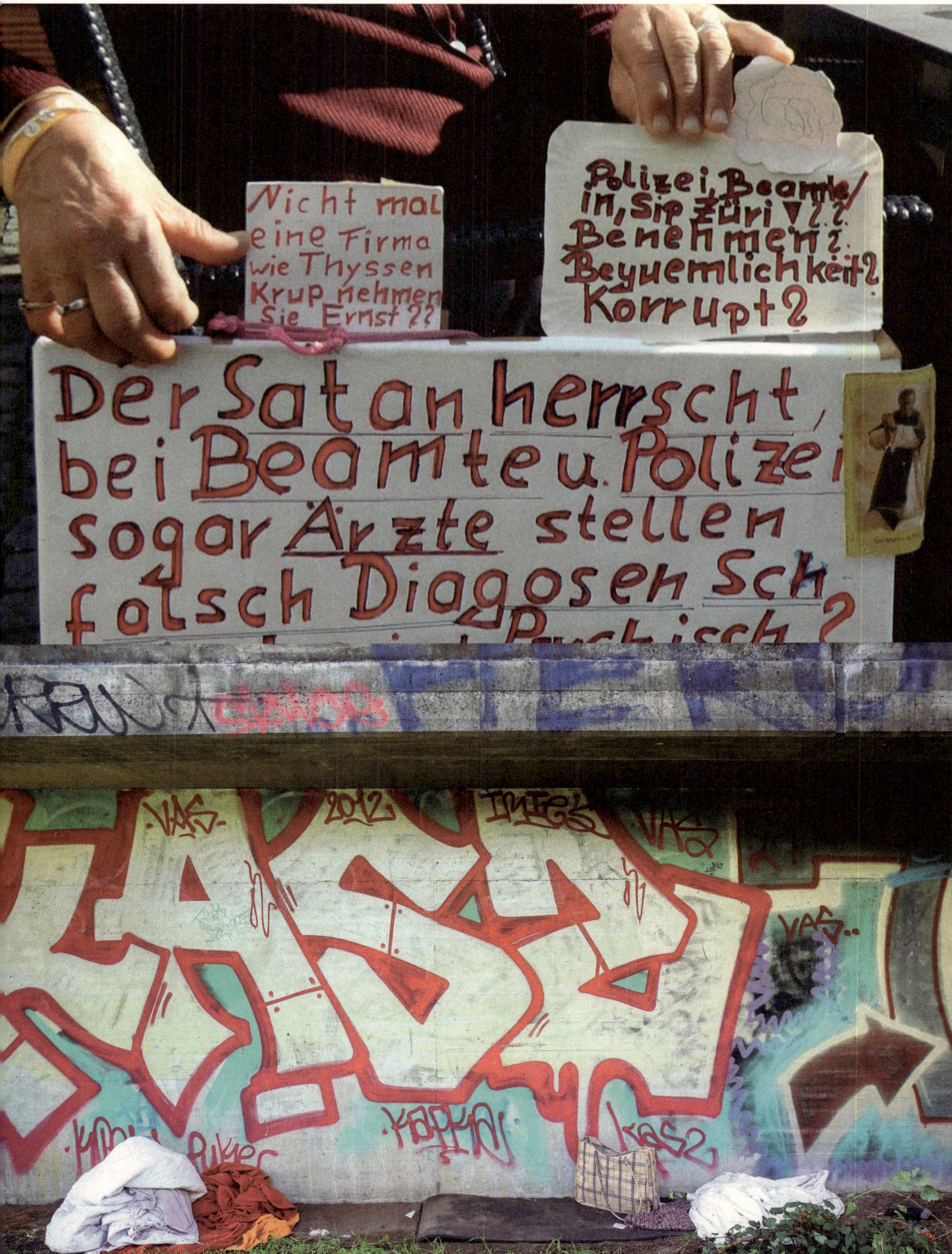

The interdisciplinary research cooperation *Computer Signals*, established in 2012, built on precursor projects to investigate aspects of producing and processing data in the biosciences. Taken together, the three project phases constitute a long-term study on the transition from analog to digital research practices based on the example of two working groups, one in Heligoland and Spitsbergen and the other in Austin, Texas.

Computer Signals II concretizes the research questions that *Computer Signals I* raised from the perspective of artistic work: Countering the common perception that digital data have always been around and were transported incorporeally through the ether from one device to the next, the art project used spatial installations to show the massive materiality of the machines and infrastructures deployed to collect, distribute, and calculate (scientific) data. They recorded the sounds of electronic research apparatus, obtained by means of induction coils, and translated them into acoustic energy, making it possible to hear, see, and sense not only the noise, but also the distinguishable sounds and rhythms of the machines. This art inverted the scientific work that consists in isolating phenomena and abstracting them into stable units of information, instead making the local conditions and environments of their production perceptible. The prism of art broke digital data work into a spectrum of physical work taking place under extreme climatic conditions in concrete locations. The devices of the internet-based *remote sensing* project on climate impact research are subjected to storms, icebergs, and often exuberant bioactivity off the island of Spitsbergen at the North Pole. Much of the enormous energy needed to cool the supercomputers and machines of the genetic and neuroresearch in Texas is extracted from the university's own oil fields through fracking.

The experiences made in the art project increasingly raised awareness of media ecology issues, which were discussed in the framework of an exhibition and a conference as well as in several scientific publications addressed to a broader audience. Subjects of debate included the societal conception of environment and how this changes when nature is understood to be the substrate of terrestrial and submarine infrastructures, and thus the ultimate infrastructure of its own observation. To take this idea even further: In this function nature is what also makes possible the individual digital media consumption of our everyday life, which, itself, is a growing driver of climate change.

Results of the work of the *Computer Signals* research cooperation, whose members included three experienced science researchers in addition to the artists and biologists, were made accessible to the public on the *Computer Signals* web platform developed especially for the project, in the form of a conversation reinforced with various data and media formats (*Rigi Discussion*). This conversation concerned not only how to look at data work and its infrastructures but also how to deepen our understanding of today's foundation of data-driven biological research through mutual exchange.

In the framework of the subsequent SNSF Agora project *Listening to Data Flows. How Art and Biology Bring the Environment into the Computer* (2021–2024), besides exhibitions in art institutions at sites of science research in Bremerhaven (Alfred Wegener Institute, climate impact research), Basel (molecular biology), and Zürich (environmental sciences), we are developing our own communication formats. We invite sound artists to produce their own art using the sound archives that have grown to become a substantial resource over the course of the long-term project, and organize soundwalks and collective explorations of digital infrastructures in urban spaces in the immediate surroundings of institutions of science and art.

Hannes Rickli

Project Title
Computersignale. Kunst und Biologie im Zeitalter ihres digitalen Experimentierens II

Project Period
1 April 2017–31 May 2021

Keywords
- Data work
- Materiality of the digital
- Digital infrastructures
- Experimental systems
- Configuration

Head of Project
- Hannes Rickli, artist

Research Team
- Jan Huggenberg, interaction designer
- Christoph Stähli, artist
- Valentina Vuksic, artist
- Birk Weiberg, art researcher

Research Partners
- Philipp Fischer, Alfred Wegener Institute, Helmholtz Centre for Polar and Marine Research
- Hans-Jörg Rheinberger, historian of science, Max Planck Institute for the History of Science
- Gabriele Gramelsberger, RWTH Aachen University, Chair for Theory of Science and Technology
- Christoph Hoffmann, University of Lucerne, Department of Cultural and Science Studies
- Hans A. Hofmann, University of Texas at Austin, Department of Integrative Biology, College of Natural Sciences

Outputs

A

B

Project Partners
- Timo Klinge, Rycote Microphone Windshields Ltd.
- Smartronic GmbH

Project Funding
- Swiss National Science Foundation SNSF

Related Projects
- Spillover, Zurich University of the Arts, 2007–2009
  P. 74
- Computer Signals I, Zurich University of the Arts, 2012–2015
  P. 118
- Listening to Data Flows, Zurich University of the Arts, 2021–2024

Project Website
- https://computersignale.zhdk.ch/en

Monograph
- Philipp Fischer, Gabriele Gramelsberger, Christoph Hoffmann, Hans Hofmann, Hans-Jörg Rheinberger, and Hannes Rickli (2020): *Datennaturen. Ein Gespräch zwischen Biologie, Kunst, Wissenschaftstheorie und -geschichte/Natures of Data. A Discussion between Biology, History and Philosophy of Science and Art*. Volume 22 of the Institute for Contemporary Art Research series, ZHdK. Zurich: Diaphanes.
  - A Open access: https://doi.org/10.5281/zenodo.5119387 (DE)
  - B Open access: https://doi.org/10.5281/zenodo.5119460 (EN)

Articles
- Priska Gisler (2019): “Artistic Research as ‘Participant Perception’: Reflecting on the Project ‘Computer Signals’ from an Arts-Inspired STS-Perspective.” In: Paulo de Assis and Lucia D’Errico (eds.): *Artistic Research 1*. London: Rowman & Littlefield International, 175–191.
- Gabriele Gramelsberger (2020): “Reenacting Science. Wissenschaftsforscher*innen und Künstler*innen in biologischen Laboren.” In: Ralf Baecker, Dennis Paul, and Andrea Sick (eds.): *Reenactments in Kunst, Art, Gestaltung, Design, Wissenschaft, Science und Technologie and Technology*. Salon Digital, Volume 1. Hamburg: Textem, 172–185.

Conferences
- Hannes Rickli, Gabriele Gramelsberger, and Birk Weiberg: “Materialität der Wissenschaften.” Panel at the 2019 annual conference: *Medien-Realitäten*. 25–28 September 2019. Gesellschaft für Medienwissenschaften, Philosophikum, University of Cologne.
- Hannes Rickli and Birk Weiberg: *Datennaturen*. International conference as part of the *Afrikanischer Buntbarsch #3* exhibition. 6–7 March 2020. Kunstraum Walcheturm, Zurich. With the research partners plus Valentina Vuksic, Peter Bexte, Simon Grab, Nils Güttler, Marcus Maeder, Astrid Schwarz, and Yvonne Volkart.

Lectures, Presentations
- Hannes Rickli: “Quasi-Objects: Nature as Infrastructure and Medium of Its Own Observation.” In: *Questioning the Non-Human Other: Political Potentials of Living Beings in Contemporary Art*. 17–19 October 2019. Institute of Art History, University of Graz.
- Hannes Rickli: “Strange Machines: Some Things Between Art and Biology.” In: *Taking Measures: Usages of Formats in Film and Video Art*. 10 January 2021. Department of Film Studies, University of Zurich. Video contribution, online conference in cooperation with Migros Museum of Contemporary Art, Zurich.
- Hannes Rickli: “Videograms of Experimentation. Animal-Human-Media Constellations in Biological Research Films.” In: *The Movement—Movement—Histories of Microanalysis at the Intersection of Film, Science and Art*. 24–26 June 2021. Artist Talk und Screening, international conference (online), Institute of Media Studies, Philipps University of Marburg.

Exhibition
- Hannes Rickli: *Afrikanischer Buntbarsch #3, Soundscape Texas*. Audiovisual installation. Participants: Valentina Vuksic, Birk Weiberg, and Christoph Stähli. 14 February–11 March 2020. Kunstraum Walcheturm, Zurich.

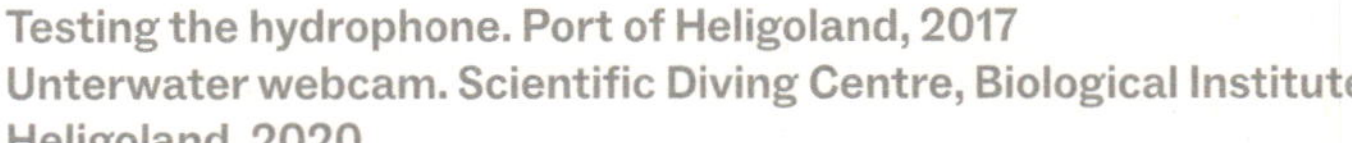

Fig. 1 Testing the hydrophone. Port of Heligoland, 2017

Fig. 2 Unterwater webcam. Scientific Diving Centre, Biological Institute Heligoland, 2020

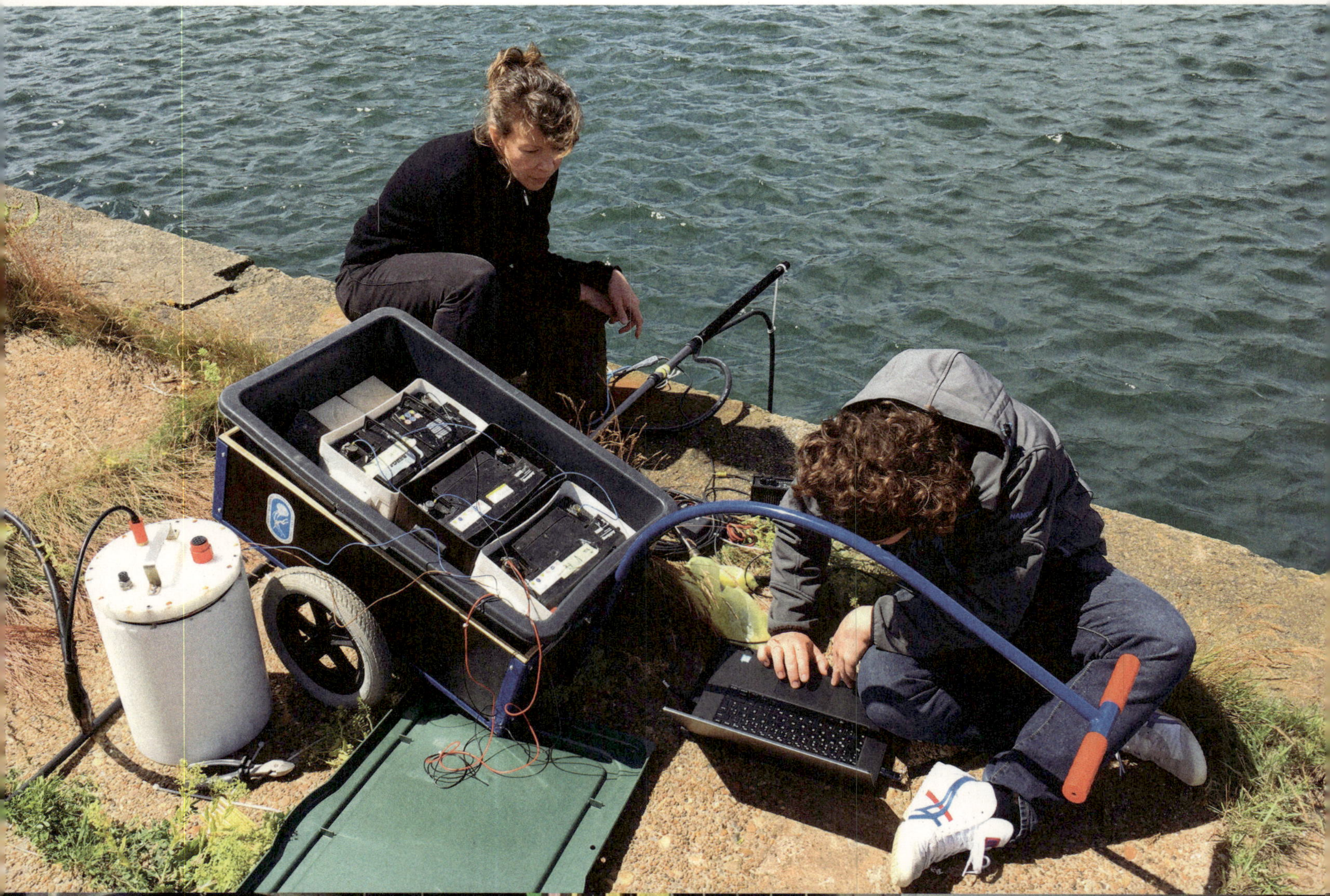

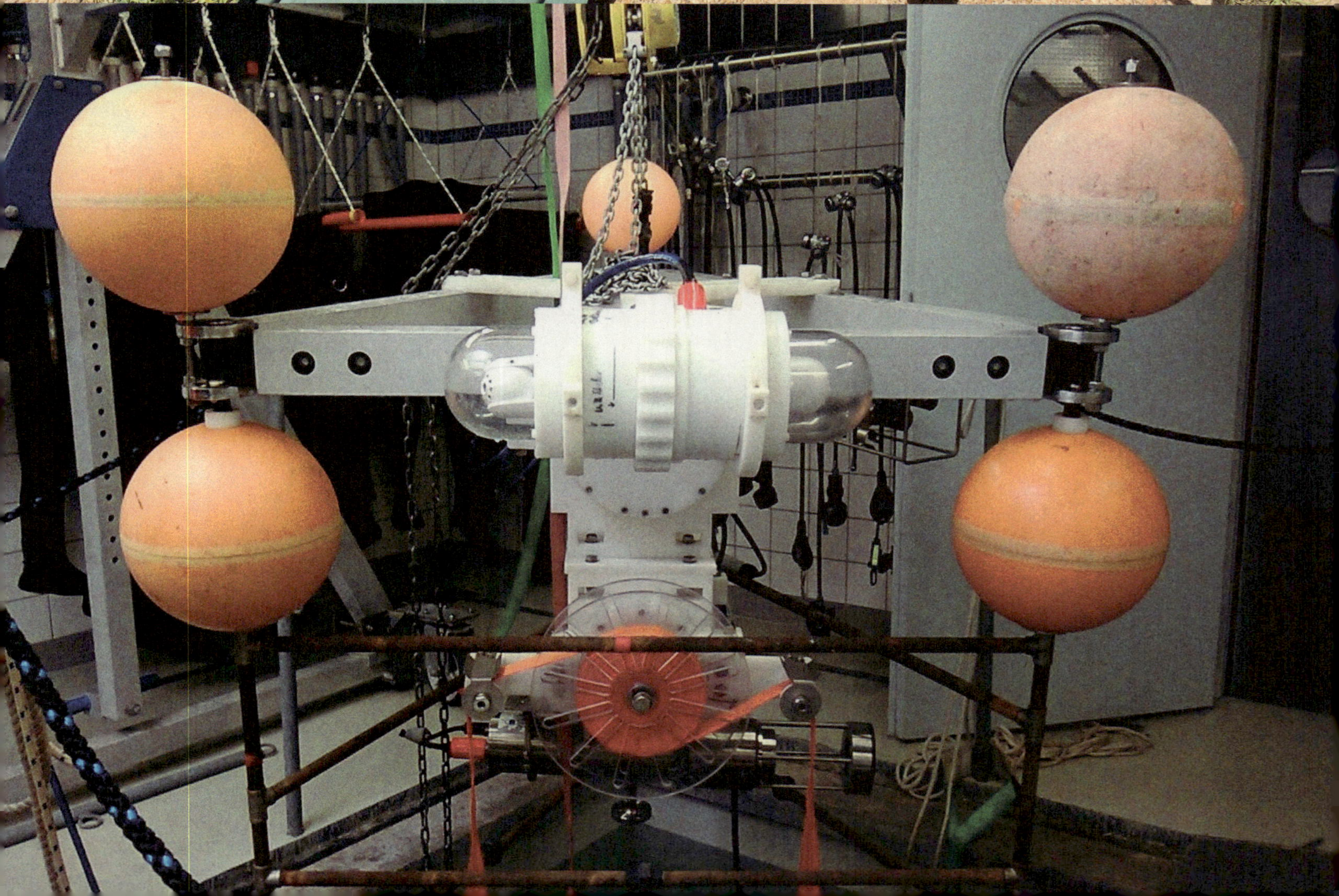

Fig. 3–4 Implementation of the electromagnetic pickups in the main housing of RemOs3. Scientific Diving Centre, Biological Institute Heligoland, 2020

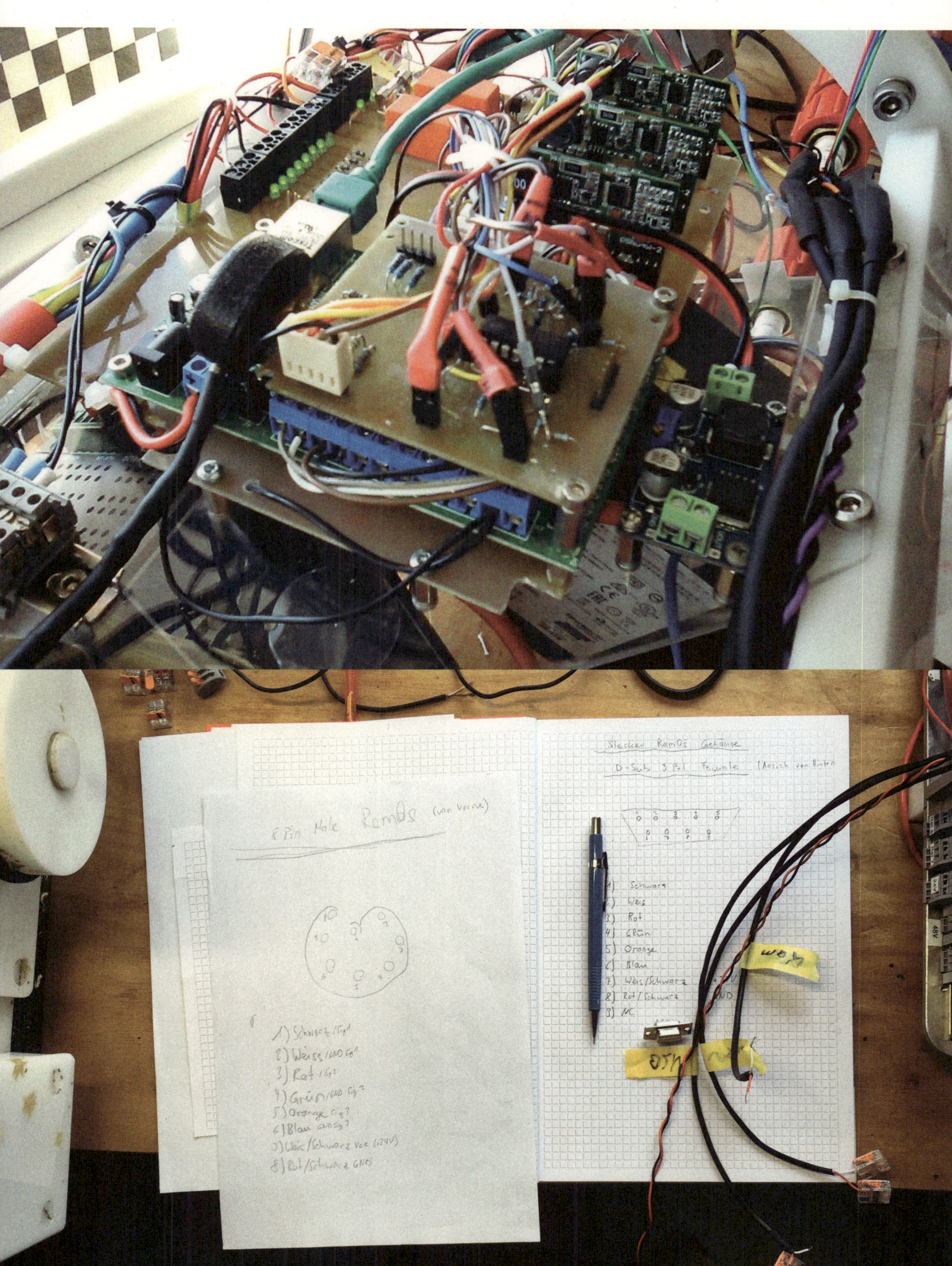

Fig. 5 RemOs2 with hydrophone. Biological Institute Heligoland, 2017
Fig. 6 RemOs3 support structure. Scientific Diving Centre, Biological Institute Heligoland, 2021

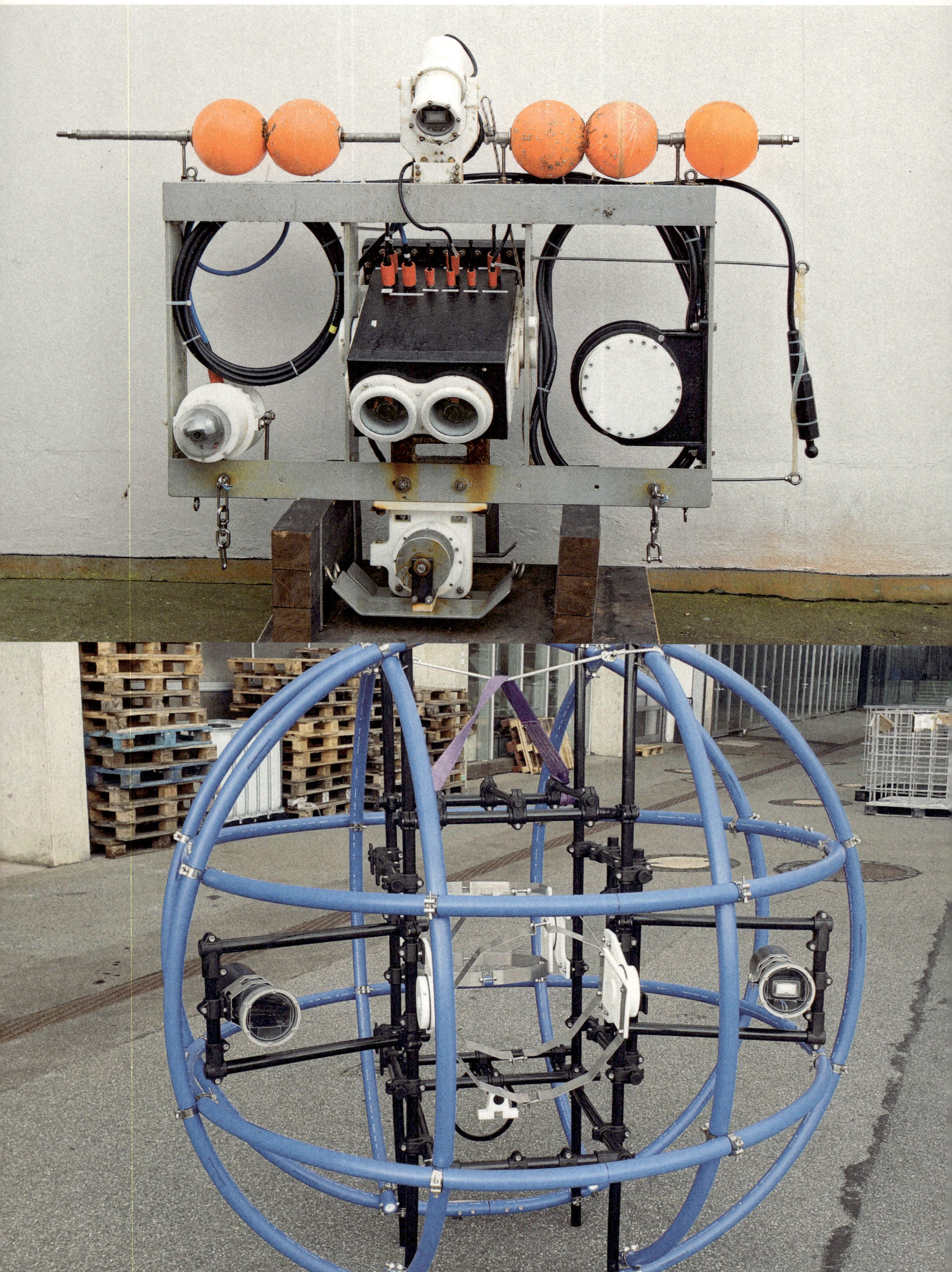

Fig. 7 *MarGate* underwater testing ground. RemOs2 installation plan, Biological Institute Heligoland, 2017

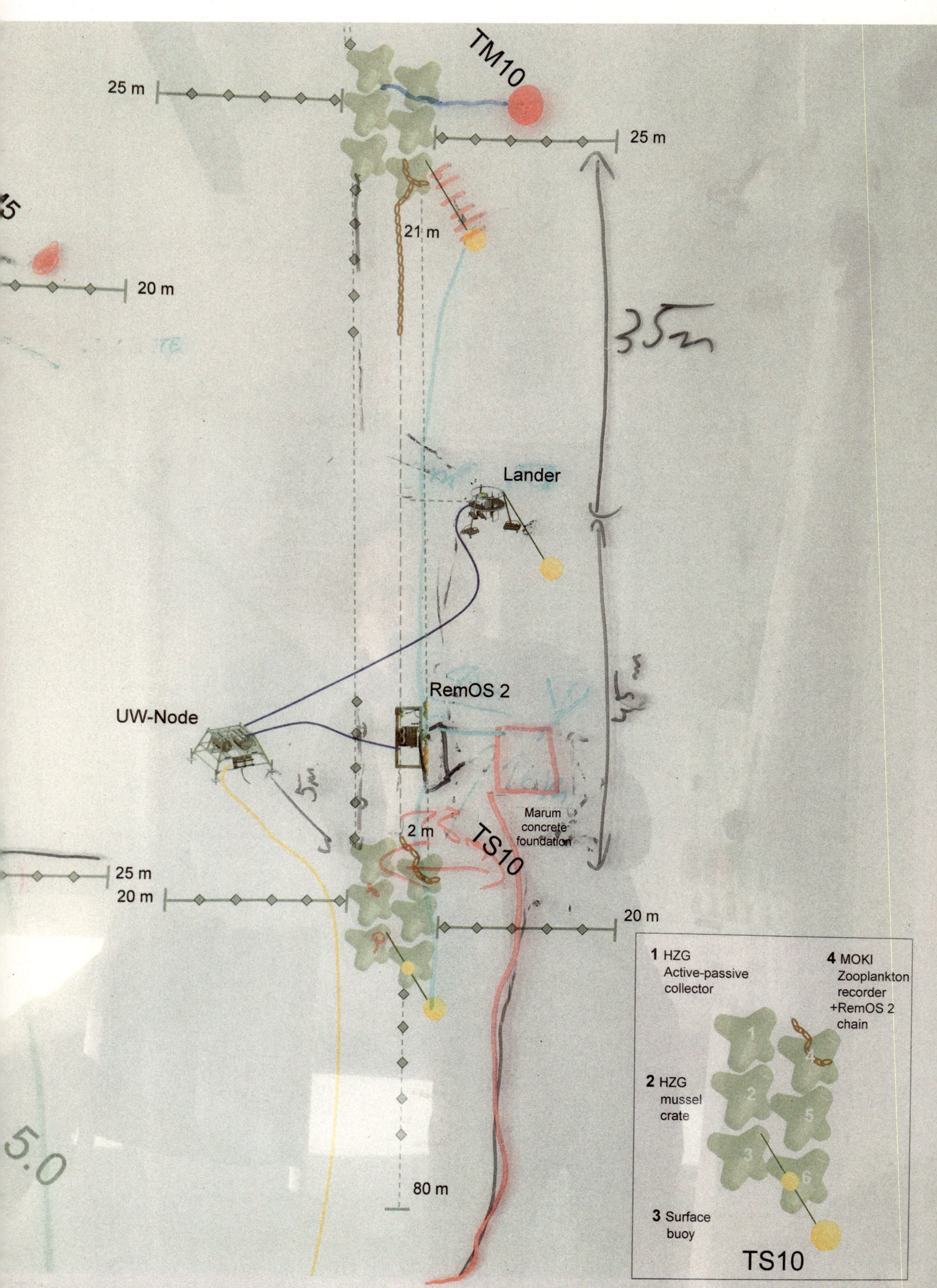

When do you work? What are you paid for? How do infrastructures, apparatuses, and forms of life influence our work? How do we influence them? What don't you capitalize in your life? Who determines funding policies? Does a PhD make one happy? Who is allowed to do research? How *white* is your research community? Where does your work stop? What goes into your CV? Which currencies does our work circulate in? How is your enterprise doing? How many projects can one pursue at the same time? Can "work done out of love" be paid for? How do we change our working conditions by talking about them?

Art Research Work. SARN (Swiss Artistic Research Network) Conference 2017 explored the working conditions prevailing within artistic research. In the last twenty years, artistic work known as artistic research has been institutionalized and found its place in the academy. Arts universities are establishing research institutes, promoting PhD programs, and competing against universities for funding. Most artists have only small workloads of institution-based research. As much time is spent on projects and exhibitions as on teaching and earning a living. Although much of this work receives great symbolic recognition, it remains largely unremunerated. Working in such diverse contexts demands great flexibility regarding methods, skills, and the ability to reconcile multiple roles. The two-day SARN Conference reflected on the processes involved in institutionalizing the changing material and ideological preconditions of artistic research in recent years from the perspective of artistic researchers. While drawing on a feminist and intersectional approach, the contributing artists and researchers reflected on the current situation of artistic researchers, outlined concrete ideas for future work-life strategies and for other funding and job opportunities, and formulated demands for self-determined artistic research.

The conference took place at Zurich University of the Arts (ZHdK). The cascading staircase—the most central and most public space at ZHdK—served as a conference forum. Participants met there to provide input, talk, draw, share conclusions from group work, and for meals and recreation. The conference was structured by three panels: 1. Episteme: Working Toward Findings, 2. Secret Currencies—Writing CVs, and 3. New Economy and New Economies—Changes in the Education System and in Art Institutions. The workshops related to the panels were held in small groups in locations beyond the reach of the central reservation system. The groups moved around the spaces with folding chairs and mobile working instruments.

In her workshop *Crip Modes. Radikalisieren des Fragens über den Alltag hinaus*, Eva Egermann addressed historical documents via Disability Studies and critiques on normality and normativity. The workshop took place at the historical design collection of chairs at the Museum für Gestaltung. *Night Shift—Precarious Sweat Music* invited participants to join a ninety-minute party that took over a service elevator. In their workshop, Amal Alhaag and Maria Guggenbichler played the game of randomly uplifting and downgrading bodies—just as it sometimes happens to us, our salary, and CV at the workplace. Raju Rage discussed with participants how QTIPOC (Queer, Trans* Intersex People of Color) survive Art School. The aim of the workshop was to challenge institutional racism and *white* supremacy within a cultural framework. The SARN Library was a place to recover from the discussions, to meet for a chat, to browse SARN publications, and to find information on SARN activities. The SARN Table Talks turned the participants' attention to their own personal relationships to work.

Barbara Preisig and Romy Rüegger

Project Title
Art Research Work. SARN Conference 2017

Project Period
8–9 December 2017

Keywords
- Artistic research
- Working conditions
- Feminism
- Intersectionality
- Love

Heads of Project
- Barbara Preisig, art historian and art critic
- Romy Rüegger, artist

Project Team
- Christoph Schenker, art theorist
- Cynthia Matumona, communication

Visual and Spatial Concept
- Riikka Tauriainen, artist
- Sarah Solderer, artist
- Hannah Horst, art educator
- Chantal Küng, artist and art educator

Contributors
- Amal Alhaag
- Gabriyel Bat-erdene
- Mirjam Bayerdörfer
- Marina Belobrovaja
- Flavia Caviezel
- Teresa Chen
- Hans Christian Dany
- Camille Dumond

- Eva Egermann
- Benjamin Egger
- Ipek Füsun
- Priska Gisler
- Maria Guggenbichler
- Marianne Halter
- Julie Harboe
- Ronny Hardliz
- Swetlana Heger
- Frank Hesse
- Michael Hiltbrunner
- Christian Huebler
- Luzia Hürzeler
- Ursula Jakob
- Pekka Kantonen
- Petra Köhle
- Lucie Kolb
- Franz Krähenbühl
- Bojana Kunst
- Rachel Mader
- Federica Martini
- Hansuli Matter
- Tine Melzer
- Doreen Mende
- Maya Minder
- Rena Onat
- Siri Peyer
- Barbara Preisig
- Raju Rage
- Irene Revell
- Hannes Rickli
- Christian Ritter
- Romy Rüegger
- Hinrich Sachs
- Jovita dos Santos Pinto
- Vincent Scarth
- Johanna Schaffer
- Christoph Schenker
- Giaco Schiesser
- Franziska Schutzbach
- Markus Schwander
- Milena Sentobe
- Cornelia Sollfrank
- Anne-Catherine Sutermeister
- Zoe Tempest
- Sophie Vögele
- Valentina Vuksic
- Yamu Wang
- Yvonne Wilhelm

Project Funding
- SARN Swiss Artistic Research Network
- Zurich University of the Arts

Conference Booklet
- Barbara Preisig and Romy Rüegger (eds.) (2017): *Art Research Work. SARN Conference*. Zurich: Zurich University of the Arts.

Fig. 1–4 Workshops and table talks, Zurich University of the Arts, 2017

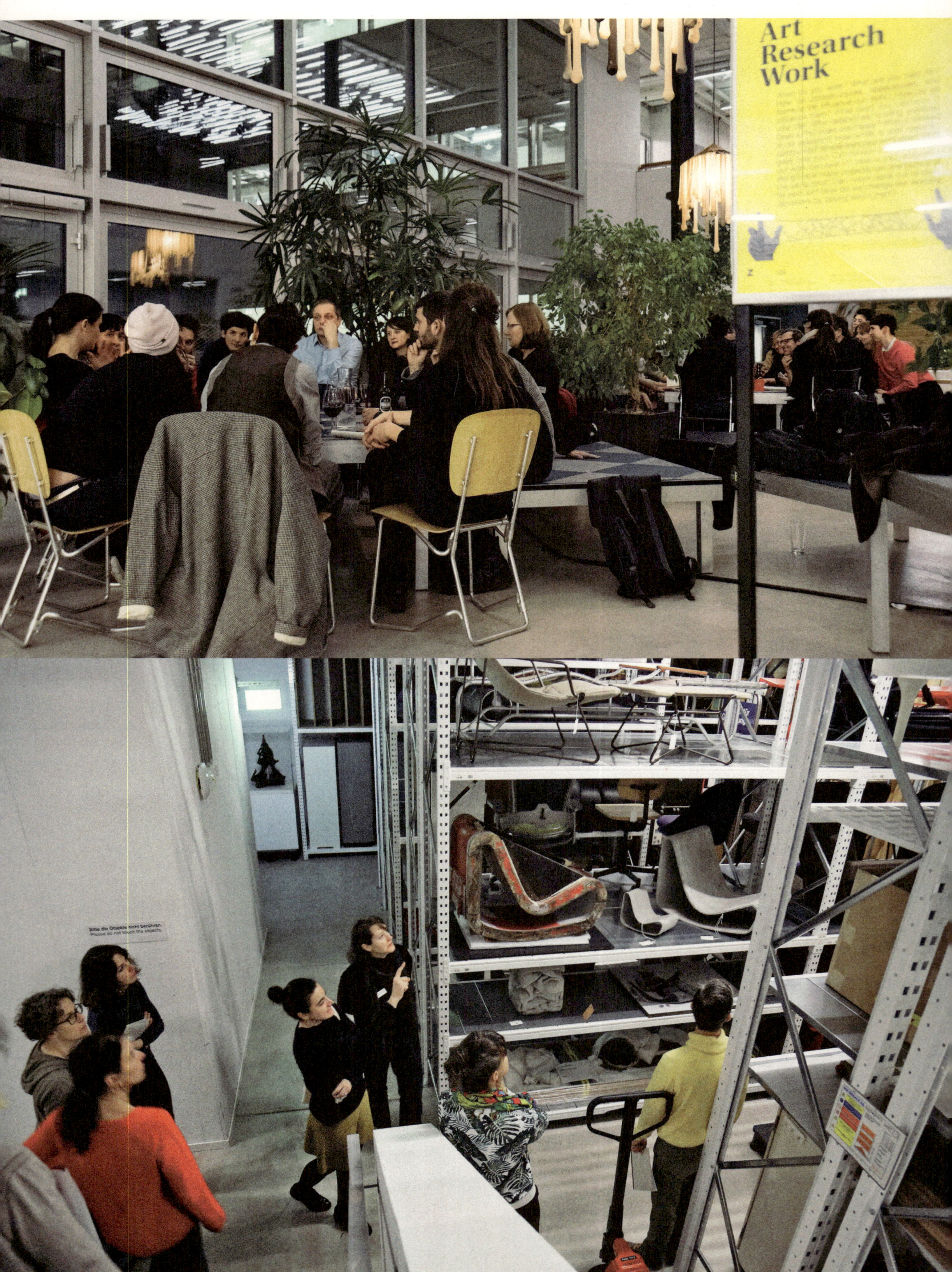

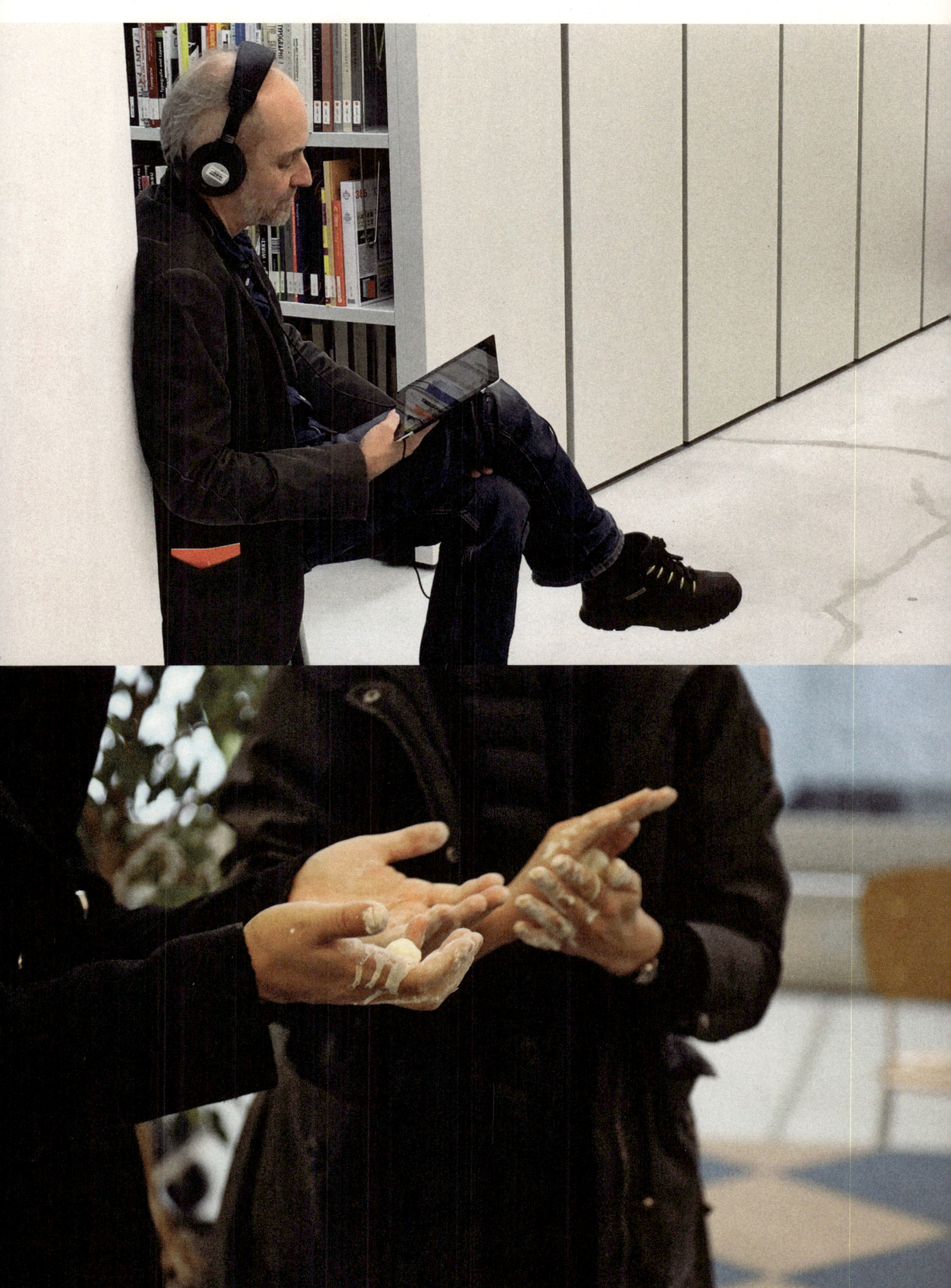

Fig. 5 Valentina Vuksic: Performance. Zurich University of the Arts, 2017

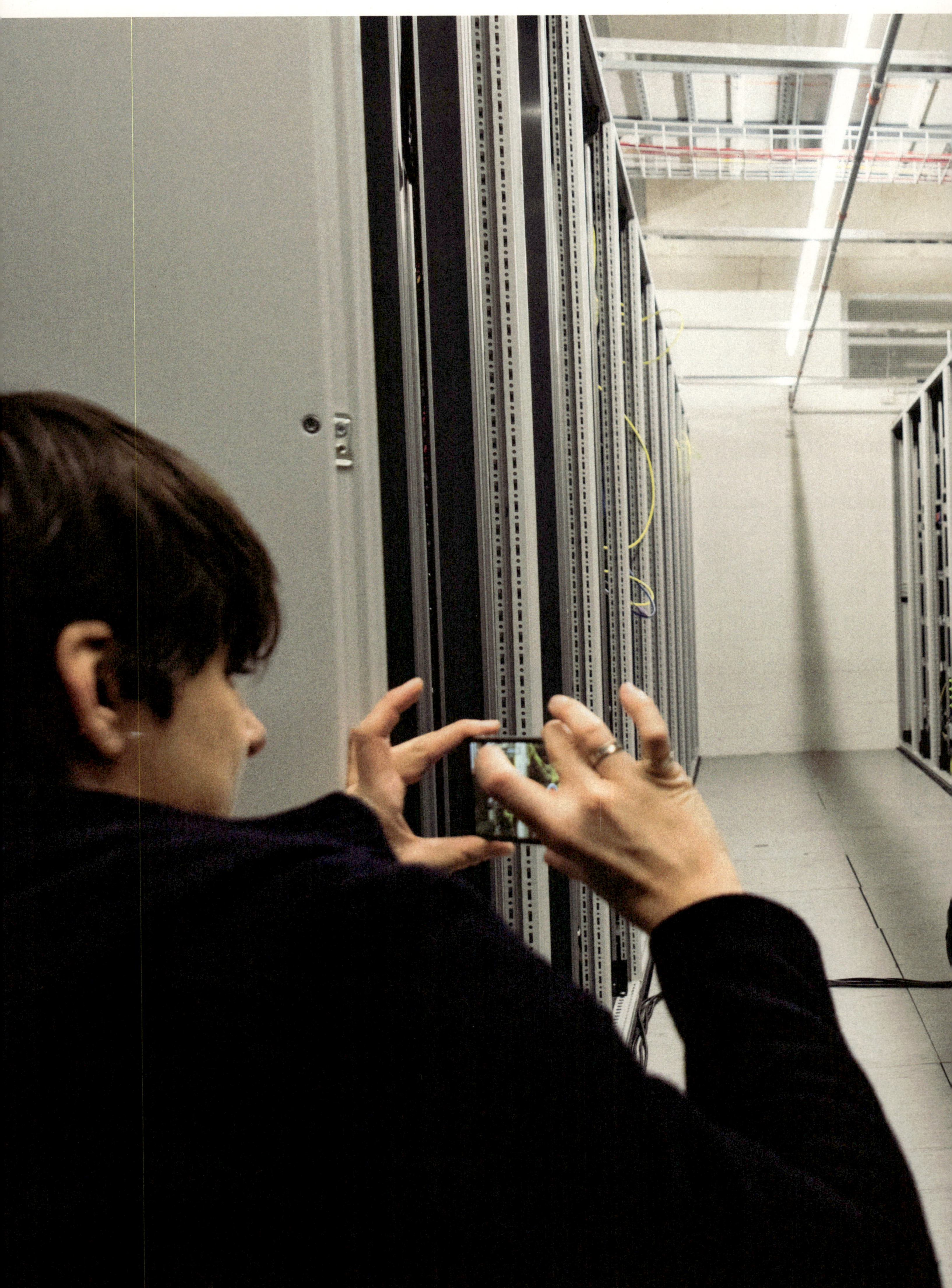

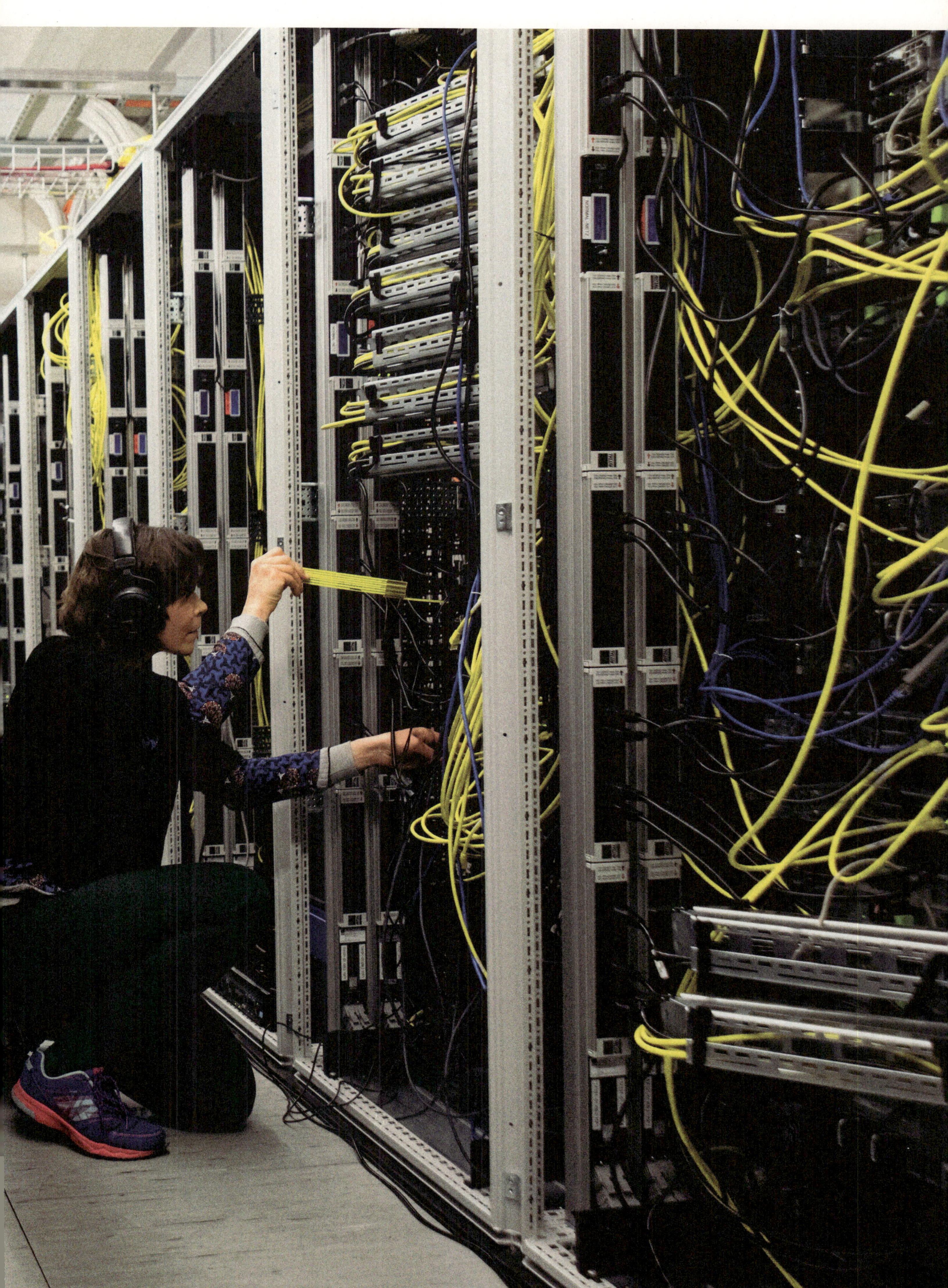

Establishing philosophy in instruction at art academies is a mark of distinction. Under the aspect of artistic research, this poses the question as to whether philosophizing in images and in nonverbal signs is conceivable, and whether such philosophizing exists. Fruitful work for addressing this question is taking place in the context of Visual Studies, where images are analyzed that were relevant in the history of philosophy and are currently regaining popularity in the form of illustrated introductions to philosophy. One of the most popular images shows "Lady Philosophy" in the *Consolation* by the ancient philosopher Boethius. This manuscript was copied and illustrated over a period of at least 1000 years. The *Iconography of Consolation* project investigated eight images in four editions of this text to examine how historical images from the history of philosophy can be addressed by contemporary image production. The first step of the project entailed Barbara Ellmerer, Sarah Burger, and Nils Röller developing the concept of image protocols.

The image protocols differentiated between the historical source image, formular, intermediate steps, and what was called a "target image," which the project team defined as the conclusion of the artistic-creative confrontation with the source image. This included research beforehand, consultations in specialized libraries, taking notes and photographs there, and drafting work in the studio. In the studio, the perceptions while producing the target images were analyzed anew, thus reciprocally interacting with the production of the target image. All source images were taken from the iconography of the *Consolation* by Boethius. In collaboration with the Zurich University of the Arts Media and Information Centre and the prometheus digital image archive, the iconography for the project was recorded digitally.

The image protocols by Barbara Ellmerer and Dominic Neuwirth showed that the process from the source image to the target image was characterized by interruptions, restarts, and abrupt shifts, and proceeded intermittently. Phases of perception overlapped with processes of production. Processes of image production were accompanied by adjustments and examinations of means of representation and their suitability for a target image. The image protocols by Barbara Ellmerer, for instance, can be read as documents of a dialog which the artist organized between her familiar means of representation (paint, ink, ice, monotype, scan, inkjet) and the representation in the target image. The conclusion of the dialog was arbitrary, eruptive; it was also determined by the artist's decisions about what means of representation she decided to use. The dialog could have been resumed just as arbitrarily. Thus, the research design was able to confirm that the artistic examination is constitutively and self-reflexively coupled with the utilized materials. At its conclusion this led to a discussion about how strongly moments of material experience are involved in this process, and to the further research question as to whether artistic production is a form of experience that cognitively undermines the separation between the sensory and the cognitive, or whether it operates independently of this separation. These findings open the door to a field in which philosophy and artistic activity can encounter each other without mutual assimilation. In order to prepare the image protocols and their discussion during the workshops and the closing symposium, the project focused on developing the relevant terminology and iconographic references. To facilitate communication within the team, these terms and iconography were saved weekly in an online glossary and an online gallery. A landing page and a blog presenting the image protocols, views of the exhibition, and information on the symposium were published in fall 2018 and have since served to communicate the project to the public. This platform was supplemented by regular posts on Instagram.

Nils Röller

Project Title
Ikonografie der Trostschrift. Verschränkung von Text und Bild

Project Period
1 January 2018–31 May 2019

Keywords
- **Image protocol**
- **Boethius**
- **Pictorial science**
- **History of philosophy**
- **Iconography of Consolation**

Head of Project
- **Nils Röller, philosopher**

Project Team
- **Barbara Ellmerer, artist**
- **Vera Kaspar, artist**
- **Dominic Neuwirth, artist**

Research Partner
- **Dieter Mersch, Institute for Theory, ZHdK**

Project Partners
- **Richard Tisserand, Kunstraum Kreuzlingen, Thurgauische Kunstgesellschaft**
- **Susanne Schumacher, ZHdK Media and Information Centre**

Outputs

A

Project Funding

- Swiss National Science Foundation SNSF/DORE

Related Project

- Indirect Experiences, Zurich University of the Arts, 2010–2011
  P. 104

Website

- www.iconographyofphilosophy.ch

Article

- Nils Röller (2021): "Interfacing Philosophy." In: *Text-Image Parergon. KOKO—The Next Generation Journal*, issue 1, 1–25.
  A Open access: https://doi.org/10.5281/zenodo.4923681

Lecture

- Nils Röller: "Bildprotokoll – Diskussion von Darstellungen der Philosophia." In: *Verkoppelungen, Verlinkungen, Verschachtelungen: Mediale Eigenlogiken – Raum/zeitliche Dimensionen*. Workshop. 5 October 2018. University of Zurich, Center for Historical Mediology.

Conference

- *Abständiges – Gegenwartskunst in Wechselwirkung mit Philosophie*. 16 May 2019. Kunstraum Kreuzlingen. With contributions by Richard Tisserand, Thomas Jürgasch, Andreas Kirchner, Barbara Ellmerer, Vera Kaspar, Dominic Neuwirth, Dieter Mersch, Nils Röller, Arno Schubbach, Katharina Zimmermann-Hohmeyer, Daniel Irrgang, Robert Preusse, and Beat Streuli.

Exhibition

- *Zellenleben*. 12 April–19 May 2019. Kunstraum Kreuzlingen. With exhibits by Nils Röller, Barbara Ellmerer, Judith Albert, Beat Streuli, and Dominic Neuwirth.

Works

- Eight target images (2019) in various media by Barbara Ellmerer, Vera Kaspar, and Dominic Neuwirth.
- Barbara Ellmerer: *Zielbild Nr. 7*. Illustrates the contribution by Christian Vogel (2019): "Mit Mathematik zum Seelenheil. Boethius im Porträt." In: *Der Blaue Reiter – Journal für Philosophie*, vol. 44. 111.

Archive

- Nils Röller and Dominic Neuwirth (2019): "Ikonografie der Trostschrift."
  Online in www.prometheus-bildarchiv.de and https://medienarchiv.zhdk.ch

Fig. 1 Boethius: *Consolatio Philosophiae*. Austrian National Library, Latin, quarto, 10th century

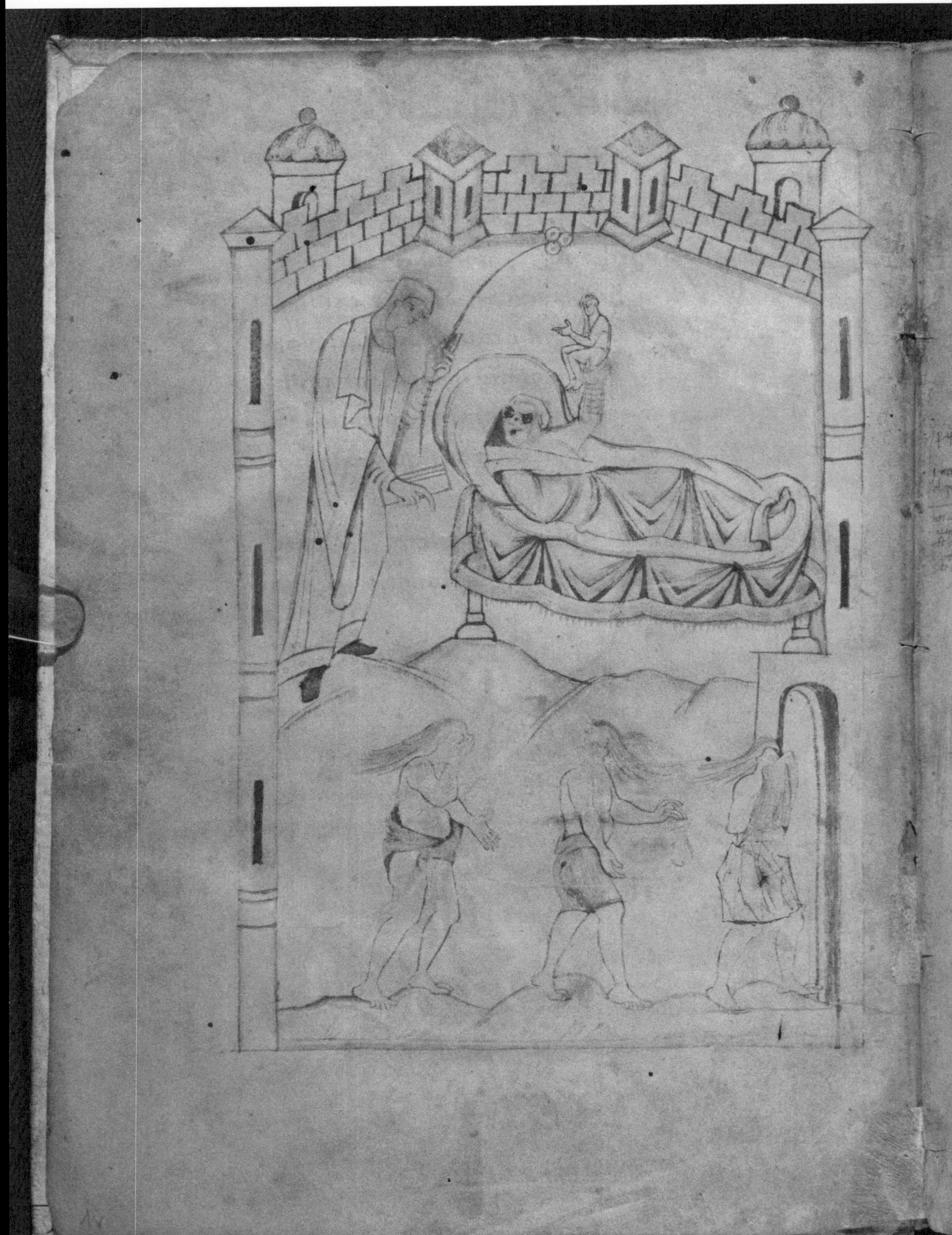

Fig. 2 Barbara Ellmerer: Sketch. Image protocol no. 2, 2018

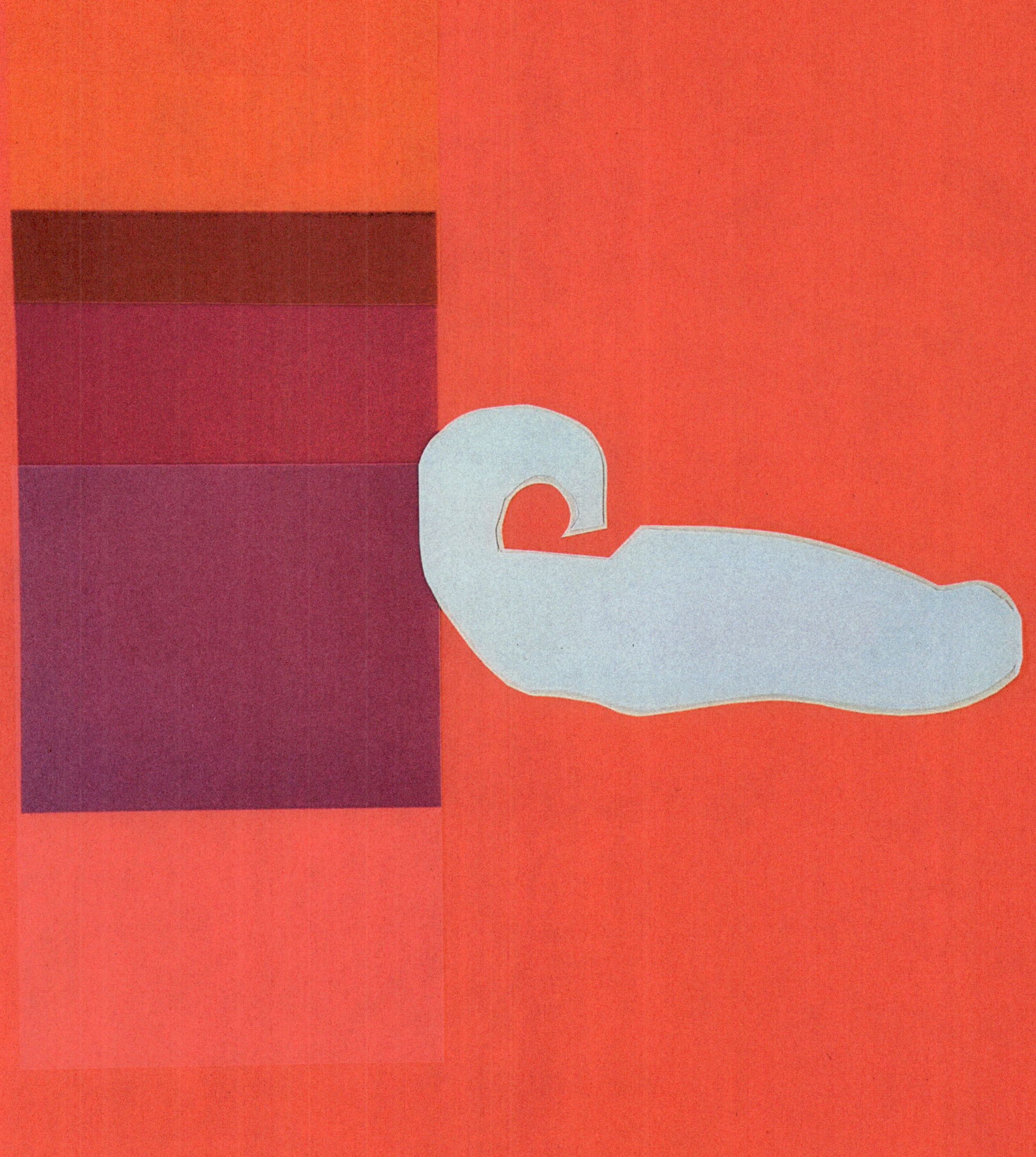

Fig. 3 Barbara Ellmerer: Sketch. Image protocol no. 8, 2018

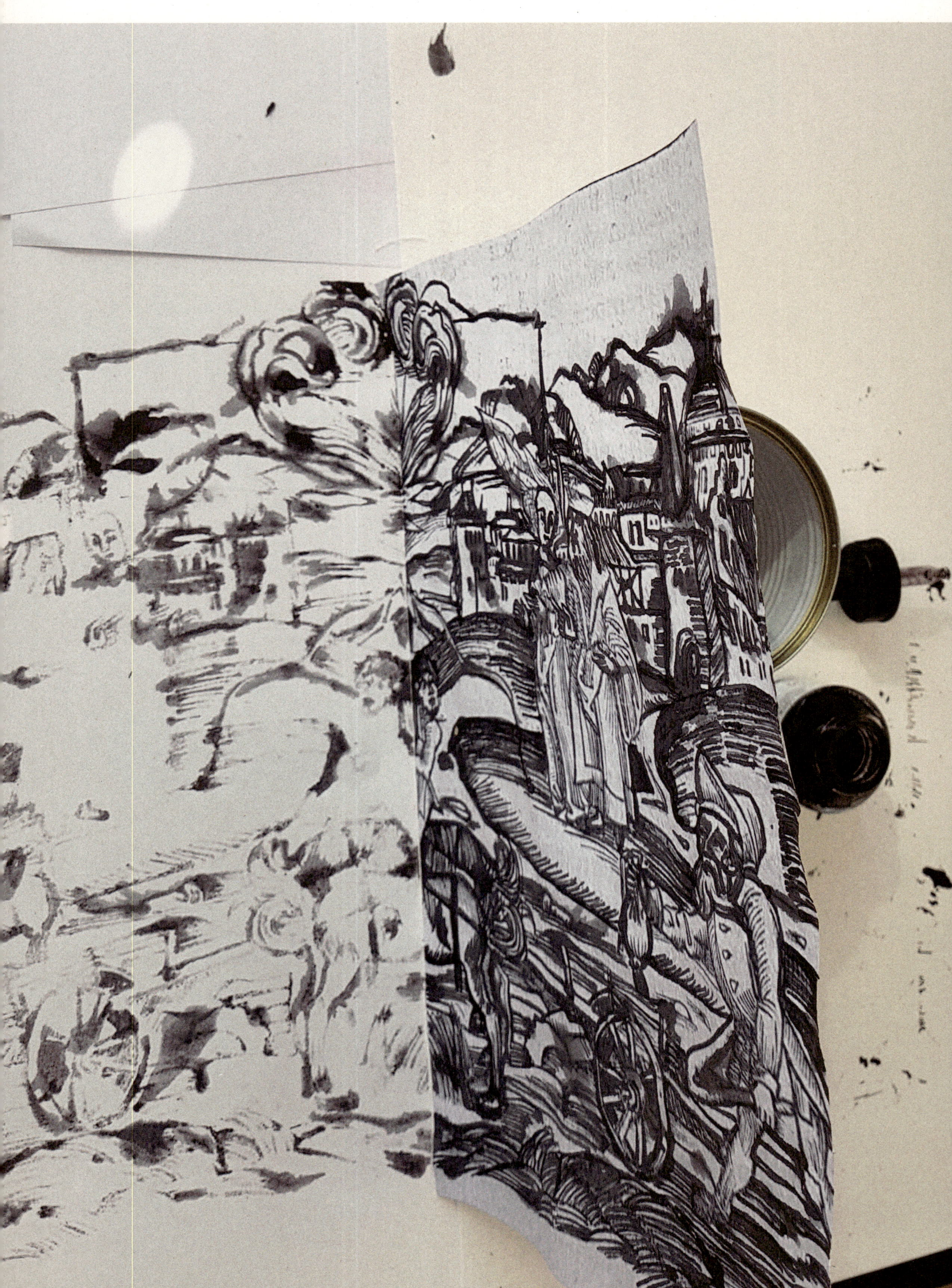

Hic incipit Quintus liber Boetij de conſolatione philoſophie.

Cuius hec eſt prima proſa. In qua phĩa vult ſoluere quedã dubia ſuã determĩationẽ cõſequentia de fato & prouidentia. Videtur enim ex dictis ꝙ caſus nõ ſit quia ſi omnia ſunt ꝓuiſa ita ꝙ nihil eueniat preter ordinẽ prouidentie diuine videtur ꝙ nihil caſualiter eueniat quia caſus importat euentũ inopinatum. Item videtur ex dictis ꝙ liberꝫ arbitrium non ſit quia omnia diſponunt̃ ſecundũ ordinem fatalis neceſſitatis. Liberũ autem arbitriũ neceſſitatem excludit. Videtur ergo ſi non ponitur prouidentia & fatum ꝙ omnino excludatur liberum arbitriũ. Philoſophia ergo in preſenti libro inquirit. Vtrum caſus ſit & quid ſit. Et inquirit vtrũ liberũ arbitrium ſit ponẽdo argumenta quibus liberum arbitrium cum ꝓuidentia diuina nõ videtur poſſe ſtare poſt hoc ponit falſam ſolutionem quorundam quã improbat & ponit ꝓpriam quã rationibus confirmat & de eternitate determinat: & alia plura ſicut patebit. Et diuiditur iſte liber in vndecim partes quia ſex ſunt ꝓſe & quinqꝫ metra eius: que partes & q̃ in ipſis determinant̃ patebũt in ꝓceſſu libri. In prima ꝓſa determinat de caſu & primo Boetiꝰ tãgit acta phĩe cõmendans eius exhortationẽ factã & mouet queſtionẽ de caſu. Scd̃o phĩa excuſat ſe ab eiꝰ determinatiõe & Boetiꝰ illã excuſationẽ remouet. Tertio phĩa determinat de caſu. Secunda ibi. Tum illa feſtino. Tertia ibi. Tum illa morem. Primo dicit philoſophia dixerat hec predicta ꝛc.

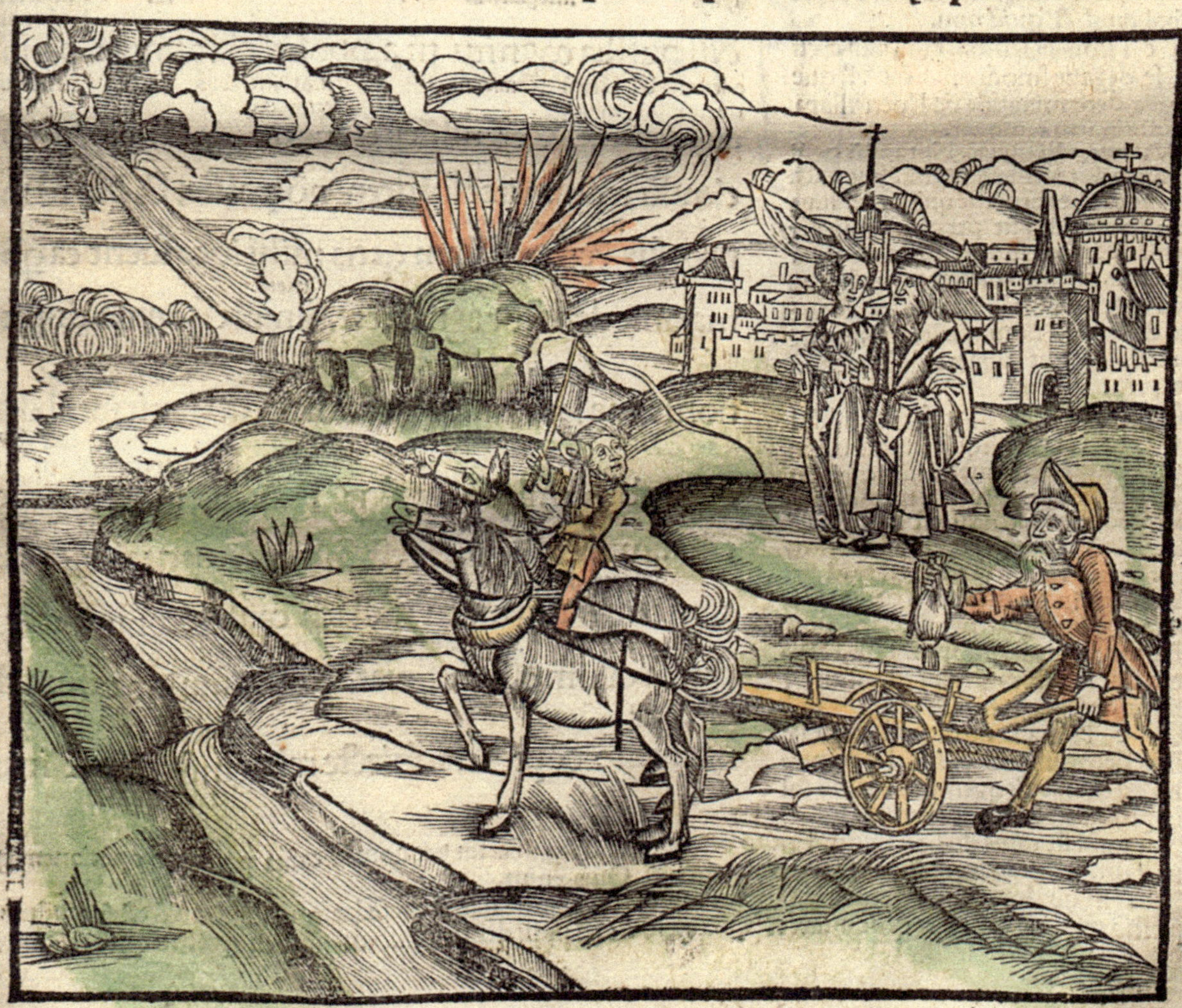

V ii

Fig. 5 Barbara Ellmerer: Sketch and target image. Image protocol no. 4, 2018

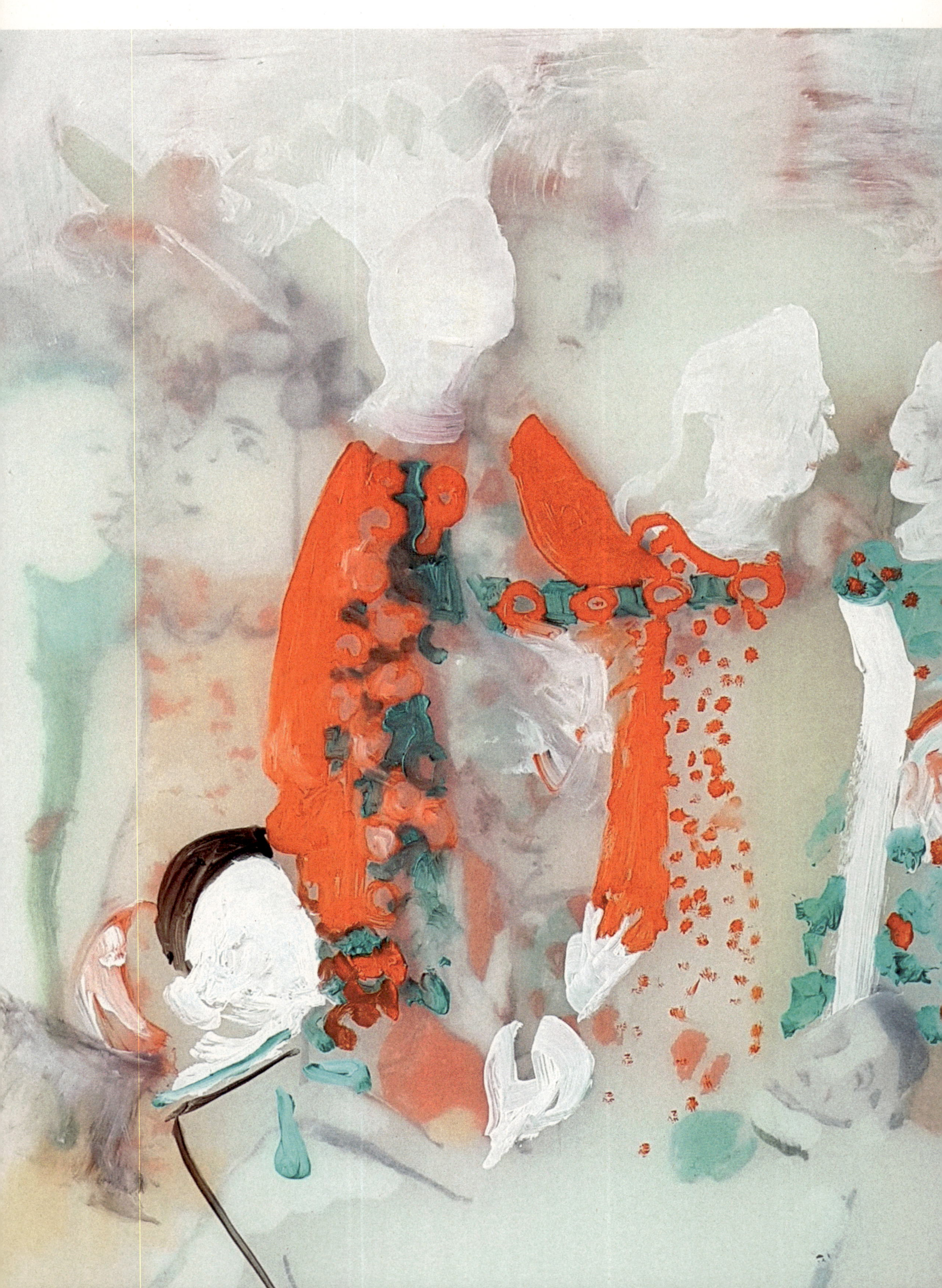

Fig. 6 Barbara Ellmerer and Vera Kaspar: Image protocols. *Ikonografie der Trostschrift*, blog, 2018

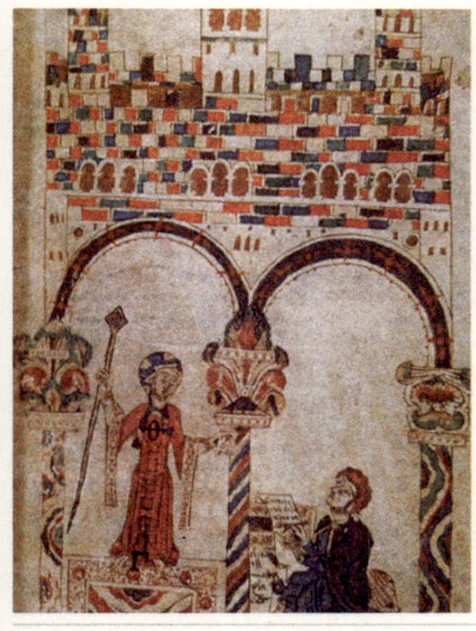
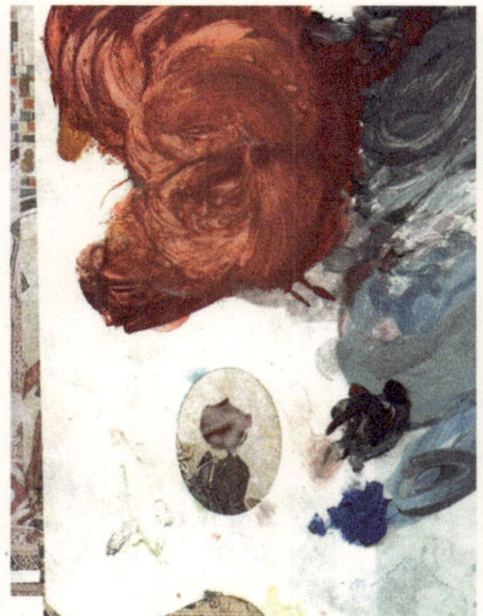
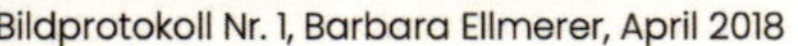

Bildprotokoll Nr. 1, Barbara Ellmerer, April 2018

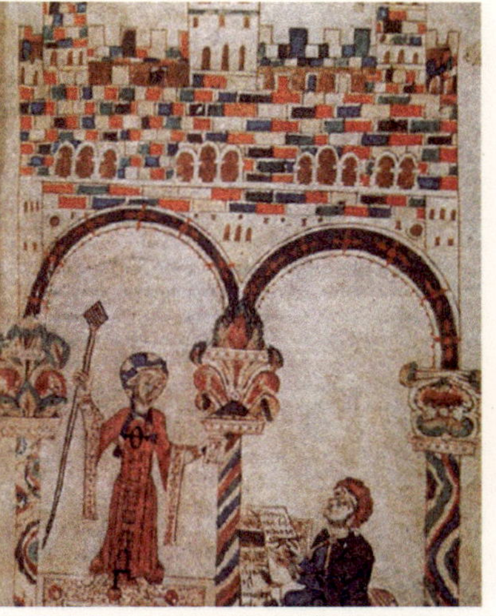
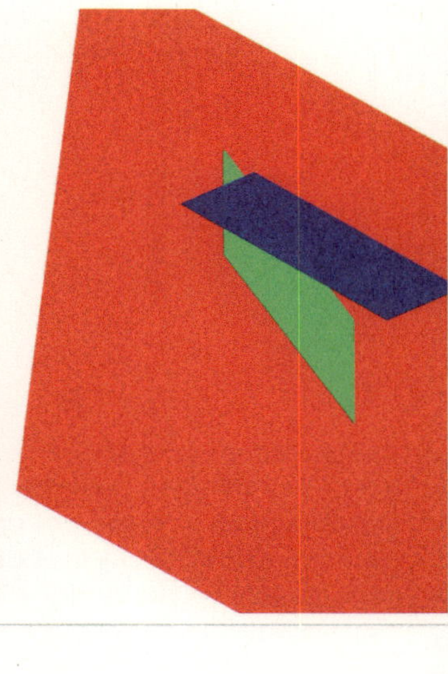
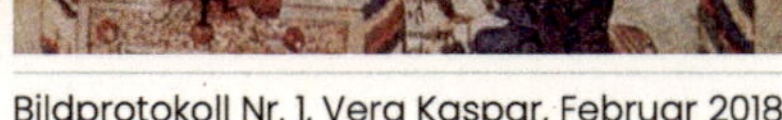

Bildprotokoll Nr. 1, Vera Kaspar, Februar 2018

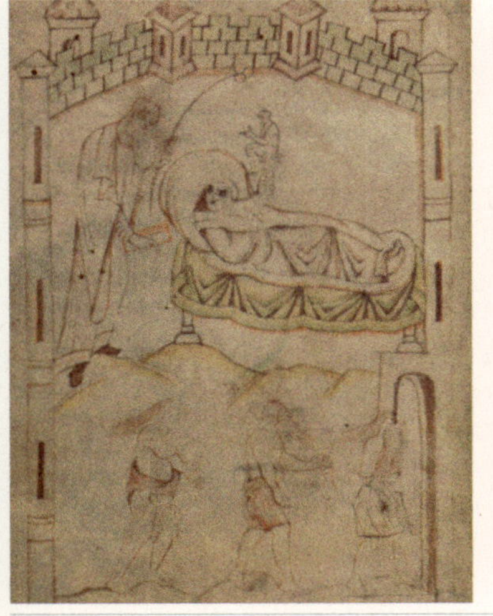

Bildprotokoll Nr. 2, Barbara Ellmerer, Mai 2018

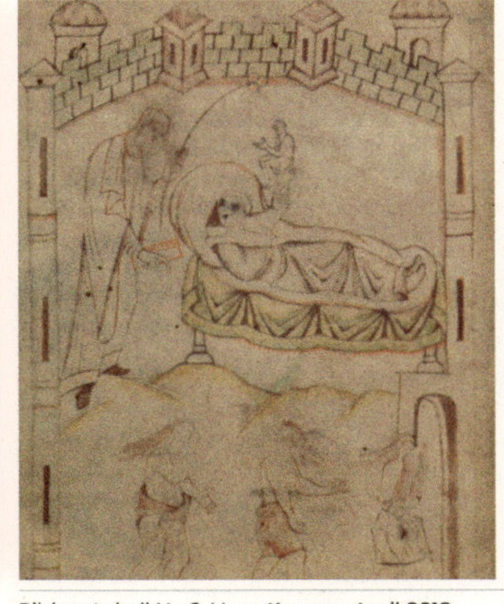

Bildprotokoll Nr. 2, Vera Kaspar, April 2018

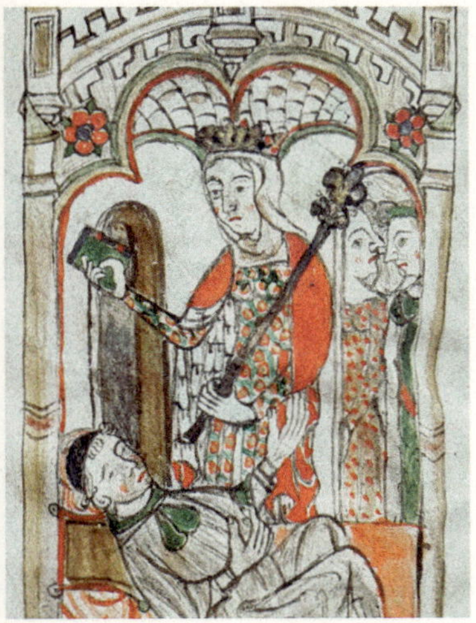
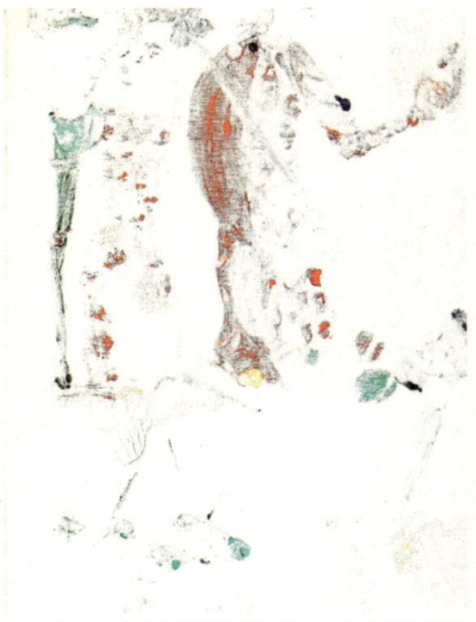

Bildprotokoll Nr. 3, Barbara Ellmerer, Mai 2018

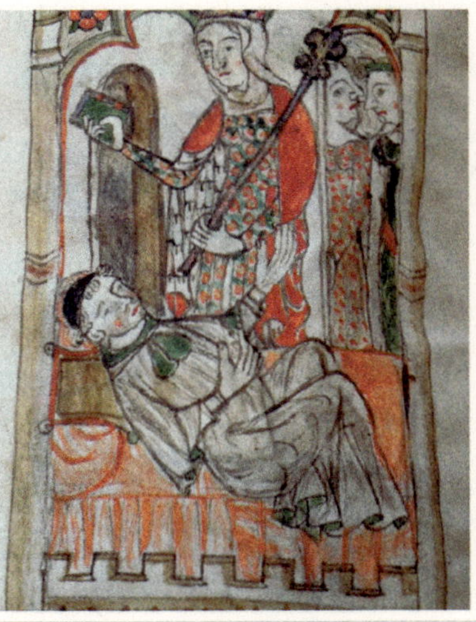
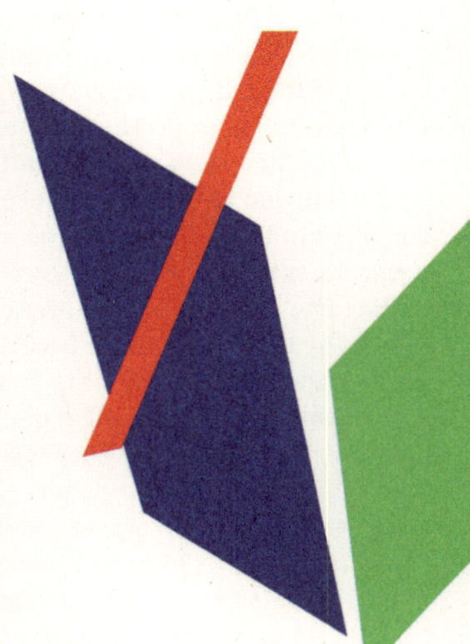

Bildprotokoll Nr. 3, Vera Kaspar, Mai 2018

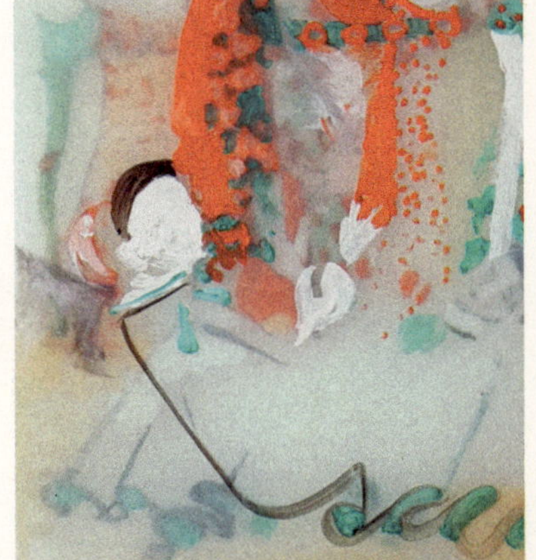
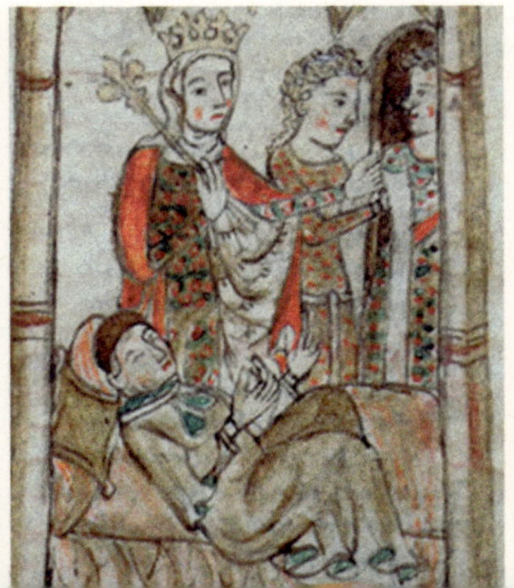
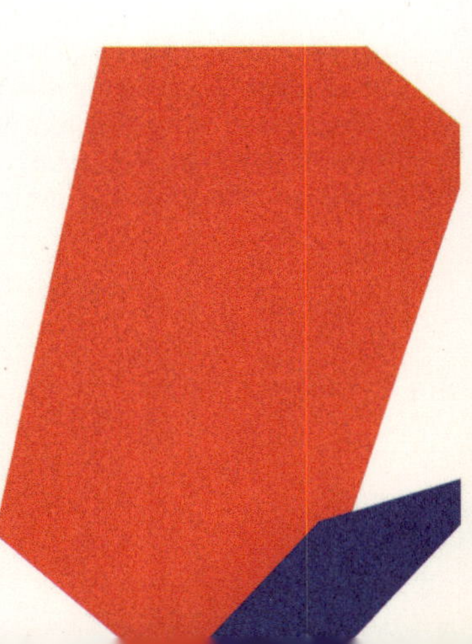

Trading Zones was concerned with camera-based practices at the interfaces of artistic and ethnographic research. It focused on practitioners who critically investigate their cinematographic and photographic means of production and how they are socially embedded. The project started as a series of events which we held with artists, anthropologists, and documentary filmmakers at Zurich University of the Arts between 2018 and 2020. The thematic emphasis emerged from a practical need: Many artistic researchers in our circle deal with how they can use the camera as a tool, based on the methods of research, observation, and oral history, to find out about ways of living together. The wide spectrum of topics addressed by the projects made it difficult to recognize that a shared object of discussion could emerge from this series. With the series of events, we not only stimulated discussions among the researchers; in the screenings, lectures, and workshops we also followed the methodological problems across disciplinary boundaries and sought dialog with researchers in the fields of ethnography and visual anthropology.

The contributions to the events were further developed for the volume *Trading Zones—Camera Work in Artistic and Ethnographic Research* (2022) and reflected in the form of conversations, essays, and artistic works. In this book artists, anthropologists, and documentary filmmakers think out loud about the practical side of their camera work, about the pitfalls and potentialities occurring before and during recordings in the field, in postproduction or presentation. What all contributions have in common is that the camera is also an actor, not a mere recording instrument. But how does the camera help shape the relationship to the field, to the research object, and to the participants? How can its social function be described? How does it enable, compel, and determine the action? What does the camera see that the camerawoman does not? How is it interwoven with the narrative position of the author, and what representational share is the camera image unable to shake off?

The book collects projects that can be understood as trading zones in the broader sense. They are places where working with the camera also enables negotiation: about common issues of artistic and ethnographic research, about the interests and expectations of the filmmaker, the filmed, and the viewers, about different narrative positions, and about translocal entanglements. These negotiations open up a shared field of artistic and ethnographic investigation whose potential is far from exhausted.

Barbara Preisig

Project Title
Trading Zones. Working with the Camera at the Interface of Art and Ethnography

Project Period
6 June 2018–25 February 2020

Keywords
- **Visual anthropology**
- **Ethnography**
- **Artistic research**
- **Camera**
- **Agency**
- **Film**

Heads of Project
- **Barbara Preisig, art historian and art critic**
- **Jürgen Krusche, artist and urbanologist**
- **Laura von Niederhäusern, artist (co-editor of publication)**

Project Funding
- **Cassinelli-Vogel-Stiftung**

A

Project Website

- https://blog.zhdk.ch/tradingzones/archive

Publication

- Barbara Preisig, Laura von Niederhäusern, and Jürgen Krusche (eds.) (2022): *Trading Zones. Camera Work in Artistic and Ethnographic Research*. Volume 26 of the Institute for Contemporary Art Research series. Berlin: Archive Books.
  A Open access: https://doi.org/10.5281/zenodo.5734214

Lecture Series: Screenings and Talks at Zurich University of the Arts

- Zheng Mahler (Royce Ng and Daisy Bisenieks): "From Ethnographic to Virtual World Making." 6 June 2018. Moderated by Barbara Preisig.
- Goran Galić and Gian-Reto Gredig: "'Ma Biće Bolje' und 'Put Mira' – Dokumentarismen zwischen Kunst und Wissenschaft." 26 September 2018. Moderated by Jürgen Krusche.
- Lorenzo Tripodi: "Urbiquity. Situated practice in contested spaces and the awkward body of the author." 17 December 2018. Moderated by Jürgen Krusche.
- Michael Oppitz: "'Wort gegen Bild' – Wechselbeziehungen zweier Medien in der Beschreibung fremder Welten." 17 January 2019. Moderated by Jürgen Krusche.
- Laura Coppens: "Die Kunst des filmischen Beobachtens im anthropologischen Film 'Taste of Hope'." 27 January 2019. Moderated by Barbara Preisig.
- Uriel Orlow: "Camera Dialogues." 5 March 2019. With Uriel Orlow, Bärbel Küster, and Barbara Preisig.
- Heidrun Holzfeind: "The Time is Now." 26 March 2019. Moderated by Jürgen Krusche.
- Artur Żmijewski: "Glimpse." 8 May 2019. Moderated by Jürgen Krusche.
- Lena Maria Thüring: "Future Me. Erinnerung, Narration, Fiktion." 5 June 2019. Moderated by Barbara Preisig.
- Shirin Barghnavard: "'Profession: Documentarist.' A Poetic Auto-Ethnography of Seven Iranian Filmmakers." 30 September 2019. Moderated by Barbara Preisig.
- Daniel Kötter: "Camera Walk as Urban Analysis." 14 October 2019. With Daniel Kötter, Johanna Rolshoven, and Jürgen Krusche.
- Bina Elisabeth Mohn: "Fokussieren – Zerlegen – Verknüpfen: Kamera-Ethnographie als epistemische Strategie." 19 November 2019. Lecture. Moderated by Jürgen Krusche.
- Anette Rose: "Capture, record and play." One-day exhibition and talk. 3 December 2019. Moderated by Christoph Schenker.
- Silvy Chakkalakal: "Kreative Figuration. Die Verknüpfung von Kunst und Wissenschaft in der frühen US-amerikanischen Kulturanthropologie." 13 January 2020. Moderated by Laura von Niederhäusern.
- Louis Henderson: "Dialect of hurricanes. Patois of rains. Language of storms. Unfolding of life in a spiral." 25 February 2020. Moderated by Nina Kerschbaumer.

Fig. 1 Lena Maria Thüring: *How to decide what to do with your life*. Two-channel installation, performance, Le Foyer, Zurich, 2016

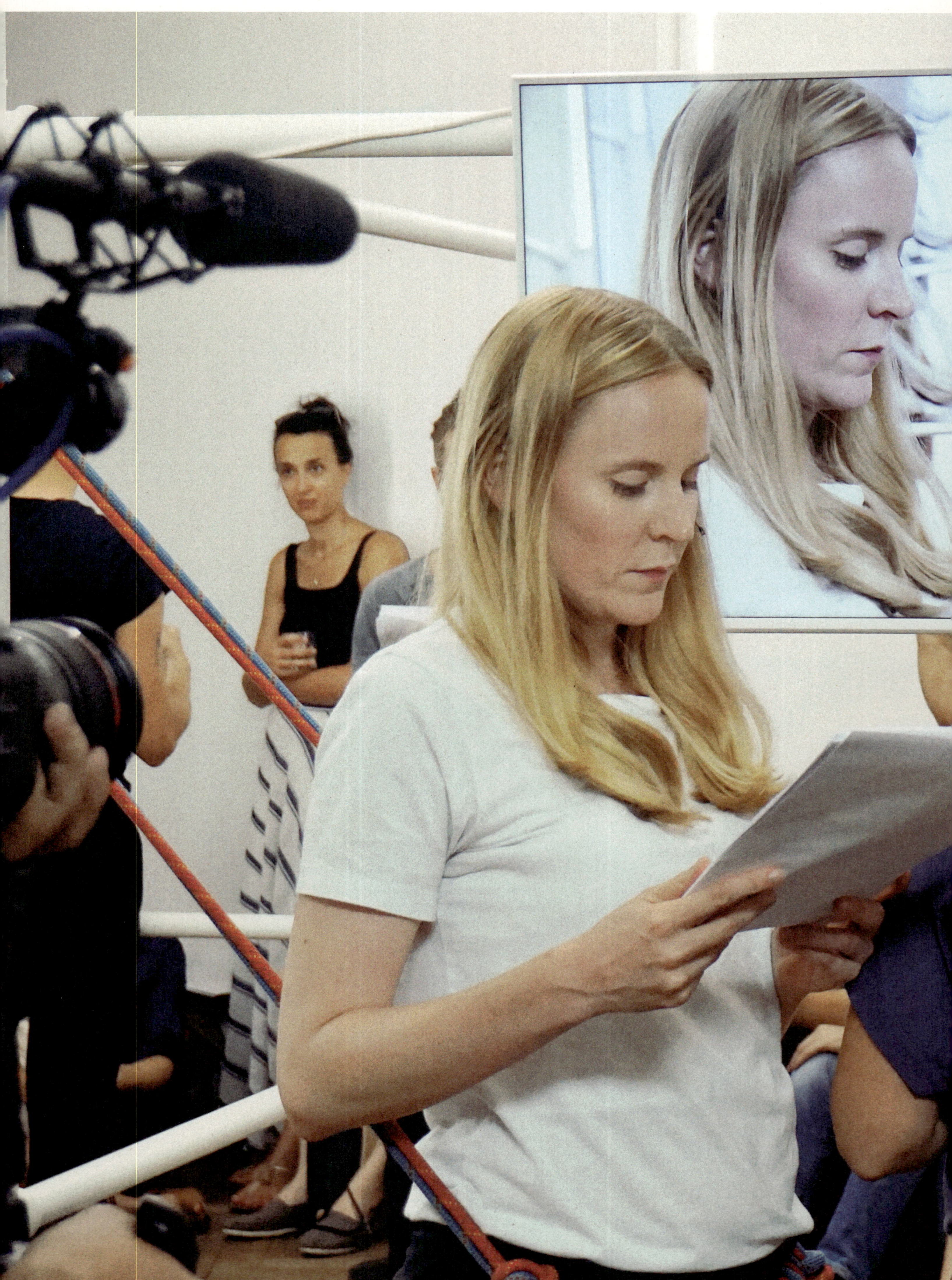

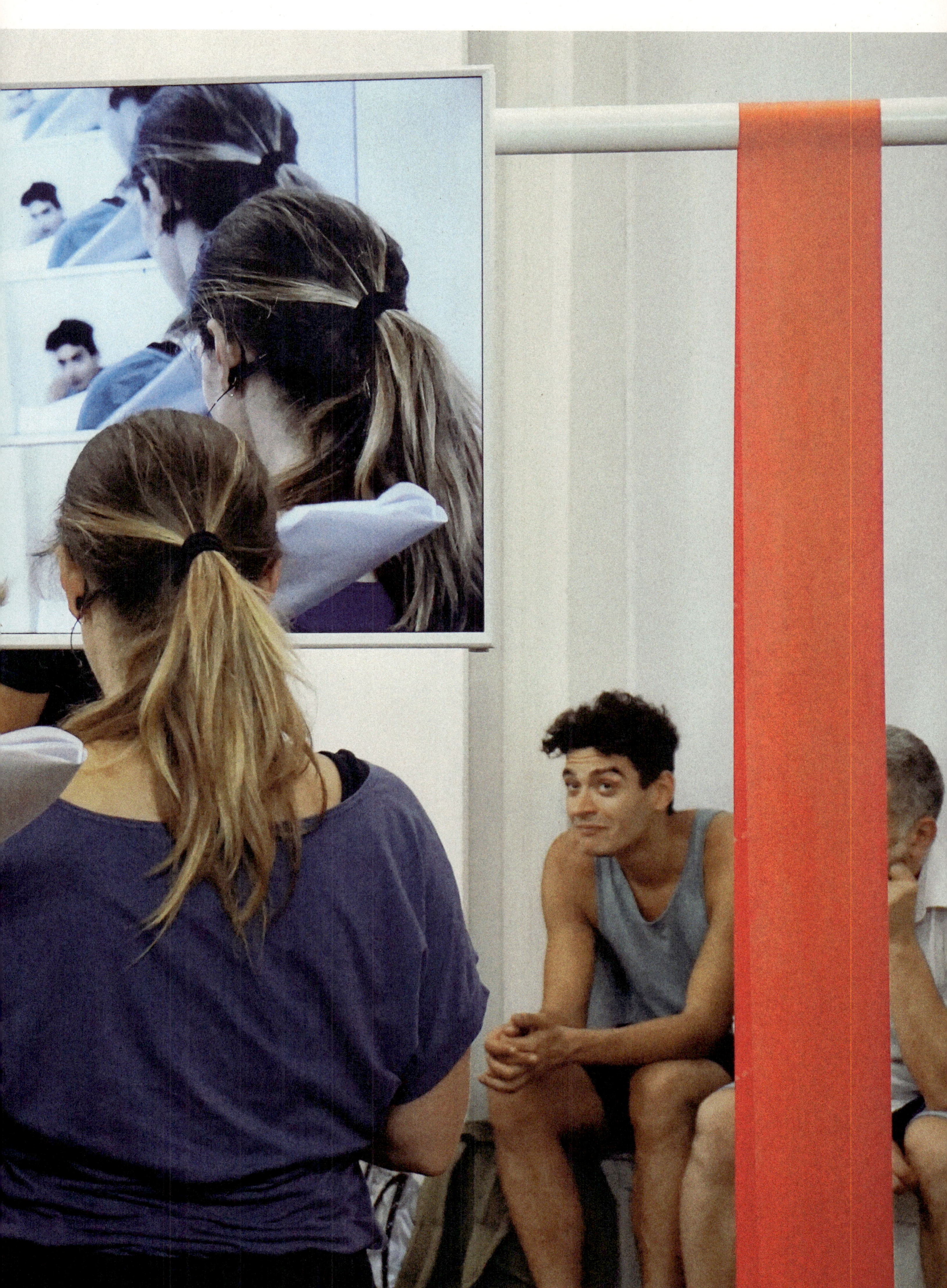

Fig. 2 Anette Rose: *Enzyklopädie der Handhabungen*. Set photo #2, 2009/2010

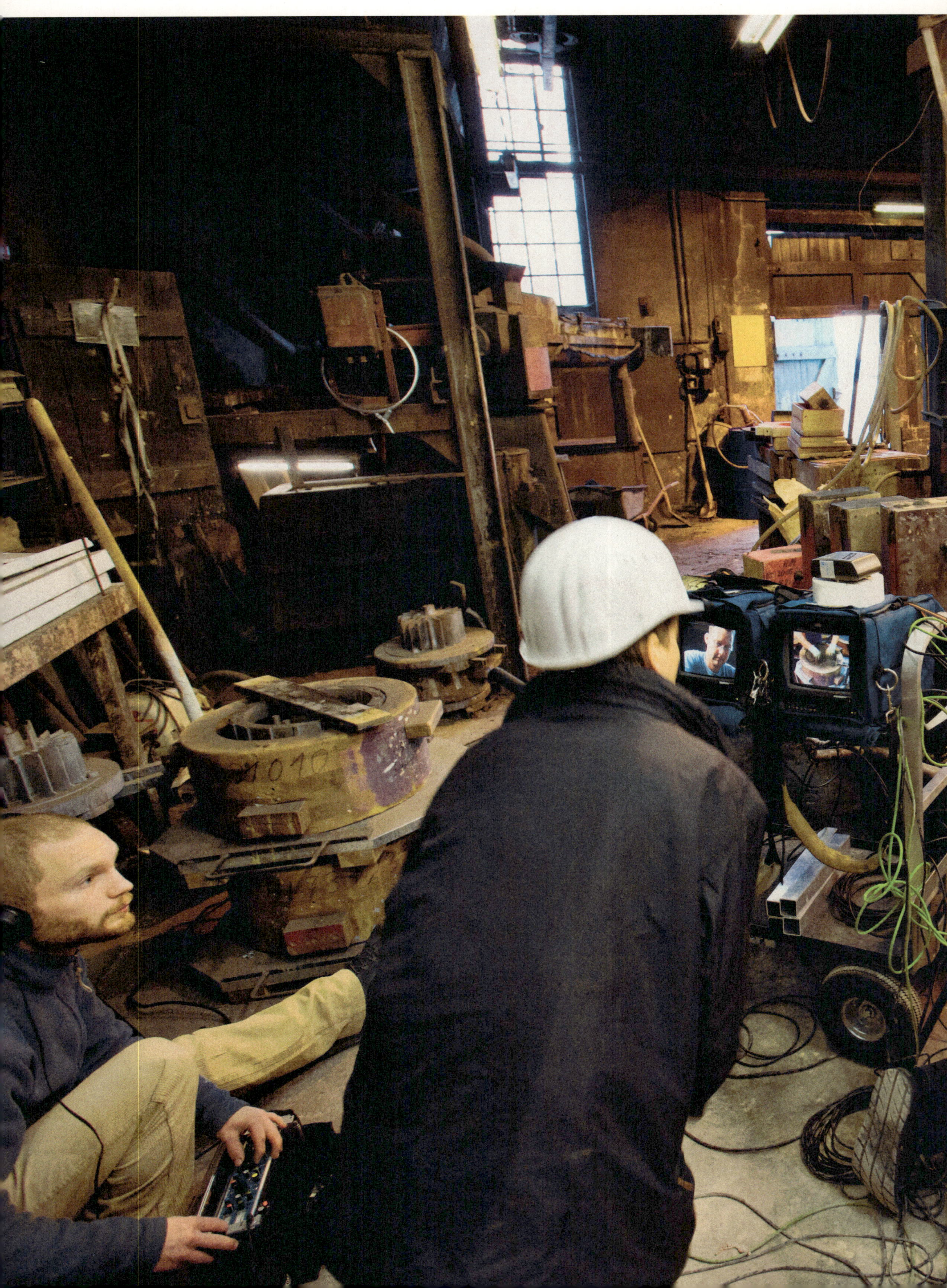

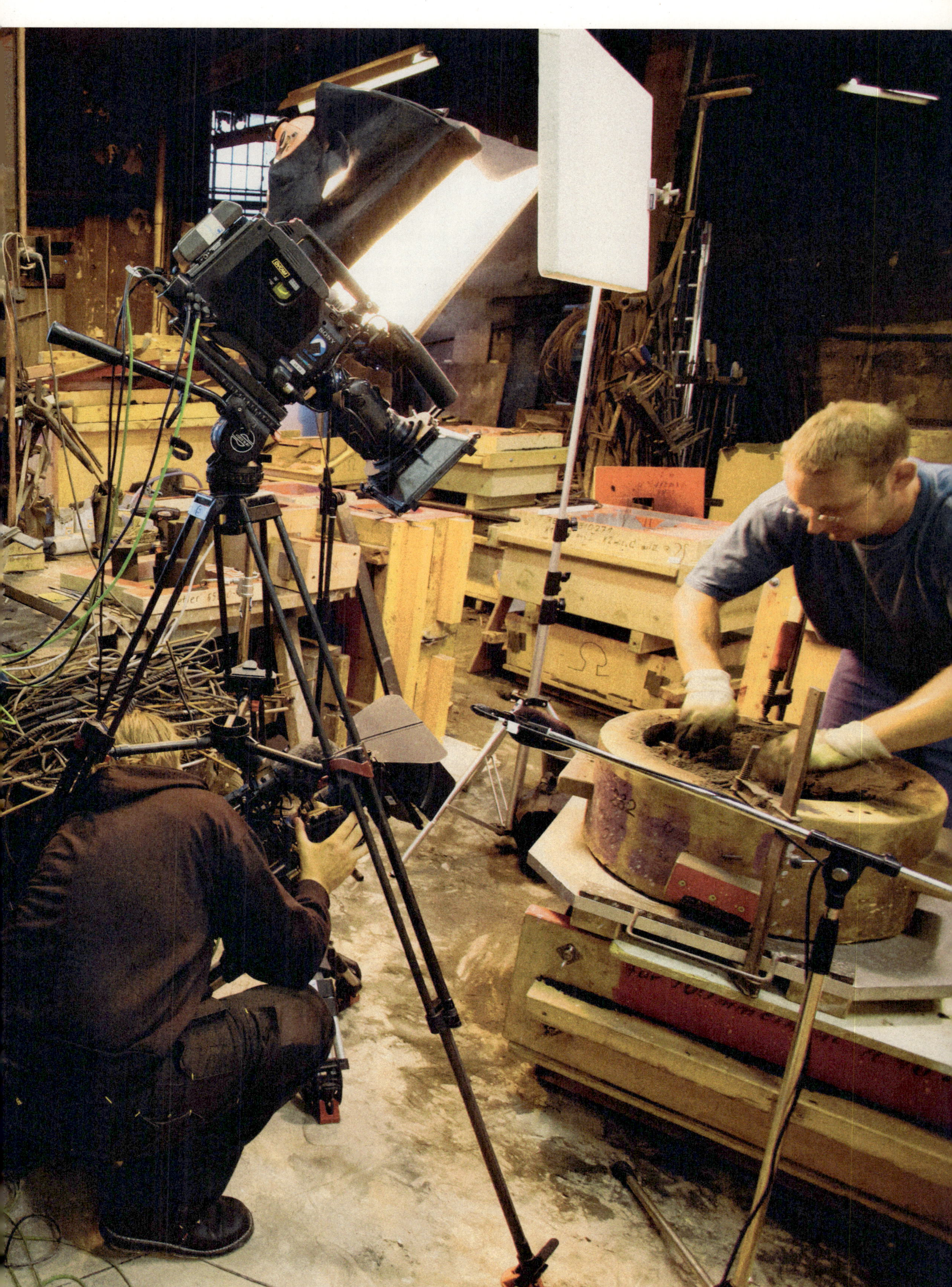

Processes of artistic creation are a frequent subject in film, literature, and history of art. Works from these disciplines generally pay insufficient regard to the kind of detailed and systematic observation that focuses on the practices of creating and their technical and material aspects. Such a focus is achieved in other fields—especially in laboratory studies (science and technology studies), but it is also of the interest of epistemology, art history, art technology, artistic research, and printing practice.

This was the starting point for the *Hands-on* project. It developed a method of systematically recording the artistic-technical processes in the print workshop from multiple perspectives—detailing all work steps, subtasks and hand movements, accounting for the whole spectrum of materials, tools, and machines used in production. This allowed the construction of a prototype for a potentially comprehensive documentation that records not only action processes but also the infrastructure closely linked to them. All this information was captured on the one hand on video, in written notes and interviews, and on the other by taking a digital inventory of everything that was used or created in the work process, including artifacts and traces. The acquisition and cataloging complied with methods of qualitative research established in social science and ethnography, as well as archiving practices.

The research project also developed a special user interface that features two adjacent frames which display synchronous video documents showing the artist and the printer at work in the workshop. At each moment during the filmed process of creation, access to the database allows the viewer to open all linked media files, recordings, and contents of the digital inventory. The links were created using a coding method that requires inventory entries much more abundant and differentiated than those in standard museum inventories. Accordingly, the coding achieves the status of scientific acquisition as understood in the context of traditional inventories. A special process vocabulary was created and introduced in order to capture the functions of the individual work steps, hand movements, and spoken interactions.

Components from three workshops flowed into the user interface. First was the lithography workshop, in which the object of observation—and what is shown in the user interface—took place. The second, the ethnographic workshop, was where the processes of observation were developed (keywords: technical-ethnographic film, observation protocol). The third workshop, finally, was the digital workshop. Its content was the data engineering which transformed and amalgamated the data for the user interface.

A user interface resulting from these three workshops contains a wealth of important information that was not previously available to the fields of art technology and history of art. It is also invaluable for artists and printers, since it helps to preserve and convey a cultural technology that is in danger of extinction.

The technical arrangement of the printing workshop embodies a knowledge that is expressed in the figure of the printer. The artist's implicit knowledge is also made visible, displayed as practical knowledge shown during the activity of creating art. The original plan for the project design intended to map out this sedimented knowledge and relate it to the discourses of science and technology studies. Unfortunately, the position which was to perform this work from the research program was not granted SNSF funding. Yet the results of the project do offer a solid empirical foundation upon which further science and technology studies will be able to build. *Hands-on* is related to other research at the IFCAR that can be understood as quasi artistic science studies, especially that of Hannes Rickli.

Christoph Schenker

Project Title
Hands-on. Dokumentation künstlerisch-technischer Prozesse im Druck

Project Period
1 September 2018–31 December 2021

Keywords
- Lithography
- Observation methods
- Process documentation
- Data engineering
- Science studies

Head of Project
- Christoph Schenker, art theorist

Research Team
- Michael Günzburger, artist
- Mara Züst, art historian
- Piet Esch, cameraman and film director
- Almira Medaric, information scientist
- Kris Decker, science studies scholar

Personnel
- Sabine Schlatter, artist
- Dominik Stauch, artist
- Maya Rochat, artist
- Lena Maria Thüring, artist

Project Partners
- Thomi Wolfensberger, printer, Steindruckerei Wolfensberger AG
- Astrom/Zimmer & Tereszkiewicz, Design & Code
- Dorothea Spitza, art technologist, Bern Academy of the Arts, Materialität in Kunst und Kultur
- Joachim Sieber, art historian

Outputs

A

- Patrick Wagner, printer
- Graphische Sammlung ETH Zürich
- Schweizerisches Institut für Kunstwissenschaft (SIK-ISEA)
- Institute for the Performing Arts and Film, ZHdK
- Verein Material-Archiv
- Archive of the ZHdK
- Media archive of the ZHdK Media and Information Centre

Project Funding

- Swiss National Science Foundation SNSF

Website

- https://hands-on.zhdk.ch

Publications

- Almira Medaric (2020): *Erstellung eines kontrollierten Vokabulars für die Prozesse im Rahmen des Forschungsprojekts "Hands-on. Dokumentation künstlerisch-technischer Prozesse im Druck."* Internship report, University of Applied Sciences of the Grisons (unpublished).
- Kris Decker (2022): *Maschinen unter Druck*. Vol. 28 of the Institute for Contemporary Art Research Series. Berlin: Vexer Verlag. English edition published as open access.
  - A Open access: https://doi.org/10.5281/zenodo.7024598

Presentations and Workshop

- Kris Decker, Michael Günzburger, Christoph Schenker, Thomi Wolfensberger, and Mara Züst: Presentation of "Hands-on. Dokumentation künstlerisch-technischer Prozesse im Druck." Research Day, 30 November 2018, Zurich University of the Arts.
- Michael Günzburger and Mara Züst: "Ortsspezifisches Vokabular: Herstellungs- und Produktionsprozesse." *Kunst Produktion Sprache*, workshop series on site-specific vocabulary, 31 March 2021, Stiftung Sitterwerk, St. Gallen.
- Michael Günzburger and Mara Züst: Workshop "Hands-on" in a seminar by Dorothea Spitza, 27 May 2021, Bern University of the Arts.

Exhibition

- *Hands-on*, 7 December 2022–5 March 2023. Graphische Sammlung ETH Zürich. With a series of talks during the exhibition.

Archives

- Media Archive of the Arts, Media and Information Centre ZHdK: Videos and documents realized in the project.
- ZHdK Archive: All artifacts created in the project.

Fig. 1 Observation situation at Steindruckerei Wolfensberger AG. Zurich, 2021

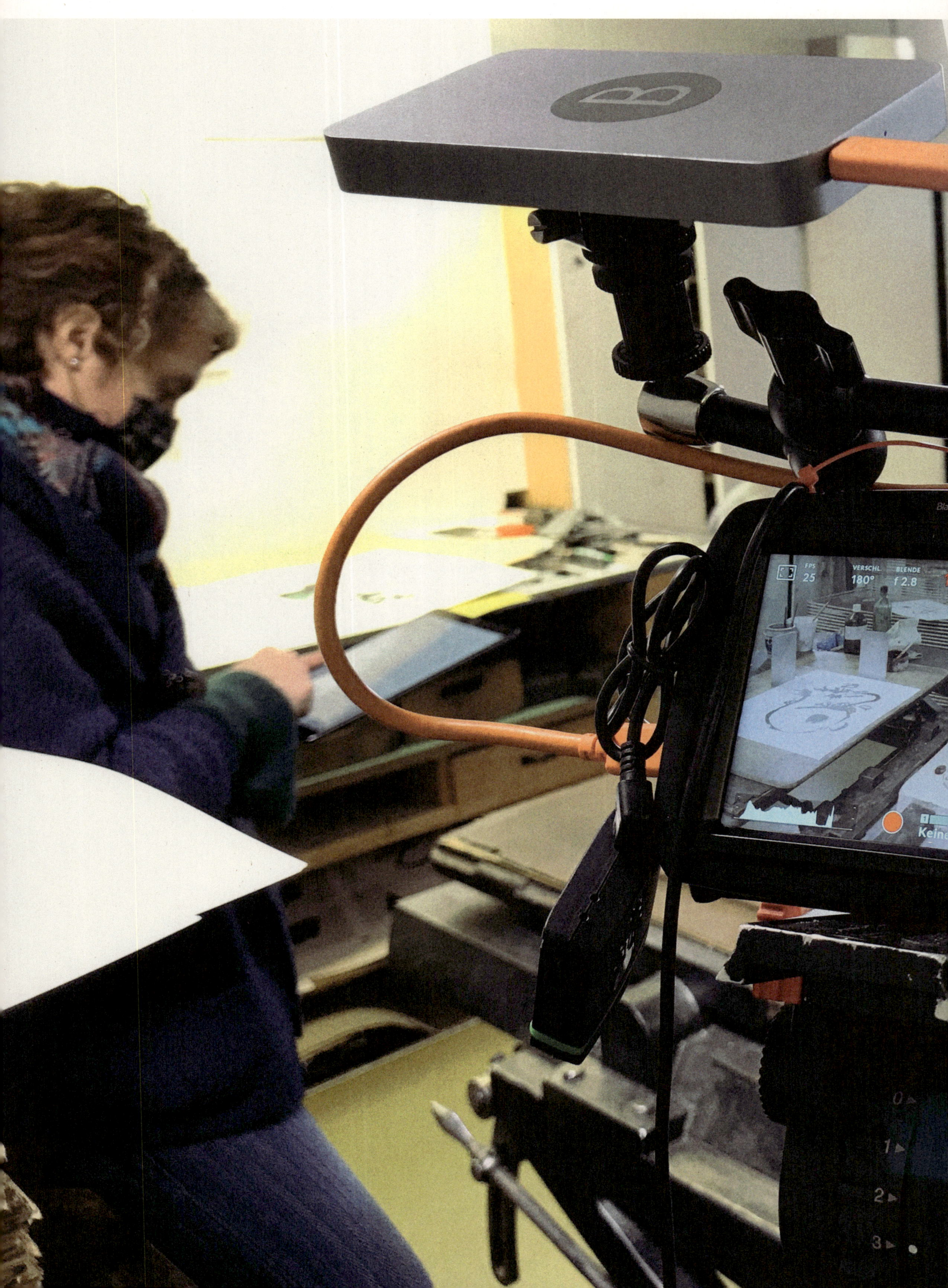

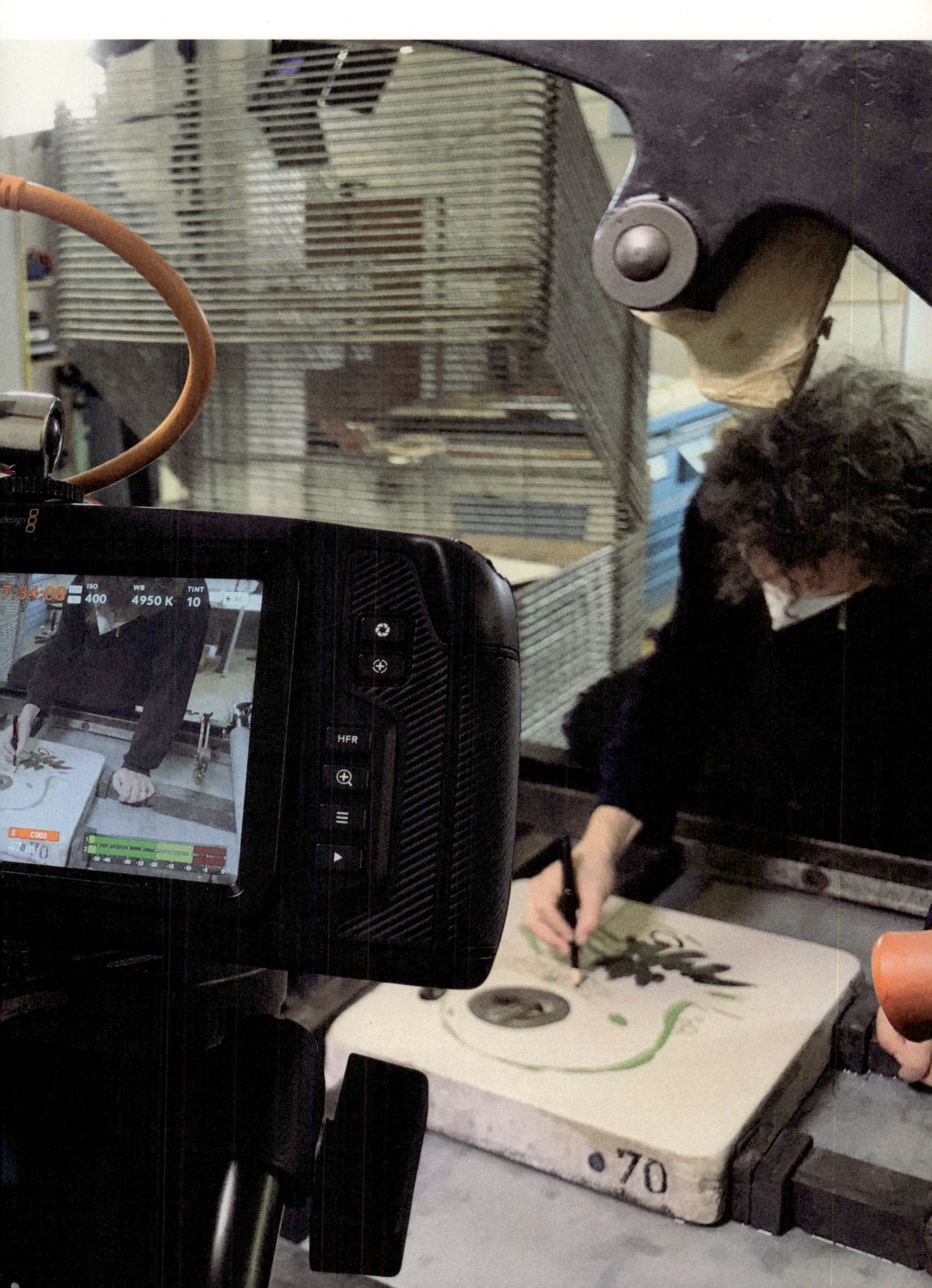
7:34:08
ISO
400
WB
4950 K
TINT
10
HFR
70

Fig. 2 Tap-outs, Steindruckerei Wolfensberger AG. Zurich, 2019
Fig. 3 User Interface https://hands-on.zhdk.ch, 2022

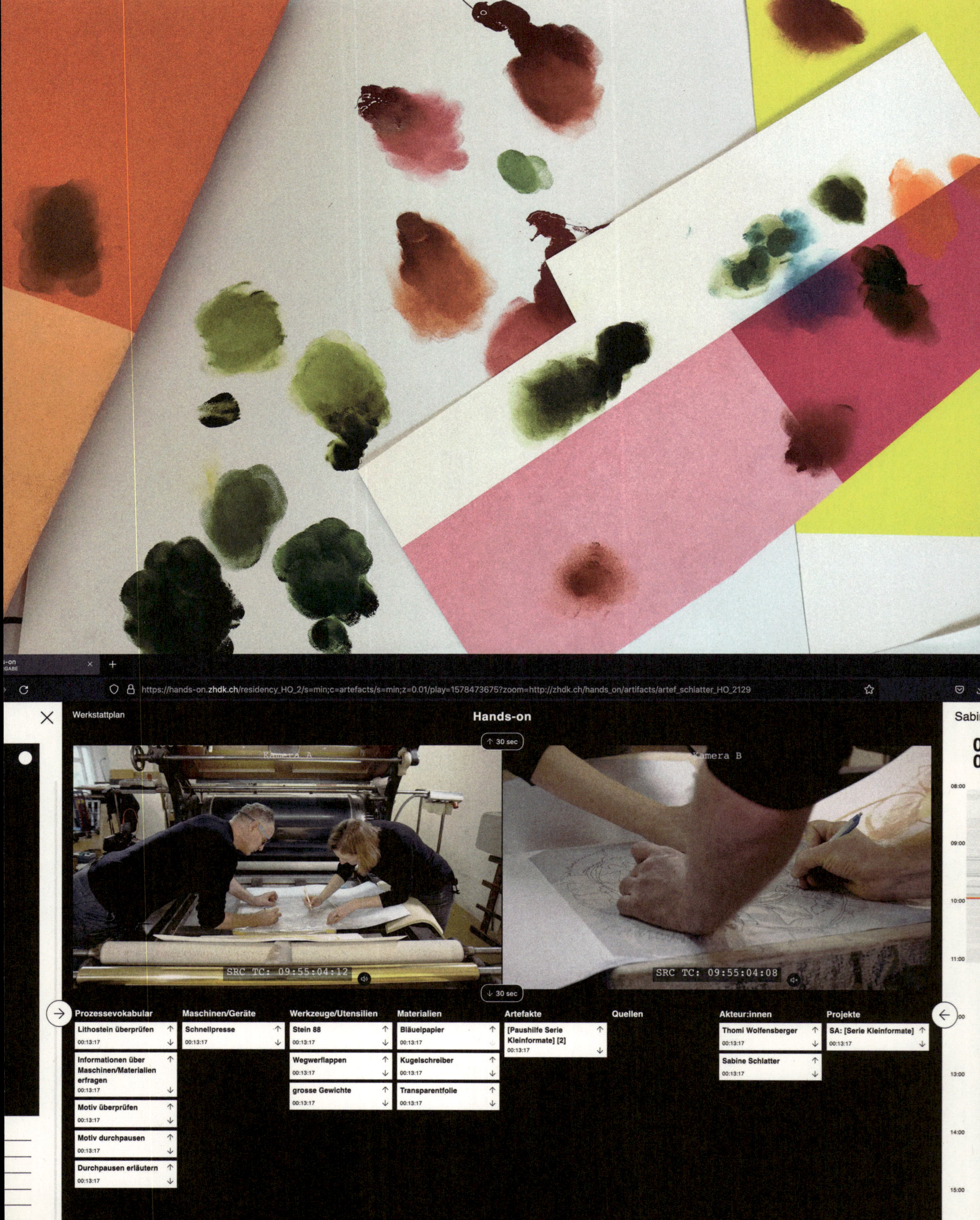

Fig. 4–5 The research team at Steindruckerei Wolfensberger AG. Zurich, 2021 and 2019

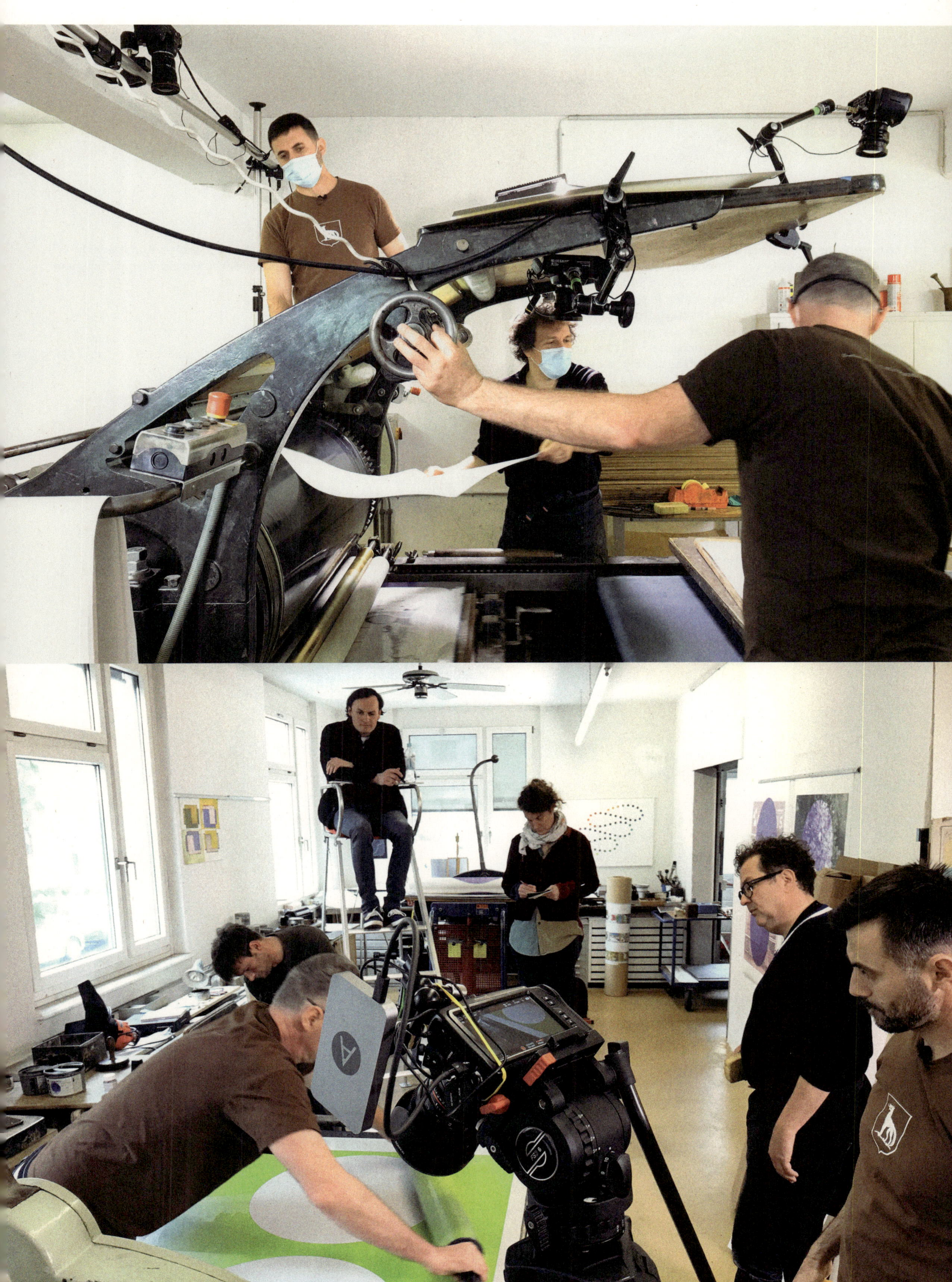

The artistic-scientific pilot project investigated the conditions, processes, and criteria of how artistic research can make latent knowledges of the translocal aesthetically perceptible and epistemically negotiable. Translocality in this context means a globally interconnected structure composed of heterogeneous actors, practices, and dynamics, which is characteristic for the globalized present yet simultaneously difficult to perceive and comprehend. Closely integrating the practice of artistic research with a critical methodological discussion, our project asked under what conditions and in which constellations translocal interrelationships can be traced, activated, and negotiated through artistic research—and how this could be discursively differentiated in the sense of a critical methodology.

Since the specific aesthetic-epistemic potential of artistic research consists precisely in the inextricable interrelationships between form and content, the methodological aspiration of the project was clearly not aimed at the prescriptive formulation of universalizable methods in the strict sense. Instead, it sought possibilities of differentiating between the semiotic-material and the relational-ethical conditions of artistic research focused on translocality, which would account for their particularities.

For this reason, the project closely interlaced artistic research practice and aesthetic-epistemic theoretical work through constant exchange. Within this interlacing the project team pursued:

I Two artistic focus studies, each of which was dedicated to specific global, historical, biosocial, and techno-ecological constellations, namely:
   a The medicinal plant Artemisia afra, which is cultivated in the Congo (Orlow), and
   b Techno-ecological transformations of an upland moor in North Sutherland, Scotland (knowbotiq);

II Art theoretical-philosophical contextualization and definition of terms (Kleesattel); and

III Critical-methodological reflections in the team and in exchange with external experts from art and science.

Provisional research findings of the pilot project flowed into a set or question cards, compiled as a critical-methodological tool entitled *Untooling*. It served primarily to differentiate between two of the central imperatives which our study worked out for response-able encounters in translocal research: deceleration and increasing complexity. The tool exists in a physical and an online version, and can be used for research and instruction. Research in art and other fields draw variable combinations of the cards to answer questions that are related to each other in translocal contexts in complex ways. The question on the front of each card is framed, expanded, or turned around by different contextualizations and additional (counter-) questions on the back. The card set promotes reflection oriented towards the complexity of translocal research as an accompanying process—and thus criteria-based artistic research —without imposing a strict set of rules. Neither strict rules nor selective distinctions between terms are suitable for negotiating latent knowledges in terms of their opacity, local particularities, and translocal process qualities. The questioning character of the critical-methodological tool, its playfulness and openness towards potential uses, and its fundamental unfinishedness allows it to open up horizons of responsivity and sensitivity to situations. The cards speak to the users of their own responsibility rather than offering universalistic recipes or conclusive solutions. In this way they can contribute to an approach to research on translocal contexts that is more ethically and epistemologically responsive.

Ines Kleesattel and Uriel Orlow

Project Title
Ästhetik des Translokalen. Künstlerisch forschende Methoden zur Verhandlung von latenten Wissen

Project Period
1 March 2019–31 August 2020

Keywords
- Artistic research
- Translocality
- Situation
- Methodology
- Response-ability

Head of Project
- Uriel Orlow, artist

Project Team
- Christian Huebler, artist
- Ines Kleesattel, philosopher and art theorist
- Yvonne Wilhelm, artist

Project Funding
- Swiss National Science Foundation SNSF

Related Projects
- Translocal Practices, Zurich University of the Arts, 2006–2007
  P. 68

A

Publication

- Ines Kleesattel, knowbotiq (Christian Huebler, Yvonne Wilhelm), and Uriel Orlow (eds.) (2021): *Untooling*. Volume 27 of the Institute for Contemporary Art Research series. Set consisting of 56 cards and supplemental sheet in folding box. Zurich University of the Arts.
  - A Open access: https://doi.org/10.5281/zenodo.6344282

Workshop

- *Ästhetik des Translokalen: Response-Able Encounters*. 6 December 2019. Institute for Contemporary Art Research, Zurich University of the Arts. With contributions by Karin Harasser and Emma Wolukau-Watanambwa.

Works

- Uriel Orlow: *Learning from Artemisia*. 2019–2020. Installation with three-channel video, 14:18 min, painting, photographs, chairs, tea set, Artemisia afra tea.
- knowbotiq: *thulhu thu thu, before the sun harms you*. 2019–2020. Raffia objects, digital film, digitally printed foulard, sound objects, growing lamps, dimensions variable, in collaboration with Ira Wilhelm, Pablo Alarcón (raffia braiding), Daniel Ranwick (camera) and incantations by Lamin Fofana, Ayesha Hameed/Elvin Brandhi, Pedro Neves Marquez/Raw Forest, Fundacion Mareia, Odete, and Romy Rüegger. Commissioned by: Timespan Arts Center, Helmsdale/Scotland.

Fig. 1 Ines Kleesattel, knowbotiq (Christian Huebler, Yvonne Wilhelm), Uriel Orlow: *Untooling*, 2019–2021
Fig. 2 Workshop. Zurich, 2019

Where else are you? Where are you not?

How do you position yourself in this encounter?

Who or what enables this encounter?

What don't you know?

How does the situation notice you?

What can you learn from feeling awkward or uncom-fortable in a situation?

What can you learn from feeling overwhelmed or exhausted in a situation?

What aspects of yours can be perceived otherwise?

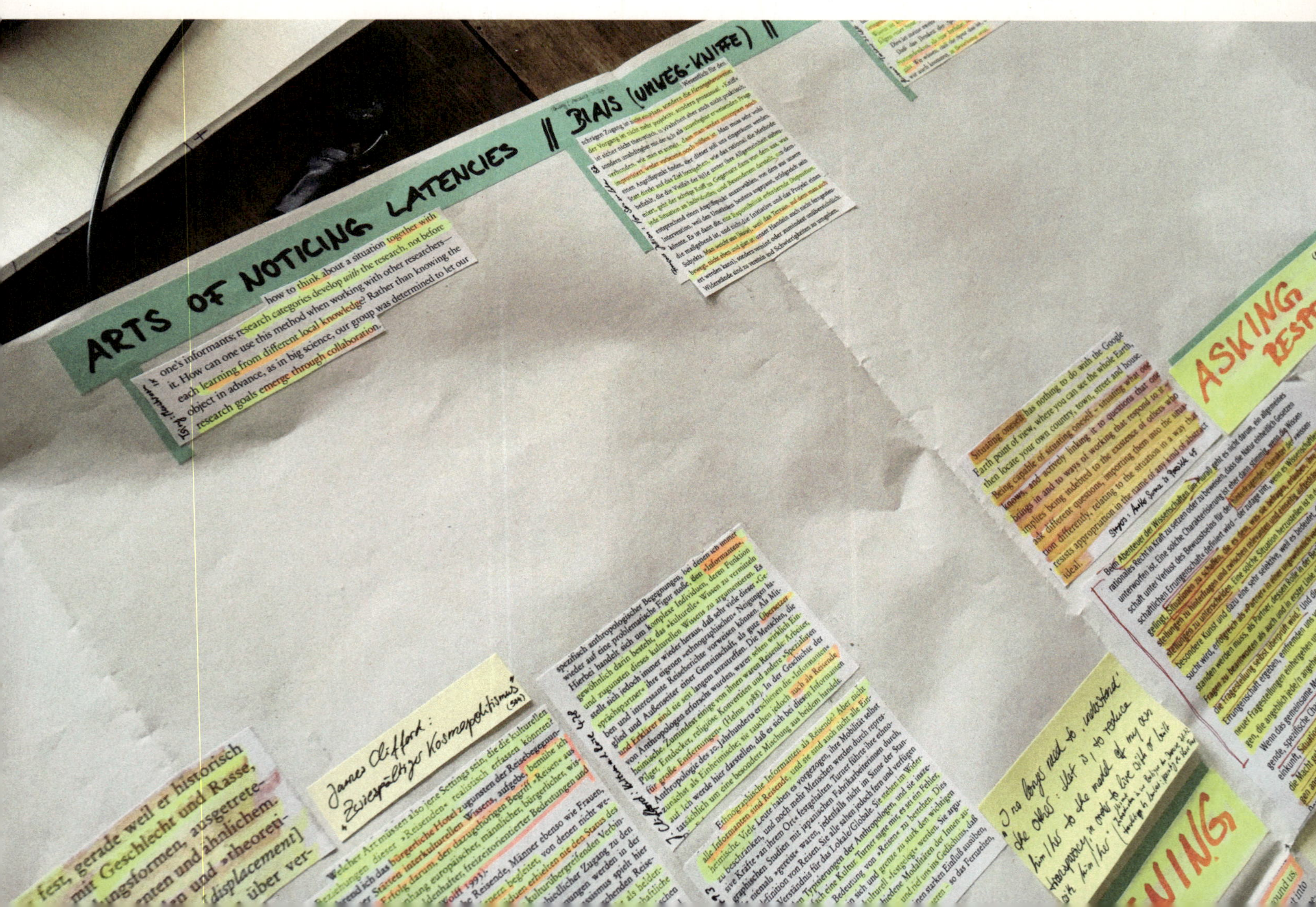

Fig. 3 Uriel Orlow: *Soil Affinities*. Kunsthalle Mainz, 2020
Fig. 4 Uriel Orlow: *Learning from Artemisia*. Kunstmuseum Lichtenstein, 2021

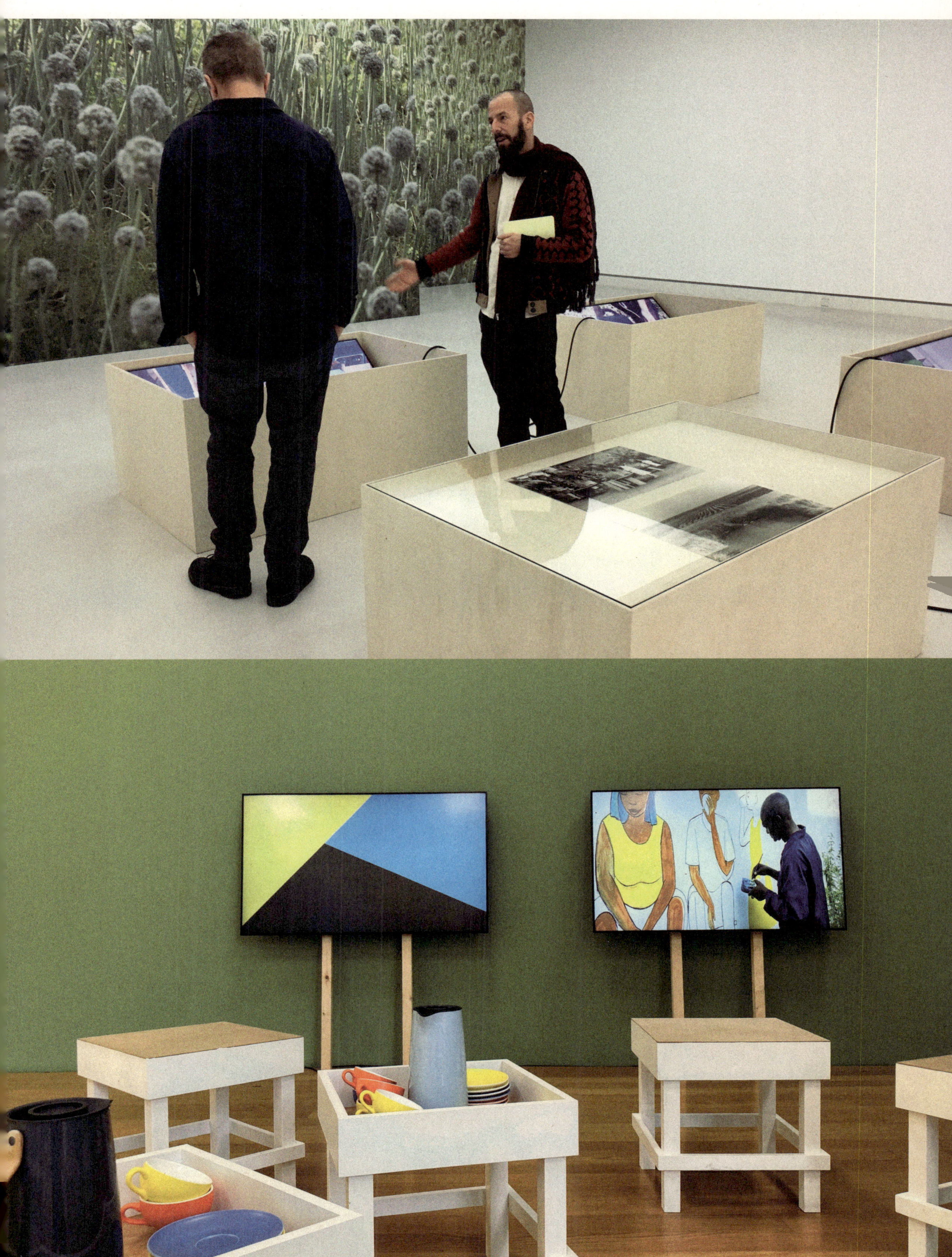

Fig. 5 Uriel Orlow: *Wishing Trees*. Kunsthalle Mainz, 2020

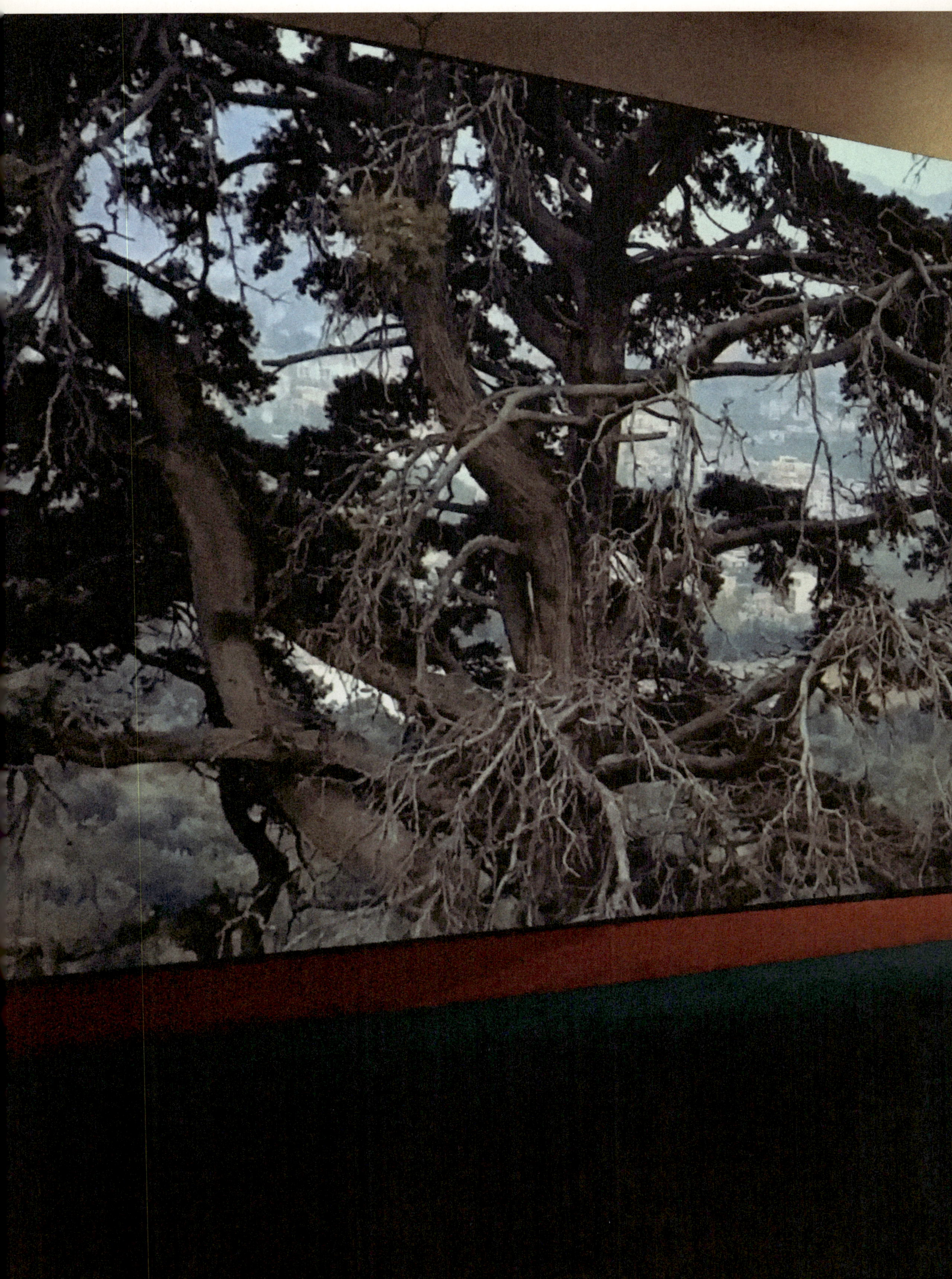

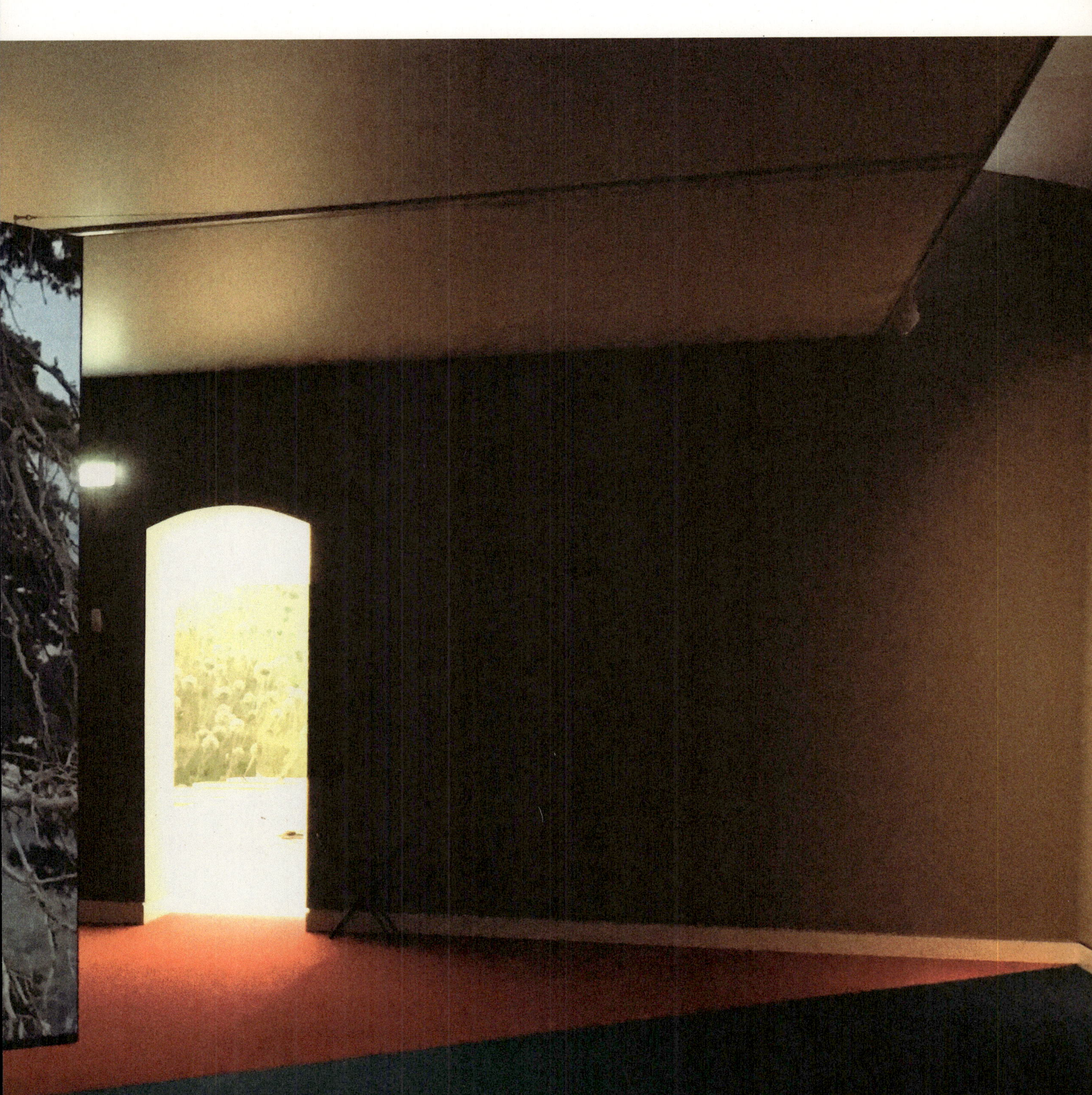

The *F+F 1971* project constitutes the first comprehensive documentation of the history of the F+F School of Art and Design Zurich—from its beginnings in 1965 as class F+F at today's Zurich University of the Arts, through its founding as a school starting in 1971 as the F+F School of Experimental Design, all the way up to today. By indexing the archive of the F+F School for the first time, and by merging the inventories of various archives, including those of Serge Stauffer, Doris Stauffer, Hansjörg Mattmüller, Liliane Csuka, and Peter Trachsel, the *F+F 1971* project has created an important historical record of radical education in Switzerland.

Today, the F+F School is the largest private school for art and design in Switzerland. Founded in 1971, F+F became an important hub for experimental design throughout Europe. The school set itself apart from other applied arts schools (universities of the arts today) through a radical democratization in its organization and its teaching methods. This democratization included the elimination of grading, allowing the students a say in the instruction materials and methods, and the conversion from ex-cathedra teaching to participative processes. The document "Skizze einer demokratischen Schule für Gestaltung" (Outline of a Democratic School for Design), written shortly before the school's founding in 1970, lays out the pedagogical principles of F+F: "The basis of the work is the experiment [...] in this sense the school performs creative research. [...] every student determines their own course of education."

The contents of instruction also defected from those of other schools. Instead of genre-specific courses, the syllabus included titles like "Teamwork" and "Witches Course," which focused on issues of cooperation or a feminist understanding of art. As the representatives of the Fluxus movement or performance art had done before, work at F+F increasingly deployed processual formats like happenings and events to connect everyday life and art. Everyday objects were transformed into sculpture, familiar surroundings conceived as a playground, one's own body deployed as a form of expression.

The school's approaches lured guest lecturers like Stephen Willats, Dan Graham, and Ulrike Rosenbach, but were also subjected to constant critique. Instruction was accused of being determined by inactivity and lacking any objective. Teamwork in the classes was also a challenge, for, as Doris Stauffer wrote, resistance had to be overcome first, as "anti-authoritarian, free activity overtaxes a majority of the students."

The documents about the history of F+F are an important, previously untapped source on Swiss art and design since the 1960s. Part of the *F+F 1971* project was the realization of an online archive exhibition of a wealth of material. Photographs, texts, films, and sound documents on F+F, which are distributed among various public and private archives, were digitized and, in cooperation with contemporary witnesses, described and made accessible. The information was deepened through a crowd sourcing initiative and oral history interviews. The website went online on the occasion of F+F's fiftieth anniversary in 2021, is being expanded and revised during the subsequent year, and will remain publicly accessible upon completion. The website was launched at the F+F School exhibition in the Kunsthalle Zürich in May 2021 and was accompanied by many collaboratively organized events: In an exhibition at the Kunsthalle Bern, for example, today's students at F+F dealt with their predecessor's work, presenting interventions with documents, works, performances, workshops, and documents on the history of F+F. Numerous workshops in Switzerland, in Europe, and in the US reflected on the historical approaches of the F+F School. They also served as the point of departure for a festival on radical education at the Migros Museum für Gegenwartskunst in Zürich.

Michael Hiltbrunner and Geraldine Tedder

Project Title

F+F 1971. Online Archiv-Ausstellung zur Geschichte der F+F Schule

Project Period

1 June 2020–31 October 2022

Keywords

- Radical education
- F+F School
- Design education
- Feminist education
- Experimental art

Head of Project

- Michael Hiltbrunner, art researcher and cultural anthropologist

Research Team

- Geraldine Tedder, art historian and curator
- Johanna Müller, artist and art educator
- Riccarda Naef, artist and art educator
- Kira van Eijsden, artist and drama educator
- Jessie Fischer, filmmaker
- Pooja Khadgi, artist

Collaborators

- Docuteam Baden
- Furbo Zurich
- Studio NOI Zurich
- Videocompany Zofingen

Project Partners

- The Swiss National Library's Prints and Drawings Department
- Stadtarchiv Zürich
- Staatsarchiv Graubünden
- Zurich University oft he Arts, ZHdK Archive
- Kunsthalle Bern
- Migros Museum für Gegenwartskunst
- Kino Xenix

Outputs

A

- Peter Jenny, Birgit Kempker, Ursula Niemand, Moshé Wessely (for oral history videos)

Project Funding

- Swiss National Science Foundation SNSF, Agora
- Casinelli-Vogel-Stiftung
- Dr. Adolf Streuli-Stiftung
- Else v. Sick Stiftung
- Ernst Göhner Stiftung
- Kulturförderung Kanton Glarus, Swisslos
- Kulturförderung Kanton Graubünden, Swisslos
- Gemeinnütziger Fonds Kanton Zürich
- Memoriav, Verein zur Erhaltung des audiovisuellen Kulturgutes der Schweiz
- Stadt Zürich, Beitragsfonds Finanzdepartement
- Volkart Stiftung

Related Projects

- Serge Stauffer, Zurich University of the Arts, 2011–2014
  P. 110
- Archives on Research-based Art, Zurich University of the Arts, 2013–2020
  P. 152

Website

- https://ff1971.ch/en

Guest Editorship

- Ric Allsopp and Michael Hiltbrunner (2016) (eds.): *On Radical Education. Performance Research*, vol. 21, Issue 6.
  A Open access: http://dx.doi.org/10.1080/13528165.2016.1251147

Articles

- Michael Hiltbrunner (2018): "Drop out of art school. 'Research meant trying new things.' The F+F School in Zurich around 1970 and artistic research today." In: *Fucking Good Art*, no. 38, 2018. Zurich: International Edition, 102–130.
- Michael Hiltbrunner (2022): "F+F School for Experimental Design. Democratic and radical learning on the edge of avant-garde art." In: Beatriz Colomina et al. (eds.): *Radical Pedagogies. Why human intelligence still beats algorithms*. Cambridge MA: MIT Press.

Events

- *F+F Festival: Radical Education*. 23–24 September 2021. Migros Museum für Gegenwartskunst, Zurich. Realized in cooperation with F+F. With contributions by Ursula Palla, Peter Jenny, Monika Dillier, Walter Pfeiffer, Mike Hentz, and Katrin Murbach; with guests from self-organized projects like Louis Ashley of AltMFA London, Piero Golia of MSA^ Los Angeles, Stalker from Rom and an "Unlearning Workshop" with Ying Que and Annette Krauss of Casco Utrecht.
- *12 Stunden F+F Schule*. 10 November 2021. Kino Xenix, Zurich. Film program realized in cooperation with Kino Xenix and F+F. With guest appearances by JOKO connected, Bianca Gadola, Emanuel Halpern, and others.

Workshops on F+F 1971 and Radical Education

- 20 August 2021. Schule Neftenbach, Zurich, advanced training for secondary school teachers
- 11 February 2022. Dynamo Jugendkulturhaus Zurich
- 23 February 2022. Bündner Kantonsschule Chur
- 16 March 22. Zurich University of the Arts (ZHdK).
- 24 March 2022. Lucerne University of Applied Sciences and Arts
- 1 April 2022. HyperWerk, University of Applied Sciences and Arts Northwestern Switzerland
- 14 April 2022. Werkplaats Typografie ArtEZ Arnhem
- 23 May 2022. Kaiserin-Theophanu-Schule, Cologne, secondary school
- 24 May 2022. HFBK University of Fine Arts Hamburg, chair Michaela Mélian
- 16 September 2022. The Mountain School of Arts Los Angeles MSA
- 18 September 2022. Public School Los Angeles
- 19 September 2022. CalArts, Valencia
- 22 September 2022. SFAI San Francisco
- 26 September 2022. Swiss Institute, New York City
- 27 September 2022. Princeton University, School of Architecture

Exhibition

- *51 Jahre Experiment F+F*. 24 December 2021–30 January 2022. Kunsthalle Bern. Exhibition with action day and workshops, realized in cooperation with F+F and run by students of F+F School of Art and Design.

Archive

- *Archive F+F School*. Stadtarchiv Zürich. Collection received 2021–2022.

Fig. 1 Foundation course with Hansjörg Mattmüller: Performance in the tram. F+F Schule, Zurich, 1977

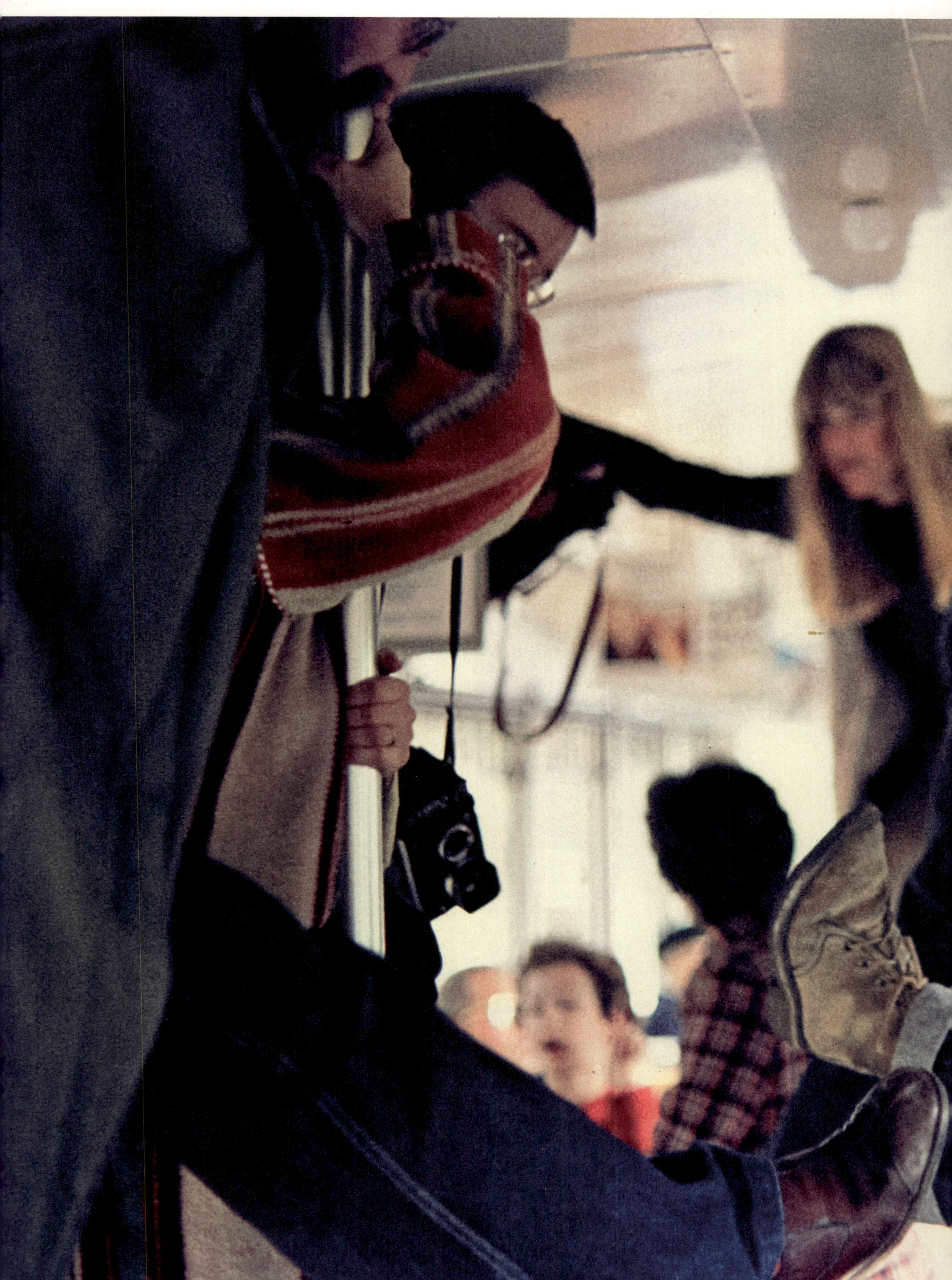

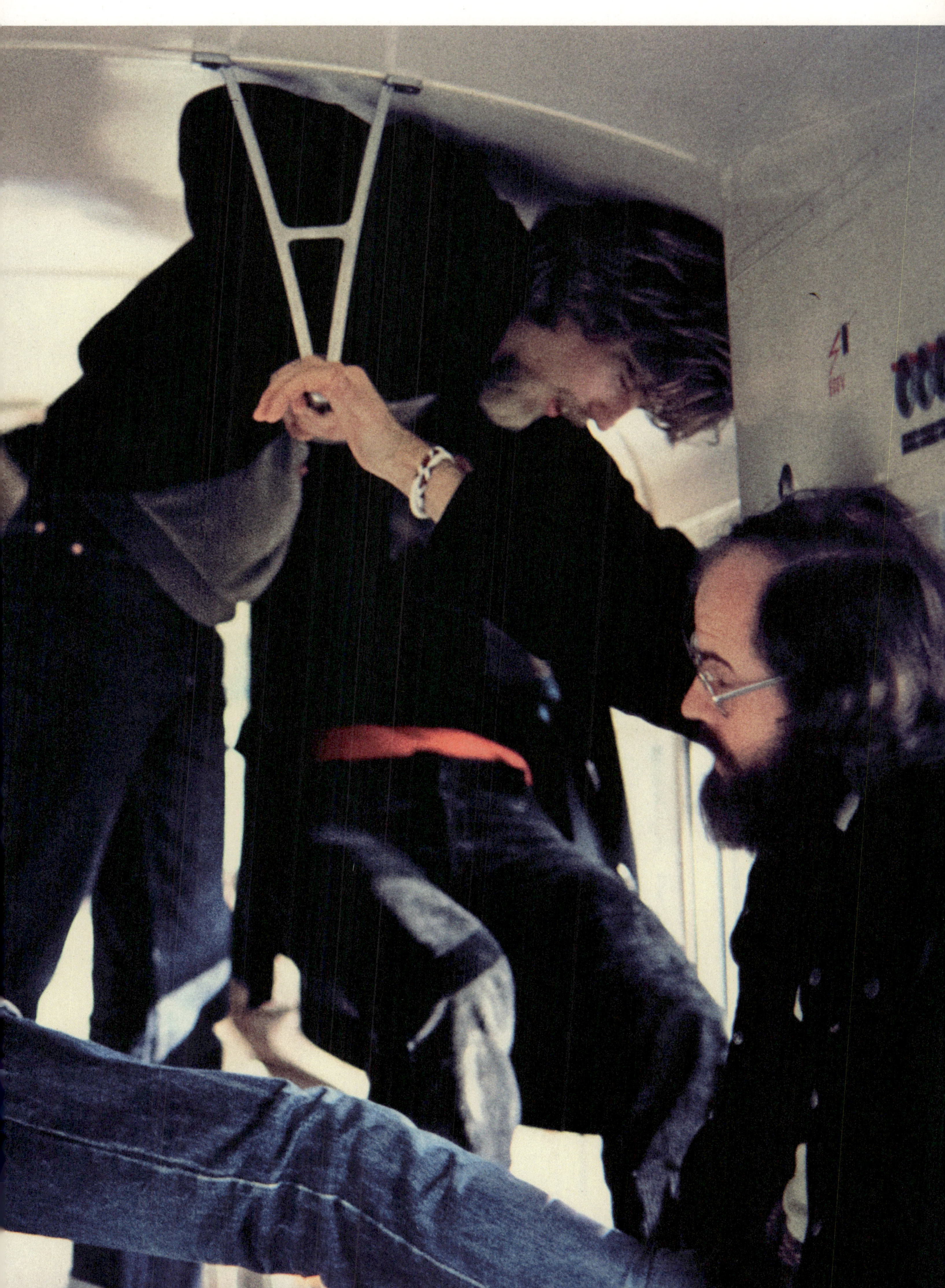

Fig. 2 Workshop with Peter Jenny and Kira van Eijsden: *Kaugummiskulpturen*. Kunsthalle Bern, 2022

Fig. 3 Teamwork with Doris Stauffer: Happening in the forest. Poliklinik Zürich, 1976

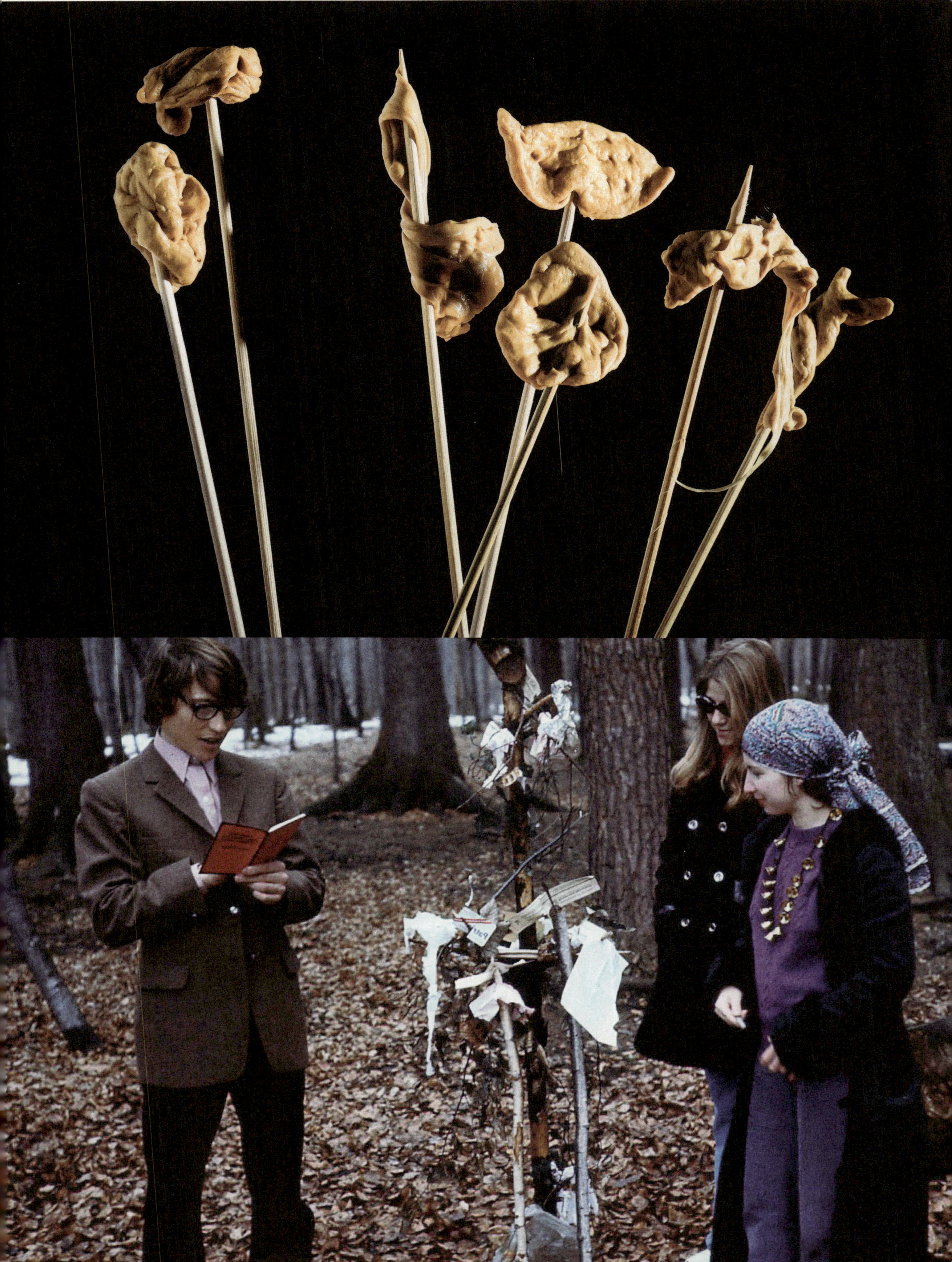

Fig. 4 Class with Doris Stauffer: Group picture with drawings in front of faces. F+F Schule, Zurich, 1973/1974

Fig. 5 *F+F 1971.* Online archive exhibition on the history of F+F School, 2022

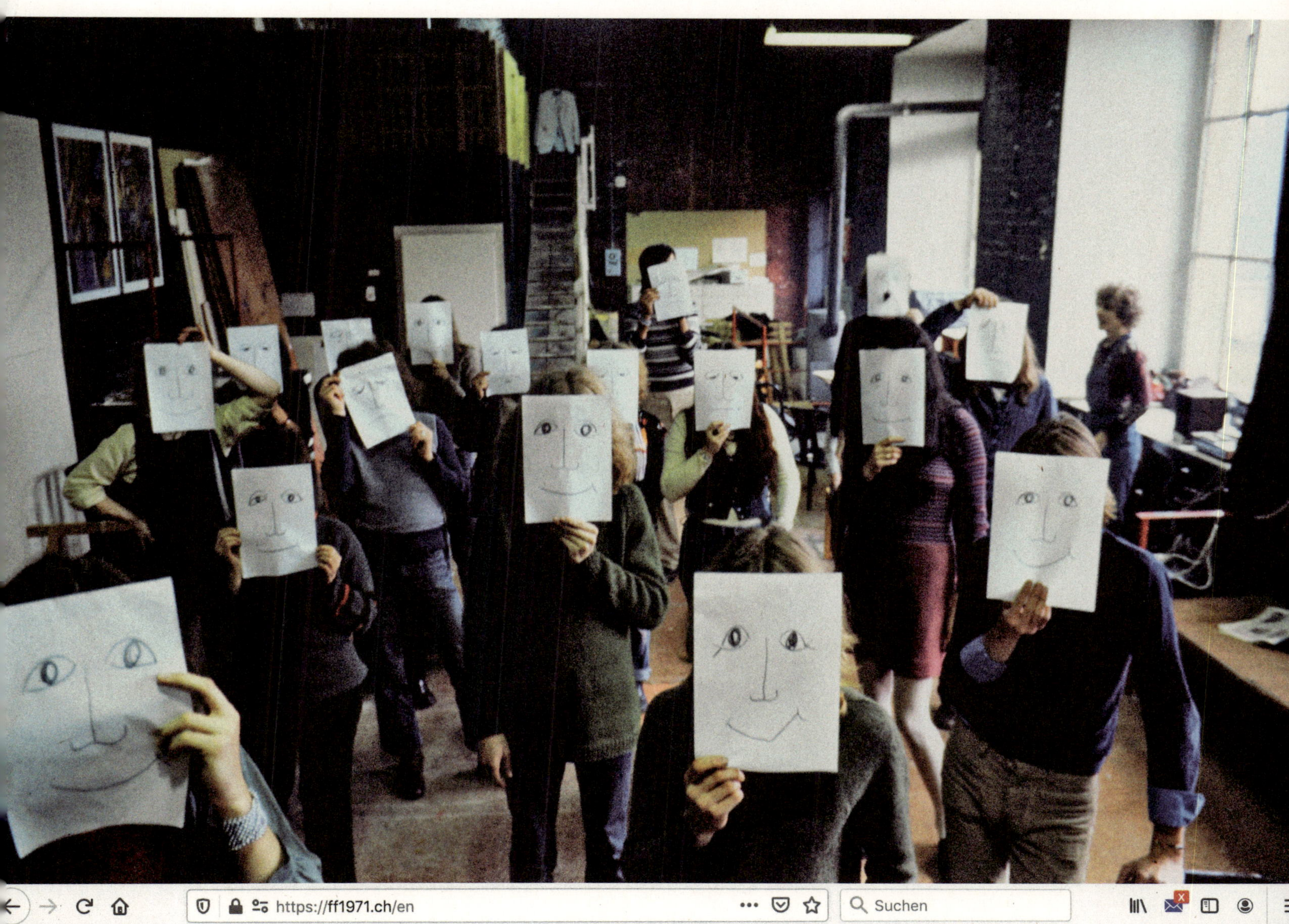

https://ff1971.ch/en Suchen

Meistbesucht Citrix Zeiterfassung... Kulturmanagement: ... WOZ Die Wochenze... ZHdK (Projektdaten... Niev vocabulari Sur... Weitere Lesezeiche

DE EN

F+F 1971

PLATFORM ON THE HISTORY OF THE F+F SCHOOL

ORAL HISTORY, ACTIVITIES, ABOUT

Reproduction rights
In order of appearance
P./Fig.

Zurich University of the Arts
14/1–19/3
30/1–31/1
46/1–47/1
52/1–59/13
62/1–67/8
70/1–73/5
76/1–79/5
80/7–81/8
84/1–85/1
86/3–87/4
100/1–103/6
106/1–109/3
120/1–124/4
126/6
128/1–133/7
136/1–138/3
142/1–145/5
148/1–151/8
156/5
160/1–165/6
176/2–176/3
177/5
180/1–183/5
186/1–189/6
198/1–199/1
202/1–203/1
204/3–205/5
208/1–213/7
216/1–219/7
222/1–225/5
228/1–233/6
242/1–245/5
248/1–251/5

Walter A. Bechtler Stiftung
22/1–23/1
24/3–25/4

The artists/authors
24/2
32/2–35/6
86/2
87/5–89/6
96/7–97/9
108/3–109/3
154/1
170/2
171/4–171/5
236/1–237/1

Pro Litteris and VG Bild-Kunst
26/6–26/7
48/2
48/3–49/5
94/5–96/6
177/4
238/2–239/2
256/2

Philipp Fischer
79/6
125/5

Kulturarchiv Oberengadin Samedan
92/1
93/4

Archiv der Vereinigung für Heimatfreunde Schlieren
92/2
93/3

Monika, Salome, and Veit Stauffer
112/1–113/4
116/6–117/12
155/3–155/4
156/6
256/3

Helmhaus Zürich
114/5–115/5

Berlin University of the Arts
139/4

Staatsarchiv Graubünden, Archiv Peter Trachsel
154/2

Stiftung für fliessenden Kunstverkehr
157/7

University Museum of Contemporary Art, Mexico City
168/1–169/1
170/3

Sigg Collection
174/1–175/1

InOctober
192/1–195/5

Tokyo Photographic Art Museum
204/2

F+F Schule für Kunst und Design
254/1–255/1
257/4–257/5

Photo credits
In order of appearance
P./Fig.

Project teams of the Zurich University of the Arts
14/1–19/3
23/1–25/5
27/9
41/3–41/4
46/1–49/5
52/1–59/13
62/1–67/8
70/1
71/4
72/5–73/5
76/1–79/5
80/7–81/8
92/1–93/4
100/1–103/6
106/1–109/3
120/1–124/4
125/6
128/1–133/7
136/1–139/4
142/1–145/5
148/1–151/8
156/5
160/1–165/6
174/1–177/4
181/1–183/5
186/1–189/6
192/1–195/5
198/1–199/1
202/1–203/1
205/5
208/1–213/7
216/1–219/7
222/1–225/5
228/1–233/6
242/1–245/5
248/1–251/5

The artists/authors
26/6–27/8
30/1–34/4
35/6
79/6
84/1–89/6
125/5

Lars Hellmann
34/5

Eilane Rutishauser
38/1–40/2

Stefan Altenburger
42/5–43/6

Rainer Schlautmann
70/2

Jorit Aust
71/3

Max Wagner/Montabella Foto+Verlag
94/5–96/6

Paul Furrer/Vereinigung für Heimatkunde Schlieren
96/7

Comet Flugaufnahme/Mercedes-Benz Automobil AG
97/8

Hans Steiner/Dokumentationsbibliothek St. Moritz
97/9

The Swiss National Library's Prints and Drawings Department, Serge Stauffer archive
112/1–112/2
116/6–116/11

The Swiss National Library's Prints and Drawings Department, Serge Stauffer archive, Dölf Preisig
113/3

The Swiss National Library's Prints and Drawings Department, Doris Stauffer archive
113/4
117/12
155/3–155/4
156/6
256/3

FBM Studio
114/5–115/5

Joy Largo
154/1

Linus Bill
157/7
Enrique González Careaga
168/1–169/1
170/3
Arai Takaaki
204/2
Alexia Manzano
204/3–205/4
Jörg Wagner
238/2–239/2
Stadtarchiv Zürich, Archiv F+F Schule
254/1–255/1
257/4
Jeff Spörri
256/2

Inventory and Hinge
Entangled Fields of Research in the Arts
Institute for Contemporary Art Research
2001–2022
Published as Volume 29 of the Institute for Contemporary Art Research series, Zurich University of the Arts

Editor
Christoph Schenker

Editorial team
Franz Krähenbühl
Barbara Preisig

Translator
Susan Elizabeth Richter

Proofreading
Michael Turnbull
Hendrik Rohlf

Graphic design
Hubertus Design, Zurich
Kerstin Landis
Jonas Voegeli
Valentin Kaiser
Nathan Meyer
Scott Vander Zee

Lithography
Widmer & Fluri GmbH, Zurich

Typeface
ABC Social, by Dinamo

Paper(s)
Holmen TRND 2.0 80 g/m²

Printing and binding
DZA Druckerei zu Altenburg GmbH
Germany

ISBN
978-3-0358-0568-0